PRAISE FOR ASCENSION MA

"Perhaps no one of his generation has said it better. Christopher Penczak's *Magick* is a groundbreaking, bridge-building, life-affirming adventure—an ascent 'home' between darkness and light through the sacred spectrum of human consciousness."

—Lon Milo DuQuette, author of *The Key to Solomon's Key*

"This book teaches the techniques of ascension magick in a clear, step-by-step manner. Highly recommended."

—Richard Webster, author of *Spirit Guides & Angel Guardians*

"Christopher Penczak's *Ascension Magick* offers a well-researched and holistic view of the occult as practised since the time of the Theosophists. He demonstrates how the principles that originally defined the term 'New Age' may be integrated into a modern and magickal lifestyle. Another wonderful read from one of our most talented contemporary teachers of the esoteric!"

—Kala Trobe, author of *Invoke the Gods* and *Invoke the Goddess*

"A pioneering book for both witches and New Agers, *Ascension Magick* weaves a bridge between two valuable modern traditions that have long allowed language and perspective to obscure their shared beliefs. Bravo to Christopher Penczak for this ground-breaking work!"

—Michelle Belanger, author of *Psychic Dreamwalking*

"In *Ascension Magick*, Christopher ably explains and provides examples of blending diverse traditions within the framework of ascensionism in a modern and appealing manner that reminds us that life is a blend of light and dark."

—Roger Williamson, author of *The Lucifer Diaries*

ABOUT THE AUTHOR

Christopher Penczak is an award-winning author, teacher, and healing practitioner. Beginning his spiritual journey in the tradition of modern witchcraft and Earth-based religions, he has studied extensively with witches, mystics, shamans, and healers in a variety of traditions from across the globe to synthesize his own practice of magick and healing. He is an ordained minister, herbalist, flower essence consultant, and certified Reiki Master (Teacher) in the Usui-Tibetan and Shamballa traditions. Christopher has been involved with the Gifts of Grace Foundation and is a faculty member of the North Eastern Institute of Whole Health, both in New Hampshire. He is the author of many books, including *Magick of Reiki*, *Spirit Allies*, *The Mystic Foundation*, *Instant Magick*, and *The Inner Temple of Witchcraft*.

ASCENSION

MAGICK

Ritual, Myth & Healing for the New Aeon

CHRISTOPHER PENCZAK

Llewellyn Publications
Woodbury, Minnesota

First Edition
First Printing, 2007

Book design and layout by Donna Burch
Cover design by Kevin R. Brown
Edited by Andrea Neff
Interior illustrations by Llewellyn art department
Magician card from the *Universal Tarot* by Roberto de Angelis © 2000 by Lo Scarabeo and reprinted with permission from Lo Scarabeo

The ascended master symbols in chapter 8, taken from Edwin Courtenay's *The Ascended Masters' Book of Ritual and Prayer*, ISBN 978-3-929345-08-7, are © 2000 Verlag Hans-Jürgen Maurer, Freiburg, Germany, and are used with kind permission.

The version of the Great Invocation in chapter 7 used with permission from the Lucis Trust.

Llewellyn is a registered trademark of Llewellyn Worldwide, Ltd.

Library of Congress Cataloging-in-Publication Data
Penczak, Christopher.
    Ascension magick : ritual, myth, and healing for the new aeon / Christopher Penczak.
       p. cm.
    Includes bibliographical references and index.
    ISBN-13: 978-0-7387-1047-1
    ISBN-10: 0-7387-1047-4
    1. Magic. 2. Ascension of the soul. I. Title.

    BF1621.P38 2007
    133.4'3—dc22
    2006048762

Llewellyn Publications
A Division of Llewellyn Worldwide, Ltd.
2143 Wooddale Drive, Dept. 0-7387-1047-4
Woodbury, Minnesota 55125-2989, U.S.A.
www.llewellyn.com

Printed in the United States of America

ALSO BY CHRISTOPHER PENCZAK

FORTHCOMING BY CHRISTOPHER PENCZAK

ACKNOWLEDGMENTS

Special thanks to all my dear ones. This is for all the walkers between the worlds who traverse many paths and traditions, and seek balance in them all. Thank you to Steve, who thought I was going crazy when I started this new path, but gave me time to explore and ground. Thank you to Rosalie and Ronnie for always supporting me in everything. Thank you to my sweet soul sister Laura Gamache for walking into the abyss with me and keeping me sane. Special thanks to my teachers, including Joanna Pinney-Buel and Hari Das Melchizedek, for guiding me. Thank you to Laurie Cabot for the approach of applying analytical skills to magickal theory. And a special thanks to my friends, loved ones, and students who turned me on to new ideas, kept me from getting too zealous, and asked me really tough questions, including Christina Colangelo, Chris Giroux, Kala Trobe, Edwin Courtney, Orion Foxwood, Wendy Fogg, Lisa Davenport, Christine Tolf, Leandra Walker, and Duirin.

contents

EXERCISES

CHARTS AND FIGURES

Charts

Figures

introduction

Home. If ascension spirituality can be summed up in one word, it is the word *home*. But the word home has different meanings for different people. Most people think of their physical dwelling as home, but that is not our spiritual home. Home can refer to creating paradise on Earth, living in true harmony with our home. For some, the spiritual home described by ascension is shifting our consciousness to another level, a new dimension of awareness, leaving the world of matter behind for a world of spirit. Another interpretation is finding the true home within oneself, the shelter of the soul. For many in ascension spirituality, the ultimate home is reunion with the source of all, merging with the godhead in eternal bliss.

When I was first introduced to ascension spirituality, the word *home* was literally the first word that came to my mind. When working in Cambridge, Massachusetts, I wandered through an esoteric bookstore in Harvard Square. On the front table I came across an interesting book by Bob Frissell titled *Nothing in the Book Is True, but It's Exactly How Things Are*. I thumbed through it and saw a picture of a strange geometric form called a star tetrahedron—two interlocked tetrahedrons (four-sided Platonic solids) forming a three-dimensional Star of David. As soon as I saw that shape, the word *home* immediately popped into my head.

Home?! What did that mean? Where did it come from? I had already had enough psychic and spiritual training in Earth-based magick to know that I should heed such a strong message and trust my intuition, so I started to read the book in the store while on my lunch break. I got through only a few pages, declared it the work of a madman, put it down, and left.

I visited the bookstore often, and there was something compelling about the image of the star tetrahedron. Each time I would pick up the book and read a little more, still leaving it there. Eventually I felt honor bound to buy the book because I had read so much of it in the store. I took it home and read it cover to cover, and learned this strange shape that triggered a longing for home in me was the basis of a meditation known as the merkaba. I had some knowledge of the merkaba from my study of Qabalistic magick, but this seemed unlike anything I had previously learned. The story and information found in the book, based on workshops that would later become the two volumes of *The Ancient Secrets of the Flower of Life* by Drunvalo Melchizedek, seemed too fantastical for me to believe. I wrestled to understand these teachings.

When the student is ready, the teacher truly does appear, and soon I found a teacher who taught the merkaba meditation, though in a different form than outlined in the books I had read. I had amazing experiences with the meditation itself, yet found myself between two worlds, with one foot in this exciting-yet-scary paradigm known as ascension. During these workshops I was bewildered because I felt that everybody had some secret knowledge I lacked and they approached it with a certainty that amazed me. Our discussions were of angels, aliens, government conspiracies, and lost civilizations, not in a mythical or archetypal sense but in the literal meaning. The best science-fiction shows seemed tame by comparison. I had come with a strong foundation in Western magick, and I perceived many inconsistencies in these new doctrines. They seemed to lack a cohesive center. Yet the techniques worked. They were healing. They were transformational.

A sense of home manifested through the techniques, a home in myself and my soul, if not in the ascension community. I felt chastised by certain lightworkers, as practitioners of the ascension paradigm sometimes call themselves, for pursuing what they considered to be dangerous occult studies in magick and witchcraft. Many lightworkers believe the craft of the witch to be evil, though in the heart of a witch, nothing could be further from the truth. I was told that "black is not a healing color" and the pentagram is a sign of evil, yet they had always worked well for me. Some lightworkers were surprised to hear of the metaphysical principles supporting the idea that both this color and symbol are forces of life and healing, not harm. Even during this stressful time, I got to know some lightworkers who completely understood and supported my path as a witch. One amazing and well respected woman in the group made a bold statement by wearing all black and sitting next to me. Amid the struggle, I continued my new studies, along with the old. I wanted to know more. I wanted to see how they all fit together.

I initially pursued the merkaba meditation because all this new information had me almost convinced that the end of the world was near, and those who knew this new meditation could "ascend" to the next level. The process triggered a lot of fear in me, but showed me just how much fear I had left to heal. Love, however, is the true purpose of the merkaba meditation, and through diligent practice of it, the entire focus of my life and spiritual practice shifted to love. It reinforced the basic teachings I had learned as a part of witchcraft and ceremonial magick—that love is the true source of magick—and completely refocused my magickal practices. If *home* was the first word I associated with ascension practices, *love* was the next word, even more important than the first. My life began an amazing transformation. I left the business world and found myself in the strange position of pursuing metaphysics full time—writing, teaching, healing, and doing psychic readings as my main source of income.

As I continued my practice, I found people from similar Earth-based spiritualities coming to me for teaching in ascension work. They wanted my point of view. They, too, were drawn to the techniques and concepts, but wanted to know how I reconciled all this seemingly new lore with more traditional material. The path of the mage or witch is not contrary to that of the lightworker. In fact, in ages past, those who practiced what we today call lightwork would have been hunted and killed for being witches. If you look in the New Age section of a modern bookstore, you will find works on everything from witchcraft and crystals to aliens, astrology, and angels. These subjects have more in common than most practitioners realize. Anyone devoted to the divine, to the healing of people and the world, and to enlightenment is involved in the work of ascension, though we might each have our own personal definition of that ultimate homecoming.

As a witch, an inheritor of the European shamanic traditions, I felt the call to be a bridge between the two worlds. Shamans are the bridge between their tribe, their community, and the spirit world. My own point of view on ascension was one of an outsider looking in who eventually became an insider looking out, which gave me a unique perspective. I soon discovered that serious magickal practitioners in pagan and ceremonial magick communities viewed lightworkers as "fluffy bunny New Agers," while many lightworkers saw pagans, Wiccans, and magicians as Satan worshippers, hastening the end of the world through black magick. Having a foot in both camps, I knew that these were horrible stereotypes and that each community had something valuable to offer the other. New Agers are not dumb, and magick wielders are not evil. In the end, they take different roads to the same spiritual destination.

The more I researched the paradigm of ascension, the more I realized that it is just that—a paradigm, a spiritual model, just like the Qabalistic Tree of Life, the shaman's world tree, or the witch's Wheel of the Year. Ascension is one lens through which we can look at the universe, and it's just as valid as any other.

I discovered that many lightworkers rely so heavily on intuition and channeled material that there is not a great understanding of the literal, historical roots of ascension. In the context of history, it becomes an eclectic-yet-intricate, expanding system of metaphysical beliefs, distilling some of the most important spiritual truths for the modern age, not un-like modern magick. Ascension is a synthesis of world wisdom. It incorporates mysticism from the pagan civilizations, particularly those of ancient Egypt and Greece, with Jewish, Christian, Hindu, and Buddhist thought, with a bit of shamanism and holistic medicine thrown into the mix. Historically, ascension practices have a rich magickal, even occult, flavor to them.

In the final analysis, ascension is a magickal paradigm for enlightenment that draws on the world's ancient wisdom. Through your thoughts, words, and deeds, you create your reality and determine the world in which you live. Magick is the process of continually re-creating your reality to manifest your true divine will. Will you use magick to "ascend" to the highest possibilities of our global home, or get stuck in the mire?

When I'm asked to speak on ascension, lightwork, and the merkaba, I feel that my call-ing is to be a bridge between new and traditional spiritual communities. I am called by the divine to reveal the love and wisdom of both worlds in a grounded, practical manner. A lot of assumptions are made in these communities, so I assume very little and explain multiple points of view. When you borrow from many cultures, you have to make sure you define your terms. There is no "official" ascension theology accepted by all lightworkers, just as there is no one magickal theology accepted by all witches, magicians, and shamans.

My magickal training helps me bridge the gaps, fill in blind spots, and point out and explain seeming inconsistencies when viewed from a literal, not magickal or symbolic, paradigm. I came to magick and psychic development as a skeptic, and grounded myself in timeless metaphysical theory. When I first approached ascension material, I had many of the same doubts and questions, but I had a more mystically educated background. I didn't get swept away in the fervor of the experience, and I continued to ask questions. I saw similarities between ascension and traditions that were not embraced by lightworkers, such as paganism and ceremonial magick. They are also part of the world's wisdom, and a necessary part of this global synthesis. I wondered why they were not strongly present in the ascension paradigm. I integrated these pieces into my own ascension teachings.

Now the same questions I once posed are asked of me. I am asked to show how all of these spiritual traditions flow from the same fount, the same divine source. My answers are based on my own experiences and understanding, as well as my research. The teachings that form the basis of this book are certainly rooted in my perspective as a gay, male, American witch practicing lightwork. Included are many views and traditions that I see as influences on the ascension paradigm, though my emphasis will be quite different from that of other lightworkers. Some might even consider these traditions controversial in relation to ascension. I strive to make sure the contributions of the Western ways, of magick, are included in this amalgam of world wisdom. I wrote a book that would answer my own questions and explain the things I didn't understand when I began this new path. My life as a witch influences my worldview of ascension, just as Christian mystics paint a portrait of ascension with a strong Christian-centered flair, or Eastern mystics color it with Hindu and Buddhists tones.

As you read *Ascension Magick*, or, in fact, any spiritual book, keep in mind the source of the material, and the author's background and perspective, to see if the information suits you and your traditions. I know that some students and fans of my more traditional teachings of witchcraft and magick might find this information disturbing, silly, or overly complicated, but I ask those readers to keep an open mind and be open to the experience, even if it's not ultimately for them. I'm still a witch at heart. This is simply one aspect of my spiritual practice that I feel is important to share with others. Remember that all the world's wisdom flows from that same divine fount, and it is through that source, through that love, that we all return home.

PART ONE

THE PATH OF ASCENSION

I

WHAT iS ASCENSION?

What is ascension? That's what I asked when I first got involved in these teachings, and I never got a clear answer. It's kind of like asking "What is enlightenment?" or "What is heaven?" A lot of people have strong opinions about their spirituality, but when they try to put them into words, those words no longer seem adequate. Words lack the power of experience.

Ascension is a mystery—a mystery not in the sense of a riddle to be solved, but an experience found in the heart of the mystery religions. Mysteries are experiences. We can talk about the mysteries, but words always fail to explain them. Those who have directly experienced the mystery have an understanding of it. When these people come together, words are not necessary. There is simply an understanding shared by those with the same experience.

People talk about ascension as if it is one absolute philosophy, yet everybody seems to have a different idea of what ascension is and how it will manifest. Some look at ascension as a global event that will happen to everybody simultaneously in the same way. Others look at ascension as a part of the personal path of enlightenment, with multiple manifestations and meanings. When I began on this path, I didn't even have an understanding that there are many different interpretations of ascension. I heard hints and whispers about ascension, with no clear idea of what we were talking about.

My own definition of ascension encompasses a wide range of interpretations, allowing for many other views. I fall on the side of personal ascension—everybody's understanding of it will be personal, yet perhaps there will be a global shift that will affect everybody. Let's examine some of the most common beliefs about ascension.

LITERAL ASCENSION

Literal ascension means the literal shift of our bodies and souls from this physical plane of existence (the third dimension) to another plane of reality. This new level of existence is not necessarily physical in the same manner that we now understand physical life. In this new dimension, many of the ills of the current physical world—illness, pollution, crime, even death—will be left behind. Within this view, both literal personal ascension and literal global ascension are possible.

The full-body ascension of Mother Mary in the Christian tradition, moving into heaven without the mortal body passing into death and decay, is cited as an example of literal personal ascension. Many saints, gurus, and holy people from various cultures are said to leave this world without mortally passing. They return to the divine, taking their bodies with them into the next world. Yet they are still linked to the mortal world, available to us through spiritual contact in prayer, ritual, and meditation.

As for a literal global ascension, many people believe that some pivotal event will change the world. Some view it as a cataclysm in which those who are spiritually prepared will ascend from the danger of the material world. Others believe a peaceful, inspiring event will trigger a global ascension. Some think the world will literally change its vibration, and physical existence will cease as the whole third dimension of physical reality literally transforms, shifting to light. Others believe reality will exist on all levels, but we will no longer live on the physical level, leaving room for another race to develop physically. We will ascend to a more subtle spiritual vibration, referred to as a higher dimension. Lightworkers believe several ancient civilizations that seemingly disappeared, such as the Anasazi and the Mayans, literally and physically ascended en masse, and are still living as a community on another plane of existence.

Literal physical ascension is one of the most prevalent belief systems in the lightworker network and tends to dominate much printed and online material.

POSTHUMOUS ASCENSION

Posthumous ascension occurs when an individual completes all necessary experiences in the physical world and no longer needs to return to the cycle of reincarnation. The doctrines of reincarnation and karma have been widely accepted in most New Age communities, influencing our views on life, death, and the afterlife. When one clears karma and breaks from the wheel of rebirth, a new level of consciousness is achieved. Rather than return from the spiritual state of existence to be reborn into the material world, these souls remain at this ascended level of consciousness, beyond the physical world. They have a different perspective from other deceased ancestors who are simply resting between lives, because they no longer need to return to the world for their own evolution. The material world has taught them all they need to know, and they are ready for new challenges. These enlightened beings act as guides and intermediaries to the physical, living beings on Earth. Great spiritual figures in history are seen in this category.

LIVING ENLIGHTENMENT

In the most conservative and symbolic view, ascension is a euphemism for enlightenment, a continual state of consciousness in which an individual is in communion with the divine. Mortal, or ego, consciousness "ascends" to a higher level of consciousness where there is no separation from the divine. Those in the world who are believed to be enlightened masters or gurus, capable of great healing and miracles, have achieved this level of ascension. Although physical beings, these masters are said to be free from karma and the wheel of rebirth, and have voluntarily chosen to stay incarnated in the world to share their teachings. Many believe this enlightenment confers great mystical powers, including physical immortality and the perfection of psychic gifts. Many living masters are said to live far longer than ordinary mortals to continue their teaching and healing work.

ASCENSION TO THE NEXT AGE

We are entering the New Age, but what does that mean? Besides being a convenient marketing label for a section of books, the New Age refers to the Age of Aquarius. In the systems of astrology, each period of roughly two thousand years is dominated by a zodiac sign, and the signs move backwards through the cycle. We are leaving the Age of Pisces, characterized by the twelfth zodiac sign, and moving to Aquarius, the eleventh sign. Mystics believe the Age of Aquarius will be one of global peace and enlightenment, though it might manifest through swift and sudden change. Many other cultures and mystical systems have a similar teaching, echoing the sentiment that we are entering a new aeon of peace and enlightenment. Some prophesy a cataclysm with little hope of survival as a culture, while others predict a golden age of peace, prosperity, and enlightenment.

Ascensionists believe that our level of consciousness will determine how easily we make the transition to the Age of Aquarius. The shift in the ages will reflect back upon us our hopes and fears. If we are in a state of loving consciousness, then the transition will be easy and peaceful, creating a golden age based in love. If we are full of anger or fear, then it will be difficult, fulfilling our more apocalyptic prophesies.

This transitional period is the opportunity for spiritual global ascension. Our consciousness, individually and collectively, will rise to ease the transition between the ages and create paradise on Earth. The world will not literally disappear, but we will leave behind a mode of consciousness based on the previous Age of Pisces, and the global culture it created, and begin a new era, with new lessons and challenges. We will ascend to a new level of life where the foundation of our consciousness will be rooted in an awareness in which we are in constant communion with the divine, transforming our current values, ideas, and resources. We will become rooted in a more spiritual dimension. We will not necessarily shed the physical realm, but it will no longer be the sole realm of importance to the vast majority of the population.

RETURNING TO THE SOURCE

This paradigm of ascension—the return of creation to its divine source—is possibly the truest. Many mystic traditions, both Eastern and Western, believe that all things created are manifestations of the divine. As humans, we go through the cycles of creation, like all life. We too must return to the source of life.

The ultimate end in the ascension model is not only the end of the world but the end of the universe, folding back into the divine. We "ascend" through the various levels of existence to merge with the force that initiated creation.

On a personal level, this means enlightenment leading to nirvana, to the ultimate union with the source. This is the final initiation of the mystic, the final achievement of what is known as the Great Work. A more cosmic view of this paradigm is not simply individual sparks or souls returning to the source, but the entire universe folding back to the point from which it sprang, completing the great cycle of creation and possibly initiating a new cycle.

PERSONAL Initiation

When practitioners say they have "already ascended," yet they are in a physical body and don't appear to be particularly enlightened, they might be referring to the levels upon levels of consciousness expansion a mystic goes through while on the spiritual path. If they reach a certain level of enlightenment, but are not necessarily capable of unearthly miracles or free of all karma, they have "ascended" to the next level on their path.

Such experiences are referred to as initiations. Although you can be initiated into various groups and traditions through rituals, personal initiation refers to the initiations of spirit, ordeals of life that can only be conferred in a personal way, through communion with the divine. The challenges of life, from personal interactions to physical illnesses, as well as the spiritual crisis known as the "dark night of the soul," are all forms of personal initiation. Mystics have intricate systems to gauge levels of expanded consciousness based on their cultural models and life experiences. These systems act as maps, to help them reach the next destination in a healthy and balanced way. By understanding the personal initiations, and the lessons they have conferred to those who have walked the path before you, you can better understand and observe your own enlightenment process.

UNKNOWN AND UNKNOWABLE

Many lightworkers believe the exact form of ascension, both personally and on a planetary scale, can't be truly known while we are in mortal form. Our senses, even with our mind-expanding and spiritually uplifting rituals and meditation techniques, can only comprehend glimpses and shadows of ascended consciousness.

Our perceptions are colored by our personal belief systems, so everybody has a different "truth" about ascended consciousness and enlightenment. A traditional Christian who touches higher consciousness may come back with a popular image of heaven, with clouds, harps, and white robes, or of ascension achieved through a relationship with Jesus Christ. A native shaman might return with an image of a paradisiacal hunting ground aided by the ancestors, while a priestess of the Goddess traditions may get an image of the Isle of Avalon and its otherworldly priestesses. Each is a symbolic interpretation of the ascended higher consciousness. Each represents a facet of the greater whole of ascension, but none contains the complete picture for everyone.

SYMBOLIC ASCENSION

Symbolic ascension looks at the lives of the masters and saints as inspiration for how best to live our lives. By emulating those whom we claim have ascended, we come into a greater sense of our own spirituality. Ascension is not about going anywhere; it is simply a deeper expression of the spiritual life on a daily basis. The view of ascension as a journey to another dimension, a heavenly utopia, is a symbol of what is truly possible when humanity works together for the good of all to create that utopia here and now. We don't have to look far to see living examples of ascended consciousness in modern times, transformative individuals who inspire others through their actions and teachings. Gandhi, Mother Teresa, and Peace Pilgrim were but a few. Imagine how many others are quietly working their magick every day, side by side with us, and never drawing attention to themselves. Perhaps you are doing it already, without realizing it. Perhaps at different times in our lives we are all inspiring others to ascend and shift their consciousness to a higher, more enlightened view.

There are a lot of varying ideas about ascension, and this chapter simply scratches the surface of the most basic, common beliefs. Each of these views has its merits, based in traditions and theologies that are rooted in older wisdom, and each has its own biases and cultural contexts.

The biggest discrepancy among these concepts is the debate over external physical ascension versus internal personal ascension. Understanding the paradox between our internal and external views is one of the biggest struggles mystics face. The struggle is one of the mysteries, like ascension itself. When you have experience with the spiritual reality in both the transcendent, internal world, through a vision, and the immanent, physical world, through nature or people, you start to understand that there is little difference between our internal and external realities. They are two views of the same thing. Reconciling the truths of both transcendent and immanent divinity is the challenge of the next age, as we recognize divinity is both beyond us and within us and everything else. Inner and outer realities are a reflection of each other. In the end, there is nothing separating the inner and outer worlds but our own perception. With that in mind, all these views on ascension and more are possible.

2

THE ROOTS OF ASCENSION

Where do the philosophies of ascension come from? At first glance, they seem to be very modern. Much of the most popular ascension literature is considered to be "channeled," divinely inspired writings credited to a variety of otherworldly sources. Though this new channeled material has inspired and evolved the ascension paradigm, using modern images ranging from futuristic utopian societies to benevolent alien contact, the fundamental spiritual principles of ascension are found in the religions of the world.

The paradigm of the lightworker is a potpourri of creed and beliefs. Each practitioner and teacher focuses on the teachings and cultures that have been most helpful on his or her own personal path. Some people assume that ascension is based solely on a Judeo-Christian view of mysticism, but that is not true. Because many people in the West are raised in that spiritual lineage, the mystical teachings of Judaism and Christianity may be the most appealing and the closest to their established beliefs. But ascension has just as strong of ties to Eastern mysticism. In fact, many look at ascension as a fundamentally Eastern philosophy developed in the Western world. Many practitioners feel a kinship to the ancient traditions of the pagan world as well. Each of these traditions brings a piece to the new ascension movement.

Since the dawn of the New Age movement, which truly began with the occult revival of the late 1800s, various teachings have been blended together to form the ascension paradigm. Starting conservatively, the first New Agers blended the mysticism of Eastern and Western traditions. In recent years, core shamanism, futuristic science, holistic health, Goddess reverence, and alien lore have been melded into the mix. To understand ascension properly, one must know where its roots are found.

THE LAND OF THE BLACK SAND

I find it funny when I speak to people about magick and healing and they say, "Isn't that one of those wacky New Age things?" I always respond with, "Well, technically it's more of an old age thing, ancient really." The New Age involves taking a lot of mysticism from the ancient world and putting it in a modern context. The oldest foundation stones of our ascension paradigm come from the most ancient civilizations—those of the Middle East. The cultures of both ancient Egypt and Sumer play a role in our mystical thinking. Traditional and radical avant-garde scholars disagree as to which culture came first. Most look at the fertile crescent of Sumer as the cradle of civilization, though some more unusual and controversial evidence dates the sphinx of the Giza Plateau far earlier than many believe, linking Egypt to mythical prehistoric civilizations.

Ancient Egypt was a magickal culture, and the mystical lore played an important role in Egyptian life. Though magick played a role on all levels of Egyptian culture, there was an intricate system of priesthoods and temples. Egyptian cosmology has several creation myths and a large pantheon of divine beings, gods referred to as the Neteru, each ruling a specific personality and aspect of creation.

Though nothing can be said about the ancient world with absolute certainty, we believe some of the ancient Egyptian initiation rites were encoded in the story of the deities Isis and Osiris and their family (figure 1). Their story has greatly influenced the ascension paradigm. Four divine siblings were born, two female—Isis and Nephthys—and two male—Osiris and Set. Isis took Osiris as her husband, while Nephthys took Set. The first couple embodies the creative and formative powers of nature and the Nile, while the second is aligned with more the destructive and decaying powers.

Although originally the story was not necessarily one of good versus evil, it was portrayed that way in later versions. Set became an archetypal adversary figure, being a god of the desert and wild animals, while Osiris was the force of civilization and agriculture.

In their constant conflict, Set tricked Osiris into a box designed specifically to Osiris's measurements—the first sarcophagus. Osiris was later found and resurrected by Isis. Set dismembered Osiris and scattered the pieces. Isis retrieved the pieces, with the help of her sister Nephthys. Temples were later built on each of the sacred sites where the body parts were found. Only the phallus remained missing, but using her magick, Isis was able to mate with Osiris and conceive the child Horus, who later battled his uncle Set for his

Figure 1: Isis and Osiris

rightful rule of Egypt, and eventually succeeded. Thoth, the Egyptian god of wisdom and learning, also played a role in aiding Horus in his struggle with Set.

This Egyptian tale definitely influenced later Christianity. Looking back on the ancient Egyptian sculptures of Isis with her child Horus, we see a strong parallel to the art of Madonna with child. Osiris, a vegetation god, was sacrificed and resurrected in a new role, as lord of the dead. A child savior god, not born through normal means of conception, and his divine mother battled the forces of destruction and triumphed to aid civilization. Set is seen archetypally as a Satan figure, the adversary in the story, though he is also the god of the destructive aspect of nature. For the ancient Egyptians, this natural destruction is embodied by the powerful desert sandstorms, and Set ruled the deserts outside of Egypt. Some see Set as the intrusion of outside cultures and foreigners, while mystics see him as the initiator, the shadow, and in many ways the harsh teacher of Osiris and Horus, who makes them greater through his actions.

The scribe deity known as Thoth, or Tehuti, is considered to be the all-father and patron of the alchemist's arts (figure 2). The root of the word alchemy—*chem*, or *khem*—comes from a name for Egypt, the Land of Khem, or the Land of the Black Sands, referring to the dark, fertile soil of the Nile River. Since that time magick has been associated with the color black, even when used in pursuit of the loftiest ideals. In the Middle Ages most magick was referred to as the "black arts," and modern magicians see this as a link to the magick of Egypt.

Many people on the ascension path have strong past-life memories and connections to ancient Egypt, and believe they were initiated in the temples and pyramids. Modern magickal traditions draw upon the rich imagery of Egypt, from its architectural forms to its sculpture, hieroglyphics, mythology, and sacred texts. Many see the Egyptian gods, with their very human dramas, as the ascended beings of the ancient world.

THE FERTILE CRESCENT

The tales of ancient Sumer, and later Babylon, play a big role in modern metaphysical thinking. Considered to be two of the oldest civilizations, we find their influences in most Western mythology, from the development of the goddess image of Inanna, later known as Astarte and transformed into the image of Aphrodite of the Greeks, to references of Sumerian practices in the Old Testament of the Bible.

Figure 2: Thoth

Like the story of Osiris, the descent of Inanna through the seven gates of the Under-world to face her dark sister, Ereshkigal, is a tale of initiation and rebirth. From Jungian therapists looking intellectually at the feminine side of the shadow to mystics describing the dark night of the soul, Inanna is the archetypal initiate, descending into the depths to truly claim the title Queen of Heaven and Earth. The story of her consort, Tammuz/Damuzi, the sacrificed vegetation god, also forms parallels with Osiris's tale.

Sumerian lore contains some of the oldest versions of primal mythological concepts. A younger generation of gods, lead by Marduk, defeated the elder race of gods, in particular the goddess Tiamat, creating the world from her remains. Subsequent gods brought civilization to humanity through gifts of fire and technology. Though some look at this story as the rise of the patriarchy in our modern civilization, we can also look it as the triumph of modern civilization over the primal tribal ways. The Sumerians were known for their lore of not only gods, but spirits and entities we would think of as angelic and demonic. Modern scholars have linked the rise of the Sumerian culture to the ancient astronaut theory, believing their gods were otherworldly alien visitors. Many of the well-known biblical stories that most modern readers assume are Jewish actually originate in much older tales of Sumer. In the Sumerian version, Noah's name is Utnapishtim. You will find variations of the flood myth, which many believe to be far more than a myth, in the folk tales and mythologies of people across the globe. The distant civilization of Sumer influenced our modern culture more than most people realize, as a cradle of not only human life, but culture, arts, philosophy, technology, and religion.

THE MEDITERRANEAN PAGAN

The cultures of ancient Egypt and Sumer influenced the mystery cults of the Greeks. Many of the philosophers from ancient Greece were influenced by Egyptian thought, and some, such as Plato, even traveled to study with the priests of the black lands.

The myths of Greece evolved in several phases, but one main point was the formation of the universe by generations of gods. Each generation gave rise to the next. The first primal creators, Gaia (who is the material universe but is now more often seen as Mother Earth) and Uranus (who is the generative principle seen as Father Sky), created the Titans, Cyclops, and other monsters. Uranus hid his children in the womb of Gaia, until his son, the Titan Chronos, freed himself and his sibling by castrating Uranus with a sickle. The Titans interbred and created the race of Olympian gods. Chronos followed in his father's footsteps and began swallowing his children whole, as it was prophesied that one would usurp his rule. Like his father before him, Zeus led his siblings in a revolt against the Titans and eventually formed the pantheon of Olympian deities. They finished creation and interacted with humanity as patrons and guides.

The mystery schools of Greece explored the primal myths. In particular, the stories of Persephone, Dionysus, Orpheus, and Apollo were vital. Much like the story of Osiris, they are about light and dark, and the fall and rise from the Underworld. Persephone was the maiden who was brought to the Underworld by the dark Underworld king Hades. The earlier versions had Hades seducing her, while the later versions depicted a kidnapping and rape. In both tales, she became his bride and queen of the Underworld. Her mother, Demeter, the goddess of grain, refused to let the plants grow, preventing humanity from having grain and foods, ushering in the first winter. Eventually a deal was struck in which Persephone would spend half of the year with her husband and half with her mother, during the growing season. Persephone is the herald of life and death. She stands between the worlds, and life and death are her mysteries. We can see similarities to the stories of both Inanna and Isis. The very popular and secretive Eleusinian mystery school was founded in honor of Demeter and Persephone, opening the initiate to their teachings of life and death.

Dionysus, in the many versions of his myth, is a sacrificed god, associated with the vine and vegetation, as well as the land of the dead and the power of resurrection. In this aspect, he's much like Osiris and Inanna's mate, Dumuzi. Apollo is linked to Dionysus, and both are patrons of the arts and theater—later myths saw Apollo as the light and smiling face of the theater masks, while Dionysus was the tragic face. Orpheus was a human figure, made divine by his descent into the Underworld to seek the spirit of his deceased wife, Eurydice, and his second tragic loss of her, by mistrusting the gods of the Underworld. His Orphic schooling was to teach the mysteries of the dead through the arts and music. Mystery schools were built up among all these figures, as well as the philosophical schools of Plato, Socrates, and Aristotle.

The later Roman culture identified greatly with the Greeks, borrowing liberally from their arts, sciences, and religions to the point of identifying their gods with many of the better-known Greek deities. Many Roman citizens took part in the Greek mystery schools. The growth of the Roman Empire, as it expanded its reach, brought together many different cultures, religions, and philosophical ideas. Through Roman travel routes, deities from remote areas were mixed with native figures. The Romans were diverse in their religious practices and education, having contact with the Celts, Egyptians, and even the new

Christian cult growing in the Middle East. The Christians were persecuted at first and then embraced. Without the Roman Empire, the rise of Christianity as a dominant force in the Western world would not have been possible.

One of the most significant mystery schools of Rome, Mithraism, possibly influenced the growing Christian religion. Mithraism was from Persia, and various forms of this religion grew in Asia Minor, as the worship of Mithras was intertwined with the myths of Babylon and Greece. Under the Romans, Mithraism was primarily a secret religious cult for men and enjoyed popularity with the military. Initiations and temples were in underground chambers and caves. Scholars assumed Mithraism came to Rome from Iran, but new research has brought into question the actual source of Roman Mithraism. Very few documents relating to Mithraism in Rome have survived to give us a complete picture of the religion, as many of its inner teachings were reserved for initiates, as in the other mystery schools. Mithraism was eventually overrun by Christianity, since Christianity welcomed all people and actively sought out converts, while Mithraism was a graded initiate system that excluded women, as did many other mystery traditions. The Catholic Church saw Mithraism as a perversion of its holy rituals, but many believe it still adopted some of the outer aspects of Mithraism, including the birth of the savior god on December 25 and the title of "Father" for members of the priesthood.

PERSIAN DUALISM

The classical pagan myths of the Middle East were not the only ones to influence world mysticism and the later ascension paradigm. Some of the most influential but least known religious traditions among modern seekers are the practices of ancient Persia. The dualism of Persia, or old Iran, forming theologies of light versus dark, spiritual versus material, and eventually good versus evil, influenced Zoroastrianism. Zoroaster, or Zarathustra, the legendary prince of the Magi, left a variety of "oracles," or scriptures, reconstructing this dualistic religion of Persia. Credited as the founder of this movement, Zoroaster may not, in fact, be one individual, but several men, with the name Zoroaster attributed as a title to a variety of philosopher-mages.

In Zoroastrianism, the supreme creator, Ahura Mazda, or Ohrmazd, the "wise lord" associated with fire and light, is in conflict with Angra Mainyu, or Ahriman, the "destructive spirit" and ruler of all material things. Though the material world is not inherently evil, as it is a creation of Ahura Mazda, it needs to be purified from the evil influence of Angra Mainyu.

Zoroastrians believe that Asha, or the way of the righteous, is embodied by light or fire, and many services are done in front of a fire. Asha leads to happiness and away from evil. Compassion, equality of the genders, charity, and hard work are basic tenets of the religion. The concepts of heaven and hell are embodied in Zoroastrianism, as it is believed that the soul will be judged by the good and evil performed in life and will ascend into heaven or descend into hell. Reincarnation is not part of traditional Zoroastrian theology, though some branches of the traditions in India have adopted a belief in reincarnation due to exposure to Hinduism. On the final day, evil will be defeated, and those in hell will be purified and rise into heaven.

Though some look back and claim that Zoroastrianism was a monotheistic religion, while others think of it as a more sophisticated version of fire worship, it laid a foundation for many of the dualistic themes in later Judaism, Christianity, and Islam. Zoroastrianism still survives in the world today, particularly in parts of Iran and India. Scholars and mystics speculate that the wise men who visited the newborn Jesus were Zoroastrian magi. Others feel they were Chaldean magi, as Chaldea was an area of the Babylonian empire that was right near Persia. Ancient Persia and the surrounding lands were well-known for their magicians. There was a definite cross-pollination in the beliefs and cultures of Babylon, Persia, and the emerging Jewish and later Christian cultures.

When Zarathustra reformed the Persian mythologies, many gods became part of a hierarchical system of immortals gathered between the two deities Ahura Mazda and Angra Mainyu. Mithras, whose name means "contract" in Persian, became a divine representative of Ahura Mazda in the world, fulfilling the sacred contract between Ahura Mazda and his followers by protecting the righteous from demonic forces. Mithras is associated with the Sun and the growing powers of light, as well as kings and soldiers. He was said to have been physically incarnated in a human body through a virgin mother and ascended into heaven in 208 BC, sixty-four years after his birth. Persian Mithraism is an outgrowth of Zoroastrianism, with the focus of worship on Mithras, though the cult of Mithras in Persia seems very different from the cult of Mithras in the Roman empire. The theologies of Mithras were also absorbed into neighboring Babylon, as many of the figures in Zoroastrian lore became identified with Babylonian gods. Looking at the story of Mithras, it's easy to see similarities to the now better-known story of Jesus.

ROOTS OF THE TREE OF LIFE

The tradition of Judaism was influenced by, and some say also influenced, the teachings of Egypt and Babylon. Abraham, father of the Jewish tradition, was born in Ur of Chaldea. Moses, a great prophet of the Hebrews, was raised in the Egyptian royal court before leading his people out of Egyptian enslavement. The Hebrews were also held in captivity in Babylon, creating opportunities for a rich, mystical melting pot despite the social injustice. The Persian Zoroastrians also had a tremendous influence on Hebrew philosophy.

Hebrew mysticism is embedded in the system known as the Kabbalah, which was primarily an oral tradition embedded in the Jewish texts until it was written about in the *Sepher Yetzirah*, or *Book of Formations*, dating between the third and sixth centuries AD. Though primarily a Jewish system, with possible influences from Egypt and Chaldea, the numerical associations with the creation of the universe have similarities to the neo-Pythagorean teachings.

Modern magicians speculate as to the source of this lore, and wonder if either the practitioners of the magickal traditions of Egypt and Babylon absorbed information from their Jewish captives, or the Jewish rabbis took this foreign lore and embedded it into the Kabbalah. Kabbalah means "to receive," though some say it means "law" or "tradition." According to the writings of most Jewish scholars, the Kabbalah was given to Moses on Mount Sinai when he received the Ten Commandments. Modern magicians state that the angels gave the Kabbalah to Adam in the Garden of Eden. The information most likely came from the tradition known as merkavah mysticism, a form of spirit travel in which the practitioners "mapped" out the spheres of creation, which eventually led to the formation of the Kabbalah and the later Tree of Life glyph.

Although Kabbalistic studies have been an underpinning of the more esoteric branches of Jewish faith, the system branches off into several traditions, sometimes denoted with different spellings, though many teachers and authors are not consistent with the spellings. There remains the primarily Jewish tradition, Kabbalah, traditionally reserved for Jewish men of good standing, over forty years of age, and with a family. The study of the Kabbalah was considered dangerous for those without such grounding.

Another branch fuses Kabbalistic thought with alchemy and Hermetic magick, and is usually spelled Qabalah or Qabala. Primarily a vehicle for ceremonial magicians throughout the ages, many images and symbol systems have been grafted to it, as the system seems able to absorb almost any other symbol system. Qabalah has influenced modern neopaganism because ceremonial magick has influenced the pagan revival.

A third branch of this system fuses Kabbalistic lore with Christianity, creating a Christian Cabala. Central to the mysteries of this line of Cabala are the death and resurrection of Jesus Christ. Historically there has been a great deal of crossover between Cabala and Qabalah, as many medieval magicians were also Christian. Kabbalah, Qabalah, and Cabala all have many similarities in their teachings, making the differences in the traditions difficult to discern.

THE PEOPLE OF THE CROSS

Through the teachings of Jesus of Nazareth, Christianity grew out of the foundation of Judaism. Jesus of Nazareth is seen by Christians as the Messiah, the son of God, who died to redeem the sins of all on Earth, and all to come. He was not recognized as the Messiah by all, as most assumed the anointed one would be a king of military might, not a humble carpenter.

Esotericists see Jesus not as deity incarnate but as a great master, performing miracles others would see as magick. Like a magus, he used simple objects, from bread and water to mud, spit, and fish, as the tools of his magick. He taught in story and parable, reducing the deepest teachings to the simplest of symbols that everyone could understand. Jesus was said to have traveled with at least twelve others, his inner circle, much like a witch's coven or a magician's lodge brothers. He taught his esoteric mysteries to this inner circle of disciples. His primary doctrine was one of love and compassion. To the esotericist, it doesn't matter if Jesus's death and resurrection were literal events. More importantly, his resurrection symbolizes his ascent to a higher level of consciousness. Christian scriptures are really a map to show others the way.

Many await Jesus's second coming, though much like his first coming, nobody agrees on what form it will take, predicting anything from a golden age to apocalyptic doom. If the first time was any indication, his next coming will not be what we expect either.

After the death of Jesus, many early Christians were influenced by a mystic tradition known as Gnosticism. The term Gnostic comes from the Greek word *gnosis*, meaning knowledge. Gnostics seek knowledge of the world through direct mystical experience. Though not all Gnostics were Christian, Gnosticism flourished in the early eras of Christianity and has now become predominantly associated with Christianity.

Gnostic Christians, influenced strongly by Zoroastrianism, believed the creator of the material world, the biblical Yahweh, also known to the Gnostics as the Demiurge, was an evil being, while the god of the Christians was the true God, loving and benevolent but beyond the material world. Through a direct, mystical experience, knowledge of the true God, beyond the material world, would be granted and salvation would be possible. Gnostic Christians differed from what were known as traditional, orthodox Christians. Different sects held different views, but basically worked within similar frameworks. Some looked at the material world and the body as evil, as creations of the Demiurge and prisons from which to escape. This differed from the belief of the Zoroastrians, who saw the world as basically good, as a creation of Ohrmazd but corrupted by Ahriman. Judaism and the Old Testament were rejected, and the serpent in the Garden of Eden was sometimes perceived as a hero, a giver of knowledge. Hierarchy and control were not emphasized, because the personal, mystical revelation was the primary goal of Gnostic worship. Other groups honored women and the role of the divine feminine.

Some paint the early Gnostics as the inheritors of pagan mysticism under the veil of Christian symbolism. There was not one church of Gnostic Christianity, but several different cults, each guided by its own direct experience of God. When the Bible (the New and Old Testaments) was codified into a single book, the most esoteric and unusual Christian texts were left out to suppress the mystical Gnostic Christian teachings. Eventually Gnosticism was replaced with the dominant branches of Christianity, yet the esoteric principle survived in the arts and among the esotericists. One could say that the concepts of ascension and the ascended masters derive their Western roots from Gnosticism and Zoroastrianism. Here we have the first concepts of achieving personal enlightenment to "escape" the material world and "ascend" to a union with the divine. The ones who have successfully used their esoteric knowledge to rise above are the models to follow for those remaining here in the world.

Due to internal disagreements, Christianity branched off into many denominations. The church split into the Western Roman Catholic Church and the Eastern Orthodox Church. The Roman Church underwent further schisms during the Protestant Reformation and its various offshoots. It is interesting to see how many of these branches of Christianity, particularly in the United States, while never being occult, have revived the ecstatic aspects of Gnostic Christianity, through hands-on healing, snake handling, trance work, and speaking in tongues.

For a time, the Celtic Christian Church survived in the British Isles in a form that was very different from the Roman Catholic Church that imported Christianity to the Isles. Some feel that the Celtic brand of Christianity reconciled aspects of Celtic and Celtic-Romano paganism with Christianity. Many ascensionists believe that the Druids, the priest and priestess caste of the Celtic people, recognized the teachings and wisdom of Christianity. Rather than be persecuted by the church, they joined it, transforming it into the Celtic Christian Church as they became priests, brothers, and nuns. Some believe the Holy Grail, as defined by Christian mythology, was brought from the Middle East to the British Isles by Joseph of Arimathea. Although there is no historical evidence, some New Age mystics with a Celtic Christian slant think that in childhood, Jesus visited with the Druids of Europe, learning their mysteries and magick.

The pagan people of Europe, and in particular Britain, didn't easily convert to Christianity, keeping alive pagan festivals, folk magick, and the faery faith. Goddess reverence was transferred to reverence for Mother Mary in both the Celtic and Roman churches. The church had to absorb pagan holidays into the Christian calendar, and went about vilifying pagan godforms, such as the horned god, transforming them into images of the Devil. Still, the practices of the Old Faith survived under the dominion of European Christianity. This folklore provided fertile ground for the rebirth of occultism and paganism in the late nineteenth and early twentieth centuries.

THE POWERS OF THE EAST

In the East, mystical systems were codified in the Vedas, forming the basis of Hinduism. Unlike in the West, there never was a great revolution in which the texts of previous eras were suppressed and burned. Yes, other religions have sprung up in the East and produced various conflicts, but none with the social and political power of the Catholic Church in Europe. The teachings, legends, and metaphysical terminology of India were preserved in various documents and through continuing spiritual traditions of prayer, yoga, and ritual.

Hindu lore has played a huge role in our New Age movement, particularly in our vocabulary. The words chakra, karma, mantra, tantra, yoga, and reincarnation are well-known by Western mystics. If indigenous Western cultures had definitive words for the chakra energy centers, or a word for the concept of karma, they are not well-known to us now. We have adopted the Eastern terms. Hinduism is associated with the five elements of earth, air, water, fire, and the fifth element they call akasha. Hindu knowledge contains lore on astrology, astronomy, the great ages of humanity, the balance of the body, diet, herbs, exercise, sex, and the virtues of gemstones. All these topics are a part of Western esoterics, yet do not stem from any unified system or teaching, save perhaps the Qabalah in its later forms.

Spiritually, Hinduism seems to straddle a line between polytheism and monotheism, stating that the material world is a maya, an illusion, where things are separate. The true reality is that all is one. In sacred Hindu texts and rituals, there is a plethora of gods and spirits, yet an underlying assumption that all is one. This unity through diversity is a key concept adopted by ascensionists. Some see this as a hidden teaching in the pagan mystery schools of Egypt and Greece.

Buddhism began in India in the sixth century BC. It was founded by Siddhartha Gautama, a prince from a northern Indian state who left a home of luxury to discover the nature of suffering. He traveled and practiced with ascetics, though their severe practices provided him with no answers. Eventually he sat beneath a fig tree, determined not to move until he knew the answer to suffering. Mara, the evil one, tempted him with demons, storms, lust, and even the satisfaction of his own ego, but Gautama prevailed. Eventually he did become the "Buddha," meaning "he who is awake." At age thirty-five he awoke to this level of consciousness and began teaching others his philosophy, based on the Four Noble Truths and the Eightfold Path. Buddhism later made its way into China, Tibet, and Japan. Tibetan Buddhism, perhaps more than any other form, has had the greatest influence on ascension practices, as it mingled with the native religion and magick of Tibet. Buddhism in its various forms eventually made it to the Western world and is now even better known due to the visible media presence of the exiled Dalai Lama.

Another religion in China that has influenced New Age mystics is Taoism. The Tao, pronounced "dow," means "the path" or "the way." The founder of Taoism is traditionally believed to be Lao Tzu, a contemporary of Confucius, and Taoism and Confucianism, along with Buddhism, existed side by side as religions of China. The goal of Taoism is to become one with the Tao, the primal force of the universe. In Taoism there is no deity, as in other religions. Problems are resolved through meditation, the movement of personal life energy through esoteric exercises, and the observance and acceptance of the facts of the situation. Taoism has influenced the West through meditation, martial arts, acupuncture, herbalism, and holistic medicine. Both Confucianism and Taoism claim the divination system known as the I Ching. In China, Taoism developed into a system of magick using willow wands, wax dolls, mirrors, geomancy, and special symbols. One of the most

Figure 3: Yin/Yang Symbol

famous symbols of Taoist philosophy is the yin/yang, representing the balance and complementary relationship of opposites (figure 3). When Buddhism arrived in China, it absorbed aspects of Taoism as well. Taoism influenced the development of feng shui. The principles of feng shui have become popular in the Western world, through interior design and decorating, and in the New Age communities, to promote health and good fortune.

THE QUEST FOR THE PHILOSOPHER'S STONE

Alchemy, like ascension, is a paradigm that crosses the borders of both East and West. Alchemy is the art and science of transformation. Though explored in the laboratory paradigm, with chemicals, beakers, and test tubes, the true alchemy was a change of the inner consciousness. Exoteric alchemists were the ancestors of modern-day chemists, but they lost the secret inner teachings of the esoteric alchemists. The outer transformations, most notably the goals of turning lead into gold, healing disease, and becoming immortal, were byproducts, or perhaps simply symbols, of the inner transformation. The lead was said to be the spiritual heaviness that we all experience, the karma of the Eastern traditions. Alchemy transforms our inner consciousness, refining it until it becomes like the incorruptible metal gold. Though the fabled Philosopher's Stone is thought by most to be a synthesized mineral or compound capable of transmuting base metals into gold and granting immortality, it is also an allegory for the inner enlightenment of the alchemist, conferring health, wealth, and happiness on all levels.

The alchemist was capable of unusual chemical feats in the laboratory due to his spiritual qualities rather than any chemical formula. An alchemist of a different spiritual awareness would not achieve the same results, even with the same ingredients, preparations, and conditions, because the most important component, the alchemist himself, would be different. This concept echoes a similar theory found in modern quantum physics. Quantum physicists have discovered that the person observing an experiment can actually affect the outcome of the experiment. Different observers yield different results, just as different alchemists, based on their own level of spiritual consciousness, yield different results.

Modern alchemists trace their mythical lineage to the Emerald Tablet (chart 1), a text attributed to the Egyptian god Thoth. Our term alchemy comes from the name of Egypt, *Khem*, but the practices are universal and are also found in the works of Chinese philosopher Lao Tzu and Islamic scholars. Some believe the Emerald Tablet dates back to the root civilization of Atlantis and was brought to Egypt by Thoth. In fact, many notable figures in both Eastern and Western history are associated with Thoth. Though Thoth is most popularly associated with the Greek Hermes, and his Roman counterpart, Mercury, alchemists also believe that Thoth incarnated as Seth, the son of Adam and Eve; Moses, the prophet; Athothis of Sumer; Imhotep, deified scribe and healer in Egypt; Hiram Ibif, who was the first Hermes according to Masonic tradition; Zoroaster; Enoch of the Old Testament; the Islamic prophet Idris; and Siddhartha Gautama, the Buddha.

Alchemy was not one specific tradition agreed upon by all practitioners. It developed differently in different areas, shaped by the region and culture where it grew. All alchemists shared the desire to understand the divine mysteries through studying nature. Alchemical philosophy included the four basic elements and their corresponding inner properties, as well as three basic principles, described as salt, sulfur, and mercury. To the alchemist, astrology, herbalism, and medicine are interrelated disciplines. The laboratory became both a sanctum and a temple, where prayers were offered and meditation was performed before experiments. The processes of chemical change were also symbols of the inner change of the alchemist, and corresponded with metals, planets, and energy centers within the body. Eventually the lore of the alchemist blended with the growing system of Qabalah, until it became difficult for many to see the two as separate practices. Although modern

The Emerald Tablet

In truth, without deceit, certain, and most veritable.

That which is Below corresponds to that which is Above. And that which is Above corresponds to that which is Below, to accomplish the miracles of the One Thing. And as all things have come from this One Thing, through the meditation of One Mind, so do all created things originate from this One Thing through Transformation.

Its father is the Sun; its mother the Moon. The Wind carries it in its belly; its nurse is the Earth.

It is the origin of All, the consecration of the Universe. Its inherent strength is perfected, if it is turned into Earth.

Separate the Earth from Fire, the Subtle from the Gross, gently and with great Ingenuity. It rises from Earth to Heaven, and descends again to Earth, thereby combining within Itself the powers of both the Above and the Below.

Thus will you obtain the Glory of the Whole Universe. All Obscurity will be clear to you. This is the greatest Force of all powers, because it overcomes every Subtle thing and penetrates every Solid thing.

In this way was the Universe created. From this come many wondrous Applications, because this is the Pattern.

Therefore am I called the Thrice Greatest Hermes, having all three parts of the wisdom of the Whole Universe. Herein have I completely explained the Operation of the Sun.

Chart 1: The Emerald Tablet
(This version found in The Emerald Tablet *by Dennis William Hauck.)*

ascensionists don't usually look to Islam for spiritual inspiration, preferring the traditions of Hinduism, Buddhism, and Christianity, the golden age of Islam highly influenced the mysticism of alchemy, numerology, and sacred geometry.

Alchemy grew to its best-known form in cities of Europe, borrowing from Middle Eastern and Far Eastern lore, until many forgot what the true pursuit of alchemy was, and instead coveted the fabled transformation of lead into gold for the sake of riches. They became known as "puffers." One who truly found the Philosopher's Stone within was a being of ascended consciousness, of great power, and had no real need to amass material wealth. The art of alchemy gave way to the rise of chemistry in the West, and not until the occult revival of the late nineteenth century did anything resembling the true spiritual art of alchemy begin to resurface in popular consciousness.

As we look at each of these spiritual traditions of the ancient world, it is easy to find a thread from each that has been woven into the tapestry of ascension. In the end, all mystical religions seek to answer the same basic questions about life and find the same fundamental truths.

3

THE DAWN OF THE
NEW AGE

People use the term New Age a lot, but aren't really sure what it means or when this age began. The New Age is a general term for the convergence of several ancient calendars and prophecies, marking our entry into the next epoch of human evolution. Many believe this next aeon will be a golden age of peace and enlightenment. In chapter 20 we'll explore these calendars and exactly when the next age is believed to begin, but the New Age movement—the underlying thoughts, paradigms, and wisdom behind this shift of the ages—has already begun. The New Age is really about the old age, taking ancient spiritual principles and making them accessible to the modern world. It is a return to our forgotten roots.

Some think of the late sixties, with our hippie counterculture of free love and esoterics, as the dawn of the New Age movement, but in reality it began much earlier, in the late 1800s, and was stalled only by the coming of the two great world wars.

Four heralds of the New Age appeared in the form of the Spiritualist movement, the Theosophical Society, the Hermetic Order of the Golden Dawn, and Edgar Cayce. They created the dominant currents that would serve as common threads throughout the metaphysical movements of the twentieth century. From these four founts came the nourishment of the Western esoteric systems, creating fertile ground for other seeds of spirituality to grow, eventually becoming the paradigm of ascension. Beyond these four sources, ascensionists have also found inspiration in the mystic traditions of indigenous shamanism, Eastern mysticism, and neopaganism.

THE SEERS OF SPIRITUALISM

The Spiritualist movement grew out of interest in mesmerism, somnambulism, and other psychic movements, though it wasn't formally recognized until the emergence of the famous Fox sisters of the United States in 1848. Truly, though, the origins of Spiritualism can be traced to Emanuel Swedenborg of Sweden, who began his work in 1744. Swedenborg traveled through the spirit world psychically and acted as a translator for spirits, becoming one of our first modern examples of a spiritual medium, or what is more commonly known today as a channel. He wrote many books, but believed they were inspired by the angels and spirits from the other world. He communicated with the spirits of the dead and demonstrated this impressive ability to Queen Louisa Ulrika of Sweden. He published several books at his own expense, as his books were not warmly received at the time of writing and were opposed by the church. Strangely enough, his theology became more codified after his death, when Andrew Jackson Davis began channeling Swendenborg's spirit, allowing Swendenborg to speak through him. Davis gave lectures in trance that were later published as *The Principles of Nature, Her Divine Revelations, and a Voice to Mankind*. We can see the influence of Swedenborg in the New Age concept of humans creating their own heaven or hell through their thoughts and intentions. With his Christian framework, Swedenborg didn't believe in the traditional images of angels and archangels as nonhuman entities, but considered all angels to have once been human.

Spiritualism became well-known in its modern form in 1848 due to the actions of Catherine and Margaretta Fox, of Hydesville, New York. Living with their parents in what was believed to be a haunted house, the sisters devised a system to communicate with a spirit by making "raps" or noises, with specific numbers of raps denoting yes, no, or letters of the alphabet. They were speaking to the spirit of a man whom they later learned had been

murdered by the previous owner of the house. The public found out about this communication, and though some people felt the sisters were frauds, many visited with them,
as other spirits began to communicate through them. Eventually they became mediums
and traveled, practicing their craft. The sisters had their ups and downs. At one point Margaretta renounced Spiritualism, claiming she and her sister were frauds who used "toe
cracking" to create the raps, while Catherine continued to act as a medium with success.
Margaretta later recanted her "confession." The two inspired many with psychic and me-
diumistic skills to pursue their talents, and Spiritualism as a movement began to grow in
the United States and Britain. In 1853 the first Spiritualist church was founded. A variety
of Spiritualist organizations grew from this inspiration. Though the Spiritualist movement
reached its peak in the 1920s, many Spiritualist churches continue to function in the United
States, Britain, and Brazil.

Spiritualists believe in life after death and that the dead can communicate with the living through a medium. Mediums use their gifts to prove to the living that the afterlife
really exists. Some mediums shun contact with the dead in favor of communication with
"higher" entities, guides, and masters who offer advice and messages. Spirits, deceased relatives, and angels guide us in life, whether we know it or not. Though the Spiritualist movement is not explicitly Christian, most of its members come from a Christian background,
and the church structure is based somewhat on the Protestant church, though there is an
openness to other belief systems and cultures. Another Spiritualist belief is that one's soul
can develop and advance through loving God, doing good works, and shunning evil. Spiritual healing, both distance healing and in-person laying-on of hands, is an important aspect
of the tradition. Those with mediumship abilities are called to share them when appropriate. Spiritualism has contributed to the New Age movement, Theosophy in particular, and
the current Spiritualist churches have in turn been influenced by Theosophy.

THE RISE OF THEOSOPHY

The Theosophical Society was founded in New York City in 1875 by three unusual indi-
viduals: Madame Helena Petrovna Blavatsky, known as HPB, a mystic of Russian descent;
Colonel Henry Steel Olcott, an American lawyer and government official; and William Q.
Judge, also an American attorney. Theosophy comes from two Greek words: *theo*, meaning
God, and *sophia*, meaning wisdom. Sophia has a connotation of feminine wisdom. Bla-
vatsky was the main mystic and author influencing the budding Theosophical movement,

with her seminal works *Isis Unveiled* and *The Secret Doctrine*. The feminine aspect was honored, as by the very title of *Isis Unveiled*, named after the most popular Egyptian goddess. An avid world traveler and mystic influenced by modern Spiritualism and mediumship, Blavatsky, with the aid of Olcott and Judge, used these gifts as the path of Theosophy unfolded before her.

Blavatsky claimed that Theosophy had roots into the third century AD, though she offered little proof of a literal direct connection to any historical organization. In Theosophy, Blavatsky sought to reconcile the doctrines of the East and West, and she felt that earlier civilizations, such as the those of the ancient Egyptians and Greeks, as well as the Hindus and Tibetans, had a much better understanding of spirituality. She believed the true root of the world's religions came from a single source. Many of our classic New Age terms, borrowed from Hinduism, were made popular in Western metaphysical circles by Blavatsky.

HPB claimed to have been taught by the "masters," ascended beings from a brotherhood that guarded and guided humanity's evolution and spiritual progression. From her writings it is unclear if these masters were fully incarnate in a body, discarnate (existing in the spiritual worlds), or able to traverse both states at will. The concept of such a "brotherhood," as it was known then, was an extension of the Rosicrucian concept of a spiritual brotherhood. Blavatsky believed that by aligning with this spiritual hierarchy of masters, one could become closer to the Creator and understand the enfoldment of the universe through vast cycles of time. She was a vocal critic of Darwin's theory of evolution, though many don't see that her argument was one of spirit, not of genetics. She believed that we, as spiritual beings, descended into matter, and did not evolve from apes. Our bodies may have evolved from the animal kingdom, but our spirits did not. Our bodies are simply the vehicles for our spirits.

Through the masters, Blavatsky expounded on some advanced esoteric concepts, though she also became mired in charges of scandal and fraud. Her texts are brilliant, albeit dense, and she is not often given the credit she is due. Some think that she, like many other occultists, purposely wrote in a obscure manner to prevent all but the most devout seekers from understanding her writings. Many feel that she was a fraud and plagiarist, while others see any potential fraudulent activity on her part as either a joke or a means to separate those looking for stage-show mediumship tricks from those seeking true spiritual knowledge. The Theosophical Society continues today, although it, too, has had its share of scandals and splinter groups.

Alice Bailey is the next notable voice of the masters of Theosophy. She began her spiritual journey at age fifteen, when she "met" an ascended master, Kuthumi, who psychically materialized before her and told her they had much work to do, after she had proven herself to him. Before this, Bailey's experiences had fallen well within the norms of her Christian upbringing, without any exposure to Eastern customs of spirituality. She was more startled by Kuthumi's turban than by his sudden appearance to her alone in her home, as she had never seen a man in a turban before that day.

It wasn't until after some time spent in India and a failed marriage that Bailey received a second vision from Kuthumi. In 1917 she was introduced to students of H. P. Blavatsky and joined the Theosophical Society. In 1919 she received contact from the ascended master Djwal Khul, whom she referred to as "the Tibetan." He indicated that he wished to write books through her. Djwal Khul appeared in Blavatsky's teachings. Though she was initially reluctant to pursue this telepathic contact, Bailey received from Djwal Khul a method to contact "her" master, Kuthumi, who assured her this contact with Djwal Khul was safe, and suggested that D. K., as Djwal Khul is sometimes known, contact Bailey directly for this work. Together, through a method we would now call conscious channeling, they wrote numerous books, including *A Treatise on White Magic*. Written at a time when the concept of magick was not taken seriously, or inspired fear, these works provided another link between the Theosophical current and the traditions of ritual magicians. These books were inspired by the masters, much as had been the case with Blavatsky, though it was clearer with Bailey that these were nonphysical masters appearing to her in vivid psychic visions. She always saw herself as a sort of "psychic secretary," taking no credit for the complex esoteric systems involving psychology, astrology, and healing that developed from these sessions, though she did write six books on her own.

The Theosophists and Bailey eventually parted ways, though the Theosophical teachings continued to play a pivotal role in her work. Alice Bailey is credited as the first to coin the term the "New Age" for the coming Age of Aquarius, though there is also a Freemason journal and a London newspaper both bearing the title *New Age*.

Bailey's work further explored the Theosophical concept of the masters, along with the science of the seven rays, adding both a Tibetan Buddhist bent to the material (as Djwal Khul was associated with the Tibetan Buddhist religion in his last physical incarnation) and a Christian slant (as Bailey came from a Christian background). Though her teachings are a far cry from authentic Tibetan Buddhism, the Eastern slant merged with her Christian background, as Christ played a pivotal role in her cosmology. In 1923 Bailey founded the Arcane School, dedicated to teaching these spiritual truths and helping individuals evolve. Her work is perpetuated today through the Lucis Trust and through many individual study groups dedicated to unlocking the secrets of these teachings.

The Theosophical current of the masters has continued through various teachers and channels. The most notable was the "I AM" movement of Guy W. Ballard and Edna Ballard. Guy reported that he had "met" the ascended master Saint Germain while hiking Mount Shasta in California. Most assume that this was a profound psychic meeting, like Bailey's first experience with Kuthumi. Germain had explained that he was searching for a person to receive his teachings, and had chosen Guy. Through several meetings, Germain taught Guy and Edna, who later established the I AM Religious Activity, the Saint Germain Press, and the Saint Germain Foundation in 1932. Under the name Godfre Ray King, they also wrote several books, including *Unveiled Mysteries* and *The Magic Presence*. They also published supplemental materials, including the *I AM Discourses*, a series of lectures by Saint Germain channeled through Guy. The Ballards began teaching this material publicly.

The I AM movement was said to be a direct reaction from the spiritual hierarchy of masters to counterbalance the complex esoterics of the Theosophy of Blavatsky and Bailey. The tone of the material was much simpler yet still profound. An emphasis was placed on Jesus as well as Germain, and Christianity. During his time with Germain, Guy learned that he was George Washington in a past life, and emphasized both America's value in the world and its role in the coming New Age. Patriotism was encouraged. A key teaching of the I AM movement is the use of the violet flame (associated with Saint Germain) to transmute unwanted energies, heal, and protect.

Like many peers and others before them, the Ballards were plagued with difficulties. When Guy died in 1939, after teaching that ascension meant that one would not die a physical death but instead would ascend into heaven, Edna announced to their students that Guy had ascended even though he had experienced an apparently typical physical death. Once the news became public, many students became disillusioned and left the organization. Edna continued on and began to channel both Germain and Guy. Students filed lawsuits for fraud, but the convictions were overturned, and in 1957 the U.S. government granted the I AM movement tax-exempt status, like any other formal religion. Although Edna died in 1971, the movement continues, as control was passed to a board of directors with operations in Illinois and Colorado.

In England in 1936, Grace Cooke founded the White Eagle Lodge, a nondenominational Christian church, on the advice of her spirit guide White Eagle. The channelings, books, and tapes of White Eagle and the lodge caused a major shift in our perception of the "masters" first made popular by Theosophy. White Eagle was a part of the Theosophical brotherhood. Now we had an image of an ascended mystic not from an Eastern or European background, but a Native American one. He espoused a doctrine of the universal Father, Mother, and Son, and taught that healing was a primary concern to the lodge. White Eagle's teachings included many nature-based ideas along with Christian and Eastern lore. His work is known primarily for the teaching that life is governed by five cosmic laws: reincarnation, karma, opportunity, correspondence, and equilibrium and balance.

Rudolf Steiner broke away from the Theosophical movement, yet retained many of its principles. Steiner was the secretary of the German branch of the Theosophical Society from 1902 until 1912, but left to form the Anthroposophical Society. He absorbed much of the esoterics and Eastern lore of Theosophy, including beliefs in Atlantis and psychic ability, but felt that Christianity should have a more prominent place in its worldview. He also believed that the Theosophical Society had entered a period of scandal and disrepute.

Steiner was the author of several books, including *The Philosophy of Spiritual Activity*, *Occult Science: An Outline*, *Investigations in Occultism*, and *How to Know Higher Worlds*. He felt that Anthroposophy was a spiritual science, and used this spiritual science to transcend aspects of the material world, to gain insight into life, nature, and children in particular. He is best known for his controversial contribution to children's education through the establishment of the Steiner schools, also known as Waldorf schools, with a curriculum designed around the stages of a child's spiritual development. Steiner has also been controversial due to an unsubstantiated link to magician Aleister Crowley and his organization of sex magicians, the O.T.O., or Ordo Templi Orientis, with some people believing that Steiner was secretly a grand master of the O.T.O.

Other authors and teachers who have continued the traditions started in Theosophy include Mark and Elizabeth Clare Prophet, founders of the Church Universal and Triumphant and authors of numerous book about and inspired by the masters. They too had a strong connection with Saint Germain, as well as many other masters. Dr. Joshua David Stone created a very popular series of ascension handbooks. Stone believed that Blavatsky's work was the first wave of information released to the public by the masters. The second was the work of both Bailey and the Ballards. He considered his work the third dissemination of teachings from the masters, though most of his work is a synthesis of many other systems and teachings into a harmonious yet sometimes inelegant whole, rather than brand-new revelations and systems. Unlike the writing of Blavatsky and Bailey, and other previous teachers, Stone's work is far more accessible to the general public and considered a great place to start in ascension study, as he distills the teachings of the masters into a more comprehensible form, in plain, easy-to-understand language.

THE LIGHT OF THE GOLDEN DAWN

The Hermetic Order of the Golden Dawn was by far the most influential organization in the revival of Western magick. The focus of the group was on the Great Work, what might be considered enlightenment or ascension, through the study and application of the Qabalah, tarot, alchemy, psychic development, and magickal ritual.

The group was brought together by a work known as the Cipher manuscript, discovered by Rev. A.F.A. Woodford, a Mason and member of the Hermetic Society. Though the manuscript was believed to be from antiquity, modern critics now consider it to be a forgery. Woodford sent pages of it to Dr. William Wynn Westcott and Dr. William Robert Woodman, officers in the Rosicrucian Society of England. Later, Westcott consulted with Samuel Liddell MacGregor Mathers and his clairvoyant wife, Moina. A letter with the manuscript said anyone deciphering it should contact a "Fräulein Anna Sprengel in Hanover, Germany." Westcott did so, and claimed Sprengel gave him permission to establish a branch of the "Rosicrucian Order of England." Together this group of budding magicians founded the Isis-Urania Temple of the Hermetic Order of the Golden Dawn in 1888. They soon attracted a following, and membership included William Butler Yeats, Arthur Edward Waite, Florence Farr, Dion Fortune, and Aleister Crowley.

The group reconstructed rituals with imagery from Jewish, Christian, Eastern, and pagan sources, synthesizing common elements to create a harmonious though complex whole. The magicians of the Golden Dawn drew upon medieval manuscripts and the works of previous magicians, including Eliphas Levi, Cornelius Agrippa, and Francis Barrett, and revived the Enochian magick first received by John Dee and Edward Kelley.

Mathers claimed to be in contact with the "Secret Chiefs," which some believe was a reference to the order's invisible or ascended masters guiding the group, much like Blavatsky's ascended masters guiding Theosophy. In fact, many would argue that the two terms ascended masters and Secret Chiefs describe the same group of beings operating in different spiritual traditions. Mathers stated that the Secret Chiefs named him the "Visible Head of the Order." Like the Theosophists, the members of the Golden Dawn also believed that inner-plane adepts guided their tradition.

The Golden Dawn was riddled with internal conflict and eventually dissolved into splinter groups, but its members left a body of lore and a magickal influence (what some magicians call a "current") on both the material and spiritual planes that subsequent aspiring magicians have tapped into for their own practices. Though much of the material was meant to be kept secret, it was eventually made available to the public, most notably by magician and author Israel Regardie.

The most famous breakaway from the Golden Dawn was the controversial figure Aleister Crowley. He rose quickly through the ranks of the Golden Dawn as the protégé of Mathers, but the two had a rather spectacular falling-out punctuated by magickal battles where each would send spirits to attack the other. After his expulsion from the Golden Dawn, Crowley dove into Eastern mysticism. His most famous contribution to the magickal world was the formation of Thelema, his own religion. Though he didn't set out to create a new religion and spiritual paradigm, he found himself as the prophet of the New Aeon. During a trip to Egypt, his first wife, Rose Kelly, received messages from the Egyptian god Horus, though she had no real background in Egyptian myth or mediumship. At first, Crowley did not quite believe her, but upon questioning her, he felt something of importance was truly happening. While in the Great Pyramid, he received and transcribed *Liber AL vel Legis*, or *The Book of the Law*. This text is the foundation of Thelema and is said to hold the spiritual principle of the next age, based on *thelema*, the Greek word for will. This magickal system is one of finding and enacting your divine will.

Crowley wrote many volumes of magick, magickal plays, and some fiction as well, exposing the rituals of the Golden Dawn and adapting them to the Thelemic practice. One of his most famous works is *Magick in Theory and Practice*, considered a classic among ceremonial magicians around the world. Crowley made the spelling magick (versus magic) more popular in the ceremonial and pagan world, to differentiate it from sideshow magic and stage illusion. His view on the tarot is encoded in *The Book of Thoth*, and he created the Thoth tarot with artist Frieda Harris. His later years were plagued with difficulties, but his work has endured as an inspiration to modern practitioners.

Crowley played up his image as the "wickedest man in the world." The people of the Victorian era didn't understand the depths of his explorations of consciousness, going beyond the boundaries of polite society, much like a tribal shaman living on the outside of the village, not understood by the typical villager. Crowley was bisexual, indulged in drug use (though in his era many substances considered drugs to us today were commonly prescribed pharmaceuticals), and practiced sex magick. He became involved with the Ordo

Templi Orientis (O.T.O.), an occult order of sex magicians, and eventually became their head in 1922, leaving his mark on the order forever. Regardless of reports, Crowley never was a Satanist, nor would he have thought of himself as a Satanist. Though often cited as a "black magician," Crowley actually saw himself as an agent of the Great White Brotherhood, another term for the ascended masters, working for the greater good and devoted to the Great Work.

Dion Fortune was one of the most influential occultists to come out of the Golden Dawn. Born to Christian Scientist parents and named Violet Mary Firth, she chose her magickal name and motto, *Deo, non fortuna*, meaning "By God, not chance," creating the magickal name Dion Fortune. She studied psychology and eventually joined the Golden Dawn, and then left to form the Fraternity of the Inner Light, which is now known as the Society of the Inner Light. She wrote esoteric texts, such as *The Mystical Qabalah*, as well as fiction with a metaphysical and occult bent, such as *The Sea Priestess* and *The Goat-Foot God*, teaching metaphysical principles through story. Like Theosophy and Thelema, the tradition of Fortune, too, includes a belief in the invisible chiefs and hidden masters. While both the Theosophists and Crowley mixed Eastern and Western mysticism, Fortune was firmly rooted in the Western mysteries and Christianity. She brought together the mysteries of the British Isles (the Grail and the Round Table) with Christianity and Atlantis. She mixed Goddess reverence and European myth with Christian mysticism and magick. Mediums of the Society of the Inner Light have channeled her as a guide and aid. Fortune's last book, *Moon Magic*, was incomplete as of her death on January 8, 1946, but a medium channeled the last section of it, as Fortune dictated it, with no apparent differences in style from the sections she had written in life.

The magick of the Hermetic ceremonial magicians continued onward, inspired by both the Golden Dawn and the Thelemic branches and drawing upon other cultures and manuscripts for inspiration. Some work in the avant-garde Chaos magick paradigm. Others have focused on the magick reportedly practiced by King Solomon. Several branches focus on the work of angels and archangels. Many forms of what claim to be purely Rosicrucian philosophy have surfaced. Ceremonial magick is a very broad practice, but those drawing from the Golden Dawn styles of ceremonial magick place an emphasis on the Great Work—communion and eventual union with the divine Creator.

THE SLEEPING PROPHET

Edgar Cayce is known as the "sleeping prophet." Born in 1877, he had no apparent interest in healing or the metaphysical world, but due to persistent throat issues in his early twenties that defied conventional treatment, he sought the aid of a hypnotist. In one session he learned to diagnose the affliction and prescribe a cure, which worked. With this success, the hypnotherapist suggested he do the same for others in trance, and Cayce reluctantly began readings for people on medical issues, even though he had no background or education in medicine. He could name specific physiological and medical conditions, which astounded others. Eventually his talents became well-known, and many sought him out. In 1911 his readings took a turn, when he attributed an illness to a karmic influence. In his readings he eventually drew in past-life information, as well as unusual information on the ancient civilizations of Atlantis and Lemuria. Cayce was from a traditional Christian background and had no education in such topics, but eventually he came to believe in past lives. He formed the Association for Research and Enlightenment (A.R.E.) in 1931. His readings became more prophetic, including information on the rise of Atlantis, the Second Coming of Christ, and cataclysmic Earth changes. His cases continue to be studied and combed for wisdom and information, and several books have been compiled on his healing techniques, remedies, prophecies, and knowledge of Atlantis.

EASTERN EXPLOSION

The rise of Theosophy and Hermetic magick encouraged the introduction of more esoteric lore in the modern Western world. Over the next century we saw an influx of yoga, Buddhism, Zen, and martial arts into Western society. The practice of Chinese medicine and Indian medicine (Ayurveda), as well as a variety of energetic healing techniques such as Reiki, coming from Japanese Buddhism, made their way to Western shores.

Spiritual seekers, feeling bereft of personal experience and meaning due to the dominance of dogmatic religions, turned to the exotic traditions from the East for fulfillment. Because of the strong health benefits of martial arts and yoga, many adherents don't even realize they are pursuing something with a spiritual root. The principles of health are inherent in the tradition, and are not a religion. They represent a way of life. You don't have to convert to Hinduism to practice yoga. You need only to practice yoga, and you will start to integrate yogic philosophy into your life, without even realizing it.

Paramahansa Yogananda, while not considered to be radically New Age, brought many of the teachings of the East into easy grasp of Western people. He founded the Self-Realization Fellowship in 1920, and was a pioneer of yoga in the West, bringing Kriya yoga to America and beyond. His emphasis on "mission" and service to humankind was strikingly powerful, as was his recognition of the common themes underlying all world religions. Through his techniques, he encouraged direct, personal contact with the divine. His own journey to experience the divine was chronicled in his book *Autobiography of a Yogi*, published in 1946. Because of his belief in the universality of all world religions and in the importance of seeking a direct experience with God, Yogananda is particularly important in the history of ascension, as those are two aims of the ascension movement.

Unfortunately, many Westerners have taken some Eastern concepts and misinterpreted them by looking at the teachings through the lens of Western culture. The concept of karma often gets fused with a sense of Christian morality and divine retribution. The concept of *dharma*, or true purpose, is usually left out of the equation. Other people have looked at certain energy centers, or *chakras*, as "good" or "spiritual," while considering the lower ones to be of lesser value, even though all are necessary components of the system. Others use Eastern teaching to encourage the psychic powers, known as *siddhis*, even though in such teachings the siddhis are not a goal unto themselves but a side effect of spiritual advancement. The siddhis can be distractions on the path to enlightenment if one focuses on them. Now, hopefully, Western spiritual seekers will delve more deeply into the lore and culture of these teachings, to fully understand their depth and significance.

GOING NATIVE

The search for a meaningful, personal spirituality didn't end with the influx of East mysticism. Western practitioners, particularly those in the United States, sought out the spiritual lore of the people indigenous to the land on which they now lived. Spiritual seekers sought out Native American medicine people. The rituals and customs of Native people, in an Earth-based tradition, became prime ways for seekers to experience divinity directly. Through nature, the Earth, and animals, people experienced their own divinity. The term shaman technically applies to those of the Siberian tribes, and their genetic relatives. Soon the term was being used not for a specific tradition but for a set of techniques and general ideas found in many cultures. Anthropologists and seekers alike applied the term to many different cultures.

The shamanic traditions, of not only North America but those across the world, became a focus, as shamanism is a form of healing not only the body but the spirit, and the spirit is what ails most modern people. Shamanism as a holistic model of healing teaches that there is a partnership between the spirit world and the physical world. Both must be in balance to have harmony.

The study of shamanism became vogue, particularly starting in the sixties, as the concept of exploring a nonphysical reality went hand in hand with the use of psychedelics. The magickal reality of the shaman and the world of the spirit complemented more martial explorations of the body and ascetic practices of the East. Despite some criticism from the Native community, certain teachers, such as Sun Bear, made Native teachings available to the public at large.

In 1968, Carlos Castaneda printed his first book, *The Teachings of Don Juan: A Yaqui Way of Knowledge*, based on his apprenticeship with a Yaqui sorcerer while in Mexico. The book was both his master's thesis and an underground bestseller, introducing many to the concept of a non-ordinary, or extraordinary, reality underlying what we all accept to be physical reality. He also talked frankly about the use of plant hallucinogens in his spiritual work. Critics claim that there was no Don Juan, and there is a question as to whether the books are fact, fiction, or something in between.

Another white Westerner, Lynn V. Andrews, was led into an initiatory experience in the Sisterhood of the Shields, a secret medicine society of forty-four female shamans from many different tribes. Through a journey after her divorce, she found herself in contact with Native teachers, experiencing trials, tests, and healing, as chronicled in her books, including *Medicine Woman*, released in 1981. She was told to be a bridge between the tribal cultures and the industrial world, to help reinstate the feminine consciousness and heal the Earth. Andrews teaches workshops and seminars. She too has received much criticism from Native Americans due to certain factual and linguistic inaccuracies, yet she stands by her accounts and teachings.

Eventually, the techniques for entering altered states of consciousness and communing with the spirits used by shamans worldwide were separated from the cultural religious rituals of indigenous people. The techniques themselves became known as core shamanism and, divorced from their tribal religions, became accessible to many "modern" people in the West because they could practice these techniques without leaving their own religion. Seekers started to explore their own ancestry, and apply the term shaman to it, creating such interesting disciplines as Celtic shamanism and Norse shamanism. Core shamanism safely introduced the spiritual practices of indigenous cultures to the Western world. Michael Harner, founder of the Foundation for Shamanic Studies and author of *The Way of the Shaman*, was pivotal in introducing the concepts of core shamanism and encouraging modern Westerners to apply these techniques to healing and problem solving in everyday life. Unlike Castaneda, who focused more on the warrior aspect, Harner focuses on healing both the self and others.

Elders in traditions of North America, as well as those in the Aztec, Mayan, and Peruvian shamanic traditions, have come forward, teaching their prophecies, rituals, and healing techniques to those outside of their culture, to bring healing to the world.

THE NEOPAGAN RENAISSANCE

The practices of the pre-Christian cultures of Europe experienced a resurgence, similar to the revival of shamanic techniques. Although first brought to light through more scholarly works, such as Margaret Murray's *The Witch-Cult in Western Europe*, and through thinly veiled fiction, the practice now known as Wicca made its public debut, most notably in the form of a man named Gerald Gardner in the 1950s. Even with the public appearance of Gardner and his contemporaries, it wasn't until the 1970s and 1980s that Wiccan spirituality became widespread.

Wicca, a revival of the religion of witchcraft, has its basis in the ancient mysteries of the Greeks, Romans, Norse, and Celts. In fact, many believe the ancestors of Wiccan practitioners can be found in the Stone Age shamans of Europe and the Middle East. From these cultures grew the ancient civilizations and their mystery schools. Though much of the traditional oral lore associated with witchcraft is believed to have been lost through the persecutions by the church, modern Wiccans draw upon the rituals of ceremonial magicians, in the style of the Golden Dawn and Thelema, to supplement their ritual texts and materials, usually omitting the Judeo-Christian references, as the members of the Golden Dawn were drawing upon similar European cultural roots.

Wiccans see divinity as having both masculine and feminine, or God and Goddess, aspects. The popularity of Wicca gave rise to the neopagan movement, a broad group of practitioners reclaiming the nature-based spiritual traditions of Europe, as the Latin *paganus* roughly translates to "country dweller" or "of the land." Pagan eventually became a term to describe rural practitioners of the old religion in early Christian times, since Christianity first gained popularity in the urban centers. Wicca, or modern witchcraft, is a subset of paganism, much as the Catholic religion is a subset of Christianity. There are specific traditions and lineages within Wicca, much like the different orders of priests, brothers, and nuns in the Catholic Church. Gardnerian Wicca, named for Gerald Gardner, is one of the best-known Wiccan traditions.

With the widespread publication of books and training manuals, Wicca grew from the more formal hierarchical traditions to freeform eclectic practices. The image of the divine as both God and Goddess, with a particular emphasis on the Goddess, combined with controversial archaeological evidence supporting the belief in Stone Age matriarchal civilizations, marrying the old religion with the upsurge in feminist spirituality. Some traditions focused primarily on Goddess reverence and the divine feminine. Many continued as Wiccans, while others cast off that name. There was an even greater return to freeform ritual and non-hierarchical leadership. At times, political, social, and environmental activism blended with this growing spiritual tradition, as in the work of Starhawk, author of many books, including the influential *The Spiral Dance*. Others focused on a personal and eclectic practice of the craft, as in the work of Scott Cunningham, best known for his book *Wicca: A Guide for the Solitary Practitioner.*

More recent scholarship has discredited many of Margaret Murray's ideas, and called into question the ancient roots claimed by Gardner and the traditional "history" taught to most Wiccan initiates. Still, it's easy to see the influence of witchcraft (and the image of the witch) throughout history, regardless of what it has been called or whether a specific lineage has remained intact. Modern seekers have reconstructed the tradition from these ancient cornerstones, adding liberally from many other sources, yet there is something distinctive about witchcraft that continues to draw people to its practice.

Though a lot of the metaphysical ideas of Wicca, paganism, and Goddess worship have crossed over into the general metaphysical community, nicely accenting material in the shamanic and Eastern traditions, misunderstandings about the true nature of these Earth-reverent practices have prevented many in the ascension movement from truly recognizing them. Still, we can see the influence of modern witchcraft and ceremonial magick on ascension practitioners in their discussions of the faery realm, mythical beings, and elemental entities.

mainstream metaphysics

While most of our ascension lore comes from ancient esoteric systems, many ascensionists look for inspiration in the academic world. The ideas from this realm are no less powerful, yet the environment from which they come lends them a credibility to be absorbed by the mainstream society as potential truths. These new strands of information are coming from the more respected segments of society. Our other strands come from those the mainstream might consider a little wacky. When those who aspire to be modern-day witches, shamans, magicians, and yogis attempt to share and explain ancient truths, most people take their teachings with a grain of salt, if at all. But when similar truths are couched in the terminology of academia, spouted by people who are well respected in traditional institutions, then the information is given more weight.

The weight of mainstream science actually helped me come to accept the spirituality of the New Age. I started as a skeptic, wanting to disprove psychic ability and magick. Thankfully, my first teachers were heavily involved in the science of metaphysics, comparing the principles of magick with the principles of what at the time was considered the most cutting-edge thought in science—quantum physics. Through an understanding of quantum physics, I came to believe in the possibility of psychic phenomena. The weight of the academic world, with its emphasis on critical thinking and controlled laboratory experiments, was more persuasive to me than the wisdom of the ancient sages. Once I let my skeptical mind entertain the possibilities, I began to have firsthand experiences that were quite powerful. After my first experience with psychic healing, I became a believer, exploring the frontiers of psychic ability. Only then was I able to go back to the timeless wisdom of the ancient sages and realize that they were stating the same facts as the quantum physicist, but in a more artistic, elegant, and timeless fashion.

A major shift in the scientific paradigm was the concept that the observer of a phenomenon was just as critical to the outcome of the experiment as all the "controlled factors" of the experiment. Previously in science, we believed that we could observe something and have no effect on the outcome. By isolating all the factors under laboratory conditions, we thought that we could screen out all other influences.

Through quantum physics, scientists came to the conclusion that the observer affects the outcome of an experiment on the level of the *quantum*, the smallest discrete bundle of energy that can be measured, where energy can sometimes be observed as particles and other times as waves. Previously, energy was considered to be only a particle or only a wave, but not both, depending on the observer. This new fluidity in the perception of energy changed everything. If our observation can affect things on such a tiny scale, then it can possibly influence all events.

The interconnection of all things became an emphasis for those scientists exploring the frontiers of physics. Holographic models of the universe, in which reality is simply a constructed image based on how we process information, became an alternative to previously accepted scientific models, echoing the Hindu teachings on the *maya*, or the illusion of reality in which we all seem separate yet are all one. Similar teachings are found in Hermetic magick and tribal beliefs. This was a major paradigm shift from the mechanistic, scientific view of life, in which each of us was seen as a discrete part of the mechanical whole, like a cog in a clock, rather than a holistic part of the universe, affecting everything else in the system.

The development of quantum theory began in the early 1900s through the work of six scientists: Niels Bohr, Paul Dirac, Albert Einstein, Werner Heisenberg, Max Planck, and Erwin Schrödinger. They were not seeking to create a new form of physics, but to find explanations for odd results of experiments that did not conform to the laws of traditional physics. New scientific paradigms were explored, looking at how life, consciousness, brain function, memory, and reality are all connected. In his 1980 book *Wholeness and the Implicate Order*, quantum physicist David Bohm proposed the most comprehensive theories on the holographic nature of the universe. Since then, other theories of the universe have been proposed, continuing to explore the interface of our consciousness with reality.

On another academic front, we have the highly influential work of Joseph Campbell. A scholar inspired by his childhood fascination with Native American and primal cultures, Campbell not only pioneered a new and insightful way of looking at myth and art through his numerous books, but brought his work to the public in a new way, through a series of PBS shows with Bill Moyers called *Joseph Campbell and the Power of Myth*. He became an intellectual who embraced the experience of spirituality through art, and was able to explain it to the general public, those without his intellectual background. In particular, Campbell compared many cross-cultural myths and stories, showing similarities in basic story cycles. His book *The Hero with a Thousand Faces* is a well-known classic. His ability to synthesize mythology from all around the world has had a great impact on modern seekers looking to decode the myths of the past as potential road maps for the future. Though his work is not discussed frequently in metaphysical circles, Joseph Campbell made a great contribution to the New Age community that cannot be overlooked.

On the religious front, Matthew Fox is another great contributor to our new paradigms, particularly through his visionary and controversial reconciliation of many Christian views with Earth-based and personal mystical spirituality. He is a theologian with master's degrees in both philosophy and theology from Aquinas Institute of Theology and a doctorate in spirituality from the Institut Catholiques de Paris. He was dismissed from the Dominican Order and later received by the Episcopal Church.

Fox is the founder and president of the University of Creation Spirituality in Oakland, California, and the author of many books on spirituality. His work, and the work of Creation Spirituality, integrates Hebrew and Christian spirituality with the wisdom of tribal societies, women's wisdom, medieval mysticism, ecological and social justice, art, and science. Fox has re-created forms of worship and ritual, emphasizing the Cosmic Christ principle, as well as the Goddess force, through the Cosmic Mass, or Techno-Cosmic Mass. In 1983 he partnered with Barbara Hand Clow and Gerry Clow to form the influential publishing imprint Bear & Company, specializing in alternative health and Creation Spirituality. His best-known book is *Original Blessing: A Primer in Creation Spirituality*.

Some basic tenets of Creation Spirituality include the belief that the universe (and everything in it) is a blessing, and we are all capable of relating to and interacting with it. We are all mystics. We are all prophets. We are all divine. We are all artists, and each of us must seek our true self. All of these tenets, in essence, are accepted by those following the path of ascension.

As these mystical and esoteric tenets make their way into mainstream consciousness via the more academic paths, they are eventually absorbed by pop culture. Actress Shirley MacLaine brought many of the New Age concepts to the mainstream through her 1983 book *Out on a Limb*. Though known primarily as an actress, through this book and the subsequent movie, she shared her experiences with the paranormal, soul mates, channeling, reincarnation, extraterrestrials, and spiritual teachers. For most of America, it was the first time such concepts had been openly discussed. She received a lot of ridicule for it from the mainstream media and society in general, but stood in her truth and continued to write. Recently, she released a book titled *The Camino*, a narrative of her explorations in Spain walking along an Earth energy line—known as the Camino—that stimulates spiritual awareness. She continues to be controversial, yet acclaimed. The works of Deepak Chopra, Jane Roberts, Brian L. Weiss, Ram Dass, James Redfield, Gary Zuvak, Wayne Dyer, and Caroline Myss have all helped bring spiritual concepts to a wider mainstream audience.

THE CUSP OF THE NEW AGE

Soon these varying strands of wisdom congealed into the overall metaphysical community labeled "New Age." Along with these broader spiritual traditions, a variety of practices and ideas have been added into the mix. Metaphysical sciences such as astrology and crystal healing, associated with the ancient world's magickal traditions, became part of the movement. Tarot cards, also popularized by modern magickal traditions such as the Golden Dawn, continue to experience popularity. The chakra system, which was originally Hindu, has been expanded, revised, and adapted by Western practitioners and has become a foundation stone of most magickal traditions. Other types of Eastern lore, from yoga and acupuncture to feng shui, have surged into the Western seeker's world. Herbalism, homeopathy, and natural healing have also become part of the New Age paradigm, due to their association with shamans, magickal traditions, and alchemy, and due to traditional science's failure to address the mind-body-spirit connection. With inspirational writings, channeling, and new metaphysical research, new paradigms have been added to the New Age, building upon and refocusing the ancient wisdom.

The New Age community has no consensus of beliefs. There is no one central authority. There is no New Age "pope," though many claim to be a world guru, world teacher, or enlightened master and believe that their way should be followed exclusively. New Age lore is a collection of theories, beliefs, and traditions under the umbrella of world wisdom. Explorers can focus on any given set of principles, and can ignore any other set. There is a wide range of beliefs, rooted in all the traditions discussed, so many practitioners of New Age spirituality are not well versed in the diverse beliefs that fall under the banner of New Age. Above all, those in the New Age community—from those who peruse the shelf in the local bookstore to those who attend workshops and book clubs—are seeking to move beyond traditional religions and into a personal spirituality that prepares them for the shift to the next age.

Ascension-based spirituality is a smaller sect within the New Age community. While many New Agers are seekers and explorers, tasting a variety of different traditions, most ascensionists are focused on the process of enlightenment, of ascension, or the Great Work, to embody their divine purpose here in the world. A big part of this process is service, including public and spiritual service to the greater community, emulating the example of the ascended masters. Many people take on the role of healer, ritual leader, or teacher, formally or informally. Ascension practitioners work to awaken others to the spiritual realities existing side by side with the material reality. Sometimes the most important teaching a person can give others occurs not in the classroom or workshop but through example, by modeling a healthy, balanced, spiritual life. As the ascended masters light the way for us, we too become beacons on the path, to light the way for others to come. We create a reciprocal chain of beings, each helping others and in turn receiving help on the spiritual path.

PART TWO

ASCENSION COSMOLOGY

4

PRINCIPLES OF ASCENSION

W hat do ascensionists believe? That's a good question, and one I often asked at the workshops and community gatherings I attended when I started on this path. First of all, there really is no formal ascensionist organization. *Ascensionist* is an umbrella label I like to use for those in the New Age who believe in the concepts and ideals of ascension, even if they don't agree exactly on what those concepts and ideals are. Though many people use the term lightworker instead—a term I do like, meaning one who works with light, the psychic spiritual light of consciousness—some practitioners claim the name without having any understanding of or background in ascension. Because of this, I prefer the more descriptive term ascensionist for those involved in ascension practices.

Like any eclectic spiritual path, ascension is filled with strong personalities hailing from a variety of backgrounds and belief systems. Practitioners draw from the esoteric lore of both the East and the West, but individuals can pick and choose what philosophies and techniques resonate with them. Ascension is not a religion in the traditional sense, but a synthesis of many different principles and universal truths as described by the world religions. Individuals do not have to subscribe wholeheartedly to any one religion, but instead can draw upon the principles that resonate with them on an intuitive, emotional, and logical level. Those on the ascension path are creating the new paradigms of the next age, using the philosophies of world mysticism as their building blocks. Sadly, as many practitioners pick and choose, they discard important parts of the philosophies simply because these teachings involve subjects that are difficult for their egos to incorporate. They abandon the lessons of discipline, ethics, and facing their own repressed emotions, believing that these parts do not resonate as truth. But they are simply truths that are difficult to hear.

Many ascensionists continue to practice their birth or chosen religion, and hope to manifest its highest and best aspects in their lives. Many ascribe to Christianity, seeing Christ as a great master, and the core teachings of the Christian tradition as the heart of their ascension practice, though they might not agree with all of Christian doctrine. Some will separate the wheat from the chaff, so to speak, and work with the core truths, possibly even making room for other deities such as Buddha or the Goddess in their personal tradition.

Other people leave the religion of their birth and base their tradition in another religion or spiritual path, such as modern neopaganism, tribal shamanism, or one of the many Eastern paths. I still wholeheartedly identify as a priest in the tradition of witchcraft, but incorporate many ideas of ascension into my practice. The wide range of ascension lore gives me a strong education in world religions, so I can more easily communicate with others about religion. Regardless of the tradition, all religions seek the same universal truth. Spiritual truth—however it is expressed through religions—is the most important principle of ascension.

THE LIMITATIONS OF LANGUAGE

One problem in explaining the beliefs of ascension is that most practitioners believe that the languages of our three-dimensional world are limiting and cannot accurately describe the ascension process. Although all language is sacred, and to the magician, language contains the codes for transforming our reality, our words are not always clear. The common earthly languages, particularly modern English, often lack the proper words to describe the spiritual dimensions of experience. So we look to the languages of cultures with a stronger spiritual dimension, particularly the ancient cultures of the East and West, borrowing terms to describe spiritual philosophies and experience. Terms such as karma, chakra, astral light, Hermetics, third eye, meridian, chi, vibration, feng shui, yin, yang, energy, and vision quest have become more common in our vocabulary, yet many of these terms are used differently in the New Age than in their original cultures. Variations in the meanings of these words develop from the different time periods and teachers. The difficulty of verbalizing spiritual experiences and concepts, as well as the use of imprecise borrowed terms, add to the confusion about what it means to be an ascensionist.

Many ascensionists feel that any earthly language is too limiting, and some, through their mystical experiences and otherworldly past-life memories, believe there is a light language that transcends the limits of normal communication. Through sounds and symbols, higher dimensional concepts are encoded, and the receiver of this information understands it on a multitude of levels. Unfortunately, it's hard to write a book in the language of light, at least in this dimension, though some people have created their own pictorial symbol systems of the language of light. Many believe that human attempts to render this pure language of light in the third dimension resulted in the development of the ancient sacred languages. Ascension lore refers to five sacred languages: Sanskrit, Egyptian, Tibetan, Chinese, and Hebrew. One could argue that languages and systems such as the runes, Greek, Gaelic, Enochian, Mayan glyphs, and even English have magickal and sacred qualities to them.

Even with the limitations of language, we can review the basic beliefs accepted by most, if not all, in the ascension paradigm.

CORE BELIEFS

The core ascension beliefs have their roots in the Theosophical material, with its strong Tibetan Buddhism flavor. As the ascension movement grows, there is a desire to be as inclusive and multicultural as possible, looking at an overview of world religions, past and present, to create the future. Many use the image of climbing a mountain as a metaphor for the spiritual journey. There are many paths up the mountain. Each major religion cuts its own path, yet they all have the same final destination—the top of the mountain, where you can see the whole picture, with all the roads leading there. An individual might follow a general path, but stray off it, exploring the woods and wilds of human consciousness, walking on other paths for a bit or blazing entirely new trails.

I think of the image of the spiral for the ascension path. If you follow a spiral path up the mountain, you cross all the other major paths several times. As we move from life to life, we are spiraling up the mountain, spending our time on different paths, but eventually we will walk all paths. Some souls find a home on one particular path, returning to it time and again, but we each taste and experience all the paths at some point.

Now let's examine some common points of ascension spirituality.

Divine Creation

Everything is divinely created, coming from one source. Some call this source God. Others call it Goddess. Those who wish to be politically correct in terms of gender identity use genderless names such as the First Cause, Godhead, Universal Soul, Great Spirit, Tao, Cosmic Logos, Divine Mind, or the inclusive Mother-Father-God. Some believe the divine is *transcendent*, meaning separate from the material world and beyond our understanding. Others feel the divine is *immanent*, or existing within the physical world, and through the physical world we can have a direct experience with the divine. Most ascensionists would see that both views are correct. All things in creation are expressions of divinity and are therefore inherently divine, and all things emanate from one source, and that source is transcendent from our current level of consciousness.

Light and Vibration

Ascensionists believe that everything in creation is constructed of energy. Physical matter is simply energy perceived in its densest form. Though the concept that everything is energy was once taken to be a symbolic truth, referring to spiritual energy, science is now telling us that matter is not as solid as we think. We now have scientific models of reality based on the concept of the hologram, a three-dimensional construct of light. A hologram is created when two beams of light are used to "photograph" an object with a holographic plate, capturing the interference pattern of the two beams with the object. When the beam is shined through the plate, it creates a three-dimensional picture that appears to be a solid object, but is really made of light. Everything is made of energy, not just our physical world. Our thoughts, emotions, and words have an energy to them as well, which ascensionists refer to not as literal light, but as a spiritual or divine light coming from the creative source. The quality of this energy, this light, is determined by its vibration. All energy, including spiritual energy, has a vibration to it. Higher vibrational energies are said to be more uplifting and consciousness-expanding, while lower energies are more grounding and focused. Some would see the higher energies as "good" and the lower energies as "bad," but it depends on the purpose of the energy. Still, harmful or unwanted energies are often described as "lower" or "denser."

Nonphysical Realities

Ascensionists, like most mystics before them, believe that physical reality is only one of many potential dimensions. Energy exists on a variety of levels. Many of these levels cannot be scientifically measured by humans, yet they are referred to in the spiritual lore of traditions across the world. Places like heaven, the astral plane, the dreamtime, Asgard, Tartarus, and Duat exist in the nonphysical worlds. They exist in the energy of divine consciousness, and although they don't exist in the objective, physical world, their subjective reality is still as valid to the ascensionist. Spiritual traditions throughout the ages have divided the energetic worlds using different names and labels. Modern traditions refer to the energetic worlds as dimensions, or density levels, and number them.

Nonphysical Beings

Just as reality exists on many levels, so does life. According to the modern scientific definition of life, humans are simply physical, biological beings, but those who have been the keepers of ancient mysteries have always been aware of other, nonphysical beings. Life manifests in a variety of forms, and our tales of spirits, faeries, elementals, angels, demons, and gods are recollections of nonphysical beings who have interacted with humanity on some level. People with psychic talents can use their gifts to perceive and communicate with these beings. Shamans, witches, and magicians seek out and forge partnerships with these unseen beings. Ascensionists are most concerned with the ascended masters, the wise sages who walked the Earth before and continue to guide us. They also look to those beings who have physical bodies but are different from humans, searching for allies among the spirits of animals, plants, trees, stones, and the planet itself. Many look to Mother Earth, sometimes referred to as Lady Gaia, as a guide and teacher.

The Multidimensional Self

The divine manifests in a variety of dimensions. Ascensionists believe that we are made in the divine image. This doesn't mean that the creative source is humanoid, though we often perceive transcendent divinity as human in order to relate to it better, but it does mean that we, too, exist in many dimensions. Each of us has not only a personal self existing in this physical dimension, but also many other "selves" existing in all dimensions. We are not consciously aware of these other selves most of them time, and the pursuit of the ascension path is to consciously awaken to your multidimensional self and widen your perspective. We have an energetic, or soul, anatomy that is just as complex as, yet more subjective than, our physical anatomy. When we fully integrate the perspective of our higher self into our daily life, many believe that we then ascend to the next level of consciousness. Though we use the metaphor of "ascending" upward, we are really bringing the perspective of our higher self down to the physical world.

Reincarnation

Ascensionists believe that our consciousness is immortal and survives after physical death, with the potential to return to physical life with another body. Most of us believe in the concepts of reincarnation and karma. We return to the world to work out our karma—to learn from and balance the energies of our actions, from this life and previous lifetimes. When we no longer have any karma to work out, then we are able to leave the cycle of death and rebirth. Though many think of reincarnation as a strictly Hindu concept, we find similar beliefs in many time periods and places in the ancient world, including Greece, the Celtic territories, and some shamanic cultures, though their beliefs may not align exactly with Hinduism or even popular modern beliefs on reincarnation. One view of ascension is the clearing of karma—no longer returning to the physical world for spiritual growth, yet continuing to exist in another spiritual dimension where the ascended act as guides, teachers, and healers for others.

The Importance of Love

One of the cross-tradition currents focused upon in ascension is the concept of spiritual love, of true divine compassion being a key to unlock the mysteries of spirit. Ascensionists believe love is the underlying cause of creation, and it is through this love that we will awaken to our multidimensional nature and be consciously connected to the divine. Love is not an ideal or an abstract concept, but a literal energy. The spiritual love of ascension is not meant to be the sentimental or romantic kind of love, nor does it always manifest in the way we expect or want. It is a transformative power. Love is often paired with light, though both are aspects of each other. A common New Age farewell or sign-off in missives is "In Love and Light," which seems simple, yet it evokes the most powerful twin forces we know—compassion and illumination.

Psychic Awareness

Ascensionists believe that as our consciousness opens to realities beyond the linear physical world, we touch dimensions not bound by space and time and have access to information beyond that which can be perceived by our normal senses. Often called intuition, psychic ability, or a sixth sense, we can perceive information about other people, places, and events from the past and future and use this knowledge to aid us in daily life and further our own spiritual development. Some people receive this information through the traditional senses, having an inner psychic vision (known as clairvoyance), an inner psychic voice (clairaudience), or simply a sense of knowing the information (clairsentience). Some use tools, such as pendulums, tarot cards, or runes, to focus their abilities, while others work directly with nonphysical entities to receive this information, performing channelings. Meditation—whether quieting the mind through focus or through guided visualization—aids our ability to find peace and clearly tune in to the messages we receive, and translate those impressions in the most helpful manner. The best psychics are those who have done a lot of personal development work and have cleared enough of their own issues that they can discern their own egos, hopes, and fears from the messages they receive. We develop our psychic senses to have "proof" that we are all connected, as well as to be of service to others and the world.

Magickal Co-Creation

As everything is made of energy, including our thoughts and words, ascensionists believe that energy can affect our reality and change our experience. By changing your energy, you can attract certain beneficial forces into your life, and repel other forces by making your personal energy incompatible with them. Through your intentions, you can manifest the life you want. In many traditions this skill is called magick. In the modern day it is known as co-creation, manifestation, creative visualization, or positive thinking. It truly is co-creation, as you are partnering with your divine energies, your higher self and divine connection, to manifest the life that fulfills your soul's hopes and dreams for this incarnation.

You can change your energy through your thoughts, words, and actions, which can be simple daily rituals or more elaborate and esoteric rites. Both techniques work, depending on what sets the mood best for you and how each personally shifts your consciousness. Most people think you have to be special to do magick, that you have to be born into it or have great skill to do it effectively. I think we are all magicians. Our reality, both personal and collective, is shaped by our thoughts, words, and deeds. The only difference between magicians and everybody else is that magicians consciously use their thoughts, words, and deeds to create their desired reality. Most people create their lives unconsciously, feeling they are a victim of circumstances and not seeing the direct link between their energy and their reality. Even in situations seemingly beyond our physical control, we can control how we react and respond. Through magick, we can create outward changes, but the most important change we can create is the inner shift of consciousness that transforms us and leads us further along the ascension path.

Shift of Ages

Ascensionists believe that the Earth is in a critical stage, and that all we do affects our collective reality as we prepare globally to shift our consciousness from one age to the next. Ascensionists disagree on when, how, and how quickly this shift will occur, but we believe we are on the cusp of an exciting new time in human development when we have the potential to manifest a paradise on Earth, if we so choose.

Though we could add endlessly to the list of core concepts of ascension, as many pioneers continue to contribute to the literature, philosophies, and terms through their experiences and channelings, these ten points cover the foundation quite well. Another way of looking at these spiritual ideas is through the lens of the spiritual principles from the ancient world.

SPIRITUAL LAWS

Just as the physical world is governed by specific laws, such as those in the model of Newtonian physics, ascensionists believe that the nonphysical realities, and their interaction with our physical reality, are also governed by specific spiritual laws, though these laws are not as easily perceived as the laws of physics. Mystic traditions have spent generations exploring, defining, and codifying these spiritual laws. Though most people set in the mold of Newtonian science would scoff at such laws, it's interesting to note that Isaac Newton himself was a mystic, an alchemist, and a believer in many unseen forces.

One esoteric document that elegantly sums up many of these spiritual laws is known as the Hermetic principles, a classic of the Western magickal traditions that parallels and is complementary to Eastern mysticism. The version presented here is a modern interpretation, distilled into seven principles, that was first made widely available at the beginning of the twentieth century through the Yogi Publication Society's printing of *The Kybalion.*

The Principle of Mentalism

Everything in existence is a "creation of THE ALL," or a thought in the Divine Mind. We are all one in the Divine Mind of the Creator. Since we are all made of this divine mental energy, we are also creators. As divine thought is the basis of creation, our minds, our thoughts, are the basis of our own creation. Our thoughts have energy; they have power to manifest. Our thoughts, words, and actions affect everything, because everything is connected through THE ALL. We are all one mind, giving rise to many different creations, different beings with individual points of view who think they are completely separate. In many ways, time and space are illusions, perceptions of our consciousness.

The Principle of Correspondence

"As above, so below; as below, so above." Patterns repeat on all scales imaginable. Microcosms and macrocosms are maps of each other. The inner and outer worlds are intimately connected. We observe the patterns of the stars and find correspondences in the actions of people. We see the structure of the solar system, with the planets orbiting the Sun, and see a similar shape in the structure of an atom, with electrons circling the nucleus. By studying the universe on one scale, we can gain insight into mysteries on another scale. Herbs, gems, and symbols all correspond to larger forces, and can be used in magickal traditions to tap into these larger forces.

The Principle of Polarity

"Everything is Dual; everything has poles; everything has its pair of opposites." The attraction and repulsion generated by two oppositely charged poles creates a flow of energy. On a spiritual scale, it is this flow that keeps the universe is motion. Many look at the creative power as the interplay between masculine and feminine energies, with the Divine Mind manifesting as a male father god and a female mother goddess. Their power together is what creates, sustains, and destroys reality, to create again. While polarity describes a wide range of pairs, in recent history and particularly in ascension lore the Principle of Polarity has been described almost exclusively in terms of good versus evil rather than as two complementary forces working in partnership. Some practitioners take a Gnostic view of polarity, seeing the polarity between a perfect spirit and a corrupt material world. They see divinity only as transcendent and see lightworkers in a constant struggle against a dark brotherhood seeking to prevent personal and planetary ascension. Such views create an exclusionary and inherently conflicted worldview. Ascensionists seek to move beyond the limits of this style of polarity consciousness, remembering that we are all part of "THE ALL," as stated in the Principle of Mentalism.

The Principle of Vibration

"Nothing rests; everything moves; everything vibrates." With the discovery of the atom, and the later theories of quantum physics, science has proven this principle beyond a shadow of a doubt. Everything physical has a vibration. Even intangible energies, both measurable and immeasurable, have vibration. Your thoughts and feelings have a vibration. By learning to work with and change vibrations, you can change your reality.

The Principle of Gender

"Gender is in everything; everything has its Masculine and Feminine Principles." Everyone and everything contains a mixture of feminine and masculine attributes. All pairs of complements can be described in terms of male and female, projective and receptive. No one has complete male or complete female energy, but rather a unique mixture of traits and potentials. Ultimately we learn to blend and balance those traits, knowing that as divine beings we contain all potentials.

The Principle of Rhythm

"Everything flows, out and in; everything has its tides." The universe works in cycles and patterns that repeat, like the cycles of nature and the stars. The Principle of Rhythm teaches us that knowledge of the cycles gives us an advantage. We know how to flow with the peaks and valleys of a cycle, rather than fight against the natural flow. Even the nonphysical worlds have their own cycles of life, perhaps less perceptible to us but nonetheless present.

The Principle of Cause and Effect

"Every Cause has its Effect; every Effect has its Cause." This law is similar to our modern belief that every action has an equal and opposite reaction. Everything that occurs has an effect on everything else. Events occurring now are the effects of previous causes. Many look at this as the law of karma, but without the moral implications often assigned to it. Like the law of gravity, it simply is. There is no judgment, but only results, which become the causes of future events.

Though not a formal part of ascension lore, the Hermetic principles sum up many world wisdoms clearly and succinctly. As we are all extensions of the Mother-Father-God, we will all eventually return to the source of creation. If a tree grows an acorn, and that acorn develops into a new tree, both trees will eventually decay and return to the Earth. The Earth, too, will eventually return to its source. Even though we see this return as a process, time is an illusion. There is no time but now. It is the infinite now. All time is one. The past, present, and future are not linear; we only perceive them as such. We have the ability to psychically retrieve information from the past, the present, and the future. We perceive ourselves as being separate and having to undergo a process of spiritual learning. Through this learning we gain greater self-mastery and reunite with our spiritual source. Through this mastery and union with spirit, we realize that we always were in union with the divine; we just forgot. Ascension is the process of remembering.

5

ASCENSION ANATOMY

We exist in many dimensions, and the process of ascension is to become more aware of all our "selves" on these levels. Many of these selves that are not apparent on the physical plane are the parts of us that are immortal, that exist after our physical death and incarnate again in a new body. It is these selves that ascend to a new level of consciousness when we complete our cycles of growth in the physical world. These selves have a great spiritual awareness of the cosmos and our purpose in it. By making contact with these "higher selves," we can co-create a life that fulfills our true will. How can we become more aware of these aspects of our consciousness and walk the path of ascension if we don't know where to look for them?

Mystic traditions have spent a lot of time exploring these parts of consciousness, mapping out our spiritual anatomy and creating systems to both understand and explore these other selves. Though the terms and levels of complexity of these systems vary, there are quite a few similarities across the traditions.

THE HIGHER SELF

Most people believe in some form of higher self, often referred to as the soul—the divine essence of a person, guiding his or her incarnation. Ritual magicians call it the Holy Guardian Angel, or HGA for short. It's not a protective spirit, as most people think when they hear the term guardian angel, but rather a person's divine essence. The magician's Great Work involves, in part, merging with this self, and implementing its divine work in the world. Magick, meditation, ritual, and prayer are all ways of connecting with this divine self. Ascensionists believe in a chain of higher selves, like octaves on a musical scale. These higher selves are fundamentally the same being, but each is in a different range of reality. Each of these selves is guiding the one below it.

THE FOUR-BODY SYSTEM

Many in the magickal and New Age world follow a simple four-body system (figure 4), modeled after the four elements of magick—fire, air, water, and earth. The elements of magick are symbolic and archetypal energies of creation. The mystic philosophers chose the natural phenomena of these four elements to represent the archetypal energies.

Earth

Physical Body—The earth body encompasses our physical self and our state of health and strength, as well as our physical weaknesses. We must care for our physical body through proper diet, exercise, and rest. It is the vehicle of our soul in the physical world, capable of manifesting changes in objective reality.

Water

Emotional Body—The water body consists of our astral self, which is related to our self-image, emotions, and dreams.

Air

Mental Body—The air body is the energy field that contains our mind, thoughts, memories, and reasoning skills.

Fire

Soul Body—The fire body holds our divine will, as well as our spiritual energies, passions, and drives. The fire body drives us to create and, through our creation, learn more about who we really are and what we are here to do in the world.

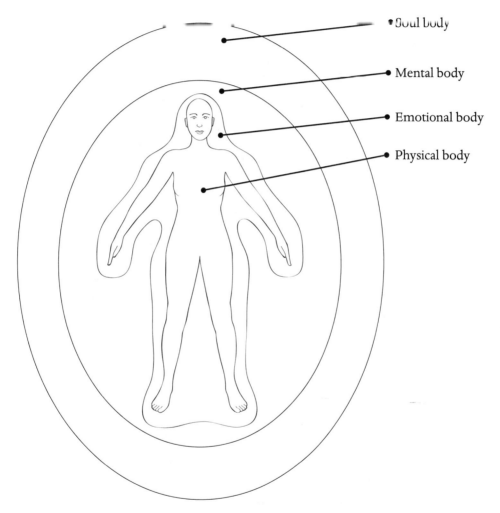

Figure 4: Four-Body System

More complicated systems divide the subtle energy of the human body into seven, nine, ten, or twelve bodies. Where we draw the lines is arbitrary, as when attempting to measure the depth of an ocean. The field of energy interpenetrating the human body is like the ocean—a spectrum with no clear-cut boundaries. Names and symbols just help us talk about and work with the subtle reality.

Changes in one of these subtle bodies can lead to profound changes in the others. Mystics learn to control the energy of the subtle bodies through a variety of disciplines, from meditation to ritual. By shifting the thoughts or emotions that are the root of an illness, one can completely transform the illness on the physical level. By making adjustments in the physical body, one can create profound shifts on the mental and emotional levels, as documented in the yogic tradition. By aligning the energy of the subtle bodies, you allow an uninterrupted flow of energy from the higher self, or fire body, to move through the mind and emotions, to manifest in the physical body.

The wisdom of the four bodies, and the four elements, is encoded in the rituals of magick, from the magick of the tribal shaman to that of the witch and the magician. We find the elements in the four classic "weapons," or tools, of magick encoded in the tarot. The pentacle represents earth and the body, the chalice embodies water and the emotions, the blade is linked to air and the mind, and the wand is the tool of fire and the soul. Yet there is a subtle and unseen fifth element, known as ether, or akasha, that rules the other four. In many ways this fifth element is symbolic of our higher self, and it is this fifth self that rules the lower four bodies. The secret teaching of the Magician card of the tarot (figure 5), and of any ritual altar space, is that there is a divine higher self that "owns" the lower powers. Magick is the art and science of mastering these elemental forces within us and learning to identify with this fifth essence. We are not our body, emotions, mind, or even will. Those are four sacred tools that we use, but our true self is something beyond all of them.

The pentagram (the five-pointed star) and the pentacle (the five-pointed star within a circle) are both universal symbols of magick and wisdom (figure 6). Both are forms found in the teachings of sacred geometry. The five-pointed stars are considered sacred symbols of the Goddess traditions, though they are often misunderstood by the general public. The five points of the star represent the four elements ruled by spirit on the top point. The pentagram is symbolic of a gateway, of opening to new energy, and can act as a shield to close us off from harmful energy. That is why many witches wear a pentagram as an amulet of protection. Some people interpret the reversed pentagram as evil, with spirit being subjugated by the four elements of matter, but others see that the spark of spirit is in the center of all matter and use the reversed pentagram as a symbol of ritual initiation.

Figure 5: Magician Tarot Card

Figure 6: Pentacle, Pentagram, and Reversed Pentagram

Though many in the ascension paradigm focus on love and light, there are four *L* words, related to the four tools and their elements, that must be kept in harmony and balance. They are law, love, life, and light, which correspond to earth (pentacle), water (chalice), air (blade), and fire (wand), respectively. Aleister Crowley replaced law with liberty in his teachings, though I prefer to keep law and add to it liberty, for the fifth element, giving us five *L* words to use in ritual and to remember in daily life.

EGYPTIAN SOUL ANATOMY

Egyptian mysticism gives us one of the most complex and complete looks at soul anatomy. The soul itself is not one single entity, but is divided into several distinct components, each with its own function in our spiritual lives. Many different systems of Egyptian soul wisdom exist, based upon different interpretations of the ancient texts. The model presented here is a common interpretation in ascension lore.

Khat (or Khabs)
The Khat is the physical body. It is what becomes the corpse or, if preserved, the mummy.

Ka
The Ka is the spiritual double, sometimes thought of as a spirit guide to the physical being. It is the part of the soul that remains in the tomb and receives offerings. It can wander about at will independently of the person and can dwell in statues. The Ka is sometimes viewed as dualistic, with a lower and higher aspect. The lower Ka contains the wisdom gained from the individual's experience on Earth. The higher Ka is akin to the higher self, inherently wise and all-knowing. The Ka is analogous to the concept of the astral body.

Ba
The Ba is the soul (figure 7), connected with the Ka. Some practitioners think it dwells in the Ka, while others believe it dwells with the gods. It appears as a human-headed hawk and can assume material form. According to some lore, the Ba is the part of the soul concerned with freedom and speaking the truth, as its image is a bird with a human head, the face of the individual from which it springs. In modern terms, we can think of the Ba as an aspect of the higher self.

Figure 7: Ba

Ab

The Ab is the heart. It represents the conscience and is associated with the animal nature and the good and evil one is capable of performing in life. At the end of life, the Ab is weighed on scales against the truth of Ma'at.

Khaibit

The Khaibit is the shadow, the primal darkness of the self. Some think of it as the repressed, unconscious emotions.

Khu (or Akhu)

The Khu is the spirit. It is the spiritual body that is the opposite of the Khat. It is radiant and shining and never decays. Upon death, it dwells with the gods. Some think of the Khu as the union of the Ka and Ba. In ascension terminology, this is referred to as the lightbody.

Achieving the union of the Ka and Ba (see Chapter 21: Merkaba Mysticism) is a vital part of the ascension process.

Sekhem

Sekhem is the vital life force—the energy of the individual. Some relate it to the life energy known in various cultures as prana, mana, ki, chi, pneuma, or rauch.

Seb

The Seb is the ancestral soul. It is the energy passed on from parents through the genetic lineage.

Ren

The Ren is the name—the secret spirit name or true name of the individual. One who knows the true name of an individual has power over that individual. For this reason, many magicians take a private spiritual name, identifying it with their soul, and do not reveal it to anyone but their most trusted allies and family members.

Sahu

The Sahu is the spiritual body, which appears after the individual is deceased and judged. It is the immortal imprint or image of the Khat.

SOUL, OVERSOUL, AND MONAD

In many strands of ascension belief, particularly in the works attributed to the ascended master Djwal Khul, there is the concept of souls extending out from a central source, in a web of increasingly greater complexity. As part of the ascension process, you travel toward the center, identifying and merging with these selves "above" you. As you do, your true spiritual self fills your earthly persona, magnifying more of your virtues and correcting your faults.

Though more recent practitioners, such as Dr. Joshua David Stone, have added to our understanding of this system and renamed some terms to simplify the original material, Djwal Khul's system contains three basic parts that today we call the soul, oversoul, and monad (figure 8).

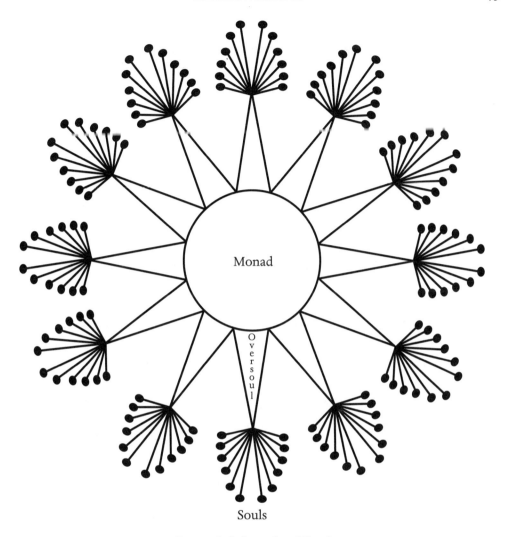

Figure 8: Soul, Oversoul, and Monad

Soul

The soul is our individual self. The consciousness of our soul is the aspect of our divinity with which we most readily identify, as it is the immortal essence that incarnates time and again in different bodies. In earlier versions of this system, the soul was called a soul extension, because this individual essence extended out from the level before it.

Oversoul

The oversoul is the larger energy from which the soul extends. Many think of the oversoul as a "soul family" or "soul group," as twelve souls extend out from the oversoul. Those individuals with whom you feel a kinship and share a similar purpose in the world may be a part of your oversoul group. Some think of the oversoul as the higher self, or at least one aspect of the higher self. In the earlier terminology, this level of consciousness was referred to simply as the soul.

Monad

The oversoul is rooted within the monad, the central core of consciousness that extends out from the source of creation. The monad is like the higher self of the higher self, closest to the source of creation. The monad creates twelve oversouls, who likewise each create twelve individual souls to potentially become incarnate beings. So each monad has 144 souls extending from it. The monad is also known as the monadic body, and is said to hold the monadic blueprint, or the patterns of perfect health and one's divine purpose. The term *monadic blueprint* can also be used in place of *true will* in ceremonial magick or *dharma* in Eastern traditions. The more you tune in to your oversoul and then monad, the better able you are to fulfill your purpose in the world and aid in the ascension process of all life.

Djwal Khul created the monadic mantra, or monadic prayer, to help one align with this divine self through daily meditative repetition:

> *I Am the Monad.*
> *I Am the Light Divine.*
> *I Am Love.*
> *I Am Will.*
> *I Am Fixed Design.*

"I Am" is the phrase associated with the monad, as the monad is often called the "I Am Presence," "Mighty I Am Presence," or "I Am Source." By using a form of the verb "to be," we link our being, our consciousness, with the monadic level. We seek to identify with the monad. "I Am that I Am" is used as a meditation mantra in ascension, either by itself or following "I Am" with whatever quality you want to identify with, such as "I Am Health," "I Am Love," or "I Am Prosperity."

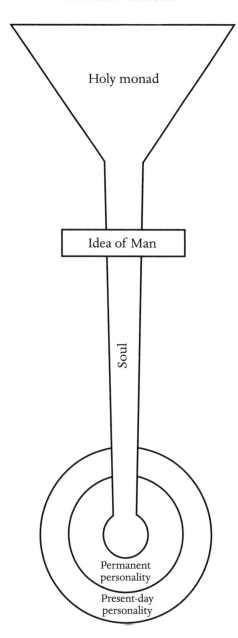

Figure 9: Present-Day Personality, Permanent Personality, Soul, Idea of Man, and Holy Monad

The phrase "I Am that I Am" has its origin in the Old Testament, when Moses was working with the Creator through the image of the burning bush. When Moses asked God for his name, God simply replied, "I am that I am," identifying with the pure source of creation. Moses was to go to the children of Israel and say, "I AM sent me unto you." The passage is found in Exodus 3:14, though some interpretations translate it as "I am who I am" or "I will be who I will be," using all tenses simultaneously, but the simpler "I Am that I Am" is favored by modern ascensionists. The Creator is sometimes referred to as the "I Am Source" and is described as a flame of white light pouring out into the universe.

In the teachings of Greek Christian mystic Daskalos, as outlined in Kyriacos C. Markides' book *The Magus of Strovolos*, a similar soul anatomy is given, though with different terminology, to help us better understand the role of our personality in the ascension process (figure 9). We usually identify with our present-day personality, which we might identify with our body, ego, and self-image. We develop a present-day personality during each incarnation. Our permanent personality is our inner self, our core, which holds our identity beyond this life and includes our sense of self from many incarnations. As we evolve, our present-day personality joins with our permanent personality. It is as if our permanent personality is at the core of our being, and as we grow spiritually, it is allowed to expand and fill more of us in our current incarnation, shining through our present-day personality. Our soul is our individual spiritual essence radiating out from the monad, through the Idea of Man. It is our perfect, spiritual ideal self, beyond corruption and any form of personality. In these teachings, souls are said to emanate from the holy monad, like rays of light emanate from the Sun. Those beings who emanate from the same monad share an affinity for each other.

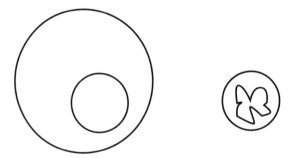

Figure 10: Expanded Consciousness and Contracted Consciousness

EXPANDED CONSCIOUSNESS

The process of aligning with these higher, or more expanded, levels of consciousness is the process of ascension. All of these models—the four-body system, the Egyptian soul lore, and the triune of soul-oversoul-monad—are just that—models, or maps, to help us expand our consciousness and better understand the process. They are three separate perspectives, and none is wholly correct. Each can inform and guide you. You can be working with the four bodies or studying the Egyptian soul parts, yet still be working to align your soul with the oversoul and monad.

Regardless of the model or tradition, a person who aligns with this expanded self and resolves karmic attachments shifts into spiritual alignment with his or her divine purpose, becoming an ascended master, an enlightened one, or a fully realized human being. By expanding your consciousness, you are able to see other people's points of view, and your own, without distortion. Those without an expanded consciousness have difficulty accommodating a larger point of view without distorting it (figure 10). Since ascensionists seek to expand their consciousness, it makes them more capable of including a variety of worldviews and religions in their own lore.

VIBRATION AND LIGHT QUOTIENT

How do we ascend to the next level of consciousness and merge with a higher level of self? What are the tools that can aid us? One of the first concepts I learned as I entered this new realm was the pairing of vibration and light quotient.

Vibration was familiar to me. We've already learned that everything seen and unseen has an energy, a vibration. It's one of the Hermetic principles. Everything vibrates. We can enter a room and pick up on the energy present, the room's "vibes," and determine whether we are compatible with the energy, whether our own vibration resonates with it or not. We might label this energy "good" vibes or "bad" vibes, but those are human qualifications. Sometimes energy that is incompatible with one person (bad vibes) is perfectly good for another.

Ascension is often described in terms of "raising our vibration." Some see this as a symbolic truth, as we describe things that we find compatible or good as having a higher vibration, and those things that are incompatible or unwanted as having a lower vibration.

To say that we are raising our vibration means that we are raising our consciousness, expanding our awareness.

Others see ascension as a literal truth, believing that the energy of our bodies, both physical and subtle, is vibrating faster. The way we interact with reality is altered as we alter our vibration. At these higher rates, we can no longer hold on to the vibrations, the energies, associated with fear, anger, hatred, or jealousy, all of which we consider to be lower-vibration emotions. The base vibration for the New Age, the Age of Aquarius, is very different than that of the previous Age of Pisces.

You can consciously choose to change your vibration through techniques such as magick, meditation, and ritual. If everything has a vibration, then you can align yourself with the vibrations you favor, that will be most helpful to your spiritual development, immersing yourself in those vibrations. This is the secret science behind many forms of esoteric healing and magick. Crystals and minerals all carry a vibration. If you want to have a vibration similar to that of one of the stones, carry the stone with you to integrate its qualities. Herbs and flowers all carry a vibration as well.

Foods have particular vibrations, and certain diets align the physical vehicle with specific vibrations. Many ascensionists favor a vegetarian lifestyle, feeling that meat products have a vibration that is too dense, and that most animals are killed in a state of fear or unhappiness, so you absorb that dense vibration when you eat them. Other ascensionists favor an omnivore lifestyle, for it is a part of our natural evolution, and many body types do not thrive on a vegetarian diet. Spiritually, one can see the choice to be an omnivore as the ability to take in and identify with all things. Christian scripture (Luke 24) tells us that the first food Jesus ate after his resurrection was a piece of broiled fish and part of a honeycomb.

Affirmations, chants, prayers, and mantras all have their own vibration. Chanting, singing, praying, or doing ritual infuses a new vibration into your energy field, altering your consciousness. Sacred sites carry a vibration, and when you visit a holy place, your vibration is changed when your energy field intersects with the vibrations of the site.

Although the concept of vibration was familiar to me, the term light quotient was not. Light quotient is the body's ability to hold "light frequency" in both the physical and subtle bodies. What does that mean? I asked around and few people could explain it to me. No one could define light quotient to my satisfaction, but everybody around me was doing everything they could to increase their own. Why? It's said that your light quotient is directly tied to your level of spiritual initiation, of spiritual advancement.

One teacher told me that if you raise your vibration but not your light quotient, you will spontaneously combust. That's what happens when you read about someone just going up in flames. The person's physical body couldn't handle the new energetic vibration. Though I'm not a big believer in spontaneous combustion, it's an interesting idea. It wasn't until we discussed light quotient and vibration with spontaneous combustion, literal or symbolic combustion, that I truly understood what this teacher meant by light quotient.

Light is a symbol for consciousness. Quotient is a count, a number, a measurement. Light quotient is the measurement of expanded consciousness you can hold in a stable manner. We all have peak experiences, where our consciousness expands. Sometimes we can integrate these changes and become more evolved and more aware. Other times we awaken and then it seems like we go back to sleep. We can't hold on to the new experience and the changes it brought. It's too big. The light quotient is our ability to hold light, to hold consciousness, in an active and stable manner. As we raise our vibration, our ability to relate to and resonate with higher energies and a higher reality, we must raise our ability to anchor, to ground, this vibration and expand our consciousness. Without this ability, we can reach peaks and valleys in our vibration, but never stabilize, never ground, the new level of consciousness permanently in our life. Some metaphysical researchers measure light quotient using a percentage system, and have measurements for each level of spiritual advancement, though these measurements are not based on objective constants, like those used to measure distance, weight, or temperature. My husband describes light quotient as the spiritual equivalent of the intelligence quotient, but instead of measuring our ability to comprehend information, it measures our ability to comprehend "light," to be "in lightened."

We can increase our light quotient much the same way we increase our vibration. Meditation, ritual, and prayer, and particularly working directly with our otherworldy allies, especially the ascended masters, all increase our light quotient. The most important action we can take to increase our light quotient is to walk our talk. This means we must act upon our spiritual insights and teachings in our everyday, physical life. We must shine in every moment we can. Only by grounding these spiritual principles in our deeds can we hope to hold on to our expanded state of consciousness.

meditation

The key to all of these mysteries—expanding consciousness, getting in touch with your other selves, raising vibration, and increasing your light quotient—is simple: meditation. Through the monadic mantra, Djwal Khul reminds us of a very important tool stressed within all the mystic traditions. Meditation simply means contemplation. You focus and direct your attention, and through this focused attention you are capable of experiencing greater insights and awareness. You have the ability to experience your true spiritual nature.

Many think meditation is sitting cross-legged on the floor, having no thoughts at all. They try it and fail within the first few minutes, and give up. Meditation can be experienced in many ways, and those who seek to have "no thought" usually have a technique to help them reach a level of pure consciousness. Some techniques have you focus your mind on a single thing, such as a phrase, called a mantra, that is repeated over and over again. The mantra is often in a foreign Eastern language, such as Sanskrit, but it doesn't have to be. Performing the prayers of the rosary could be considered a Western mantra. Other techniques have you focus on counting your breath, or stare at a sacred symbol known as a mandala or yantra. More popular meditations are based on specific visualizations and guided imagery. They are called pathworkings or guided journeys. All of these techniques help you focus your attention and allow you to experience an expanded state of awareness.

All meditation techniques help you alter your consciousness. They literally change your brain waves. At certain levels of brain-wave activity, you are more capable of accessing an expanded consciousness and other dimensions of reality. Meditation helps lower your brain-wave frequency from beta level (13 to 16 cycles per second) to alpha level (8 to 13 cycles per second), the state you enter when you daydream. The difference between meditation and daydreaming is that in meditation you are conscious, focused, directed, and able to take full advantage of the benefits of this level of consciousness. Meditation can help you enter the light trance state of alpha, but with practice you can learn to go consciously into even deeper states of consciousness.

I use a very simple meditation technique to enter a trance state. Once I get physically comfortable and prepared for meditation, I imagine a blank screen in my mind's eye. Then I draw or visualize on that screen a series of numbers, starting at twelve and counting down to one. It's like drawing on a chalk board or white board. Then I let the screen fade from my mind, and silently count down from thirteen to one. Keep in mind that some people are more visually oriented, while others are more auditorily oriented. This technique works with both senses and stimulates both parts of the brain—the linear, logical side and the intuitive, emotional side. Twelve is a number associated with masculine energy and with the Sun, for the twelve solar months of the year. Thirteen is a number associated with the feminine and with the Moon, for the thirteen months of a lunar year. The combination of both is a sure-fire method to get you into a meditative state.

Practice this basic meditation exercise. Learning a reliable meditation technique will help you with subsequent exercises in this book.

EXERCISE 1:
BASIC MEDITATION TECHNIQUE

1. Make sure your environment is conducive to meditation. Turn off and block out all distractions, such as the ringer on the phone. Dim the lights, or turn off all the lights and light a few candles. Incense can help set the mood. I prefer combinations of frankincense and myrrh, as well as lavender and sandalwood. Turn on some relaxing, ambient music suited for meditation.

2. Sit in a physically comfortable position. You can sit cross-legged on the floor, back straight and wrists resting on the knees, palms up and open. This is a traditional Eastern pose. If you can put your feet on your thighs, forming a lotus position, that's great, but it's not necessary. You can also sit in a chair, with your feet flat on the floor and your hands in your lap, palms on your thighs, in the pose known as the Egyptian sitting position.

3. Relax your body, from the top of your head to the tips of your toes. Go through each section of your body and mentally give yourself permission to relax. Feel waves of relaxation moving through your muscles, as you become more and more relaxed.

4. Imagine a screen in your mind's eye. This is your window to the psychic world. You control everything on it. Draw or visualize the number twelve on the screen. Hold it for a moment, then let it fade or erase it like a blackboard. Then draw or visualize the number eleven. Continue this pattern until you reach one.

5. Release the screen of your mind, and silently count from thirteen to one in a slow, even pace, as you slide into a deeper meditative state.

6. You are now at alpha level. Sit for a moment, feeling the difference between this trance state and your normal waking state. At this point you would continue on to any meditative workings to expand your awareness. For now, continue on to step 7 to learn a visualization that will help you develop better skills of focus and concentration.

7. When you are ready, call forth the screen of your mind again and visualize a candle burning before you. Take notice of the candle. What color is it? What shape? How brightly does the flame burn? Can you feel the heat it gives off? Notice all the details of the candle. Focus all your attention on the candle.

8. When you are done, which could be anywhere from a few moments to ten minutes or even longer (we often lose track of time at this level of brain-wave activity), erase the candle from the screen of your mind. Wipe it away until the screen is blank.

9. Now count up from one to thirteen without visualizing the numbers. Then count up from one to twelve without visualizing anything. You are now back to a state of normal waking consciousness.

10. Ground yourself. Being grounded means you have your energy, your consciousness, fully anchored in your body and the physical world. Many people who are drawn to ascension practices are often naturally ungrounded and have to work at being present in the world. Imagine a beam of light descending from the base of your spine into the Earth, as if you were a ship dropping anchor. Imagine your anchor descending into the core of the planet.

If you are not a visual person and don't see anything during this meditation exercise, don't worry. Focus on expanding your entire awareness, not just your visual ability. Meditation exercises are usually described in visual terms because most people in our society relate best to visual instructions, but in this work it's just as important to learn how to feel, how to sense, and how to know. You might not clearly "see" in your mind's eye the numbers or the candle, but instead feel them. Know they are present because you are intending them to be there. Use your imagination and all your senses. Feel the warmth of the flame. Hear it crackle as it burns the wick. Hear the drip of the wax. Imagination is an important skill in magick. It is through our imagination that we direct energy and manifest change.

———————————————

6

THE STRUCTURE
OF REALITY

Mystics in the ascension paradigm spend a great deal of time and thought trying to understand the unseen worlds and humanity's place in them. Mystics throughout the ages have developed models of reality to describe these unseen worlds. Many people use these models, described in hierarchical terms, as spiritual road maps, charting their path and guiding their ascent back to the source of creation. The basic Principle of Correspondence is often expanded to "as above, so below; as below, so above; as within, so without," and many mystics see parallels between our spiritual anatomy and these unseen dimensions. The many selves of our multidimensional consciousness exist in these realms.

The concept of multiple dimensions of reality is a common point of almost all mystic traditions. Each tradition recognizes that reality, consciousness, and life are not limited to the physical plane. One quote attributed to Jesus in the New Testament has been interpreted as Jesus's own teaching on the dimensions and ascension: "In my Father's house are many mansions: if it were not so, I would have told you. I go to prepare a place for you."—John 14:2. Each dimension is a different mansion, a different room, in the structure of reality.

Mystic traditions have attempted to map reality, and many have succeeded. Each map is a tool and a symbol of a truth that often defies language. These symbol systems help us relate to concepts that are beyond our human understanding. No system is the absolute truth. Each system expresses things in terms of its culture, psychology, and spiritual traditions. Even though the systems are all different, it's not surprising to find so many common themes, because the human perspective is a common denominator in all of them.

THE WORLD TREE

Shamans were the first to use their otherworldly journeys to create maps of the nonphysical worlds, the unseen roads. Through trance-inducing techniques, including drumming, dancing, herbs, and meditation, shamans can send their awareness out from the body to explore the etheric realities. There they encounter a vertical axis, which takes shape as a mountain, ladder, or most popularly a tree, known as the world tree, the center of the universe (figure 11). The world tree is found in many mythologies, including those of the Norse, Celts, and Siberians. Many modern shamanic practitioners continue to use the image of the tree, as the roots give access to a realm below and the branches give access to a world above.

Middle World

The middle realm is the physical world of mortals, the land of humanity. It is the realm of cycles, seasons, and change. The Middle World contains the entire time-space continuum—not just the present moment, but also the past and all potential futures we can experience.

Lower World (Underworld)

Below the Middle World is an inner earth, an underworld that truly has nothing to do with the Christian concept of hell, but is a place of the ancestors and primal beings. This Lower World is a place of testing and facing fear. Beings of the Underworld are emotional and personal, and have strong feelings.

Figure 11: Shaman's World Tree

Upper World

Above the Middle World is the realm of the gods, the heavens, the sky heroes and star gods. These beings are detached in their viewpoint and give guidance and information from their perspective above, seeing the greater picture, but they are unattached to the personal details. This Overworld is said to be the home of those who are no longer attached to the Earth through reincarnation, but continue to offer their guidance and wisdom to those in the Middle World.

Each of the three worlds of reality corresponds to an aspect of the self. The Middle World corresponds to the middle self, the ego and physical body. The Upper World is connected to the higher self, the superconscious. The Lower World is linked to the lower self, the intuitive or psychic self. By exploring all three of these realms, you build a relationship with these three parts of yourself.

THE TREE OF LIFE

Another tree model used in our effort to map reality is the Tree of Life, a glyph drawn from Jewish Kabbalah and used extensively in Hermetic Qabalah. It is not a literal tree (and some have difficulty seeing a tree image in the symbol), but is more like a ladder, with ten spheres, each representing a different level of consciousness, both in the universe and in ourselves (figure 12). The ten spheres are known as sephiroth (sephira, sing.), which translates to "emanations," referring to emanations of energy from the divine source creating our reality.

Each sphere corresponds to a number, an aspect of astrology, an archangel, and a spiritual experience. Magickally there are also associations with animals, stones, plants, and scents. The sephiroth are arranged in a specific pattern of sacred geometry that visually describes the relationships between the ten spheres, which are connected by twenty-two paths. Each path corresponds to a tarot card and a letter of the Hebrew alphabet. These associations map the process, spiritual and psychological, needed to move from one level of consciousness to another, and the system of Qabalah provides texts, rituals, and meditations to facilitate this process.

The ten spheres are numbered in order from the least dense and most spiritually pure sephiroth to those that are more dense, more personal, and more human in scope. Some think of the Tree of Life as being rooted in the bottom, tenth sphere (Malkuth), but the

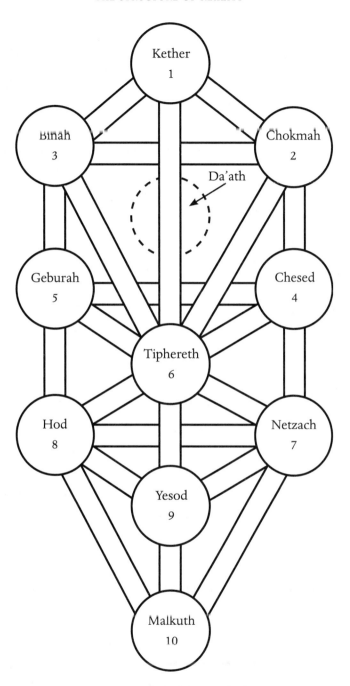

Figure 12: Glyph of the Tree of Life

older depictions actually describe an upside-down tree, with its roots in heaven. There is a similar image of an upside-down tree in Hindu texts such as the Bhagavad Gita: "The blessed Lord said: 'The wise speak of an eternal Asvattha tree (sacred fig) with its roots above and its branches here in this world. Its leaves are the Vedas (holy scriptures). Whoever understands this tree knows the most sacred wisdom.'"—chapter 15, sloka 1. The material world is the manifestation, the fruit, of this heavenly tree. Within the fruit is the seed to grow a new tree, a new root, into the divine. Each of us is the tree. Each of us contains the mystery, the seed, that will lead to a continual connection with the source.

From a Qabalistic perspective, ascension, at least the first stages of it, is the climbing of the path from Malkuth to Yesod, ultimately making our way to Tiphereth. Ascension is not a simple meditative projection up the tree, but a true fundamental shift of consciousness, of reality, up the path. Instead of human consciousness being rooted in Malkuth, it moves a step higher, to Yesod, or even Tiphereth. In the process of ascending the tree, we do not necessarily lose our physical body; we simply find our awareness centered on another level of consciousness. The physical world of Malkuth is no longer the sole priority. We still have our body in Malkuth, but the root of our consciousness is centered in another, higher realm.

THE SEVEN PLANES OF EXISTENCE

In some esoteric lore, the universe is divided into seven planes of existence (figure 13). Much like the Qabalah, the higher we go up the ladder, the further away we move from human experience through the subtle layers of reality, until we reach the divine source from which the planes emanate. These planes are also said to relate to our own personal subtle anatomy, as we have a "body" on each of these planes of existence.

Physical Plane

The first plane is not a subtle plane at all, but is physical, dense and solid. It is the material world and all things measured by the material senses. It is the place of space and time, solid form and function. It is the Middle World of the shamans and the sephira of Malkuth in the Qabalah.

Etheric Plane

The etheric plane closely resembles the physical plane, providing an energetic spiritual template upon which the physical world is based. The etheric realm is considered the blueprint, or working model, for the physical world.

Figure 13: Seven Planes of Existence

Astral Plane

The astral plane is the realm of idealized form. While the etheric plane is the template for the physical plane, the astral plane is the idealized template for the etheric plane. Sometimes the etheric body, the template of what is, doesn't match the astral body, the idealized form. On the astral plane is your self-image, which can be very different from your physical body. Everything physical has an astral form, but not all things astral have a physical form. Astral forms are affected by energy, intention, and emotions, whether directed at them consciously or unconsciously. The astral correspondence of a place of war or violence can still be scarred energetically even if it has been cleaned up on the physical plane. Other places don't look special on the physical plane, but their astral energies, unseen, can be felt and create a sense of harmony or peace. The astral plane is the first realm of spirits, from beneficent spirit guides to ghosts. It is related to the dream plane and the collective consciousness. The astral plane responds to strong emotions, as the emotions influence the shape and form of astral energy.

Emotional Plane

The emotional plane is sometimes called the higher astral plane. It is part of the astral, but is responsive to our highest and best emotions, including love. Here we move beyond the lower astral forms, of unwanted entities and ghosts, and have greater contact with the more compassionate guides, including the ascended masters, who can aid our spiritual evolution.

Mental Plane

The mental plane is the realm of ideas and concepts. To create something, one must first have an idea and then give it emotional energy to manifest a form on the astral, etheric, and eventually physical levels. The mental plane is the realm of information, abstract concepts, and communication.

Psychic Plane

The psychic plane contains the divine vision—of where you are, where you were, and where you wish to be. Here is the connective plane where seers and psychics have visions to understand the past and to plan the future. Everyone can operate on the psychic plane. When you remember something, or when you project an image, from a wish to a fear, into the future, you are working on the psychic plane.

Divine Plane

The divine plane is the Divine Mind, the field of energy that surrounds and interpenetrates the other six planes. It is the container and source of all creation. The divine plane is where our highest self resides.

Mystic traditions use a variety of names for the seven planes. Some traditions describe them using the terms physical, astral, mental, buddhic, atmic, monadic, and logoic. Another version is physical, elemental, emotional, mental, spiritual, divine, and ultimate. Yet another variation is physical, etheric, emotional, mental, Christ, causal, and divine. Each of these systems uses terms for the seven planes that correspond to the seven bodies in our spiritual anatomy.

Each of the seven planes can be subdivided into seven dimensions. Each plane has a denser aspect that corresponds to the physical, plus an etheric aspect, an astral aspect, and

Figure 14: Forty-Nine Planes of Existence

so on. Together, they create forty-nine planes of existence (figure 14), though for all practical purposes, esotericists use only the seven main ones.

Some simplify the system, and rather than divide creation into seven planes, they use only four, based on the four elements and the four-body system of our spiritual anatomy. The earth element is the densest level and encompasses what we previously have called the physical and etheric planes. The water element contains the astral and emotional planes. The air element corresponds to the mental plane, and the fire element embodies the psychic and divine planes.

THE DIMENSIONS OF LIGHT

Though ascensionists can refer to the shaman's world tree, the Qabalah, or the seven planes of existence, the model favored by modern practitioners is the dimensions of light. Received mostly through channeled information, this new cosmology is quickly becoming the standard map. Many ascension practitioners use this dimensional terminology, casually referencing the third dimension, fourth dimension, or fifth dimension in conversation or teaching, though not all agree on the exact definitions of each dimension. That's part of the problem, and yet part of the beauty, of being on the cusp of the ages, where new paradigms are being developed and there is no one standard understanding. We all have the chance to explore the new frontiers together.

While we can call these planes of existence *dimensions*, that word is confusing. Most ascension practitioners refer to this world that we all currently share as the third dimension, but scientists would also refer to it as the third dimension because of the fact that we have height, length, and width—three dimensions. We are not two-dimensional, flat forms or one-dimensional points. A fourth dimension, which we do not currently understand, is the subject of much speculation and is often described as our concept of time.

In ascension lore, the dimensions could be better described as density levels. Dimension doesn't refer to length, width, and height in this case, with a position or place in space, but rather to a resonance of energy. Those who resonate with a particular level of energy, referring to their vibration and light quotient, exist in that dimension. The third dimension is a particular resonance, the vibration of the physical, measurable universe. In this paradigm, that is a very small portion of the universal "spectrum." The other dimensions represent mostly nonphysical levels of consciousness. Each dimension has its own qualities, assets, drawbacks, and rules of existence, which are very different from our own. Our physical world intersects with these other dimensions, and we have access to them during expanded states of consciousness. Several things or beings can exist at the same point in space but be in different dimensions, unperceived, much as radio waves, television waves, and light waves can all exist at the same point in space yet in different frequencies. There is overlap between dimensions, but as humans we are based mostly in this third level, while other forms of life are based in other levels. Under the right circumstances, they, too, can interact with our world. Our consciousness exists on all density levels, but we are not usually aware of these other levels.

With enough personal mastery, you can change your energy to resonate with a different dimension and project your consciousness into that level of awareness. Shamanic practitioners do this when entering an altered state and visiting the worlds above or below. A magician involved in a pathworking to climb the Tree of Life is using ritual, invocation, and the images of tarot cards to alter his or her energy and reach a new dimension. Spiritually visiting the dimensions of light is the same process, just with a different paradigm. And like some practitioners in the other traditions, many ascensionists believe that if you have sufficient mastery, you can move your entire self—soul, mind, emotions, and body—between dimensions, though it's not necessary to become a discarnate entity to attune with other dimensions. You can attune your awareness to the upper dimensions and still have a physical body. The ideal of ascension is to be incarnate, yet fully conscious in all dimensions.

If creation (the physical and subtle dimensions) is a spectrum, then where we draw the lines between the dimensions is rather arbitrary. This is similar to the rainbow spectrum, where there is no neatly placed line dividing red and orange or orange and yellow. One color blends seamlessly into the next. Where we draw the lines is up to us. Dimensions are somewhat like that. Occultists have created these reality maps as mandalas, to help us understand our experiences, to understand where it is useful to draw the lines. Though we could divide the rainbow into twelve colors, the easiest and most useful model is divided into seven. The descriptions of the dimensions are attempts to create familiar rainbows. The most popular systems use a scheme of seven, nine, or twelve dimensions, and limit the scope of dimensions to the realities of this galaxy and/or the universe. Those whose maps move beyond this universal consciousness say there are 352 "levels," or dimensions, through higher and higher universes, that lead back to the divine source.

Within each dimension of light are multiple levels of awareness, or subdimensions, referred to as overtones. Each of the twelve dimensions is divided into twelve overtones, creating 144 levels of reality (figure 15). Many ascensionists believe the entire planet is moving so gradually from third-dimensional consciousness, and vibration, to fourth-dimensional

Figure 15: Dimensions

consciousness, overtone by overtone, that we are not generally aware of it. Some speculate that we are in the higher overtones of the third dimension, or even higher. As a species we could still be physically in the third level, but hopefully our group consciousness is moving into an awareness that includes the fourth dimension or even higher dimensions. We exist in all dimensions, and are simply becoming more consciously aware of this.

Each dimension of light has a life form, a consciousness, that acts as its guardian or caretaker. From our perspective, we are the keepers of the third dimension, though we've been doing a poor job of protecting our earthly world. Other nonphysical beings are the keepers and guides of the other dimensions. When we contact other planes, we can interact with these nonphysical beings. In the ascension paradigm, these beings are often associated with other stars, reminiscent of the shaman's star spirits and gods. Modern teachings on the dimensions abbreviate their names, with the number of the dimension followed by a capital *D*, such as 3D for the third dimension.

The following description of the dimensions is a synthesis of my own experiences and several different teachings. Barbara Hand Clow is one of the front runners of exploration in the dimensional model of reality. Her pioneering books *Alchemy of Nine Dimensions: Decoding the Vertical Axis, Crop Circles, and the Mayan Calendar* and *The Pleiadian Agenda: A New Cosmology for the Age of Light* are some of the most complete and helpful guides to this material, focusing on the first nine dimensions. In *Alchemy of Nine Dimensions*, Clow compares this vertical axis of reality (figure 16) to the Tree of Life in other cultures.

First Dimension

The first dimension is the sphere of planetary consciousness. It relates to the planetary being we call Mother Earth, or Gaia, from the Greek myths. Many, but not all, of the ancient myths describe the Earth as feminine, as the mother. She gives us our bodies, our homes, our food, but eventually, like any good child, we must form an adult relationship with her, based on love and mutual respect. People today are learning how to rebuild and repair their relationship with the Earth, looking to the lore of cultures that have a strong relationship with the planet, such as ancient paganism and the surviving indigenous cultures.

The first density level is the first level of consciousness that connects us all, because we all live in the biosphere of Mother Earth, even if we don't consciously recognize it. According to the Gaia theory of scientist James Lovelock, we human beings, along with all species on the planet, are like the specialized cells and organs within Gaia's body. We are all part

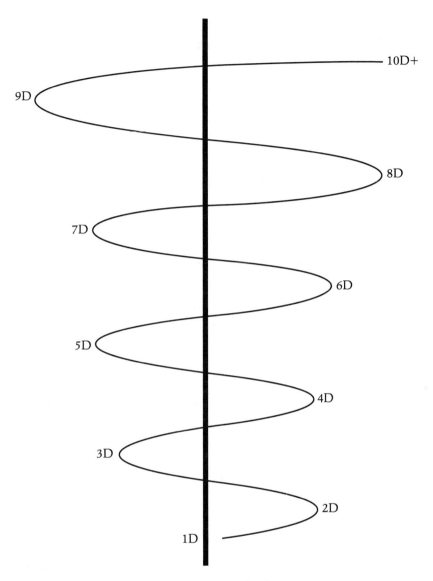

Figure 16: Dimensions of Light

of the planetary being, as she is a part of the solar being. In no way does this diminish our own individual spiritual journeys, or our personal wants and needs, but it does put those individual needs into a larger perspective.

Clow relates this level of consciousness to what she calls the "iron core crystal" in the core of the planet. Because of our blood, which is filled with iron, we resonate with the heart of the Earth. Priestesses have been her voice, touched by women's Moon time, shedding blood to connect with the Mother. But we all contain the blood of the Mother, and can attune to her through it, through our bodies.

If we think of the first dimension in terms of space, being a single point, the first dimension would be the single point in the center of the Earth. The center holds the records of what has been. Many people experience the patterns of former life forms on Earth, including extinct species of animals and plants, passed cultures, and dearly departed loved ones. Some might call these the planetary akashic records, manifesting out of the magnetism of the planet, though others would locate the akashic records (the energetic recording of all that is, was, and will be) in a higher dimension. Theoretically, those on other planets would experience a different first dimension because their world core, their Underworld, would be different from ours.

In the shamanic worldview, the first dimension would have less to do with the terrestrial, material Earth, the nature aspect of the Goddess, and more to do with the depths of the Underworld, the realm of the ancestors and the Dark Goddess, whose actions transform us. In a Qabalistic model, some would see the bottom black quarter of Malkuth in the first dimension, while others might include the "higher" spheres, such as Binah, in this dimension. Binah is the void, the cosmic ocean from which form springs. In the Greek myths, Gaia rises from the darkness of the void to create reality. She is seen as both the living spirit of the planet Earth and the spirit of all matter everywhere. On this level, she exists in all things as the Prime Mover. While many current creation myths naturally assign a male pronoun to the First Cause of creation, the oldest pagan myths assume creation is a feminine force. Some faery traditions envision a Dreamer in the heart of the Earth, shining brightly like a star within the womb of the Goddess. He is the one who dreams reality into being, while she manifests it. As mystics have the philosophy "as above, so below," many traditions believe that the heart of the Earth is really a star, and if you travel deep enough, you will find yourself in the heavens again.

We attune to the consciousness of the first dimension to understand our primal nature and our relationship with the planet and all the other life forms on Earth. Through the first dimension, we see the entire spectrum of life—past, present, and a potential future. We are in relationship with the planet, as our Mother, and she has called our souls here for a reason. The Earth wants us here at this time for a purpose, and by knowing our past, we can better plan our future in harmony with the planet.

The first dimension holds many secrets about the Mother and the history of her children. Those attuned to this dimension can have great insight. In Greece, Gaia was the giver of prophecy, as her priestesses guided kings and commoners to make the most appropriate decisions for the future.

Second Dimension

The second dimension is the consciousness level between the core of the planet and the surface, between Mother Gaia and humanity. The forces of nature that mediate between the heart of the Earth and the world of humans are the beings who are the guardians of the second density level. They are the telluric beings, known by many names. We call them elementals, nature spirits, and faeries, though in other times they have been known as imps, goblins, and gremlins. Barbara Hand Clow also includes viral beings, as a form of mineral life, as well as bacteria, in the second dimension of consciousness. From a shamanic view, this is a "higher" realm of the Underworld, closer to the Earth, much like the mantle is closer to the crust than is the core of the planet. From a Qabalistic view, the second dimension might relate to the realm of Netzach, as some equate the nature realm with the green sphere on the Tree of Life.

The elementals are the spirits who embody one of the four classical elements of earth, air, fire, and water. They guide and harness the energy of their particular element. Nature spirits are more complex than elementals, and have the power to influence more than one element. They bring the patterns of nature into manifestation. They are the workers of the natural realm. Faeries are the last beings in the telluric order of consciousness. They act as primal guardians of land, and as the gateway between our third-dimensional world and those below. Faeries are sometimes mistaken for elementals or nature spirits, but they are really the guides and guardians of the nature spirits.

In modern ascension lore, Pan is the guardian of the second dimension and the guide to the telluric beings. Pan, whose name is translated as "all," is the masculine guardian of nature and creation, working in harmony with Mother Earth. Pan was originally a Greek god of Arcadia, a god of woodlands, shepherds, music, and sexuality. He is depicted with the upper body of a man and the hindquarters and horns of a goat. His name is said to be the root of the word *panic*, because like nature he is both beautiful and terrible, as forces of nature cannot always be controlled. Despite this, he has nothing to do with the Christian Devil. He is simply a primal force and leader of the natural realm, guiding the elementals and spirits specifically to manifest the world we know. Many modern pagans call upon Gaia and Pan as the manifestations of the Mother and Father in the terrestrial world.

Ascensionists work with the second dimension through ritual. Rituals align us with our body and nature, particularly if the ritual involves tools from the natural world, such as stones or plants. These rituals help us attune to nature and heal ourselves, each other, and the planet.

Third Dimension

The third dimension is the easiest of the density levels to explain. The different levels become more difficult to describe the further away you get from the third dimension. The third dimension is the level of human consciousness. It is the surface of the planet, but more importantly, it is the collective consensus physical reality that has not only height, length, and width, but also linear time, cycles, seasons, and the physical laws of Newtonian science.

In the shamanic cosmology, the third dimension is the Middle World, the world of humanity, as the base of the world tree, between the branches and the roots. In Qabalistic lore, it is most definitively Malkuth, the densest of the sephiroth.

The third dimension is the bridge between the lower realms and the higher realms beyond the planetary consciousness on the vertical axis of reality. Humans are supposed to be the guardians and keepers of the third dimension, to align the vertical axis. From a higher dimension, our third dimension is like a vertebra out of place, a slipped disc preventing alignment. Many myths, from pagan Teutonic myths to those of current indigenous cultures, talk about those who must perform the ancient rituals to keep the cycles of life going. Without these rituals, the world would be destroyed. Thankfully, there are people who continue to perform the rituals, and many more are returning to the old ways and learning to integrate their wisdom in daily life. At one time, only priestesses and priests (mystics, shamans, and witches) were concerned with this work, and although they can be our teachers as keepers of this knowledge, we are all involved in this work in the New Age. Our task now is to integrate our spirituality into the physical world, to be the true guardians of the third dimension and fully participate in the vertical axis, aligning with the other worlds above and below.

Fourth Dimension

The fourth dimension is the space of the collective unconscious, the archetypal realm that links the thoughts and mind, conscious and unconscious, of not only humanity but all the beings of Earth. Here we are beyond time and space. We experience this dimension as the dream world, or the astral plane. We can go anywhere or do anything here, limited only by our imagination. Our thoughts and ideas manifest much more readily in the fourth dimension, because unlike the third dimension, the fourth is not dense, not bound by the rules of space and time. This level is associated with the realm of Yesod in the Qabalah, and has similarities to both the Upper and Lower Worlds of the shaman. One of the secrets of true magick is that for something to appear in the physical world, it must first manifest on the

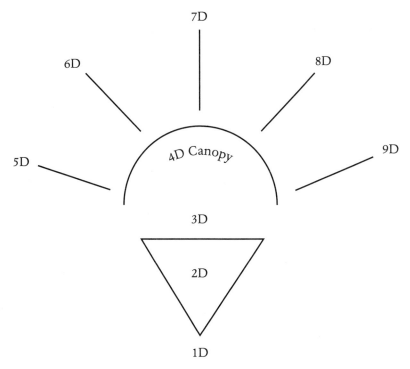

Figure 17: Fourth Dimensional Canopy of Light
(This figure is based on an illustration from Barbara Hand Clow's Alchemy of Nine Dimensions.*)*

astral plane. Magicians are adepts of the fourth dimension, practicing the skills of astral travel, remote viewing, and building astral thoughtforms to manifest physical results in the third dimension.

The fourth dimension forms a screen to the higher dimensions (figure 17). As we ascend beyond this dimension of light, we move further and further away from human experience. We have more difficulty understanding the pure energies of the higher dimensions and require a method to translate them into forms we can better understand. Our minds translate the energies of the higher dimensions, using the symbols found in the collective fourth-dimensional consciousness. We relate to higher energies as colors, sounds, pictures, feelings, and archetypal imagery.

The keepers of the fourth dimension are the gods—not the ultimate creative source, but the many archetypal manifestations of divinity, recorded in our pagan mythologies as the pantheons of the gods. Like humanity, the gods exist on multiple levels at once. Just as we have found the gods Gaia and Pan in the first two dimensions, they can also be found in the higher dimensions.

Gaia is not just the Earth and its core, but all matter everywhere. She is the starry goddess whose body is the entire universe. Pan is not just a nature god. Pan, as "all," is one face of the male form of creation, the spurting seed to the goddess's cosmic womb. His seven-reed pipe symbolizes the seven planetary powers of the ancients, and the spots on his furry cloak are the stars of the heavens. On another level, he is the inspiring force of poetry and music, the god of inspiration. On yet another, he is the god of shepherds and woodlands, making the world grow, guiding the spirits of plants and animals. All of these different entities are connected through the figure of Pan. Each is a manifestation of Pan in a different dimension, like the same musical note being played in different octaves.

The gods of mythology manifest in all these dimensional octaves, depending on what aspect of the divine we are seeking to understand. But one of the most important ways in which the gods have manifested to humanity is through this canopy of the fourth dimension, through story, song, myth, and ritual. The gods manifest through our dreams and psychological images. Their power is translated into archetypal images, common to humanity, to help us better understand them and the mysteries of the cosmos. Even when we are not looking for divinity, we see their faces in our popular culture, in our books and movies. In the fourth dimension, the gods manifest in various guises, known as godforms. There is an almost universal image of the Moon goddess, but she wears a different mask for different cultures and people. She is Artemis in one form and Diana in another. She is Isis and she is Arianrhod.

It is through the fourth dimension that the gods become the most human and personal, but don't make the mistake of thinking that they are limited only to the fourth dimension. The fourth-dimensional manifestation is simply one expression of the gods.

Other teachings on the dimensions assign the star tribe of the Nibirians, also known as the Anunnaki of Sumerian myth, to the fourth dimension, as their speculative dealings with humanity have been very archetypal and have been equated with the Sumerian gods. The Nibirians will be discussed more fully in chapter 11.

Fifth Dimension

The fifth dimension is the dimension of unity. The individuality of consciousness merges harmoniously with the group identity of the collective consciousness. "You" and "I" identities more easily flow into "we," yet individuality is not completely sacrificed. This strange paradox is difficult for those of us in the third dimension to understand. There is still a sense of individuality, yet there is a much greater awareness of group identity on the conscious level. Where the fourth dimension is characterized as the collective unconscious, the fifth dimension is the collective consciousness. At this level we truly experience unconditional love and a commitment to that love. The fifth dimension is called Christ consciousness in some teachings, though we could easily describe it using the name of any other mystic who has reached this same level. To avoid a Christian bias, some purposely call the fifth dimension Krishna consciousness or Buddha consciousness, though in traditional Theosophy the functions of the Christ and the Buddha are considered separate (see chapter 7). Attainment of the fifth-dimensional consciousness is a major goal of people on the ascension path.

In the fifth dimension, we are truly conscious of the paradox of duality and separation. How can we all be one? Each of us is an individual, with a distinct sense of self and free will, yet we are all part of the greater whole. We are all strands in the web of life, woven by one weaver. We are all thoughts in the Divine Mind. We are all aspects of the Creator.

All paradoxes are resolved at this level. All dualities are understood. "Me" versus "you" consciousness shifts into "we" consciousness, and issues of balance between male/female, light/dark, good/evil, and material/immaterial are all transcended. Now we truly understand that these forces were never really in conflict to begin with, but were complementary. Even the paradox of time is resolved in the fifth dimension. In the third dimension, we consciously experience linear time—the past, present, and future—yet we know that other times are accessible. We touch other times through the use of divination tools, to predict the future or recall past-life memories. Mystical teaching says that time is really an illusion, and in the fifth dimension we truly understand this. We become conscious of ourselves in all times and all places. As we go higher in the dimensions, they become less linear and harder to put into words. I think we must accept the fact that some concepts are confusing and, like a Zen koan, something to be reflected upon. All versions of you—your current life, past lives, and all future lives—exist in the infinite now. When you are in fifth-dimensional consciousness, you exist in the infinite now, in touch with all of your selves.

There is quite a jump from the intellectual understanding of an idea that you hope to be true to the firsthand experience of the spiritual reality. We have glimpses of this higher fifth-dimensional reality when we awaken through the heart, experiencing the sense of divine union with another. It is through these heart awakenings that we come to the higher dimensions. In many spiritual traditions, the focus on love, on being a loving, compassionate person, is said to be the key to heaven. Love is the key to breaking through the canopy of the fourth density level and moving to the fifth. Ecstasy is a hallmark of many mystic traditions, when the practitioner is enraptured by divine love and hopefully comes to embody it in the physical world. When a person is rooted in the fifth dimension, it is said that he or she can manifest heaven on Earth.

Initiation and spiritual training bring us to the heart space, the middle point between the energy centers (known as chakras) above and below the heart. Through these spiritual experiences we awaken to the heart, to the place of balance. This is the point the bodhisattvas, or ascended masters, reach, where they are so filled with love for humanity that they consciously choose not to merge with the divine source, but instead to ascend to this point, where they can remain behind to be available to all, to share their love, so that in love we may all reach this point and find union with the source together.

Nature is one of the keys to awakening the heart. Many spiritual traditions encourage us to forge a balanced relationship with the natural world, animals and plants, to find this state of union. The natural world, unlike the human world, is not out of balance. Plants and animals instinctively know they are part of a greater whole, while humans, not having the same instinctive nature, intellectually feel they are separate.

Plants are particularly important in our healing. It is no coincidence that the color we associate most with the heart, green, is the same color as most plant life. Both plants and our heart centers convert the divine light (which is embodied in our solar system as the golden light of the Sun) into the green, growing, expansive, loving energy of nature. If love is stressed in many world religions, until fairly recently a reverence for nature was equally emphasized, particularly in pagan and Native traditions. By understanding, appreciating, and working with nature, we understand ourselves and the universe and open to a higher level of awareness. Some lightworkers believe that the Stone Age cultures that we look at as technologically inferior to our modern-day culture were actually more advanced because they were living, through their connection to nature, in a natural, intuitive, fifth-dimensional state of being. Some tribal people still live on this level of consciousness. A hallmark of both these ancient peoples and our modern indigenous tribes is a strong relationship with nature, both physically and with the spirits of nature, those we might call the faeries, devas, and nature spirits. Through partnership with them, we come to better understand the fifth dimension.

Our strongest allies in reaching fifth-dimensional consciousness are the ascended masters. The first image I was taught of the ascended masters was that of Shamballa. They were called the Lords and Ladies of Shamballa. Though in most lore Shamballa is seen as either a hidden city somewhere in Tibet, populated by true spiritual masters, or an etheric city, floating in the higher dimensions above Earth, I learned that Shamballa is really a diamond.

The image of the city of Shamballa is a tool to help those of us in the third dimension understand it. There isn't really a city. Even the image of the diamond is a symbol. There isn't really a diamond either. Those truly anchored in the fifth dimension are beyond shape and form. The diamond is just a better symbol now than the city. The diamond of Shamballa is an expression of the collective consciousness of the ascended masters of Mother Earth. Each facet of the diamond is an expression of a single master, one of the Lords or Ladies of Shamballa. In fact, they are truly beyond physical gender, but manifest in ways that we can understand or be comfortable with. Most people would have difficulty identifying with a group of ascended hermaphrodites, but can relate more easily to the familiar images of Jesus, Saint Germain, and Quan Yin. The image of Shamballa is Eastern, but the concept can also be found in the Western traditions. In ceremonial magick, Shamballa is similar to the Inner Temple or Inner Convocation of the Withdrawn Adepts, the spiritual beings who guide the traditions of magick.

In the paradox of individuality, each Lord or Lady has a face, a facet that is his or her area of expression, yet each is undeniably part of the whole. In human terms, we can think of Shamballa as holographic, with each piece containing the whole, just as each piece of holographic film, when cut, contains the entire image. We used to view the city as a whole identity, but each building, each home, in the city belonged to an individual master. In the image of the city, there was group identity and individual identity. The diamond is just a better way of showing both individuality and group consciousness. This diamond of light is a good symbol not only for the masters but for the fifth dimension.

The diamond of Shamballa is a focus for the fifth dimension, but it is said to have the bottom point anchored in the first dimension, our planetary consciousness, and the top point anchored in the divine Creator, the highest dimension possible. I learned that Shamballa stretches from the first level to the 352nd level, to the Godhead. It not only acts as a structure of the collective consciousness in the fifth dimension, but is available to us on all levels, in all dimensions, much like another model of the axis of reality, the Tree of Life. Although their consciousness is anchored in the fifth dimension, the masters often make themselves known to us through the canopy of the fourth dimension, appearing in visions, meditations, and dreams, and they embody archetypal qualities. Many masters have been devoted to particular deities and are thought of as deified humans, blurring the line between god and ascended master.

Barbara Hand Clow identifies the Pleiadians as the extraterrestrial intelligences, the star spirits, that guard and guide the fifth dimension. They will be described in more detail in chapter 11.

Sixth Dimension

The sixth dimension is the realm of geometry. It isn't the realm of the Pythagorean theorem, though Pythagoras had a strong connection to this level of consciousness. It is the realm of sacred geometry, teachings that were part of the Greek mystery schools, where Pythagoras was a teacher. Though sacred geometry has been omitted from most classroom teachings, it is the language of life and light, from which all things manifest.

Sacred geometry is the study of form and structure. All material things in the third dimension have an energetic template. According to traditional occult principle, in order for anything to exist in the material world, it must first exist on the astral plane. But how does something come together on the astral plane, what we would relate to as the fourth dimension? Its pattern, its basic components, must be fashioned from the geometry of light in the sixth dimension. All form precipitates down from the sixth dimension, through the diamond of Shamballa in the fifth dimension, to the astral archetypes of the fourth dimension, to physical forms in the third, second, and first dimensions.

While the fifth dimension is emotional in nature and based on love, the sixth dimension is mental in nature and based on ideas and information. Thoughts first take form in the sixth dimension before they manifest on the astral plane. Spiritualists and occultists would call the sixth level the mental level. Ideas take "shape" here through sacred geometry. All shapes are said to be based on combinations of the Platonic solids—five shapes, each resonating with a different element. The Platonic solids are expressions of elemental energy on a higher plane. Their "discovery" is credited to Plato, the Greek philosopher and spiritual teacher. Plato studied with Aristotle, who was a student of Pythagoras. The Platonic solids, and their relationship to your own energetic body, will be explored in detail through the teachings of the merkaba in chapter 21.

The morphogenetic fields, the geometric structures of energy theorized by biologist Rupert Sheldrake, exist in the sixth dimension. They are the patterns of energy that hold our template, that hold the geometry of not only our bodies but also the collective information of our species. When you were conceived, you were one single cell, with a variety of instructions encoded in your DNA. That single cell divided into two, four, eight, and so on, forming an embryonic human. But how do certain cells know to become brain cells, bone cells, muscle cells, or nerve cells? Most people would say that the DNA tells them to do so. But if all cells start out exactly alike, how do certain cells know how to "activate" nerve-cell instructions while others activate muscle-cell instructions, and then develop accordingly and in the right location? According to the theory of morphogenetic fields, it is these invisible geometric fields that are guiding the process. According to the ascension paradigm, it is the sixth dimension guiding the process, for all shape and form are rooted there.

Morphogenetic fields are also associated with the concept of consciousness grids, which evolved out of a controversial theory known as the hundredth monkey effect. According to this theory, each species has a field of energy, low in energy but high in information, connecting all members in that species, and this energy field transfers information to the members in a nonlocal fashion. Every member of the species is linked through an invisible force.

This theory was initially based on the discoveries of researchers studying the Japanese snow monkey on the island of Koshima in 1952. They noticed that one female monkey learned to wash the dirt off her potato in the water. She began to teach potato washing to other monkeys on the island. Soon, all the monkeys on the island (about a hundred) were washing their potatoes. Researchers on other islands noticed that immediately all the monkeys of the same species on the other islands began to wash their potatoes. They didn't learn the skill slowly and teach it to each other, as on Koshima. No monkey from Koshima swam over to teach them. They all spontaneously knew how to wash their potatoes, and made it a part of their culture.

It was theorized that when a certain "critical mass" of a species, about one hundred for the Japanese snow monkey, learns something, the information is suddenly transferred into the consciousness of every member of the race. It's as if enough members of a species have to do the work to create a psychic "circuit" in the collective field of consciousness. When the circuit is solid and fully formed, the entire consciousness of the species can flow through it. The story of the hundredth monkey phenomenon is found in Lyall Watson's 1979 book *Lifetide*. Experiments with other types of animals and people have been done to explore this theory. The fields of energy in the hundredth monkey theory are like racial morphogenetic fields as described by Sheldrake.

The human race's morphic field is much like a racial oversoul or monad connecting us all genetically, culturally, and spiritually. This concept is very important in ascension because it is believed that once a critical mass of people reaches a level of ascension, then the rest of the species can automatically ascend in what is called a global ascension, aiding in the creation of a golden age on Earth, as has been prophesied. The consciousness of the planet can radically shift with the ascent of a relatively small number of people. Ascensionists believe that if they can individually reach this level of enlightenment, then they are aiding the entire planet. A human civilization operating at fifth-dimensional harmony can truly create heaven on Earth.

Ascensionists believe that normal human consciousness is one grid, and that there is a second human consciousness grid, known as the ascension grid or Christ consciousness grid, that the enlightened connect with and ascend to in their process of spiritual evolution. This second grid was created by the ascended masters who have gone before, but it is not yet the dominant human consciousness grid. It is this geometric structure that manifests the unconditional love of the fifth dimension. Beyond the Christ consciousness grid are further levels of ascension that might be termed solar consciousness, galactic consciousness, universal consciousness, and cosmic consciousness.

While we associate archetypal beings with the fourth dimension, the sixth dimension contains the first thoughts that are the basis of all archetypal patterns. This level holds purer forms of those specific expressions. The true power beings exist as pure concepts on this sixth level of density, moving through the harmony of the fifth, to express themselves individually and make contact through the fourth. Beings who are truly rooted in the sixth level can mediate the love of the fifth dimension to bring it to those in the lower realms. Practitioners of spiritual traditions working with the various gods of creation find that the archetypal gods act as gateways to expanded consciousness in the other dimensions. Sometimes the fourth-dimensional expression of a being, particularly a goddess or god, distorts the being's higher nature. Many of our myths (our fourth-dimensional expressions of these beings) portray cruel gods, distorting their true sixth dimensional nature because they are being translated through human story.

For example, in the sixth dimension we have the all-encompassing love goddess. She manifests in the fourth dimension in many godforms, such as Aphrodite, Venus, Ishtar, Astarte, Inanna, Freya, Isis, Hathor, Aine, Branwen, and Gwynhwyfar. Each expresses a different kind of love. The myths of Inanna are not just of love, but of the mysteries of life, as Queen of Heaven and Earth. The myths of Aphrodite are more specifically of love, passion, and sexuality, and many of them do not portray her in the best light. Part of that distortion is due to how those in later Greek culture, particularly the male-dominated myth recorders, chose to portray her.

Along with the gods, the devas are also associated with the sixth dimension. Most think of the devas only as plant spirits, but they are considered the "little gods" of nature. They act much like the higher self, oversoul, or monad of nature, holding the perfected, purer forms of nature. They hold the morphogenetic fields of nature. Through the devas' patterns and blueprints of sacred geometry, nature manifests in the lower dimensions. We see their work as the plants and stones of the third dimension.

The power animal is like the deva of the animal species. We might consider it to be the oversoul or monad of animal life. When shamanic practitioners are working with the spirit of an animal ally, they often don't view the ally as one of many spirits of the same species, as a wolf spirit, for example, but rather as Wolf, the spirit of all wolves. Through Wolf, the wolf oversoul/monad manifests wolves in the physical world. The process begins on the sixth density level, with each subsequent dimension acting like a transformer, until the wolf manifests in physical form on the third level.

When we are out of touch with our sixth-dimensional energies, imbalance occurs. Many arts and sciences are used to connect us with our sixth-dimensional geometry. Anything that aids our connection with the sixth dimension aids the process. The practice of yoga, martial arts, and other physical disciplines bypasses the mind entirely and brings our body into alignment with our sixth-dimensional energies. The study of geometry—understanding intellectually and intuitively how all things are connected through pattern and form, and how our own proportions are perfected—is a powerful tool. Something happens when we study sacred geometry. Not only can we assimilate the intellectual information, but it triggers a connection to the higher dimensions. The study of any pattern, from genetics to weather or fine art, can help us tune in to the sixth dimension. The study of crop circles, manifestations of sacred geometry from the sixth dimension to the third, also activates this awakening.

Ascension lore tells us that the star beings associated with the star Sirius act as guardians of the sixth dimension for those of us currently on Earth. The Sirians, along with the Pleiadians, have been the most active of the star beings in aiding the development of humanity. The role of the star beings will be discussed in detail in chapter 11.

Seventh Dimension

As we enter the higher dimensions beyond the sixth, we lose shape and form. The dimensions become more abstract and less easily described in human language. We are still trying to comprehend what consciousness could be like at these levels, and have created ideas and models, yet nothing can be very concrete because reality at this level is not concrete. Many practitioners believe that the lines between the higher density levels become even more vague, as they overlap each other.

The seventh dimension is the realm of cosmic sound—not the vibratory patterns that we hear in the physical dimension, but the harmonics of creation. If the Principle of Correspondence teaches us that patterns repeat on every level, then this dimension is the higher expression of what we know as sound. This is the sound of creation.

Many traditions look at creation through sound imagery. We think of the universe as the song of creation. We each play our own note, our own pattern and melody, in the song. We each have our part. We even use the octave and overtone imagery in our model of the dimensions, with twelve dimensional "notes" in our scale, like the twelve tones in Western music. Hermetic magick references the "music of the spheres," the heavenly tones created by the movement of the planets, theorized in days past to be the "rings" of their orbits rubbing together. This music was audible only to those mystics with the ears to hear it, those in tune with the higher dimensions. The seventh dimension isn't just the realm of planetary sounds; it is the realm of the galaxy itself, as the orbits of the stars create a music of the heavens.

In the traditional mystic faery teachings, such as those of faery seer Orion Foxwood, the Creator is sometimes referred to as the Utterer, and the seventh dimension could be thought of as his uttering. The Utterer speaks or sings the world into creation. As many traditions link creation with the power of words, it shows how important our own words are in creating our own reality. Language has power. Magick is the study of words and thoughts to create reality.

In Judeo-Christian myth there is the concept of "the Word," also known as the Word of God or the Logos. In the biblical creation stories, it is the Word of God that creates the universe. Later, the concept of the Word was identified and equated with Jesus Christ, as the Word of God incarnate on Earth. "In the beginning was the Word, and the Word was with God, and the Word was God."—John 1:1. "And God said, Let there be light: and there was light."—Genesis 1:3. Through God's act of speaking, the world was created. God called for what he desired through words, through sound.

Barbara Hand Clow relates the seventh dimension to modern superstring theory, which is a model in which all the particles and fundamental forces of the universe are seen as tiny strings that vibrate at resonant frequencies. In a symbolic sense, I think of these infinite strings of energy as the "fabric" of reality. I see the Creator as a great weaver goddess, who takes the vibrations, the threads, and weaves them together into our reality. In the study of the science of semantics, terrestrial sound waves are used to create visible forms in sand, dust, and jellies. The more complex the sound played through the medium, the more complex is the shape created, including images of sacred geometry. On this cosmic creative scale, the cosmic-sound dimension creates, or "weaves" together, the structure and reality of our universe. The first step it takes is to form the sacred geometry of the sixth dimension. Magick is becoming conscious of our own weaver nature, our own ability to weave the strings, to pluck out the right notes and to change our part of the song of creation, to create the life we want. Clow also relates this dimension to the galactic highways of light, looking at a theory on the variable nature of the speed of light. Light moving faster than the standardly accepted speed of light exists in this higher dimension, acting as the connecting threads between galaxies, as information highways of light connecting us all. From a magickal perspective, these are the strings in the web of life, moving beyond space and time and connecting all things.

Working with sound helps us align with the seventh dimension. As we vibrate sonically in the physical world, we resonate with our power in the seventh dimension. Healers can use sound to restore the divine pattern of health within a person. Sound healing is a powerful art, and many claim that practitioners in ancient civilizations effectively used sound and music to treat illness by restoring a person's perfect patterns of sacred geometry, just as the cosmic sound creates the perfect geometric patterns of the universe.

The guardian spirits of the seventh dimension are said to be those star spirit intelligences from the Andromeda galaxy. Little is known about these Andromedans, and I've often wondered why they are keepers of the seventh dimension of this galaxy, at least from Earth's perspective, when they are in another galaxy. Dimensions one through nine are said to be in our Milky Way galaxy. When I asked my own guides about this, they said that much as other star systems act like a higher self to our solar system, the Andromeda galaxy acts as a higher self to our Milky Way galaxy. As the sacred sounds and strings of light act as highways of light connecting galaxies in the universe, this galaxy is the one we have the strongest higher connection to, and it and its inhabitants help us rise in our evolution. According to channels, the Andromeda galaxy is much like our own, with a solar system like ours, and a planet like Earth. The Andromedans have maintained a sense of harmony and interconnection with the divine that we have forgotten, so they are the perfect teachers to help us reweave our interdimensional highways of light and reestablish our connection to all things. Ascensionists see this "forgetting" of our divine connection as the archetypal "fall" mentioned in so many mythologies. Ascension therefore includes all the practices that help us "rise" and reconnect consciously to our true divine and magickal heritage.

Eighth Dimension

The eighth dimension is the realm of the Divine Mind, or at least the aspect of the Divine Mind that manifests our galaxy. Some describe this as the divine light, but it is not simply light; it is the consciousness of our creation. In the faery traditions, there is the Utterer who speaks the world into creation. If his utterances are the actual "sound," or seventh dimension, then the Utterer, the being doing the uttering, is the manifestation of the eighth dimension. The eighth dimension is the mind of the galactic god, beyond real shape and form in the way we think of divinities. Because of this lack of true shape or form, we describe this dimension as the divine light, though any lightworker knows that divine light permeates all dimensions. Within this Divine Mind are all the possibilities of the galaxy. We are all thoughts in the Divine Mind, according to the Hermetic principles.

The divinity of the eighth dimension is the source of our experience of the various godforms—the various faces of God, such as the solar and lunar goddesses and gods and the other archetypal beings—through the lower dimensions. These beings act as guides and gateways to the transcendental aspects of divinity. The light of the Sun has been a symbol, an interface and gateway, for the divinity of the eighth dimension. The Sun is our solar source of life, a lower "octave" of this divine light. Teachings that focused on the unity of monotheism, of the single Divine Mind, the single Creator, would use the Sun as the focal point, such as the work of the Egyptian Pharaoh Akhenaton, who tried to convert Egypt's polytheistic people to a monotheistic Sun worship. For other cultures, primal divinity resided in the Moon, the reflected light of the Sun. In truth, the light of the eighth dimension is of a higher vibration than that of the Sun or Moon or any stars. It is the source of all other light in the galaxy. When we look at the eighth-dimensional mind of light, the seventh-dimensional cosmic sound, and the sixth-dimensional geometry, these levels have parallels in the lower dimensions—in the unity of the fifth dimension, the archetypes of the fourth dimension, and the form of the third dimension. In the third dimension there is the manifestation of the visible light spectrum and the sonic spectrum, and the physical manifestation of the world.

According to the model of dimensions given by Barbara Hand Clow, the spiritual guardians of the eighth dimension are the beings from the constellation Orion, also known as the Hunter. This constellation plays strongly in human mythology, and channeled sources give information about both helpful, advanced beings in Orion and destructive ones, like the dual nature of divinity and all energy. All potential exists in the eighth dimension, though our choices govern how this potential manifests in the lower dimensions. The eighth dimension is not inherently good or evil, but rather is neutral, with the potential for both good and evil.

Ninth Dimension

The ninth dimension is the galactic center, metaphysically described as a black hole that acts as the gravitational linchpin of our system. From a multidimensional view, the heart of the Milky Way is a gateway, an interface and transformational point, into the next realm, which some describe as a new universe. The ninth-dimensional time waves emerge from this point, aided by the guardians whose name we draw from Mayan lore—the T'zolkin. The ninth-dimensional time waves are like the fertile soil in which our third dimension grows. Some would say that it is a "stargate" to the Great Central Sun of the universe, which is the true gateway to the next realm and new universe.

Tenth Dimension

The tenth dimension is the vertical axis that aligns the previous nine dimensions. It is the shaman's world tree, the Qabalistic Tree of Life, and the spire running through the dimensions. When a person's consciousness is simultaneously aware in all nine dimensions equally, it is in the tenth dimension. We use the tenth-dimensional axis all the time, to ascend and descend the vertical axis of reality, but the mastery of the entire axis gives us access to tenth-dimensional consciousness.

Eleventh Dimension

The eleventh dimension is the all-encompassing energy field that manifests and contains the previous dimensions, one through ten. This is the first realm of universal consciousness. If we could envision the ever-expanding boundary of our universe, in all dimensions, the eleventh dimension would be that boundary and container.

Twelfth Dimension

The twelfth dimension is the Great Central Sun of our universe, the source from which all the galaxies in our universe emanate and around which they all revolve. It is the source of universal consciousness, and a higher aspect of the Divine Mind and Creator. It is the Universal Logos, the universal creative source. Some look at the twelfth dimension as Melchizedek consciousness, while others feel that Melchizedek consciousness is one step beyond the twelfth.

Thirteenth Dimension

The thirteenth dimension is the gateway to the universes beyond our own universe. This is the level of cosmic consciousness, the Cosmic Logos, and the source of all the other universes in the multiverse. It is through the thirteenth dimension that we are able to access other universes. Many see the thirteenth dimension as a new universe that humanity is ascending to, because mastery of the thirteenth dimension allows travel between universes.

The dimensional model works in even and odd numbering, at least for the first nine dimensions. The odd-numbered dimensions have a more intuitive and emotional feeling to

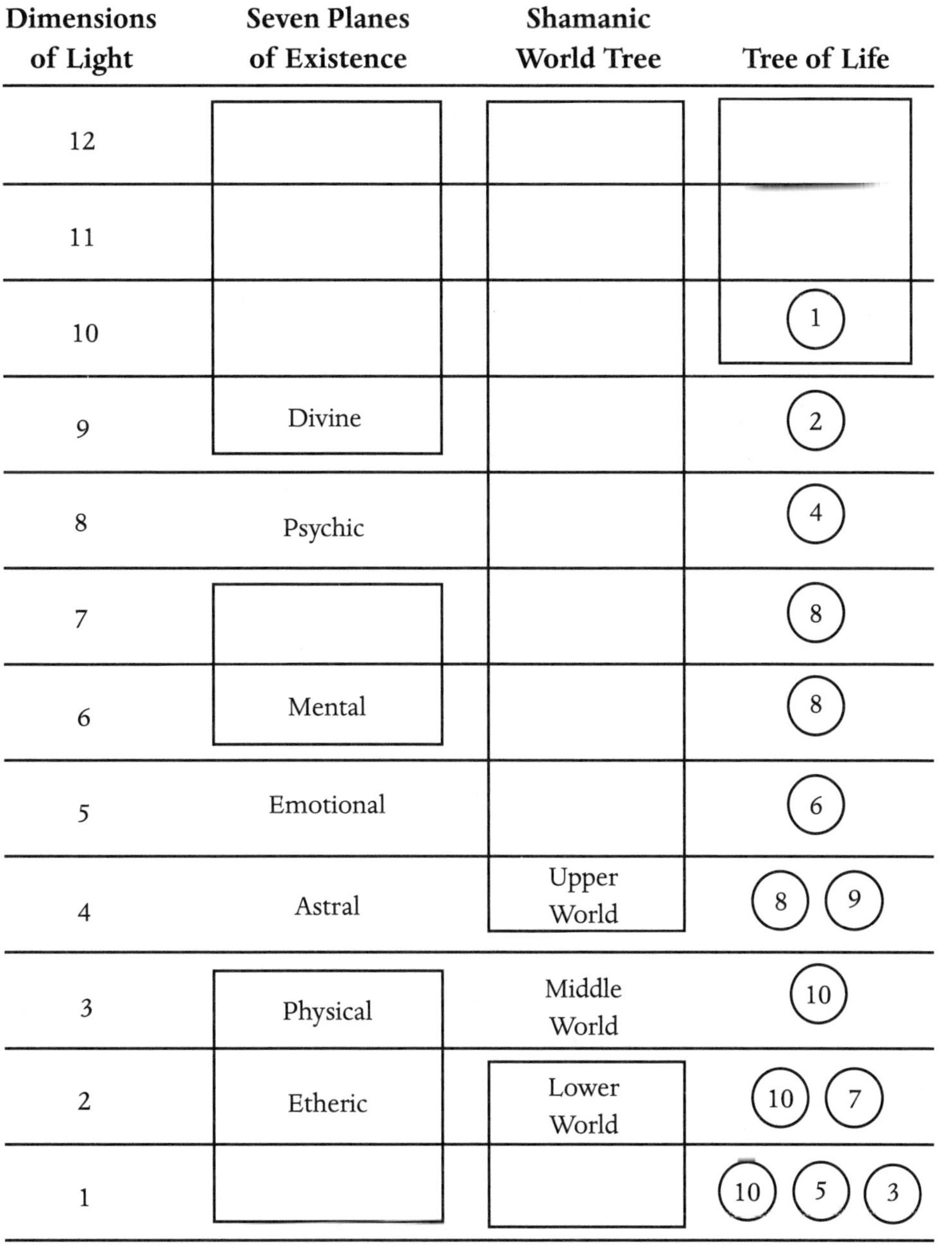

Dimensions of Light	Seven Planes of Existence	Shamanic World Tree	Tree of Life
12			
11			
10			(1)
9	Divine		(2)
8	Psychic		(4)
7			(8)
6	Mental		(8)
5	Emotional		(6)
4	Astral	Upper World	(8) (9)
3	Physical	Middle World	(10)
2	Etheric	Lower World	(10) (7)
1			(10) (5) (3)

Figure 18: Dimensions of Light, Seven Planes of Existence, Shamanic World Tree, and Tree of Life

them and are often described as more feminine, while the even-numbered dimensions are more analytical and intellectual, having a more masculine flair.

TRANSLATING DIMENSIONAL MODELS

These models—the dimensions of light, seven planes of existence, shamanic world tree, and Tree of Life—show a wide range of interpretation of the structure of reality (figure 18). Each is like a language, with its own context and frame of reference. None represents the literal truth, but all express a symbolic truth. Our reality models are ways of trying to take something subjective and subtle and make it into something more objective and overt. They aid in our personal understanding and ability to communicate our experience, but we must find the models that work best for us. Some are far too complicated for most of us, while others are too simple to express the complexities of life. We must find a balance and realize that in the end, these maps are simply symbols. The map itself is not the terrain. By putting a mountain onto the graph of a map, one does not completely express the majesty of the mountain. By putting the unseen realms into a two- or three-dimensional model, one loses the beauty, the true expression, of what those realms embody. Like the map, these models can only help us climb the mountain, but once it is in our view, we can enjoy its beauty directly.

EXERCISE 2:
Dimensional Travel—First Dimension

Though many ascension mystics feel that the higher dimensions are not accessible to humanity unless the person is of a sufficient spiritual vibrational level, the lower, more earthly dimensions are available to all. We all exist on the Earth and can more easily connect with Mother Earth and the first and second dimensions while rooted in the third dimension. Once we have a firm understanding and awareness of the lower dimensions, we can rise higher with greater ease and safety in our meditative journeys. This is one reason that many traditions focus on a reverence of nature—spending time outdoors and being in tune with animals, plants, stones, and the cycles of the Earth. Nature aligns us with the first and second dimensions. We then look to the stars, to the constellations, to be the archetypal patterns to give us greater access to the fourth and fifth dimensions. In this meditation, we will focus on going within the Earth, to the Underworld consciousness of the first dimension.

One of the "keys" to opening to multidimensional consciousness is aligning yourself with the sacred directions. Native American shamans, witches, and ceremonial magicians all have rituals to create sacred space by honoring the four directions. In addition to the traditional four directions, many practitioners also acknowledge the space above as the heavens, the space below as the shaman's Underworld, and the space in the center, the heart, as the place of balance. This orientation aligns you with the vertical axis and helps you traverse the dimensions.

When working with the sacred directions, it can be helpful to have an altar. The altar is simply a magickal workspace and a focus. By giving your sacred space a physical presence, the space is anchored in the physical world and can be a place to begin and end your magickal experience. On their magickal altar, most practitioners use the magician's tools (see chapter 5) to embody the four elements, and assign them to the four directions. The pentacle for earth is placed in the north. You can also use a stone, crystal, or bowl of salt for your earth tool. The blade for air is usually placed in the east or south, depending on the tradition. A feather, incense burner, or aromatic oil can also be used as an air tool. The wand for fire is placed in either the south or east, again depending on the tradition. A candle is another acceptable tool for fire. The cup for water is placed in the west. A seashell, open gourd, bowl, cauldron, or other container of liquid can also be used as a water tool. Many practitioners put a white candle for spirit in the center of the altar.

The altar itself is simply a flat surface that can hold these tools. A cloth is usually placed on top of it, then the tools are arranged according to direction. The altar usually faces either north or east, and can be a permanent structure in your home or something assembled and disassembled as needed. You can perform your meditations and rituals before the altar, so it can act as a focus for your magickal practice. Traditionally, items on the altar are "cleansed" of unwanted energies by smudging them, or passing them through the smoke of a purifying incense, such as sage, lavender, or a frankincense and myrrh combination. You can also smudge yourself and the room, too, before meditation and ritual to purify yourself and focus your energy. You can anoint the tools with a weak solution of water and sea salt to purify them in addition to, or instead of, smudging them with smoke. Next, the tool is "charged" by placing an intention into it. If the tool, such as a candle, is a symbol of elemental fire, you would hold it in your hands (once it is purified) and think about fire, and imagine the power of fire entering and charging the tool. A properly cleansed and charged altar helps you focus your energy during spiritual practices. You don't have to cleanse and charge all your tools before every exercise, though you should cleanse and consecrate them periodically, at least once a year.

With your altar in place, you are now prepared to traverse the dimensions of light. For our first journey, we will focus on visiting the first dimension.

1. Sit before your altar in a comfortable position. Call upon the divine, in whatever form you prefer—God, Goddess, Great Spirit, Divine Mind, Mother-Father-God. Ask to be consciously connected to your source, for guidance and protection, and to all your spirit allies who are appropriate for you at this time. Do Exercise 1: Basic Meditation Technique up to step 6 (see page 81) to get into a meditative state.

2. Acknowledge the power of the four directions. Bring your attention to the north, then the east, south, and west. Bring your attention to the heavens above and the space below you. Then bring your awareness to your heart. You are now oriented to the dimensional axis.

3. Return your focus to the space beneath you. Imagine that beneath you there is a tunnel guiding you down to the lower dimensions, to the core of Mother Earth, to the first dimension. Imagine yourself descending deep into a hole, into a tunnel of moist soil. Descend into the earth beneath you. Though it is dark, you feel you know your way perfectly. You are not frightened.

4. Enter the telluric realm of 2D, the realm of the elementals and mineral beings. Feel the spirits that cause the soil to grow rich and the plants to grow tall. Feel the power of the elemental world. As you descend, the moist, rich soil gives way to more solid stone, with veins of minerals and crystals that reflect slightly in the dim light. Feel the presence of all the mineral and crystal spirits that reside in this realm. As you go deeper, the red, warm glow of the Earth's mantle and core shines through, guiding you, warming you, yet never harming your spirit self. You feel like you are traveling home again.

5. Your journey brings you to a reflective surface, like a polished iron wall. Perhaps the wall is cut into facets, like a gem, or is smooth, like the surface of a

crystal ball. This is the central core of Mother Earth. Place your hands on this outer wall, and sincerely ask to gain entrance to the inner mysteries of the first dimension. If the time is right, Mother Earth will grant you this request, and you will find yourself "phasing" through this iron wall. You match its vibration and are no longer barred from entering. You pass through the wall as if it were a phantom barrier, as if it were not there.

6. As you enter the first dimension, you find an underground world, like the primal first lands of Earth. It is like a primordial jungle or forest that humanity has never touched. Here within the first dimension are all the animals that have ever lived in the world, all the species that are extinct and all that reside in the world now. The same holds true for all plants, as you find all manner of flora and fauna that you might never have seen in the third dimension. Explore the realm of the inner Earth. Many think of this as the true Garden of Eden.

7. Eventually you hear the pulse, the beat, of the Earth's heart, in the center of this dimension, if you don't already hear it. It's a low, powerful frequency that resonates throughout your entire being. Move toward the pulsing. Move toward the heart of the first dimension. There you will see the central core crystal, the memory of all that was, is, and shall be on planet Earth. It dazzles and shines with an inner light, as if a star were encased in the crystal, radiating streams of light.

8. When you reach the center of the first dimension, the core might take shape and form to speak to you directly as Earth Mother, or you might simply feel her presence all around you. When she takes a form, it is often a simple one, similar to our own ideal mother archetype. She may appear as a cook, in her nourishing aspect, or as a weaver, as the goddess of fate. Sometimes she is a gardener, though it is important to realize that Mother Earth is both the gardener and the garden itself. She is nature. While you are in the first dimension, you might even find the Dreamer who sleeps in the heart of the planet, and be able to commune with him.

9. When you are done communing with the Earth Mother, thank her and say your farewells. Return the way you came, through the primordial land. Know you can return to the first dimension whenever you desire. Pass back through

the iron wall and ascend through the tunnel, passing through the realm of 2D, of nature and elemental spirits. Slowly move through the moist earth, knowing that it is part of the 3D expression of Mother Earth.

10. Acknowledge the four directions around you again, north, east, south, and west, then above, below, and center. Thank the divine Creator for guidance and protection. Thank your guides and allies. Perform steps 9 and 10 of Exercise 1: Basic Meditation Technique (see page 82) to return to normal waking consciousness. Ground yourself by imagining an "anchor" dropping down, or a beam of light descending, from the base of your spine, deep into the Earth. This line tethers you to the material world and, like a grounding wire, releases into the Earth any excess energy from the meditation that is unhealthy for you to retain. This grounding technique can be used at the end of any meditation or ritual. Write down any impressions or messages you received, before you forget them. The return to 3D consciousness can make them fade quickly, like a dream.

Once you have mastered traveling to the first dimension, you can begin to explore the other dimensions. When you have conscious contact with your ascension allies and an understanding of the spiritual hierarchy, you can call to your spirit guides to consciously guide your dimensional travels in safety.

———————————————

7

THE SPiRiTUAL HiERARCHY

O ur spiritual anatomy begins with a central source—the monad, acting like a seed, with tendrils of energy expanding outward in increasingly complex branches, creating the oversouls and individual souls. Our universe is structured in much the same way. During the rise of Theosophy, there came about the idea of a cosmic and planetary hierarchy of beings, starting from a central source and extending outward in greater and greater complexity. Like the progression of union from soul to oversoul, and oversoul to monad, the spiritual hierarchy defines a series of roles on our spiritual evolutionary ladder.

This isn't a new concept. We find hierarchical structures in all spiritual cosmologies, and in an effort to re-create them in the human world, we have devised the structures of training, degrees, and levels of clergy within each tradition. The gods of the pagan world had their own hierarchies, with each one sovereign over a specific range of creation, a specific domain. The less powerful deities deferred to and respected the more powerful ones, who ruled over larger domains. When one hierarchical structure became outmoded, in both human thought and cosmically, the change was reflected in the myths, as with the Greek Olympians' overthrow of the elder Titans. We find hierarchy in the shaman's world tree, the Qabalist's Tree of Life, and the ascensionist's dimensions of light. The hierarchy represents the progression from primal expressions of the spirit world to more complex ones.

The Theosophical hierarchy describes a series of beings in positions on an ascending structure. Each being occupies an "office" in the hierarchy and has certain duties and responsibilities in the structure. Many act as guides, teachers, and healers to incarnated beings, or help guide natural forces on planets and solar systems. Beings can ascend through these offices, following various paths of spiritual development.

The term hierarchy has become outmoded. It has a negative connotation to most of us now, denoting bureaucracy and red tape. Originally, the hierarchical model was developed by the Theosophists in an attempt to make complicated esoteric subjects easier to understand, using a very human structure. Unfortunately, this model is pretty complex and at times even silly. It's hard to imagine spiritual masters as corporate employees, getting promotions and advancing through the universe. My friend Lisa and I used to joke about the cosmic boardroom flow chart, as neither of us resonated with corporate culture. We both escaped the corporate world to embrace a more metaphysical lifestyle. We wanted to find new models for understanding the relationships between spiritual beings and humanity.

As we enter the next age, one of its hallmarks is the end of hierarchy and the rise of lateral relationships and equal partnerships. The hierarchies of the world's political, social, and religious organizations will give way to more equitable forms of rulership, such as democracy, councils, and coalitions. Our spiritual models must also follow suit. The spiritual hierarchy is not a literal truth, but rather a symbol, a human interpretation of the complex relationships between spiritual beings. In the last age, we organized these relationships in terms of a vertical hierarchy (figure 19). Now we are struggling to create new, simpler models. I like to look at things in terms of circles, wheels, and spirals (figures 20 and 21), rather than linear levels. This removes the sense of authority and creates a holistic pattern in which everybody's role in the hierarchy is crucial. Changes comes slowly, and many of the older models and terms are still ingrained in metaphysical literature.

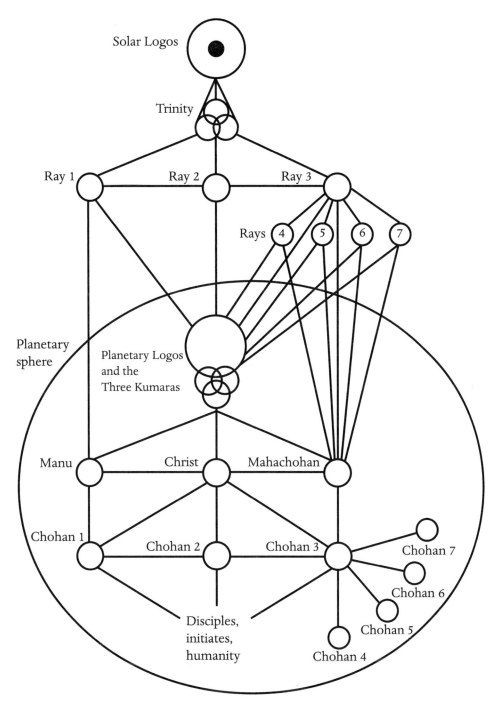

Figure 19: Traditional Model of the Spiritual Hierarchy

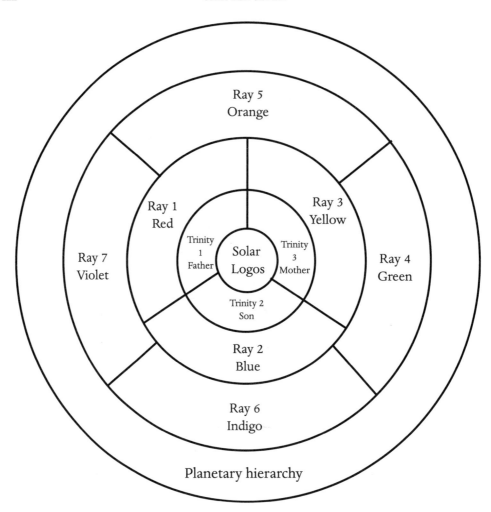

Figure 20: Modern Model of the Spiritual Hierarchy

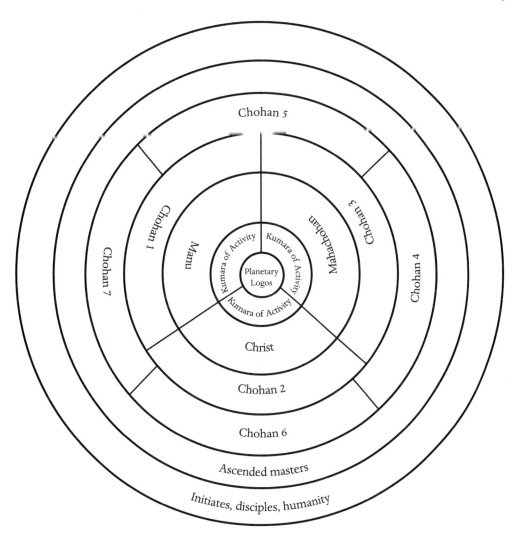

Figure 21: Modern Model of Earth's Spiritual Hierarchy

THE LOGOS

The Logos is a term that was used by the Greek philosopher Heraclitus to describe the underlying force of the universe. Logos translates to "word" but can also mean "principle" or "order," and is associated with the laws of nature. To the Greeks, logic was the guiding force of the universe, giving it structure and form. The Logos could be said to be a precursor to our concept of the collective consciousness. In much later periods, it has been compared to the concept of the Tao in Chinese mysticism or the Om sound of creation in Hinduism.

By the time of the classical Greek scholars Socrates, Plato, and Aristotle, the Logos was personalized as the individual's reason and faculty for knowledge. Plato believed that the soul was divided into three parts: the *epithymia*, the desire, which resides in the belly; the *thumos*, the will, which lives in the heart; and the immortal *logos*, the divine self, which is associated with the head and intellect. Plato personified the logos, describing it as a living being.

For individuals, the Logos can be said to be the higher self, the oversoul or monad, the divine wise part of the self. The Logos is the higher aspect of creation, what to the Greeks was the guiding logic of the universe, the divine intelligence guiding creation, similar to the Hermetic concept of the Divine Mind.

In other traditions, the Logos is seen less as pure reason or logic, giving structure and form to the universe, and more as the wisdom and redemptive quality of the universe. In Christianity, the Logos is equated with Jesus Christ, as the Word of God incarnated. The creator god of Judaism and Christianity is also considered to be the Logos, for this Creator creates reality through the power of his words. The Logos is the creative power emanating from the prime Creator. We can relate this concept to the seventh dimension. The Logos is responsible for the manifestation of all reality. In Christianity, the Logos, or Word, is said to be the second part of the divine trinity, yet in ascension, the Logos is, or contains, the trinity.

In ascension lore, the Logos is the higher self of creation. As there are many levels of each individual being paralleling the many levels of creation, the Logos manifests on many levels. Each Logos is responsible for the development of life in its domain. The concept of the Cosmic Logos is the closest thing we can understand as the creator of all universes, and all reality (figure 22). From the Cosmic Logos flows the Universal Logos. The Universal Logos is epitomized by the Great Central Sun of our universe. It is the holy, formless fire in the center of the universe, or the mythical "Secret Fire" in Tolkien's fictional tale *The Fellowship of the Ring*, which the wizard Gandalf describes as his true master. Gandalf, as a force of harmony, serves this Secret Fire and uses its power to stop the demonic Balrog. The universal fire is found in many traditions, myths, and stories. The flow continues to the Galactic Logos, the Solar Logos, and finally the Planetary Logos level. Each universe has its own prime higher self, as does each galaxy, solar system, and planet.

Each Logos is the prime center of power for that structure's hierarchy. The Universal Logos has its own hierarchy, as does the Galactic Logos of our galaxy, and so on through the cycle to the planetary level. Each Logos has several beings in charge of various functions of its being, the administrators of that part of reality. Each is responsible for shaping that level of creation.

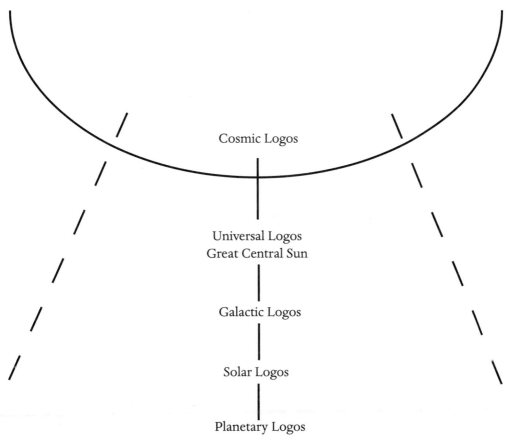

Figure 22: Logos Expansion

One can think of the structure of each system in a manner similar to the model presented in the Gaia hypothesis. We are like cells in the body of the Earth, as are all living things. Each has its own purpose for the greater functioning of the being, just as the cells within the organs of our body have their own individual purpose. Each planet is like an organ in the solar being's body. Each star is a part of the galactic being's body. Each galaxy is a part of the universal being's body, and each universe is a part of the cosmic being's body. One can take the model of offices and the cosmic hierarchy boardroom flow chart and replace it with the image of anatomy, organs, and cells in varying levels of complexity, in bigger and bigger beings. But we know that each "cell," each "organ," is alive, and each level of beings has a higher self, a spiritual Logos, guiding this level.

Humanity is more concerned with the Solar Logos and Planetary Logos on a personal level. Our planet, along with the others in the solar system, is said to be one of the chakras, or spiritual organs, in the Solar Logos's body. In ascension lore, the Solar Logos is known as Helios, named after the Greek Titan of the Sun, a precursor to the solar figure Apollo. Perhaps the old myths of Helios show the ancient Greeks had knowledge of the Solar Logos, or perhaps the new ascension models are simply borrowing names from Greek mythology. From the Solar Logos emanates the hierarchy associated with our planet.

THE TRINITY

The first emanation from the Logos is a trinity of forces. Each Logos manifests its own trinity. The Solar Logos is said to manifest a solar trinity. The Planetary Logos manifests its own trinity as well. Much of the ascension lore from the time of Alice Bailey is filled with Christian terms, including the use of the Father, Son, and Holy Spirit to describe the trinity of the Solar Logos. Some know the third aspect as the Holy Ghost or the Holy Sophia, the feminine wisdom aspect of creation, bringing balance to an otherwise male-dominated image. Many think of the aspects as father, child, and mother principles, as one aspect is the impetus to create, the second is the redeeming or connecting force, and the third, the Holy Spirit, is the spark of the divine residing in all things, material and nonmaterial.

Though we can think of the trinity principle in Christian terms, the concept of triune powers is universal. In Hinduism, the concept is embodied by the gods Brahma, Vishnu, and Shiva. Brahma is the generative force, Vishnu is the preserving force, and Shiva is the dissolving force. The Hindu form of the "Word," or an interpretation of the Logos, is the mantra Om, or Aum, as the trinity manifests through the three letters A-U-M. In astrology, the three powers manifest in the energies of the cardinal, fixed, and mutable signs. In ceremonial magick, the forces are personified as Isis, Apophis, and Osiris, borrowing symbolism from Egypt. Others see a parallel between the Egyptian trinity of Osiris, Horus, and Isis and the early Christian church that looked at the third aspect of the trinity as the mother wisdom principle, or Holy Sophia. In alchemy, the three creative principles are described as sulfur, mercury, and salt, the combustive, absorbing, and materializing forces. In witchcraft and paganism, the triple goddess or the three fates are the triune powers. Many modern mystics use the term GOD as an acronym for generating, organizing, and destroying. The three-ray teaching has parallels in the Celtic lore of the Druids and bards, with the symbol of *awen*, or divine inspiration, manifesting as three rays of light emanating from three dots (figure 23). The three rays correspond to the three worlds of the Celts; the three parts of the soul; the earth, sea, and sky; the letters I, O, and U; and the principles of love, wisdom, and truth.

Figure 23: Druidic Symbol of Awen

In the Theosophical system, the trinity manifests as the three Rays of Aspect, the first three of the seven rays. The divine energy, viewed as light, is said to be divided into various "rays," or frequencies, of divine energy, each with specific attributes. The divine light first manifests from this trinity into three rays that we associate with the primary colors—red, blue, and yellow. The three principles of these rays are will, love, and intelligence. The principle embodied by the first ray, the red ray, is will. The second ray, or blue ray, embodies the power of love. The third ray, the yellow ray, manifests the power of active intelligence.

The trinity of three rays manifests in the various orders of beings in the cosmos. Angelic beings are said to be a primary manifestation of the red ray, enacting the will of the divine and having no free will of their own. The spirits of the natural world—plants, animals, stones, and the entities that guide them—embody the heart and love of the Creator and are aligned with the powers of the blue ray. Humans—or any humanoid, incarnate race—manifest from the mind of divinity, aligned with the yellow ray. The Principle of Mentalism shows us that the nature of creation is mental, and we, having minds like the Creator, are able to create. We are like creator gods, made in the divine image. But we also have difficulty learning to master the mind. Spiritual technologies such as yoga, meditation, and magick are techniques to give us greater mastery over the mind and bring it into harmony with will and love. Though we have a strong mental nature, we also have free will and the capacity to love—a trifold nature.

The power of the Logos is said to manifest through the second ray, with the first and third flanking it, as it is through the Logos and the second ray that we become more aware of our divine nature and reconcile the two other aspects of creation. The second and third rays, seen as embodying the "son" and "mother" principles, share a unique relationship that is often overlooked. Though the mother aspect is strongly associated with love, the mother rules the third ray of the mind and humanity, which at first glance seems more male oriented. At first we would probably see the mother principle as being more in tune with the ray of love, until we see that she is the spark, the life force, in all of creation, and creation is but a construct of divine mental energy. The son principle, which we might think of as being more closely aligned with the mind, is really ruled by the second ray of love. Through the choice of love, humans find their way to spiritual awakening and empowerment.

In ascension teachings, all humans have a triple flame within their heart, manifesting the blessings of these three principles. Sometimes described as power, love, and wisdom, or power, love, and intelligence, they are the three core principles of ascension. The three principles work together to create a balance. Love without intelligence and power is ineffective. Power not tempered by intelligence and love is harsh. Intelligence without power and love to put it into action is useless. Getting in touch with all three principles is an important step in remaining grounded and stable on the ascension path, giving you the ability to act, discern, and love in equal measure. When you lack one, it's easy to stray off your path and become unbalanced.

Meditation on the threefold flame will help you open to the powers and blessings of the will, love, and mind. Perform this exercise to develop these powers.

Exercise 3:
Threefold Flame Meditation

You can perform this meditation whenever you want. Many practitioners suggest you do it every day. I do this at my altar, either at the start of my day or right before bed. You can be as ritualistic as you'd like, perhaps lighting a red, a blue, and a yellow candle on your altar before you perform the meditation. Once you are comfortable with this exercise, you can do it quickly in a light meditative state, standing up, to harmonize yourself, rather than getting into a deeper trance.

1. Sit before your altar in a comfortable position. Call upon the divine, in whatever form you prefer—God, Goddess, Great Spirit, Divine Mind, Mother-Father-God. Ask to be consciously connected to your source, for guidance and protection, and to all your spirit allies who are appropriate for you at this time. Do Exercise 1: Basic Meditation Technique up to step 6 (see page 81) to get into a meditative state.

2. Bring your attention to your heart. Imagine that your heart space (what people call the heart chakra) is like a door that is opening up. Some imagine it like the shutter iris of a camera, opening in a circular fashion. Feel a light pour out from your heart, radiating all around you. With your inner vision, look within your heart. See, sense, feel, and know that there are three flames there.

3. The first is the red flame of power. It is the principle of applied will—not your ego's will, but your soul's will, your higher spiritual will. How does it feel? Is there anything that keeps you from manifesting this power in your life? If so, ask for it to be revealed now, and to have the intelligence and love to deal with it. Ask the divine to stoke the fire of power, and make it stronger within your heart. Feel the flame grow.

4. The second is the blue flame of love. It is the principle of divine, unconditional love. How does it feel? Is there anything that keeps you from manifesting this love in your life? If so, ask for it to be revealed now, and to have the intelligence and will to deal with it. Ask the divine to stoke the fire of love, and make it stronger within your heart. Feel the flame grow.

5. The third is the yellow flame of intelligence. It is the principle of applied logic, knowledge, and discernment. How does it feel? Is there anything that keeps you from manifesting this intelligence and wisdom in your life? If so, ask for it to be revealed now, and to have the love and power to deal with it. Ask the divine to stoke the fire of intelligence, and make it stronger within your heart. Feel the flame grow.

6. Ask for all three flames to be drawn together, as if they were braided, within your heart. Each supports the other two. Feel your various selves come together in the harmony of love, wisdom, and power. Feel your ability to radiate it into the world, into your manifested life. Feel yourself with the power to fulfill your divine potential, whatever it may be.

7. Thank the divine Creator for guidance and protection. Thank your guides and allies. Perform steps 9 and 10 of Exercise 1: Basic Meditation Technique (see page 82) to return to normal waking consciousness. Write down any impressions or messages you received, before you forget them. The return to 3D consciousness can make them fade quickly, like a dream.

Alternate versions of this meditation use the color combination of pink, blue, and gold or violet, silver, and gold, but the original red, blue, and yellow combination is truest to the original Theosophical principles.

THE SEVEN RAYS

The Logos refracts the light of divinity much as a prism refracts light, expressing it in a spectrum of seven colors emanating from the source. Each ray is an archetypal energy representing a form of consciousness and development in the world. These emanations are much like those of the Qabalah, as the divine descends into ten colored spheres, each manifesting one aspect of creation. The science of the rays—using them to understand the universe and our place in the universe—is much like the study of the Qabalah.

The rays play a large part in our ascension cosmology, but they are not to be confused with the dimensions, for the rays shine through and permeate all the dimensions. Mystics can connect to these manifestations of consciousness in any dimension. There are "higher," or more enlightened, expressions of each ray, and lower, or baser, expressions of each ray, based upon the consciousness that is expressing the ray into form. The lower expression of the first ray, the red ray of will and power, can manifest as simple survival or as a craving for power. At a higher level it manifests as the spiritual warrior and guardian of truth and divine will.

The three primary rays, known as the Rays of Aspect, are the manifestation of the trinity, as previously discussed. According to Theosophical teachings, the remaining four rays, known as the Rays of Attribute, manifest from the third ray. They have more to do with human realms and the concerns of civilization, although in meditative vision, my guides have shown me a new model, in which the rays manifest like paints from the three primary colors swirling together. The seven rays of light, much like the colors of the rainbow spectrum, express seven different facets of divinity. One thing that is difficult for new students to understand about the rays is the order of their colors. When compared to the order of the colors in the rainbow spectrum (red, orange, yellow, green, blue, indigo, and violet), the order of red, blue, yellow, green, orange, indigo, and violet seems illogical. If you think of the order of the rays in terms of primary and secondary colors (first the primary colors and then the secondary colors), then it makes more sense.

The seven rays are attributed to specific forces and realms, as shown in chart 2.

Ray	Color	Title	Purposes
First ray	Red	The ray of will	Will, power, action, force
Second ray	Blue	The ray of love and wisdom	Compassion, understanding, benevolence
Third ray	Yellow	The ray of active intelligence	Logic, reason, ideas, communication
Fourth ray	Green	The ray of harmony through conflict	Art, creativity, nature, love
Fifth ray	Orange	The ray of concrete science	Science, technology, advancement, invention
Sixth ray	Indigo	The ray of devotion	Devotion, religion, spirituality
Seventh ray	Violet	The ray of ceremonial order	Magick, ceremony, ritual, healing, transformation

Chart 2: The Seven Rays

The light of the seven rays reaches us through the Sun, the Solar Logos. In channeled material it is often stated that such high-vibrational celestial energies have to be modified as they move down through the various dimensions, much like an electrical current moving through a series of transformers, in order to reach us at the appropriate frequency. The various energy transformers are associated with the star systems around us, linking our spiritual evolution to other stars and the spirits residing in those star systems. The rays are said to be focused through the stars of Ursa Major, Ursa Minor, Polaris, the Pleiades, and Sirius before reaching our Sun. As they move from these stars into the Sun, they continue to move through the body of the Solar Logos by passing through the seven sacred planets of the ancients, the chakras of the Solar Logos's body. According to the ancients, these seven planets were the Sun, Moon, Mercury, Venus, Mars, Jupiter, and Saturn. The rays are further transformed as they move through the planetary energy centers, the chakras of the Earth, and then they resonate with our own individual energy centers.

THE PLANETARY HIERARCHY

The planetary hierarchy is the extension of this divine pattern of life in the sphere of our planet. Though we will learn that there are many cosmic beings taking an interest in the affairs of Earth, the Earth has its own spiritual council that works with the solar and celestial councils. Those in the Earth council are primarily beings who have lived lives upon this planet, in the third dimension. In fact, every human is said to be a part of the planetary hierarchy. Disciples, mystics, seekers, and even those who are not consciously concerned with spiritual development are a part of the planetary hierarchy. We might not be aware of it, but our own thoughts, feelings, and actions affect the direction of our planet as much as, if not more than, those of discarnate entities such as the ascended masters and angels, who seek to guide us.

As in any Aquarian political system, the true power belongs to the people, who are seemingly at the bottom of the planetary hierarchy but who can change the course of events. Those at the top can guide, yet because of our free will, we might not listen. Though the planetary hierarchy was founded in love, and the beings at the top of the hierarchy have the best interests of the people at heart, only the formation of a partnership between the unseen masters and the people will bring about the New Age.

The Planetary Logos and the Three Kumaras of Activity

The planetary hierarchy is headed by the Planetary Logos, also known as the Lord of the World, the Ancient of Days, or the One Initiator. The Planetary Logos is seen as the spirit of the world. Our planet has two primary beings that work together in partnership. Mother Earth, or Mother Gaia, is partnered with the Planetary Logos, also known as the Dreamer of the World. He is usually described in terms of a male identity and, to a pagan, might be seen as the Son of the Mother Goddess. He is the manifestation of the divine heavenly man, and could be related to our concept of the Sky Father, the Greek Uranus to Mother Gaia. It is his dream that sustains and guides the world and, in particular, humanity's role in it. He keeps the human collective consciousness together. He does this in harmony with the Mother. As the embodiment of the planet, Lady Gaia is the most important entity in the planetary hierarchy, and works closely with the Planetary Logos.

The Planetary Logos is the Lord of Shamballa, the ultimate guide and teacher to all the ascended masters of Earth. He guides the spiritual initiation process and aids in the evolution of human consciousness. He regulates the contact of Earth with solar and other stellar forces. Through the Planetary Logos we receive the energies from the Solar Logos and beyond. He is the prism that disseminates the rays of light. He guides the process of incarnation into the physical world. Physical life is not a manifestation of the Planetary Logos, but the Planetary Logos is the being who guides the manifestation of all physical life. One could see him as the closest embodiment of God the Father on the planetary level.

According to Theosophy, the Planetary Logos at this time is known as Sanat Kumara, an enlightened being who came to us from our sister planet Venus. He is known as the Lord of Venusian Love. Another title is the Solitary Watcher, as he has been guiding us for a long time. Sanat Kumara is known as the first hierophant, the first initiating priest or guru, and is considered to be the greatest of all gurus, the greatest of all teachers, leading humanity's evolution. His name has been translated as "always a youth," as his presence is immortal and available throughout the ages. He is also known as the Youth of Eternal Summers and the Youth of Timeless Aeons.

At one time Sanat Kumara was known to be more actively involved in humanity, but he was most likely not physically incarnated, although the description of the Ancient of Days, in the Book of Daniel, is attributed to him by ascension teachers: "I beheld till the thrones were cast down, and the Ancient of Days did sit, whose garment was white as snow, and the hair of his head like the pure wool: his throne was like the fiery flame, and his wheels as burning fire."—Daniel 7:9. It's also important to remember that not all see Sanat Kumara as the

Ancient of Days referred to in this passage. Many Qabalists see the sphere of Kether, the crown of the Tree of Life, as the Ancient of Days. As part of the planetary hierarchy, Sanat Kumara is only a reflection of that sphere of consciousness, not Kether in totality. But one could say he is a reflection of Kether on Earth. Some feel that Sanat Kumara has recently ascended to a new role, guiding the evolution of not just Earth, but of several planets, and that the Buddha, Siddhartha, has replaced him as Planetary Logos.

The Planetary Logos works closely with a trinity of beings known as the three Kumaras of Activity, or the three Buddhas of Activity. Though the term Buddha can be used for any of the ascended masters, particularly those who have ascended from a life in a Buddhist tradition, here it refers to three specific offices in the planetary hierarchy. In the Hindu tradition, the Kumaras are "the mind-born sons of Brahma." Sanat Kumara governs their activity, as they guide the other kingdoms, or realms, of planetary life, while he focuses on the human realm. Sanat Kumara aids in the spiritual initiation of humanity and helps humans find their path in relationship to all other life. The three Buddhas guide and inform Sanat Kumara. These three Kumaras can be seen as "positions" or "offices" for various beings to occupy in their evolution. Their role in the planetary hierarchy is that of mediator between the various offices of the hierarchy, facilitating communication. Their hallmark is the teaching and manifestation of wisdom. There are also said to be three other "hidden" Kumaras in various realms working beneath Sanat Kumara, but usually they are not outlined in the planetary hierarchy. Sanat Kumara works to unite the visible, exoteric Kumaras/Buddhas of Activity with the hidden, esoteric Kumaras/Buddhas.

The three main Rays of Aspect manifest through the three Buddhas. Each of the three primary rays has its own "office," or area of expertise, to guide the planet. The first office is known as the Manu, the second is the Planetary Christ, and the third is the Mahachohan.

The Manu

The Manu manifests the first ray, the ray of power, or the will of the Planetary Logos in the world. The Manu puts into action the Planetary Logos's purpose, primarily by guiding government, founding and dissolving countries, and forming and dissolving racial, social, and cultural groups. The Manu is also said to be in control of the movement and formation of the Earth's crust. The Manu guides the formation of the various "root races" outlined in Theosophical teaching, as each being who holds the office of the Manu is marked to rule for an epoch of a root race's evolution (see chapter 20). The root races form the perfect vehicle for a planetary age's challenges and lessons. It is fitting that the head of the first department, of the physical world and its governance, guides the evolution of the physical vehicle, the physical body. The Manu and those in his council guide the working of political systems, the founding of new governments, and the transformation of governing bodies. As the Planetary Logos is the Lord of Shamballa, but oversees the entire planetary hierarchy, the Manu rules Shamballa as a governor of sorts, as the head of government systems, both physical and spiritual.

Though the Manu can be seen as an "office" in the planetary hierarchy, the being currently occupying this office is usually known just as Manu, though this being's name has been referred to as both Allah Gobi or Vaivasvata in various texts. Manu has little direct personal contact with ascensionists. Manu was originally a figure in Hindu mythology, known for the sacred text the *Laws of Manu*, but he does not have the same connotations in the ascensionist view of the office of the Manu. Manu is like the Eastern equivalent of Adam from the Book of Genesis, the first man. As the first man, it makes sense that he would govern the development of physical bodies and races. Perhaps the Hindu Manu was the first being from Earth to ascend to this position in the planetary hierarchy, and he left his "laws" to guide the way of his own passage. Ascensionists and Qabalists alike refer to the perfected body of light as the Adam Kadmon body, and perhaps both the myth of Manu and the being in this office have teachings to offer us on the perfection of the body to rise to the level of light. It is said that the ascended master El Morya, the lord of the first ray, will ascend to the office of the Manu for the next root race, being its primary template in the next age.

The Planetary Christ

The second office in the planetary hierarchy is that of the Christ, the Planetary Christ. In mainstream literature, Christ is a title for a master known as Jesus of Nazareth. Traditionally, the Christ refers to the anointed one. Christ is seen as the messiah figure whose arrival is anticipated in Judaism, and who already appeared (as Jesus) in Christianity. To the ascensionist, Christ is a level of consciousness, a title or office. The Planetary Christ is the second aspect of the trinity, ruling over the second ray, and fulfills the function of the child/redeemer in the triad, forging a personal link between the Planetary Logos and those below. Christ consciousness, also known as Christos consciousness or simply the Christos principle, is named for Jesus Christ, because we aspire to reach the level of enlightenment and unconditional love that he achieved. We can all be anointed ones, anointed by the spirit of the Creator, to embody this love and wisdom. We can all become our own saviors, our own redeemers. Rather than looking at one individual, such as Jesus of Nazareth, as our redeemer and our doorway into the next level, we can use his example to transform ourselves and our world. Jesus's true message was one of example; to be Christian, one must be "Christlike," not subservient to a regime. By entering this level of fifth-dimensional consciousness, we become more Christlike and assume a new awareness and new challenges.

The office of the Christ is reserved for the one who has assumed the role, in the planetary hierarchy, of bringing a level of Christ consciousness to a specific area of the spiritual hierarchy. The one in the office of the Christ guides the development of Christ consciousness, and creates the needed patterns to bring it to fruition. Just as the Logos exists on all levels, so too does the Christ exist on all levels. One can speak of the Christ in terms of the Cosmic Christ, Universal Christ, Galactic Christ, Solar Christ, and Planetary Christ. There are many Christs and many levels of Christ consciousness, just as there are many levels of the Logos. When you ascend to one level of consciousness, you have another to reach, until your consciousness becomes so expansive that it is one with the divine Creator.

The Planetary Christ is the guiding force of the second ray and the areas of religion and philosophy. This being mediates the love in the heart of the Planetary Logos. The office of the Christ is known as the World Teacher, or the Bodhisattva. Though all ascended masters could be called bodhisattvas, the office of the Christ is said to best embody the journey of the bodhisattva as a path of love and wisdom. While the Manu rules Shamballa, a place (although it is a place manifested only in the ethers of the fifth dimension), the Christ is said to rule the planetary hierarchy itself, the masters of Shamballa. The current holder of the office of the Planetary Christ is the Lord of Compassion, Lord Maitreya. According to some teachings, Lord Maitreya was the master who etherically overshadowed Jesus during his life on Earth. Maitreya's teachings in that lifetime focused on the aspect of the second ray of love, or compassion for others. His predecessor in this office was the first being known as the Buddha, Siddhartha, who was known as the Lord of Wisdom. Together, they grounded the teachings of the second ray—love and wisdom—into the world of humanity.

The Mahachohan

The last office of the planetary hierarchy is known as the Mahachohan, or Lord of Civilization. The Mahachohan rules over the seven masters of the seven rays, as this office oversees the "mother" ray, or third ray of civilization and humanity. The third ray gives birth to all of civilization and higher ideas. The Mahachohan also oversees the development of the natural world, working closely with the Manu and all manner of devic and telluric forces in the second dimension. As the department head of the third ray of active intelligence, the Mahachohan manifests the intelligence of the Planetary Logos. The Mahachohan guides the development of education, science, art, culture, magick, and ritual. The identity of the Mahachohan is under dispute, though most sources say that Saint Germain, also known as Master Rakoczi, assumed the post, leaving his position as the lord of the seventh ray to assume the mantle of Mahachohan sometime between World War I and World War II. Others feel that Saint Germain is still the master of the seventh ray and will assume the position of Mahachohan at the dawn of the New Age. The seventh and third rays have much in common.

As there is a Solar and a Galactic Christ, it is possible that there is also a Solar and a Planetary Manu and Mahachohan, though no one talks of working with such beings on a personal level. They are not directly involved in the process of human evolution. The second office of the Christ (and the second ray) seems to be the direct line to the higher realms of the universe. Through the Planetary Christ and the Planetary Logos, we reach the Solar Christ and the Solar Logos, and move onward and upward.

The Lords of the Rays

The seven rays manifest in our planetary cosmology through seven special ascended masters known as chohans, or lords or masters, of the seven rays. Each lord of a ray guides the ray's energy as it interacts with humanity and the hierarchy of Shamballa. In traditional Theosophy, the third ray is said to "mother," or manifest, the fourth, fifth, sixth, and seventh rays. The Mahachohan guides the lords of the seven rays, with a particular emphasis on the chohans of rays three through seven, as the Manu plays a role in guiding the chohan of the first ray and the Planetary Christ guides the chohan of the second ray. The Mahachohan is concerned primarily with the chohan of the third ray. Though the chohans of rays four through seven are placed beneath the Mahachohan in the popular hierarchy charts based on the work of Alice Bailey, the colors of these rays are a mix of the three primary colors, so these rays are also involved with the Manu and Planetary Christ.

The seven chohans have access to any being of the three offices of the Kumaras of Activity as needed to fulfill their functions and purposes. Though we delineate them as separate beings, there is a point at which a group consciousness, the nature of the fifth dimension, takes hold when we talk about the ascended masters. They are in a group synergy

Ray	Master (Chohan)
First	El Morya
Second	Kuthumi
Third	Serapis Bey
Fourth	Paul the Venetian
Fifth	Hilarion
Sixth	Sananda (Master Jesus), Nada
Seventh	Saint Germain, a Discipline of Saint Germain, Portia

Chart 3: The Masters of the Seven Rays

and are not able to be put neatly in little boxes, slots, or offices. The definitions and diagrams we use simply help us better understand their roles and relationships. The masters of the seven rays are listed in chart 3.

As we enter the shifting of the ages, various channels report a reshuffling of the ascended masters in the chohan positions to match the changing energies. Many feel Saint Germain is moving from chohan of the seventh ray to assume the position of Mahachohan, though he, or his disciples, will still respond if you petition him in conjunction with the seventh ray. Serapis Bey was the chohan of the fourth ray, and recently moved into rulership of the third. "New" masters, unnamed in the spiritual hierarchy, are now making themselves known through psychic contact with channels. Their new information has been the source of conflict and disagreement in our ray lore.

Through the work of Alice Bailey, the masters of Shamballa have introduced a spiritual guide now known to humanity as "the Plan." Though there are many interpretations of it, and the original version of Bailey's channelings was definitely colored by her Victorian-era upbringing, the Plan basically refers to the higher or divine will manifesting on the planet, rather than a specific political, social, or spiritual agenda. Lightworkers, ascensionists, and other mystics, whether they use the term or not, are custodians or keepers of the Plan, meaning that as we live our lives to fulfill our spiritual will, we contribute our part to the Aquarian Age. The Plan is a path of service to divinity, to the greater good, and to the world.

The Great Invocation

From the point of Light within the Mind of God
Let light stream forth into the minds of men.
Let Light descend on Earth.

From the point of Love within the Heart of God
Let love stream forth into the hearts of men.
May Christ return to Earth.

From the center where the Will of God is known
Let purpose guide the little wills of men—
The purpose which the Masters know and serve.

From the center which we call the race of men
Let the Plan of Love and Light work out
And may it seal the door where evil dwells.

Let Light and Love and Power restore the Plan on Earth.

Chart 4: The Great Invocation
(used with permission from the Lucis Trust)

The Plan doesn't refer to destiny (with no free will) or the loss of individual responsibility. We are each called to manifest our divinity, our part of the Plan, through the actions of our lives. Sometimes our manifestation of the Plan falls short of the ideal. Bailey's channelings give us the Great Invocation, a prayer or spell to "restore" the Plan upon Earth. It's a magickal call to awaken to higher will not only our individual selves, but the entire planet. It can be used in daily prayer and devotion or in ritual.

The text of the Great Invocation is given in chart 4. In modern circles, God is sometimes replaced with Creator or Mother-Father-God. The concept of Christ's return is now interpreted not as the return of an individual savior, but as the attainment of Christ consciousness by all, so some people substitute Christ consciousness for the word Christ in the Great Invocation.

THE FOUNDATION OF THE PLANETARY HIERARCHY

Beneath the seven chohans in the planetary hierarchy are various other ascended masters who are not in charge of a specific ray, though many of them are devoted to a particular ray in following their soul's path. They are training on the path to possibly assume the role of chohan of that ray. Other masters mix and match their work in the rays as they did in physical life, and are on other ascension paths. Many act as guides and healers to humanity, making contact with mystics of all traditions. Some partner with humans to create new systems of philosophy, healing, and spirituality. Some ascended masters act as guides to departed souls, taking on the role of "Lord of Karma," through which the master helps the soul review the past lives and plan the next one. Since this occurs beyond the bounds of conventional time and space, the soul can reincarnate instantly or wait a certain amount of time. Though only one "lord" is said to exist for each of the seven rays, the term *dhyan chohan* has been used to refer to any of the ascended masters in the hierarchy, though originally the term was reserved for those masters who were thought to be fully incarnated in a physical body, and at the lowest level.

Beneath the masters are the levels of incarnated life, which form the foundation of the planetary hierarchy. In the human kingdom, or human garden, there are four groups. These groups include spiritual initiates, or those who have achieved a measure of success on the path of ascension in this lifetime or a previous one; disciples, or those actively working toward their first initiation; those on the probationary path or skirting the edges of initiatory spiritual development; and average humanity. Personally, at this time I think we are all on an initiatory path toward ascension, and there is no such thing as "average" humanity. These modes of thinking are outdated. Every human—in fact, every being—is a shining star seeking to remember his or her true nature. Flanking the human kingdom is the multitude of beings in the animal, plant, and mineral gardens. Each of these beings has its own course of evolution and spiritual purpose. Like the angels, nature has its own structure. Though this structure is described as a hierarchy, it really is a web of life, a vast and complex chain of relationships, in which everyone and everything affects everything else. Different beings might take up larger or smaller portions of the web, or have different responsibilities, but if any part is missing, there is a hole in the web. Each being is vital to the continued, evolving pattern of the web of life.

PART THREE

ALLIES ON THE ASCENSION PATH

8

THE ASCENDED MASTERS

The ascended masters are a very special group of beings dedicated to the spiritual development of humanity. Though each incarnated human has many different guides available, the ascended masters are uniquely suited to guide our Earthwalks. This is because the ascended masters have also been incarnated on Earth and have lived through many of the same joys and difficulties we experience on the spiritual path.

Ascended masters are basically humans who realize their full potential, who realize their innate god selves, either while incarnated or just after death. They merge their consciousness with their own divine template, what is sometimes known as the lightbody, and are released from the wheel of karma and the cycle of rebirth. They come into conscious mastery of themselves and their relationship with the divine. They merge with their higher selves and monads, uniting themselves with their true spiritual will and purpose. They reach a level of what we call enlightenment, which is really to be "filled with light," the light of consciousness.

Rather than move on to the ultimate merger with the divine, the ascended masters remain in a state of union with all of creation while still retaining an individual essence and persona. The masters choose to make themselves available, on the spiritual planes, to all of humanity, and guide forces on the planet and in the universe, as a part of their new level of awareness and growth. Being discarnate, they are available to many people simultaneously, regardless of time and space, which increases their ability to help others. If they had chosen to remain enlightened but incarnated, they would have had only one place of physical presence on Earth. The masters mediate divine energies, acting as conduits, as connective forces, between the higher powers and their human family. Just because they have grown up and moved out of the house of physical existence, as some teachers describe it, doesn't mean they have forgotten their brothers and sisters back home. Like good siblings, they look in on us and guide us when we choose to listen.

The ascended masters have had many lifetimes devoted to spiritual practices and come from a variety of religious backgrounds, showing that all religions serve the purpose of aligning us with our true spiritual essence. We find the concept of the ascended masters in many traditions.

In the East, the masters are known as bodhisattvas. Though bodhisattva is a term for the second office of the Planetary Christ in the later New Age material, generally it stands for an Eastern mystic who reaches a level of enlightenment but forgoes the bliss of nirvana, of union with the divine. The mystic knows that others have not made the same leap in consciousness to nirvana, and seeks to remain behind, in compassion, to guide others until we can all achieve that blissful union with the divine together. The bodhisattva seeks not only self-enlightenment, but the enlightenment of all. A bodhisattva wants to release all people from suffering and is motivated by love and compassion. The concept of the bodhisattva is the closest ideal we have to the New Age concept of the ascended master in our Theosophical works, starting with those of Blavatsky and Bailey.

In the West, we don't have the same concept of a bodhisattva as in the East, although a close equivalent would be a saint. Though from a doctrinal view a saint must be recognized by the church, in a purely spiritual sense a saint is one who has become so close to God in life, and after death, that he or she acts as a conduit to the Creator, passing prayers and requests to God on behalf of the prayerful. Usually a saint will embody an aspect of divine energy that he or she manifested in life. In terms of Christian magick, each saint has an archetypal quality and a specialty of prayer. Certain saints are prayed to for certain actions, from healing to safe travel to finding lost objects. Relics of the saint, including finger bones and shrouds, help mediate this divine energy. Pictures, statues, and medallions are also ways of connecting to the saint's energy, and have been popular in forms of Christian prayer and magick for almost two thousand years. Some saints, such as Mother Mary, are said to have ascended into heaven with full body and soul, without having experienced a physical death.

In Jewish lore, there are the Tzaddikim. The Tzaddikim are thirty-six righteous individuals who are said to shoulder the world upon their backs. It is due to their offering that the world as we know it continues to exist. They are the secret and selfless kings and queens of the world. Each generation is said to have thirty-six of these individuals. Though the Tzaddikim are thought to be flesh and blood and not ascended into the ethers like the bodhisattvas, their "ascended" consciousness, devoted to the continuation of the world for their fellow humans in accord with the will of the Creator, makes some interesting parallels to the concept of ascended masters. Many of the characters of the Old Testament, such as Elijah, are considered ascended masters, ascending into the heavens.

Though most in traditional Islam would not consider the prophet Mohammed an ascended master, one could look at his story in much the same light as those of many Jewish and Christian holy people who are now considered ascended masters. It was said that Mohammed did not to die bodily in the world, but instead ascended with full body into heaven, much like Mother Mary.

With this archetypal quality and god-self realization, one can see the ascended masters in the pagan and tribal traditions. The power of the ancestors is evoked in shamanic tribal custom. All ancestors are honored in a family or tribe, but the particularly powerful ones, those who were healers, priests, warriors, and rulers, stand out in history and hold a special place in religious services. Their larger-than-life status is much like that of a saint or bodhisattva. In fact, many would consider special ancestors, with larger spirit "jobs" to do in the other worlds, to be like "enlightened ancestors" or "mighty dead," whose power and status grow as more people pay attention to them after their death. Native American tribes look to the wisdom of the grandmothers and grandfathers, the aunts and uncles, who have gone before them. Certain chiefs, warriors, and shamans throughout history are honored for their historic and spiritual contributions, but they also seem to be guides to those in the physical world, making spiritual contact through ceremony and vision.

Some Asian traditions also have a process of deification of the ancestors and family line through reverence, rituals, shrines, and altars. The status of the ancestors in the spirit world reflects on the blessings of prosperity and health they can bestow upon their living relatives. In fact, the ancestor reverence of the Eastern, African, and original pagan traditions may be one of the first forms through which the ascended masters manifested. Practitioners of these traditions think that their reverence of the ancestors elevates the departed spirit to a higher plane, to be closer, or become one, with the creative source. Our reverence feeds the departed spirits energy to rise in consciousness, and they in turn help guide our material life and spiritual evolution. This traditional teaching fits in well with the concept that the Theosophical masters work with us because it is a part of their own current learning to work with those of us who are physically incarnate.

African diasporic traditions, such as Voodoo and Santeria, have special spirits—called loa/lwa and orishas, respectively—that act as intermediaries between the remote divine Creator and humanity. They are not gods, ancestors, or angels, but have qualities of all three. Certain ancestors become loa over time and are called upon in ritual. Famous practitioners, such as Marie Lavou of New Orleans, are honored as something more than an ancestor in the tradition but not quite one of the ancient loa. Modern figures such as politicians and musicians have even started to make their way into the pantheon of loa. The archetypal qualities of the loa made it easier for the African practitioners to equate them with the Catholic saints when they were forced to adopt Christianity in the New World.

Pagan traditions are less clear on the theology of ascended masters. Coming from a polytheistic background, many would think that the pagan gods and goddesses are simply the deified ancestors. When we look at many of their stories, they do have a very human quality, and many, such as the Norse god Odin or the Celtic Lugh, seem to grow in enlightenment and power, as if they are on a path of magickal ascension. To a pagan, the divine Creator manifests in many faces, and the deities of pagan myth are not seen as humans rising toward divinity. Their stories are humanity's attempts to understand the nature of the divine.

Pagan myths do, however, have quite a few examples of what we might consider demigods. These are humans who seem to ascend to the heavens in a variety of ways. In Greek myth, they are symbolically elevated to the realm of the constellations, so their stories will be remembered forever, etched into the stars. In Celtic myth, the line between gods and mortals is quite a bit blurrier. The Christian scholars who recorded the pagan myths reduced the role of many of the gods in the myths. Many, such as the god Lugh, seem to transform over time, from human to immortal and divine. Lugh begins as a talented youth knocking on the door of Tara, at the home of the Irish gods known as the Tuatha de Danaan, or children of the mother goddess Danu. His tale ends with him being a powerful warrior, king, and leader of the gods. He ascends from a more human world, where he is remarkably gifted, to the realm of the gods, where his talents are put to good use.

In some Celtic belief systems, you can see the process of enlightenment and ascension in their cosmology. The universe is described in terms of concentric rings, starting with the Underworld cauldron of life known as Annwn. Annwn gives rise to the ring of Abred, the realm where the human soul is perfected. Those who are not perfected, freed from anger, fear, and dishonesty, go back to the Underworld of Annwn. Those who reach a state of perfection move to the realm of Gwynedd, the realm of purity. Those in this realm are free from reincarnation. The final outer ring, Ceugant, is the infinite dwelling place of the powers of creation, beyond the reach of all those in the previous realms. Some modern neopagans see this theology as influenced by Christianity and Eastern traditions and not purely Celtic, particularly with the concept of Ceugant, but it shows that the Celts had some concept of enlightenment and perhaps even of ascension.

Many of the names of the ascended masters are related to pagan gods. Humanity's views of the various gods have changed and transformed over time, affecting our relationships with these powers. The goddess Brid became known as Bridget, and later Saint Bridget, and many now see her as an ascended master. Similarly, the Eastern Quan Yin was depicted as a goddess, then as a bodhisattva, and now as an ascended master.

In the Norse pagan traditions, we see the possibility of ascended humans in the myths of the Valkyries. The name means "choosers of the slain" and refers to a divine troupe of warrior women riding winged horses. They work for the Norse all-father god Odin, and upon his direction, ride over battlefields and "choose" the brave and distinguished heroes of the battle to become one of the Einherjar. The Einherjar are brave warriors who died in battle and now reside in Odin's hall, Valhalla, feasting and drinking in a warrior's paradise until the end days and the battle of Ragnarok, the Norse Armageddon. In this society, the qualities of battle prowess, bravery, and honor are as much the tools of enlightenment as are quiet contemplation and a peaceful attitude.

Valhalla is only one of the "zones" for spirits who leave the material world. The Middle World of Earth and humanity, known as Midgard, our third dimension in ascension terms, is the land of the living. Most of the dead go to Hel. In Norse cosmology, Hel is not a place of torture or fire, but simply where the dead go. There is no devil there, but there is a goddess named Hel. Her name and the name of the land were later associated with the Christian Underworld, but the concepts are quite different. There was a land for those who did evil and died with dishonor, sometimes known as Niflheim, that separated them from the honorable dead and those who simply died of illness or old age. The chosen warriors went to Valhalla, and some Norse traditions also describe the realm of the lights elves, called

Alfheim, as a realm of enlightened ancestors who live with the elf spirits. One might see the light elves of Norse myth as either ascended beings, angels, or benign faeries. Those who work closely with these divine beings might spend their afterlife with them.

In Italian folklore, the figure Aradia could be seen as an ascended master. The details of her life, if indeed she was a living person, are hotly debated. She was said to be born in 1313 in Italy, sent by her mother, the goddess Diana, to revive the traditions of witchcraft. Aradia taught magick, and her testaments eventually were collected by Charles Leland and made into the book *Aradia, or the Gospel of the Witches*. Other witches would point out that Aradia is more properly an *avatar*, to borrow a Hindu term, of the goddess Diana, meaning that she is a physical incarnation of the goddess. Aradia is an incarnation of Diana and is referred to as her daughter, similar to how in Christianity, Jesus is considered both the son of God and an incarnation of God. Celtic witches would look to the Irish hero Cuchulain as a potential avatar of the god Lugh, as Cuchulain is often thought of as an incarnation of this powerful god. In the ascension paradigm, each of these beings would be considered an ascended master devoted to, and enlightened through, a particular archetypal energy.

Practitioners of witchcraft traditions believe that the spirit of a powerful witch can live on in the spiritual planes and influence the world. Witches see their spiritual ancestors as the Mighty Ones or Mighty Dead on the inner planes, or the Wise Ancestors, and believe they guide the craft of the wise from the Summerlands, acting as spirit guides to new witches and guiding the modern evolution of paganism. Doreen Valiente, in her book *An ABC of Witchcraft Past & Present*, compares modern witches to the Stone Age practitioners of cave art. She describes a ritual reported by Robert Cochrane in a magazine article in the publication *New Dimensions*: "It gave a vivid description of a rite in West Country cave, when chanting and dancing took place round a fire, until a spiritual presence, that of a master witch of long ago, manifested itself." It appears that the purpose of this ritual was to summon what we might consider an "ascended witch." Today, practitioners of a non-Wiccan traditional craft refer to the powerful ancestors as the Hidden Company, as they feel the presence of hidden beings at the edge of their rituals, guiding them.

Those who have completed what they call the Great Work in ceremonial magick traditions, or alchemists who have made the Philosopher's Stone or completed the "operation of the Sun," reaching the Western equivalent of enlightenment, are available to provide spiritual guidance to seekers on the path. They form a spiritual order on the inner planes that is connected to the magicians of this age. The priests and priestesses of the ancient world, particularly the spiritually empowered ones, guide their tradition after their passing. Various lodges and magicians have reported having secret masters who are not clearly humans or spirits, but are perhaps humans who have ascended to a higher plane. These masters manifest a presence when they need to be heard or seen, to guide those within their order.

WHAT'S IN A NAME?

In the modern age, the ascended masters are known by many names. My first introduction to them was less than auspicious. I met someone who was a channel for a master, like Blavatsky and Bailey. I had no real knowledge of New Age terminology, and he introduced himself as a "channel for the Great White Brotherhood." The term frightened me just a bit, and I felt like I was joining a meeting of the Klu Klux Klan, waiting for white sheets and torches. The name Great White Brotherhood was coined at the turn of the twentieth century, with the concept of white being a combination of all colors and brotherhood seen as a universal brotherhood/sisterhood of the human family and Aquarian ideal. No one realized that by the end of the century the term would be considered potentially racist and sexist. The name has led to some misunderstandings of New Age practitioners and Theosophists in particular. Another older term for the masters is the Great White Lodge, as the lodge is the organizational system, the body, of such spiritual traditions as the Masons and Rosicrucians. The Rosicrucians referred to their secret masters as part of an Invisible College. The term lodge also has associations with Native American lodge traditions. Lately, the inheritors of the Theosophical lore have emphasized the title "Lords and Ladies of Shamballa," hoping to diffuse the sexist or racist overtones of the other name. Others simply refer to the ascended masters as the hierarchy, the mahatmas, the bodhisattvas, or simply the masters.

The Theosophists were not the only ones who were in contact with the ascended masters at the turn of the century. The Hermetic Order of the Golden Dawn claimed contact with the "secret chiefs," beings who had completed the Great Work of the magicians and now guided those traditions. In fact, the highest offices of the Golden Dawn were said to be occupied not by incarnate individuals but by the ascended. The visible head of the order simply took his orders from the secret chiefs. Contact with these secret chiefs gave many others in the Hermetic magick traditions license to begin their own lodges and branches. Aleister Crowley, who split with the Golden Dawn and later formed his religion of Thelema, created the Order of the Silver Star, or Argenteum Astrum, and took over the existing group known as the Ordo Templi Orientis, or O.T.O., which also claimed to be in communion with the secret chiefs.

Soon others founded organizations under the direction of the secret chiefs and ascended masters. Other names and titles for these beings that have come to popular attention include the Order of Blessed Souls, the Withdrawn Order, the Inner Plane Adepts, the Secret Masters, the Enlightened Ancestors, the Invisibles, the Buddhas, the Christed Ones, and the Illuminated Ones. Shamballa is also known by many names, such as the Great Lodge, the Starry Lodge, the Inner Convocation, the Invisible College, the Academy, the School of Shadows, Solomon's House, and the House with Wings. More references to Shamballa can include the underground city of Agartha, the Russian-Mongolian tales of Belovodia, the Kirghizstanian Janaidar, the Islamic Hurqalya, the Hindu Aryavartha, the Chinese Hsi Tien, the Hawaiian Pali Uli, the Samoan Bali Hai, and the legendary Spanish golden city of Cibola.

One of the earliest teachings on the ascended masters that I received said that once you make a connection to them, you can call them anything you'd like. I was introduced to them as the Great White Brotherhood, but that name still bothered me. In my own perverse way, I decided to call them the Big Black Sisterhood, and they responded. The name doesn't matter as much as the spiritual connection. Now I prefer the Lords and Ladies of Shamballa, but in the end, use the name that works best for you.

WORKING WITH THE ASCENDED MASTERS

In our three-ray model of existence (the rays of will, love/devotion, and active intelligence), humanity is rooted in the third ray, the mind of the Creator, which grants us our greatest strengths and biggest challenges. We focus so much on our mental body, our thoughts, ideas, and words. Though we can use the power of the mind to create, we can also use our mental faculties to overanalyze and become distracted from our spiritual existence, getting lost in our thoughts. The ascended masters are also rooted in this mental aspect of creation, but through it they have found not only balance, but harmony. Mentally, they are able to come to the transcended point of equanimity, and then step off that point, rising above it, and identify their core identity with their highest aspects. They are still involved in the world of form, but they are untouched by it. They embody the spiritual saying "Be in the world, but not of it." While incarnated, they can enjoy the pleasures of life, but not be swayed by the illusions of the material world, knowing that the very nature of the physical world is change, not permanence. The only permanence they find is in the spiritual worlds and higher dimensions. Through this balance of mind they unlock their own divine powers.

Contrary to popular belief, not all masters pursued an earthly life of asceticism and denouncement of material pleasures. Many enjoyed all that the world had to offer. Saint Germain, in particular, during his incarnation as the Count de Saint Germain, was known to enjoy the company and pleasure of many beautiful ladies of the courts of Europe, and lived a lavish lifestyle as he taught among the nobility, impressing them with his acts of alchemical transformation. He even used alchemy to perfect gems with flaws in them, thereby increasing their value. The difference between Saint Germain and most of us who might seek such powers is that, as an ascended master, he was not seduced by power or fame. He knew that those pleasures were simply the enjoyments of the world, not the ultimate goal of the spiritual seeker.

Ascended masters succeed in manifesting the highest ideals of the mind when so many of us struggle, because they learn the art of inner alchemy. Regardless of the religion or tradition, they learn how to unite and fuse their mental aspect with both their divine will and their divine devotion. Through their spiritual alchemy, the three aspects of creation become one harmonious whole. Humans, or any incarnated sentient beings, have a fairly unusual ability in the universe to bridge the gaps between these three principles and unite them.

We have free will. We are not rooted in divine will. We can be in divine will, but we must choose it. We can work with our personal will, our ego's wants and desires, but that is very different from divine will. We see the secret of divine will expressed in the Christian prayer Our Father: "Thy will be done on Earth as it is in Heaven." Divine will is done in the heavenly realms, in the angelic realms, automatically. There is no choice. On Earth, we must partner with it to make divine will, or at least our part of it, occur. We must choose it.

We can feel love and devotion. We can experience divine wisdom, but it is not ours automatically. Though we have a great capacity to love, again, we must choose to do so. We must choose to be open to divine love, to receive it, and to express it to others. When we are stuck in the mind, we forget our capacity to choose love.

The mind is the bridge between us and both divine will and divine love. It is through the tool of the mind that we choose. It is through our thoughts that we create our reality. If we get caught up in our day-to-day thoughts, we may forget our great capacity to create through the power of the mind. When we not only remember our capacity to create but also choose divine will and divine love, we create in harmony with the universe.

The ascended masters are special guides. They teach us how to unite these three principles—love, will, and intelligence—because they have already done so, and they know the challenges we face in life. They unlock the divine alchemy in us by teaching through example. Each has had different struggles in life, different archetypal challenges, and different religions, techniques, and magick to aid their spiritual mastery. As they have climbed the mountain, they can show us their path. We might follow their path all the way, or walk with one master for part of the time and another master for the second leg of our journey. Each will show us something new.

The masters often assume the persona of the last physical lifetime from which they ascended. Though they are beyond space and time, physical human shape, and ego, they take on very human characteristics in order to relate to us. One could describe an ascended master as a diamond of light, with each facet of the diamond representing a previous lifetime. The facet that we are most familiar with, or that has the most to show us in its reflection, is the window through which this being shines light to us. So we see a familiar face we can relate to and understand, often one with a historical background that we can recognize, and a culture or time period we can relate to, in our own spiritual journey. Those drawn to Egyptian magick will be called by Egyptian ascended masters. Those drawn to Buddhism will connect with Buddhist ascended masters. Each master is beyond these religions, using the universal principles in each, but the masters will meet us on the road we are walking, to help us find the top of the mountain. We will work with the masters who are in harmony with our current spiritual path. Though we work with individual masters as "specialists," all of the ascended masters are joined together in one large diamond, the diamond of Shamballa, and to work with one is to work with them all.

It has become popular to trace the soul histories of the various masters. Channeled material gives a list of famous personas that each master has had through the course of his or her soul development, though there is disagreement among the various sources. I'm not sure I believe all the soul lore, but it presents interesting ideas to contemplate when looking at the evolution of a master. Unfortunately, studying the histories of the masters can be discouraging, too. One of the first thoughts I had was that I didn't think I was anybody that famous in my past lives. I discovered no continents. I did not lead a people through the desert. I wasn't a disciple of Jesus. Or if I was, I don't remember it. Is this a requirement for ascension? If so, I have a long way to go.

I think it's important to realize that once a master ascends, he or she becomes part of the collective consciousness. We all are part of it, but we are not conscious of it when we are at the linear, human, third-dimensional level. The lives of the masters are very archetypal. Their roles and functions are archetypal. They might work through the stories of the past, finding familiar archetypes with which we can identify. It gives us some alternate names and myths to help us connect with the energy. I know I have an affinity for the master El Morya, although initially I had no idea who El Morya was or what he would look like. I resonated with his description and the function of the chohan of the first ray, but I couldn't quite connect on a personal level. When people described him as King Arthur or King Solomon in a past life, I then had an understanding of his kingly, warrior energy and could connect to him more easily, though scholars could debate if there ever was a physical person attached to either of those personas, as the historical evidence is scant. Perhaps one of these highly archetypal lifetimes has been imprinted on your soul, too.

Part of the archetypal nature of the master is in working with the seven rays and the various offices of the planetary hierarchy. Not all masters hold an office, though many seem to be connected to one of the rays in terms of their nature and work. If you are drawn to a ray, you might be drawn to masters of that ray. Do not be alarmed if your meditations yield masters who are not listed in any book. There are far more masters than are currently known. It's just that the popular names give us something to latch onto when we call to them in ritual. Go with your first impression.

Some masters are said to have ascended past the planetary hierarchy. They have moved to higher dimensions and systems, or even out of this universe all together. The star system Sirius is said to act like a higher self to our own system, and our Great White Brotherhood is like an outpost for the Brotherhood of Sirius. Many of the ancient Egyptian and Old Testament ascended masters are said to have ascended to a galactic, universal, or cosmic level, and people question whether they are still available if we "call" on them in meditation and ritual. I have found that although the "core" of a master might ascend further and further up, his or her consciousness is beyond shape and form, and now available in many dimensions. The fact that the master has ascended higher means he or she is available as a guide in an even greater understanding and scope. I have found that all the old masters still respond to my call, or perhaps their disciples, taking over certain functions, respond in their guise. Either way, I am connecting to a loving, wise, healing master. If you want to connect with a particular master, and it serves your higher will, the master will connect with you.

One of the most striking teachings about the archetypal universality of the ascended masters came from a Shamballa Reiki master who was teaching a more traditional Native American healer. As the Reiki master led a meditation introducing each of the masters to this student, she evoked each one silently, allowing the energy of each master to surround them both. The Native American student described each master's energy as she felt it, but she named each according to her tradition. She would say, "We call that being . . .," and then name a figure from her Native shamanic tradition, rather than using the Eastern names preferred by the Reiki teacher. Archetypally, her descriptions matched quite well.

I think the masters are active in all cultures and traditions, throughout time. We just recognize them as different beings. In fact, our current view of them as Lords and Ladies of Shamballa is only the latest view, through our modern multicultural lens. Who knows how they will manifest in the coming age?

THE MASTERS

Traditionally, the male figures are called Lord or Master, while the feminine masters are called Lady, not ascended mistresses. These beings are beyond gender and have had past incarnations as both genders, but they choose to manifest in a particular gender so we can relate to them in our current life.

The following is a list of ascended masters and some information on each. It is drawn mostly from modern New Age sources, and is not a complete list. Most of these masters are part of the planetary hierarchy of Shamballa, but some are cosmic masters, or their station is not fully clear. You should feel free to work with other masters and research your own inner-plane contacts.

Adonis

Though Adonis is a name from classical mythology, in ascension lore Adonis is a cosmic master who has acted as teacher to Sanat Kumara and Vywamus. He trains Planetary Logoi. Adonis helps us align our heart with our spiritual will and ideals. He helps us expand our perspective to be inclusive and work for the good of the universe rather than just ourselves.

Afra

Afra is said to be one of the first ascended masters of Earth, from a land we would consider to be a part of the African continent today. She helps us attune to the rhythms of life, through nature-based spirituality, to find our true purpose. Afra helps us relate to all Earth-based spiritualities and the spiritual nature of the seasons.

Alizor

Functioning as a part of the Great White Brotherhood's medical program, Alizor is available to help in our healing work, for ourselves or when working with others. Alizor can help us commune with our medical guides and work healings on the physical, mental, emotional, and spiritual levels.

Aradia

Aradia refers to a historic figure of Italian witchcraft, reportedly born in 1313. Aradia is said to be the daughter or avatar of the Moon goddess Diana. She came to Italy during the Burning Times, the Christian persecutions against witches and pagans, to teach others the religion of the Goddess and the mysteries of magick. *Aradia, or the Gospel of the Witches*, a text used in the modern neopagan revival, is said to be based on her teachings. Some forms of Wicca honor her as the Goddess.

Atlanto

Atlanto is a cosmic master whose function is to sustain the Cosmic Day of Brahma, or the Day of Brahma, in Hinduism. He is not focused on accelerating the New Age on Earth. His focus is broader and more cosmic, and it is said that if he focused his energy directly on us for healing or magick, its cosmic force would be too intense for us. He is available for guidance and wisdom through meditation and channeling.

Averan

Averan is a cosmic master who finds his home in the center of our galaxy. He oversees the evolutionary process of the entire galaxy. He works with the light of creation, disseminating it out into the planets of this galaxy

Babaji

According to lore, Babaji is an incarnated ascended master who was born in 203 AD and is currently living in the Himalayas in a perfectly healthy sixteen-year-old body. He has remained physically incarnate on Earth to continue his teachings and, through his initiations and lineage, is said to be responsible for the start of the Self-Realization Fellowship of Yogananda.

Bridget

The image we have of Saint Bridget actually started with the Celtic goddess Brid. The daughter of the father god the Dagda, she is considered a triple goddess, with the aspects of healing, inspiration, and metal working. The February 2 celebration of Imbolc is sacred to her, as the goddess of light. The goddess Brid eventually became Bridget, and then was transformed into Saint Bridget by pagans who converted to Christianity. Her priestesses, keepers of the sacred flame, were transformed into an order of nuns. Saint Bridget is thought of as a figure who bridged the gap between the pagan magick of the old world and Celtic Christianity. Many wells in Ireland are sacred to her and are used for healing.

Christian Rosenkreutz

Christian Rosenkreutz is the mythical founder of the Rosicrucians and a patron of all the modern orders of ceremonial magick that have been influenced by the Rosicrucians. According to myth, he was a descendant of nobility, and a Jesuit in his youth, who traveled to the Holy Lands of the Middle East and further still, learning healing and magick from Arabian magi, Egyptians, and Spanish Cabalists. He returned to his homeland and founded the Rosicrucian Order, or Rose Cross Order. Members traveled the world, doing their healing work. They met once a year and kept the order secret for one hundred years. Later, a "manifesto" brought the order to light. This manifesto described the discovery of the full preserved and uncorrupted body of Christian Rosenkreutz. After the manifesto, another text appeared, called *The Chemical Wedding of Christian Rosenkreutz*, which described the initiation process through the imagery of a wedding. Some feel Rosenkreutz is one of the "secret chiefs" guiding the ceremonial magick renaissance of the Golden Dawn.

Cuchulain

Cuchulain is a hero of Irish mythology, often viewed in the modern era as an avatar, or embodiment, of the Celtic solar figure Lugh. Cuchulain means Irish wolfhound, and upon his journey of warriorhood and heroism he was given two geisha, or sacred prohibitions. One was to never refuse hospitality from another. The second was to never eat the flesh of his namesake. He spurned the advances of the goddess known as the Morgan, and she later appeared to him as the washerwoman at the ford, washing blood out of his clothing, a prophecy that he would soon die. Cuchulain was later invited to feast with someone who was eating dog meat. Forced to accept the man's hospitality and eat the meat, he broke his sacred taboo, losing his magickal power and dying in battle. Modern pagans look to Cuchulain as a hero and warrior figure, one who teaches us how to battle with honor and to work in harmony with the gods.

Djwal Khul

Djwal Khul works in the second ray, assisting Kuthumi in his work. Known as the Tibetan, he, along with Kuthumi, was responsible for contact with Alice Bailey, and then much of the writing she produced. He also figured in the works of Madame Blavatsky and the Theosophical Society.

El Morya

El Morya is the chohan of the first ray and carries the power of an enlightened, or sacred, king. He is a warrior, protector, and guide to those in government office and political life. Some claim that El Morya's past lives include the magician-king Solomon, Abraham, and King Arthur.

Gwydion

Gwydion is the Welsh wizard detailed in the tales of the *Mabinogion*. He is the uncle and mentor to Lleu and brother of Arianrhod. A magician, trickster, shapeshifter, and sage, he can be called on to learn magick, shamanism, and cunning. Gwydion is also associated with the seventh ray.

Gwynhwyfar

As the queen and wife of King Arthur, Gwynhwyfar (Guinevere) is an embodiment of the sacred goddess of the land. As many of the figures in Arthurian myth manifest as ascended masters, Gwynhwyfar can be contacted to understand the sacred feminine mysteries and to enter into a spiritual relationship with the land where you live. Some think of her as a past incarnation of the ascended master known as Lady Miriam

Hilarion

As the chohan of the fifth ray of concrete science and knowledge, Hilarion is doing one of the most important jobs of the New Age. In a dual approach, he stimulates scientific development among the traditional academic institutes, but is also responsible for psychic research and is a patron to Spiritualists, the Spiritualist movement, and all those seeking higher knowledge and exploring this knowledge through experimentation. In addition to advancing technology to help heal the world and create a utopia, Hilarion guides psychics, mediums, and all manner of psychic explorers in the proper use of their power. Some believe that Hilarion has a historical root in the personage of Saint Hilarion. Saint Hilarion was born to pagan parents and was sent to study at the libraries of Alexandria, where he eventually converted to Christianity. He is known for his healing cures and exorcism of demons, though some historians think of him as a fictitious person. An early incarnation of Hilarion was Paul the Apostle.

Isis

Isis is usually thought of as a great mother goddess of the Egyptian pantheon, but many in the ascension paradigm believe the gods of Egypt were actually the heroes and royalty of the Atlantean continent, and the tales of their adventures and battles are what we have left of Atlantean history. Perhaps the ascended master Isis is a priestess of the great Goddess, and through her devotion to the Goddess, she ascended. In both ascension and Egyptian magick, Isis is known as a great magician and healer, with the ability to transform herself and others. She learned the secret name of the creator god Ra, tricking him into revealing it to her, and she used that knowledge in her troubles against her brother Set. Isis used her magick, along with Thoth's help, to resurrect her husband-brother, Osiris, and conceive their child, Horus. We can call upon Isis to understand the Egyptian and Atlantean mysteries and to learn the arts of healing and magick.

Khunda

Khunda is a master and medicine man with lives in many different native traditions, including the Hawaiian, African, Native American, and Australian Aboriginal traditions. He is an excellent shamanic healer and teacher of nature and the spirit worlds.

Kumeka

Kumeka is a cosmic master who has never incarnated physically on Earth. He is the chohan of the eighth ray, the first of the new rays descending into the world. His work is focused on manifesting more intense, higher vibrational cleansing energies on Earth to prepare the world for more powerful initiations of spiritual energy. By preparing the world for a higher initiation of energy, Kumeka is readily available to those who want to work on preparing for the New Age.

Kuthumi

Kuthumi is the master of the second ray. His work on Earth deals primarily with performing spiritual initiations for those who walk the path of ascension. Although a spiritual initiate might have leanings toward a particular ray for study, Kuthumi guides the overall process of ascension and spiritual progress and initiation. He aids us in finding and implementing our life purpose. In life, he may have been a Sikh spiritual leader. Some researchers believe he was a physical teacher of Blavatsky, and that Kuthumi, or Koot Hoomi, was the pseudonym she gave him to protect his identity in the West. It was only after he passed that she and others began to channel messages from him. Like much information about the early Theosophical Society, the story is shrouded in mystery. Other teachings state that Kuthumi's past incarnations include lives as Pythagoras, Galileo, Shah Jahan, John the Apostle, Melchior, and Saint Francis of Assisi. Some call upon Kuthumi to form a spiritual bridge between humans and elementals, so they can more easily communicate with each other.

Lanto

Lanto is the master associated with all forms of education, from traditional education to spiritual education. He can be called upon by teachers of all traditions to aid in the process of imparting information and experience to students.

Lao Tzu

Lao Tzu is reportedly the founder of Taoism and the author of the book Tao Te Ching. His main teachings focus on how to live in harmony with the Tao. We can call upon him to learn the Way of the Tao and to balance yin and yang energies.

Lenduce

Lenduce is the higher self of Vywamus, who is the higher self of the Planetary Logos, Sanat Kumara.

Lo Chi

Lo Chi was said to be a great spiritual master and leader of ancient Lemuria. He is credited with initiating the spiritual development of the people of Lemuria and anchoring the concepts of love, wisdom, and courage in the earthly plane. At the end of his reign in Lemuria, he oversaw a mass ascension of many of his people. Call upon Lo Chi when you desire to get in touch with the wisdom of Lemuria.

Lorporis

As the head of the healing teams of the ascended masters, Lorporis guides the work of the masters in the physical, emotional, mental, and spiritual healings of people in the world.

Luciar

Luciar is a healer in the ascended master healing program.

Maitreya

Maitreya is the current holder of the office of the Planetary Christ. He was said to over-shadow, or directly guide, Sananda in his life as Jesus of Nazareth. The history of the figure of Maitreya is a bit clouded, though he is associated with a compassionate monk named Sthiramati. He is also linked with a monk from the T'ang dynasty named Hotei. Others think he was in the era of Krishna, as Rishi, while others believe he was incarnated during the time of Buddha. Many Buddhists believe Maitreya is the inheritor of Siddhartha's role as Buddha and will lead the world to accept the teachings of Buddhism. To Theosophists, he is the world teacher and embodiment of the Christ principle. Call upon Maitreya to transform and heal yourself through unconditional love. He is the embodiment of the Christ principle of love and wisdom for the planet Earth and works closely with the Plan-etary Logos and Manu. Maitreya was also said to be incarnated as Krishna, the teacher of Arjuna in the Bhagavad Gita. Maitreya is referred to as the fifth Buddha or the next incar-nation of Christ, and many believe he will incarnate in the world and lead us into a new era of enlightenment. Some people have even claimed to be Maitreya, though the world hasn't recognized the leadership of any of these individuals.

Marie Lavou

Though she is not usually considered an ascended master in traditional Theosophical lore, Marie Lavou, the Voodoo Queen of New Orleans, has a presence in the spiritual lives of Voodoo, Vodou, and Hoodoo practitioners that is as strong as that of any ascended mas-ter. Though her story appears dark (like much of Voodoo), she was a spiritual leader who helped liberate many from slavery and empowered the free people of color through rit-ual and magick. Her spirit and persona have survived as an honored ancestor. Every year, many people visit her grave in New Orleans to pay their respects and ask her for help with their magick. Marie Lavou actually refers to both a mother and a daughter of the same name, who were often thought to be the same person. Although most people look to the mother as a spiritual guide, the daughter is also available for guidance and aid. Marie is called upon to grant all sorts of wishes, but she specifically aids those who want to learn the spirituality of Voodoo, those who seek knowledge in root work, herbalism, beauty, love, and money. I have a friend who asks Marie for help in gambling every time she visits New Orleans, and offers to give half of her winnings to the Catholic Church in Jackson Square in the French Quarter. She always wins.

Marko

Master Marko assists Hilarion in the fifth ray, just as Djwal Khul assists Kuthumi in the second ray. Specifically, Marko guides the development of higher mental capacity, logic, reasoning, and discovery. He works closely (although intuitively) with those engaged in scientific pursuits and technological development. Marko is also associated with the galactic masters and acts as a liaison between members of the Earth hierarchy and beings from beyond.

Mary Magdalene

Though not always popular among Theosophists, Mary Magdalene as a spiritual leader and teacher resurfaced at the turn of the twenty-first century. Some believe that Mary Magdalene was not a simple prostitute, as many would have you believe, but a sacred priestess and consort to Jesus. They were both involved in a type of sexual tantric magick, and she was one of his most trusted and honored disciples. Mary Magdalene was perhaps an Essene mystic, and keeper of sacred knowledge, a magician and priestess in her own right. Her texts, including the feminine mysteries, were not included in the traditional version of the New Testament, but are just as valid, if not more so, in understanding the mysteries of the Christ. After his resurrection, Jesus first appeared to Mary Magdalene. Some consider the Holy Grail to actually be Mary Magdalene, rather than a chalice. They also believe that Mary Magdalene had a child with Jesus, and their bloodline has survived to this day. As an ascended master, Mary Magdalene can be called upon to understand the mysteries of the Christ, of feminine wisdom and the Holy Sophia, and the Holy Grail.

Melchior

Two figures have the name Melchior. The first is one of the wise men, the Eastern Magi, who visited Jesus upon his birth. That soul is said to be the ascended master now known as Kuthumi. Others say it is the master El Morya. Another Melchior is believed to be a galactic master, assisting the Galactic Logos yet available on a personal level to those in this galaxy, including the people of Earth. Melchior's "sector" of responsibility is said to include Earth, so when you desire information or insight on a galactic level, call upon him.

Merlin

Though many see Merlin as a previous incarnation of Saint Germain, others believe that the Merlin energy manifests separately and distinctly from that of Germain. From a traditional magickal or pagan perspective, Merlin is not one particular being in history, but an office or order of magicians considered to be the high priests of Albion, or Britain. These priests have inherited an Atlantean tradition of magick, and their duties include guiding the current king of the land in his sacred duties to maintain spiritual peace and balance and guiding the genetic bloodlines of the royal families, to make sure the future rulers will be capable of fulfilling their duties. We see this in the stories of Merlin guiding Arthur and orchestrating his parents' union. Most view Merlin as the old wizard of King Arthur's court, but in other tales Merlin is portrayed as a prophetic child or crazed warrior. In reality, the archetype of this magician is less that of a civilized sage, with a blue robe of stars and moons, and more that of a Celtic shaman, a wild man wearing animal skins and living in the woods. We can call upon any of the Merlins to learn magick, Druidism, shamanism, Celtic lore, counseling, leadership, or cunning wisdom.

Miriam

Lady Miriam is best known for her past incarnation as Gwynhwyfar of the Arthurian court. She was much more than a queen; she was also a priestess. She was also possibly an oracle priestess at the Temple of Delphi, when it was devoted to Gaia. Miriam mediates the energy of the Earth Mother, and can be called upon for all Earth Mother mysteries and magick. She helps in matters of the heart and in choosing our partners wisely.

Mother Mary

Mother Mary, virgin mother of Jesus, is seen as a master in her own right, reaching a level of consciousness and purity that enabled her to bring Jesus into the physical world. Though many believe her to have been a simple girl, some sources say she was an Essene mystic, fully prepared to be the mother of Christ. Mary was also said to have ascended directly into heaven, full body and soul, rather than suffering a physical death and leaving a body in a tomb to decompose. Along with Jesus, she is the best example of a mythical full-body ascension into the heavenly realms. Mary is the keeper of divine compassion and mother energy, and has been called upon for healing and intercession as both a Catholic saint and an ascended master. Many in the pagan traditions see her as the vestige of Goddess reverence in Catholicism. Mary is the protector of women and children, much like the pagan virgin goddess Diana. Many believe her past incarnations include lives as Isis, White Buffalo Woman, and Quan Yin, though I tend to think of those as different beings. Some see Mary as the persona for the Planetary Mother or even Cosmic Mother.

Nada

Nada is associated with the sixth ray of devotion, and works closely with Sananda. She helps spiritual seekers find the truth of religion, and is particularly devoted to those who feel they have been misled by religion or by spiritual teachers and ministers. Nada is a teacher of joy. Some believe she is the spiritual partner of Sananda, and that during Sananda's lifetime as Jesus Christ, Nada was Mary Magdalene.

Nightingale

Lady Nightingale is called upon in rituals of awakening and healing. Though there is little information available on her, I wonder, with the name, if there is any connection to the story of Florence Nightingale.

Orpheus

Orpheus is a mythical Greek figure who was the son of the solar god Apollo and the muse Calliope. He was a great magician and musician, with a magickal voice that could charm beasts and heal the sick. He was one of the Argonauts, and after his adventures, he married Eurydice. When she was killed by a serpent bite, he went to Hades to rescue her. He met with Hades and Persephone, and they eventually agreed to let his wife return with him, but first as his shade as he ascended from the Underworld. If he looked back, he would lose her forever. He agreed to this arrangement, and just as he made it to the cave entrance to the world of mortals, he feared he had been played for a fool and looked back, losing her forever.

Orpheus never recovered from the loss of his wife. Blaming himself, he spurned his friends and the company of all but the animals. Eventually he came across the frenzied followers of Dionysus, the Maenads, who, in their zeal, tore him to pieces. His head floated down the river and, some say, ended up on the Isle of Lesbos, still singing about his loss of Eurydice. Orpheus is considered to be the founder of one of the great Greek Mystery schools, and his poetry is still used in ritual and teachings today. His teachings and his myth demonstrate the powers of the Underworld, of loss and attachment. Even though his myth ends in sadness and death, many believe that Orpheus is an ascended master of the highest order, available to all who seek to understand the mysteries of death.

Osiris

In Egyptian mythology, Osiris is considered to be the pharaoh god who ruled over an age of peace, prosperity, and civilization. Along with his sister-wife, Isis, he taught the ancient Egyptians agriculture, magick, and religion. In ascension lore, Osiris is looked at as a wise and powerful king, of either Atlantis or early Egypt. It was not until the conflict with his brother Set, and his murder by Set, that his rule of peace was disrupted. Isis resurrected Osiris in what could be considered a posthumous ascension, and he assumed his role as Lord of the Underworld, guiding his son, Horus, into eventual victory over Set. We can call upon Osiris to learn the mysteries of life and death, agriculture, civilization, victory in conflict, wisdom, tantric sex magick, and healing.

Pallas Athena

Pallas Athena is the name of a Greek goddess of wisdom. Of all the Greek deities, Pallas Athena is most strongly associated with the ascended masters of Shamballa. Some believe that she was a priestess of the goddess Athena who reached enlightenment while on the goddess's path to wisdom. Pallas Athena can be called upon in all matters of wisdom, intelligence, and ingenuity. Though a great warrior, she learned how not to fight when it was not necessary, and how to use diplomacy, intelligence, and strategy to defeat one's enemy.

Paul the Venetian

Paul the Venetian is master of the fourth ray and is dedicated to improving human life through the encouragement of the arts. Said to be the former head of the third ray, Paul eventually moved to the fourth to focus on the arts and artistic expression for humanity.

Portia

Lady Portia is a match with Saint Germain, as co-ruler of the seventh ray. She is said to rule the silver violet flame, what some consider the more feminine version of the violet flame, while he rules the traditional violet flame. In the past, she was Morgan le Fay, the Celtic sorceress, to his Merlin of Camelot. Portia empowers and initiates us into the feminine mysteries of magick and connects us to the Goddess. She is a tester, and a gate keeper to the mysteries. Those who are unworthy do not get by her and learn her secrets of magick.

Quan Yin

Quan Yin is considered a goddess of compassion and mercy in the Asian traditions, and a spiritual guide, or bodhisattva, along with Buddha, in the Buddhist traditions. To those in the New Age, Quan Yin, also spelled Kwan Yin, is the epitome of the divine mother. She is said to be one of the lords of karma, guiding souls in the choice of their next life. In a historical context, some research indicates that, ironically, Quan Yin was originally a male figure, and was absorbed into Buddhism. Quan Yin's images were altered to be more feminine to complement Buddha but not compete with him. To some, Quan Yin could be considered the first spiritually transgendered master recognized in ascension lore. Historically, Quan Yin might be a merger of the figures Tara and Avalokitesvara.

Quetzalcoatl/Viracocha/Kukulcan

In the legends of Central and South America, a white-bearded god of light skin visited the land, bringing culture, art, science, and magick. Known as the feathered serpent, this renowned being was prophesied to return to the land in the future. When Cortes and his men arrived in 1519, the natives mistakenly believed that the Spanish invaders were the descendants of Quetzalcoatl. Many believe that Quetzalcoatl is an ascended master, or perhaps, paralleling some of the theology of the Mormons, this was Jesus visiting the Americas after his death and resurrection.

Ra

Like Isis and Osiris, the sun god Ra is considered to be an ancient Atlantean king in ascension lore. Ra is both powerful and wise, and some myths credit him with the creation of the universe. As a solar figure, Ra teaches us about light, power, inspiration, healing, and creativity. The Egyptian sun was considered both destructive and life giving, and Ra's power can be called on to remove obstacles and illness or to grant life and healing.

Sai Baba

Some say the Indian master Sathya Sai Baba is a physical incarnation of the Cosmic Christ here on Earth. Sai Baba is a teacher who is surrounded in controversy, and some consider him to be a great master incarnated. He demonstrates his mastery over the material world through feats of psychic ability, manifesting objects as needed and healing the sick. Many people all over the world use his name, image, and photo as a focus to connect with the divine, and are devoted to his work. Others are less inclined to believe that he is a living master.

Saint Germain

Saint Germain is one of the most beloved of the modern masters. Though many think of him as a saint in the Catholic sense, approved by the church, during the lifetime in which he ascended he was actually the Comte de Saint Germain, an alchemist and magician known in the royal courts of Europe as the man who never died. He is also known as Prince Rakoczi, or Master R, and that was believed to be a past identity or past incarnation of Germain. It is said that through his alchemy he kept himself alive far longer than any mortal could live and often had to fake his own death and then "reappear" as a descendant or in a new identity. He would travel around the courts to perform "miracles," changing lead into gold, removing flaws from jewels, and offering prophecies. It's hard to separate fact from fiction in his tales. He was occasionally seen as rowdy and was arrested at least once.

Now Saint Germain is the chohan of the seventh ray, the ray of ceremonial order, and guides all those involved in magick, ranging from his traditions of alchemy and ceremonial magick to shamanism, witchcraft, and the lodge traditions of Freemasonry. All secret societies that work toward the evolution of humanity are under the influence of his ray. He is particularly important in the work of this book, as the patron of magick and alchemy. Saint Germain, along with El Morya, Kuthumi, and Djwal Khul, was responsible for the dissemination of teachings to Blavatsky and the Theosophical Society. He later released the I AM Discourses through Godfrey Ray King. Some believe Germain is transitioning from the seventh ray to the office of the Mahachohan, or Lord of Civilization, as we approach the next age. Many also see him (and the seventh ray) as the gateway to the higher rays. The seventh ray is the ray of alchemy and transmutation, and Germain can be evoked for transforming any energy into its highest form.

In past incarnations, Saint Germain was said to be Samuel the Prophet, Joseph of Nazareth, Proclus the Philosopher, Christopher Columbus, Sir Francis Bacon, and the Merlin of King Arthur's court. In one of his earliest incarnations, he was High Priest in Atlantis, and responsible for the prototype initiation system that eventually developed into Reiki and Shamballa Reiki in the modern era. Many believe Saint Germain, in his last physical life, was completely aware that it was his last physically incarnated life, and extended his life not only to further his teaching but also to enjoy the material plane. He encourages us to enjoy life, regardless of our incarnational development. As the patron of the New Age, he teaches us about freedom and liberation, to not accept restrictions or dogma imposed upon us by other people or religions. As long as we harm none and follow our magickal will, we are free to do as we choose.

Sananda

Sananda is the spiritual name of the master known as Jesus Christ in the physical world. During that lifetime, Sananda was overshadowed by Lord Maitreya. Sananda was also said to be Adam from the Garden of Eden, Enoch, Joshua, Joseph of Egypt, and possibly Apollonius of Tyana. He is now the chohan of the sixth ray, and works with priests, mystics, and all those devoted to the ideal of making the world a better place.

Sanat Kumara

Sanat Kumara is the Planetary Logos of Earth. According to channeled lore, he ascended on another planet that was very much like Earth. He then trained in the ethers of Venus to be a Planetary Logos and was directed to Earth. His union with the earthly body started the hierarchy of Earth. Though often viewed as a human, his body is in union with the Earth, and the planetary energy grid is like his aura. In more traditional myths of India, Kumara is a demon slayer and a leader of gods in times of darkness.

Serapis Bey

Though Serapis Bey is usually thought of as an Egyptian master or a solar bull deity of the Underworld, some believe he is actually an angel who incarnated on Earth in ancient Egypt. Some feel that one of his incarnations was as the pharaoh Akhenaton. Serapis Bey is now the chohan of the third ray of active intelligence. He is the keeper of the white flame of ascension. He is a patron of both science and art, encouraging a balance between both aspects of human existence.

Seshat

Seshat is the wife of Thoth and an ascended master of wisdom and magick in her own right. Like Thoth, she is said to be a keeper of the mysteries of Atlantis and Egypt, of ancient alchemy, and of working magick through words and symbols.

Solomon

Solomon, the king and mage of the Old Testament, is known for his unorthodox wisdom. He is credited with the wisdom of knowing which of two women claiming to be the mother of a baby cared for the child more, when he threatened to cut the child in two. Though many consider him to be a past incarnation of El Morya, the chohan of the first ray of power and will, Solomon often manifests individually, because many people resonate more with the Solomon figure than with El Morya, just as many people resonate more with Merlin than with Saint Germain. Solomon is not only a powerful king and warrior, but also an excellent magician. He is said to have built his temple with the aid of spirits or demons, and is credited with binding the seventy-two demons of the Goetia, as well as authorship of many manuscripts that appeared in the medieval period. Though he probably wasn't the author of such grimoires, assuming that there was a historical Solomon, the grimoires may have been based on his magickal tradition. The physical person of Solomon was most likely a magician training in the magick of the ancient world of the Middle East, and possibly involved in sex magick with Bathsheba and even pagan practices in honor of Astarte. We can call upon Solomon when seeking knowledge of ceremonial magick, demonology, angels, leadership, strength, courage, and magickal willpower.

Taliesin

Taliesin is considered one of the greatest Celtic bards. In Welsh myth, he started life as the servant Gwion Bach, until he tasted the potion known as greal, brewed in the cauldron of the goddess Ceridwen. The potion contained all the wisdom and knowledge of the world. Ceridwen charged Gwion to stir the potion for a year and a day, as she brewed it for her son Avagddu. Gwion accidentally tasted the potion and was filled with wisdom. Knowing Ceridwen would be furious, he used his newfound magick to escape. Ceridwen followed him, and through a shapeshifting duel, Gwion turned into a grain and Ceridwen into a chicken, and she devoured him. Like the dark mother goddess that she is, Ceridwen gave birth to a child nine months later, from the seed of Gwion Bach. She was still angry but could not kill such a beautiful boy, so she set him afloat in a leather bag. He eventually found his way to Elphin, who raised him. The child retains the magick and wisdom of the potion, and he is named Taliesin, for his "shining brow." Like the Merlin, many feel that Taliesin is an archetypal power, and not restricted to any one single person, incarnation, or time period.

Thoth

Thoth is the ascended master of ancient Atlantis, considered a priest and magician, and author of *The Emerald Tablet*. He is an alchemist credited with the foundation of Western magick and spirituality. Some feel he took on the form Hermes Trismegistus in ancient Greece, teaching the mysteries in both Egypt and Greece. Some feel he was a priest-king of Atlantis, and took his teaching, and his tablets, to Egypt after the sinking of the motherland. In Egyptian mythology, Thoth is the scribe of the gods, a sage and counselor of the ruling gods, and is immensely powerful. Thoth is associated with the Moon, and his steady power keeps the universe in alignment. Thoth can be called upon when seeking to understand the mysteries of Egypt and Atlantis, for all study and learning, and for writing, magick, spiritual advancement, alchemy, and healing. Some ascensionists think Thoth was a past incarnation of Buddha.

Venus

Lady Venus is usually linked with Sanat Kumara in ascension mythology. As Sanat Kumara is said to have come from the planet Venus before becoming the Planetary Logos of Earth, Lady Venus is his counterpart. In Roman mythology, she is the goddess of love. In Greek mythology, she is Aphrodite, goddess of love, fertility, and sexuality. Modern ascensionists call upon Venus in matters of romance, love, marriage, and relationship.

Vywamus

Even though he is the higher self of Sanat Kumara, Vywamus is still accessible and available to humanity as a guide and teacher. He is considered a master psychologist and counselor, and his healing helps us rewire our energetic circuitry to hold a higher level of consciousness and activate the higher chakras. Vywamus helps us dispel the self-created illusions, doubts, and dramas that block our path.

White Eagle

White Eagle was one of the first tribal masters to make himself known in the New Age to nontribal people. His channeled teachings were responsible for the founding of the White

Eagle Lodge in the 1930s. White Eagle can be called upon to respectfully understand tribal ways and integrate the Native wisdom with Western traditions.

Wottana

Wottana/Wottona/Wontanna is a Native American ascended master. Wottana is said to be from the Anasazi tribe, a mystical group that achieved mass ascension as a civilization. Wottana is still available to us now, and can be called upon for both personal and planetary healing. He works closely with Mother Earth and her energy lines.

Yohannan

Yohannan is the manifestation of the master who was Jesus's apostle John, guiding a branch of disciples of the Great White Brotherhood known as the Researchers of Truth, as taught by the mystic Daskalos. Yohannan is possibly an expression of Kuthumi.

Zoroaster

Zoroaster is the founder of the Zoroastrian religion and a Persian magi. Many look to this powerful figure as a guiding light and master. Zoroaster teaches us about the power of spiritual light and about the perils of dualism.

The ascended masters are always increasing our knowledge and perspective of them through channeled contact, revealing more about their own teachings and paths. "New" or at least previously unknown masters make themselves known. If you make contact with a master who wasn't listed here, have no fear. There are too many to list in any one book. If you want more details about the lives of the ascended masters on Earth and their past incarnations, I suggest books such as Dr. Joshua Stone's *The Ascended Masters Light the Way*, Doreen Virtue's *Archangels & Ascended Masters*, and Edwin Courtenay's *Reflections: The Masters Remember*.

EXERCISE 4:
Visiting with the Masters

> 1. Sit before your altar in a comfortable position. Call upon the divine, in whatever form you prefer—God, Goddess, Great Spirit, Divine Mind, Mother-Father-God. Ask to be consciously connected to your source, for guidance and

protection, and to all your spirit allies who are appropriate for you at this time. Do Exercise 1: Basic Meditation Technique up to step 6 (see page 81) to get into a meditative state.

2. Acknowledge the power of the four directions. Bring your attention to the north, then the east, south, and west. Bring your attention to the heavens above and the space below you. Then bring your awareness to your heart. Feel a shaft of light descend from the heavens, from the highest dimensions, surrounding you in a column of light and finding its anchor in the heart of the planet. You are now aligned with the twelve dimensions and are capable of interdimensional contact and journey.

3. Ask your higher self and guides to bring your awareness to the fifth dimension, the realm of Shamballa, the collective consciousness of the ascended masters of Earth. Feel your consciousness rise from your body, from your third-dimensional consciousness, and ascend to the heavens. You might feel like your spirit is ascending in a glass elevator, climbing higher and higher, as if each dimension were a floor. Feel yourself enter a crystalline structure, the structure that is the Shamballa diamond itself. Take a look around. Perhaps you see a matrix of shining light and geometry. Perhaps it manifests as a city of the ancient world. However you see Shamballa, know that you are in a place of light and healing.

4. Call out to the ascended masters. Ask for the master who is most perfect for you at this time to make his or her presence known. Be open to the form and identity of whatever master appears. If you desire an audience with a specific master, request that master. If you are not sure of a specific master but are seeking a teacher from one of the rays of light, evoke that ray of light, by color or number, and ask for a master of that light.

5. Spend as long as you desire with this master. Allow the ascended one to communicate with you through words, pictures, and feelings. Keep an open heart and mind. Ask whatever questions you have. Bring your problems and issues to the master. The master might take you on a journey away from Shamballa, into other dimensions, or even into your own past or future. Go with it. Know that once you connect to the realm of Shamballa, you are in good hands, connecting with the collective consciousness that is in harmony with the source of life.

6. When you are done, say your farewells. Your master might give you a gift or symbol, to help establish the link between the two of you. Then return to where you began. Imagine yourself descending through the tunnel of light, riding the cosmic elevator from the fifth dimension down to the third. Ground yourself in your body and relax. Take a few breaths. Open your eyes.

7. Acknowledge the four directions around you again, north, east, south, and west, then above, below, and center. Thank the divine Creator for guidance and protection. Thank your guides and allies. Perform steps 9 and 10 of Exercise 1: Basic Meditation Technique (see page 82) to return to normal waking consciousness. Write down any impressions or messages you received, before you forget them. The return to 3D consciousness can make them fade quickly, like a dream.

The purpose of this contact is to develop a relationship with the master, much as you'd develop a relationship with a mentor, teacher, or friend. A devotee or disciple of a particular master is known as a chela. Some ascensionists believe that becoming a chela to a master is a pivotal part of the ascension path. Use this meditation to develop a relationship with the masters. You will find that they are instrumental in guiding you on your path.

Speak to the masters about your metaphysical questions, and seek practical spiritual advice for your everyday life. I confer with these teachers and guides when I have a problem and don't know how to apply my spiritual values and knowledge to the situation at hand. I also work with them to better understand my mind, will, and love, so I can unite the three in every aspect of life. Some masters can help guide us in healing both ourselves and others. They guide me both in meditation and in life, sometimes leading me to others who resonate with them.

As great as the masters are, sometimes we need a flesh and blood counselor, teacher, or healer to help us truly understand the messages we receive in meditation. Sometimes the master will ask you to be his or her instrument in the world, introducing teachings and ideas through you. Through such partnerships we have the works of Blavatsky and Bailey, as well as modern traditions of mysteries and healing.

DISCERNMENT WITH THE MASTERS

Modern psychics and channels now make contact with a variety of deceased people and put them in the same category as the ascended masters. Many of these new masters come from the founding spiritual traditions, such as Madame Blavatsky, Alice Bailey, Yogananda, Dion Fortune, and Aleister Crowley. Others are considered to be akin to saints because of their social work on Earth, such as Mother Teresa, Mahatma Gandhi, and Peace Pilgrim. Even more are from popular culture, including John Lennon, Princess Diana, Walt Disney, Eva Peron, and Jim Morrison. Some of these people might not be true ascended masters (meaning they did not achieve enlightenment in their last lifetime), but they can still be valuable guides. For all we know, in the last moments of life on Earth, they could have reached a state of enlightenment and truly ascended. Many ascended masters exist who were not famous in life and won't be found in any book, but they are still valuable guides and teachers if they should make personal contact with you. I suggest that you make contact with a master you trust, and then decide what other spirits are helpful guides. If you get good guidance and information from Princess Di, she can be a great guide and aid, but it doesn't necessarily make her a "master."

When looking over the history of ascended masters, particularly their active contact in the early Theosophical movement, it appears that these masters either manifested to their disciples physically, precipitating a body from the ethers, or they appeared so strongly in psychic vision that they were mistakenly believed to have appeared in the physical realm. Perhaps I'm just not as psychic as those who have met with the masters before me, but I always "see" the masters with my inner vision, and although these interactions are very real to me, I never mistake them for physical contact. Some say that the masters manifested physically at the beginning of this new age to get our attention, and now it is no longer necessary to do so, that enough of us have developed our inner faculties, and the masters need not expend energy in manifesting a physical presence. They can focus their energies on other tasks and make sure their messages are as clear as possible.

There are also incarnated individuals who claim to be ascended masters. They claim to be fully realized and enlightened beings on par with any in the planetary hierarchy, yet they live normal lives like you and me. Though I don't doubt that this is possible, I think more people make this claim than have actually manifested it. I think few masters are running around telling everybody that they are ascended and don't need to eat, drink, or defecate anymore, or shave, cut their hair, or wear deodorant, but that they choose to, while in the

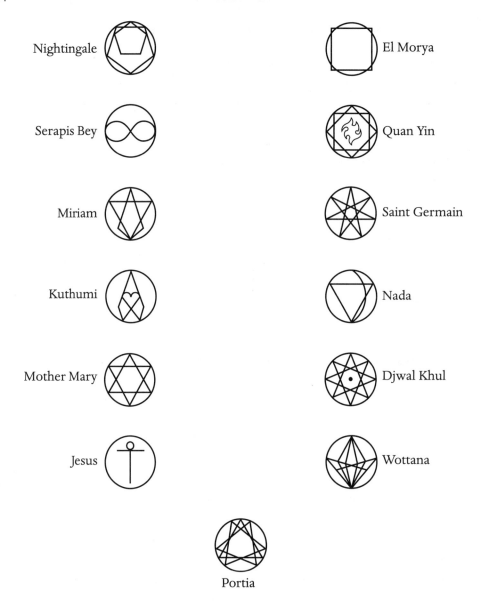

Figure 24: Ascended Master Symbols
(All rights reserved. Used with permission. Depicted for personal, not commercial, use only.)

world, to not lose touch with regular people. I think the true masters are doing their work, and could be teachers in the New Age world, but I don't think they claim to be special or make any big deal about their level of awareness. Many who claim to be masters say they don't need to do the miracles attributed to the masters of old. They don't have to turn water into wine, bilocate, or even repair flaws in gems, because it's not necessary in this age. Perhaps this is true, but I don't think it's necessary to claim that you're an ascended being if you're not going to live up to the reputation. I think many enlightened souls are teaching, healing, and modeling a healthy, whole, happy life, and letting the people who contact them come to their own conclusions about the nature of their ascension state. In the end, use your own discernment when dealing with these living "masters."

THE MASTERS' SYMBOLS

The use of geometric symbols to represent spirits, gods, and angels is a long-standing magickal tradition. Magicians use various "seals" to summon the aid of angels and spirits. The geometry of a symbol resonates with the name and purpose of the spirit. Sometimes the ascended masters will give you a symbol in meditation that will connect you to a particular master. Other times they will give you sacred magickal symbols for healing, manifestation, and other purposes.

Edwin Courtenay, author of *The Ascended Masters' Book of Ritual and Prayer* and the *Ascended Master Symbol Cards*, received a variety of symbols from the masters, to be used in ritual with them. I have found that you can use these symbols in meditation, ritual, and daily life to connect with the energy and wisdom of the master you seek. They are presented here as black-and-white line drawings (figure 24), though Courtenay gives some more specific, detailed color associations for them in his works.

Like Courtenay, you can make personal contact with the masters and receive their symbols. Your symbol for a master might be different from the ones pictured here. Follow your own guidance and use the symbols given here as inspiration.

To work with these symbols, you can choose one and:

- draw the symbol in the air in front of you with your finger, hand, or magickal wand and/or blade.
- draw the symbol over your body or the body of another. In particular, draw it over the palms, heart, or brow.

- visualize the symbol in your mind's eye and think of that master's name.
- draw the symbol on a candle with a pin or pen knife. Every time you light the candle, you are asking for the presence of the master. This is particularly useful to do before meditating on that master. You can use the candle flame as a meditation focus.
- anoint yourself with water or oil, tracing the shape of the symbol on your skin.
- outline the symbol on the ground in stones or crystals.
- make a talisman of it by writing the symbol on paper, card stock, or wood, carving it into a tablet of wax or wood, or etching it into metal. When you carry the talisman, you are asking for the guidance, protection, and blessing of that master in your life. The talisman becomes a touchstone to constantly remind you of the master's teachings.

There is no wrong way to use the symbols as long as you do so with respect. Experiment to see what techniques connect you to the masters in ways that work best for you. Ask the masters how they want you to use their symbols. If you don't see your favorite master's symbol here, ask your master for a symbol.

THE MASTERS' ASHRAMS

Many of the ascended masters are said to have "ashrams," or teaching temples, on the etheric planes. Their disciples travel to these ashrams through their spirit bodies while their physical bodies sleep. The disciples study and evolve while their bodies rest. Some have conscious memories of the lessons upon waking, while others do not. Through this dream work, it is as if the master is running a night school for sleepers. Those who attend this school seem, by some unconscious or intuitive mechanism, to know things that they weren't consciously taught, appearing to advance much more quickly than other people around them. This dream work is no substitute for actually learning the tradition of your chosen path while fully conscious and in the physical realm, but it does help quite a bit. You can also ask the masters to help heal you, build your light quotient, raise your vibration, solve a problem, provide artistic inspiration, or anything else you can conceive of. If your request is for your highest good and in the province of the master's work, then all things are possible.

Chart 5 lists the masters' known ashrams, which are said to exist in the ethers near various power spots around the globe. Sometimes when you feel a calling to a particular place in the world, you will find yourself spiritually attracted to the master associated with that place.

Ascended Master	Ashram(s)
El Morya	Darjeeling, India
Lanto	Grand Teton, Wyoming, USA
Paul the Venetian	Southern France
	Statue of Liberty, New York City, USA
	Washington Monument, Washington, DC, USA
Serapis Bey	Luxor, Egypt
Hilarion	Crete, Greece
Nada	Saudi Arabia
Saint Germain	Transylvania, Romania
	Table Mountain, Wyoming, USA
	Mount Shasta, California, USA

Chart 5: The Masters' Ashrams

EXERCISE 5:

DREAM WORKING

1. Go to bed and relax your body from head to toe. Give your body permission to relax fully, as you sweep your awareness from the top of your head down to your feet. Keep a notebook and pen or pencil by the bed for when you wake up in the morning.

2. Before you fall asleep, take a moment to think about what kind of dream working you would like to do, and what master would be appropriate to call on for this work. In your mind, or out loud (if you are alone), ask for the presence of the master while you sleep. If you use a symbol with that particular master, envision it now, draw it on your body before going to bed, or have a talisman with it near you. If you want to go to a specific ashram, think about that location and try to envision it in your mind. Ask the master to help you, and state clearly and specifically what you want to do in your dream. Are you simply seeking spiritual knowledge and advancement? Are there specific topics you wish to study? Do you want to heal, be inspired, or solve a dilemma? Be specific. Ask that it be for your highest good, harming none, in accord with your true will. Then go to sleep.

3. When you wake up in the morning, write down the first thing you remember. It may reflect the dream work you did that night, or it may not. Much of the work you do will be intuitive and unconscious, so don't expect profound dreams to be the benchmark of how much spiritual work you did in your dreams with the masters.

I recommend not using this technique every night. Even though your body is resting, your mind may come back weary and lethargic, which will have a negative effect on the rest of your day. Use your intuition as to how often to use this technique.

9

THE ANGELIC FORCES

In the primary triad of the divine, the angelic kingdom manifests through the will of the divine, implementing divine will on the many levels of the cosmos as guardians and guides of creation. As instruments of divine will, angels are said to be devoid of free will. They have no ego or personal desires. They simply execute the will of divinity. The word angel comes from the Latin *angelus*, derived from the Greek *angelos*, meaning "messenger." In the Hebrew tradition, the word that translates most closely to angel is *mal'akh*, meaning "messenger," though many words, titles, and names are believed to refer to the angels of Hebrew lore. Other words associated with angels include the Persian *angaros*, or "courier," and the Sanskrit *angeres*. Angels are the messengers, couriers, and executors of divine will. Though in modern times we see angels as benign beings, historically they were as likely to destroy as to bring good news, and were considered fearsome beings as well as guides and helpers.

Humanity can work with the angels because, like the Creator, we too have divine will. The will of our higher self, of our oversoul or monad, is in perfect alignment with the divine. Humans who explore magick learn to find their true will. Angel magick is a form of theurgy, of divine magick, putting divine will into action. Though in many old texts it appears that the angels are being commanded or bound by the magician, they are in fact carrying out the magician's will, because they are in alignment with the magician's will, which, at that point, is the same as divine will. Some magicians believe angels to be automatons, with no free will, so they can be bound by the will of whoever summons them. Though that might be true for some spirits, I don't believe that is the case with most angels. I've found that angelic magick either works spectacularly well or not at all, even when I'm confident that the angels were properly summoned. I believe my success or failure is proportional to how well I am aligned with my divine will, and when I am not, the results of my magick make that fact very apparent.

Familiar angelic lore is drawn primarily from the Abrahamic religions (Judaism, Christianity, and Islam), but most mystics believe that angels are a universal force, available to all traditions and religions. Many modern ceremonial magicians and Wiccans use angels to call upon the four directions. Many believe the seeds of angelic lore in the Old Testament actually come from the Jewish contact with the other magickal cultures of the Middle East, including Persia, Babylon, and Egypt.

Our modern-day images of angels differ greatly from those in the ancient world. The descriptions and images of angels in the Old Testament are quite fearsome and not altogether human, in contrast to our modern depictions of angels as benevolent and human, as seen in everything from Renaissance art to contemporary greeting cards. Though many biblical passages describe angels as humanoid and often indistinguishable from humans unless their nature is revealed by the divine, other orders of angels appear in monstrous and elemental forms. The burning bush of Moses was not a manifestation of God, but an angelic messenger: "And the angel of the LORD appeared unto him in a flame of fire out of the midst of a bush: and he looked, and, behold, the bush burned with fire, and the bush was not consumed."—Exodus 3:2. Angels are also associated with fire in the book of Psalms: "Who maketh his angels spirits; his ministers a flaming fire."—Psalms 104:4.

Scholars have speculated about the size, shape, and nature of angels, giving us the famous question, "How many angels can dance on the head of a pin?" By their very nature, angels are beyond the manifested world, and as the executors of the Creator's will, they can do anything willed by the Creator. They can be any size or shape, and have any ability needed. Though they are usually depicted in artwork as male, angels of all orders, even when in human form, are said to be neither male nor female. They hold all potentials and are beyond gender, duality, and polarity. Yet most people use the pronoun *he* in angelic traditions, just as they usually assign a male pronoun for the divine.

Old pagan images of winged beings from the Middle East are construed as angelic forces from our modern perspective. These images mix human, animal, and mythical characteristics together to form the image of a spirit that acts as a guardian or teacher (figure 25). These "angels" are not described in human terms at all, but are more akin to the mythical beasts of our ancient tales and more in alignment with what tribal shamans might see.

Figure 25: Angelic Being

We find other angelic images across the world, as spirits don't fall into separate and neatly defined categories. In Western magick, angels are clearly defined as specific races of beings, with specific attributes differing from those of other aspects of creation. But in Tibetan Buddhism, the sky spirits referred to as the Dakini are often equated with Western angels. Some believe the Hopi's Kachina spirits are related to the angelic realm. The shining ones of the Hindus, the devas, are sometimes considered akin to angelic spirits. But the Dakini, Kachina, and devas, with their cultural attributes, have also been linked to the faery beings and the starry ones (which we will discuss in the coming chapters). In the modern age, angels don't belong to any one culture, tradition, or background. Their energy is available to all who seek to align themselves with divine will and make magick. I have found the angels to be quite responsive when the call is sincere and the heart is open.

ANGELIC HIERARCHIES

Angelic scholars and theologians of the past have spent much of their lives debating and detailing angelic lore, but we still have no real consensus on how the angelic realm is structured or which angels belong to what group. Even the spellings of the angel names, from Hebrew to English, are debated, with multiple versions of one angel's name mistakenly seen as multiple angels. The most popular groupings come from Christian, Jewish, and New Age sources, yet there is little agreement on which, if any, is correct. Great effort has been made to correlate the many systems into one harmonious whole, with little success.

Christian sources have a division of nine angelic orders, also known as choirs. This lore was first outlined by Pseudo-Dionysius the Areopagite of the fifth century, and has become the standard basis of Christian angelic lore. The nine choirs are divided into three spheres, of three choirs each.

The First Sphere

The first sphere consists of angels who serve as heavenly counselors. They are known as the angels of contemplation. They have little or no contact with humanity and are concerned with the workings of the universe.

1: Seraphim—The angels of the Seraphim are at the throne of the Creator, singing the music of the celestial spheres. They contemplate divine order and providence. The Seraphim are known as the "burning ones," for they are aflame with the love they feel for the Creator. They give off so much light that even other divine beings cannot dare to gaze upon them. The Seraphim are described as having six wings, with two covering their face, two covering their feet, and two for flying. They are said to stand at the throne of the Lord, chanting, "Holy, holy, holy is the LORD of hosts; the whole earth is full of his glory."—Isaiah 6:3.

2. Cherubim—The Cherubim are the angels of wisdom, contemplating divine essence and form. They are said to be the guardians of the light and the guides of the stars. Though often associated with our modern images of childlike cherubs or cupid-like angels, they are traditionally described as fearsome, with four wings. The Cherubim were the guardians of the Ark of the Covenant and the guards at the gates of Eden, holding flaming swords: "He drove out the man, and at the east of the garden of Eden he placed the Cherubim, and a flaming sword which turned every way, to guard the way to the Tree of Life."—Genesis 3:24.

3: Thrones—In the first sphere of angelic life, the Thrones, too, are angels of contemplation, but they are said also to be angels of action, connecting them to the next sphere. The Thrones are also known as the Many-Eyed Ones, sometimes associated with the four living creatures of Ezekiel's vision, ascending to the throne of God. Some portray them as the angels of divine justice, while others see them as the planetary angels, though the Virtues (in the second sphere) also have planetary associations.

The Second Sphere

The second sphere of angels is made up of those beings who work as heavenly governors, keeping the universe in order. They are also known as angels of the cosmos.

4: Dominations—The order of Dominations, also known as Dominions, consists of the managers and architects of the angelic orders beneath them. They are an organizing force in the cosmos. The Dominations are described as having long albs, or gowns, reaching to their feet, with golden belts, green soles, and a gold staff, scepter, or orb in the right hand and the seal of God in the left.

5: Virtues—The Virtues are said to literally infuse the world and all in it with spiritual energies, or what we call virtue. They are the angels of miracles, encouragement, and blessings, particularly for those who are struggling with their faith. They bestow grace and valor upon humans. The Virtues are also known as the Malakim, Dunamis, or Tarshishim, as well as the Brilliant Ones or Shining Ones. Some think of them as the forces of the stars and planets, and they could be associated with the planetary spirits and archetypes. The Virtues are said to be the angels who aided Jesus's ascent to heaven after the Crucifixion.

6: Powers—The order of Powers comprises the angels who maintain the harmony of the universe. They are said to be angelic record keepers and historians, and the guides of religion and consciousness development. Out of all the angels of the second sphere, the Powers have the most interaction with humanity. Also known as the Dynamisms, Potentiates, or Authorities, the Powers are responsible for maintaining the barter and balance between heaven and the material world. They also guide lost souls who have left the body and cannot find heaven. The Powers were the first order of angels created by the divine.

The Third Sphere

The third and last sphere consists of angels who have the most contact with humanity. They function as messengers and guides. Because of this, they are known as angels of the world.

7: Principalities—The Principalities act as guardian angels to large collectives, including nations, communities, and religious organizations. They protect and guard these groups and their leaders. The Principalities are described as wearing a soldier's uniform with a golden girdle. They are the managers of the members of the last order in the third sphere, who are simply known as angels. One Principality aided David in his task of slaying Goliath.

8: Archangels—Archangels are the guides and guards of larger areas of human activity. Each one rules a different province in life, from protection and healing to mercy or death. Archangels are in charge of the armies of angels in heaven.

9: Angels—Angels make up the order that is most closely associated with humanity, acting as protectors, healers, companions, teachers, guides, and intermediaries. When most people think of angelic beings, they are usually thinking of the members of this order.

In the Qabalistic methodology, a different angelic order is associated with each sephira on the Tree of Life (see chart 6). Each order rules a particular sphere. In the Qabalistic system, the archangels are a separate order of beings from the ten angelic orders on the Tree of

Life, and reside on a higher plane of existence. Each archangel rules a sephira on the Tree of Life, and rules one of the ten angelic orders (except for Uriel, who rules Da'ath, which doesn't have an angelic order). Mystics have sometimes described the various individual angels in each of the orders as cells in the body of the ruling archangel, working in total harmony with the direction of that archangel, whose body extends across the cosmos, available to any and all, anywhere and at any time.

Here is a description of the ten angelic orders and the number of the corresponding sephira on the Tree of Life for each order.

1: Chaioth ha-Qadesh (Holy Living Creatures)—The Chaioth ha-Qadesh are on the highest of all the angelic orders, save the archangels, who are on another plane. It is the task of the Holy Living Creatures to bear the throne of God in the heavens.

2: Auphanim (Wheels)—The Auphanim are the whirling forces, described as wheels within wheels with many eyes. They are associated with merkaba lore and the vision of Ezekiel.

3: Aralim (Mighty Ones)—The Aralim are the angels of understanding. They are sacred to the cosmic womb or void, the great mother of creation.

4: Chashmalim (Shining Ones)—The Chashmalim are the angels associated with mercy as well as magnificence. Many older traditions of magick look to the gods of the world as the Ancient and Shining Ones, and the Chashmalim are the forces highest on the part of the Tree of Life that is still below the abyss.

5: Seraphim (Burning Ones)—Known as the angels of severity and justice, the Seraphim carry out the destructive will of God.

6: Malakim (Kings)—These angels are associated with the center of the Tree of Life, and are angels of harmony, beauty, and healing.

7: Elohim (Sparkling Ones)—Known as the angels of victory, the Elohim are sacred to the spheres of Venus, the planet of beauty and love.

8: Beni Elohim (Children of the Divine)—Known as the angels of glory, the Beni Elohim are associated with the forces of the mind and memory, as well as creation.

9: Kerubim (Strong Ones)—These angels are known to lay the foundation of the material universe.

Sephira	Archangel(s)	Angelic Order	Angelic Choir	Planet(s)	Day of the Week	Color(s)	God Name	Incense(s)	Stone(s)
Kether (1)	Metatron	Chaioth ha-Qadesh	Seraphim	Pluto, Uranus	None	White	Ehieh	Ambergris	Diamond
Chokmah (2)	Raziel, Jophiel	Auphanim	Cherubim	Neptune, Zodiac	None	Gray	YHVH	Musk	Star ruby, jade, turquoise
Binah (3)	Tzafkiel	Aralim	Thrones	Saturn	Saturday	Black	YHVH Elohim	Myrrh	Star sapphire, pearl, jet, onyx
Da'ath	Uriel	(Serpents)	None	Uranus, Pluto	None	Violet, prismatic	(YHVH Elohim)	Wormwood	Synthetic and altered stones
Chesed (4)	Tzadkiel	Chashmalim	Dominions	Jupiter	Thursday	Blue	El	Cedar	Amethyst
Geburah (5)	Chamuel	Seraphim	Virtues	Mars	Tuesday	Red	Elohim Gibor	Tobacco	Ruby, carnelian, bloodstone
Tiphereth (6)	Michael, Raphael	Malakim	Powers	Sun	Sunday	Yellow, gold	YHVH Eloah Va Da'ath	Frankin-cense	Topaz, citrine, yellow diamond
Netzach (7)	Haniel	Elohim	Principalities	Venus	Friday	Green	YHVH Tzabaoth	Rose, sandalwood	Emerald, lapis, tourmaline
Hod (8)	Raphael, Michael	Beni Elohim	Archangels	Mercury	Wednesday	Orange	Elohim Tzabaoth	Storax	Opal, agate, hematite
Yesod (9)	Gabriel	Kerubim	Angels	Moon	Monday	Purple, silver	Shaddai El Chai	Jasmine, mugwort	Quartz, pearl, moonstone
Malkuth (10)	Sandalphon	Ashim (humanity & ascended masters)	Ascended masters	Earth	None	Black, olive, citrine, russet	Adonai Ha Aretz	Dittany of Crete	Rock crystal, tiger's-eye

Chart 6: Qabalistic Correspondences with Angels

Ray	Color	Elohim	Archangels
First ray	Red	Hercules and Amazonia	Michael and Faith
Second ray	Blue	Apollo and Lumina	Jophiel and Christine
Third ray	Yellow	Heros and Amora	Chamuel and Charity
Fourth ray	Green	Purity and Astrea	Gabriel and Hope
Fifth ray	Orange	Cyclopia and Virginia	Raphael and Mary
Sixth ray	Indigo	Peace and Aloha	Uriel and Aurora
Seventh ray	Violet	Arcturus and Victoria	Tzadkiel and Amethyst

Chart 7: Ray Correspondences with Elohim and Archangels

10: Ashim (Human Beings)—These are the angels of the material world. Sometimes referred to as the Order of Blessed Souls in modern terminology, the Ashim are now associated with the ascended masters.

New Age Theosophical lore based upon the seven rays focuses primarily on the angelic forces of archangels and the Elohim (chart 7). Both are seen as the primary forces of creation in contact with humanity at this time. The archangels sit on the right-hand side of God, said to be the spiritual side of God, administering to the forces and energies of the universe, while the Elohim sit on the left-hand side of God, the material side, administering to the creation and maintenance of the physical universe. The seven positions on each side of God correspond to the seven major rays of Theosophy. Some think of the archangels as the more heavenly, refined entities, and see the Elohim as somewhat similar to the Titans of ancient myth, the more chthonic gods and creators of the material world. Though ascensionists don't make those associations to the Elohim directly, their pairings (of one male and one female) remind me of the twelve main Greek Titans (six male, six female) led by Chronos.

The Elohim are the creative gods. There is a controversial belief that the term Elohim is a plural, multigender word, so when it is used in the book of Genesis, it was not God the Father who created the world in seven days, but a group of creator gods, both male and female. Because of this, we find the Elohim and the archangels, in pairs of male and female, borrowing names and titles from modern and ancient myths. Though the pairs are quite complementary, they are, at least for the archangels, completely nontraditional, as the archangels are said to be of both or neither gender, beyond the divisions of male and female.

ARCHANGELS

Whether looking at the Christian, Jewish, or Theosophical models, most magicians are concerned with the archangelic forces. The archangels are either one of the lowest orders of angelic beings, yet readily available for human contact, as in the Christian model, or they are one of the highest angelic orders of beings, beyond the ten orders, or equal in power to the worldly creative forces of the Elohim.

The archangels are the best known and most beloved group of angels for Christian, Jewish and ascensionist mystics. The four that rise above all the others are the archangels of the four directions, called upon in ritual magick as the watchers and guardians, administering the four elements. These four archangels are Raphael, Michael, Gabriel, and Uriel. Manifesting on a higher level are said to be the seven archangels of the classical magickal planets, which are cited as Michael, Gabriel, Raphael, Uriel, Chamuel, Jophiel, and Tzadkiel. Other sources give us Michael, Gabriel, Chamuel, Raphael, Tzadkiel, Haniel, and Cassiel. One could also look to the archangels of the Qabalistic Tree of Life as the primary powers, including Metatron, Raziel/Jophiel, Tzafkiel, Tzadkiel, Uriel, Chamuel, Raphael, Haniel, Michael, Gabriel, and Sandalphon.

Michael

Archangel Michael is the divine warrior and protector. In ritual magick, he is associated with the element of fire and the direction of south, as he is the keeper of the flaming sword or flaming spear. Michael teaches about the development of will, to stand fearless in the face of danger when doing our divine will. Modern practitioners call upon him to release unwanted spirit attachments during healing sessions. Qabalistically, Michael has been associated with both the sphere of Tiphereth (the Sun) and of Hod (Mercury). Most texts say he rules one sphere and co-rules the other, jointly with Raphael, showing his association with healing. I prefer the solar attributes myself, as Michael is a leader among angels, and many consider him second only to God and perhaps Metatron. His name means "he who is like God." Some believe it was Michael who appeared to Moses in the burning bush to deliver the divine message. The Koran states that the Cherubim are formed from Michael's tears. His colors are red and sometimes blue.

Gabriel

Archangel Gabriel is the archangel of the direction of west, the element of water, the Moon, and the Qabalistic sphere of Yesod. With all the water associations, which occultists link with love, emotions, and healing, Gabriel is the messenger and is best known for delivering the news of Jesus's upcoming birth to Mother Mary. He is also said to have dictated the Koran to Mohammed. Gabriel is also associated with Joan of Arc. Why then, does he have a water association, when metaphysically he seems more linked to air? I asked this question while meditating, and received the answer that Gabriel is the messenger of the heart, and all these messages come through the heart first, to be translated later by the head. Gabriel's name means "God is my strength," but this may refer to the emotional and spiritual strength of God, rather than the physical. Watery colors, such as blue and sea green, as well as the lunar colors of silver and violet, are appropriate for Gabriel.

Raphael

Archangel Raphael's gifts are well-known in the realm of healing, as he is the divine physician. His name means "God heals" or "healed by God." He is the archangel of the eastern quadrant, the element of air, and either the sephira of Tiphereth (the Sun) or Hod (Mercury). I prefer the Mercurial associations, as the archangel of air. Raphael's colors are yellows, blues, and oranges. He is said to have healed Abraham's pain after circumcision, as well as Jacob's thigh, and he gave Noah a book of medical knowledge. Raphael even personally gave King Solomon his magick ring to bind spirits to build his grand temple. Air is associated not only with the knowledge of healing, but also the knowledge of magick. Most Mercurial figures are magician archetypes.

Uriel

Of the four main archangels, Uriel is one of the most mysterious and interesting. Though all are androgynous, Uriel, sometimes spelled Auriel, is the most feminine of the four, with the feminine pronoun most often used in angelic literature and ritual. Uriel means "light of God" in most translations, yet is associated with the north and the element of earth in ceremonial magick. Sometimes she is described as dark winged, and as an angel of death, interring the body back to the earth. Teachings on grounding, being secure in the material world, and prosperity are her domain, as the archangel of earth. Uriel's other associations are with Uranus and, in some Qabalistic systems, the hidden sphere of Da'ath, which means "knowledge." Da'ath is the gateway between the day side and the night side of the Tree of Life, and is the mysterious center in the abyss separating the three upper powers from the rest. With the Uranian associations, Uriel is connected to sudden and swift knowledge, like a burst of lightning awakening the intuitive mind to divine truth. Uriel was said to give to humanity the knowledge of alchemy and, some say, the Qabalah itself. She gave secret arcane lore to Ezra, warned Noah of the flood, and lead Abraham out of Ur. With the Uranian connection, which rules sudden changes, disasters, and revolutions, as well as Earth changes, Uriel helps protect us from disasters, humanmade or otherwise, by giving us advance warning and insight so we can take appropriate action. She also has an association with electricity, and can be called upon to help repair any type of electrical device. Uriel's colors are greens, browns, and black for Earth, and electric blue, yellow, and ultraviolet for Uranus.

Chamuel

This archangel's name means "he who seeks God" or "he who sees God." Most strongly associated with the power of Geburah (Mars), Chamuel is a protector, though he is seen as harsher or more direct than Michael. Chamuel was said to appear at Gethsemane to aid Jesus with the promise of eternal life through resurrection. In modern lore, he is associated with the third ray of active intelligence. Though most often associated with Geburah, some use Samael (sometimes equated with Chamuel) as the archangel of the warrior sphere.

Tzafkiel

Occasionally confused with Tzadkiel, Tzafkiel is the archangel associated with the sephira Binah and the planet Saturn. Tzafkiel is an immense being who will not fit entirely in our spirit vision, and usually manifests simply as a body part or two. He is associated with both beginnings and endings, and most angelic workers think of him as one of the archangels of death. Tzafkiel can bring a swift end to a situation and start another when requested.

Tzadkiel

Tzadkiel, also known as Zadkiel, is the archangel of benevolence. His name means "the righteousness of God," and he is associated with the planet Jupiter, the sephira Chesed (which means "mercy"), and the violet flame of transmutation. Tzadkiel was the angel who stopped Abraham from slaying his son in God's name. He is also an angel of memory, called upon to improve our human faculties of memory whenever we need his aid.

Haniel

Haniel is the archangel of the planet Venus and the sephira Netzach. Haniel is another angel with a more feminine energy and association, and her name means "grace of God." She teaches humanity about the stars and the powers of nature, herbalism, and beauty secrets. She aids with fertility of all kinds, from human fertility to that of the land, or even that of the imagination. The true and deep teachings of Haniel are on the nature of love, true unselfish love, and the proper balance in a romantic or family relationship.

Jophiel

Jophiel is the archangel of beauty, and his name means "beauty of God." Modern practitioners call upon this being to aid in all artistic and beautifying projects. Jophiel is the companion to Metatron, but is also one of the angels who drove Adam and Eve from the Garden of Eden.

Raziel

Raziel, also known as Ratzkiel, is the archangel of mysterious lore, and his name means "secret of God." He said to be the author of a mythical book of magick known as the *The Book of the Angel Raziel*, or *Sefer Raziel*. This book was said to have been given to Adam and Eve after their expulsion, and copies were handed to Enoch and Noah. Though historians do not credit Raziel with authorship, many who read it feel that you need Raziel's aid to understand it. In magick, Raziel helps us understand secrets and explore the mysteries of the occult to our fullest capacity.

Metatron

The lore of Metatron is one of the strangest for angelic mages. The meaning of his name is unclear, because, unlike the other angels' names, Metatron does not end with the "el" suffix, which translates to "of God." His name has been translated to mean "measurer," "guide," or the "one who sits at the throne next to the throne of God." Metatron is considered the most divine of all the angels. He is called the archangel of the presence, and is associated with the top sphere on the Tree of Life, acting as an intermediary between the Creator and all of creation. He has two common images—either that of a creature described as the tallest of all beings, with thirty-six wings and countless eyes, or that of a small, peaceful child. Though Metatron is not listed in any of the traditional scriptures, occultists see him as trumping all other angelic beings. Some say Metatron is far removed from the human plane, having no interface with humanity, while others say he was once human, the scribe and prophet Enoch, who ascended to heaven with the aid of the *Sefer Raziel* and transformed into Metatron, and is still keeping watch over his human brethren. Magicians sometimes call him in ritual for the center of the circle and the element of spirit. If and when Metatron does make contact with humans, his presence is said to mark a pivotal spiritual shift in the life of that human, and his wisdom should be heeded, despite his appearance.

Sandalphon

Sandalphon is the only other archangel besides Metatron who is associated with a human life on Earth. Most strongly associated with Elijah, but also with John the Baptist, Sandalphon is the archangel of Malkuth, the earthly realm, and some see him as having a place in the planetary hierarchy of ascended masters, as humanity's first link to the angelic realm. His name is said to mean "brother," referencing his association with his "twin," Metatron. Many think of Sandalphon and Metatron as two sides of the same coin, as Malkuth is simply the Kether of a lower Tree of Life. Sandalphon appears in the world as a wise old man, but his feet are said to be in the earth and his crown in the heavens. His other forms include the classic Qabalistic Princesses (or Pages) of the tarot—the Princesses of wands, swords, cups, and pentacles.

GUARDIAN ANGELS

In both the traditional Christian and Jewish systems, the lowest orders of angels are the ones most closely aligned with humanity. The term *guardian angel* is used for such a being, with the belief that an angel is "assigned" to an incarnated human at birth, and will protect and watch over that person. This is similar to the shamanic belief in a totemic or tutelary spirit, protecting, guiding, and watching over a human on the path of life. People with a stronger conscious connection to their guardian receive more direct guidance.

The nature of angels, of guardian angels in particular, is the subject of great debate. A common belief in the modern lore is that ancestors, deceased loved ones, act as guardian angels for individuals. Tribal cultures have always seen the ancestors as guides and guardians, as intermediaries between the living and the divine. According to traditional angelic lore, however, angels are not, have never been, and will never be human. They emanate from the will of God, having no free will of their own, and thus could not be former humans who had free will. They are beyond gender and duality, and by their very nature cannot descend into duality, or they will cease to be angels. Modern channeled lore and Spiritualists' information defy these traditional angelic teachings, not only with the concept of deceased relatives acting as guardian angels, but also with the concepts of angelic walk-ins and incarnated angels (see chapter 19).

The bridge between these two systems of thought can be found in the teachings of ceremonial magick. In *The Book of the Sacred Magic of Abramelin the Mage*, the term Holy Guardian Angel is found. Though the text does not clearly define it, leaving some to think of it as a separate, independent entity, magicians of the Golden Dawn and their related groups equated the entity, also known as the HGA, with one's own divine genius or higher self, keeper of one's true will and purpose. This terminology equates our core nature with the angelic realm. Our divine will is equated with the will of the Creator, even though, as humans in the world, we create through the mind of God and have free will. These teachings show us that humanity's purpose is to be the bridge, the uniting force, between the three divine rays of heart, mind, and will.

Those who successfully unite heart, mind, and divine will, the ascended masters, are known in some angelic lore as the Order of Blessed Souls, and are seen as an order of angels in their own right. The Lords and Ladies of Shamballa consist of Earth's own angels, united with the will of God through love and mind. Many think of Earth as an angelic training ground and the masters as the new angels.

FALLEN ANGELS

No discussion of angels would be complete without speaking of the fallen angels. The lore of the fallen angels is quite muddled, but the basic theology is that there was a war in heaven, begun by a group of angels who rebelled against God's will, seeking to fulfill their own. The angels were ultimately cast out of heaven. We can find parallels to the angelic fall from grace in history, including a human fall from grace as related in the story of Genesis, or even in the more mythical tales of the demise of the civilizations of Atlantis and Lemuria.

As angels are traditionally in harmony with the will of God, those angelic beings whose focus has shifted from the will of God to one of the other two aspects, the mind or the heart of God, are transformed into something else, and are no longer true angelic beings. According to traditional lore, they became the demons and devils of the Underworld. The spirits of the Goetia (a book of unsavory spirits often considered demons, summoned by magicians to do their will) are often related to fallen angels and pagan gods.

Older, lesser-known lore doesn't paint such a tortured picture of the fallen angels. Some say a group of angels, traditionally lead by Lucifer, the angel of the Morning Star, of Venus, and the light bringer, volunteered to fall, to descend, and bring the spark of light to the material world. These angels moved to the heart of God, animating nature and becoming what we think of as the devic, or nature, realm. Lucifer is traditionally associated with the emerald, a heart stone, and with Venus, the planet named after the goddess of love and fertility. Lucifer has been linked to the Theosophical Sanat Kumara, and Madame Blavatsky's journal was known as *Lucifer*, showing her lack of fear for the concept of Lucifer, unlike many of her spiritual descendants, who would equate Lucifer with the Christian concept of the Devil. Others see Lucifer's rebellion as just that—a rebellion based on ego and personal desire rather than divine will. But if the angels were truly angels, then wouldn't this rebellion still be a part of divine will and a greater plan or pattern?

AΠGELIC WORKIΠGS

To work the theurgy of angelic magick, one simply has to align with the divine will to work in cooperation with the angels. Though some medieval manuscripts show magicians summoning the angels to do whatever they desire—good, evil, or indifferent—most modern angelic magicians believe that the angels will minister only in divine will, and that if you ask them to do evil, they will refuse to work with you. Other magicians find this view naive and believe angels will go about fulfilling whatever instructions you give them.

The following exercises will help you develop a relationship with the angelic realm, and prepare you for more complex forms of magick and ritual with the angels.

EXERCISE 6:
FIΠDIΠG YOUR AΠGELS

The first step in working successful angelic magick is to make contact with the angelic realm, and the beings most attuned to your purpose and nature. You might find, particularly among the archangels, a specific angelic being who resonates with you and your path, who will develop a special relationship with you as a guide and aide, even though all the archangels are available to you. Sometimes such angels will make contact with you spontaneously. I began my own exploration into angelic magick when I was visited by a being who appeared as a pyramid with a single eye and two feathery wings. He was burning with violet flame and announced himself as Tzadkiel. Since then he has been a guide and companion to me. Other times, the magician is the one who initiates contact.

Particular minerals are said to facilitate contact with the angelic kingdom, including the following.

Angelic Stones and Crystals

Amethyst

Angelite

Azeztulite

Calcite, Blue

Calcite, White

Celestite

Petalite

Quartz, Celestial

Quartz, Clear

Quartz, Rose

Quartz, White

Seraphinite

Try holding one of these stones in your hands as you do the following exercise. You can cleanse the stone first, and charge it with the intention of angelic communication. (See exercise 2 in chapter 6 for instructions on how to cleanse and charge the stone.)

1. Sit before your altar in a comfortable position. Call upon the divine, in whatever form you prefer—God, Goddess, Great Spirit, Divine Mind, Mother-Father-God. Ask to be consciously connected to your source, for guidance and protection, and to all your spirit allies who are appropriate for you at this time. Do Exercise 1: Basic Meditation Technique up to step 6 (see page 81) to get into a meditative state.

2. Acknowledge the power of the four directions. Bring your attention to the north, then the east, south, and west. Bring your attention to the heavens above

and the space below you. Then bring your awareness to your heart. Feel a shaft of light descend from the heavens, from the highest dimensions, surrounding you in a column of light and finding its anchor in the heart of the planet. You are now aligned with the twelve dimensions and are capable of interdimensional contact and journey.

3. Ask to be taken to the angelic realm. If you desire to meet a specific angel or archangel, hold that intention. If not, simply ask for the angelic guide who is correct for you. Feel yourself rise through the interdimensional spire, ascending through the dimensions. You might find yourself rising to the fourth, fifth, sixth, or seventh dimension or even higher. You might find yourself climbing the Tree of Life, ascending to the sphere of a specific archangel, if that is your intention. Allow your vision to awaken to the angelic realm. In my experience, I have seen angels more as geometric figures than as the traditional cherubs surrounded by puffy clouds and playing golden harps. Angels have manifested to me as complex fractal forms and balls of light, or three-dimensional geometric shapes with semi-human appendages. Allow the vision to take place in whatever way is necessary for you to interface with the angelic realm. Do not judge. Simply go with the process. Ask whatever questions you have, and allow your angelic guide to impart any messages to you.

4. When you are done, say your farewells. Your angel might give you a gift or symbol to help establish the link between you. Then return to where you began. Imagine yourself descending through the tunnel of light and back to the third dimension. Ground yourself and relax. Take a few breaths. Open your eyes.

5. Acknowledge the four directions around you again, north, east, south, and west, then above, below, and center. Thank the divine Creator for guidance and protection. Thank your guides and allies. Perform steps 9 and 10 of Exercise 1: Basic Meditation Technique (see page 82) to return to normal waking consciousness. Write down any impressions or messages you received, before you forget them.

Build a relationship with this angel as a guide and spiritual helper, much as you are developing a relationship with the masters. When you desire to make contact with a specific angel, you can request that angel. In traditional magick, the archangels

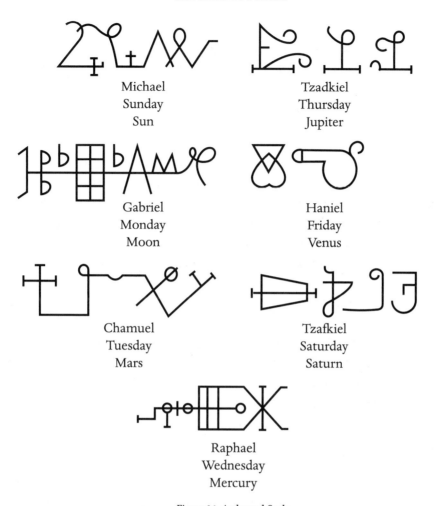

Michael
Sunday
Sun

Tzadkiel
Thursday
Jupiter

Gabriel
Monday
Moon

Haniel
Friday
Venus

Chamuel
Tuesday
Mars

Tzafkiel
Saturday
Saturn

Raphael
Wednesday
Mercury

Figure 26: Archangel Seals

have seals, or sigils, that are used to evoke them (figure 26). You can use these symbols much as you would use the ascended master symbols (see figure 24 in chapter
8), on talismans, carved into candles, or visualized in your mind.

EXERCISE 7:
PROTECTION WITH ARCHANGEL MICHAEL

Of all the archangels available to humankind, Archangel Michael seems to take the
greatest role in guiding and protecting humanity. He can be called upon in rituals
and healings to protect, remove unwanted forces, and guide us on our path. Michael
is an invaluable ally to have as a lightworker. As a warrior of the light, he is a great
role model to help us understand the ways of the peaceful warrior.

Michael is so readily available that we can make contact with him simply by
speaking. Elaborate rituals are not necessary. Two important techniques I've
learned are his pillar of light and his suit of flame, both of which confer a similar
level of psychic protection.

Ask Michael for a pillar of light whenever you are having difficulty separating
your energy from what you perceive as harmful forces, be they mundane sources,
such as family, coworkers, or people on the street, or more esoteric sources, such as
harmful practitioners and unhealthy spirits. Simply state, out loud or silently, "Archangel Michael, give me a pillar of light to protect me from all harm." Imagine a pillar of pure light descending from the heavens, from Michael, surrounding you and
your aura, and grounding itself into the heart of Mother Earth and the first dimension. You are now protected from harm on all sides, above and below, in all dimensions. If you are still having difficulties, the energies inside the pillar are yours, so if
someone triggers feelings of pain, anxiety, or fear in you, you have to deal with your
own emotions and learn to process them, but you are protected from the "outside"
influences. The pillar of light will move as you move and will fade eventually, when
the crisis passes. You might need to call for it several times during a stressful period.
Generally you don't need it every day, but only in cases of stress or fear.

Alternately, you can ask Michael for a suit or shirt of flame and then imagine
his flame, either red or blue, moving around you and purifying all that doesn't
serve your highest good as it blocks and burns away all unwanted energies directed
toward you. Like the pillar of light, the suit will eventually fade, but it moves as you

move. The suit of flame is something that many people evoke every day, at the start of the day, to prepare for the outside world and to purify their aura of anything that has been picked up over the course of the night.

Exercise 8:
The Lesser Banishing Ritual of the Pentagram (LBRP)

The Lesser Banishing Ritual of the Pentagram, known as the LBRP for short, is one of the foundation rituals of modern ceremonial magick. The purpose of the ritual is to banish all unwanted energies and forces, connecting you to the universe through the image of the Tree of Life. Particularly powerful, the LBRP bolsters and heals your auric field, preparing you for deeper actions of magick, and evokes the power of the four primary archangels of the quarters to protect you from all directions.

Unlike other circle-casting rituals, which create a stationary sacred space, the protective shield of the LBRP moves as you move, as you are working with your own energy field in ritual. The cleansed space, protective boundary, and angelic aid are part of your own energy field, and will last for several hours after the ritual. Repeated use of the LBRP transforms your energy field so you always have these qualities. The LBRP does not create the same type of magickal container that the magick circle ritual does (see chapter 12), but is primarily a preparatory ritual used before meditation or more complex rituals or as a daily practice to strengthen the aura and basic magickal skills. It is performed at the beginning of ceremonial magick operations, to prepare the space, and is then repeated at the end, to make sure everything summoned has been properly dismissed.

Though more detailed pentacle rituals exist, the basic LBRP, which is taught with many variations to it, has become a staple in many modern magickal traditions, from branches of Wicca to ascension. I even know a yogi who clears his studio with this ritual and teaches it to his students. Unfortunately, he doesn't teach them that the sacred words chanted are in Hebrew and that the ritual is based on the symbolism of the Tree of Life, which can create a lot of confusion.

The LBRP can be divided into four basic parts: the Qabalistic Cross, the Banishing, the Angelic Call, and a repeat of the Qabalistic Cross. Ceremonial magick is much like yoga or martial arts in the sense that many smaller ritual movements compose the greater rituals. This is one reason that the Qabalah has been known as the "yoga of the West." The ritual presented here is a simplified version of the LBRP. For more traditional and detailed versions, with more specific body positions, consult a formal text on ceremonial magick. The benefit of performing this ritual regularly, if not daily, is a stronger connection to the four archangels of the elements.

Qabalistic Cross

Face the east and take a few deep breaths. Imagine that you are firmly anchored to the Earth, but your body is expanding upward infinitely. The Earth beneath you is like a firm volleyball. Your body is in the cosmos.

Above your head descends a ball of pure, brilliant white light, right above your crown. Reach up with your right hand and touch the sphere of light above you, drawing its light down, and then touch your forehead. Intone: **Atah**. Chant it out loud, using full breath and full voice, extending each syllable. As you tone the symbol (also known as vibrating the words of power), put your will, your energy, behind the sound as you speak. Imagine that the crown of your head is the top sephira of the Tree of Life, Kether.

Visualize the beam of light descending from your crown, down through your body (as the Middle Pillar on the Tree of Life), as you move your right hand from your forehead to point at your feet. Intone: **Malkuth**. Imagine that the "Earth" beneath your feet is the bottom sphere on the Tree of Life, Malkuth. Feel the connection between your crown and the Earth.

With your right hand, touch your right shoulder. Imagine the beam of light that is running through your body extending a beam out to your right shoulder and then out to the right side of the cosmos. Intone: **Veh Gebura**, for the fifth sephira on the Tree of Life, Geburah.

With your right hand, cross over and touch your left shoulder, imagining the horizontal beam of light extending to your left shoulder and then out to the left side of the cosmos, infinitely. Intone: **Veh Gedula**, for Chesed (also known as Gedulah), the fourth sephira on the Tree of Life.

Figure 27: Banishing Pentagram

Bring your hands to your heart center in prayer position, palms pressed together. Intone: **Le Oh Lam.**

Focus on the cross of light running through the middle of your body. Feel yourself grounded and balanced. Intone: **Amen**.

Banishing

Face the east, and with your right hand, index finger extended, draw a banishing pentagram (figure 27). Imagine it in electric-blue light. The size of the pentagram should be anywhere from the size of a large dinner plate to the width of a standard door frame. Intone: **Yud Heh Vahv Heh**, one of the names of God in the Qabalah. Then, with your arm and finger extended, move clockwise, tracing one-quarter of a circle visualized in blue or white flame at shoulder's height above the floor, until you are facing south.

Draw a second banishing pentagram in blue light, the same size as the first. Intone: **Adonai**, another name for the Creator from Qabalistic lore. Again, move clockwise, tracing one-quarter of a circle in the same color of flame, until you are facing west.

Draw a third banishing pentagram in blue light, the same size as the first. Intone: **Eh Heh Eh**, another name for God from the Qabalah. Again, move clockwise, tracing one-quarter of a circle in the same color of flame, until you are facing north.

Draw a fourth banishing pentagram in blue light, the same size as the first. Intone: **Agla**, an acronym for a phrase that is considered to be another name for God in Qabalistic lore. Move clockwise, tracing one-quarter of a circle in the same color of flame, until you are facing east, where you began. You are now surrounded by four pentagrams interconnected by a ring of flame.

Angelic Call
Facing east, speak or chant the following:

Before me, Raphael.
Behind me, Gabriel.
On my right hand, Michael.
On my left hand, Uriel.
Before me shine the pentagrams.
(Be aware of the ring of light and four pentagrams around you.)
Chant: **Within me shines the six-rayed star.**
(Visualize a hexagram, a six-pointed star, in your chest, symbolic of the cosmos. The angelic names, like the names of God, can be toned and extended out. For example, Raphael would be RAAF-EYE-EEL.)

Qabalistic Cross (Repeat)
Repeat the Qabalistic Cross.

With the conclusion of this ritual, you have cleared your aura of unwanted forces and created a protective seal, invoked angelic protection and guidance, and energized yourself with divine energy. Many magicians highly recommend performing the LBRP as a daily ritual.

10

THE REALM OF THE FEY

If angels stem from the will of God, to execute divine will in all worlds, and human beings come from the mind of God, with free will and creative capacity, then those from the faery realm are rooted in the heart of the Creator, and help us tune in to the love of the heart. Associated with both the blue ray of love and the green ray of nature, the realm of the faeries has come back into popular consciousness stronger than ever with the New Age movement, after centuries of being considered evil by the dominant religious authorities. Now many seek to know the wisdom and love of the faeries, working in partnership with them, as did the nature magicians of old.

Most modern magicians of the New Age don't look to the traditional lore to learn how to work with the faeries. Since faery lore comes from a variety of cultures and lands, the information can appear conflicting. Modern sources seem to be describing something different from that of classical sources, which can make the serious seeker of the fey confused as to what is respectful, proper, and true about these allies.

I always suggest that first and foremost you trust in your own experience of the other worlds, but you should also approach these non-ordinary states of reality with respect. Like the world of humans, the world of the faeries is a material one, connected to great love and healing, but also illusion and danger. One could say that all the worlds hold such dangers for the spiritual seeker, but the myths of faeries come with many particular customs and warnings. The teachings and myths of the past are the road maps for those of us in the present. Our elders left them for us to use. Eventually, we will become the elders, adding our knowledge to the tradition and passing it on to the next generation.

WHAT ARE FAERIES?

The term faery is now most popularly spelled *faery*, as opposed to *fairy*, to differentiate it from the stereotypical Tinkerbell images found in popular culture. It comes from the English word *fee*, which finds its roots in the Roman *fata* and the Greek *fatua*, both of which refer to fate. In days of old, the faeries were said to play a role in human fate. The term fey, or fay, traditionally meant one who is enchanted, often by one of these otherworldy beings, but now the term is used interchangeably with faery.

While most modern seekers of faery lore think of the fey as the spirits of nature, they have many other associations as well. Carvings of small-winged figures on Etruscan tombs have been found, connecting them to the dead, to the ancestors. In Celtic lore, the land of the faeries and the land of the dead were both beneath the ground, and the faeries were often considered the kin and guardians of the dead. Faeries had a special kinship with mortals who were considered witches. These humans had great magickal power, like the faeries, for they were said to have faery blood in them. Others associated that blood with the blood of angels or gods, two other depictions that have been associated with the fey. In fact, our image of tiny winged beings flitting about in nature didn't become popular until the Victorian era. Although there are ancient images and stories of tiny beings, they constitute only one race of the faery realm, as many faeries are considered to be human size, or taller, and depicted as the "bright and shining ones" or the "people of the dawn," having more in common with majestic gods than tiny beings.

Faeries have been associated with many different beings in folklore, including elves, dwarves, brownies, sprites, pookas, pixies, leprechauns, and nymphs. These beings might be different types of faeries, or their names might represent different ways that people understand them. Other beings associated with nature, such as satyrs, fauns, dryads, goblins, hobgoblins, gremlins, giants, and banshees, may or may not be part of the faery lands as we know them. In Celtic lore, it was taboo to refer to the fey as faeries. They had names such as "the kindly ones," the "good folk," the "fair folk," the "good people," or even "them" or "that lot," because in some traditions it was believed to be unlucky to mention the faeries by name. To the Celts, they were forces of nature and of what we might call the shamanic Underworld, and were not good or evil. Faeries are attracted to love, so to mention their name in association with anyone you love, such as a partner or child, might invite them to steal away your loved one. That brought about the custom of nicknames. If you did not refer to your loved ones by their true names, the faeries could not find them and steal them, not knowing to whom you were referring. Those in Ireland have an almost symbiotic relationship with the fey to this day, as even in the modern age, the old customs are kept. Though the old ways are almost never spoken about and are not seen as New Age forms of mystical empowerment, new roads are still constructed around faery mounds and paths out of fear that the faeries will cast ill those who disturb them.

Keeping track of the many different kinds of faeries and how they work can be confusing. Typically, several different orders of spiritual beings have been considered faeries by humans, ancient and modern, including the following.

Elementals

Mystic philosophers have stated that the four classical elements found in both Eastern and Western lore—earth, air, fire, and water—are embodied by "spirits" that organize and direct the energy of the elements. Though these are not physical beings, they reside in substances that resonate with the four elements. Fire elementals live in the flame, and earth elementals live in the rocks and soil. Water elementals live in the oceans, rivers, and lakes, and air elementals live in the sky, wind, and breath. Elementals are associated with the second dimension, to help manifest the third.

Mystic scholars have assigned images to these elementals that are much in keeping with our concepts of faery lore. Earth elementals are described as gnomes or dwarves who live in the earth and value the precious metals of the land. Their king is known as Ghob, a name that some believe is the root of the word goblin. The fire elementals are known as salamanders, though some modern traditions call them "fire faeries." Classically, they are seen as tiny lizards, also known as fire drakes. Their ruler is Djinn, from the root term *djinni*, also known as the Middle Eastern *gennie*. Many see the Middle Eastern races of djinn as forms of elementals or nature spirits in the desert. The air elementals are called sylphs, being light of form and looking like lithe pixies with gossamer insect wings. Though their appearance is more like that of our image of a classic Victorian faery, sylphs are associated more with mountaintops and winds than plants. The ruler of the air elementals is Paralda, who is often depicted as a shining knight. Water elementals are undines, also known as merfolk, and their ruler is Niksa.

Some lightworkers feel that their own souls have evolved out of one of these four elemental kingdoms and have a particular resonance with one of the four elements. More traditional teachings state that every elemental spirit either ascends the hierarchy of its own elemental kingdom and evolves beyond the element world to become an angelic being, or it masters each of the four elements in turn. Once the elemental spirit has mastered all four elemental powers, it evolves beyond the elemental world and becomes a more complex entity. Traditions disagree on what final form the elemental assumes, but possibilities include a dragon spirit, a nature spirit, or a human soul.

Nature Spirits

Nature spirits are literally the spirits, the consciousness, of nature. They are the conscious energy and life force in the flowers, trees, and herbs, but also in the stones, clouds, dirt, and seas. When you talk to your plants, it is the nature spirits of those plants that listen and respond. It is the personal consciousness of nature. Everything in nature has a nature spirit associated with it. The nature spirits work with the elementals, but are more complex than the elemental beings. Sometimes nature spirits are personified as little people in the land, but often they are felt as vortexes of energy and light. Like elementals, nature spirits are associated with the second dimension, but have more of a presence in the third dimension, as they are the consciousness of manifested nature.

Devas

The term deva comes from the Hindu teachings and refers to a "god," "little god," or "shining spirit." In Hinduism, everything—from every blade of grass to every grain of sand—has its own god. Some gods are just bigger than other gods, or more universal. The smaller gods, these devas, are the spirits of nature that oversee nature. Unlike the traditional nature spirits, which are more personal, devas are described as the architects of nature. They keep the blueprints of everything in nature. Plato taught that everything has a perfect form that underlies it, based in its sacred geometry. The devas are the guardians of these perfect forms and operate from the sixth dimension.

There is a deva for every perfect form. There is a deva for pine trees and for squirrels. There is a deva for emeralds and quartz, dandelions and rivers. The deva is like the collective higher self of nature, the oversoul or monad. The deva holds and maintains the perfect pattern, while the nature spirits seek to implement the pattern. Sometimes things in nature turn out perfectly in the material realm, and other times less so, but there is still an underlying pattern to everything. Devas are often equated with angels, and the term "overlighting deva" has come to describe special devas, much as the term archangel signifies special angels. An overlighting deva is like the leader, or organizer, of many other devas. The human body has an overlighting deva, and each deva for the lungs, liver, bones, blood, etc., is under its charge. In healing, this special deva is referred to as the Overlighting Deva of Healing.

Material from Djwal Khul separates the devic order into two primary groups: the solar pitris, or great builders and extensions of the Solar Logos, and the lunar pitris, or the lesser builders, associated with the work of nature spirits. Perhaps this is why so many lunar goddesses are associated with nature, faeries, and the wild woods. In some Theosophically inspired models, faeries, nature spirits, devas, and angels are all from the same order of beings, but the devas are on the lower end of the spectrum while the traditional angels are on the higher end of the spectrum, less immersed in the physical world. While I think devas and angels are closely related, I believe they are different, fulfilling different purposes in the universe.

Underworld Spirits

In most traditional faery lore, the fey are not nature spirits or devas, but spirits beneath the earth, under the hills. Underworld spirits are connected to nature and guard nature, but are something different and broader in scope than the traditional nature spirits. They often act from more human motivations—feeling anger and jealousy, love and compassion. While Underworld spirits are most noted for their mischievous pranks, they are also known for their blessings and curses. Some think of these spirits as the old gods, retreated into the land. In Ireland, the race is known as the Tuatha de Danaan, or children of the goddess Danu. They arrived in Ireland and vanquished the Fomorians, who represented the powers of blight and illness. The Tuatha de Danaan, in turn, faced an invasion by the Milasians, the ancient ancestors of the Irish. They decided that rather than fight this noble race, they would disappear, and found themselves in a land that mirrored the surface world in many ways, going beneath the land, where everything is perfect. In the Underworld, everyone is beautiful, the trees are in fruit and bloom at the same time, and everything is magickal. In Celtic lore, the seasons and times are reversed in the land of the faeries when compared to the seasons and times in the mortal world. When it is summer here in the human world, it is winter in the faery world. When it is day in the world of humans, it is night in the world of the fey.

Eventually, our understanding of the gods evolved into a reverence for them as faeries, the guardians of the land. To some neopagans of the Irish traditions, thinking of the gods as faeries and not gods is sacrilege, much the same way Christians and Jews take offense when the god of the Old Testament is referred to as a minor tribal god. In Golden Dawn lore, there was a distinction made between Arch-Fey, or High Elves, associated with the Tuatha, and lower forms of nature spirits. The concept of the People Under the Hills developed further with the introduction of the Christian religion in the Celtic territories. Like the ancient Etruscans, the Celts associated these spirits with burial mounds and, later, graveyards. Norse traditions have two realms of "elves," one above and one below, with light and dark elves. The light elves are associated with the noble ancestors, with what we perhaps would consider the ascended masters. In Ireland the Underworld faeries became known as the Sidhe (pronounced "She"), while in Scotland they were known as the Sithe. The faery society in the Otherworld was patterned after a medieval court system, with kings, queens, fools, and heroes. The "good" faeries, or those favorably disposed toward humans, were known as the Seelie Court, while the "bad" faeries, or those unfavorably disposed toward humans, were the Unseelie Court.

Faery scholars categorized many different kinds of faeries. Various wise ones who worked with humans directly became faery seers and faery doctors or healers. Many believe the old traditions of Celtic witchcraft were, in part, rituals to balance the energy between the human and faery worlds. Native American teachings make references to the "little people" in their lore. There are stories of these beings acting as guardians among the Chickasaw, Muscogee, and Cherokee tribes. The Muscogee also referred to "docktors" working with these beings, who would take and train children in their arts, much as in the Irish tales. In the Cherokee tradition, these beings are sometimes called Taliloquay. You'll find tales of the faeries in all lands that honor the Earth and the realms of nature. Faery magick today is an attempt by both sides to rekindle this practice.

Angels

Faeries are often called the angels of nature, and some people think of faeries, or perhaps the devic aspect of the faery realm, as angels of a "lower" vibration, tied to the land, to the material plane. Because of this affinity for the material world, faeries are depicted as less than straightforward when compared to the angelic realm, giving rise to our thoughts of mischievous faeries. In some Christian lore, in its attempt to vilify faeries, faery angels are seen as fallen angels. Some are seen as the angels who fell with the Morning Star in the story of Lucifer, making them demons or imps. Gnostic Luciferians see Lucifer as the heart of the Earth, glowing like a brilliant sun and radiating rays of Earthlight. Each ray is a faery being guiding the development of nature and the world. Lucifer is the Dreamer in the heart of the world, and the guardian of nature. Such traditions might equate the Theosophists' Sanat Kumara with the benevolent vision of Lucifer in the Earth. The Earthlight shining from the heart of the planet shows that the wisdom of the stars can also be found in the heart of the Earth. Our enlightenment is not just a matter of reaching up for celestial fire, but also finding the same celestial fire of enlightenment within nature.

All of these beings are part of what we consider the faery realm. While each is separate and distinct, they all have a place in our vision of the faery. Each type of being can be called upon in our own spiritual workings.

I once asked my faery guide to explain to me the structure of the faery world and its relationship to humanity, and she gave me a model of the faery realm in terms of the three worlds of the shaman. The nature spirits are in the Middle World and the third dimension. These are the spirits that consciously manifest nature. They are the spirits of the plants, stones, and trees. Also in the Middle World are the elemental spirits—the gnomes, salamanders, sylphs, and undines. They are developing into nature spirits, but have not yet mastered all four elements. They do not fully live in the physical part of the Middle World, but are said to reside in the four elemental worlds that encircle the material world. The devas are the higher selves, the oversouls and the monads, of nature. They act as guides to the natural world, holding all the information about each aspect of nature. They are in the Upper World and the fourth, fifth, and sixth dimensions. The Underworld spirits, the Sidhe, are the lower selves of nature. The Underworld faeries are the guardians and protectors of nature. They are the ambassadors of nature, building a relationship with humanity through dreams, visions, and inspiration. They exist in harmony with the Earth, through the first and second dimensions.

FAERY WORKINGS

As a mystic, you might personally feel drawn to one or more aspects of nature. Some people are drawn to the devic realm, while others feel called by the elemental or Underworld realm. You might not be called by all three, and that's fine. The purpose of humanity's interaction with nature and these faery forces is to build bridges between the realms, and we are each called to different missions.

Learning all you can about the faeries is the first step in engendering their goodwill, but you have to go beyond book learning. Books will help you learn proper etiquette in the faery world, but if you want to work with the faeries, you have to be brave and dive into their world, and invite them into yours. Here are some ways the modern practitioner can work with those in the faery realm.

Exercise 9:
Faery Offerings

Traditionally, the first step in building a relationship with the faeries is to make them an offering. Offerings of traditional natural substances, said to be sacred to the faeries, resonate with their nature. Making offerings with love is like sending bursts of energy to the faery world, to attract their attention. These offerings invite them into your life. Though this can attract all types of faeries, it particularly attracts Underworld faeries.

You start by building a faery shrine. Though this can be done in your home, most practitioners, myself included, suggest that you build your first one outdoors, if possible. My faery shrine is simply a flat stone in my garden. Around the stone are several upright stones, forming a semicircle around the flat stone. The flat stone acts as my offering plate. Shiny things are said to attract the faeries, so I have some small stones and crystals near my shrine. The following minerals have associations with faeries.

Faery Stones and Crystals
Apatite
Apopholite, particularly Green
Aventurine
Barite
Calcite, Green
Dioptase
Emerald
Fluorite, particularly Green
Holey Stone (a stone with a natural hole in it)

Moss Agate
Quartz
Staurolite
Topaz
Tourmaline
Tree Agate
Turquoise
Wulfenite

These minerals can be used in a faery shrine or held when doing meditations and rituals with the faeries. Some people believe that bells frighten away the fair folk, but this legend comes from church bells, loud and heavy, not tiny bells or wind chimes, which I personally think they like. Decorate your shrine in whatever manner you feel called, keeping in mind the old legends of the faery folk.

I make my faery offerings during the holiday celebrations of the pagan year, such as the solstices and equinoxes, because they are the "in-between" points of the year. Faeries are "in-between" creatures and respond best at in-between times. During the day, the liminal, or in-between, times are dawn, noon, dusk, and midnight. Dawn and dusk are neither night nor day, and noon and midnight are neither morning nor evening, but are in between. You can also make offerings at the full or new Moon.

Traditional faery offerings in the Celtic traditions include milk, honey, bread, butter, cheese, and grain. In the Native traditions, grain, cornmeal, and tobacco are proper. Modern offerings include chocolate, caramel, candies, cake, shortbread, cupcakes, nuts, and seeds. Some people cook whole meals for the faery folk, as they do in ancestor rites. Some offer liquors such as rum, brandy, or wine. Not only is an offering a token of love and respect, but the energy you imbue it with forges a link across worlds to commune with the faeries.

When making a faery offering, sit or stand before your altar. Think of the faeries. Open your heart. Then say this or something similar:

I invite those faeries who come in love and trust, completely for my highest good, into my life. I seek to know you and, if I'm worthy, know the ways of nature through you. Welcome.

Hold your offering. Infuse it with your intention and love, and then leave it on the offering site. Some practitioners will instruct you to bury it the next day if no animal, acting as an emissary of the faeries, comes by to eat it.

I know many practitioners who make "faery homes" for the otherworldly ones. Though critics say that offering these diminutive houses only reinforces the Victorian-era stereotype of faeries, and doesn't take into account the fact that many faeries are quite large beings, those faery-house builders seem to get good results. I think of these tiny homes, crafted of wood, cardboard, paper, and other materials, as offerings that are as loving as honey and chocolate.

As you make your regular offerings, be mindful of faery contact in your life. You might feel their presence in your home or garden. Things could be a little chaotic and unusual. You might feel an attunement with the land. If you watch, listen, and feel, the faeries will most likely make themselves known to you.

Exercise 10:
Visiting the Faery Realm

In the myths, faeries of the Underworld or Otherworld are notorious for bringing others into their realm. They are the keepers of the gateways. Etruscan faeries are said to have vials of a magickal potion. One drop heals any illness. Two drops reveal the mysteries of nature. Three drops transform spirit into matter or matter into spirit, to facilitate crossing from one world into the next. Several stories exist of learned men and women who, instead of ascending to the heavens and angels or simply passing into the land of the ancestors, walk full body into the realm of the faery folk without dying, and spend eternity as companions to the fey and teachers of humans who visit this realm.

Many faery mounds in the British Isles, also known as Sidhe mounds or faery hills, are actually Stone Age burial chambers that were associated with faeries by the Celtic people. Time passes in a different manner in faery land. You can be gone for only a night, but experience years with the faeries. Or you can be gone for years, and feel as if only one night has passed with the faeries. Our sense of time is skewed in faery land, much as in dreams. Intense magickal training can occur in a short time in the faery land due to this time shift. It is recommended that one put an iron nail in the gateway to the faery world, to prevent it from closing completely, as the fey cannot bear to touch iron. Iron acts as a lightning rod to ground a spirit's manifestation in the material world. Medieval sorcerers summoning angels, spirits, and demons would use a sword with a reach beyond the circumference of the magick circle to "stab" and disrupt unruly spirits, dismissing them back to their plane of origin.

From a lightworker's perspective, the various types of faeries are associated with different dimensions. We can use the dimensional axis to attune to the faeries with whom we desire contact.

1. Sit before your altar or faery shrine in a comfortable position. If you can do this journey outside, it will help you connect with nature, though once you have made a connection to the faery realm, you can commune with them anywhere. To aid you in the journey, you can cleanse and consecrate any of the faery stones listed on pages 210–211, as you did with the angelic stones in exercise 6. Call upon the divine, in whatever form you prefer—God, Goddess, Great Spirit, Divine Mind, Mother-Father-God. Ask to be consciously connected to your source, for guidance and protection, and to all your spirit allies who are appropriate for you at this time. Do Exercise 1: Basic Meditation Technique up to step 6 (see page 81) to get into a meditative state.

2. Acknowledge the power of the four directions. Bring your attention to the north, then the east, south, and west. Bring your attention to the heavens above and the space below you. Then bring your awareness to your heart. Feel a shaft of light descend from the heavens, from the highest dimensions, surrounding you in a column of light and finding its anchor in the heart of the planet. You are now aligned with the twelve dimensions and are capable of interdimensional contact and journey.

3. Ask to be taken to the faery realm of your choice. If you seek contact with the devas, then bring your attention to the devas and the sixth dimension. If you seek the wisdom of the nature spirits or elementals, then think about the spirits of the second and third dimensions. If you seek to commune with the Underworld faeries, then attune to the first or second dimension. You can ask your ascended masters or angelic guides to aid you.

4. Feel yourself journeying to the faery realm as the gates are opened for you. You might find yourself spiraling quickly downward or upward through tunnels,

arriving at your destination like Alice in Wonderland through the rabbit hole. Notice how the realms manifest for you. They are often lush and green, glowing with an inner light. Faery myths are filled with otherworldly imagery, from rivers of blood, tears, and honey to trees with golden or fiery apples. Castles, courts, and villages are also common. In Celtic folklore, there are four sacred cities in the four directions, for the four elemental realms. In the center is the Glen of Precious Stones, or the Garden of Precious Stones, where the faeries congregate. I envision a garden of fantastic plant life, adorned with large minerals and gems.

5. Make contact with the faery beings. Converse with them, and allow them to respond through words, images, and feelings. Connect with the love of nature. Ask any questions you have about the faery realm, and learn how you can partner with these allies. Enjoy their company. They might even take you to meet the faery king or faery queen, or to see the faery court.

6. When you are done, say your farewells. Your faery ally might give you a gift or symbol to help establish the link between you. Most myths warn against accepting faery food, and say to decline it, but be sure to do so politely, or you will be trapped in their land forever. Others think the warnings about faery food were church propaganda, to prevent those who had faery contact from experiencing their own empowerment and awakening from the food. In any case, if you are offered faery food in your journeys to their land, use caution and discern what is right for you. Ask your masters or angels if accepting the food would be beneficial for you. Personally, I am always cautious about accepting faery food, but the decision is up to you. Then return to where you began. Imagine yourself descending through the tunnel of light and back to the third dimension. Ground yourself. Relax. Take a few breaths. Open your eyes.

7. Acknowledge the four directions around you again, north, east, south, and west, then above, below, and center. Thank the divine Creator for guidance and protection. Thank your guides and allies. Perform steps 9 and 10 of Exercise 1: Basic Meditation Technique (see page 82) to return to normal waking consciousness. Write down any impressions or messages you received, before you forget them.

Build a relationship with your faeries as guides and spiritual partners. They may teach you mysteries of magick and healing that you couldn't learn from any book.

FAERY GARDENING

One of the ways in which faery teachings entered popular consciousness again was through the work of the Findhorn Community. Based in northern Scotland, near the Arctic Circle, the Findhorn Community was a spiritual and social experiment in creating community. At first glance, it was one of the worst places to start a garden, with soil that was no more than sand and gravel. The founders of Findhorn, in contact with the intelligences of nature, were able to grow truly amazing specimens, much greater than normal size, including forty-pound cabbages. Founded by Peter Caddy, his wife, Eileen, and friend Dorothy Maclean in the 1960s, the Findhorn Community began with Maclean's meditation, making contact with a deva. Peter Caddy, who started the garden, would consult the devas, through Maclean, for advice on the garden. The results were phenomenal. Soon the team was visited by Caddy's friend R. Ogilvie Crombie. While meditating in the garden, Crombie had a vision of a nature spirit named Kurmos, who appeared as half man, half animal. Kurmos's job was to prepare the group for contact with the most important nature spirit, Pan. Pan taught them about working in partnership with nature, and saw Findhorn as a way to renew contact between humanity and the natural world. As it grew in size and purpose, Findhorn became a model for New Age communities to live in cooperation with nature. As the next generation of Findhorn took over, plants returned to their normal size, yet still flourished in this desolate environment.

Following in the footsteps of Findhorn is Machaelle Small Wright, the founder of the Perelandra Gardens in Virginia. She is also in contact with the devas and nature spirits, and has become one of the pioneers in making this information available to the public. In addition to creating a line of flower essences and manuals on co-creative gardening, Wright works with the Great White Brotherhood and brought forth the MAP healing protocol.

Like those at Findhorn and Perelandra, you, too, can work directly with the nature spirits. Before you decide to start a garden, I suggest you consult with the faery allies. If you already have a garden, and want to work in partnership with nature, you can still consult the spirits. By working in conscious communion with nature, you develop a spiritual rapport with the faery realms and with Mother Earth.

When planning your garden, there are various traditional plants and trees associated with faery lore that are said to attract faeries and bring harmony in our relationship with them.

Faery Plants
Clover

Cowslip

Daisies

Elecampagne (Elfwort)

Fennel

Foxglove

Goosefoot

Hollyhock

Lily of the Valley

Marigold

Milkweed

Nettle

Rose

Rosemary

Thyme

Wood Anemone

Yarrow

Faery Trees
Alder

Beech

Elder

Elm

Hawthorn

Silver Birch

Walnut

People who want to work with the nature realm may feel excluded if their meditations don't include detailed communications from the plant world, as the founders of Findhorn and Perelandra were able to receive. You don't necessarily have to be psychically gifted to work with nature. Systems of divination using yes/no answers can serve as an interface for your communication with nature.

Pendulum

A pendulum is a weight on the end of a length of cord. There are fancy crystal pendulums on silver chains available, but you can also use a necklace, or a needle on the end of a cotton or silk thread. I've used a simple piece of string with a washer on the end of it. Through the movement of a pendulum, you can determine a yes or no response. Many people erroneously assume that it is the pendulum itself that is giving a response to their question, when in actuality the pendulum is a method of divination that interfaces with other spirits. You can use it to connect to your higher self, the ascended masters, angels, and faery nature spirits and devas.

To use the pendulum, first cleanse it as you would a ritual tool. Intend that it be free of all unwanted vibrations. Consecrate it by holding it with the intention that it be a device to communicate with spirits, who will answer you clearly and truly. Traditionally, a yes answer is a clockwise motion, while a no answer is a counterclockwise motion. But I suggest you first connect to a spirit, and ask to see a yes answer, then a no answer. This is what I state:

> I, (state your name), ask to connect to (state the spirit's name) through this pendulum, with the guidance of my higher self, for the highest good, harming none, with ease, grace, and gentleness.

Once the yes and no responses are clear, I formulate my questions as yes/no queries, until the meaning of the spirits is clear to me. As with all communications, I then thank and release the spirits summoned. I cleanse my pendulum each time I use it, and always start with that statement, so it is completely clear to the universe who I want to answer my questions through the pendulum.

Muscle Testing

Another method for communicating with nature is to use applied kinesiology, or muscle testing, to get yes/no answers through your body. Applied kinesiology is used to test the

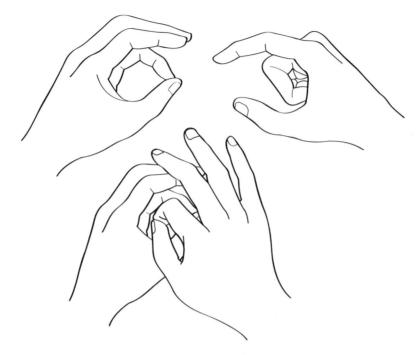

Figure 28: Muscle-Testing Positions

body for helpful or harmful substances, determining if a substance energetically strengthens or weakens the body. The same technique has been applied to spiritual communication, using the weakened response as a no answer and the strengthened response as a yes. The technique is based on the belief that the spirit can easily put a signal into the energetic system of a person's body.

Though muscle testing is traditionally administered by a second person, you can also use the technique on your own arm. With both methods, you begin with an intention, just as in the pendulum work, to make it clear to the universe who you want to communicate with you through your body. For the first muscle-testing position, you make rings with the thumb and first finger on each hand, and link the rings like a chain. Ask your question and then try to pull the rings apart. If the chain breaks, the answer is no, because your body is weakened. If the chain holds, the answer is yes. Though most people prefer this simple method, if you are prone to sweaty hands, you will find that all your answers are no. You might want to test your answers in any muscle-testing situation by first asking a simple question to which you know the answer is yes, such as "Is my name (state your name)?" Then feel the yes energy. Next, ask a question for which you know the response is no, perhaps by using another person's name, and then feel the no energy.

For the second muscle-testing position, take your nondominant hand (if you are right-handed, your nondominant hand would be your left) and form a loop with your thumb and pinky. Take your dominant hand and form a pincer shape with your index finger and thumb. Place the pincer in the loop (see figure 28), and ask your question. Then try to open your pincer while keeping the loop closed. If the loop breaks, releasing your nondominant pinky and thumb, then the answer is no. If it remains tight, the answer is yes.

Use your meditation techniques along with muscle testing or the pendulum to enter into a conscious relationship with your land. Try this exercise with the spirits of your garden to partner with them and create together. You may want to have a notebook handy to write down your answers as you go.

Exercise 11:
Co-Creative Gardening

1. Sit in a garden or a potential garden site. Do Exercise 1: Basic Meditation Technique up to step 6 (see page 81) to get into a meditative state. Use the sounds in nature to attune your awareness to the vibration of nature.

2. Call upon the spirits of nature with whom you wish to communicate. Call upon your own higher self and your guides and masters to aid you. Call upon the deva of the garden, as well as the nature spirits. Call upon the Underworld faeries of the land. I like to call upon Mother Earth and Pan as well. Ask them to work together in harmony and communicate in a way that you can understand, with one clear voice.

3. Out loud, or silently in your mind, communicate your desire to create or develop your garden, and ask to partner with these beings. Ask for their desires and needs to be made clear to you. Start by listening, and you may hear voices, see images, or have a strong intuition. If not, ask yes/no questions using either the pendulum or muscle-testing technique. You can take notes, if you choose. The spirits may give you a detailed schematic as to how the garden should be developed.

4. When done, thank all the spirits you have called and say farewell, ending the session. Perform steps 9 and 10 of Exercise 1: Basic Meditation Technique (see page 82) to return to normal waking consciousness.

As the co-creative process continues, I check in regularly with the spirits of my garden, testing out things that I intuitively or intellectually feel are needed. I speak to the garden plants before planting a new one, making sure that both the new plant and the existing plants want the new plant there. I check in about watering times and amounts, as well as adding fertilizer, crystals, flower essences, and decorations to the garden. Through muscle-testing and pendulum work, I add crystals and remove them from the garden. Sometimes a crystal is healing for a short period of time and then needs to be removed. Other times the faeries instruct me to bury crystals and leave them in the garden. For a more detailed understanding of co-creative gardening, I highly suggest reading *The Perelandra Garden Workbook* and *The Perelandra Garden Workbook II*, both by Machaelle Small Wright.

———————————————————

One of the most important lessons the faery folk can teach us is to not take ourselves, or life, too seriously. Faeries, at their best, often want to play, to enjoy life to the fullest. They are spirits of the material world, and want us to enjoy the material world. They want us to embrace singing and dancing, eating good food, making love, and running around acting silly. You can embody the playful attitude of the faeries in your daily life by bringing more of their joy into your own life. Through us, they learn more about the material world, and what it's like to be human, and from them, we learn more about the realm of the fey, and how to reconnect to our childlike innocence and the primal power of nature.

11

THE STARRY OꞀES

Out of all the concepts presented to me on the ascension path, the one I've had the
most difficulty with is the star nations. Star brothers and sisters, the starry ancestors,
the cosmic brotherhood, E.T.'s . . . whatever you want to call them, they just didn't fit into
my worldview. Oh, I believed in the potential of life on other planets. I even believed that
such life might have visited our world in the past, or might even be here today, but I didn't
think the tarot reader and crystal healer in my local New Age store were in telepathic
communion with them. That just seemed rather far-fetched to me. I still struggle with the
concept of the star nations, but understanding the historical background of such teachings
can make the idea not only more plausible, but also more spiritually helpful.

When I first got involved with the community of lightworkers in my area, I signed up
for the pivotal merkaba workshop that would change my view of spirituality. When I was
registering for the class, the woman on the phone who took my information made reference to Sirius and the Pleiades, and any number of other stars. I gathered later that she
was telling me that she believed she was an ascended master from Sirius. She talked about
humanity having to get its act together collectively before it was too late. She ended the
conversation with, "Well, what do I care, really? I'm not even from this planet!" It was at

that moment that I wanted to ask her to rip up my credit card information and cancel my registration, because she was obviously a crazy person and I didn't want her having my financial information. But I was too dumbstruck by the whole thing to say anything. My first thought was that I must have misunderstood her. But I didn't. And I didn't cancel my registration. I showed up anyway.

The workshop took place the weekend after the Hale-Bopp comet cult, Heaven's Gate, made the news. The group of cultists had been taught that the comet Hale-Bopp was really a spaceship, or perhaps a spaceship was flying behind the comet, sent to "pick up" a chosen few. They could enter the ships by freeing their souls from their bodies by ending their physical lives through suicide. And the entire group did. Most of the world looked at the event in horror, as I know I did, and thought it was a mind-controlled cult led by a charismatic yet crazy person. Looking back on it, I'm not sure I feel any differently, but I do believe people have choices. And if that is how they chose to use their lives, then as long as they did not take other people with them who had not agreed to die, I'm not sure if I should judge.

At the merkaba workshop, I was introduced to flower essences. The participants, all of whom seemed to know each other, passed to me a small blue vial of what I later learned was yarrow flower essence made in moonlight. They told me it would help "activate my light vehicle and help me fly." With the Hale-Bopp incident in mind, I was understandably skeptical. I passed on the essence that day, and decided not to eat or drink anything in the presence of those folks. People talked about ascended aliens and teachings from the stars, from Sirius, the Pleiades, and Andromeda. I was blown away by it all. Here was a meditation and healing technique, the merkaba, that was having an obvious and profound effect on me when we used it, but the concepts of extraterrestrial life that I was hearing from my peers were just so bizarre that I didn't know what to think.

It was only after I learned the historical context of what they were saying, beyond the immediate channeled information, that I could properly digest what I had heard.

ULTRATERRESTRIALS

The first thought I had to digest was the possibility that perhaps these beings from the star nations are not extraterrestrials in the classic sense, as most people, even those in the lightworker community, assume, but rather that they are ultraterrestrials.

What is an ultraterrestrial? The term consists of the prefix *ultra*, meaning beyond space, limits, or range, and *terrestrial*, referring to Earth, terra, the land or planet and its inhabitants. To me, an ultraterrestrial is a being that comes from beyond the terrestrial chain of life. This includes beings not defined in terrestrial terms. They are not necessarily physical, cellular beings in the way we know life to be. Spirits of all kinds could be considered ultraterrestrials. In the paradigm of ascension, we believe that those of us in physical life can ascend to a higher plane of existence, possibly transforming our whole body. We are then no longer cellular beings. The ultraterrestrials, those that are perceived to be aliens by many, could be beings who have already achieved various states of ascension, or those whose life forms originated on those higher levels of reality and have no need to ascend to them, just as we humans begin our conscious journey on the physical, third dimension. Their sense of origin and home has nothing to do with the process of life on Earth. They were never humans ascending from a human point of view, or spirits linked to life on Earth, such as the faeries, but are life forms that are alien to us.

Seen in this light, the alien lore starts to make more sense. This is not the only interpretation of the starry ones, as many believe these beings do have a physical existence somewhere in the universe. But when viewed as spiritual entities that are not intimately linked to the life forms on Earth—not our terrestrial ancestors, gods, spirits, or elemental forces—they appear alien. Yet, experiences with these alien forces are quite similar to shamanic initiations and awakenings—sometimes frightening, sometimes beautiful and loving, but always life changing. They appear to the participants to be very real beings, yet little physical evidence can be found to prove their physical reality.

If the starry ones are of a different vibrational level than humanity, then their favored means of contact—visions, sensory experiences, and now, channeled telepathic communication—are the same methods that have been used by spiritual beings throughout the ages to make contact with human consciousness. I've known many mystics, shamans, and witches who have had alien contact and seen flying saucers, though most don't like to talk about it for fear they will be perceived as even crazier than they already appear to the general population. But perhaps it is those who have the eyes to see, or perhaps the eye of spiritual sight developed, who can best detect these forces.

The perceived "technology" of the aliens is not necessarily technology in the mechanical sense, but an inner, spiritual technology. Modern channelers refer to such alien ships as "lightships" or "living vehicles," as they are constructed from energy and intention rather than metal and wire. Many describe the sightings of such flying saucers moving in a manner in which no terrestrial ship could move, such as making a fast, ninety-degree turn. The patterns of UFO flight seem to align with "ley lines," or energy lines on the Earth's surface, connecting sacred sites. In days past, ghosts, spirits, and deities were said to walk or fly over these pathways. Many make the comparison between the traditional lore of faery abductions and modern alien-abduction scenarios, as both have much in common in terms of experience and location. Both are traditionally sighted in places of geological stress or areas considered sacred by the indigenous populations that live nearby. Both the gray "aliens" and the faeries are said to abduct people into their world, and the abductees describe the experience as either blissful or torturous. Both aliens and faeries are small and inhuman and seem to have magickal powers. Though most faery seers and UFO enthusiasts will say that the two groups are totally separate phenomena, there could be a link. Perhaps a nonhuman consciousness is making contact with us, using the cultural imagery of the time. When the dominant imagery was from folklore, they manifested as faeries. Now, when the dominant imagery is from science fiction, they appear to be aliens.

Those in the drug culture taking ethogens, or psychedelics, report visits from tiny people—faery-esque or alien-esque, depending on the "tripper" and the drug. Experiences of such "space elves" are more common with the use of DMT, the active ingredient of ayahuasca tea, a psychedelic preparation that contains the jungle "spirit" vine *Banisteriopsis caapi*. Pivotal to our understanding of this phenomenon was writer and philosopher Terence McKenna, who studied and espoused the universality of certain drug trips, believing they opened other levels of consciousness and lead to communion with beings of an objective existence in another dimension. Those who encountered these beings, dubbed "hyperdimensional machine elves," experienced a flying-saucer or alien-abduction scenario. Perhaps it is through these plants that higher alien intelligences are communicating with us.

As advanced beings, ultraterrestrials will not always manifest in ways that we clearly understand. Perhaps we cannot truly comprehend these nonlinear beings from our linear point of view. We see this concept in our more advanced or lofty science fiction literature. We find the concept of the Q Continuum in the *Star Trek* series. Though they do not always appear to be spiritually advanced, beings from the Q Continuum possess a relationship with time and space beyond human understanding at this time, which results in difficult relationships. In the 1997 film *Contact*, the main character is transported in a geometric structure quite similar to a mechanical merkaba (see chapter 21) and travels through a tunnel of light, ending in a tropical paradise where she is visited by aliens manifesting as her deceased father. This contact with alien life is not like anything she had expected, and in some ways her experience proves to be both surreal and mundane in terms of our science fiction expectations. Alien contact, in the New Age, might not be like anything we are expecting.

THE STARRY ANCESTORS

One of the most interesting yet simultaneously disturbing theories about the ancient origins of humanity is the ancient astronaut theory. It's a popular theory among those in the lightworker community, yet is not accepted with any credibility by any in the mainstream scientific community. It's an expansion of the more basic paleocontact theory, which was taken seriously as a possibility by a number of scientists, though as more outlandish information was added to it, the greater scientific community dismissed most thoughts on the topic. As a fringe theory, the ancient astronaut theory is the belief that the ancient civilizations of humanity arose out of contact with extraterrestrial beings. These beings taught us art, science, writing, mysticism, and agriculture and are responsible for our "leaps" in cultural evolution. Some even believe that these beings mated with, or genetically experimented with, early humans, resulting in our current race.

Many myths and legends report gods, angels, or spirits descending from the sky and bringing civilization. We have many mythical gods who "gave" civilization to humanity, from Prometheus of the Greeks, who stole fire from the gods to aid humanity and then suffered for it, to Ea of Sumer, Osiris and Isis of Egypt, Quetzalcoatl of the Aztecs, and Viracocha of the Incas. In biblical lore, there is a "race" of angels known as the Grigori, the fallen angels, who mated with mortal women who then gave birth to the race of giants known as the Nephilim. The Grigori taught the arts and sciences to humanity and are often thought of as the "Watchers" in modern magick. These Watchers were called the teaching angels, and the stars in the heavens were said to be their campfires. They were known as the "sons" of God and were considered giants to ordinary humans, though their exact proportions are not clear, particularly if they were able to mate with human women. Some speculate that these were not angels at all, but a race from the stars.

Most people see these stories as myths, as allegories for the shaman's journey into the sky realm, bringing back new ideas that shaped civilization by connecting with spiritual forces. Those promoting the ancient astronaut theory believe that ancient alien contact was a literal physical event, rather than a shamanic experience, and that their landing and exchange began our ancient advanced civilizations. Based on our ultraterrestrial theory, perhaps shamanic contact and literal contact with a starry race are the same thing, as both would put us in contact with an intelligence beyond our current human understanding.

Proponents of the ancient astronaut theory look at many examples of early pictographs and statues, some of which look like people in modern-day spacesuits, and see an apparent "alien" influence. In ancient literature, we have passages cited as "proof" of ancient accounts of modern technology. Ezekiel's vision in the Old Testament can be seen as a spacecraft, with its fire and light, a chariot ascending to the heavens. The flying machines in Vedic lore, called Vimanas, are seen as spacecraft by some. In fact, many Hindu legends describe great battles with these flying machines, and some believe the destruction described in these legends is an account of a nuclear war that occurred in Earth's ancient past. Mystics would say that these flying machines were not vehicles of metal and wire, but the spiritual chariot of the merkaba, a vehicle of light and consciousness generated by a magickal individual.

Skeptical mystics would argue that the ancient Stone Age shamans were perhaps seeing things in the future in their psychic vision, and not depicting ancient astronauts and flying ships in their present-day lives. Either way, it is an interesting argument. Proponents of the ancient astronaut theory say that it is the only way to account for the number of civilizations that simply spring up, with advanced concepts and technology, and then seem to decline. There is no clear build-up of complexity. It is as if these cultures bloom like a desert oasis and then crumble away when the higher influence leaves, seeding ideas for future cultures. Proponents view the existence of ancient structures such as the Egyptian pyramids, Easter Island, and Stonehenge as evidence of such advanced, off-world technology. The root races of Theosophy (see chapter 20) are said to hint at the influence of aliens, and possibly spiritually oriented aliens, in the origins of humanity.

The main proponents of the ancient astronaut theory include Erich von Däniken, a German author who wrote *Chariots of the Gods,* published in 1971, and Zecharia Sitchin, author of numerous books on the topic, including *The 12th Planet,* published in 1978. Sitchin is the most widely known author on the ancient astronaut theory in the ascension community, and he attributes humanity's origin to a group of deities called the Anunnaki, from a planet called Nibiru, or Marduk, which lies beyond the orbit of Pluto. The Anunnaki influenced ancient Sumerian culture. Lightworkers generally see the Anunnaki as a malevolent, or at least selfish and misguided, influence upon humanity.

The legends of the Dogon tribe of Africa also lend support to the controversial ancient astronaut theory. The Dogon tribe lives in the central plateau of Mali, south of the Niger bend. The Dogon are said to have migrated from ancient Egypt and are keepers of particular mysteries in the Egyptian tradition. Though this is the folk history associated with the Dogon, their true origin is unknown. The most startling fact about the Dogon is their mythology surrounding the star Sirius.

When interviewed by a Westerner, the Dogon revealed information about Sirius B, a white dwarf star in a system with the visible Sirius A. Sirius B is not visible without a powerful telescope. When asked about their knowledge of Sirius B, they told of an oral tradition dating back to contact with beings known as the Nommo. The Nommo had advanced astronomical information about Sirius B, including the fact that it moves in a fifty-year elliptical orbit around Sirius A. They described it as white in color, and as the smallest thing there is and the heaviest thing there is. Though Sirius B is not really the smallest thing in existence, the Dogon did a good job of describing its properties. Sirius B is very small when compared to other stars, such as Sirius A, and it is incredibly dense, or in other words, heavy. The Dogon's calendar is based on the rotation of Sirius B, a fifty-year cycle.

Some have described the Nommo as twins, like the archetypal yin and yang, though others describe them as an aquatic extraterrestrial race that came from Sirius and started an ancient civilization from which the Dogon are descended. The Nommo are said to be similar to mermen and merwomen or to cetaceans, which parallels some of the descriptions of the Sumerian god Ea, who emerged from the primordial waters to teach humanity the arts and sciences of civilization. Many ancient gods of civilization have fish associations.

In the mythology, the Dogon describe stars in the inner system of stars (including Sirius, Orion, and the Pleiades) that greatly affect Earth and its inhabitants, as opposed to the stars in the outer system. The Dogon have an intricate language and religion, involving the ancestors, the Earth, and agriculture, using ritual, divination, and dance in ceremonies. The imagery and cycles of Sirius play a strong role in their religion and culture.

Skeptics of the Dogon theory think that the advanced extraterrestrial contact was the product of the interpretation and imagination of Robert Temple, author of *The Sirius Mystery*. Proponents of the extraterrestrial theories state that the Dogon's knowledge of Sirius B predates contact with Robert Temple, and was given to anthropologists who didn't realize the significance of the information they were given. It's also possible that knowledge of Sirius B was integrated into their mythology through contact with the modern world, as the Dogon were very interested in astronomy and would talk to visitors about it, or through ancient cultures that knew about Sirius B, referring to it as a dark companion to the star. But even if other ancients knew about Sirius B, how did they learn of its existence?

Along with the information of the Dogon, we have teachings from the living traditions of Native Americans. Proponents of the alien astronaut theory, in its various forms, believe the Native wisdom is an additional verification of the theories of alien contact. Some Native elders are sharing this information, while others do not support or corroborate these ideas. Many Native cultures, including the Hopi, Navaho, Cherokee, Mayan, Aztec, and Inca, have been associated with alien contact, past and present, by those in the New Age movement. Each culture is said to have secret knowledge of the true history of the world, and the origin of the races. Author Nancy Red Star has done much to reveal this controversial information to the general public, sharing stories of Native elders "visited" by what she refers to as the Star Ancestors. In her opinion, this contact is extremely beneficial and a part of our transition to the next age.

Other ancient cultures have been associated with the secret knowledge of alien visitors. When we examine ancient cultures, it's hard to distinguish a belief in alien life, or even contact, from their concepts of gods, angels, demons, and other spiritual visitors. From the mystic's point of view, perhaps all are one and the same.

American horror author H. P. Lovecraft, in his Cthulhu mythos, touches upon this archetypal concept of ancient alien contact. Directly inspired by his own nightmares (and many magickally oriented fans feel that he was latently psychic and in tune with the primal forces) and writing a new mythology based on an ancient truth, Lovecraft wrote about a pantheon of primal alien "gods" and creatures of a dark and malevolent nature, originating from beyond the stars, influencing humanity and worshiped by insane cults. These gods are alien in the sense of being totally unknown and unknowable to the human mind without the person being driven insane, rather than an enlightened race of happy, humanoid people living in a paradise on another planet. They are multidimensional in nature, beyond the physical realm and normal human comprehension.

The first and foremost of these alien gods is Cthulhu, a monstrous being who sleeps in a city named R'lyeh on a sunken continent in the Pacific. In the theology of the mythos, it is speculated that the arrival of the alien gods triggered evolution on Earth from single-cell organisms to multi-cell organisms. Cthulhu is the most powerful of these beings residing on Earth, with various followers and rivals. Other beings exist on other planets. The magick of this mythos is stellar in nature. It is said that Cthulhu will be awakened when the stars are in the correct alignment. Other creatures can influence Earth only when their star shines down visibly upon the planet. Though Lovecraft originally created an amoral setting for his stories, with no overall theological meaning for humanity beyond the random harness of the universe, subsequent writers have adapted the mythos and ascribed to it their own moral themes, often Christian in nature, in conflict with Lovecraft's original vision. The Cthulhu mythology has taken on a life of its own, and inspired many magicians and metaphysicians to use it as a modern paradigm to commune with archetypal forces that are alien to human consciousness.

We even find mention of such spiritual extraterrestrials in the teachings of modern Christian mystic Daskalos. In *The Magus of Strovolos*, by Kyriacos C. Markides, the magus Daskalos relates his experience with these beings, whom he encountered while psychically trying to alter the trajectory of the Skylab space station descending into Earth's atmosphere in 1979, to prevent it from crashing in a populated area. His extraterrestrial allies were also attempting the same feat. On page 150 he says: "They seemed as if they were working groups which gave me the impression of flying saucers. I asked them whether they in fact were flying saucers but they seemed to ignore any question. Their response instead was that they are 'space people.' They live around our planet . . . They truly love us."

Though the lore of alien visitors is filled with accounts of benign contact, many in the New Age take the view of the tribal people, and think of the star spirits as the ancestors, who should be honored and respected. They are the Nations Beyond the Stars, our Brothers and Sisters in spirit, if not flesh. I believe that any group—be they people, angels, spirits, or yes, even aliens—should be judged individually. Modern mystics should not be naive and assume that all entities mean us well, or be paranoid and think that all mean us harm. Each case is individual. I've had spiritual contact with beings that I would consider ultraterrestrials, and although the outcomes were ultimately positive for me, not all of the entities I've encountered are beings that I would trust or like to see again. As with people, sometimes those we consider the "enemy" can be our greatest teachers, but I still don't want to give them the keys to my house.

THE COSMIC HIERARCHY

Modern mystics not only have ancient mythical ties to the stars, but they also look to the heavens for guidance. When we speak of the Hierarchy of Masters on Earth, there is an implication that the hierarchy extends far beyond Earth. With levels of awareness ranging from the terrestrial to the solar, galactic, universal, and cosmic, we have various beings aiding the evolution of life. The Great White Brotherhood of Earth, the Lords and Ladies of Shamballa, is said to be an "outpost" for the true lodge coming from Sirius. The star system of Sirius has played an important role in our ancient cultures. Sanat Kumara is said to descend from Venus. Many people believe that at some point there was life on Mars, being a sister planet to Earth, and that we humans are following in their destructive footsteps. The concept of life on other planets has fascinated humanity, from writers to mystics, for ages.

Those in the lightworker community have identified a variety of "races" of aliens, associated with different planets and star systems. They are often identified, through channeled information, as masters and teachers within the cosmic hierarchy. Beyond Earth's ascended masters are masters of a galactic level, who do not interact with humanity as much on a personal level. These galactic masters are the next step in evolution for our current ascended masters, while the Lords and Ladies of Shamballa represent the next leap in consciousness for humans. Other "space masters" between the planetary and fully galactic levels do have contact with the people on Earth. Here is a list of the best-known star races, working with, or sometimes against, the evolution in consciousness of the inhabitants of Earth.

Alpha Centaurians

The star system Alpha Centauri is said to resonate with violet light and is home to a very advanced civilization. Alpha Centaurians seek to improve humanity's understanding of science and scientific theory.

Altairians

Altair is home to a quiet, contemplative, and peaceful civilization colonized from the Vegans. Altairians are not involved in exploration beyond their own planet.

Andromedans

Andromeda is a galaxy spiritually connected to the Milky Way, and is home to many advanced civilizations currently taking an interest in the Milky Way. The Andromedans are the guardians of the seventh dimension.

Antarians

Antares is a binary star system that resonates with the colors red and green and is home to a highly evolved spiritual civilization. Antares itself acts as a bridge, interdimensionally, with Andromeda.

Anunnaki

The Anunnaki are an offshoot of a Sirian race that settled on Nibiru and was part of humanity's development in ancient Sumer. Some equate the Anunnaki with the Dracos, Reptilians, or Grays, but it appears that they are something else. The Anunnaki were equated with the Sumerian gods, and possibly the later Greek gods, of ancient mythology.

Arcturians

Arcturus is home to an advanced fifth-dimensional civilization. Those Arcturians who are involved in Earth affairs are interested in our emotional, spiritual, and mental healing. They are said to have many technologies that are available to us if we contact them spiritually and request such aid, including protection shields, an electronic "plate" in the third eye to aid in spiritual and psychic development, an information exchange chamber, a synthesis chamber to build our light quotient, a love and joy chamber, a future chakra system, and a pranic clearing device to clear the physical and energy bodies of debris. Arcturus is said to be the ideal model of the civilization into which humanity is evolving.

Ashtar Command

Members of the Ashtar Command, a branch of galactic ascended masters, act as spiritual protectors from any harmful alien involvement on Earth. The command is led by the master Ashtar, a being channeled by many on Earth.

Ataien

The Ataien are a race of beings that look like insects, specifically like praying mantises. Though their appearance can be frightening to many, they have a vision of the future based in love, harmony, and a collective consciousness.

Cessnans

Cessna is a planet of humanlike beings. The Cessnan culture is oriented around the study of alien cultures and peace with all other races.

Dracos

The Dracos are the races originating from the star Draco. See *Reptilians* and *Grays*.

Essassani

The Essassani are a race residing in a star system near the Orion constellation. This system is not visible to humanity from Earth because it is in a higher dimension.

Grays

The Grays, also spelled Greys, is a nickname for a large group of aliens coming to Earth from various star systems, including Rigel, Zeta Reticuli, Ursa Major, Draco, and Orion. Opinions on the Grays differ among various groups of lightworkers. Most see the Grays as a destructive force, responsible for abductions, and feel they have physiological problems that they are trying to cure by abducting and doing experiments on humans and cattle. They seek to colonize or subjugate the planet and are depicted as "hive mind" oriented, with little emotion. Those who see the Grays as strictly biological entities believe they have made contact and treaties with various factions of the world government.

Others see the Grays in a beneficial light, as beings who are assisting humanity and initiating or healing future mystics. In Nancy Red Star's *Legends of the Star Ancestors*, Ana Brito, a Cuban-Basque writer and medium, states that the Grays are benign and the keepers of our genetic code, returning to us in this time of transition. Some even think the Grays are not aliens at all. One teaching that rings true for me comes from a scene in a comic book series known as *The Invisibles*, written by chaos magician Grant Morrison. In *The Invisibles: Counting to None*, when it appears that the main characters might be experiencing something like an alien abduction and experiment, their leader, King Mob, states to his lover, Ragged Robin, "They're not aliens. They never were aliens. They're anti-bodies." The Grays of Grant Morrison's writings appear to aid and heal, and are said to appear when the universe itself is sick. Another main character from *The Invisibles*, Jack Frost, has the Grays show up in his initiatory experiences in the form of shamanic teachers who take the initiate apart and put him back together, this time with a "stone" in his third eye, to awaken him. Jack Frost goes on to become the future Buddha, the Maitreya of the next age. The Grays are the race most closely associated with the frightening or malevolent faeries. In general, lightworkers tend not to initiate contact with the Grays.

Hathors

The Hathors are a group of fourth-dimensional beings on Venus and are depicted as "cow-like." Their civilization is based on the principles of sound, and they use sound and vibration in healing. Associated with ancient Egypt, and the goddess Hathor in particular, the

Hathors are said to be depicted in Hathor's temple in Dendera. Many lightworkers believe that the Hathors had contact with the ancient Egyptians and helped them develop systems of sound healing and ritual.

Iargans

The Iargans are a race of beings from the planet Iarga who are advanced in technology and spirituality. Their goals are selfless service, cosmic integration, and immortality.

Inxtrian

The Inxtrians are another highly evolved race, hailing from the planet Inxtria in the star group of Beta Andromeda. They have been involved in gathering information on Earth and its species, and express great concern for us regarding our use of nuclear, chemical, and biological weapons.

Lyrans

The Lyrans, from the star system Lyra, are the original ancestors of the human race. Though they have a history of conflict, the Lyrans are now said to be beyond the need for aggressive conflict resolution. Through their history, they have played a role in seeding places such as the Pleiades, the Hyades, and the Vega system. The Lyrans have an exploratory nature and can adapt easily to other environments. They are the original root race of humanity in this galaxy.

Maldekians

According to channeled sources, Maldek was a planet located in this solar system, where the asteroid belt currently is. Maldek was destroyed, resulting in the formation of the asteroid belt. Some feel the spirits of the Maldekians incarnated on Mars and then Earth, and some are currently available as guides and teachers.

Nibirians

Nibiru, also known as Marduk to some who look at Sumer through the eyes of the ancient astronaut theory, was home to the Anunnaki. The Nibirians are sometimes equated with the fallen angels known as the Nephilim. See *Anunnaki*.

Nors

The Nors are an elder race who act as guardians to those on Earth. They are associated with the planet Venus.

Orions

The Orions are a variety of races from the Orion system. Some Orions are predisposed to aid humanity, while others are not so inclined. Some are said to be actively working against humanity. The wars of Orion play a role in our collective consciousness and humanity's own conflicts (see chapter 20). Ascension myths tell us that Orion became a battleground in the conflict of polarity, the conflict between good and evil, in this galaxy.

Pleiadians

The Pleiadians are a race of spiritually enlightened beings from the Pleiades who have been involved in the evolution of Earth for aeons and continue to aid us through telepathic communion, teachings, and healings. They have played a role in the Mediterranean, Chinese, and Mayan cultures, and are involved in the arts and poetry. Their civilization is very heart-oriented and is thought to be rooted in the fifth dimension. The Pleiadians are said to be one of the main root races of humanity and the keepers of the living libraries of Earth. They are also said to have a vast living library of light in the star Alcyone. The works of Barbara Hand Clow, Barbara Marciniak, and Amorah Quan Yin detail the teachings of the "P's," as they are affectionately called by these channels. Though the Pleiadians are generally considered beneficent, some are thought to be renegades and to not have humanity's best interests at heart.

Procyonians

The Procyonians are a highly evolved humanoid race with a beneficent view of humanity. They are able to travel through time and dimensions and have been trying to protect Earth from harmful alien influences. Some lightworkers believe that the Procyonians have been in contact with the governments on Earth.

Ra

Though some lightworkers see Ra as an ascended master and priest-king of Atlantis and Egypt, others see Ra as a race of discarnate beings who had contact with ancient Egypt and the Mayan civilization. Some believe this race to be responsible for the teachings of Akhenaton.

Reptilians

These humanoid reptilian beings are said to be aligned with the Grays, though some think of the Grays as a subspecies or worker caste of the Reptilians.

Rigels

The Rigels are the Grays originating from the star Rigel. See *Grays*

Sirians

The Sirians are a variety of alien races from the Sirius star system. Some are considered physical beings, while others are seen as strictly spiritual entities. The Sirians are descendants of the Lyrans and have played a role in Earth's evolution, including the Egyptian and Mayan civilizations. Though loving, the Sirians are more intellectually oriented, particularly in contrast to the Pleiadians, as they were very involved in the structure and architecture of the ancient civilizations. Some believe that the Sirians' involvement in human affairs in the 1970s "saved" Earth from imminent destruction.

The Great White Brotherhood is said to be an extension of the Sirian hierarchy, led by Lord and Lady Sirius, ascended beings much like our own Solar Logos. The cetaceans, dolphins, and whales are also said to be linked strongly with Sirius, as we have found in the teachings of the Dogon. Their Nommo could be extraterrestrial or ultraterrestrial beings from Sirius. Another intriguing and inspiring quote about the Nommo comes from page 97 of Grant Morrison's *The Invisibles: Counting to None*: "The Nommo ain't gods; the gods are to the Nommo what our shadows are to us. Gods are the traces of the Nommo's passage through our world." The Nommo are later described as the Shining Ones, manifesting to us through time, not space.

Ummites

From the planet Ummo comes this advanced yet humanlike civilization that is very knowledgeable about the "science" of the soul. The Ummites are active on at least ten dimensions of reality.

Vegans

Vega, a star within the Lyran star system, was one of the first places colonized by the Lyrans. The battles between the Lyrans and the Vegans started the first conflicts between those souls who would eventually incarnate as humans. The Vegans battling against the

Lyrans soon embodied the opposite traits of the Lyrans, creating a split in consciousness in which one side assumes it is completely correct and demonizes the other side, rather than looking for resolutions in which everyone is satisfied.

Zetas

The Zetas are the Grays originating from the Zeta Reticuli star system. See *Grays*.

At first, you may look at this information quite skeptically, and I must admit that I did. But when I look at it in the context of ultraterrestrials, as stellar and sky spirits, like the sky heroes of the shaman's Upper World, aiding the evolution of humanity, then such contact fits in quite well with my more pragmatic magickal worldview. I'm not certain how I view the information on government conspiracies and secret alien bases, but I've found various groups of very loving, very healing spirit guides and guardians through workshops, rituals, and books by proponents of these stellar traditions. Archetypally, we could interpret the story of helpful aliens and evil invaders like the conflict of angelic and demonic forces, aiding and thwarting humanity's efforts.

Magickally, these star spirits open us to a range of possibilities. With this list of races in mind, if you were having trouble in school with science, you might do a meditation to call upon the aid of the Alpha Centaurians. Those seeking artistic inspiration or simple healing could call upon the Pleiadians. Those seeking healing with sound, or simply to find their voice, might find aid with the Hathors. If you wanted to know more about the nature of the soul, or to travel to your past for healing or to your future for knowledge, the Ummites would be your best allies. Even the darker forces, such as the Orions, can teach you about being a warrior, and the "negative" extraterrestrials can teach you about courage and facing your shadow and personal fears. I know many people, myself included, who have had communications with the Grays that resulted in an overall positive experience. Admittedly, the useful correspondences of these different races are limited, as most are oriented toward peace, science, and exploration, but there are some archetypal variations. The more experiences you have with these entities, the more ideas for partnership will be suggested to you.

It's also important to realize that we are generalizing about what could be considered entire races. Is there any one phrase that would describe all humans on Earth? I don't think so. When working with any individual intelligence, physical or discarnate, I think it's important to judge the entity as an individual.

HOME STARS

Many people in the ascension paradigm feel a longing to "go home" to the stars, as if they truly belong there and not on Earth. Though this may seem far-fetched to many grounded mystics, the concept is found in various mystical teachings. We have it from the Greek mystery schools of Orpheus and Pythagoras, recorded on a funerary plate:

Thou shalt find to the left of the House of Hades a spring,
And by the side thereof standing a white cypress.
To this spring approach not near.
But thou shalt find another, from the Lake of Memory
Cold water flowing forth, and there are guardians before it.
Say, "I am a child of Earth and starry heaven;
But my race is of Heaven (alone). This ye know yourselves.
But I am parched with thirst and I perish. Give me quickly
The cold water flowing forth from the Lake of Memory."
And of themselves they will give thee to drink of the holy spring.
And there after among the other heroes thou shalt have lordship.

—From the Funerary Gold Plates from Petelia, Italy, fourth–third century BC

I've always found one particular line in that verse quite inspiring: "But my race is of Heaven (alone)."

We find the same concepts in the poetry associated with the mythical bard figure Taliesin:

Primarily chief bard am I to Elphin,
And my original country is the region of the summer stars;
Idno and Heinin called me Merrdin,
At length every king will call me Taliesin.
I was with my Lord in the highest sphere,
On the fall of Lucifer into the depth of hell;
I have borne a banner before Alexander;
I know the names of the stars from north to south;
I have been on the galaxy at the throne of the Distributor;
I was in Canaan when Absalom was slain;

I conveyed the divine spirit to the level of the vale of Hebron;
I was in the court of Don before the birth of Gwydion.
I was instructor to Eil and Enoc;
I have been winged by the genius of the splendid crosier;
I have been loquacious prior to being gifted with speech;
I was at the place of the crucifixion of the merciful Son of God;
I have been three periods in the prison of Arianrhod;
I have been the chief director of the work of the tower of Nimrod;
I am a wonder whose origin is not known.

In this excerpt from "The Introduction of Taliesin" in the *Hanes Taliesin*, or *Book of Taliesin*, we find that Taliesin's original country is "the summer stars." He's been to the center of the galaxy, and his true origin is "not known." This era of text mixes pagan and Christian symbolism, as the historical and the biblical references show us that this is beyond a purely Welsh tradition.

Concepts we might think of as pure escapism or science fiction have a place in mystical teachings. I was first exposed to this concept in the more modern teachings of witchcraft, from my own teacher, Laurie Cabot:

I see a future in which the current interest in science fiction among so many Witches and neo-pagans will prove to have been a wise study of things to come, not the escapist fantasy that many detractors think it is. Witches have always tended to think in terms of the galaxy as whole, to see all time and space in the present moment, as they divine the future. Our natural interest in space and the "times beyond time" will result in Witches being among the first to understand and accept extraterrestrial visitors, for we have already contacted them in our dreams and visions. We know that the universe is so structured that anything might be true at some time and in some place, so we are free to speculate and dream. The plans and projects that we instill in our children today may became the nucleus for life in space and in other galaxies tomorrow. Out of our dreams will come the communities and ways of life that will reach beyond the planets and lead us back to the stars.

As Plato taught, as many Native Americans knew, as ancient people around the world surmised, and as Witches have always believed, we are sky people who have come from the stars. Birth is a kind of "Forgetting" of all the knowledge that we held while living among the galaxies, and life is a remembering of who we are and for what we are destined. The root races, the ancestral beings, the original life force that populated our planet so many aeons ago, are waiting for us in the times to come. They will welcome us back.

—Laurie Cabot, *Power of the Witch*, pp. 300–301.

Such teachings show that the ancient lore, the material of witches and shamans, doesn't conflict with the concepts of Theosophy, but actually reinforces some of them. Did one get the ideas from the other? And if so, which came first? Or are they archetypal truths that cut beyond place and time, and find a role in all mystery traditions?

You might find that you resonate with a particular stellar group. This experience is akin to the shamanic belief that we each come from a "home star," and that upon fulfilling our purpose in the world, we can return to it. This belief builds on the concept of star ancestors, being associated with our roots and early civilizations. I feel a kinship with the Pleiades. I'm not 100 percent sure if that is my "star" system or if I just like them because my Sun sign is Taurus and the Pleiades are stars in the horns of Taurus. I resonate with their message. As a practitioner of an Earth-based religion, the Pleiadian material seems the most "green" to me, and I've found it quite healing.

Through your dreams and meditations, you can commune with the starry ancestors. Use this exercise to connect with your own stellar allies.

EXERCISE 12:
COMMUNING WITH THE STARRY ONES

1. Sit before your altar in a comfortable position. Call upon the divine, in whatever form you prefer—God, Goddess, Great Spirit, Divine Mind, Mother-Father-God. Ask to be consciously connected to your source, for guidance and protection, and to all your spirit allies who are appropriate for you at this time. Do Exercise 1: Basic Meditation Technique up to step 6 (see page 81) to get into a meditative state.

2. Acknowledge the power of the four directions. Bring your attention to the north, then the east, south, and west. Bring your attention to the heavens above and the space below you. Then bring your awareness to your heart. Feel a shaft

of light descend from the heavens, from the highest dimensions, surrounding you in a column of light and finding its anchor in the heart of the planet. You are now aligned with the twelve dimensions and are capable of interdimensional contact and journey.

3. Ask to be taken to the starry realm of your choice. You might ask to be guided to your own home star realm and meet with your spiritual star ancestors. You can ask your guides to bring you to the star of your origin in this universe. Imagine your consciousness rising through the shaft of light. You find the beam of light branching out in many different directions, to many different stars, like the branches of a tree. Follow your own path to your star.

4. Find yourself entering a big glowing star of light. What color is it? Are there other stars near it? Is it a single star, or a multiple star system? Is it a cluster? When you mentally ask its name, what do you intuitively know? You might get our earthly name for the star, or another name. What dimension does it feel like to you? Are there any other beings of light there? Do you see/hear/feel/sense anyone? You might meet beings, starry ancestors, to guide you in this experience and inform you of your heritage. In the light, you might see the brilliance recede to reveal an entire form of civilization that may not conform to your expectations of alien life. Be open to whatever you experience.

5. When done, thank all the spiritual entities you have visited, knowing you can return here again using the same method. Find yourself returning to where you began, through the tunnel of light and the vertical axis of reality.

6. Acknowledge the four directions around you again, north, east, south, and west, then above, below, and center. Thank the divine Creator for guidance and protection. Thank your guides and allies. Perform steps 9 and 10 of Exercise 1: Basic Meditation Technique (see page 82) to return to normal waking consciousness. Ground yourself as necessary. Write down any impressions or messages you received, before you forget them.

Keep in mind that you might originate from more than one star system, or you may have traveled to many systems before your soul ended up here on Earth. So the first answer you get for your home star in this exercise might not be the most ancient one for you, but the one you consider most to be "home" right now from your earthly perspective.

PART FOUR

THE MAGICK OF ASCENSION

12

ASCENSION
RITUAL MAGICK

The traditions of magick permeate the roots of ascension, from the Egyptian priests and Greek oracles to the Taoist wizards and tribal shamans. All of our ancestors harnessed unseen energies and created change, healing, and transformation.

But what is magick? It's an unseen power, a subtle energy that binds and unites all things. Magick is divine energy, found in all things manifest and unmanifest. It's a lot like Yoda's description of the Force in the 1980 movie *The Empire Strikes Back*: "For my ally is the Force. And a powerful ally it is. Life creates it, makes it grow. Its energy surrounds us and binds us. Luminous beings we are, not this crude matter. You must feel the Force around you. Here, between you, me, the tree, the rock, everywhere!" Though the *Star Wars* series is seen as a product of popular culture, there is a lot of inherent esoteric wisdom in it for those with ears to hear.

Modern magicians define magick not in terms of an energy, but of a process. The popular definition for many comes from the well-known but often maligned magician

Aleister Crowley. His teachings state that "magick is the art and science of causing change in conformity with your Will." Magick is the process of creating intended change. That's a pretty broad definition, when you think about it. It could just as easily mean getting up from your chair and moving a cup of tea from one end of the table to the other. You willed something to occur, and it occurred. Most people in the mindset of movie magick would think of such an act as true magick only if the magician didn't get up, but moved the cup of tea solely through the power of his mind, telekinetically. True magicians know that every action, even a seemingly mundane one, is a form of magick.

Most people see magick as the ritual that puts into motion unseen forces that manifest a person's will. In the modern era, magick goes by the names of creative visualization, positive thinking, affirmations, prayer, and manifestation. Each has a variety of protocols, a process, a ritual, to set into motion subtle energy that will manifest a person's need or desire. Some rituals are formal, such as the Catholic High Mass, while other rituals are spontaneous and eclectic, such as the rituals of a modern witch out in his or her garden.

Magicians usually feel they have superior methods for manifesting their will because they have studied the theories and concepts behind magickal operations, and draw upon a whole host of techniques from many ages that modern nonmagicians would discard as superstitious or barbaric. There are reasons that such traditions have survived, and that they became traditions in the first place. They have power. They work.

A lot of our modern magickal techniques work, too, but they sometimes leave out vital parts of the equation that transform the process into a spiritual awakening. Modern techniques often make the process so mental that the practitioner doesn't realize it's sacred. Without any kind of physical ritual involved, it's easy to forget to honor the sacred aspects of the physical world. Anybody in a modern corporate boardroom can learn the techniques of creative visualization and have success. In a sense, they are doing magick, but divorced from any ritual, they might not have any idea that in doing the visualization, they are communing with the forces of the universe, with divinity. They can just walk away with a sense of power, a sense that they can create anything they want, but not have any devotion to divinity, the source of their power, or any training in a moral code on the correct use of power.

THE SPECTRUM OF MAGICK

In an effort to understand the nature of magick, practitioners divide it into many different categories. You can divide magickal processes according to the goals of the magick, creating traditions such as love magick, prosperity magick, healing magick, and protection magick. You can divide magick into broader groups, such as spirit magick, which would include the practices of Spiritualist mediums, shamanic journeyers, and magicians summoning spirits; sorcery, or the process of creating a physical change, including manifestation of wealth or healing; and divination, or divination magick, using psychic ability to learn about the past and present in order to predict the future and receive guidance. Magick can also be divided according to tradition. Practitioners of many traditions would not consider themselves practitioners of magick, yet they are still doing magick. We can look at witchcraft, shamanism, hermetic magick, alchemy, mediumship, folk magick, and even arts such as feng shui as traditions of magick.

In terms of our stereotypical Hollywood images, the most popular way to divide magick is into black and white magick. White magick is defined as "good" magick, helping people, while black magick is "bad," harming people. Most magicians do not subscribe to these terms because they are too polarized and absolute. Those who use them also include gray magick, and have different definitions for each kind of magick. White magick is any magick used to know your divinity, your true will or monadic blueprint, and your relationship with the divine and the cosmos. Black magick is used to harm another, or interfere with another's will, to control or manipulate someone. Gray magick is any magick of manifestation used to create a tangible, physical change that you desire. Most people would think of healing as white magick, but according to this system, it is gray magick. If you heal someone without the person's permission or knowledge, it can be considered black magick, even though you have the best of intentions. Most mages acknowledge that magick comes in more colors than black and white, and a magician, when deciding whether to do magick, must always consider the intention and the outcome. Magick is no simple task, but requires a deep connection to your own divinity and a sense of purpose before you set things into motion.

When we look at all the divisions of magick, we find that they are arbitrary, based on a particular point of view. Magick is a force, an energy, though magick also refers to the various systems used to harness that energy. There is much overlap between the various systems of magick. Magick is a spectrum of energy. Our labels are arbitrary, much like our names for colors. If we look at a prism refracting light, and look at the familiar rainbow of colors, the colors are not neatly separated as they would be in a cartoon. They blend together. We define seven distinct colors (red, orange, yellow, green, blue, indigo, and violet), yet when we look at real refracted light, it's hard to see where, for example, red ends and orange begins. Ideally in our society, we would have a distinct notion of red-orange, and a specific name for this color that everyone agrees upon. We might recognize lime and sea foam as parts of the color spectrum. But we look at the rainbow more simply, through a lens of seven colors. The specific color choices are not important, but create a common base of knowledge. When someone says "red," we all know exactly what that means.

High and Low Magick

Another, slightly more refined approach to categorizing magick is the use of the terms high and low magick. I don't like this division either, because it implies that one is better, or more spiritual, than the other, but these terms do indicate two very important aspects of magick.

Low magick is also known as thaumaturgy, and is the magick most people are familiar with. Rituals that create immediate and tangible changes in very small and very large ways are forms of low magick. Examples include a spell to get the parking space by the door of a shop, a ritual to cure a person of cancer, a love spell to find a partner, or a ceremony to stop a psychic attack.

Rituals designed to awaken you to the divine spark within, to align you with your divine will, and to embody your relationship with the divine and the universe are forms of high magick, which is also known as theurgy, or the magick of the divine, of God. High magick rituals might not produce immediate results, but are a spiritual practice to bring personal enlightenment. You might have to practice them regularly, over a long period of time, before you see any results, and the results will not be as tangible as a physical healing or manifestation of money. You will notice changes in how you feel, your connection to divinity, your sense of peace and purpose. The LBRP is one of the first rituals aspiring high magicians learn, to prepare them for deeper workings. Skeptics who don't believe in magick will probably never see the value in doing rituals of high magick, and might see them as empty religious practices. With our understanding of high magick, we could include not only the practices of Western ceremonial magick, but also the regular practice of yogic exercises, mantra meditation, and even Christian prayers. In our system of white /

gray/black magick, high magick is white, while low magick is gray with the potential to be black.

Some see theurgy not as high magick, but as a form of manifestation based upon asking divinities (gods, angels, masters) for results, rather than fueling the spell with your own personal energy or the energy of nature. The source of your success or failure is the transcendent divine. Theurgy and thaumaturgy are closely linked, and are both associated with "miracle working." Theurgy can produce practical results in the end, such as clearing your consciousness, clearing a space, or creating a sense of peace, and thaumaturgy can produce very spiritual results. You cannot continually manifest your will without contemplating the force that connects all things, that allows you to do magick. You can't do the "low" magick of thaumaturgy for long and not think about the effects that your actions and other people's actions—thoughts, words, and deeds—have upon you.

By exploring our personal desires, we find out more about our divine will, the desires of our higher self. By aligning more closely with our higher self, we find that our personal desires and needs manifest more quickly, to support our divine purpose in this world. To a true practitioner, all magick is a blend of high and low magick, as all magick has both spiritual and practical ramifications.

MISUNDERSTANDINGS ABOUT MAGICK

Many people, particularly those from a traditional religious background, are suspicious of magick. They have been taught to fear their birthright. Many think that their religion prohibits magick, but even the mainstream religions have had a rich magickal tradition. Some Christians fear that magick is against the teachings of Christ, but when you look at Christ's life, you see the story of the archetypal magician. Jesus's teachings went against the orthodox status quo of his time. He encouraged his followers to be like him, not just follow him. In the Gospel of John, Jesus said that those who believe in him shall do the same or even greater miracles. "Verily, verily, I say unto you, He that believeth in me, the works that I do shall he do also; and greater works than these shall he do; because I go unto my Father."—John 14:12. By following his path, we would become magicians, like him. He set a path of both high and low magick, eventually returning to the source and doing healing magick for others.

Everybody does magick to some extent, whether they realize it or not. The difference between a magus and everybody else is that the magus consciously knows he is doing magick. If you are already doing magick, as a divine being in this worldly drama, I think it's far more responsible to realize your power and take responsibility for your actions, and your creations, as they affect you and others.

Every thought, word, and deed affects your reality. Each one creates your reality. The thoughts, words, and deeds of today pave the path of tomorrow. Your path can be made only with whatever materials you have created. Still, magick is scary. Magick is powerful. Magick is dangerous, just like life. When you become conscious of your magick, you realize there is nothing you cannot do, which is both empowering and frightening. Because of the fear and responsibility associated with magick, many people have renounced their personal power. They fear that magick is manipulation of others, interfering with another's free will, or that magick will interfere with the other person's destiny, which brings up a few excellent points. Most magicians don't believe in an immutable destiny. Non-magicians use a lot of words to describe a person's destiny, borrowing terms from other cultures and traditions. When referring to your karma, your soul's contract or God's plan for you, magicians would call this your true will, and know there is not one immutable destiny. Your future is what you create. You can choose to align with your true will and manifest your life in partnership with the divine. Nothing is completely destined. There is always choice, and many different ways to manifest your divine will. By following our intuition and direct guidance, by being in tune with the divine currents of life, we find ourselves in the right place, at the right time, doing the right thing. But it's our choice to act. We can sit helplessly on the sidelines and not take advantage of the opportunities that come our way, but then we wouldn't be magicians. Many people miss out on what appears to be their "destiny" because they saw an opportunity to fulfill their higher will, but did not take action.

Magicians are known by many names in other cultures. Some are shamans and medicine people. The change they create is primarily healing, at least from our outside observation. They are the sorcerers and seers of the Otherworld. In some cultures, the term sorcerer means a harmful practitioner, while in others, it is a holy person, a spiritual warrior of the light. I like the term because it reminds me that the power of the sorcerer is from the source, the divine. Witches and wizards are the names used most often for practitioners of the European traditions of magick. As with the term sorcerer, witches and wizards may be seen as forces of good, or as harmful practitioners, because the Christian churches maligned the European magick traditions in their effort to convert the pagan populations. Originally, the witches and wizards were considered holy ones, priestesses and priests of the old religions, and spiritual healers.

Names can cause a lot of trouble. Many people are troubled by the word magick because their religious training has told them it's evil, but they are already doing it. I know one woman, a Reiki teacher, who teaches her students "Reiki manifestation." On the new Moon she writes her "wish list" for the month, and every day she does Reiki on the list, drawing the power symbols (see chapter 15) on it. On the full Moon, she reads the list again in the moonlight, periodically looking up at the Moon as she does so. She then burns the list and scatters the ashes. Most, if not all, of her desires manifest within the next Moon cycle. I informed her that she was practicing witchcraft. She was aghast and insisted it was Reiki. She was using Reiki to power her magick, but the ritual she was using was a classic bit of folk magick found in many witchcraft traditions. She couldn't handle that name for her practice because it was frightening to her. We have come up with many other words for magick that describe it without any of the occult significance.

Magick often works through seeming coincidence, comes in many forms, and doesn't always resemble the popularly known movie magick. I am always reminded of the story of the religious man on the river, awaiting the predicted flood and praying to God to save him. A news report comes across his radio and warns all residents to leave now, because the flood is coming. But he continues to pray, believing that because he is a religious man and his faith is strong, God will save him. The waters come, and he goes up to his roof. A man in a boat comes by, willing to rescue him and take him to dry land. The man on the roof tells him, "I'm a religious man. My faith is strong. God will save me." The man in the boat leaves. The waters continue to rise. A person in a helicopter comes by, lowers a ladder, and yells down to the man to climb up. He yells back, "I'm a religious man. My faith is strong. God will save me!" The waters climb, and the man dies. At the pearly gates of heaven, Saint Peter looks at him and says, "You aren't supposed to be here yet. What happened?" The man explains the situation to Peter and asks why God didn't save him, as he is a religious man and his faith is strong. Peter says, "We sent you a radio report, a boat, and a helicopter. What more did you want?"

Magickal manifestation can occur in the most ordinary of ways, through other people, as emissaries of the divine, showing that we are all connected, that when the divine hears our needs, all people hear our needs and everybody assumes their correct position on the field of life. But we must take action once everything is in place. One of the four laws of the magus, also one of the four points of the witches' pyramid, is "to dare." We must dare to take action, to manifest our true will in the world. The other three laws are "to know," "to will," and "to keep silent."

Those of an Eastern spiritual bent sometimes use the perception of Eastern traditions as having a solely receptive and non-aggressive attitude toward life as an excuse to simply let things happen and not take any action, yet one of the pivotal spiritual texts of the East, the Bhagavad Gita, urges us all to do our duty, to show up and take action. The main character, the mortal prince Arjuna, must partner with his charioteer, the god Krishna, acting as guide and teacher, to go out on the battlefield of life and perform his duty. Many people think magick, or psychic development, is a distraction from true spirituality, but to the magician, nothing could be further from the truth. Magick is the secret science of the universe. By studying it and applying its laws to your life, your spirituality, your sense of connection to everyone and everything, is deepened. You find the power that connects us all, like the Jedi knights working through the Force. Yoda says, "You must feel the Force around you; between you, me, the tree, the rock, everywhere." There is nothing that is not divine, that is not from the source of creation.

Through the power of creation, you identify more with your divine spark, and know that you and the godhead come from the same source. By exploring mundane matters with magick, you explore the avenues of life—prosperity, health, love, romance, protection. The moral magician asks that all spells be "for the highest good, harming none" or "in accord with divine will." By using this intention or something similar, you are asking that all actions be aligned with your higher will. In Wicca, we say, "An' let it harm none, do what you will." By finding the spells that work well for you, you learn what is in alignment with your higher will. By finding spells that do not work at all, or go awry, you learn where your true will does not support you, or where you have not effectively communicated your will to the universe, and need to be more introspective in your magickal process. Most magicians of all sorts will do either a divination or a meditation, will go inward, before doing a spell, to make sure it has the support of their inner guidance and higher will.

SACRED SPACE

One of the most powerful ways to blend thaumaturgy and theurgy in your spiritual practice is through the creation of sacred space. All space is sacred, as all of space and time is a manifestation of the divine, but performing a ritual that formally declares an area a sacred space, a temple between the worlds, aligned with the dimensional spire, opens you to higher divine guidance and a greater possibility of aligning with your divine will. You can perform all forms of magick, meditation, and journey from sacred space.

In the exercises in this book so far, we have created sacred space by acknowledging and honoring the four directions, but an even more powerful and focused ritual for creating sacred space is known as the magick circle. The use of the geometric form of the circle is found across the world, including the Native medicine wheel, the circular mandalas of the East, the witch dancing in a circle, and the magician's circle drawn on the floor, circumscribed with the holy names of God. The circle acts as a container for magickal forces, blocking out all things that would distract or harm, and creating a space to gather and grow your energies.

Though there are many forms of circle casting, the most common one comes from the traditions of neopaganism. Here are the steps involved in casting a circle.

Altar Setup

Make sure you have all the ritual tools you will need for the working. Place the four consecrated elemental tools in each of the four directions. Traditionally, the pentacle goes in the north for earth, the wand goes in the east for fire, the blade goes in the south for air, and the chalice goes in the west for water. Many traditions switch the correspondences and the placement of the wand and blade. Next, arrange on the altar any spellcrafting tools necessary for your specific working, such as candles for illumination, anointing oil, incense, and sacramental cakes. As you learn more about spellcrafting, you can coordinate your altar decorations, such as candles and altar cloths, to match the intention of your ritual.

Cleansing the Space and Self

The next step, typically forgotten, is to cleanse the space prior to creating the circle. This removes unwanted energies, so they do not become a part of the circle. The circle acts more like a bubble, a sphere, and blocks out unwanted forces, but if those unwanted forces become incorporated into the sphere before you even begin, then your magick will be less effective and your sacred temple will have a lower vibration. To cleanse the space, you can burn a purifying incense or sage to remove the lower vibration, just as you would cleanse ritual tools. Some practitioners sprinkle salt water in the space. You can also imagine it filling with violet flame (see chapter 13). You should also cleanse and purify yourself. Smudging, ritual bathing, or removing mundane clothes or dressing in clothes reserved only for ritual, such as ritual robes, are all effective ways to purify yourself. The LBRP is another effective way to cleanse both yourself and the ritual space (see chapter 9).

Casting the Circle

Casting a circle creates an energetic boundary for your ritual. Begin by standing at the center of your soon-to-be circle. Take your wand and breathe in deeply. Imagine drawing energy from the heavens down through your head and into your body, while drawing energy up from the Earth and into your feet and body. Feel the energies mix in your trunk, and use your will to "push" the energy from your shoulders and arms out of your hand and into your wand. Imagine a beam of light radiating from the tip of your wand, extending in front of you. Practitioners of most traditions begin ritual in either the north or the east, drawing upon either the magnetic pole of the Earth or the place of the rising Sun, respectively. When the beam of light from your wand reaches the point where the circumference of the circle will be, begin turning clockwise, tracing a ring of energy. Most people imagine this beam and circle of energy in electric blue, but violet, white, silver, or gold are also acceptable colors. Sometimes the color depends on the type of magick to be done and can be based on your knowledge of the rays of light. Retrace this circle, making a total of three complete rings of light around you. Your circle is cast.

Calling the Quarters

Calling the four quarters anchors your circle between the worlds with the power of earth, air, fire, and water. Each element is said to be ruled by a "watchtower" and an order of beings whose purpose is to guide the elemental powers. These beings are often envisioned as the archangels, elemental kings, pagan divinities, or animal totems. Oftentimes the ritual pentacle, also known as a peyton or paten, is held aloft toward each direction, to open the gateway to each elemental energy. Other times a star shape is drawn in specific ritual motions, with the wand, blade, or hand, to open the gateways. Some practitioners simply hold out their left hand, the five fingers like the five points of the star, to open the gateways.

As you call the quarters, you can draw a basic invoking pentagram to open the elemental gateways. If you are uncomfortable with the pentagram image, you can use the image of the Celtic cross (figure 29).

Calling Upon the Divine

Call upon your conception of divinity, including any masters, angels, and guides whom you want to be present in the circle, aiding you. Divinity is present in all things and at all times, but a specific evocation of divinity attunes your awareness to the form of the divine that is most appropriate for your magick. At this time I also light a black candle on the left

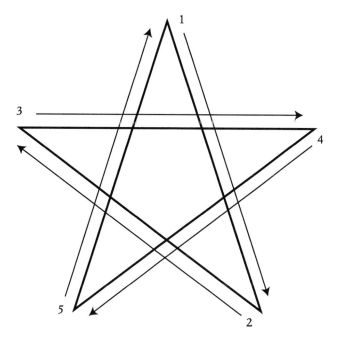

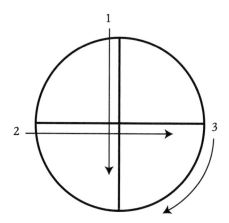

Figure 29: Invoking Pentagram or Invoking Celtic Cross

of the altar and a white candle on the right. The two candles symbolize the forces of female/male, Goddess/God, night/day, Moon/Sun, and the two outer pillars of the Tree of Life. By lighting them both, I am opening the gateway between the worlds and recognizing the polarity of life that is used to create in this world.

Naming the Work

Naming the work makes your purpose clear to all members, physical and nonphysical, in the circle. If you are casting the circle for a specific purpose, such as healing, prosperity, meditation, or knowledge, state it as clearly as possible. If you are doing several acts of magick in a circle, then you do not have to name the working. I also light any incense for the ritual if it's not already burning from cleansing the space. Sometimes I use an incense that is specific to the working, or a general sacred space incense, such as a temple incense or kyphi (see chapter 14).

Anointing

Traditionally, the magician anoints herself or himself and all present in the circle with an anointing oil or potion, or simply a mixture of sea salt and water. This anointing sanctifies the participants, preparing them for the work, and also helps dispel any remaining unwanted energies that they might have brought with them into the circle, before any magick is performed. This is why the anointing potion is known as a protection potion—because it protects all participants from harm. The leader of the circle (considered the high priest or high priestess) or other designee can anoint everyone, or each person can anoint the person to the left, moving clockwise. In general, you should always move clockwise in a magick circle, to build the energy. In Masonry they call it keeping the altar to the right, meaning that if the altar is in the center, and you are moving clockwise, it will be on your right-hand side.

Here is one of my favorite protection and anointing oil formulas.

Protection and Anointing Oil

 5 drops myrrh essential oil

 5 drops frankincense essential oil

 10 drops base oil, such as jojoba, grapeseed, apricot kernel, or olive oil

Add the drops of essential oils to the base oil, and gently swirl them together by moving the mixing bowl or bottle clockwise. Store in a glass bottle.

An anointing oil favored by Thelemites is known as Abramelin oil. The following is a traditional formula found in the initiatory magick known as the Abramelin operation, designed to aid the magician in communion with the Holy Guardian Angel. It is also said to hold the spiritual vibration of the next aeon.

Abramelin Oil

> 8 parts cinnamon oil
> 4 parts myrrh oil
> 2 parts galangal oil
> 7 parts olive oil (or other base oil)

Modern mystics usually make Abramelin oil with essential oils. Cinnamon essential oil is caustic to the skin and usually carries a label warning not to apply it to the skin. I've used this formula and experienced only minor irritation, though I've known people to anoint their brow and, with the sweat running down their face, get it into their eyes and burn them. You can dilute the formula by using a larger amount of olive oil, potentially doubling the amount. A variation is to skip the essential oils and instead use cinnamon bark, myrrh tears, and sliced galangal root, macerated in the olive oil for at least one Moon cycle (one month). Grind the herbs. Fill a jar with the herbs in the right proportion, then cover them with olive oil. Seal the jar and shake it frequently. Then strain out the herbs and bottle the oil. The oil will be scented and have magickal properties, but will not be as caustic or as strong smelling as the essential oil version. Commercial preparations of Abramelin oil are also available at most occult shops.

I'm also a fan of using rose water, lavender water, or Florida Water as an anointing liquid. These are available at occult shops, metaphysical stores, and ethnic botanicas. Each of these waters has an uplifting vibration.

Sacrament

After the anointing, most magickal rituals have some form of sacrament, in which a substance is blessed with the power of the divine. Participants consume this sacred substance, thereby identifying themselves with the divine. The sacrament helps connect them with their own true will, and they are able to manifest magick more readily because they are acting as embodiments of the divine in the ritual. In witchcraft, we enact a ritual called Drawing Down the Moon and infuse the power of the Goddess and God into the chalice through a ritual known as the Great Rite. The Great Rite is symbolic of the sexual union of the divine masculine and divine feminine. The cakes and the ale, wine, or water in the chalice are blessed and consumed by the group. Sometimes the cakes are reserved until the end of the ritual, to aid the participants in grounding, but the liquid is consumed during the ritual.

The sacrament of wine and some form of cake or bread can be found the world over. The concepts of the Catholic Eucharist come from older pagan traditions. Modern pagans now celebrate "cakes and ale" as a part of their rites. Some ceremonial magicians have the more complex "mystical repast," while Thelemites have a type of cinnamon cookie known as the cakes of light. The following is a recipe for the cakes of light that can be used in any ritual working, particularly as the sacrament of a circle ritual. If you don't wish to use this recipe, any wheat or corn cake can be used, as well as cinnamon or honey cookies. Use your own judgment and discretion. As for the wine, many people do not wish to consume wine for various reasons. An appropriate fruit juice can be used, of a variety that can be easily distilled into an alcoholic "spirit," such as grape or apple juice, to keep the spirit association.

Cakes of Light

The cakes of light are a traditional Thelemic sacrament used in the Gnostic Mass and have been adapted for a variety of ritual purposes. I love the elemental associations of this recipe, and the use of the magickal oil.

1½ cups flour (earth)

6 tablespoons extra virgin olive oil (water)

7 tablespoons honey (air)

1 tablespoon wine leavings (spirit)

7 drops Abramelin oil (fire)

Mix together the flour and olive oil, then add the honey, wine leavings, and Abramelin oil. If you cannot use the actual wine leavings from the bottom of a bottle of regular wine, then you can use the leavings from a bottle of good port, or simmer some ruby port until it leaves a thick, syrupy residue. Pre-heat your oven to 300 degrees F. Mix all the ingredients together and knead them until you get a thick, doughy consistency that holds together but does not stick to an oiled rolling pin. Oil your cookie sheets. Take a small ball of dough and press it flat, using the oiled rolling pin if necessary. At ⅛" thick, cut a cookie shape from the dough, roughly the size of a quarter. Bake for 4–7 minutes. Cakes can be refrigerated or frozen to store.

Some practitioners use a few drops of menstrual blood, or Moon blood, in the dough, as suggested in Crowley's *The Book of the Law*. I know others who use a few drops of semen. In the modern age of good hygiene, many people suggest that if you do so, you consume only your own cakes. If going to a group ritual, bring your own cakes of light, clearly marked. Many practitioners who are not performing the Thelemic rituals still use this recipe, usually minus the blood.

Sometimes the sacrament is skipped in less formal magick circle rituals, though I find it to be one of the most empowering aspects of ritual, even if only a liquid is consumed, and not cakes. The sacrament helps us identify with the divine light within all things, including ourselves.

The Working

The heart of the ritual is the working—the spells, meditations, journeys, or prayers performed in the sacred space after the participants have identified with the divine by consuming the sacrament. Rituals in the working can be solemn or lively. Concentration, spell-craft, singing, and dancing are all ways of raising energy in ritual. An increasing number of modern mystics are exploring circle dancing, with mixes of both traditional percussion and modern techno music. Such rituals are fresh and inspiring.

If energy is raised and imprinted with a specific intention to manifest, a "cone of power" is released through the top of the circle. With the arms raised and feet spread apart for balance, the magician enters what is known in Wicca as the Goddess position (figure 30), to send forth the cone of power. When the energy is released, the magician assumes the God position—arms crossed over the heart, head bowed slightly, and feet together, reminiscent of an Egyptian statue or sarcophagus, as well as a skull and cross bones. The mage reflects upon the intention. When all spells are done, participants ground themselves, usually by touching their hands to the floor to release excess energy into the land and return the body to a normal energy level. Those who can't bend down can simply send the energy down through their feet, imagining energetic roots, or they can use a staff, cane, or sword to touch the floor, creating a connection to release the energy downward.

Figure 30: Goddess and God Positions

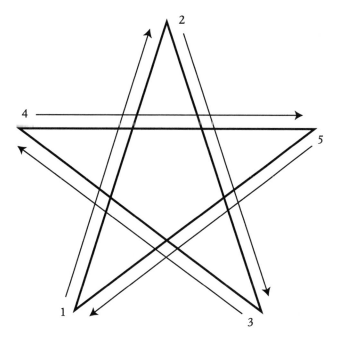

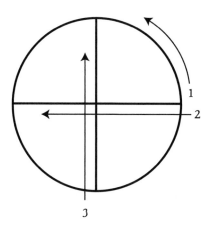

Figure 31: Banishing Pentagram or Banishing Celtic Cross

Releasing the Quarters

Next, the four quarters are thanked and released. Start with the same direction, and release counterclockwise until all four quarters have been thanked and released, so the circle is no longer anchored between the worlds and can be completely deconstructed. The gateways to each element are closed as they were opened, either by holding up a ritual pentacle, holding up the right hand to release, or drawing the specific pentagrams with the wand, blade, or hand.

When you release the quarters, you can draw a basic banishing pentagram or a banishing Celtic cross to close each elemental gateway (figure 31).

Thanking the Divine

At this time, all divinities, spirits, and guides are again recognized, thanked, and released from the space. Remember, although divinity is present in all things and cannot be released, we are releasing our attention from a particular aspect of divinity in an effort to return to a normal state of consciousness.

Releasing the Circle

Just as the circle is cast, it is released. Starting in the same direction and moving counterclockwise, trace the boundary of the circle with the wand. Some magicians imagine sucking the rings of energy into the wand, while others imagine it more like opening a circular curtain or expanding the rings out infinitely. Once the circle is released, participants are urged to ground themselves and return fully to normal waking consciousness. Feasting can follow ritual, because eating grounds your energy into the physical body.

Keeping this basic format in mind, you can alter the steps in casting the magick circle to change the flavor and feel of the ritual. The most common way to cast a circle in both Wiccan and Hermetic traditions involves calling on the four archangels to act as watchtowers for the four elements. For more detailed information on casting a circle according to the Wiccan traditions, refer to my book *The Outer Temple of Witchcraft: Circles, Spells and Rituals*.

The following exercise will take you through all the steps needed to cast your own angelic magick circle. In this sacred space, you can meditate, pray, perform spiritual journeys to other dimensions, and perform spells.

EXERCISE 13:
THE ANGELIC MAGICK CIRCLE RITUAL

1. Prepare the altar and make sure you have everything you need present.

2. Cleanse the space and yourself before beginning the ritual. Light your candles and incense to set the tone for the ritual. Remain standing, and do Exercise 1: Basic Meditation Technique up to step 6 (see page 81) to get into a meditative state, but don't go so deep that you can't speak or move in the ritual.

3. Face the north. Cast the circle, holding your wand in your dominant hand.

   I cast this circle to protect us from all harm on any level.
   I charge this circle to draw all the necessary forces for my magick and block out all unwanted energies.
   I create a space beyond space and a time beyond time, a temple of perfect love and perfect trust, where the highest will is sovereign.

4. Face the north. Call the quarters.

   To the north, I call upon the element of earth and the archangel Uriel, keeper of the earth mysteries and the treasures of the lands. Hail and welcome.

   Feel the power and presence of Uriel, grounding, solid, and safe. When ready, turn to the east and call the next quarter.

   To the east, I call upon the element of air and the archangel Raphael, keeper of the healing mysteries and the sacred caduceus. Hail and welcome.

   Feel the power and presence of Raphael, the divine physician. When ready, turn to the south and call the next quarter.

   To the south, I call upon the element of fire and the archangel Michael, keeper of the warrior mysteries and the flaming sword. Hail and welcome.

   Feel the power and presence of Michael, the sacred warrior. When ready, turn to the west and call the next quarter.

   To the west, I call upon the element of water and the archangel Gabriel, keeper of the heart mysteries and the sacred grail. Hail and welcome.

   Feel the power and presence of Gabriel, the divine messenger. Turn to the center, facing the altar once again.

5. Call upon divinity in a manner that is appropriate for you and your traditions.

   I call upon the powers of the divine, the Goddess, God, and Great Spirit, Mother-Father-Creator, to be present and guide this work. Hail and welcome.

6. Anoint yourself and all others present with an appropriate substance. I anoint with a five-pointed star motion, but a cross motion can also be used.

   I use this oil to protect us from all harm on any level, and to bless us in this working. So mote it be.

7. For the sacrament, if you are not familiar with more formal consecrations, simply bless the liquid in your chalice and whatever cakes you are using. Wave your hands over the items to be consumed as you say this or something similar:

   In the name of the divine, we awaken the divine light within these substances, to nourish not only our bodies, but our hearts, minds, and souls. Through consuming this sacrament, we awaken the divine spark within us, and fulfill our divine magickal will, for the highest good, harming none.

   Consume the sacrament, and reflect on the divine power that is aligned with you.

8. Perform your spellcraft, meditations, or other rituals. For now, you can simply meditate or recite the Great Invocation. Enjoy the sacred space, and commune with the divine. I complete the workings by sending any remaining energy in the circle for a general healing either into the Earth or to those who are then named into the circle, using words such as these:

   I place (name the person) into the circle, to receive healing and blessings for his/her highest good.

   When done, I say:

   We ask that all those named in this circle receive the healing and love needed for their highest good. So mote it be.

9. Face the north and release the quarters.

   To the north, I thank and release the element of earth and the archangel Uriel. I thank you for your guidance and protection. Hail and farewell.

   Move to face the west.

To the west, I thank and release the element of water and the archangel Gabriel. I thank you for your guidance and protection. Hail and farewell.

Move to face the south.

To the south, I thank and release the element of fire and the archangel Michael. I thank you for your guidance and protection. Hail and farewell.

Move to face the east.

To the east, I thank and release the element of air and the archangel Raphael. I thank you for your guidance and protection. Hail and farewell.

10. Thank and release the divinities. Move back to the altar, facing the center.

    I thank all the divinities, guides, and angels who have joined with us. Stay if you will, go if you must. Hail and farewell.

11. Release the circle. Face the north, with your wand in hand.

    I release this circle out into the cosmos. The circle is undone, but never broken. So mote it be.

You can alter the tone of your magick circle ritual and sacred space by calling upon the four rulers of the elemental realms, instead of the archangels. Though both fulfill a similar function, the elemental rulers have a denser energy that those attuned to Earth religions and faery traditions might resonate with them more strongly. Just because they are terrestrial forces doesn't mean that they are not spiritual. Each ruler is the pinnacle, the true master, of that element, and working with the ruler in your personal life can help you master the element. The elemental rulers can be great teachers. Use the same circle format, but replace the angelic quarter calls with these or something similar:

To the north, I call upon the powers of the realm of earth. I call for the blessings of Ghob, ruler of the earth elementals, keeper of the treasures of the material world. I call forth the gnome spirits to aid me in this working. Dig deep within to find the resources necessary for my magick. Hail and welcome.

To the east, I call upon the powers of the realm of air. I call for the blessings of Paralda, ruler of the air elementals, keeper of the treasures of the mental world. I call forth the sylph spirits to aid me in this working. Fly freely, releasing the powers of mind and memory necessary for my magick. Hail and welcome.

To the south, I call the powers of the realm of fire. I call for the blessings of Djinn, ruler of the fire elementals, keeper of the treasures of the spiritual world. I call forth the salamander spirits to aid me in this working. Burn brightly in the darkness, illuminating the powers of spirit for my magick. Hail and welcome.

To the west, I call the powers of the realm of water. I call for the blessings of Niksa, ruler of the water elementals, keeper of the treasures of the emotional world. I call forth the undine spirits to aid in me in this working. Swim strongly in the currents of the astral to reveal the powers of the heart for my magick. Hail and welcome.

To the center, I call upon the divine as Gaia, the Great Goddess of the Earth, and as Pan, master of all nature spirits. I call upon you both as the keepers of all life on this planet. Open me to your creative force, so together we can manifest this magick. Hail and welcome.

Through the powers of the five elements, I manifest their highest attributes. I call forth the powers of law, life, light, love, and liberty. I stand in the circle, in the center of the cosmos, ready for this work.

Though the five-pointed star is strongly associated with the natural realms, some people feel that the seven-pointed star is strongly aligned with the faeries. Sometimes called the Elven star, it is also associated with the seven magickal planets and, in some ceremonial magick traditions, with the goddess of nature and love, such as Venus, Inanna, and Ishtar. Lightworkers also associate the seven-pointed star with the Pleiades, one of the star tribes most strongly associated with nature. You can use these basic drawings for invoking and banishing stars (figure 32).

When done, reverse the quarter calls, releasing the powers you've summoned.

To the north, I thank and release the element of earth. I thank and release the spirits of earth, the gnomes. And I thank and release your ruler, Ghob. Thank you for the many treasures of the Earth. Hail and farewell.

To the west, I thank and release the element of water. I thank and release the spirits of water, the undines. I thank and release your ruler, Niksa. Thank you for the many treasures of the heart. Hail and farewell.

To the south, I thank and release the element of fire. I thank and release the spirits of fire, the salamanders. I thank and release your ruler, Djinn. Thank you for the many treasures of the spirit. Hail and farewell.

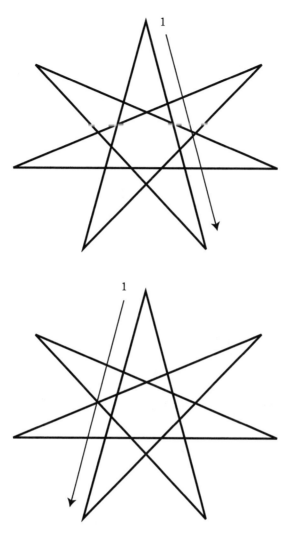

Figure 32: Invoking and Banishing Elven Star

Direction	Element	Zodiac Sign	Image
East	Fire	Leo	Lion
South	Earth	Taurus	Bull
West	Air	Aquarius	Human
North	Water	Scorpio	Eagle

Chart 8: Elemental Associations for Stellar Ritual

To the east, I thank and release the element of air. I thank and release the spirits of air, the sylphs. I thank and release your ruler, Paralda. Thank you for the many treasures of the mind. Hail and farewell.

As you are released from the circle, within me I hold the powers of law, life, light, love, and liberty. So mote it be.

To the center, I thank and release the great gods of nature. I thank Pan, master of the nature spirits. I thank Mother Gaia, Earth Mother. I thank you both for your blessings. Stay if you will, go if you must. Hail and farewell.

Another variation of the traditional angelic magick circle is oriented to the stars. In ceremonial magick, rituals oriented to the pentagram have a terrestrial and elemental association, while rituals of the hexagram have an association with the planets and the macrocosm. The hexagram rituals orient the four elements differently than most other ritual circles, and often use the imagery of the four fixed signs of the zodiac—Taurus, Leo, Scorpio, and Aquarius (chart 8). The images of the four fixed zodiac signs—a lion, bull, human, and eagle (a higher expression of Scorpio)—are the elemental beasts on the tarot cards, the four beasts of the apocalypse in the Bible, and are associated with the four apostles of the main gospels. Many classic rituals, from the Golden Dawn and other forms of magick, start in the east. For stellar or solar magick, the east is an appropriate direction.

When calling the quarters, you can use the image of the hexagram to open and close the gates. Like invocations of the elements involving the pentagram, with a set of basic invoking and banishing methods of drawing the star as well as very specific drawings of the star to invoke and banish each individual element, the hexagram has a set of basic invoking and banishing drawings as well as very specific

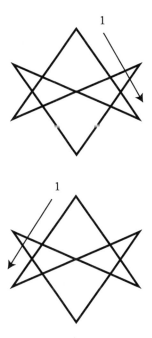

Figure 33: Invoking and Banishing Unicursal Hexagrams

drawings for invoking and banishing both elemental and planetary forces. For the purposes of this book, we will be dealing with only the basic forms of the pentagram and hexagram. I actually prefer the fluid motion of the hexagram known as the unicursal hexagram, favored by Thelemites in their version of the hexagram ritual known as the Star Sapphire, though this hexagram is not universally accepted by ceremonial magicians because of its unusual shape (figure 33).

You can work the hexagram motions and new quarter calls into the structure of your magick circle ritual, replacing the more traditional quarter calls.

To the east, I call upon the element of fire, and the sign of Leo, the proud lion. Hail and welcome.

To the south, I call upon the element of earth, and the sign of Taurus, the strong bull. Hail and welcome.

To the west, I call upon the element of air, and the sign of Aquarius, the water bearer. Hail and welcome.

To the north, I call upon the element of water, and the sign of Scorpio, the transformer. Hail and welcome.

The releases can be structured in a similar manner.

To the east, I thank and release the element of fire, and the power of Leo. Hail and farewell.

To the north, I thank and release the element of water, and the power of Scorpio. Hail and farewell.

To the west, I thank and release the element of air, and the power of Aquarius. Hail and farewell.

To the south, I thank and release the element of earth and the power of Taurus. Hail and farewell.

Another variation includes calling upon the various ancient gods or masters for each direction. For a circle in the style of Egyptian magick, you can use Egyptian gods for the four quarters. Egyptian elemental associations are often east–fire–Osiris, south–water–Nephthys, west–air–Isis, and north–earth–Set or Anubis.

Please keep in mind that these are modern adaptations of some traditional ideas, drawn from ceremonial magick and paganism but set for those practicing an ascension-based spirituality. As you explore creating sacred space, you might find that your own nature resonates with the angelic, elemental, or stellar realms, and these preferences will be reflected in your rituals. Experiment with creating sacred space, following your guidance and intuition, and see what works best for your magick.

13

THE MAGICK OF THE RAYS

As universal consciousness is refracted through the prism of our planetary hierarchy, manifesting as the rays of light to us on Earth, an understanding of the rays can be very helpful to those on the magickal ascension path. Theosophists think of the ray system as the true and ancient secrets of Tibet and India, in fact, the true secret teachings of all the world's mystery schools, finally being revealed at this time to the world. Though the concepts of the ray system might be found in certain Tibetan and Hindu teachings, they are not necessarily found in the same form described by Alice Bailey in her work *The Rays and the Initiations* and her other treatises on the rays. The basic concepts can be found in many different systems, not as "rays," but as other divisions of seven, such the seven magickal planets, the seven chakras, or the rainbow bridge of the Norse. Lore of the rays is most popular in Theosophy, but still exerts an influence on modern ceremonial magick and popular New Age thought.

The Theosophical science of the seven rays has many applications. First, it is used to understand the spiritual hierarchy, the masters guiding our development, and our place within the hierarchy. You can look at your spiritual traditions and tendencies, your personal spiritual work on Earth, as being ruled by a particular ray, or a synthesis of several rays, illuminating the spiritual psychology of your work. The work of occultist Dion Fortune is said to be a mix of the green ray, blue ray, and violet ray, reflecting her synthesis of the inner faery contacts from nature, the loving nature of Christ, and the ceremonial and Qabalistic forms of magick. The work of Gerald Gardner, on the other hand, is a mix of just the green and violet rays, as it is focused on the natural world of the folk witch mixed with the ceremonial magick of a high magus. Through understanding your personal spiritual traditions, you will know which masters to actively connect with and what practices to pursue.

On a more personal level, the rays are used in a system of modern soul psychology, to help you determine and understand your personal makeup and the energies that affect your evolution, much the same way as astrology and numerology are used today. By understanding the different parts of yourself, you can act rather than react. You can gain an understanding of your virtues to develop, and become aware of the potential pitfalls of your nature.

Lastly, the ray system is used as a magickal correspondence system, revealing what colors, stones, animals, days of the week, archangels, and masters resonate with what principles, and how to build rituals and spells based upon their correspondences. If you want to do a working involving artistic development, then knowing the corresponding symbols and tools for artistic development will help you tune in to that vibration of divinity and receive the guidance and help you request.

Due to some modern channelings, there is some dispute over the number, order, and understanding of the rays, but the information presented here is an overview of what is generally accepted, based on the more traditional Theosophical material. Some of the correspondences come from my study of the Theosophical material, while others are based on Qabalistic ceremonial magick and intuition. Some people would consider the Theosophical characteristics as the esoteric attributes, and the characteristics based on traditional magickal systems as more exoteric. I don't think that's necessarily the case, as both groups of characteristics are very esoteric. The Theosophical material is modern and channeled, creating a new paradigm, while the Qabalistic correspondences fit a more traditional system of esoteric knowledge. Esoteric astrology, based upon the book of the same name by Alice Bailey, divides the planets into two groups—sacred and non-sacred—believing that the awakened human is aligned with the sacred planet for each sign, while the average human is aligned with the non-sacred planet for each. Traditional Western astrology and Vedic astrology make no such distinctions, looking at all the planets as equally sacred. In the end, use the ray correspondences that work best for you. As you explore further in this book, you will find uses for working with the rays in healing, ritual, and meditation.

Many of the correspondences given here, including the positive attributes, negative attributes, and glamours, are taken directly from Theosophical teachings of Alice Bailey, representing the best and worst attributes of the rays, and their worldly challenges, or glamours. They are often poetic but unclear upon first examination, and should be reflected and meditated on to gain further insight into each ray and how it works in your own life.

THE SEVEN RAYS

First Ray

Color: Red.

Purposes: Will/power, politics.

Archetypes: Warrior, leader, politician, occultist, explorer, executive, king, manager, dictator.

Chohans: El Morya and the Manu.

Elohim: Hercules and Amazonia.

Archangels: Michael and Faith (Theosophical), Chamuel (Qabalistic).

Positive Attributes: Purposeful, strong, courageous, fearless, trustworthy, persistent, statesmanship, government, diplomacy, international relations, detachment.

Negative Attributes: Destructive, ruthless, hard, cold, arrogant, ambitious, tyrannical, cruel, controlling.

Glamours: Physical strength, personal magnetism, self-centeredness, personal power, ambition, control, messiah complex, selfish destiny, divine right of kings, destruction, isolation, superimposed will upon others and groups.

Religion: Hinduism.

Chakras: Crown, root.

Animal: Elephant.

Day: Tuesday.

Jewel: Traditionally diamond, but as a substitute you can use quartz or any red stone, such as ruby, garnet, red jasper, or red calcite. Bloodstone and hematite can also be used.

Oils: Black pepper, ginger, basil, bay.

Flower Essences/Herbs: Stinging nettle, hawthorn, holly, rose, garlic, thistle, yarrow.

Esoteric Astrological Attributes: Vulcan (sacred), Pluto (not sacred), Aries (main sign), Leo, Capricorn.

Qabalistic Attributes: Geburah, the fifth sphere on the Tree of Life; Mars. Also either Chokmah or Kether, as part of the supernal triad, the first three spheres on the Tree of Life.

Description: The first ray is the ray of willpower. It is the manifestation of the will to create in the physical world. Red is the color of fire, of power, of purpose. It creates and it destroys. Those who resonate with the first ray are leaders in the world. They are those who use their power to affect whole regions of territory and groups of people. The old archetype of the first ray is the priest-king, ideally the wise and enlightened ruler. The spiritual warrior is another high expression of the first ray. Qabalistically, the red sphere of Geburah is the sphere of the warrior on the chariot. This energy is fierce and sometimes destructive, yet removes the old to manifest the new. Those who don't know how to direct the red energy are often frustrated or angry or feel out of control. In modern times, the first ray manifests in lower forms, through our politicians, royalty, dictators, and even business executives and managers. An often forgotten archetype of the red ray is the occultist, one who channels the power of the mystery teachings into the forces of magick. Many of the priest-kings of ancient days, such as King Solomon, were powerful magicians.

Those with first-ray energy are able to go where others fear to tread, and are the explorers and pioneers of the world. First-ray people are working with pure power, and must be vigilant in how they apply it. Ideally they use it to serve the greater good of the community, the country, and ultimately the planet. The keyword of the first ray is will, a term that has two meanings. With a lowercase *w*, it is about our personal will, about what we want right here and now. It is the will of our ego, our desire. Through the process of spiritual initiation we awaken to the Will, with a capital *W*, and understand our higher self's Will, or monadic Will. Through understanding our higher Will, our higher purpose, we can put the power of the first ray into action in our lives.

Second Ray

Colors: Blue (some say indigo).

Purposes: Love / wisdom, education.

Archetypes: Teacher, healer, sage, scholar, humanist, philanthropist, server.

Chohans: Kuthumi and the Planetary Christ (some say Lanto).

Elohim: Apollo and Lumina.

Archangels: Jophiel and Christine (Theosophical), Tzadkiel (Qabalistic).

Positive Attributes: Inclusive, calm, peaceful, inner strength, patience, love of truth, intuitive, serene, spiritual initiation, religious and spiritual education, writing, speaking, radiance, attraction, expansion, power to save.

Negative Attributes: Coldness, indifference, dispassion, self-pity, fear.

Glamours: Love of being loved, popularity, personal wisdom, selfish responsibility, self-pity, fear, self-sacrifice, selfish unselfishness, self-satisfaction, selfish service.

Religion: Buddhism.

Chakras: Heart, throat.

Animal: Dog.

Day: Thursday.

Jewel: Traditionally sapphire, but as a substitute you can use any blue stone, such as lapis, turquoise, blue lace agate, sodalite, blue aragonite, or blue calcite.

Oils: Cedar, cinnamon, clove, frankincense, nutmeg, pine, juniper, benzoin.

Flower Essences/Herbs: Blueberry, dandelion, hyssop, oak, pine, red clover, vervain.

Esosteric Astrological Attributes: Sun (non-sacred), Jupiter (sacred), Gemini, Virgo (main sign), Pisces.

Qabalistic Attributes: Chesed, the fourth sphere on the Tree of Life; Jupiter. Also either Kether or Chokmah, as part of the supernal triad. Tiphereth, as the Christ center on the Tree, can also be aligned with the second ray, though its color is different.

Description: The second ray is the ray of love and wisdom. I was always confused by this ray, because I thought of love and wisdom as two separate things. Perhaps they are, but they come from the same root. The love of the second ray is not affection or romantic love, but the spiritual love of divinity. It is unconditional love. When you are living from a place of unconditional love, you are also using great wisdom. Those who are influenced by the blue ray are living a life of compassion, and sharing that love with others. They choose to manifest the energy through working with others in a personal yet spiritual way. Blue-ray energy can manifest as spiritual teaching and healing, but anyone who serves the public, anyone involved in humanitarian or philanthropic work, uses this energy. Blue is the color of peace and harmony. Think of how you feel when you look at the clear blue sky—both peaceful and energized. The blue light is the sky illuminated by the Sun, reflecting in the atmosphere. The light of the divine illuminates our minds, bringing a sense of peace, spiritual love, and compassion.

The sphere of the Qabalah associated with blue is Chesed, the sphere of mercy. Its archetype is the heavenly king, beneficent and loving. This is the sphere of spiritual love. Jupiter, the sacred planet of the second ray and Chesed, is the planet of expanding consciousness. Jupiter is the planet embodying the higher self. By putting love and wisdom into our daily lives, we find our higher selves and better understand our true will. With better understanding of our true will, we can more effectively use our first-ray will powers.

Third Ray

Color: Yellow.

Purposes: Active intelligence, civilization, humanity, economics/business.

Archetypes: Philosopher, theorist, astrologer, mathematician, economist, historian, business person.

Chohans: Paul the Venetian and the Mahachohan.

Elohim: Heros and Amora.

Archangels: Chamuel and Charity (Theosophical), Raphael and Michael (Qabalistic).

Positive Attributes: Intellect, abstract ideas, communication, creativity, adaptability, sincerity, patience, caution, planning, spreading money/resources, finance, power to manifest, mental illumination, perfectionism.

Negative Attributes: Mental pride, deviousness, scheming, inaccuracy, obstinacy, manipulation.

Glamours: Being busy, creative work without true motive, good intentions that are really selfish, "spider in the center," "God in the machine," devious manipulation, self-importance.

Religions: Chaldean (Sumerian/Babylonian), Neo-Platonism.

Chakras: Throat, heart, solar plexus.

Animal: Cat.

Day: Sunday.

Jewel: Traditionally emerald in Theosophical lore, but most magicians will use as a substitute any yellow stone, such as citrine, pyrite, or yellow calcite.

Oils: Peppermint, spearmint, lemon, lemongrass, melissa, patchouli, citronella.

Flower Essences/Herbs: Broom, chamomile, coltsfoot, daffodil, lobelia, peppermint, sunflower, skullcap, slippery elm, valerian.

Esoteric Astrological Attributes: Saturn (sacred), Earth (non-sacred), Cancer (main sign), Libra, Capricorn.

Qabalistic Attributes: Tiphereth, the sixth sphere on the Tree of Life; the Sun. Also Binah, the third sphere on the Tree of Life, as the mother aspect of the supernal triad.

Description: The third ray is the ray of human civilization. It is described as the ray of active intelligence, as it rules all the advances of humanity that mark our development. Anything that is not ruled by the first two rays is influenced by the third ray or one of the four remaining rays that the third ray gives "birth" to as the mother ray. The third ray is the power of ideas, and implementing those ideas to manifest in the world. The philosopher, theorist, and mathematician all have a place in the third ray. Those who follow the details of civilization, the patterns of the world, such as historians and record keepers, are here, particularly those who synthesize views of the past to help point the way to the future. Astrologers, who see the patterns of the stars take form in human civilization, also find a home in this ray. The abstract is made tangible in the third ray. In color psychology, yellow stimulates the mind and creativity. All forms of communication and exchange are ruled by the third ray. The third ray handles all the details of human civilization, and its energy is responsible for the development of economics, banking, and business. Just as money and trades are exchanges, so are ideas and cultures. All business people, economists, and entrepreneurs are in the domain of the yellow ray. This ray has promoted the development of a global identity, primarily through commerce.

The yellow ray works with global and world views, as it is often seen as the mother aspect of the three primary rays, as the mother of civilization and human development. The Earth is one of the planets associated with the third ray. As the mother aspect of the primary triad, the third ray is associated with Binah, the mother of form in the primary triad of the Tree of Life. Binah's planet is Saturn, which is the sacred planet of the third ray in esoteric astrology. Saturn is the mother of manifestation, though most people associate this planet with the Greek god Chronos or the Roman god Saturn, god of the harvest and time. The color yellow is associated with Tiphereth, which is the sphere of illumination through self-sacrifice and solar awareness.

Fourth Ray

Color: Green.

Purposes: Harmony through conflict, nature, love, faery realm, art.

Archetypes: Mediator, artist, poet, musician, psychologist, architect, Earth priest/ess.

Chohan: Serapis Bey.

Elohim: Purity and Astrea.

Archangels: Gabriel and Hope (Theosophical), Haniel and Uriel (Qabalistic).

Positive Attributes: Affection, sympathy, courage, devotion, generosity, humor, beauty, sensitivity, artistry, Masonic initiation, architectural construction, modern city planning and development, sociology.

Negative Attributes: Worrier, self-centered, cowardice, extravagance, mood swings, inaccuracy, volatile, forceful.

Glamours: Aiming for personal comfort and satisfaction, war, conflict with the idea of imposing peace and righteousness, vague artistic perceptions, psychic perception, musical perception, pair of opposites in the higher sense.

Religions: Egyptian, neopaganism, Shinto, faery faith, Masonry.

Chakras: Root, third eye, heart.

Animal: Cat.

Day: Friday.

Jewel: Traditionally jasper, but as a substitute you can use any green stone, such as emerald, aventurine, jade, green tourmaline, or green calcite.

Oils: Rose, jasmine, rosewood, lime, anise, orris.

Flower Essences/Herbs: Apple, catnip, elecampagne, foxglove, lady's mantle, motherwort, passion flower, rose, vervain.

Esoteric Astrological Attributes: Mercury (sacred), Moon (non-sacred), Taurus, Scorpio (main sign), Sagittarius.

Qabalistic Attributes: Netzach, the seventh sphere on the Tree of Life; Venus.

Description: The fourth ray mediates the energies that bring harmony through conflict. That concept always seemed so strange to me. I think of emerald-green light as healing and loving, stimulating growth and prosperity. Traditions of magick use green in love, money, and healing magick. It is the color of the growing grass and new leaves of spring. It is the color of life. And in the power of life, we understand the true nature of the emerald ray. Life involves conflict. The cycles of life are rise and fall, growth and decay, life and death. Ascension—the transmutation of the body to light within another dimension—is eternal, without the peaks and valleys of life, and is symbolized by a golden light. The golden solar light is brought into the cycle of life and rebirth through the plant life on this planet, and the plant life is green. Gold, the metal of the Sun favored by the alchemists, is incorruptible. It is solid yet malleable, and never tarnishes. Copper, the metal of Venus and Taurus, turns green as it ages, connecting it to the plant world. Plants absorb the golden energy of the sun and bring it into the cycle of life, transforming it. The plants in turn feed the animals, and animals feed other animals, creating a cycle. Life feeds life. That is the conflict of this fourth ray, but eventually we find harmony when we learn to live in balance with the cycle. The cultures that have most successfully lived in a state of harmony with the cycles of life and nature, the tribal cultures of our world, have never forgotten that life must feed life.

We don't evolve without some disharmony or disruption to the status quo. That disruption, and the effort made to resolve it, is what leads to greater manifestations of harmony and peace, because our consciousness expands to become more inclusive. Through conflict we can learn about other points of view, and accept them even if we don't agree with them. Without any conflict, everybody would be just like us, thinking, feeling, and believing as we do. We would not expand to encompass the diversity of life and become more like the Creator.

The Qabalistic sphere of green light is Netzach, associated with Venus. Venus is the planet of love, attraction, and passion, and acts as a counterbalance to the red Martian tendency toward war, putting those passions to other uses. The sphere of Netzach is one of magnetism, drawing what is needed through the power of attraction. On the Tree of Life, Venus and Netzach are associated with all the elements. In the Golden Dawn grade system, the sphere of Netzach is the level of elemental fire, the last of the four elements to be mastered before going on to the higher work of the tradition. As a sphere of emotion and relationship, Netzach can be described as a watery power. The faery realm and the green ray of nature are associated with Netzach. Lastly, in traditional astrology Venus rules both Taurus and Libra, an earth sign and an air sign, respectively. We are able to find harmony in our own lives by observing the cycles of nature. Rituals that honor the Earth have a place within this ray. We resolve many of our inner conflicts through the arts, including graphic arts, music, poetry, storytelling, and dance. Those who seek to balance the needs of the modern community with the needs of the land—such as our more enlightened city planners and designers, particularly if they are in communication with the devas and nature spirits—are part of the fourth ray. The heart chakra, which is usually described as green, mediates the flow of energy between the upper three chakras and the lower three chakras of the traditional seven-chakra system (see chapter 15). Anyone who seeks to mediate conflict and bring a greater sense of harmony to the world is working with the green ray.

Fifth Ray

Color: Orange.

Purpose: Concrete science.

Archetypes: Scientist, researcher, technician, alchemist, engineer, inventor.

Chohan: Hilarion.

Elohim: Cyclopia and Virginia.

Archangels: Raphael and Mary (Theosophical), Raphael and Michael (Qabalistic).

Positive Attributes: Analysis, mind, keen intellect, common sense, reason, logic, accuracy, esoteric psychology, modern educational systems, medicine, psychology.

Negative Attributes: Narrow-minded, harsh critic, unsympathetic, arrogant, proud, prejudiced, cold.

Glamours: Materialism, intellect, knowledge, assurance, form that hides reality, organization, the outer that hides the inner.

Religions: Zoroastrianism (Persian dualism), alchemy, neo-Platonism.

Chakras: Third eye, belly.

Animal: No traditional animals.

Day: Wednesday.

Jewel: Traditionally topaz, but as a substitute you can use any orange stone, such as carnelian or orange calcite.

Oils: Eucalyptus, fennel, orange, sandalwood, sage, clary sage.

Flower Essences/Herbs: Angelica, eucalyptus, fennel, hazel, licorice, sage, sandalwood, walnut.

Esosteric Astrological Attributes: Venus (sacred), Leo (main sign), Sagittarius, Aquarius.

Qabalistic Attributes: Hod, the eighth sphere on the Tree of Life; Mercury.

Description: The fifth ray is the orange ray, and its purpose is the advancement of science and technology. Many people believe that the New Age will be both a spiritual and technological utopia, where much of the damage we have created in the world will be healed with technology. Many of our problems regarding the scarcity of resources, environmental damage, and the needs of our economy will also be solved with advanced technology. The orange ray will play a key role in the coming transition of the ages. Anybody who works with this power has greater insight into science. I was blessed once to meet a psychic who acted as a channel, or voice, to the ascended master of this ray, Hilarion. The psychic had no prior knowledge of Hilarion or the rays before she started channeling, and certainly had no advanced scientific background. In an evening channeling session at a local metaphysical bookstore, she fielded some quite advanced questions from scientists in the audience, and they seemed satisfied and intrigued by her answers. When the channeling session ended, she had no memory of anything of which she had spoken, yet the information of the orange ray had come through her with a great amount of detail.

In ages past, when we did not have modern technology, the orange ray manifested in the arts of alchemy and engineering. Both had sacred components to them, as arts taught in the temples and performed by wise men and women. They were the forerunners of our modern scientific arts. Even now, our modern scientists, particularly those studying quantum mechanics and the holographic theory of the universe, continue to find profound spiritual insights in their scientific research. They are moving through one of the glamours, or illusions, of this ray—the outer form that hides the true inner reality. Science has always been a sacred art, even though we don't often think of it as sacred. Though many people perceive the cultures of our ancient ancestors as primitive, they were the foundation upon which we built our modern civilization. Until the step back of the Dark and Middle Ages, the world was more advanced than most people think. From the invention of the wheel to the ancient monuments of Egypt, Greece, Sumer, India, Europe, China, Central America, and South America, the orange ray has been active in humanity's development.

The orange ray is associated with the eighth sphere of the Qabalah, known as Hod, the sphere of the magician and the planet Mercury. Hod rules communication, language, thinking, and speaking. Through the explorations of the mind, we advance our inner and outer technologies. In many ways, ritual, a technique to focus energy, could be considered a form of technology. All those magicians who advance the inner and outer forms of technology, from scientists and researchers to sacred geometricians and alchemists, work with the energy of the fifth ray.

Sixth Ray

Colors: Indigo, purple, sky blue.

Purposes: Devotion/idealism, religion.

Archetypes: Minister, mystic, missionary, devotee, orator, crusader, zealot.

Chohans: Sananda, though some believe Nada was, or is, the chohan of this ray.

Elohim: Peace and Aloha.

Archangels: Uriel and Aurora (Theosophical), Raziel (Qabalistic).

Positive Attributes: Devotion, single-minded, persistent, tender, intuitive, loyal, religious, reverent, religious organizations, philosophy.

Negative Attributes: Selfish, jealous, sentimental, escapist, deceptive, fanatical, extreme, narrow-minded, zealous.

Glamours: Devotion, adherence to form and persons, idealism, loyalties and creeds, emotional response, sentimentality, interference, lower pairs of opposites, world saviors/ teachers, narrow vision, fanaticism.

Religions: Christianity, Islam, Judaism, Buddhism, Gnosticism.

Chakras: Solar plexus, third eye.

Animals: Horse, dog.

Day: Monday.

Jewel: Traditionally ruby, but as a substitute you can use any indigo or purple stone, such as amethyst or sugilite.

Oils: Frankincense, mugwort, myrrh, sandalwood, ylang ylang.

Flower Essences/Herbs: Aloe, chives, frankincense, mugwort, myrrh, willow, wisteria.

Esoteric Astrological Attributes: Neptune (sacred), Mars (non-sacred), Virgo, Sagittarius (main sign), Pisces.

Qabalistic Attributes: Chokmah, the second sphere on the Tree of Life; Neptune; the zodiac.

Description: The power of the sixth ray is that of religious idealism. The indigo-blue light manifests the qualities of devotion, prayer, introspection, and mysticism. The master of the sixth sphere is Sananda. During his earthly lifetime as Jesus, Sananda worked closely with the Planetary Christ, Lord Maitreya. Lord Maitreya was said to overshadow Jesus, working with him to bring the teachings of compassion and love to the world and give form to the Christ-consciousness grid. The sixth ray has been working strongly with humanity over the last two thousand years, manifesting as the religion of Christianity, bringing to light many of the light and dark sides of the indigo ray. All devotional religions have the indigo ray's power, and in fact one could say that all religions have an aspect of the indigo ray in them. Whenever there is philosophical belief, we have the sixth ray's power at work. While those influenced by the sixth ray are devoted to the divine and have a love and tenderness for all, there is also a propensity toward fanaticism, focusing on creeds and giving away power to teachers and institutions as savior figures.

Neptune is the sacred planet of this ray, and is associated on its highest level with spiritual love, unconditional love. Neptune brings in the power of Christ consciousness, and although it is named after the Roman sea god, the energy of the planet also appropriately fits the gods of the harvest and sacrifice, such as Dionysus. Neptune is one of the older three brothers in the Olympian pantheon, along with Zeus and Hades, and manifests to many mystics as a father figure. The second Qabalistic sphere, Chokmah, the father in the supernal triad, is associated with the planet Neptune. Lower manifestations of Neptune's astrological energy are idealism and romanticism. When Neptunian energy is put into manifesting ideals, it can be a powerful force for good, but too much of this energy can manifest as zealousness and an inability to see anyone else's vision. Lower manifestations of Neptune include disillusionment and even escapist or self-sabotaging behavior. Ideally, the mystic moves through these lower forms, devoted to the divine, and ultimately manifests the highest ideals of the seventh ray.

Seventh Ray

Color: Violet.

Purposes: Ceremonial order/magick.

Archetypes: Magician, witch, alchemist, revolutionary, builder, administrator, designer.

Chohans: Saint Germain, though some say Portia co-rules this ray as the silver violet flame.

Elohim: Arcturus and Victoria.

Archangels: Tzadkiel and Amethyst (Theosophical), Uriel and Gabriel (Qabalistic).

Positive Attributes: Creativity, organization, freedom, strength, perseverance, courage, detailed, reliable, practical, occult, spiritualism, power, protocol, ceremony, diplomacy, order, discipline, grounding spirit into matter.

Negative Attributes: Opinionated, proud, judgmental, bigoted, rules, administration.

Glamours: Magickal work, relations of the opposites, Subterranean Powers, that which brings together, physical body, mysteries and secrets, misuse of sex magick, merging manifested forces.

Religions: Ceremonial magick, witchcraft, shamanism, Freemasonry, Rosicrucianism, all religions.

Chakras: Belly, crown.

Animal: No traditional animals.

Day: Saturday.

Jewel: Traditionally amethyst, but as a substitute you can use any purple or violet stone, such as sugilite.

Oils: Lavender, melissa, rosemary, spikenard.

Flower Essences/Herbs: African violet, borage, cinquefoil, copal, datura, juniper, lavender, lemon balm, lilac, mandrake, periwinkle, rowan, spikenard, unicorn root.

Esoteric Astrological Attributes: Uranus (sacred), Aries, Cancer, Capricorn (main sign).

Qabalistic Attributes: Da'ath, the hidden eleventh sphere on the Tree of Life; Uranus; Yesod, the ninth sphere on the Tree of Life; the Moon.

Description: The violet ray is probably the most popular of all the rays. As different rays dominate time periods, the seventh ray is the ray of the New Age, and the chohan of the seventh ray, Saint Germain, has been instrumental in bringing about the New Age. The seventh ray's traditional name is the "ray of ceremonial order," another ray title I initially had difficulty understanding. Ceremonial order refers to the structure of ritual, but the seventh ray is more than just ritual. Ritual is a force that reorders consciousness and reality. Ritual creates magick, and magick is the power of change, the ability to restructure the order of one's inner and outer worlds. All the traditions of magick and ritual—from alchemy and Hermetics, to witchcraft, to the rituals of Freemason lodges and Rosicrucians—are in the domain of the seventh ray. The use of magick is empowering and transforming. The realization that you are in control of your reality is very liberating, but also somewhat frightening. Magick can also be seductive. Many people study magick not as part of a spiritual teaching, but as a method to accumulate power. Once they have the power, they might not have the morals and ethics of a spiritual philosophy to guide their use of that power. Ultimately, the magick of the seventh ray ties in to the magick of the first ray, that of will. Magick is an act of will, and understanding the nature of your true will, your purpose, and partnering your magick—your thoughts, words, and deeds—with your true purpose is what will bring the proper order to the world in the next age.

The seventh ray works with all forms of magick, including folk magick, elemental magick, angelic magick, and spirit summoning. The violet fire of the seventh ray is described as the process of transmutation, of transformation. All that does not serve your highest good, all that is dense and disruptive, is consumed by the violet flame. As violet is the highest color on the spectrum before all the colors merge into white light, violet light is used to raise the spiritual vibration of any person, place, or thing when evoked. For this reason, violet light is protective. All harmful energies and spirits must leave its presence or be transformed into something more benign. Violet light is also very healing, and is used to transmute and transform illness and injury. When using it in healing, the violet flame helps provide insight into the nature of the illness, through meditations, dreams, or a message from another, to help you integrate its lessons before fully recovering. The violet light of the seventh ray is the power of spiritual alchemy, and Saint Germain was said to be one of the world's foremost alchemists. In stories of Atlantis, it is said that the soul that would later incarnate as Saint Germain was the high priest in the violet flame temple of Atlantis.

In esoteric astrology, Uranus rules the seventh ray. In traditional modern astrology, Uranus rules the sign of Aquarius, the sign associated with the New Age (see chapter 20). Uranus is the planet of sudden and unexpected change. It is the planet of revolution and innovation. It brings new thoughts, ideas, and models of life to manifestation. Uranus is the bolt of enlightenment, the inspiration to take the highest heavenly ideals and ground them into matter, manifesting the ideals as reality. Uranus and Aquarius embody the balance between the overall good of the community versus the freedom to be an individual, and teach us that only when we manifest our individuality will we truly serve the greatest good. While the seventh ray is about order and discipline (as all magicians need a certain amount of discipline), it is also about freedom. True universal order is not rigid, but flows with the changing patterns. Qabalistically, the hidden sphere of Da'ath is associated with ultraviolet, like the peacock-colored stain of an oil slick. Da'ath means "knowledge" and is also associated with Uranus. Da'ath is found in the abyss, the break in the Tree of Life between the supernal triad and the lower spheres. The magician climbing the tree is challenged to keep focused on the full spiritual power of Kether as the godhead, rather than be seduced by the knowledge of Da'ath without higher spiritual wisdom. Magicians who are seduced fall into the abyss and can enter the reverse of the Tree of Life, a world of empty shells devoid of divinity. An adept can be enticed by knowledge and power, so crossing the abyss is the final test of the adept before experiencing the supernal power of the divine.

Though not violet in color, the ninth sphere of Yesod is lavender flecked with silver, and the violet flame of the seventh ray is often described as a silver violet flame. Yesod is the sphere of lunar magick, where a magician learns to shape thoughts on the astral plane to change reality. Part of the work of the seventh ray at this time is encouraging interest in magick and occultism. This has manifested as an interest in ancient Egypt, angels, faeries, witchcraft, ceremonial magick, shamanism, and ascended masters. We each find the aspects of magick that resonate with us. In the coming age, we will all be challenged to be magicians, to be masters of our own reality, and work together to manifest a new reality. In some way, we will all be working with the seventh ray.

An alternate system of rays lists the first ray as blue/power, the second as yellow/wisdom, the third as pink/love, the fourth as white/purity, the fifth as green/truth, the sixth as purple/peace, and the seventh as violet/freedom. I prefer the traditional correspondences.

THE EXTENDED RAYS

Modern lore has expanded the seven-ray system into a multitude of "new" rays for the New Age, said to embody the consciousness developing in the world. Channels say these new rays were grounded into the Earth during the 1970s and are now available to us all. The Solar Logos, Helios, "gives" these rays to the Planetary Logos, Sanat Kumara, who then funnels these energies through the "department" of the seventh ray. Because the information on these new rays is even less codified than the material on the first seven, there is not a whole lot of agreement on the numbers, colors, and functions of the extended rays. Here is the system that I first learned and that resonates most with me.

Eighth Ray
Colors: Seafoam green or violet green.
Purpose: Higher cleansing.
Chohans: Kumeka and Nada.
Description: The eighth ray is the first of the new rays manifesting to prepare us for the New Age. As the seventh, violet ray is a cleansing ray, the ray one rung above it is said to be even more cleansing and transformative. Though described as "seafoam green," I've heard some describe it as "violet green," which at first doesn't seem to make any sense. Think of the high-vibrational quality of violet—the bluish-red flame of true violet has a mysterious quality. Take that same quality and transpose it to the green spectrum. Violet green isn't a color we can see yet with our physical eyes, but we can see it psychically with our inner sight. Many people see the energy of healing modalities such as Shamballa Reiki as violet green. In his book *The Complete Ascension Manual,* Dr. Joshua David

Stone describes the eighth ray as "composed of the fourth ray, the seventh ray, and the fifth ray with a touch of white light, all mixed together." This ray is used to manifest the powers of cleansing and healing to prepare for the higher rays to come. The eighth ray is used to remove any unwanted thoughtforms, spirit attachments, and spiritual implants in the energetic field.

Ninth Ray

Color: Blue green.

Purposes: Joy, attracting the body of light.

Chohan: Unknown.

Description: The ninth ray brings the quality of spiritual joy or spiritual bliss. Through working with this ray, the individual attracts the "body of light," which is another way of saying lightbody, or merkaba vehicle. The person doesn't so much attract the merkaba, but rather he or she prepares the way for the manifestation of the merkaba, the chariot of light that allows people to ascend to a higher consciousness. It is important to clear your physical and energy bodies with the previous eighth and seventh rays to clear the way for the lightbody to become a permanent manifestation of your consciousness.

Tenth Ray

Color: Pearlescent.

Purpose: Anchoring the body of light.

Chohan: Some see Quan Yin as the keeper of the white, pearl, or alabaster flame.

Description: The tenth ray has the power to anchor the body of light, the higher consciousness, into physical form. The pearlescent ray is described as a combination of the three rays of activity (the red, blue, and yellow rays) mixed with white light. Through working with the tenth ray, you can come to understand your true will more clearly, by integrating the higher consciousness into your everyday life.

Eleventh Ray

Color: Pink orange.

Purpose: Bridge to the New Age

Chohan: Unknown.

Description: The pink-orange light of the eleventh ray acts as a bridge, a connection, to the New Age. This ray is very cleansing and can clear anything that was not cleared by the seventh and eighth rays. It removes anything that blocks an individual, a community, or an area from the patterns of the New Age. It is the first, second, and fifth rays mixed with white light. The eleventh ray brings the will, wisdom/love, and insight of the New Age to the planet.

Twelfth Ray

Color: Gold.

Purpose: The anchoring of the New Age and Christ consciousness.

Chohan: Unknown.

Description: The twelfth ray is the power of Christ consciousness. It is a mixture of all eleven rays with white light, to form the golden light of Christ consciousness, all in perfect balance and harmony for any given time or place. This is the highest power that can be used to integrate the Aquarian principles into your life and the world. The only higher vibration that can be accessed here in the third dimension of the Earth is the energy of the Mahatma, who is known as the avatar of synthesis.

RAY EVOCATION AND DECREES

The energies of the rays can be used in meditation and prayer, evoking their power directly into your life. You can gain an understanding of each ray's mystery through personal experience. If you feel you are already working with a ray, then evoking it through meditation will help you bring out the best qualities of that ray in your life, so you can work with the energy consciously. If you feel you are lacking qualities of a ray that you desire, evoking the ray will bring those energies into your life. You can evoke rays in ritual and ceremony to empower your magick. When working with the energy of a particular ray, you can more easily make contact with the masters, angels, and elohim of that ray.

You can do the following exercises while in a meditative state, to be more aware of the energies, but it's not necessary. You can call upon the rays at any time, using the simple decrees and pure intention. The power of the rays is readily available at all times.

EXERCISE 14:

RAY EVOCATION

Determine which ray you wish to work with at this time. When you are ready to begin, simply choose the ray and ask for its light to descend upon you. Say something like, "I ask for the light of the (number) ray of light, the color of (color of ray), to descend and be present now." Imagine a spotlight or large laser beam of the color surrounding you. Imagine that the light emanates from the highest heavens, the Great Central Sun of the universe, and descends into the heart of Mother Earth. If you are having difficulty visualizing this, you can ask for the chohan, archangel, or elohim associated with the ray to aid you.

Feel the beam's light, and take time to notice what shifts occur in your own consciousness. How does it make you feel physically? Where are your thoughts directed? How does it feel emotionally for you? What spiritual qualities are apparent as you bathe in the light of the ray? Think of what qualities from this ray you want to assume. Then visualize/feel/believe in the qualities. Know that you are assuming these qualities in your daily life.

When done, thank the ray and all beings you have called upon. Imagine the beam of light descending into the Earth's core, where it will be disseminated as needed to the planet. Feel the new qualities enhanced and growing within you. Like seeds sprouting, they were already there, but the light of the ray simply woke them to grow within you and take root.

Ray evocation can take the form of poetry or prayer. Some practitioners use a mantra—repeating a specific phrase over and over again during a meditative practice. Some use mala beads, a string of 108 beads used for mantras, to recite a mantra or affirmation 108 times. The beads help you keep count. Repetitions traditionally are done in sets of three, nine, thirty-three, or 108. Decrees can be used by anyone and bring great benefit, but I think they are more effective when used once you have made a more meditative and experiential link with the ray in question, through the previous exercise. You can do decrees anywhere. People do them in deep states of meditation, but also in the car or shower or at the office.

Here are some examples of traditional decrees. They often emphasize the words "I AM" to attune to the higher self or "I AM" presence, calling upon one's own divinity to guide the use of the energy. The Saint Germain Foundation, which prints the Saint Germain teachings of Guy Ballard, has trademarked many phrases associated with the seventh ray, including "I AM violet flame," so many people have added the word silver, creating the "silver violet flame," to avoid any legal disputes. The use of decrees was popularized through Elizabeth Clare Prophet's book *Violet*

Flame to Heal Body, Mind & Soul, which contains numerous examples and has been traded among ascension practitioners for years.

The most popular decree is "I am a being of violet fire. I am the purity God desires." Another is "O Saint Germain, in thy sweet name, I call upon you to fill me with the violet flame." Though the most popular decrees focus on invoking the violet ray, you can adapt these invocations, or make your own for the other rays.

Expanding upon this concept and other ray systems, various "flame evocations" have been used, based upon color if not the twelve rays. Try working with these flames, calling them forth from the divine light, much as you would call upon the violet flame. See which flames work most powerfully for you.

Flame of Purity: White.

Flame of Healing: Green.

Flame of Abundance and Prosperity: Green tinged with gold.

Flame of Mercy: Pink violet.

Flame of Comfort: White tinged with pink.

Flame of Cosmic Honor: White tinged with gold.

Flame of Peace: Golden yellow.

Flame of Fearlessness: White tinged with green.

Exercise 15:
Twelve-Ray Alignment

As a personal exercise for ascension, I like to use the decrees with all twelve rays to align myself with the powers of the universe and creation. That way, whatever energy I need for the day will be present and flowing through me, even if I was not consciously aware that I needed it when I started the day. You can be as quick or as meditative as you want with each ray, depending on your schedule and time constraints. Some people find this exercise to be a quick and powerful way to start or end the day, while others prefer to meditate slowly and take time to feel each ray.

> *I call forth the first ray.*
> *I call forth the red ray.*
> *I call forth the ray of will.*
> *I am the first ray.*

I call forth the second ray.
I call forth the blue ray.
I call forth the ray of love and wisdom.
I am the second ray.

I call forth the third ray.
I call forth the yellow ray.
I call forth the ray of active intelligence.
I am the third ray.

I call forth the fourth ray.
I call forth the green ray.
I call forth the ray of harmony through conflict.
I am the fourth ray.

I call forth the fifth ray.
I call forth the orange ray.
I call forth the ray of concrete science.
I am the fifth ray.

I call forth the sixth ray.
I call forth the indigo ray.
I call forth the ray of devotion and idealism.
I am the sixth ray.

I call forth the seventh ray.
I call forth the violet ray.
I call forth the ray of ceremonial order.
I am the seventh ray.

(You can continue this exercise with the additional rays if you desire, or stop after the first seven.)

I call forth the eighth ray.
I call forth the violet-green ray.
I call forth the ray of cleansing.
I am the eighth ray.

I call forth the ninth ray.
I call forth the blue-green ray.

I call forth the ray of joy.
I am the ninth ray.

I call forth the tenth ray.
I call forth the pearlescent ray.
I call forth the ray of anchoring the body of light.
I am the tenth ray.

I call forth the eleventh ray.
I call forth the pink-orange ray.
I call forth the ray that is a bridge to the New Age.
I am the eleventh ray.

I call forth the twelfth ray.
I call forth the gold ray.
I call forth the ray of the New Age.
I am the twelfth ray.

You can call forth the power of the rays for others, though it is considered a misuse of magick to do so for people who have not given you conscious permission. You can also evoke the power of the rays in your home or office, to bring those qualities into your environment. Simply say, "I call forth the power of the (number or color) ray for (name of the person or place)."

RAY SPRAYS

Various product lines have been created by infusing the power of essential oils, flower essences, gem waters, and herbal preparations (see chapters 14 and 15) with intention and using them in spray bottles to change the energy of an environment or person. Through working with the power of the rays and evoking the power of the chohans, I have found that you can create powerful ritual tools to attune yourself and your environment to the rays. These sprays can be used in healing, meditation, or ritual, or simply for daily use to transform your living space.

Before you mix the ingredients together as listed below, take time to meditate on the ray you are working with. You can make your spray in sacred space by first casting a circle.

Make sure you have all your ingredients with you before you do so. Ask for the aid of the chohan of that ray. As you add each ingredient, do it with intention, putting your intention and will, in alignment with the chohan, into every ingredient. You might find yourself singing or chanting over the bowl with strange words and sounds. You could find yourself toning over the bowl. If you have musical instruments, singing bowls, or tuning forks, and feel guided to use a particular one in your ritual to create your spray, then do so. I suggest that you make each spray one at a time, on the traditional day for each one, so you don't mix the energies of the rays.

After combining the ingredients, put the mixture in a spray bottle. Spray bottles are commonly available for purchase through herbal supply stores and companies. Then spray the mist liberally to evoke the power of the color of that ray in your life. Ray sprays can be used to alter the mood of an environment or person and effect change, or as a preparation for a larger working or meditation. Each spray can help put you in contact with that master and ray whenever you desire.

To make a spray, start with a base of 50 percent pure water and 50 percent high-proof alcohol, such as an 80+ proof vodka, to preserve the spray for a long time. For these recipes, I usually make an 8-ounce spray bottle size, so I would use 4 ounces of water and 4 ounces of alcohol. I prefer the spray bottles that are specially designed for aromatherapy, made of a dark amber, blue, or green plastic. Ideally, if you can find colored glass or plastic bottles to match the ray colors, then do so. If not, I prefer a neutral amber, because unlike green or blue, the color amber is not associated with one of the rays.

Start by soaking a non-water-soluble stone associated with the ray in clear water in a glass bowl in the sunlight. Make sure the stone has already been cleansed and consecrated (see exercise 2 in chapter 6). Invoke the power of the colored ray upon the liquid by decree. Ask for the aid of the chohan, archangels, and elohim associated with the ray. Keep the stone in the sunlight for at least an hour. Then pour the water into your bottle, making sure you don't lose the stone in the bottle. Add the essential oils and flower essences one at a time. Intuitively choose from the list of correspondences provided (starting on page 271), and add 5 to 20 drops of each essential oil and 3 to 10 drops of each flower essence. I like to use one essential oil and one to three flower essences. Experiment with the oils if you choose to mix scents, as not all scents combine well together. Also, be sure to purchase essential oils, which are natural plant products, instead of synthetic fragrance oils. Good oils vary in price depending on the oil. Oils that are rarer or more difficult to extract, such as rose and jasmine, cost more. Some suppliers have substitutes that are more affordable, made by either cutting the essential oil in a base oil or using a different plant with a similar quality. I usually use rosewood essential oil in place of true rose essential oil.

If you can't find a particular flower essence, but you do have the dried herb available, you can make a tea of the herb(s) you have chosen with the water portion of the spray. First boil the water, and use about a half tablespoon of dried herb to every 4 ounces of water. Let the mixture steep and cool, then strain it. Use that tea as the base of your spray, soaking the stone in it in the sunlight.

Seal the bottle and shake it up. Take a moment to meditate with it as the liquid settles. Affirm that the liquid be filled with the beneficial power of the ray you have evoked by decree. Ask the chohans, archangels, and elohim of the ray to bless it. You are now ready to use your new tool. Label the bottle as a ray spray, and be sure to list the ingredients you used. You might find that you adapt and change the formulas over time, using whatever ingredients are available.

Ray sprays are used to change the vibration of an area. If you apply the formula directly to a living being, be extremely careful, as the oils can irritate the skin, even in this dilute form. Always consult a good medicinal aromatherapy book and medicinal herbal book before applying anything to the skin or taking anything internally. Ray sprays are not meant for internal consumption, but rather are meant to be used to effect energetic change.

14

ASCENSION SPELLCRAFT

Spellcraft is the art and science of designing rituals to communicate with the divine in order to manifest your will. It is a universal language, moving beyond any one dialect or tongue, helping you interface with the primal forces of creation, and your own higher will, to co-create your reality.

All spells combine intention, directed thought and energy, emotion, and symbolic actions to communicate to the universe. With some spells you effect change by simply reading a short passage, from a chant or prayer to a magickal phrase in a foreign language. Other spells require you to draw a symbol, gather herbs, or carry a stone. Spells can be incredibly long, lasting hours to days, or very short, taking a matter of moments. They can require elaborate tools or simply your own mind and voice.

A spell is an act of ritual magick, with specific, definable goals. Unlike forms of high magick designed to spiritually evolve the practitioner without focusing on a short-term result, spellcraft almost always has a clear goal. The means by which the goal manifests might be left to fate, but the end result is specific. Magick often involves taking the easiest route possible, but you have to leave the door open. If you do a spell for a new job, then make sure you send out résumés and go on interviews. If you do a spell to lose weight, then follow up by eating responsibly and exercising. You will find that the times you tried to lose weight through diet and exercise and failed will be quite different from what you experience when you back up your will with magick.

Spells can be done for any purpose, from finding a new romantic partner to increasing money to pay your bills. You can do magick to increase your business, expand your clientele, attract new friends, awaken psychic powers, heal your body/mind/heart/soul, grow an amazing garden, or create world peace. Anything you can envision and dream about is potentially an intention for a spell, keeping in mind our ethical considerations. "Harming none and in accord with divine will" generally means that if you wouldn't want something done to you, then don't do it to anybody else. The more specific and tangible a spell is, the more likely it is that it will manifest. Intentions like world peace are so vast and affect so many people that they are hard to effect on your own unless large numbers of people are also focusing on the same intention. A more effective spell would be to create a peaceful community in your area. If everybody did so, then we could truly have world peace.

A spell that is too specific can also be difficult to manifest. You might do a spell to get a specific job, but if that job is not right for you, or if someone else is a better fit, then your spell will fail. If you do a spell listing certain qualities you want in a job and do not specify the exact position or company, then the universe has more freedom to provide for you.

Spells can be left open-ended, or locked with time-specific instructions, such as "manifest in the next month, six months, or year." What you want now might not be what you want ten years from now, so keep that in mind, as magick can move across time and space to manifest. You might want to keep a magickal journal with all your spells, so you can find what went right, what went wrong, and what simply happened far later than you expected. I have a friend, Lisa Davenport, who leaves her spells opened-ended, to her higher self, asking "for this, or something better, in partnership with my higher self." So if the spell is not good for her, or if her higher self wants to use the energy manifested for something else, then it will. Her spells usually do not work out as planned, but amazing blessings come to her after every ritual.

Spellcraft is a creative process in which you partner your intuition with a knowledge of magickal correspondences. Various substances, tools, shapes, and symbols are related to set ideas. Lists of correspondences were given in chapter 13 when we explored the rays of light. Magicians know that certain things vibrate at a similar rate. A stone, herb, sound, color, planet, or chakra may all hold a similar vibration, a similar cosmic note, but be playing in a different octave. The first is in the mineral octave, the next is in the plant octave, then the sonic spectrum, the visible light spectrum, the planetary spectrum, and the subtle-body spectrum, respectively. By using one, we can align with the others, much as when you hit a C on a piano with the pedal up and all the C's in the other octaves vibrate.

People on the ascension path look at forms of Western magick, particularly folk magick, and feel that there is too much "stuff." They feel that they are playing with props, when all that is needed is intention and will. It's true that intention and will are the key ingredients to a spell, but certain substances can focus and amplify an intention. Ritual tools are consecrated to be both batteries and gateways for the forces we seek to evoke. Some practitioners believe that special and exotic items from the tribal and Eastern cultures are holy tools, while the tools of Western magick are only silly props. Yet the Western folk-magick paradigm, in which familiar, everyday objects are used in ritual, allows us to bring that philosophy into our modern culture, and use modern, everyday objects in our rituals. From a postmodern magickal perspective, a food processor, a bird feeder, a CD player, and even a computer are all magickal tools.

In magick, the material world is a manifestation of the divine, and all substances play a role in our evolution and ascension. All things are sacred and divine. Things like herbs have chemicals in them that aid the healing of humans and animals but, to the best of our scientific knowledge, are of no use to the plant. Plants are meant to be in partnership with humanity. Those of us who have the ability to commune with nature, to explore the ways plants can partner with us, what old folk traditions call "the eyes to see and the ears to hear," know that plants are not just food or even medicine, but also spiritual allies. The same holds true for all of nature. By working with plants and other natural substances in ritual and spells, you are partnering with the natural world, with the spirits of woods, plants, oils, and stones. You create a partnership not only between you and the divine, but between you, the divine, and the natural world.

Rituals are designed by taking this knowledge and combining it with our creativity. There are no true rules for spellcrafting. If your spell transmits your intention to the universe and you experience success, then your spell was sound and no one can argue with it. Spells generally contain a clear intention, a vessel for that intention, and a method to broadcast the intention to the universe. An intention can be in words (written, oral, or both) or visuals (internal visualizations or drawings), or it can simply be pure, clear-willed intent. The vessel for an intention is a charm of some sort, a physical tool or construct. Such a tool can be destroyed to broadcast the intention to the world, such as burning or ripping a slip of paper once it has been read, or it can be kept, like a talisman or amulet, so that it broadcasts its energy when carried with you, attracting the forces to you or repelling them as desired. If you are doing a ritual circle, you can release the cone of power at the culmination of the spell or, if you prefer, the culmination of all spells, and then ground the remaining energy of the circle.

If you have been following the exercises of this book, you have already been doing spells. The decrees of the ascended masters and rays of light are one form of spell working. The petitions, the ritual languages of the angels, the ascended master symbols, and the sigils of the star nations are other forms of spellcrafting. In this chapter we will continue that exploration, with the desire to inspire you to create your own spells. As you do so, don't forget the previous tools and symbols you have learned. We'll be synthesizing from a number of different paradigms and cultures, using techniques and tools you might not find in traditional spell books.

Spellcrafters often caution against doing too many spells at one time. I was taught to do only one magick-circle ritual a day, and only three formal spells per day. Though I do lots of little magick throughout each day, I restrict myself to three formal spells a day, or often just one. I tend to do more spells only when needed, though I have a lot of pre-prepared items—such as consecrated stones, sprays, pendants, and other tools—to carry or wear when the need arises.

Use the following spells to prepare your own magickal tools and cast your own spells, either by following the directions given here or using them to inspire your own brand of magick.

MAGICK WORDS

The power of magick is deeply entwined with our words and language. The archetypal image of the magician is of one speaking a secret arcane language, the classic magick words that reshape reality. We know that the power of words, and more importantly the power of the thoughts that empower the words, creates our reality. The ability to speak, write, and imagine what we want to create, from positive affirmations to the decrees of the rays of light, is the skill of the magus. Most people don't know what they want to create, let alone have the clarity to clearly express their desires to the universe. When they do create, they do so unconsciously, using words without an awareness of their power. When we are able to clearly communicate our intentions to both our own soul and the universe, we become more like the Logos of the cosmic hierarchy, and find ourselves infused with the ability to create our reality with our words.

EXERCISE 16:

PƐTITION SPELLS

One of the simplest ways of using your words to create magick is through the use of a petition spell. By writing an intention on a slip of paper and reading it in sacred space, you are asking to align with the divine forces to manifest a new reality. The petition is read in a sacred space, such as a magick circle. Many feel the angelic magick circle is the most effective type of magick circle, as the angels act as messengers, carrying the petition to the creative source so it can then manifest in our physical reality.

The first petition format I learned was in the framework of Wicca, and it goes something like this:

> I, (state your name), ask in the name of the Goddess, God, and Great Spirit to be granted/have removed (state your intention clearly). I thank the Goddess, God, and Great Spirit for this, and I ask that this be for the highest good of all involved, harming none. So mote it be!

The petition is then burned in a cauldron to release the power as the cone of power is raised, and the ashes are scattered. Other traditions might instruct you to dissolve the petition in water, bury it in the ground, or rip it up and scatter the paper in the wind. You can coordinate your paper color with the ray color that rules your intention.

Traditionally we do magick to manifest things in our lives when the Moon is waxing, as the psychic tides are coming toward us, and do magick to banish things when the Moon is waning, as the psychic tides are leaving. You can determine the state of the Moon by consulting an almanac or astrological calendar.

You can alter the deity reference in the petition spell to reflect your own beliefs. For many lightworkers, "Mother-Father-God" would be more appropriate. Asking that your petition be for "the highest good, harming none" is really a request that the petition be in accord with higher will. "So mote it be" is much like the pagan "Amen" and means "it is so." The phrase makes the entire spell a positive statement, like a powerful affirmation, rather than a tentative query.

Though magick done in English with the Latin alphabet, or any other modern language, is quite effective, many magicians prefer to use ancient languages and magickal scripts. The shape and character of the letters in magickal alphabets are said to have inherent magickal virtue. Since the scripts are alien to our everyday culture, they lend an air of mystery, engaging our magickal minds and helping us get into the proper mood for magick.

Modern magicians have associated the various characters of these scripts with letters of the Latin alphabet. An entire petition spell can be translated into a new script, or a specific word of power from the intention—such as PROSPERITY, HEALTH, or ROMANCE—can be translated into the new alphabet. The statement can be written on paper and burned, like a traditional petition spell, or the symbols can be put on parchment, wood, stone, or wax and carried as a talisman, much as you would do with your ascended master symbols or archangel seals. The symbols can also be carved into candles or drawn over potions and remedies.

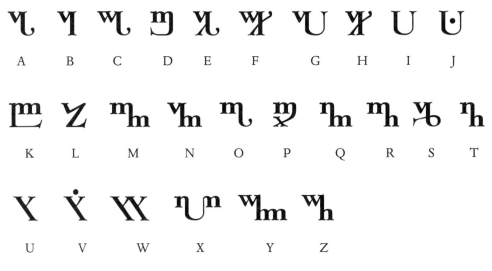

Figure 34: Theban Script

One angelic language that is popular in modern witchcraft is the Theban script (figure 34). Known as the Witches' Alphabet and attributed to Honorius of Thebes, it is used as a code for ritual books. Angelic magick teacher David Goddard claims that Theban is actually an angelic language of a lunar nature, showing the natural connection to witchcraft through lunar associations.

Another lesser known angelic language is the Passing of the River script (figure 35), which, along with Theban, was popularized in Agrippa's *De Occulta Philosophia*, or *Three Books of Occult Philosophy*. Many think of the Passing of the River script as a more pow-

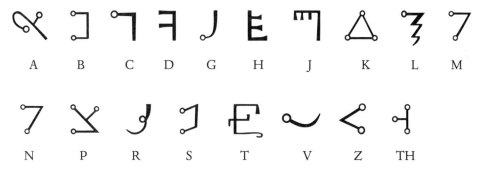

Figure 35: Passing of the River Script

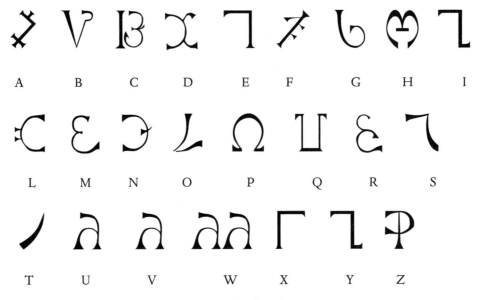

Figure 36: Enochian Script

erful system than the Theban script, as it is said to be of a more celestial nature. Rather than directly translate letter for letter, as is done in Theban, the intention is usually spelled out phonetically, using the corresponding phonetic characters of the Passing of the River script.

Lastly for the angelic languages, there is the widely popular but little understood Enochian script (figure 36). Pioneered in the Elizabethan era by controversial occultists John Dee and Edward Kelly, the symbols are the foundation of a very complicated system of ritual magick that was later absorbed into the work of the Golden Dawn and its successors.

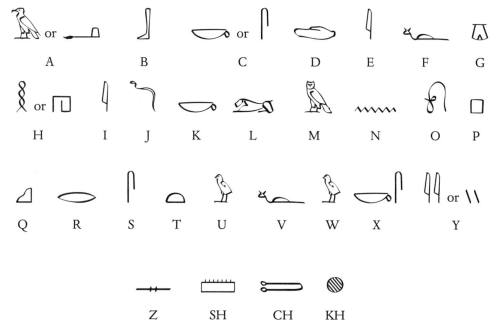

Figure 37: Egyptian Hieroglyphics

Though the entire system is far too complicated to explain here, I have personally found a benefit in translating my petitions and words of powers into Enochian script for ritual, though most traditional Enochian magicians would see that as a misuse of the system.

Another script favored by lightworkers is the system of Egyptian hieroglyphics (figure 37). Though the ancient Egyptian language has nothing to do with our modern alphabet, practitioners have associated the symbols with specific Roman letters. A popular form of jewelry involves "translating" your name to create a personal Egyptian cartouche pendant.

A variety of other sacred languages and scripts can be used, including Hebrew, Chinese, Sanskrit, Gaelic, Runes, and Greek. The detailed workings of these scripts and languages go beyond the scope of this book, but would make interesting subjects of research for an aspiring ascension magician.

CANDLE MAGICK

Candle magick is one of my favorite forms of magick. It is simple and highly effective and reminds me of the similarities between so many of the different spiritual traditions and religions. The lighting of a candle during ritual is a sacred act for so many of us. I remember going to the Catholic Church with my grandmother to light a candle for someone's health or good fortune, under the statue of Mother Mary. Today I light my candles under the statue of the Goddess, yet both are sacred and magickal.

Start by choosing a candle. The material is often a petroleum product, because that is cheap and easy to find, though many people prefer beeswax or soy when available. Choose a color that corresponds to your intention. You can use the colors of the seven rays as a guide. Black and white are all-purpose colors. In general, black is used to draw things to you or absorb energy, while white is used to send out energy or banish it.

Cleanse the candle as you would any tool. I prefer to cleanse candles in the smoke of a purifying incense, though I have a student who prefers to roll them in sea salt.

Clearly form your intention. You can do candle magick for anything you desire, as long as it is in accord with divine will. You can carve and dress the candle, but this is not mandatory. All you need is a clear intention. You can do all this work in a magick circle, but again, it's not mandatory. I feel that the magick circle helps me focus my energies, but if you are not drawn to include much ritual, then simply focus on working with your candle and your intention.

Carve the candle with a pin or the point of a ritual blade. You can carve the key words of the intention in English, or use any of the magickal scripts. If doing a spell for yourself or someone else, you can carve the astrological Sun sign symbols of those involved.

"Dress" your candle by anointing it with an essential oil, a holy water, your own saliva, Aura-Soma remedies, or any other liquid you feel is suitable. To draw things to you, generally you anoint at the top and then move down. To banish things from you, anoint at the bottom and work your way up. If uncertain, the most traditional method is to anoint from the center of the candle and work outward to both ends.

Hold the prepared candle in both hands, and think about your intention. Will the intention—in words, feelings, and mental images—into the candle. Feel the energy within you travel through your hands and into the candle. Imagine that your energy is filling the candle, just as you would fill a glass with water. When you reach the brim, stop and light the candle.

Let the candle burn down as much as possible. If you cannot let it burn out, snuff the candle, sealing in the intention, and relight it later. Repeat this process until the candle is burned all the way. I suggest using metal candle holders, as glass and crystal can crack due to the intense heat of a burning wick.

Incense

Incense magick is the use of herbs, resins, and oils mixed together for a specific intent or vibration that is released when the incense is burned. Incenses are usually used for general intentions, such as protection or love, but can also be used to supplement a specific working, such as a love spell. If you burn a love incense during a love spell, you add more energy, more of the vibration of love, to your work. Incense can be used to set the vibration of a ritual or meditation.

If you don't desire to make your own incense, fine commercial brands, from powders to sticks and cones, are available for your convenience. I suggest all-natural incense rather than synthetic brands, to form a deeper connection to the plant spirit energy.

Here are some incense recipes. A "part" in the proportions is a tablespoon. If you want to make a larger batch, adjust the proportions as necessary. After grinding together the ingredients, all incense should be stored in an airtight container and ideally allowed to "mellow" for about a month.

The first recipe is a simple substitute for the more complex formulas that follow.

Basic Temple Incense
   1 part frankincense
   1 part myrrh

Complex Temple Incense
   1 part frankincense
   1 part myrrh
   1 part sandalwood
   1 part orris root
   5 drops frankincense essential oil
   5 drops myrrh essential oil
   3 drops sandalwood essential oil
   2 drops orris root essential oil

Purification Incense

1 part sage leaves

1 part cedar wood

1 part rosemary leaves

½ part yarrow flowers

Magickal Power Incense

2 parts copal resin

1 part lavender leaves and flowers

1 part dragon's blood resin

1 pinch rose petals

10 drops lavender essential oil

Kyphi Incense

Kyphi is a high-vibrational incense that was used as an offering to the gods in the ancient temples of Egypt and Greece. Its smoke sent prayers to the Egyptian gods and was said to "feed" them, or really "feed" their link with us, for better communication and magick. It can also be used to aid the ancestors in their travel from the tomb to the afterlife.

Several formulas of kyphi exist, both ancient and modern versions, as references to it are found in the Ebers papyrus, the Harris papyrus, and the writing of Plutarch (46–120 AD), as well as on the temple walls of Isis and Horus. Modern practitioners have adapted the formulas to suit the availability of resins and woods in the modern world. There is no one correct formula, as the Egyptians and Greeks had several different versions. The following formula is an amalgam of several recipes that works well for me.

7 raisins

Red wine, enough to cover the raisins in a small bowl

Honey, about a tablespoon

Starting at the dark of the Moon (near the end of the fourth quarter of the Moon), before any light is showing, soak the seven raisins in red wine in a small bowl. I have a friend who puts all the incense ingredients, as they are undergoing preparation, in a copper-wire pyramid to amplify their energy and attune them to the powers of ancient Egypt.

When the waxing crescent Moon shows itself, grind together the following herbs, woods, and roots.

1 part cedar wood powder

1 part ginger root (or galangal)

½ part vetivert (or calamus)

½ part cardamom

½ part cinnamon

½ part juniper berries

½ part orris root powder

½ part cypress wood

½ part rose petals

Depending on how much you want to make, a "part" measurement can be anything, though I usually use a tablespoon as a part. As I add each ingredient, I bless and consecrate it, holding it in my hands, connecting to its energy and mentally asking to catalyze the spiritual properties of each substance while using my will to push a little of my energy, and intention, into the substance. Traditional rituals would have songs, incantations, and rituals to bless each ingredient.

Next, mix together the following resins and herbs, and grind them finely. Some recipes call for gum arabic rather than gum mastic, but gum mastic, if available, produces a superior incense and will aid in creating a sense of otherworldly journey, magickally creating a slightly psychedelic effect.

4 parts frankincense

2 parts myrrh

2 parts benzoin

2 parts gum mastic

Mix together all the resins and herbs, and store the mixture in an airtight container until the Moon is full.

Add about a tablespoon of honey to the bowl with the raisins and wine. Add more wine if what is left in the bowl is evaporating too quickly and the raisins are exposed.

At the full Moon, strain out the raisins and save the wine-honey mixture. Mix the raisins with the dry powdered herbs and resins, mashing them together. Add the honey and wine mixture to create a nice sticky consistency. Add more honey or wine if needed. Spread out the mixture on a clean cotton cloth somewhere warm and dry. You can also use a baking sheet reserved only for this purpose. Most recipes tell you to avoid direct sunlight, but others suggest sun drying. I prefer no sunlight, to preserve the fine oils in the mix. Let the mixture dry, occasionally turning it over to help the process. While still pliable, before the new Moon, form the mixture into small balls or pea-sized pellets, and then let them dry more. Store the pellets in an airtight container, somewhere cool and dark. The longer the incense matures, the better the smell. It's not unusual to make a large batch of kyphi and let it age for over a year before use.

To use homemade incense, obtain a pack of self-igniting charcoal discs, found in most metaphysical and occult shops. Light a charcoal in a heat-proof container. I use a brass bowl filled with sand, to absorb the heat. Place a small spoonful of the incense, or a kyphi pellet, on the ignited charcoal, and let it smolder and burn, releasing a powerful, though sometimes thick, smoke. Make sure you have some sort of container or lid to snuff out the incense if the smoke gets too intense.

STAR MAGICK

I encourage magicians of every persuasion to explore their connections to the stars. The image of the light within darkness, symbolized by the stars in the heavens, relates to the most powerful teachings of the ancient mystery schools. The classic magi of the ancient world, of Persia, Chaldea, and Egypt, were known for their associations with light, with the stars in the heavens, being expert astrologers and astronomers. We can study complex systems of magickal timing, based on the alignment of the planets, zodiac, and stars, to find the most auspicious times to perform ritual, healing, and even mundane tasks. Our magickal lore is filled with teachings on the mysteries of the stars, echoing Carl Sagan's modern observation that "we are all made of star stuff," pointing to the heavens as our place of origin.

Star symbols are used in traditional forms of magick. The three scripts presented here are said to date back to Mesopotamia and are found in occult manuscripts from the Middle Ages and the Renaissance. These runic forms are associated with hereditary forms of witchcraft, and have been brought to light in the works of author Raven Grimassi. These three scripts are from Grimassi's book *Hereditary Witchcraft*. You can use them in ritual to align with the power of a particular star, if you want to explore it in meditation or invite its beneficial forces into your life.

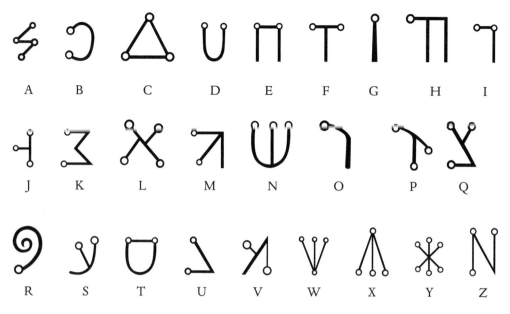

Figure 38: Runic Star Alphabet

The first script is a runic alphabet credited as a star alphabet (figure 38), but with Latin letter translations, much like the scripts presented earlier in this chapter.

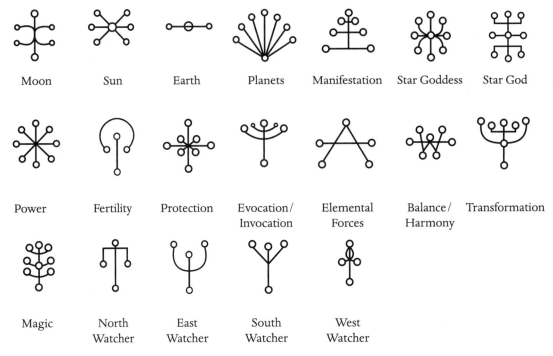

Figure 39: Magickal Star Runes

The next script is composed of general magickal symbols that can be used in your meditations, rituals, and magick (figure 39).

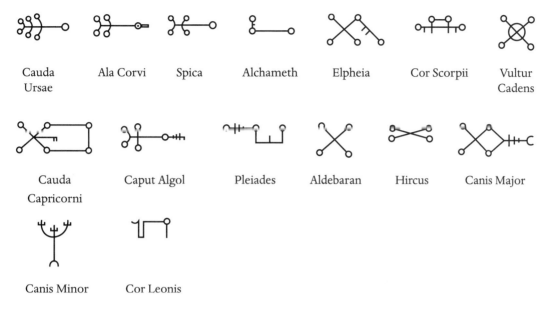

Figure 40: Talismanic Star Symbols

Lastly we have specific star symbols, to be used as amulets and talismans to connect with the blessings of specific stellar forces (figure 40). To evoke the influence of these particular stars, draw them in sand and put candles in the circles of each glyph. You can also use them as traditional talismans, crafting them in wood, stone, metal, or paper and carrying them with you.

Here are the traditional magickal associations of these stars, also taken from Grimassi's *Hereditary Witchcraft*.

Cauda Ursae

Astrology: Venus and the Moon
Metals: Silver or copper
Stone: Lodestone
Plants: Mugwort, chicory, periwinkle
Images: Bull, wolf tooth
Uses: Generate love and friendship, protect travelers, draw like-minded people together

Ala Corvi (in the wings of the crow)

Astrology: Mars and Saturn

Metals: Silver or lead

Stone: Onyx

Plants: Comfrey, henbane

Images: Raven, frog

Uses: Restrict or bind another person's magick, gives power over spirits

Spica (first magnitude star in Virgo)

Astrology: Venus and Mercury

Metal: Copper

Stone: Emerald

Plants: Sage, mandrake

Images: Bird holding a jewel, a shaft of wheat

Uses: Similar to Cauda Ursae, but also used to bind enemies and enhance telepathy

Pleiades (in Taurus)

Astrology: Moon and Mars

Metal: Quicksilver

Stones: Quartz, diodocus

Plants: Fennel, diacedon

Images: Torch, pentacle

Uses: Influence nature and the forces behind nature; can bind another's magick, particularly earth or sea magick, and give power over earth and sea spirits

Canis Major

Astrology: Cancer and Venus

Metal: Silver

Stone: Beryl

Plant: Mugwort

Image: Hunting dog

Uses: Influence the subconscious mind and emotions, develop psychic powers

Canis Minor

Astrology: Mercury and Mars
Metal: Quicksilver
Stone: Agate
Plant: Pennyroyal
Image: Cock
Uses: Bind another person's magick, bring the aid of the gods and spirits

Hircus (Capella in Auriga)

Astrology: Jupiter and Saturn
Metal: Tin
Stone: Sapphire
Plants: Horehound, mandrake
Image: Minstrel
Uses: Draw favor of authorities, heal bones and teeth

Aldebaran

Astrology: Venus and Mars
Metal: Iron
Stone: Ruby
Plant: Milk thistle
Image: An ascending god
Uses: Destruction, binding, protection, and defense

Caput Algol

Astrology: Saturn and Jupiter
Metal: Lead
Stone: Diamond
Plant: Mugwort
Image: A severed head
Uses: Protect from harmful magick, revitalize the physical body

Elpheia

Astrology: Venus and Mars
Metal: Copper
Stone: Topaz
Plant: Rosemary
Image: A crowned person
Uses: Promote chastity, generate love and goodwill

Alchameth

Astrology: Mars and Jupiter
Metal: Iron
Stone: Jasper
Plant: Plantain
Image: A leaping wolf
Uses: Heals the blood, cools fevers

Cor Leonis (Regulus in Leo)

Astrology: Jupiter and Mars
Metal: Iron
Stones: Garnet or granite
Plants: Mastic, mugwort
Image: A cat sitting on a throne
Use: Generates a positive temperament

Cor Scorpii (Antares in Scorpio)

Astrology: Jupiter and Mars
Metal: Iron
Stone: Amethyst
Plant: Saffron
Image: Scorpion
Use: Drives away evil spirits

Vultur Cadens (Vega in Lyra)

Astrology: Venus and Mercury
Metal: Tin
Stone: Chrysolite
Plant: Succory
Image: A descending vulture
Use: Influence over animals and evil spirits

Cauda Capricorni

Astrology: Saturn and Mercury
Metal: Lead
Stone: Chalcedony
Plants: Catnip, marjoram
Image: Goat
Use: Increases material wealth

A modern symbol system I love to experiment with is the glyphs found in crop circles. No longer just simple circles, these glyphs have become complex geometric designs. Crop circles are geometric patterns in fields of grain that seem not to be made by a human agency, but appear as if the plants "grew" that way—swirled on their sides, even though they were upright the day before. Investigations of crop circles show that many of them, despite a few hoaxes, were not pushed down or flatted by people, animals, or anything else physical. I have a "piece" of a crop circle, a stalk of grain from the United Kingdom that my friend Leandra gave me, and it still retains an interesting energy and a sense of power. Crop circles have appeared in many places in the world, but seem to be most active in the county of Wiltshire in England.

Many people believe that interdimensional vortexes of energy form these mysterious geometric symbols, as a means of communicating with humanity. Some think of crop circles as communications from the planet Earth itself, while others think they are created by higher dimensional beings who are trying to awaken us to higher realms of information and spirit with the energy of these pictograms. These beings are referred to as the "circlemakers."

Many spiritual symbols have appeared in the crop circles, such as the Tree of Life glyph of the Qabalah. Other crop circle glyphs are less defined in meaning. I have found meditating on the glyphs to be quite empowering, and each seems to unlock a different meaning or insight for an individual. The glyphs are said to "awaken cellular and soul memory" and accelerate spiritual growth. I believe that once a practitioner has meditated on and attuned to a crop circle glyph, and the personal meaning of the glyph is clear, then it can be used in magick. The symbols can be drawn upon a piece of paper, wood, or stone and used as a talisman. They can be carved on candles for magick, or drawn in the air before you, like any other magickal symbol. Enterprising individuals and companies have seen fit to carve or paint these glyphs on stone, or make them into jewelry designs. Cleanse and empower these tools as you would any other tool to use them in your magick.

Pictured here are only a few crop circle glyphs (figure 41). More and more are created all the time. Websites and new books are chronicling the ever-expanding library of images. Explore to find the symbols that call to you for your own magick.

Figure 41: Crop Circle Glyphs

STONE MAGICK

Though the recent mass-market commercialization of stones and minerals in the New Age world makes crystal magick look like a modern fad, we find evidence of the spiritual use of stones from many times and lands, from the Stone Age shamans with their pebbles and quartz river stones to the ancient cultures that explored the virtues of exotic minerals. People have always been drawn to the power of stones. Our most enduring ancient monuments are stone cathedrals of the old world, from Stonehenge and Karnak to those lesser known yet still powerful stone circles. Evidence of the use of stones as talismans and amulets, to draw in beneficial forces or ward off unwanted energies, has been found in ancient India, Asia, Egypt, Greece, Rome, and the Middle East. In the New Age, we are once again drawn to the power of stones, and now have access to larger collections of minerals than ever before, due to modern transport and trade.

Each stone works by virtue of its vibration, its natural, inherent energy. A stone's chemical structure, color, and quality, and the geographic location where it was formed, all contribute to its overall vibration. Each crystal naturally resonates with certain subtle forces and can be used consciously or unconsciously to tap into those forces. The difference between people who simply carry rocks and those who do stone magick is that magicians are conscious of the relationship between themselves and the stone. There is a partnership. They are allies.

From the ascension perspective, all things, including crystals, have a consciousness. I found that very hard to believe at first, thinking stones were "just" rocks and not alive. Since then I've had many experiences with the personalities of stones, and I now feel they do have a sense of life. Though their own form of devic evolution is quite different from ours, crystals have a wisdom, knowledge, and personality. A wise stone magician lets the crystal pick her as much as she picks the crystal. You should try to work with the stone allies that already want to work with you. You will be drawn to the stones that you need to partner with.

The following is a list of stones and some of their general properties. Please keep in mind that each stone is unique, and your specimen might be aligned with a different intention than what is listed here. But in general, we know a lot about specific types of stones through both ancient lore and modern psychic communication with the stones.

Agate, Blue Lace: Blue lace agate is a very peaceful stone, used to connect to spiritual love and to speak your truth. It is also associated with Jupiter and can be used in prosperity and business magick.

Amber: Amber is a powerful talisman, sacred to both the Goddess and God. The resin is energetically versatile, being both projective and receptive. Associated with solar light, amber is used to increase energy, wealth, and inspiration and is a very strong protective stone.

Amethyst: Traditionally, amethyst is used to keep a clear head, particularly when dealing with the Otherworld. It can be used to facilitate psychic ability and spirit contact, and to bring a general sense of peace and well-being. Amethyst, due to its royal color, is a stone of wealth. It also helps break addictions.

Angelite: Angelite is primarily used to contact the angelic realm and invoke angelic protection.

Apatite: Apatite is a versatile stone, used to facilitate shifts between personal energy levels. It can curb cravings and bad habits and heal addictions. Green apatite, like many green stones, is used to facilitate faery contact.

Apopholite: Clarity is a keyword for apopholite, which can be used to clear both energy pathways and, for those with respiratory problems, breathing pathways. Vision, physical and psychic, is improved with apopholite.

Aragonite, Brown: The starburst structure of brown aragonite helps keep a person spiritually open while also remaining grounded. It teaches the user about the spiritual dimensions of the body and the sacredness of the physical world.

Aragonite, White: White aragonite helps align the upper chakras and aids in lightbody and merkaba activation.

Aventurine: Aventurine is a great Venusian stone of love, prosperity, and health. It is used to facilitate contact with the natural realm.

Azeztulite: Azeztulite is used to align oneself with higher vibrations and facilitate contact with angelic beings. It can also be used to activate the lightbody to ground expanded consciousness within the world.

Black Obsidian: A form of volcanic glass, black obsidian is used for protection and grounding. Aligned with the powers of Pluto, it can be used to add power to any form of magick, and grant wishes.

Calcite, Blue: Blue calcite encourages feelings of peace and tranquility and facilitates contact with the angelic realm.

Calcite, Green: Green calcite helps one see and remove blocks to love and self-esteem, heal, and connect with nature.

Calcite, Merkaba: This white form of calcite is used in all forms of ascension practices, to increase one s personal vibration and awaken to divinity on a deeper level of consciousness.

Calcite, White: White calcite aligns the crown chakra and helps one connect to higher guidance.

Carnelian: Carnelian helps one get in touch with physical energy and intuition and become stronger in the world.

Celestite: Celestite helps open the celestial gates to communicate with and journey to the higher realms of spirit.

Citrine: This form of yellow quartz is a high-energy stone of abundance, physical strength, inspiration, and healing. It brings solar energy into the energy body of the user, which can be expressed as divine love or joy.

Emerald: Emerald is a powerful heart healer and improves eyesight. It is used in magick for love, abundance, money, grounding, and communing with nature.

Fluorite: Fluorite is a great energy cleanser and recycler, removing unwanted forces from the aura and strengthening one's energetic shield.

Garnet: Garnet mixes the energy of earth and fire, grounding the warrior energy so one can stand strong in the world.

Hematite: Hematite is a useful stone for protection, grounding, and healing blood-related illnesses.

Herkimer Diamond: This double-terminated clear quartz aids in astral travel, psychic development, ascension meditations, and prosperity magick.

Holey Stone: Holey stones (stones with a naturally formed hole in them) are used to view faeries and otherworldly beings by gazing through the hole. They are sometimes referred to as hag stones.

Jet: Jet absorbs all harmful energy, creating a powerful force for protection. It is also used for grounding and, as an organic substance transformed, for recalling past-life memories, particularly when those memories are of trauma.

Kunzite: Kunzite is used to clear the energy field of unwanted forced and attachments. It is used to open the throat chakra in particular.

Labradorite: A beautiful, high-energy stone, labradorite is used in a variety of practices to raise one's vibration, open to psychic ability, or awaken unseen forces within a person.

Lapis Lazuli: A stone of the Goddess, lapis lazuli is used to encourage prosperity, love, and intuitive ability.

Lepidolite: Lepidolite helps tranquilize nervous and traumatized people and can be used to open a person to happiness and joy.

Malachite: Malachite is an excellent grounding stone that does not close one down to psychic awareness, as hematite is prone to do. It leaves one strong but openhearted in the world. Malachite is also used for prosperity and general physical healing magick.

Moldavite: A silicon-based tektite, this green stone is used to connect the Earth to the heavens, and is associated particularly with E.T. beings.

Moonstone: Moonstone opens the psychic gates and attunes the belly chakra to the natural tides of life. It gets us in touch with our feminine intuitive and creative self.

Moss Agate: Moss agate is used to attune oneself to nature, to the faery realm in particular. It is also used to heal skin ailments.

Onyx: A powerful grounding stone, onyx also helps alleviate grief when in mourning, whether due to a physical death or a change of self or environment.

Pearl: Like moonstone and selenite, pearl is connected to the Moon and the oceans, stimulating psychic ability and one's feminine nature.

Peridot: Peridot is a strong love stone that is used to open and heal the heart chakra.

Phencite: Phencite is said to be one of the highest-vibrating stones on the planet, if not *the* highest-vibrating stone. It is used to activate all ascension and lightbody processes for consciousness evolution.

Pyrite: Known as fool's gold, pyrite helps us remove blocks to our self-esteem that prevent us from manifesting prosperity and wealth.

Quartz, Clear: Clear quartz is the great all-purpose stone. It amplifies whatever intention you put into it, like a magnifying glass refracting sunlight passing through it.

Quartz, Rose: Rose quartz holds the vibration of love and can be used in all magick with a loving intent, but healing in particular.

Ruby: Ruby is a stone of fire, conferring energy, passion, sexuality, and vitality to the user.

Selenite: A fragile stone of the Moon, selenite connects us to our Moon self beyond the veil, aiding in psychic ability, past-life recall, and working with spirits.

Sugilite: Sugilite is a powerful psychic stone, awakening us to the power of dreams, intuition, and higher dimensions.

Tiger's-eye: Tiger's-eye is a stone of grounding and abundance, helping us manifest our ideas in the world.

Tourmaline: Tourmaline directs energy in a linear fashion, following the growth of the crystal. Each color relates to clearing the corresponding chakra. Black tourmaline in particular is known to be very grounding and protective.

Turquoise: Turquoise is a great all-purpose stone, used for all forms of healing and magick. It is used to ease communication and bring peace, protection, and spirit contact.

To use a stone consciously, cleanse and consecrate it (see exercise 2 in chapter 6) as you would any other ritual tool. As with any tool, you are in partnership with the stone. Your consecration is a way of instructing it to behave in a way you require for your magick. More than any other magickal tool, crystals are described like computers, in terms of taking our programs, our thoughts and intentions, and fulfilling our instructions. Crystals take our programs and fulfill them, amplifying the energy like a magnifying glass focuses light. Here are some of the programs I use, based on information given to me by crystal teacher Hari Das Melchizedek.

I charge this crystal to work in accord with the Seed Blueprint for Life.
I charge this crystal to activate all powers upon command consciously asked for by the user.
I charge this crystal to activate all powers that are subconsciously needed by the user.
I charge this crystal to activate and deactivate upon command.
I charge this crystal to direct and amplify my will in accord with its nature.
I charge this crystal to be self-cleansing.

I charge this crystal to be "fixed" so that no one may change the programs unless they are for the highest good, harming none. So mote it be.

When I say "the Seed Blueprint for Life," I visualize the Flower of Life (see chapter 21) as the fundamental symbol of creation. It's another way of saying "for the highest good" or "in accord with divine will."

After cleansing the stone, hold it in your hands or up to your third eye and simply think each of these program commands. Wait a moment after each one, and listen to see if the stone accepts it. A stone might not accept a program, or it might make it clear to you that it doesn't want to be programmed or perhaps even work with you. You might get a clear message that you are the guardian of the stone, but you are to pass it on to someone else. The stone might even tell you whom to give it to.

Though many of us are tempted to run out and buy a large number of stones, I suggest that you choose a small number and work with them intimately before you expand your repertoire. It's as easy to have a lot of stones as it is to have a lot of friends, yet if you never take the time to develop a relationship, it will never grow deeper. A good crystal mage can do a lot with a small number of stones if they are working together in partnership. I suggest you work with perhaps five, seven, or twelve stones of different types and colors to start. Meditate with them. Carry them around with you. Feel their energy. You might be extremely sensitive to stones, or oblivious to them. I was drawn tactilely and visually to stones, but had a hard time feeling the energy everybody else talked about. I had to meditate to feel the energy more clearly, and have an understanding of what a stone could or couldn't do with me. Once you have a handle on the first group of stones, add more to your collection, unless you have a specific need and feel moved to search out a specific mineral to aid you in that need.

You might find that certain stones work exceptionally well together, finding a synergy when placed together for a common intention. Traditional folk magick charms are created by choosing a cloth bag in a color based on the intention and placing in it an assortment of stones, herbs, oils, minerals, bones, and other materials. You can create a similar magickal device with just stones. The crystal company Heaven & Earth (see the bibliography) offers specially prepared bags and necklaces of such stones in combination. If you have more herbal knowledge, you can add herbs or incense mixes to the bag. You can even modify the formulas for the ray sprays (see chapter 13) and make them into charm bags. Here are some suggestions to fuel your creativity and get you started.

Ascension/Merkaba/Lightbody Activation (white bag)

Moldavite

Phencite

Merkaba calcite

Herkimer diamond

Clear quartz

Chakra Balancing (black bag)

Garnet

Carnelian

Citrine

Emerald or rose quartz

Turquoise

Amethyst

Quartz

Energy Increase (yellow, gold, or orange bag)

Citrine

Ruby

Carnelian

Amber

Grounding (black or brown bag)

Tiger's-eye

Jet

Black tourmaline

Brown aragonite

Onyx

Malachite

Healing (green bag)

Green tourmaline

Kyanite

Kunzite

Rose quartz

Joy (pink, yellow, or white bag, or whatever your favorite color is)

Citrine

Rose quartz

Lepidolite (or lithium silicate or lithium quartz)

Love (green or pink bag)

Rose quartz

Aventurine

Emerald

Peridot

Citrine

Blue lace agate

Past-Life Remembrance (black bag)

Selenite

Fossil

Jet

Prosperity (gold or blue bag)

Lapis lazuli

Pyrite

Amber

Protection (black bag)

Hematite

Black obsidian

Black tourmaline

Jet

Turquoise

Fluorite

Psychic Awakening (indigo, purple, or violet bag)

Sugilite

Amethyst

Lapis lazuli

Moonstone

Pearl

Spirit Contact (indigo, purple, or white bag)

Selenite

Labradorite

Celestite

Warrior Energy (red or black bag)

Ruby

Garnet

Hematite

PSYCHIC PROTECTION SPELL

One of the most needed and requested spells by practitioners of magick and healing is one of psychic protection. In a desire to be of service to others, we often have poor energetic boundaries, along with a heightened sensitivity, and find ourselves taking on the energy of the people and places around us.

While other meditations have you simply visualize a protection shield as a bubble or barrier, this spell helps you really reinforce boundaries if you are having difficulties and little success with the traditional shield. Mastering the LBRP or the merkaba meditation (see chapters 9 and 21, respectively) is also extremely helpful.

Make sure that wherever you are working, you have enough space to create a circle around you physically, which will act as your boundary. If you can do it outside, all the better. For this spell, you will need something to represent the four elements. For the water element, you can use water, in a ritual cup or bowl. For fire, you can use a candle or lamp—anything that will hold a sustained flame. Black, white, or gray candles also work well. For air, any high-vibrational incense will do. And for earth, you can use stones/crystals, salt, or sand, depending on if you are outside or inside. If outside, you can use sand or soil, or salt. Don't use the salt on fertile land with plants growing on it. If inside, you can use rocks or crystals. Have at least twelve of them.

Defensive and protective magick falls in the sphere of the warriors of the first ray, the chohan El Morya, and the archangels Michael and Chamuel. Call upon them to aid you.

Ask for their help and guidance in setting your protection shield. I also like to call upon the four traditional quarter angels—Uriel, Raphael, Michael, and Gabriel—to act as guards, to anchor my shield. You can do the LBRP before starting the ritual, if you desire.

Start by cleansing and consecrating your candle for protection. Light it and walk around your area in a clockwise circle. Make the circle big enough that you feel comfortable in this bubble. Envision a ring of flames around you. Do the same with the incense, cleansing and consecrating it for protection. Light it and create a ring of smoke around you. Then sprinkle water around the circle. Lastly, either sprinkle the sand or salt, or place the twelve stones in a circle around you. Sit in the center of the circle, and close your eyes. Get into a light meditative state. Envision the angels and masters helping rebuild your energetic boundaries, out of an elastic energetic material that allows wanted energies in, yet blocks harmful energies. Imagine the material like a translucent Teflon.

When done, thank the masters and angels. Extinguish your candle and incense. Pour out your water. Dismantle your stone circle, if you made one, and go about your life confident of your strengthened energetic boundaries. If you are experiencing a trying time in your life, you might need to repeat this spell regularly until the crisis is over.

BANISHMENT OF UNWANTED FORCES

Like the psychic protection spell, banishing spells come in quite handy. Often called uncrossing spells, they are used when someone, or something, has crossed our path and put what we might consider a curse on us, consciously or unconsciously. When we feel like we are having a long bout of bad luck, depression, illness, or injury for no apparent reason, we could be the target of unhealthy energies. We might not be aware of the situation, or if the source of the problem is a specific person, that individual might not even be aware of it.

The transmutation of unwanted forces definitely falls under the jurisdiction of the seventh ray, the chohan Saint Germain, all magician and alchemist figures, and the archangels Tzadkiel and Uriel.

Place 7 drops of lavender essential oil in a bowl of pure water. Add the peels of any citrus fruit; orange is very appropriate. Then, if possible, place the petals of a white flower—any white flower—in the water. Mix in a handful of sea salt or kosher salt, dissolving it in the water. Salt is a purifying substance. Ask the spirits of the lavender, orange, white flower, and salt to aid you in the cleansing and healing of your home, office, self, or whatever it is that you wish to cleanse. Fill the water with violet flame, calling upon Saint Germain and Tzadkiel through a decree of the seventh ray (see chapter 13). If you have a seventh-ray spray, you can use that with, or in place of, this wash.

Sprinkle this water throughout the house, from top to bottom. Using your fingertips, lightly splash it on the walls, floor, and ceiling of every room. Do the basement too. End at either the front door or the back door, and imagine all the unwanted energies that will not transmute leaving the building completely. Pour the remaining water on the steps of the back door and front door, to attract balanced and harmonious forces to your home.

LiFEMATE LOVE SPELL

If protection is the main reason people visit a magickal practitioner, then love and money have to be the next two most popular reasons. Many lightworkers are searching for their twin flame, their ideal mate who matches their interest in spirituality and service. I prefer to use the term lifemate, rather than twin flame or soul mate, because I don't think such matches necessarily have to be romantic life partners. I always recommend that all love magick be done to ask for the "person that is correct for me at this time" or, when you are ready for it, "the person who is to be my lifemate in this incarnation." Please keep in mind that perhaps not everybody has a perfect lifemate in this lifetime, or that just because you are ready, your lifemate might not yet be.

Patrons to aid you in this spell are almost all Goddess figures. The Goddess embodies the receptive, magnetic aspect of creation. Our myths of love goddesses still play a significant role in our collective images of the enchantress and sensual woman. Aphrodite, Venus, Inanna, Ishtar, and Astarte are all wonderful patrons of love.

Many see Lady Venus as an ascended master, and a perfect patron for this work. The planet Venus is associated with both the fourth ray, Qabalistically, and the fifth ray, Theosophically. For love workings, the fourth ray seems more appropriate. Haniel is the archangel associated with Venus, while Gabriel is the messenger of the heart and is associated with the element of water.

For this ritual you will need rose petals, fresh or dry, 2 candles of green or pink, 1 white candle, and an oil that smells romantic, sexy, or sensual to you. Cast your magick circle, and call upon Lady Venus to aid you. Cleanse the candles. To manifest whatever you desire, hold the white candle and think about the abundance of the universe. Think about Lady Venus and her ability to bring lovers together. Light the white candle. Take the first green or pink candle, anoint it with the oil, and consecrate it for yourself. Think of all your positive attributes, and how good you are feeling about yourself. Light it with the flame of the first white candle, and place it on one side of your workspace or altar. Take the second candle, anoint it, and then think of all the qualities you want in a lifemate. Choose the most important ones, keeping it open enough to let the universe manifest the right person for you. For example, I wouldn't designate hair color or eye color, because those things are not important to me; qualities like intelligence, emotional availability, and spirituality are. Next, light the candle from the white flame, and place it on the other end of the workspace. Hold both candles, one in each hand, and imagine you and your lifemate coming together. Say:

> In the name of Lady Venus, I ask that my lifemate and I come together, for the highest good, harming none. Now. So mote it be.

Bring the candles together, and let the two flames intermingle—two separate flames that can burn as one, yet remain separate, whole, and distinct. Put the two candles down next to each other and let them burn. Sprinkle the rose petals clockwise around the two candles, making a circle of petals around them.

Release the circle, and let the candles burn out. If they need to be put out, snuff them and relight them later until they burn away.

PROSPERITY SPELL

Working on abundance consciousness in regard to money is a recurring theme among ascensionists. It seems like we tend to be on one side of the equation: having money, but feeling like we are not fulfilling our life purpose, or not having money, but following our bliss. It is possible to do both. Much of our negative programming about money stems from the idea that to be spiritual, we must be poor and renounce the world, or that prosperous spiritual people are frauds. Neither of these is true. One really has nothing to do with the other. While some paths require you to take a vow of asceticism, ascension does not, unless you personally feel it's necessary. Ascension works the wisdom of all paths. I come from a tradition that is about the middle path, having neither too little nor too much, but living a physically comfortable existence in which money should not be a source of stress. That is the ideal I try to teach to spiritual seekers. Many of us have past-life vows to poverty that we are trying to break in this lifetime.

There are no masters specifically concerned with prosperity, as that was not a concern for the early Theosophists, at least in their writings. Blavatsky's work took a definitive turn away from practical occultism after *Isis Unveiled* to the more Eastern aesthetic of *The Secret Doctrine*. The green ray is linked with prosperity and growth, as magickally green is the color of money. The prosperity flame is green with gold, which can be visualized for this magick. Saint Germain, the alchemist with the ability to change lead into gold and transmute the flaws within gems, could also be a patron. Of all the masters, he probably lived the most decadent earthly life before he ascended. In ritual magick, Jupiter is the planet of abundance and prosperity, and it rules the second ray, so Kuthumi could also be a patron to call upon in this ritual. The archangel Uriel, as the angel of the element of earth, is also a patron of material wealth.

This spell calls for the use of citrine, a stone of material abundance and wealth. Some say that citrine is of such a high energy that it never needs to be cleansed. I still cleanse it anyway, just to be safe. Citrine is aligned with the Sun, a planet for success and good fortune on all levels. The Sun's colors are yellow and gold, like the stone we will be using. The Sun is linked with Tiphereth, the sphere of beauty.

Cast your magick circle. I prefer a terrestrially aligned elemental circle, to make my wealth manifest in the physical world. King Ghob, as the ruler of the earth element, can also be quite helpful in the manifestation of wealth. Gnomes and dwarves are said to dig within the earth for riches. When you have your circle cast and you are in sacred space, cleanse your citrine and program it for material wealth. If you have a specific, tangible goal in mind, then make that part of the program.

Hold the citrine up to the sky. Chant the god name for the sphere of Tiphereth (Yud –Heh-Vavh-Heh El-oh-ah V-dah-aht) at least four times. Imagine the sacred circle filling with golden light. Feel the power of the circle grow, almost bursting at the seams. Imagine yourself surrounded with whatever material possessions and resources you desire. Make the wealth a reality in your mind.

After a few moments of intense consecration, gather up the energy with your mind and imagine pushing it out of the top of the circle in a burst of light, creating a cone of power to manifest your wish. Use the Goddess position to release the energy and the God position to reflect (see figure 30 on page 258), then ground the remaining energy of the circle. Release the quarters and the circle, and know that your manifestation will occur in a timely manner.

CAREER SPELL

One area of life that most lightworkers struggle with is career. It can be difficult having strong spiritual values and an understanding of energy, yet living and working in a society that mostly ignores the concepts of subtle energy and consciousness expansion. We often don't do well in office politics and on the corporate ladder. Even when we do, playing by the rules of the societal group, we may feel unfulfilled or inauthentic.

Unfortunately for us at times, but fortunately for the rest of the world, we are often called into situations to stimulate growth and change, even on a subconscious level. Though it can be difficult for us, bringing our spiritual life into whatever we do (not necessarily overtly, but energetically) can inspire others to live more authentically and expand their own viewpoints. When I worked in the business world, I was pretty open about being a witch, doing meditation and celebrating seasonal holidays through ritual with my coven. I know that made me seem a bit crazy to my co-workers, but eventually they saw a guy who was good at his job, together, stable, and caring, and who happened to be a witch. That helped them realize that such people are not crazy, but simply a part of society, like any sect of Christian, Jew, or Muslim. My approach to business decisions in meetings was never win/lose, but instead I tried to find a win/win situation for all involved by offering the best possible services and products. I know that made me naive in the eyes of some of my co-workers, but it was another attempt to apply my spiritual and ethical beliefs.

Career magick, as opposed to just getting a job to simply get money, is associated with dharma. Though there are different interpretations of dharma in the various Eastern traditions, to me, dharma has always been the flip side of karma. Karma is the result of your actions when you are not aligned with your divine will, your true purpose. It is described as the debt and credit you exchange with others in life. Your true will in life is your dharma. When you do your dharma, the result is more dharma. When we want to clear all karma, good and bad, we seek to be in a place of balance, in our dharma. Often our dharma can take us in a direction that our personal will and ego might not enjoy, but that direction serves our higher purpose. Discovering our true vocation in the world is a part of finding our dharma.

Esoterically, Jupiter and the Qabalistic sphere of Chesed are about our true will. While the Sun in astrology represents our personal self, the planet Jupiter is the higher octave of the Sun, manifesting our higher self. Herbs and plants like cinnamon and cloves, baking spices, are aligned with Jupiter, along with the colors blue and purple and the metal tin.

The archangel of Jupiter is Tzadkiel. In this ritual we call upon Tzadkiel to align us with our dharma, our true purpose. For this you will need a blue or purple candle, cinnamon powder, and olive oil. This spell is best done on a waxing Moon.

Cast your magick circle and call upon the four archangels of the quarters. Call upon archangel Tzadkiel to be present in your circle. Ask Tzadkiel to aid you in understanding and manifesting your dharma here and now, particularly in the area of your career and vocation. Take the candle and cleanse it. Then carve into the candle the symbol of Jupiter and the word "DHARMA," in Theban script, to align with the angels (figure 42).

Hold the candle and think about finding your true purpose and vocation. Anoint the candle with a dab of olive oil, then sprinkle cinnamon on the candle. Light it and let it burn. Make sure the surface under the candle and candle holder is flameproof, in case sparks of cinnamon fall from the candle. Release the circle as you normally would.

Figure 42: Jupiter Symbol and the Word "DHARMA" in Theban on a Candle

As with any candle spell, let the flame burn as long as possible, and if you must put it out, snuff it and relight it again later until it burns completely. You will soon be guided to your purpose in life at this time, through the messages of the archangel Tzadkiel. Meditation and journaling afterward are highly desirable, as the message might come to you during those introspective moments.

15

HEALING MAGICK

Out of all the magickal arts, ascensionists seem most concerned about the path of healing. In fact, many lightworkers who claim never to do spells, still do healing work that could be considered spellcraft. Many of us come to esoterics either through an interest in holistic health, feeling that there is something missing from conventional medicine, or through a personal healing crisis, be it physical, emotional, mental, or spiritual, and find aid through nontraditional sources. Lightworkers are called to bring light to the darkness in terms of personal healing, and study a variety of healing techniques to aid themselves and others on the healing path. Like the mystics and witches of old, they are torchbearers into the mysteries of life, helping us face the darkness within and, through this search, find wholeness.

All forms of healing are magick. If magick is creating change in accord with your divine will, then a healer helps you align with your divine self, your primal pattern of true health, restoring a greater portion of the divine perfection that is already inherent in you. Through this process, what appear to be miracles can happen, on a physical and spiritual level. In essence, a healer is truly meant to be a healing facilitator, one who empowers the individual to find healing, one who aids, suggests options, and facilitates the process. Many people come to the magician, witch, priestess, or healer in hope of finding a miracle cure, and put their faith in another individual. We do the same thing with our doctors and clinical professionals, and their words often hold a magickal weight. If a doctor tells a patient that he will die within a year, usually that is a self-fulfilling prophecy if the patient believes it. Likewise, a doctor who predicts a cure will often manifest that cure. Healers can hold the same power, yet it's our responsibility to educate our clients that the true source of healing is really our divine source. A healer, counselor, or even doctor can only help the process along, but ultimately we cure ourselves.

Through this lens, we discover that many techniques we have used before, that we don't think of as magick, really are forms of magick. Chakra balancing, energy work, Reiki, tai chi, and even conscious deep breathing can be acts of magick. If they alter your health in accord with your will, then you are doing magick. You are acting with intention.

The matter of healing is not a black and white issue. Many people assume that all healing is "good" or necessary and could never do any harm. Magick is power, a force directed by will, and unless that will is tempered by wisdom, by divine will, the best of intentions can still cause harm. In some forms of magick, divided into black and white, healing magick is considered gray, because while black magick is done to harm, white magick is done to find enlightenment, to connect to your higher self. Magick used for change, for manifestation, even healing, is considered gray. And it is a gray area for all of us.

Many healers believe that the higher self, soul, or monad of an individual, the keeper of the person's higher will, requires the individual to experience particular illnesses or injuries for personal growth. That experience is simply the best "teacher" to expand the consciousness of that individual. It's not a punishment. Healing is the process of understanding this higher will, and when the "lesson" is understood, then the healing can more easily take place. If the individual is not aligned to his or her higher nature, then nothing you do to heal the person will be of any benefit. Some healers, whose egos are invested in the cure of their clients, will force their personal will upon the client. Though they might physically cure the illness, the result will not be beneficial to the person's overall incarnation. Sometimes healing does not result in a physical cure. Sometimes healing is allowing someone to suffer, and offering compassion and support and, when necessary, aid to cross over from this world to the next. A true spiritual healer is aligned with divine will, not ego will, to create a cure.

Sometimes we get attached to the outcome of our healing magick because we are working on a friend or family member whom we love. Most healers suggest that we don't work on family and friends, just as a counselor wouldn't offer professional services to a family member or friend. In an effort to help a loved one, our ego gets involved and becomes more of a hindrance than a help. I know that was my experience when I first got involved in healing with the Reiki system. I took a Reiki class because my mother was experiencing pain in her leg from an injury, and nothing magickal or medicinal was helping her. Though the Reiki treatment gave her some temporary relief, my ego and my desire to make her better, rather than an unattached desire to facilitate her process along with my inexperience, got in the way of her healing. When she was able to work with others outside of her family, she started on a path of true healing in regard to her leg pain issues.

Like other forms of spellcasting, one way of attempting to avoid imposing your personal will on a situation is to ask that the spell be done "for the highest good" or "harming none" or "in accord with divine will." Then, in the worst-case scenario, your magick, if unneeded or unwanted from a higher level, will simply dissipate. I have a friend who says, "I ask that if the chosen recipient is not open to his healing, that these energies will go to wherever they will do the most good." Healing magick, like all magick, should be done in this spirit of divine will. Most of us have a predisposition to heal when we are ill or injured, as health and balance are our natural states of being, and most of the time, magickal energy will aid that process.

HEALING RELEASE

One of the most important aspects of the healing process to understand is that of the "healing awareness," "healing release," or "healing crisis." Healing facilitators usually describe this to a client as an awareness or release, but when you are experiencing it, it feels like a crisis.

When you embark upon a path of emotional, mental, and spiritual healing, the healing techniques don't necessarily make unresolved issues, feelings, and thoughts go away, but they do aid you in processing these emotions and memories, to eventually integrate them into a healthy self-image and reap the blessings from the difficulties. Through the process, your body, heart, and mind can struggle with the conscious desire to release an unhealthy pattern, and attempt to hold on to the unhealthy pattern. Rather than experiencing a gradual reduction of the problem to be healed, from a strong emotion or thought to physical illness and pain, the symptoms intensify. The unwanted pattern doesn't want to let go and, on some level, hopes to win a battle of wills with your conscious self. If you learn to process the pattern, the intensity of the symptoms will diminish and eventually you will be able to release the pattern completely.

If a person seeks relief from back pain, then the healing crisis might involve greater back pain, until the individual eventually experiences a release and then further recovery. If the issue involves fear, anger, anxiety, jealousy, or pride, then those feelings might intensify until they are eventually released. Many people find the most difficult and profound healing releases to be related to past-life issues, which can be worked on with a skilled regression therapist, who can help you make contact with the life and process the karmic energies from the past that are affecting you here and now. An understanding and awareness of healing release on many levels, from this life and past incarnations, is critical for those on the healing path.

Usually such a healing awareness is a sign that the modality is working and should be continued. If it involves physical or psychological issues, the expert care of a medical professional, ideally one open to alternative therapies complementing traditional ones, should be sought out. Doing breathing exercises, meditation, journaling, and traditional counseling are all ways to facilitate the release of issues on all levels.

HEALING MASTERS

The most prudent step a person can take on the path of healing is to connect with an inner-plane healer and teacher. You should have a healing guide to facilitate your own healing experiences in your personal life, and if you choose to work healing magick with others, then you should have a guide, and backup, in your service to others. The healing masters can offer not only wisdom, information, and guidance, but also pure healing energy, protection, courage, and new abilities.

Many ascended beings have experienced the vocation of healing in lifetimes past, and are capable of granting aid to us now. The Lords and Ladies of Shamballa are said to have their own "department" devoted to aiding humanity's healing. Brought to us through the work of Machaelle Small Wright, the department is known as MAP, which stands for the Medical Assistance Program of the Great White Brotherhood. Ascended masters Lorporis and Luciar are said to head this department of Shamballa. If you decide to contact this group through conscious intention, then you will be assigned a MAP team of ascended masters specializing in healing. Through this system, you connect with your team in a four-point "coning" field of energy, along with your higher self, the Overlighting Deva of Healing, and Pan with his nature spirits. For more information on this specific system, read Wright's book of the same name, *MAP*.

I've found that the most helpful experience is to meet your own healing guides and develop a relationship with them as you train in healing magick.

Exercise 17:
Meeting Your Healing Guides

Repeat Exercise 4: Visiting with the Masters, but ask specifically to meet a master of healing, or your entire healing team. Ask them how you can work with them for your own healing and, if you feel called to the path of the healing facilitator, how you can help others.

Some in the ascension paradigm experience a spontaneous "rewiring" of their energy system, either for personal healing, due to all the high energies they channel, which their body is not always physically prepared for, or to aid their ability to channel energy for others and to communicate with their healing guides more efficiently. This experience occurs in meditation, journey, or dream. They are rewired by their masters and healers. This modern sense of wires reminds me of the old faery lore of being "re-veined," with greenery and sap running through the veins, placed there by those who are initiated into the faery healing traditions. In both situations, the initiate of the inner-plane healing tradition is having something human and terrestrial replaced with something otherworldly, in an effort to create a connection, a sympathy, with the other realm from which the person draws his or her healing energies and powers. This is similar to the classic initiation of the shamanic healer, who is taken apart by the spirits of the Otherworld and put back together with some "new" component, like a stone or bone. Don't be surprised if you feel called to the healing path and experience a similar rewiring from your healing guides.

THE CHAKRA SYSTEM

Along with the ascension soul anatomy of the monad, oversoul, and soul, the four-body system, and the Egyptian concept of the soul, ascension healers work deeply with the chakra system. Chakra, a term from India, is translated as "spinning wheel" and refers to vortexes of energy, spinning like wheels in the body. Chakras act as spiritual organs, processing subtle energies much the same way our physical organs process food and waste.

Most chakra systems depict seven main chakras, starting at the base of the spine, also known as the root chakra, and moving up through the belly, solar plexus, heart, throat, brow, and crown chakras (figure 43). Like the colors of the rainbow, the base chakra is red, rising up through orange, yellow, green, blue, indigo, and (white) violet (chart 9). Other minor chakras are recognized in the hands, fingertips, armpits, soles of the feet, knees, and other joints or nerve clusters. Each of the seven main chakras is associated with a state of consciousness as well as specific glands and organs in the physical body. When an illness occurs in a particular body part, then it is believed that a corresponding imbalance will be found in the related chakra. Each chakra is also associated with a subtle body, expanding on the four-body system and dividing it into seven, similar to the seven planes of reality—physical, etheric, astral, emotional, mental, psychic, and divine.

Modern lore has expanded the main seven chakras in two ways. Some systems place additional chakras in between the seven main chakras. If you imagine the seven main chakras as the seven keys on a piano scale, from C to C, then the "new" chakras are the five black keys on the piano, giving us twelve chakra centers in all (figure 44). Some teachings say these "new" chakras have always been there, but are now playing an important role in our life as our consciousness becomes more subtle and refined. Other teachings say that they have recently come online, and had not been active and present in the human body before now.

Other chakras are visualized above and below the body (figure 45). If the central tube of the chakras (known as the sushumna, pranic tube, or antakarana) extended out infinitely, there would be chakra systems above and below us, like higher and lower octaves on the piano, representing levels of consciousness we've evolved out of below us, and are evolving up and into, above us. Many look at the antakarana, when fully formed, as connecting us down to the center of the Earth's core and up through the Sun and into dimensional gateways, to the galactic core. These higher chakras are related to the higher rays in terms of color. Some healers believe that these higher chakras will eventually "drop" into the body, displacing the traditional chakras, which will descend further down the pranic tube and into the Earth. Some ascension teachings tell us that the main seven chakras are going to unite into a harmonious whole energy center, known as the unified chakra. Though an intriguing idea, I'm not sure I agree.

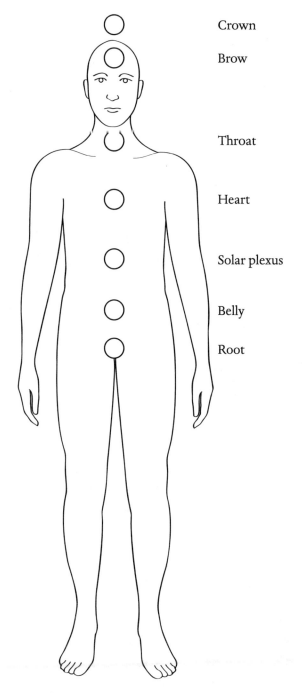

Crown

Brow

Throat

Heart

Solar plexus

Belly

Root

Figure 43: Chakra System

	Earth Star	Root	Lower Abdomen	Belly	Upper Abdomen	Solar Plexus	Heart
Functions:	Grounding	Survival	Balance	Instinct	Discipline	Power	Personal love
Subtle Body:	Physical	Physical	Etheric	Etheric	Astral	Astral	Emotional
Glands:	None	Ovaries, gonads	Ovaries, gonads	Pancreas		Adrenal	Thymus
Body Systems:	None	Reproductive, excretory	Reproductive	Lower digestive, skeletal	Connection between upper and lower digestive systems	Upper digestive, musculature	Circulatory, immune
Organs:	Legs, feet, toes, DNA	Sex organs, colon, anus, legs, feet, skin, DNA	Sex organs, kidneys	Intestines, spleen, kidneys	Stomach, intestines	Liver, stomach, gallbladder	Heart, veins, blood, skin, arteries, lymph nodes, arms, hands
Illnesses:	Genetic illness, body-wide illness, all life-threatening illnesses	Sexual dysfunction, infertility, genetic illness, colon cancer, venereal disease	Sexual dysfunction	Ulcers, kidney infection/stones, pancreatic illness, hypertension	Digestive ailments	Hyperactivity, chronic fatigue, stomach disease, liver disease	Heart disease, blood-pressure, imbalance, chronic illness, colds, flu, viral/bacterial infections, diabetes

Imbalances:	Feeling disconnected from the planet, ungroundedness, lacking a connection to history, family, or nation	Ungroundedness, depression, lack of pleasure, suicidal impulses, betrayal, sexual or gender shame	Imbalanced emotions, disconnect between sex and love	Stress, inability to trust, difficulty relating to others, sense of not fitting in, nervousness	Too low or too high personal energy, clumsiness, awkwardness	Abuses of power, fear, poor self-image, control issues, ego issues, giving away power, anger, addictions	Shame, guilt, fear, inability to form relationships, selfishness, dislike of physical contact
Learning:	Connection to the planet, evolution, learning from the past	Learn to be in the physical world, pleasure, grounding	Learn to connect sexual energy to intimacy	Learn to trust self and others, form societal and sexual relationships	Learn self-control, discipline, the proper use of power	Find personal power, learn to control self and not others, learn to express anger in a healthy manner	Learn to love, empathy, compassion, self-love
Colors:	Brown, black	Red	Red-orange	Orange	Gold	Yellow	Green
Musical Tones:	B	C	C#/Db	D	D#/Eb	E	F
Healing Stones:	Smoky quartz, black tourmaline, brown aragonite, jet	Garnet, ruby, zincite	Red calcite, orange calcite	Carnelian, moonstone	Pyrite, golden calcite	Citrine, yellow calcite	Emerald, rose quartz, watermelon tourmaline, green fluorite, malachite

Chart 9: Chakra Correspondences (continued on next page)

	Higher Heart	Throat	Brain Stem	Brow (Third Eye)	Back of Head	Crown	Soul Star
Functions:	Unconditional love	Expression	Dreams	Vision	Understanding	Spirituality	Evolution
Subtle Body:	Emotional	Mental	Psychic	Psychic	Psychic, divine	Divine	Divine
Glands:	Thymus	Thyroid	Pineal	Pineal	Pineal, pituitary	Pituitary	Not in the body
Body Systems:	Immune	Respiratory	Nervous	Nervous	Nervous	Nervous, endocrine	None
Organs:	Lymph nodes	Throat, ears, teeth, mouth, larynx, lungs, vocal cords, trachea, tonsils	Brain stem	Lower brain, eyes, nerve tissue	Upper brain, spinal cord	Upper brain, glands, skin, spinal cord	None
Illnesses:	Autoimmune disorders	High/low metabolism; hormone imbalance; throat, mouth, tooth, and lung disease; asthma; laryngitis; loss of breath; bronchitis	Nervous disorders	Visual impairment, headaches, nervous disorders	Nervous disorders, mental imbalances	Hormone imbalances, autoimmune and environmental illnesses, all body-wide illnesses	None

Imbalances:	Blocks to self-love, forgiveness, and loving others	Fear of speaking up, gossip, silence, inability to listen	Self-sabotage, letting the unconscious mind run your life	Inability to see the world clearly, lack of vision, inability to realize potential, illusions, delusions	Blocks to understanding one's true purpose, confusion about one's purpose	Feeling of separation, lack of spiritual experience, no belief in divinity domination of the physical over al	None
Learning:	Learning compassion for self and others	Learn to speak and listen, creative expression, listen to guidance, act on higher will	Conscious dreaming, intuition, opening to the true nature of reality, shadow work	Learn to access visionary and psychic abilities, intuition	Understanding sacred geometry, understanding one's personal visions and true purpose	Learn to connect to the divine, inspiration, bliss, wholeness, spiritual insight	Evolution and ascension
Colors:	Blue-green	Blue	Deep blue, indigo	Indigo, purple	Magenta, violet	White violet	Dazzling white
Musical Tones:	F#/Gb	G	G#/Ab	A	A#/Bb	B	C
Healing Stones:	Turquoise, aquamarine, blue aragonite, infinite	Turquoise, lapis, sodalite, kyanite, sapphire, azurite	Amethyst, sugilite, tektite, labradorite, spectrolite	Amethyst, lepidolite, moonstone, selenite, purple fluorite	Amethyst, selenite, labradorite, spectrolite, celestite	Quartz, opal, diamond, selenite, white calcite, danburite	All stones

Chart 9: Chakra Correspondences (continued)

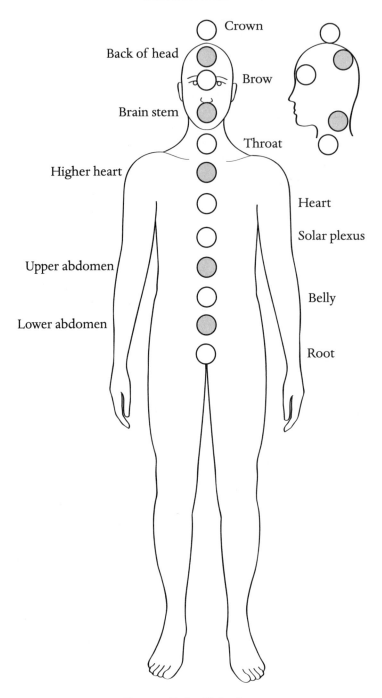

Figure 44: Twelve-Chakra System

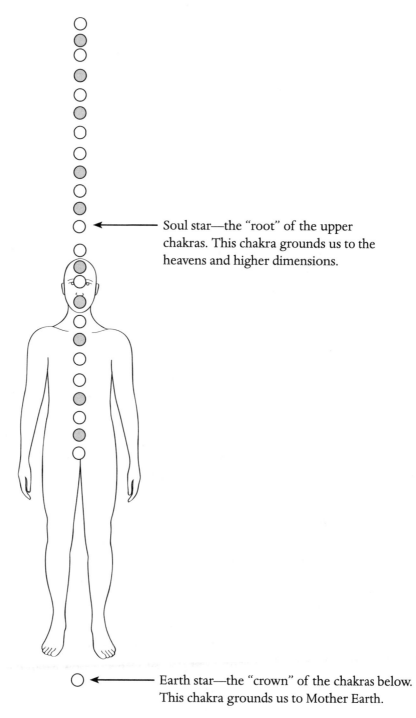

Soul star—the "root" of the upper chakras. This chakra grounds us to the heavens and higher dimensions.

Earth star—the "crown" of the chakras below. This chakra grounds us to Mother Earth.

Figure 45: Extended Chakras

Try this simple chakra exercise focusing on the seven main energy centers. You can use it to clear and balance your energy system, promoting overall health and well-being. Once you have a greater familiarity with the seven main chakras, you can expand the exercise to include chakra points in between, above, and below. Understanding subtle anatomy, and the levels of consciousness associated with each part of the body, is vital in understanding how to effectively facilitate healing.

EXERCISE 18:
CHAKRA BALANCING EXERCISE

1. Sit in a comfortable position. Once you are experienced with this exercise, you can do it lying down or even standing up. Call upon the divine, in whatever form you prefer—God, Goddess, Great Spirit, Divine Mind, Mother-Father-God. Ask to be consciously connected to your source, for guidance and protection, and to all your spirit allies who are appropriate for you at this time. Do Exercise 1: Basic Meditation Technique up to step 6 (see page 81) to get into a meditative state.

2. Bring your awareness to the base of your spine, to your root chakra. Imagine dropping a beam of light, from the base of your spine, down into the Earth, down into the heart of the planet. As you inhale, imagine that the beam of light is like a straw, and you are drawing the pure energy of Mother Earth up through the straw and into the root. Feel your root chakra become energized with scarlet-red energy. Feel the power of grounding, survival, and foundation in your life.

3. Once you feel your root chakra energized, take another breath and draw the energy up to your belly chakra, and feel it fill with orange energy. Feel your power of intuition and instinct, your ability to determine how to be safe and how to be intimate.

4. When your belly chakra is energized, take a breath and draw up energy into the solar plexus chakra. Feel it brighten with golden solar energy and awaken to personal power and self-esteem.

5. On the next breath, allow the energy to move up to your chest, to your heart chakra. Feel your heart chakra awaken and glow a dazzling bright green, filling with love and harmony. Feel your sense of emotional connection to all.

6. When your heart chakra is filled with love, take the next step by drawing the energy up to your throat with your breath. Feel your throat chakra fill with blue light, connecting you to the powers of communication and will.

7. Draw the light of the throat chakra up to the brow chakra, to the third eye, and feel it open with indigo or purple light. Feel your psychic vision, your ability to send and receive images, awaken.

8. When the previous six chakras are awakened and aligned, draw the energy up to your crown chakra, and feel it explode like a fountain of dazzling white light. Feel your connection to the divine source of all. Feel the beam of light ascend to the heavens and connect you to the center of the galaxy. Feel the flow of energy moving up through you, expanding your consciousness.

9. When you feel ready, draw another current of energy down from the heavens. Feel the current of energy enter your crown, balancing and aligning the energies of the crown. Feel the flow descend into the third eye, balancing and aligning the powers of psychic vision. Let the energy flow descend into the throat, balancing and aligning the powers of expression and communication. Witness the energy move to the heart, balancing and aligning your ability to love and be in relationship with others and the world. Allow the energy to move into the solar plexus. Feel it balance and align your sense of personal power. Feel the energy descend into the belly. Feel it balance and align your sense of intuition. Finally, feel it descend into the root, balancing and aligning your sense of survival and pleasure. The descending energy stream then moves down into the floor and into the Earth, to the center of the planet, aligning, balancing, and healing Mother Earth.

10. Thank the divine Creator for guidance and protection. Thank your guides and allies. Perform steps 9 and 10 of Exercise 1: Basic Meditation Technique (see page 82) to return to normal waking consciousness. Write down any impressions or messages you received, before you forget them.

This version of the chakra opening and balancing is based upon the traditional seven-chakra model. Once you are very familiar with the seven main chakras, you can expand this exercise, using the chakra points in between, or the chakras above the head as well.

ENERGY HEALING

Healing occurs when the body has enough vital energy to heal itself. Magickal energy is simply another way of describing energy, and spellcraft is a method to direct healing energy. Traditions of healing have different ways of describing these healing energies, and different methods of directing the energy, but in essence, all are doing the same thing.

Light

Energy can be described in terms of the colors of the visible light spectrum. Though lightworkers say they are working with light, and visualize color, these colors are simply symbols for a psychic light, readily available in the universe, that can be directed to heal the self and others. This healing method is safe and effective, as it does not drain personal energy, but directs the abundant energy of the universe and can work very quickly. Through meditation and concentration, a lightworker can visualize herself, or another, even if the recipient is not physically present, surrounded by light. The decrees and invocations of the rays of light are a method of directing these energies. Each color is said to confer a different form of healing (chart 10). The science of the seven rays is an esoteric system of understanding color and light, but the color associations can be much simpler, and are in harmony with the chakra lore.

Pranic Healing

Prana is the Hindu term for life force, and is very intimately connected to the breath. Many cultures with an understanding of subtle anatomy have terms for life force, including ki, chi, rauch, pneuma, and mana. It is the vital life force that flows through our chakra system and energy bodies. Pranic healing refers to a variety of traditions that usually draw energy from another source, such as the Earth, the sky, the Sun, or a spirit guide, through the healer's body, and the healer then directs the energy to the recipient, either through a hands-on technique or through mentally projecting it in a "beam" to the recipient. This technique requires training and a strong understanding of energy to prevent the healer or recipient from overloading or burning out.

Reiki

Reiki is a specific, lineage-based tradition of pranic healing that comes from Japan. Reiki means "universal life force" and refers to the energy that animates all things, though now we also use the term to denote the system of healing, which was originally known as the

Color	Healing
Red	AIDS/HIV, anemia, low blood pressure, low energy, parasites, sexual dysfunction, venereal disease, viral infections, lack of motivation, low energy, depression
Red-Orange	AIDS/HIV, hay fever, infections, internal bleeding, loss of blood, low blood pressure, pneumonia
Orange	Bladder infections, bowel syndromes, broken bones, memory loss, mental focus, logic stimulation
Gold	AIDS/HIV, back problems, low metabolism, nerves, sore muscles, total health, masculine energy
Yellow	Adrenal problems, bladder infections, indigestion, liver disease, low metabolism, sore muscles, stomach cramps, depression, agitation
Lime	Cleansing, nausea, pH balance, purging, stomach aches, toxicity
Green	Blood loss, colds, eczema, eye infections, flu, heart conditions, infections, insect bites, rashes, ulcers, anger, emotional lethargy, relationship healing
Turquoise	All purposes, epilepsy, fevers, menstrual problems, pain, nausea, rashes, swelling, peace, tranquility, spirituality
Blue	Anxiety, asthma, ear infections, fevers, high blood pressure, high metabolism, liver, stress, TMJ syndrome
Indigo	Alcoholism/addiction, eye infections, headaches, hemorrhoids, high blood pressure, inflammation, Parkinson's disease, pneumonia, thyroid conditions, psychic development, inner knowing
Purple	Brain swelling, eye problems, liver disease, nervous disorders, nervous tension
Violet	Abscesses, arthritis, bacteria, cancers, cleansing, cysts, infections, unwanted growths, viral infections, warts, removing all unwanted energies
Black	Eye conditions, relaxation, stress, ungroundedness
Brown	Animal healing, bleeding, open wounds, ungroundedness
Rust	Cleansing, grounding, removing unwanted material
Pink	AIDS/HIV, blemishes, breast cancer, menstrual problems, self-esteem, happiness
Silver	Emotional problems, fertility problems, maternal issues, menstruation issues, psychic blocks, feminine energy
White	All purposes, cleansing, healing, soothing

Chart 10: Healing Colors

Usui System of Natural Healing, named after its founder, Dr. Mikao Usui. I like to distinguish between the two by describing the energy as lowercase *reiki* and the system as capital *Reiki*. Through a ritual known as an attunement, the ability to practice this specific system is passed from a teacher, or Reiki Master, to a student, allowing the student to effortlessly tap into a great reservoir of pure universal life force and, through various techniques, including direct hands-on healing, project the energy to a recipient in need of healing. The recipient's own body takes the energy and uses it to create healing. Reiki energy is said to be guided by a higher intelligence, and cannot overload or harm the recipient. It also protects the practitioner from taking on any of the recipient's illnesses or pain, unlike other forms of healing.

Though Reiki originally had nothing to do with ascension practices, it has become one of the most popular forms of healing among ascensionists. In fact, it is so popular, many people assume that if you follow ascension beliefs, then you must already be a Reiki practitioner. Many say that the attunements increase your vibration and light quotient and aid in the ascension process, even if you choose not to practice the healing techniques of Reiki. Through inspiration from mostly channeled sources, Reiki has expanded into a variety of flavors, complementing the basic healing modality. Now we have forms of Angelic Reiki, the Radiance Technique®, Terra Mai™ Reiki, and Seichim. The most notable of the Reiki traditions related to ascension is Shamballa Reiki, also known as Shamballa Multi-Dimensional Healing, relating the origin of Reiki to ancient Atlantis. Symbols, which are used in both individual healing sessions and attunements, are a big part of both traditional Reiki and Shamballa Reiki and its many offshoots (figure 46).

Mahatma

Another expression of life force used by ascension healers is known as the Mahatma. Mahatma is both an energy and a being who disseminates that energy for healing and transformation. Mahatma is called the avatar of synthesis, and is said to be a being who exists on all 352 levels simultaneously. This energy was recently "grounded" into our Earth's level of reality during the Harmonic Convergence in 1987. Mahatma can appear as brilliant white light, or as a mix of silver and gold metals, with a violet gleam. Mahatma energy synthesizes all conflicts, polarities, dualities, and paradoxes, bringing harmony between any and all seemingly opposed forces. Mahatma energy brings with it a sense of unconditional love and harmony, and a balance between male god and female goddess energies. It was named the Mahatma energy for those of us on Earth because Mahatma is a term

Power symbol
(Cho Ku Rei)
General healing
and balance.

Mental-Emotional symbol
(Sei He Ki)
Emotional healing
and healing the past.

Distance symbol
(Hon Sha Ze Sho Nen)
Distance healing,
higher-self connection.

Master symbol
(Di Ko Mio)
Initiation symbol.

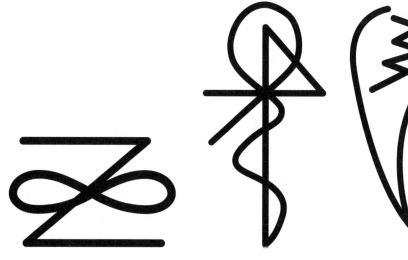

Zonar
Healing multidimensional
issues.

Mer Ka Fa Ka Lish Ma
Earth and DNA healing.

Motor-Zanon
Anti-Viral symbol.

Figure 46: Reiki and Shamballa Reiki Symbols

for which we have no preconditioned fears; we have naturally healthy associations with it. In Sanskrit, Mahatma refers to a "Great Spirit," "Great Soul," or "Adept," and can be used for religious and political leaders, such as Gandhi. Other divine names, such as Yahweh or Jehovah, have been used to harm others, and many people recoil from these names.

Mahatma energy is part of the Shamballa Reiki system of healing, but you don't have to be attuned to Shamballa Reiki to call upon the Mahatma energy. It is available to everybody. Like the ray energy, Mahatma can be called upon using a decree. Simply say as your affirmation, silently or out loud, "I am that I am. I am the Mahatma. I am the Mahatma in love." Then feel the silver/gold/violet energy descend into your crown. With each repetition of the affirmation, the energy descends into the next chakra, until it fills the body and surrounding aura. With each mantra you can move it anywhere in your body that is in need of healing love. You can fill your aura. You can imagine the energy descending into the Earth, via your grounding cord, to heal Mother Earth. When done, there is no need to dismiss or release the energy. You can keep as much of it as is comfortable in your aura and body, to raise your vibration and bring healing. If you feel there is excess energy, simply ground it into the Earth.

HEALING FROM NATURE

Nature provides a cornucopia of remedies and modalities for the modern healer. Though our pharmaceuticals find their roots in old-world herbalism and alchemy, many modern healers are going back to the old ways, feeling that the new medicines are missing something—spirit, energy, consciousness. By looking at healing from the holistic perspective, lasting cures can be found. This is not to say we scorn all forms of modern medicine. It does have a valuable place in society, but it is not the only way to heal.

The vibration, the energy quality, of the medicine is as important as the chemical constituents. In fact, it is the vibration that creates the healing. Herbalism is our first line of natural healing, and although herbs do contain powerful chemicals that scientists have learned to isolate, many powerful healing herbs have no single chemical that has been isolated. Other results are erratic, with some herbs seeming to work better for certain herbalists and patients than others. From the spiritual healer's perspective, each herb has a spirit, a consciousness, and healing with herbs is as much working with the plant's spirit medicine as it is working with the chemical constituents. Shamans and witches of the old world, and those in the new who follow the old ways, build a relationship with the spirits of nature, who instruct them in healing. The remedies work better for them, because they are treating the body, mind, heart, and spirit, unlike the mass-produced herbal capsules and tablets.

The concepts of the energies and vibrations of plants, minerals, and other natural substances have developed into a wide range of new modalities.

Homeopathy

Homeopathy works according to the principle of "like cures like," and medicines that cause particular symptoms in large doses are given in minute and diluted doses, to cure the same symptoms. For example, onions in a homeopathic dose will stop the eyes from watering. Though homeopathy is considered a fairly modern system of medicine that is still not widely recognized in the United States, the principles of homeopathy can be found in alchemy and the ancient world.

Flower Essences

Modern flower essence therapy grew out of the work of a homeopath named Dr. Edward Bach. Each flower has a spiritual healing quality that will address imbalances in the emotions, mind, and spirit. Small doses of very dilute solutions of flowers soaked in water and exposed to bright sunlight are administered to confer the flower's healing effect on the individual. By addressing issues on the mental/emotional/spiritual levels, deep and profound healing can occur. The water of the solution is said to "record" the essence, the vibrational energy, of the plant, so the remedy contains very little, if any, actual plant substance. Lightworkers consciously work with the devas, nature spirits, and faery allies to make powerful flower remedies.

Aura-Soma Remedies

Aura-Soma remedies are a system of bright, vibrantly colored liquids, often in a two-tone bottle of both oil and water consisting of herbals, oils, and gem energies. The founder of the system, Vicky Wall, was blind when she created these bright liquids and trusted her inner spiritual guidance for the combinations. She was not educated in Theosophy or the ascended masters, yet her guidance "told" her to name several remedies after specific masters, showing the masters' involvement in the creation of this complex healing system. Aura-Soma products are available at metaphysical shops, through mail order, and on the Internet, with several fine books explaining the system in detail, including *Aura-Soma:*

Healing Through Color, Plant and Crystal Energy by Irene Dalichow and Mike Booth, and *Aura Soma: Self-Discovery Through Color* by Vicky Wall.

Crystal Healing

Crystals can be carried, worn, meditated with, or placed upon the body to confer their healing vibrations. Crystal healing and layouts are a complex art and science that could fill many volumes, but in general, stones that are the color of a particular chakra are used to heal that chakra and its issues. By working with the spirits of the stones and the devas of the minerals, you can gain great wisdom and insight into how to work with the stones for your healing and the healing of others. Make sure you use cleansed and programmed stones to make the healing as gentle and balanced as possible. Start with short time periods and build up to longer sessions, as some people are overwhelmed easily by the power of stones, feeling their energy immediately.

Gem Elixirs

Gem elixirs are created the same way flower essences are created. The energy of the stone is imprinted upon the water through exposing it to sunlight. A few drops of the remedy is taken to administer the healing powers of the mineral internally. In many ways, this mimics old Celtic faery healing in which water was poured over a sacred faery standing stone, and the water was then collected and drunk to promote healing. Not all stones can be made into elixirs directly, as some are water-soluble minerals and potentially toxic.

EXERCISE 19:
MAKING VIBRATIONAL ESSENCES

To make a vibrational essence, you will need a clear glass bowl without any patterns or writing, pure water (spring or distilled), a larger dark glass storage bottle (mother essence bottle), two smaller dropper bottles, and a preservative (alcohol, cider vinegar, or glycerin).

Though you can learn the techniques of making these preparations, you really need to have a relationship with the spirits of the plants or stones, and the devas that rule them, to make truly effective remedies. Channeled material says that in the days of Lemuria and Atlantis, we were better in tune with the natural world, and flower essences and gem elixirs were used to heal on a multitude of levels.

Learning to make vibrational remedies can help you work with the devas, faeries, and nature spirits to help heal humanity's relationship with nature, as well as promote your own personal healing.

Choose a sunny day and a sunny location when making your essence. If you're making a flower remedy, make the essence in close physical proximity to the living plant and make sure the flower is blooming. Chose a day just before the plant blooms fully, or when it is blooming fully, but don't make it after the flowers have started to wither away. We use the flowers because they are the pinnacle of healing energy from the plant, but technically we could make an essence from the leaf, berry, bark, or root. Theoretically, you don't even need the plant, but only a connection to the plant deva.

1. Start with a clear glass bowl of pure water. Some practitioners insist on using quartz-crystal bowls, like the crystal singing bowls, but clear, plain glass works fine.

2. Meditate with the focus of your remedy, such as a flowering plant or a stone. Ask to connect to the spirits of the plant or stone. I like to count myself down into a deeper state of meditation and really commune with the plant or stone before making an essence. Ask to also connect with Mother Earth and Pan. Ask to know the mysteries of this medicine and its healing properties. Allow the deva of the plant or stone to communicate with you through vision, words, and feelings, revealing to you its healing power.

3. Ask the deva for permission to make a flower essence or gem elixir. Use muscle testing or a pendulum to get a yes or no answer. If you receive a yes, then place the focus of your essence in the water. For a stone, simply place the stone in the water. For flowers, ask the deva if you should pick the flowers and place them in the water, and if so, how many. Cutting the flower isn't always necessary to make an essence, particularly if it's endangered or the only one. Simply placing the bowl of water beneath the flower can be sufficient. Though some essence makers want the process to be clinical, and recommend using scissors and tongs, I pick the flowers myself and put them in the water. Ask to make a "full-strength flower essence (or gem elixir), for the highest good, harming none." If you know any particular healing symbols, such as the Reiki symbols, you can draw them over the water. If not, I think the magician's infinity loop

(a figure shaped like the number 8 on its side) is particularly powerful for this work.

4. Let the bowl sit out in the sun for at least three hours if completely sunny or five hours if partially sunny. The sun raises the vibration of the mixture and helps imprint the essence, the spirit, of the plant on the water. You might get different effects from an essence made under moonlight. My favorite essences were made all day in the sun and then left out under the light of the full Moon and collected before sunrise.

5. When you are done, and the essence is made, thank the deva and the plant or stone. Make an offering to the plant or stone, in exchange. Traditional herbalists often leave a strand of hair. Desert shamans leave spit, their life's water in a parched land. You can leave tobacco, cornmeal, or anything else that you would make for a faery offering. I also like to do Reiki and energy healing on the plant, because I just harvested a few flowers from it.

6. To preserve and use the essence, take the bowl and strain out the flowers or stone. Pour the water into a dark-colored bottle, with ¼ to ⅓ of the bottle filled with a preservative, such as an 80-proof or higher alcohol (usually brandy, vodka, or run), apple cider vinegar, or vegetable glycerin. This bottle is now called the mother essence. Alcohol will preserve the essence the longest, for possibly as much as a decade, while essences made with the other preservatives will last only a few years.

7. To use the essence, take a dark-colored dropper bottle, filled with a solution of ¼ preservative to ¾ pure water, and put 3–7 drops of the mother essence in this bottle, now labeled a stock bottle. This is the dilution you purchase from commercial suppliers. When taken at this level, the physical effects are the most potent. You can dilute the essence further by putting a few drops from the stock bottle into another dark-colored dropper bottle, filled with a solution of ¼ preservative to ¾ pure water. You can use muscle testing or a pendulum to determine how many drops to add. This is called the dosage level, and has the greatest effect on the emotional, mental, and spiritual levels. In the dosage bottle, you can mix several different essences at once, making a personal essence combination (see chart 11).

Flower/Element	Uses
Angelica	Angelica facilitates contact with the angelic realm, and provides divine guidance and spiritual protection.
Basil	Basil is a purifying herb, but is used as an essence to get you in touch with your sexuality and romantic nature.
Black-eyed Susan	Black-eyed Susan helps you commune with your shadow self and see the parts of your being that you deny.
Celandine	Celandine helps you express yourself in public.
Chamomile	Chamomile brings serenity and calmness.
Comfrey	Comfrey is used to release emotions and patterns trapped in the body, and to recall past-life memories.
Daffodil	Daffodil facilitates communication with spirit guides.
Dandelion	This herb is a liver tonic, and as a flower essence it helps you heal anger, relax the muscles, and remain grounded.
Echinacea	Echinacea essence stimulates the immune system. It also purifies the thoughts and mind.
Garlic	Garlic repels unwanted energy and dangerous forces.
Lemon balm	Lemon balm uplifts the mind and spirit.
Lilac	Lilac aligns the chakras and helps you get in touch with the truth.
Lily	All lilies help heal the pain of betrayal. The color of the lily, as related to the corresponding chakra, is connected to the type of betrayal.
Lunaria	Lunaria connects you to prosperity and abundance.
Monkshood	Monkshood encourages introspection and finding meaning and purpose in life.
Oak	Oak provides stability and support.
Peppermint	Peppermint stimulates the mind and enhances communication and creativity.
Queen Anne's lace	Queen Anne's lace awakens the third eye to open you to psychic development, yet keeps you grounded.
Quince	Quince helps you develop a healthy sense of power and the proper application of power.

Chart 11: Flower Essences

Flower/Element	Uses
Rose	Rose opens the heart to love and healing.
Sunflower	Sunflower aids in the development of a healthy ego and individuality.
St. John's wort	St. John's wort helps heal trauma and soothes difficult dreams and nightmares.
Yarrow	Yarrow heals the aura of all holes and strengthens the psychic protection shield.
Earth	Comfrey, dandelion, echinacea, garlic, oak, Queen Anne's lace.
Air	Angelica, celandine, daffodil, echinacea, lemon balm, lilac, peppermint.
Fire	Basil, chamomile, dandelion, garlic, quince, sunflower, St. John's wort, yarrow.
Water	Chamomile, lemon balm, lilac, lunaria, rose.
Spirit	Angelica, echinacea, lilac, lily, monkshood, Queen Anne's lace, rose, St. John's wort.

Chart 11: Flower Essences (continued)

You can use essences traditionally by taking them internally, usually in a 1–3 drop dose; apply them to your skin topically; use them environmentally on the floor, ground, bath water, or fountain; or even use them in ritual. When doing a healing or a faery magick circle, I like to have four bowls, for the four elements, and place a few drops of an elementally appropriate essence in each bowl, to anchor that element's energy.

In other forms of vibrational healing, the same techniques are used, but instead of imprinting the remedy with the energy of a plant or stone spirit, other energies are used, such as the energy of sacred sites on Earth, musical notes, a healing mantra, the light of a star, or the spirit of an animal.

REMOVING BLOCKS

Though much of healing magick focuses on putting energy into the body to create healing, lesser known forms of healing actually focus on removing unhealthy energies, known as blocks, from the body. Many healers believe that flushing a system with healthy energy naturally and gradually dislodges energy blockages from the system, but specific methods can be used to remove blocks as well.

Psychic Surgery

Psychic surgery is the process of moving or removing the subtle energies of an illness within the body to effect healing. From a metaphysical point of view, everything has a subtle energy supporting it, including bacteria, viruses, and illnesses, such as cancer. Removing the energy that supports these physical structures can encourage their physical collapse, letting the immune system handle them much more easily than before. Other forms of psychic surgery move the subtle energy of damaged tissue and organs back into a healthy alignment, to encourage the physical tissue to grow or move to where the subtle energy pattern is now located. Since psychic surgery involves moving the energies, or spirits, of illness and health, it is often known as shamanic surgery or spirit surgery. Shamans are known to use variations of it to "suck out" the spirit of an illness from a client's body.

Entity and Implant Removal

Some forms of psychic surgery are used to remove energy blockages that are described as implants or entities. The concept is that the blockage is not simply stagnant energy, but a spirit trapped within your energy system, or a fragment of someone else's energy that you had a traumatic experience with, either in this life or a past life. Other times, the blockages are thoughtforms—programmed energy that has taken on a life of its own, our own personally created monsters that haunt our thoughts and feelings. For some, energetic entities, implants, and thoughtforms are the basis for tales of demonic possession, but elaborate exorcism rituals are just other ways of removing this blocked energy. Various spiritual healing systems have catalogued and codified these impairments, with their own special jargon and terminology. Shamballa Reiki uses a specific meditation to aid the aspiring student in releasing these entities and implants through the direct aid of the ascended masters, archangels, elohim, devas, Pan, various star spirits, and your own monad.

Figure 47: Copper Wand

Healing Wands

Those who practice more advanced forms of psychic surgery often use ritual tools, such as healing wands, to help them focus and direct energy. A healing wand is usually a copper tube with two quartz points at the ends (figure 47). You can easily make or purchase your own wand. To make your own copper wand, take a copper tubing of the desired length, and with a hacksaw, cut two lengthwise one-inch incisions at the top end of the tube, where you will affix your crystal. Use pliers to open up the end, so your crystal can fit in, with the point facing out if it's a single-terminated crystal. Make sure you use a crystal that will fit snugly when the strips of copper tubing are returned to their normal position. You can add a few drops of glue or epoxy and then bend the strips back in, to secure the stone. You can keep the tube hollow or fill it with smaller crystals, healing herbs, or soil from a healing sacred site. On the bottom you can repeat the process and affix a second crystal, or put a cap on the end. Some makers will run a wire through the tube from the top crystal to the bottom crystal, to energetically connect them. Once both ends are secure, wrap a strip of leather around the tube, affixing it with glue at various intervals. The leather is said to insulate your hand holding the wand, so that you don't receive a shock of energy when using it.

Many people claim that copper and crystal healing tools were used in Atlantis to direct energy. They have come up with a number of other "devices" for healing and psychic development, including copper and crystal headbands, bracelets, and chestplates. Though these devices look funny to us, they are similar to the silver circlets, headdresses, diadems, armbands, and medallions worn by traditional witches and magicians, of the modern age, and ancient temple priestesses and priests, to control and direct energy.

Crystal Wands

Wands can be made out of other substances, instead of copper tubing and wire. Some people use a glass tube, such as a test tube, rather than a copper tube. They fill the tube with stones that can be easily seen through the glass, and cap each end with a quartz point. Another popular form of crystal wand is to take a long-shaped crystal, which is already a

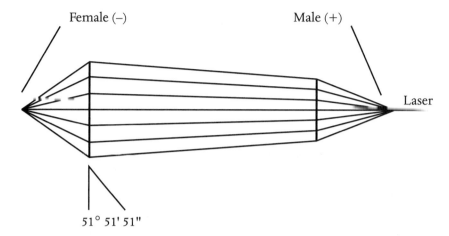

Figure 48: Vogel Wand

natural wand, and with epoxy, affix several smaller crystals that work harmoniously together. A flat selenite wand with crystals for the elements or chakras glued on it can be a
wonderful healer.

Vogel Crystal Wands

Vogel wands are double-terminated quartz crystals that are naturally six-sided, but are then
cut in a desire to focus and amplify their healing ability (figure 48). Marcel Vogel, the man
credited with inventing these wands, was both a scientist and a spiritual visionary, who
experienced a number of strange encounters with spiritual forces that propelled him to
study the healing effects of crystals. When pondering cutting the crystals, he experienced a
dream with a vision of the Tree of Life, yet he had no previous Qabalistic knowledge. He
sought to cut the crystal in the proportions of the Tree of Life, with an inner angle of 51
degrees, 51 minutes, 51 seconds, which is also the measurement of the angle of the Great
Pyramid in Giza. Over the years, Vogel has created wands of 4, 8, 12, 21, 24, and 33 sides,
though the most popular ones have been the 12-sided wands. Usually one end is larger
than the other, with the larger end being female and receptive, drawing in energy, and the
smaller end being male and projective, sending out energy. A primary teaching of Marcel
Vogel is that the crystals are used to amplify the frequency of human love, which is the
strongest force that can heal. While the users of Vogel wands report amazing success in
healing, some argue that a crystal is perfectly fine the way it grew, and needs no cutting or

fashioning. Simple quartz points, single- or double-terminated, without copper tubing or cutting, can be used to heal quite effectively on their own.

EXERCISE 20:

USING YOUR HEALING WAND

The use of a wand varies from practitioner to practitioner. Your connection to the tool will help you develop your own unique style and techniques. In general, the wand is used to direct will, to direct energy. Many people believe that the natural structure of a crystal wand automatically directs energy when held, but as a magician, it is important to use intention to direct the energy through the wand. You can visualize a beam of light extending from the point, directed to where you will it. You can also evoke the various rays by decree and use the wand to focus the colored energy of the rays.

Many practitioners believe you should hold the wand so the end is exposed, not in your palm, so that you are not directing your personal energy through the healing, unless you are attuned to Reiki or another source of healing energy to be amplified by the wand. You don't want to drain your own energy. Others say that if you focus your energy and intention on love, and let that flow through your palm and into the crystal, then nothing harmful will happen to you, as love is an infinite source of energy flowing through you. Follow your guidance and intuition to find the healing style that is right for you.

When the wand is pointed and held steady, it will direct a flow of energy. You can direct energy from the wand to a specific chakra, particularly during crystal healing. In general, a counterclockwise motion is said to diminish or remove energy. Small counterclockwise circles (a direction also known as *widdershins*, or against the path of the Sun) done around the aura can help a client release harmful energies. Clockwise circles are used to energize and amplify. You can also use the basic banishing pentagram to remove energy and the invoking pentagram to bring healing energy. If you are uncomfortable with the circular motions or pentagrams, you can use the infinity loop, which uses both motions simultaneously and is a powerful symbol of the magician. In the end, your intention to banish or amplify is the most important part of the ritual, but these symbols are recognized widely by practitioners in many traditions and healing methods.

You can also use the wand to direct energy in any way your guidance recommends. You can use a healing wand for ritual, to cast a circle, or to direct any energy. You can pass it over other stones and tools to cleanse them of unwanted energies. It can be used to draw symbols, send distance healing energy, send thoughts, open gateways to the elements, and cast spells.

DNA ACTIVATION AND GENETIC HEALING

Another popular concept among ascensionists is that we, as a species, are evolving—not just in terms of consciousness, but physically evolving, by transmuting our DNA and RNA, transforming ourselves literally on the genetic level. Ascension healers claim we are becoming beings of not two strands of DNA, but twelve strands.

When I first heard this, I found it a bit incredible. From a scientific viewpoint, the idea of twelve strands of DNA didn't make sense, for humans or anything else. I then had a long conversation with someone thoroughly rooted in the ascension paradigm, yet with one foot in the scientific world, and we talked about our beliefs in this DNA model. After much discussion, we came to the conclusion that the ascension paradigm is multidimensional, and our truths and understanding of ourselves, including our DNA, are also multidimensional, though a lot of healers, teachers, and channels are not clear in their multidimensional truths, and often state things solely as physical truths.

If we look at a twelve-dimensional model of the universe, then we have a spiritual self, a spiritual body in each dimension, with a corresponding set of spiritual DNA. Performing twelve-strand DNA activations is much like doing affirmations to be active, alive, and awake in all twelve dimensions, and as a result, becoming multidimensional. Information from one self to the next is not blocked, but connected, through this etheric DNA link. As much as the physical DNA in the third dimension holds our physical blueprint and makeup, our other-dimensional DNA holds the patterns and purposes of our spiritual selves. Meditations to activate and align these DNA patterns align our multidimensional selves with our physical self. With this alignment, we are better able to consciously fulfill our spiritual purpose on all levels, rather than have our other-dimensional selves working with no conscious connection to our physical self.

Other forms of genetic healing are not as far-fetched as the concepts of multidimensional evolution and physical mutation. In ancestor-reverent traditions, there is the teaching that we of the current generation redeem the ancestors. We carry their energy in our blood, and anything left unresolved from them is often transferred to the children, and we must then resolve the issues or pass them on generationally. Some spurious psychics will tell a naive client that he or she has a family curse, and only the psychic can remove it—for a large sum of money. Family "curses" are usually not really curses, but heavy energies that can be transmuted and healed. This does not mean that we are to blame for anything our ancestors did, but it shows that we are tied to the actions of the past. Native traditions have the saying of "seven generations," always keeping in mind how their actions will affect the next seven generations of their descendants. We should also keep in mind that we carry the blessings and gifts of our ancestors as well, and they will aid us on our paths.

We can transmute the past that we carry with us through traditional healing methods, and by understanding that the energies we carry from our families do not have to be our personal issues. By taking a stand and deciding to release the energies and heal them, we help future generations transform those issues.

Healing is an art, science, and spiritual tradition, much like ascension itself. Those of us who are called to the path of the healer—truly the healing facilitator, for all we do is help others heal—must be diligently working on our own healing as we seek to help others. All healing is a form of sympathetic magick. What we do to one person, in the microcosm, we do to the greater consciousness of the macrocosm. We are all connected, and what we do affects everybody. As we heal ourselves, we help heal others and the world.

16

CHANNELING

Channeling is the process of psychically communing with nonphysical entities to receive information for the betterment of humanity, either individually or for a community. Channeling is a relatively modern term to describe this type of communication. Though some people use the term *to channel* to refer to any act of accessing knowledge via the psychic senses, it really refers to a communication with a spiritual entity.

Though we think the roots of channeling come from the Theosophical Society and its spiritual descendants channeling the masters, the techniques of channeling have far older roots. We can look to the Spiritualist church as an influence on Theosophy. Its modern methods of mediumship are very similar to those of modern channels. The medium's ritual of séances harkens back to even older traditions of spirit interface—those of the pagan oracles, who channeled the messages of the gods. Modern pagans have revived and adapted these oracular practices of invoking the gods for guidance and wisdom. Today we see the practice of more visceral channelings in the practice of Voodou, in which the participant is ridden by, or physically channels, the loa spirit, who then communicates and celebrates with the community. Such sessions can be frightening to those who are used to the modern, sedate sessions of channeling done in a bookstore or convention hall. Channeling in the pagan world was probably more primal and shamanic, akin to Voodou, and eventually evolved into the formal rituals and ceremonies of the temple oracles.

We believe the ancients across the globe had a great reverence for the spirits of the dead. They ritualized the transition from the living to the dead, creating crossing-over ceremonies and funeral rites. They recorded the geography of the Otherworld that the newly dead experienced in texts known as bardos, or books of the dead, and presumedly received this information from the dead themselves, other spirits, and the gods. Two of the most famous books of the dead come from Egyptian and Tibetan cultures. Every culture had its own customs surrounding the burial and honoring of the dead, from Stone Age people interring bodies in stone cairns with flowers and beads to the amazing embalming feats of the Egyptians. Offerings of incense, food, water, and wine were made to maintain a link with the ancestors.

To make contact with the deceased, one classically sought the aid of a necromancer. Necromancy is another time-honored tradition found across culture and time. We still have necromancers today. Our popular television psychics, from John Edward and Sylvia Browne to our turn-of-the-twentieth-century Spiritualist church mediums, are all technically necromancers. Yes, that's right. Though our Hollywood images of necromancers deal with cadavers and bones, and, yes, that can be a part of the practice of necromancy, technically necromancy refers to any magickal art involving the dead. You don't need to dig up a corpse or reanimate a body to be a necromancer. You simply need to communicate with the dead. We can trace mediumship to the Old Testament in the story of the Witch of Endor:

> Then said Saul unto his servants, Seek me a woman that hath a familiar spirit, that I may go to her, and enquire of her. And his servants said to him, Behold, there is a woman that hath a familiar spirit at Endor. And Saul disguised himself, and put on other raiment, and he went, and two men with him, and they came to the woman by night: and he said, I pray thee, divine unto me by the familiar spirit, and bring me him up, whom I shall name unto thee. And the woman said unto him, Behold, thou knowest what Saul hath done, how he hath cut off those that have familiar spirits, and the wizards, out of the land: wherefore then layest thou a snare for my life, to cause me to die? And Saul sware to her by the LORD, saying, As the LORD liveth, there shall no punishment happen to thee for this thing. Then said the woman, Whom shall I bring up unto thee? And he said, Bring me up Samuel. And when the woman saw Samuel, she cried with a loud voice: and the woman spake to Saul, saying, Why

hast thou deceived me? For thou art Saul. And the king said unto her, Be not afraid: for what sawest thou? And the woman said unto Saul, I saw gods ascending out of the earth. And he said unto her, What form is he of? And she said, An old man cometh up; and he is covered with a mantle. And Saul perceived that it was Samuel, and he stooped with his face to the ground, and bowed himself.—1 Samuel 28: 7 14

There have always been those among us, like the village witches and cunning folk, who speak to the spirits as easily as they speak to living people. There are those with a natural gift and inclination. It is through those gifted individuals that we have reconstructed and renewed the practice for the New Age.

Modern channeling has evolved greatly from its development in the early Spiritualist church. In the modern age, the process of mediumship was initially a joint partnership between two physical beings, to successfully commune with the spirit world. The two, consciously or unconsciously, fulfilled different roles. One person acted as a battery for etheric forces, to power the connection of sessions, while the other acted as the receiver and primary communicator. One might act as "anchor" and "pitcher," asking questions, while the other was in deep trace, receiving and communicating the answers. Sometimes a Spiritualist cabinet was used to collect and store energy for the session.

The contact would manifest in a variety of ways. Sometimes the spirits would manifest through a divinatory action, such as rapping on or tilting a table, manipulating the flame of a candle, or using a pendulum or the planchette of a Ouija board. During sessions of automatic writing, one person would often guide the session, asking questions and reading answers, while the actual medium was in a trance, writing with little or no conscious knowledge of the answers. Some contacts supposedly manifested through ectoplasmic occurrences. Like much ritual involving psychic ability and the ancestors, most manifestations were reported in dim lighting, and unfortunately that encouraged many charlatans to misuse the process of mediumship for their own fraudulent aims.

Mediumship has developed into modern channeling abilities that are often performed alone, without the use of a partnership. Some people claim that this now makes mediumship less valid, but Blavatsky and Bailey also received messages directly from the masters, individually, rather than in a partnership. As mediumship moved beyond the realm of the dead and into ascended beings, star brothers, and angels, it became known as channeling. The work of the Theosophists, and then Edgar Cayce, really provided a foundation for our understanding and use of channeling, even though Cayce was not channeling a specific persona or entity. They in turn led the way for the channels of Seth, Kryon, Abraham Hicks, Ramtha, Michael, Ra, and the Pleiadians.

Channeling can be divided into two kinds: conscious and full body.

CONSCIOUS CHANNELING

In conscious channeling, the channeler makes contact with the spiritual entity, communicates questions to this spirit, and listens for the answers using clairaudience. If others are present, the channel will repeat the answers aloud, acting as a translator for the spirit. The channeler is fully aware of the situation, retains complete memory of the session, and can participate fully and consciously. Proponents of conscious channeling feel that it is safer than full-body channeling, and establishes a greater equality, trust, and partnership between both beings.

FULL-BODY CHANNELING

In full-body channeling, the channel gives up conscious control of the physical body, allowing the spirit to take physical motor control of the body and speak directly through the channel without translation. The channel usually is not consciously aware of what transpires, and will often forget the session. Experiences that are not full-body channeling but rather partial-body channeling are often known as overshadowing or blending. Advocates of full-body channeling feel that the message is purer than with partial-body channeling, because no conscious ego gets in the way. Critics feel that the ego is inherent in the body, and that you shouldn't give up your body to a being who doesn't have a body. If they were meant to have a body, they would. High-vibrational beings, no matter how well-intentioned, can burn out the energy systems of physical beings because such energy is not meant to be incarnated.

CHANNELING GUIDES

Channeling practices are categorized by the type of spirit one seeks to connect with, and the purpose the communication serves. Through communing with the spirits, the Spiritualists have developed their own theories and theologies about the other side, our guides, and how contact and healing work. Different branches of Spiritualism across the world have different views and terms, but they have quite a complete, modern system that is easy for anybody to understand. I once had a Spiritualist minister describe the various guides we have, including the following.

Departed Loved One

Departed loved ones act as our guides in day-to-day concerns, offering advice as they would in life, but because they have crossed over into the next world, they can offer that advice from a higher, divine perspective, because they have crossed the veil. People who might not have been much help in life can be of great aid after their death. They can also act as guardians, aiding us on the path. One of the ailments that afflicts humanity across cultures and times is the fear of death, of suffering and the mystery of what happens next in the journey across the veil. Many people become stuck in grief after losing a loved one, particularly those who have no strong spiritual support system or mystical experience to help them understand death. Sometimes simply making contact with a departed love one is very healing and reassuring for the living, transforming their point of view on spirituality. One might wonder how an ancestor can "answer" us if we believe in reincarnation, but modern Spiritualists believe that some aspect, such as the higher self, oversoul, or monad of the person, is truly making the connection and transmitting the information through the earthly persona of the ancestor.

Master Teacher

Master teachers are guides who reached enlightenment in their last physical lifetime, and resonate with our spiritual path, so they can offer guidance and teachings to help us reach closer to enlightenment in this lifetime. Channeling of the personal master is the most commonly sought-after experience, because it can grant both personal information and esoteric knowledge to aid the disciple on the path. Some channel master entities do not necessarily identify with the ascended masters.

Healer/Alchemist

Healers, or alchemists, are spirit guides who heal us, changing us on the physical as well as the subtle levels. They are sometimes referred to as alchemist guides, because they might guide you to a specific remedy, or change the vibration of your food or drink to accelerate your healing and consciousness expansion. For example, they might tell you to put water in a red, blue, or green glass, and leave it on your nightstand, changing the water as you sleep, so that when you drink it the next day, it is a powerful vibrational remedy. They also transmit detailed knowledge of healing when channeled.

Joy Guide

Joy guides give you a healthy perspective, and encourage you to have fun, play, and spend time recreationally, without a need to accomplish or do anything. They can be an excellent balance to the master teachers, who often take a taskmaster approach to life. Joy guides are not often purposely channeled, but usually appear in meditations and day-to-day life.

Runner

A runner is a spirit who will help you manifest things in the physical world, running and getting you things that you need. Runners are not purposely channeled.

Gatekeeper

A gatekeeper is a spirit guide whose task is to protect you from unwanted forces and energies entering your consciousness or harming your physical body. The gatekeeper controls who is let "in" to the channel during a session. Gatekeepers are never channeled. Their sole purpose is to protect you during channeling, dream work, astral travel, and any other time in which you might leave your body and consciousness psychically vulnerable. Some gatekeepers also act as guardians to protect you from day-to-day harm.

Try this exercise to help you awaken to your own channeling abilities, so you can communicate directly with your spirit allies. By developing this ability, you'll be able to find answers for yourself and better help others by partnering with your spirit guides.

Exercise 21:
Opening to Channel

> 1. Sit before your altar in a comfortable position. If you have a second person to aid you in this exercise, your partner can act as the anchor, asking you questions and writing down or recording the answers for you. Call upon the divine, in whatever form you prefer—God, Goddess, Great Spirit, Divine Mind, Mother-Father-God. Ask to be consciously connected to your source, for guidance and protection, and to all your spirit allies who are appropriate for you at this time.

Ask specifically for the presence and guidance of your gatekeeper. Feel a strong and secure connection to this being. Do Exercise 1: Basic Meditation Technique up to step 6 (see page 81) to get into a meditative state.

2. Acknowledge the power of the four directions. Bring your attention to the north, then the east, south, and west. Bring your attention to the heavens above and the space below you. Then bring your awareness to your heart. Feel a shaft of light descend from the heavens, from the highest dimensions, surrounding you in a column of light and finding its anchor in the heart of the planet. You are now aligned with the twelve dimensions and are capable of interdimensional contact and journey.

3. Ask to connect with an entity to channel. Ask for your master teacher or trusted ancestor. When you begin this work, I suggest using the technique of conscious channeling. Imagine the spirit rising or descending in the column of light before you, as if it is right there with you and you can have a conversation. As you grow more experienced and confident, you might feel called to full-body channeling, and allow the spirit to rise up through your body or down through your crown and then merge with your physical presence. Some people imagine the entity hugging them from behind, and stepping into their body from the back. The entity isn't literally in their body, but around and interpenetrating their body and energy field to merge with them. Only attempt full-body channeling if you feel strongly called to do so.

4. Ask your entity any questions you have. Some channelings might have a personal side, acting almost like a counselor, answering specific questions about your life, while others will seem more like "downloads" of esoteric information.

5. When done, thank the entity you have channeled, and tell it that now it is time to release and return to its native plane. Thank all the spiritual entities that have aided you, including your gatekeeper.

6. Acknowledge the four directions around you again, north, east, south, and west, then above, below, and center. Thank the divine Creator for guidance and protection. Thank your guides and allies. Perform steps 9 and 10 of Exercise 1: Basic Meditation Technique (see page 82) to return to normal waking consciousness. Write down any impressions or messages you received, before you forget them.

Though you can find some great information and wisdom in channeled works, I think it is far more important to learn how to make your own connections to divine guidance and find answers to your own questions, rather than rely on someone else's interpretation of the divine. Seeking out information through others can be very helpful in times of stress when we need a fresh, detached perspective, but we shouldn't grow too reliant on others. As the saying goes, "Feed a man a fish and you feed him for a day; teach him how to fish and you feed him for a lifetime." Our approach to spirituality in the Aquarian Age must echo this teaching, for we all have to forge our own relationships with the spirit world.

17

PLANETARY HEALING

While many in the ascension community are focused on individual healing, others direct their efforts toward the healing of the planet and facilitating Mother Gaia's ascension process. The true teaching of planetary ascension is to manifest the heavens, the spiritual ideals of our age, here on Earth by recognizing the spiritual in everything. As people need aid in their individual healing processes, the planet itself can use support from her children who are tuned in to her needs. Those of us aligned with Mother Earth can act as spiritual midwives to her rebirth in the next age.

LEY LINES AND THE PLANETARY GRID

Much like the human energy system, with chakras connected by lines known as meridians or nadis, the planet has an energy system that carries vital energy around and through it. This grid system is composed of major and minor vortexes of energy, often found at or near ancient sacred sites, that act much like the world's chakras. These vortexes are connected with lines of power, which are now popularly known as ley lines, though in the past they have been called dragon lines, dead roads, or faery roads.

The concept of ley lines is controversial, and not even all ley "hunters" agree on their meaning and purpose. The term originated with Alfred Watkins, the author of *The Old Straight Track*, from a Saxon word for a "cleared strip of ground." He used the word to describe his perception of straight alignments connecting ancient sites in the United Kingdom's countryside, including prehistoric stones and stone circles, barrows, mounds, moats, crossroads, river crossings, hilltops, and pre-Reformation churches. These roads were strongly associated with the old pagan religions, the spirits of the dead and the old gods, and faery beings. Watkins saw them potentially as ancient walking paths, trade routes, and astrological markers. The lines were not exclusive to England, as they can be observed both in Europe and in Native American territories.

Most of the archaeological world did not take Watkins' views seriously, and his ideas became further distanced from conventional science when they were associated with UFO sightings, alien abductions, crop circles, and Earth lights. Occultist and novelist Dion Fortune, in her book *The Goat-Foot God*, was the first in the modern era to make an overt connection between these lines and the concept of vital Earth energy connecting sacred sites. Many believe she was privy to a body of secret magickal teachings on the Earth mysteries, and chose to share it in code, through her novels. John Michell's book *The New View Over Atlantis* attempted to further codify these teachings into a whole, though the ideas are still dismissed by mainstream scientists, even though there is evidence that some ley lines have points of unusual electromagnetic activity. Traveling to ley lines for spiritual pilgrimage was made even more popular with the publication of Shirley MacLaine's *The Camino*, which reports that she traveled along such a line in Spain and received past-life information on the origin of humanity. Some would say that the occult definition of leys as energy lines and Watkins' archaeological interpretations are describing two different phenomena.

Magicians, neopagans, esoteric environmentalists, and ascensionists have built on the visions of Fortune and Michell and attempt to reconstruct a system of geomancy that they believe was practiced in the ancient world. Parallels can be found between modern thought on ley lines, and the "dragon lines" of the East, made popular in recent times by the introduction of the art and science of feng shui in the West. Though many people think of feng shui as nothing more than esoteric home decorating, the origins of the practice come from deep Asian magick to attune with and alter the flow of energy brought about through the alignments of the land, water, and wind.

Many modern practitioners see the stone circles and ancient sacred sites of the Western world as a technology to interface with the energies of Mother Earth in a reciprocal fashion. By working our magick and healing at these sacred sites, we have access to a greater amount of energy than we would personally have available to us. At the same time, we must use the energy responsibly, for whatever is done at these sites can potentially affect the entire planet. We have a duty as caretakers to maintain the energetic health and vitality of these sites, by not always just taking energy out of them, but also putting blessings and energy into the sites.

The following modern systems of geomancy share some basic points, though the execution of geomantic magick differs greatly from one practitioner to the next.

Sacred Sites

A place where two or more ley lines intersect is a sacred space, or energetic crossroads. Most ancient sacred sites are situated at the location of a large number of intersections. Like the crossroads of traditional witchcraft, such places are said to be between the worlds, and a multidimensional consciousness is more easily accessed at these sites. Profound dreams occur at these sites, and human fertility is also said to increase. Children conceived at sacred sites can be quite unusual and spiritually oriented. The lines themselves are said to be multidimensional, though each line might not be active, or "awake," on all levels. Though many powerful sites have been marked by ancient people, many other sites either were not marked, or have newly developed over the last age. There are powerful sacred sites everywhere if you know to look for them.

Energetic Differences

Not all sites and energy lines have the same type of energy. Just as different chakras in the human body are characterized by different colors, elements, and qualities, so too are sacred sites different. They are often characterized in terms of gender or element. Energy lines also carry similar connotations. The two most famous lines, the Michael and Mary Lines crossing the United Kingdom, are described in terms of male and female energies and names.

Multiple Grids

Just as the human body has many different energy systems, from the Chinese meridian and Vedic nadis to the New Age concept of modern and extended chakras, the Earth also has many different systems, not all of which will be apparent to us. Several grids can exist simultaneously, but on different frequencies. Just as we have multiple subtle bodies, so does the Earth. Some people believe there is a different grid in each dimension, or one associated with each of the elements. Some even believe that the consciousness grids of the various species are a part of the planetary grids of Gaia. We, and all beings, are a part of the collective consciousness of Mother Earth.

Health

Ley lines and sacred sites can be in various stages of health. Some are sluggish or asleep in terms of the energy flowing through them, while others are vital and awake. Some change with the seasons and astrological alignments, becoming more active near equinoxes, solstices, and new or full Moons, while others are simply blocked and unhealthy. Many people feel that the standing stones and circles were ways of performing megalithic Earth acupuncture. Much as a practitioner of Chinese medicine would use a metal needed in a person's meridians to stimulate the healthy flow of energy, of chi, the standing stones are like giant stone needles in the meridians of the Earth, and are used to promote healthy energy flow. Some unhealthy lines are considered to be toxic, and can have a harmful effect on people, animals, plants, and the environment through which they flow. They are often related to the concept of geopathic stress, which is theorized as a natural radiation that is distorted through weak electromagnetic fields, such as those created by underground water, certain minerals, fault lines, humanmade electronics, and possibly even Earth grid lines. This distortion creates a field of energy that is detrimental to the health of most beings, particularly mammals, though some plants and insects thrive in it.

Crystals

Stones and crystals are said to resonate with these Earth energies, and can be used to amplify and heal people, animals, plants, and the planet. Many of the ancient standing stones have a significant quartz-crystal content in their makeup. The power of stones at sacred sites and on such lines is increased exponentially.

Rituals

Through ritual that focuses and directs the consciousness, it is possible to interface and work with the energy of ley lines for personal and planetary transformation.

DOWSING FOR LEY LINES

Traditionally, ley lines are located through dowsing. Dowsing is a method of communing with higher guidance, similar in many ways to use of the pendulum and muscle testing. According to age-old traditions, the cunning folk dowsed for water with a hazel branch terminating in a fork, to know where to successfully dig a well. Such acts were known as water witching. Modern dowsers still find water, metal, or anything else, but more often they use copper rods, usually two. Basically, the dowser holds the intention of finding something and then walks. When the copper rods move or, when using two, cross each other, then something has been found. No one is exactly sure how dowsing works. Some believe it is based on electromagnetics, moving the metal wires, but that doesn't account for successful dowsing with wood. Others feel it is simply an interface for higher guidance, with the information bypassing the conscious mind, but subtly influencing the muscles holding the rods.

Dowsing rods can be made easily and cheaply with an old coat hanger (figure 49). Many people use a cardboard tube to hold the rod, to prevent themselves from grasping the wire too tightly and inhibiting its free movement in the dowsing process.

Dowsing rods should be cleansed and consecrated like any other ritual tool, to improve accuracy and effectiveness. I usually do a short, silent invocation before I use them, asking them to be cleansed and accurate and calling upon my higher self and masters to guide their movement for me. As I walk with the intention of finding ley lines, they will cross. By noting where they cross and uncross, I can map out how the lines flow. Though most

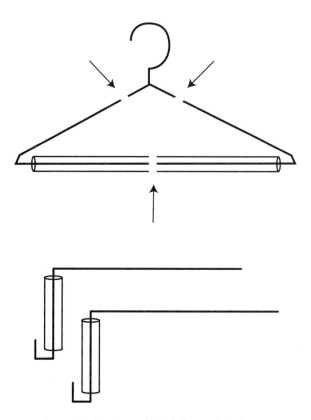

Figure 49: Dowsing Rods Made from a Coat Hanger

assume from Watkins' initial work that all ley lines are straight, most modern practitioners notice that they bend and curve, and some appear to move in the form of a spiral.

I suggest making a map of the ley lines of your home area, particularly of any places where you do ritual. You'll learn where to be when you do magick for world peace and ascension, or planetary healing, and where to stand when you want to keep things private and personal. Meditation at these sites can yield powerful information about the land, its past and its future.

EARTH HEALING

Healing on the grids and the surrounding energetic environment can be done much the same way that healing is done on a human being. Visualization, energy work, crystals, flower essences, and aid from spirit guides are all techniques to be adapted for healing.

Sacred geometry lends us a set of tools to bring healing and balance to our environments. One of the most powerful but little-known tools is one I learned from Machaelle Small Wright's co-creative gardening lessons. It involves the use of a Genesa crystal (figure 50). The Genesa "crystal" is not a crystal at all, but a geometric form usually made of copper. The Genesa crystal is a pattern of four interlocked circles, or rings, based upon the work of Dr. Derald Langham, who is said to have developed it in the 1950s. The image is pattered after the eight-cell pattern that begins all life. The shape is called a crystal because it acts much like a stone metaphysically, and can program and move energy. The Genesa recycles energy, clears unwanted patterns, and holds intentions. It is often thought of as a psychic/spiritual energy purifier. Psychic ability, communication, and dream work improve in the presence of a Genesa crystal. The energy of anything placed in it, such as a crystal, gets amplified and projected in all directions. People often put crystals, flower essences, or essential oils in the structure, to supercharge them, but also to diffuse their qualities in a large area. The larger the construct, the larger the field it projects. Though some metaphysical shops make them available in small jewelry form, or large room and garden sizes, you can also construct a Genesa crystal. For detailed instructions, see Wright's *Perelandra Garden Workbook*. By simply by putting a Genesa crystal in a disturbed environment for a time, you can heal the land significantly. I use mine in Earth healing rituals.

More complicated methods of Earth healing include full rituals to restore balance. I find such rituals particularly useful in the face of modern construction. The Earth is not opposed to human advancement, if it's in harmony with nature. Too often we tear down things in an effort to be efficient, without thinking of the consequences of our actions. I look forward to the time when everyone will respect the Earth and faery folk, and build roads and dwellings with them in mind. When we cut down trees, dig up land, or disrupt

Figure 50: Genesa Crystal

nature in any way, we upset the balance of devic and telluric forces around us. Those in tune with nature often feel this as pain, as nature feels it as pain. Many lightworkers go around "fixing" the problems generated by those who are not aware of the natural forces. Most people involved in construction do not have a belief system that takes into account the spirits of nature. Many of us who are in tune with nature see our roles as guardians and partners with the natural realm. We perform Earth healing in areas where there is disruption because we sense the need. If everybody who sensed the pain of the land and the land spirits had the tools to help heal the land and used them, then humanity might have a more harmonious relationship with the environment.

If there has been construction, pollution, violence, or any other energetic disruption of the land, then visit with the land. It's best to visit with it in person, but if the construction or other damaging agents are still present, or if it's private property and you can get arrested for trespassing, then count yourself down into a meditative state and visit it psychically. To find out what to do to help heal this land, I summon the spirits connected with it.

I, (state your name), call upon the deva ruling over this land.
I call upon Pan and the nature spirits of this land.
I call upon Mother Gaia.
I call upon my higher self and my highest guides and masters.

Then, mentally through words and pictures, I ask the spirits gathered to tell me what needs to be done to this land in order to bring healing and restore balance. Then I listen with an open heart and do whatever I am guided to do. They might give me a specific visualization, to summon energy to restore balance. Often I evoke the green ray to descend from Shamballa and bathe the area in healing light. Other times I simply visualize nature growing up around the construction in a harmonious way, as best it can around the buildings. Sometimes I get instructions, when feasible, to cleanse, program, and bury certain crystals at the site. Sometime I'm called to charge a stone that was dug up at the site, to act as an anchor for healing energy. I particularly enjoy being called to use flower essences. I often put drops of the necessary flower essences in big gallon jugs of water and then pour the liquid over the land. For those who do Reiki, you might be called to use it, or other healing techniques, upon the land. Another option is to do a magick circle ritual, either physically or mentally, to bring balance. Be open to whatever creative suggestions Gaia, Pan, and the spirits have for you. When done, make sure you thank and release any of the spirits you have summoned.

> I, (state your name), thank and release the deva ruling over this land.
> I thank and release Pan and all the nature spirits of this land.
> I thank and release my higher self and my highest guides and masters.
> I ask that all of you experience the healing and love that you need at this time.
> Hail and farewell.

If I know construction is going to start in an area, then I do this communication prior to the disturbance, to warn the spirits and prepare the land energetically for the disruption. Simply use your communication and follow your guidance. Each situation will be unique, as the land's needs will be unique. Sometimes you might feel like a counselor, trying to soothe the land spirits while apologizing for humanity's actions. We can't control our peers when they don't understand the results of their actions. Offerings, like the faery offerings, can restore peace and good will between humanity and nature spirits, when heartfelt. You might feel moved to bring a Genesa crystal to the land. The land will help you restore balance. Simply listen to it and then act.

CRYSTAL GRIDS AND PLANETARY HEALING

A modern, and much easier, method of Earth acupuncture and planetary healing is through the use of crystals. Rather than worrying about permanently erecting large megaliths, healing can be done with a set of small stones. Crystals can change the energy of any environment, when directed to do so, healing areas of pollution—physical or energetic. They can perform a form of Earth grid acupuncture, to activate an area of land into full consciousness.

Crystal grids are groups of crystals, working in harmony together as a team, set in specific geometric patterns. Any group of crystals can work as a team, but these specific alignments give them a certain power. Grids create magickal mandalas, usually out of quartz points, to direct the energy, but are sometimes accented with other minerals, whose energies the quartz points will amplify and direct.

Though grids can be made in star formations with any number of points, one of the most popular alignments is the six-point, or hexagram, configuration (figure 51). It is balanced and harmonious. It creates a merkaba vortex (see chapter 21) and can be used for healing, integration, and ascension. Hexagram configurations are the primary geometrical shapes used to do Earth healing. When the points are directed outward, they are used to project an expanding field of energy, to cleanse, clear, and renew the vibrations of the area. This configuration can be used for physical and energetic pollution. When pointed inward, the grid acts like a crystal acupuncture point, to direct energy into a specific point. This configuration can be used on ley lines, to fill them with healing energy and awaken them to all twelve dimensions. Earth healing work should be done only with the direct guidance of the masters, devas, and nature spirits. If you feel called to do this work, then the masters will guide you to do so.

To use a crystal grid, make sure your crystals are cleansed and programmed, particularly with a program to activate/deactivate upon command. Place the crystals in the correct geometric positions on the land where you want healing. Direct your energy to one point, either with your fingers or third eye, and mentally command that crystal to activate. Then mentally draw a line to the next crystal in the geometric pattern, moving clockwise. If you are doing a hexagram, the alignment would be the two interlocking triangles. Complete the geometric shape three times, each time telling the crystal to activate. Once all the crystals are active, imagine the vertical axis of dimensions descending as a pillar of light to the crystal grid and then down into the center of the Earth. If the points are facing inward, then the pillar will stay focused on that point, like an energetic needle going into it. I call upon archangel Uriel and my master guides to aid the healing of the ley line and ask that it be activated in harmony and love in all twelve dimensions. I might also draw Reiki symbols, particularly the Shamballa symbol Mer Ka Fa Ka Lish Ma, or do a Mahatma infusion into the grid.

If the points are facing outward, then imagine the energy flowing outward in waves, healing and purifying the area all around the grid, reaching out further and further.

Figure 51: Hexagram Crystal Grid

Follow your guidance as to how long to keep a grid active. You can use your muscle testing or pendulum for a clear yes/no answer. When done, visualize the beam of light descending into the Earth. Thank the angels and masters for their help. Point to each of the crystals in the reverse order, moving counterclockwise, and mentally direct each crystal to deactivate. Trace the hexagram three times. Disassemble the grid.

The hexagram grid can be used for individual healing, with the client inside the grid, or for meditation, creating something akin to a dimensional stargate and making it easy to access multidimensional consciousness. You can put other stones in the center of the grid, to add more energies to the healing. I like to use rose quartz, amethyst, and moldavite.

PART FIVE

THE MYSTERIES
OF ASCENSION

18

initiation

Initiation is a powerful term that is filled with mystery but is also the source of a lot of confusion. *Initiate* literally means "to begin," though some people think of an initiation as a completion. It's much like a graduation ceremony from school. It signifies that a certain amount of training has been done, but now the real work begins, in which you apply what you have learned outside the halls of school and use it out in the real world.

Initiation occurs on two levels. There are outer-world initiations and inner-world initiations. The outer-world initiations are rituals performed by a particular teacher or tradition. They are like formal graduation rituals. Through such initiations, you can be formally recognized as a member of that tradition after a period of training, or have a new rank or title conferred upon you. The formal traditions of Wicca and Golden Dawn–style ceremonial magick have such initiations, as do the Freemasons. Even the traditions of Reiki healing are initiatory, as a teacher uses a ritual to "attune" a new student to the system and practice of Reiki. In fact, all initiation rituals are similar to Reiki attunements, as the teacher is passing on a "current" of energy from the tradition to the student. Each tradition contains its own thoughtforms or guiding spirits made from energy contributed by all those who have been part of the tradition. The initiate receiving the energy might find herself with newly awakened abilities and an increased energy or vibration that aids her spiritual journey.

Inner-world initiations are a bit more mysterious. The purpose of many outer-world initiations is to actually trigger the experience of an inner-world initiation, though an inner-world initiation can happen spontaneously. Such initiations include any experience that utterly changes you, that marks a new beginning. Life circumstances provide initiation experiences. We feel like we are being tested. Experiences that we could describe as "if it doesn't kill you, it will only make you stronger" would be considered initiations. Times when you have had to expand your sense of self, your resources, your perspective to get through your difficulties can be initiations. From a spiritual perspective, you come away from an inner-world initiation with profound spiritual teachings about life and the nature of consciousness, even if you don't recognize them as such, and once you experience them, you can never go back to being the "old" you. Recovery from a severe accident or serious illness, change of career, death of a loved one, coming out of the closet, and changing religions are all forms of initiation, depending on how you handle the situation.

Initiation Through Non-Ordinary Reality

Magickal inner-world initiations are much like these challenges of life, but are even more intense. They involve breaking down limited notions of life or reality, and opening the initiate to a new way of looking at the universe, including the spiritual world.

In shamanic cultures, when the tribe had no shaman, often one member who might be inclined toward spirit healing work would fall sick and enter a coma. In this fevered dream, the spirits would teach this person how to be a shaman. If he recovered, then he would come back with healing power and knowledge. In other shamanic cultures, an initiate would go into the woods for an extended period of time, usually unprepared. If he survived, it was because he spoke to the spirits of the plants, animals, and nature, his own guardians and gods. When he returned, he would have the power of a shaman. If he didn't return, then he failed that initiation experience and died.

Sometimes the shaman will experience an initiation known as dismemberment, in which the shaman is torn apart by a divinity or monster during a vision. Though the shaman's self-image is destroyed, his pure consciousness survives, teaching him the mysteries of transcending death. His body is then rebuilt by a divine figure, and typically a new element—such as a stone, bone, or crystal—is added to the body to demonstrate the change, and additional power, of the resurrected self. This mystery is similar to the teachings of the mysteries of the gods Osiris, Dionysus, and even Jesus Christ. Sometimes these experiences happen spontaneously, while other times the shamanic practitioner initiates them, such as the Tibetan ritual of Chöd. Initiation traditions of death and resurrection are found at the heart of all the ancient world's mystery schools and temples, including the teachings of Inanna, the Eleusinian mysteries of Demeter and Persephone, the Orphic mystery schools, and the Mithraic cults. Each systematically taught the mysteries, using rituals to induce the inner-world transformation. We can even look at the root of many of our life-passage rituals, from tribal rites of passage to Catholic sacraments, as forms of initiation ceremonies.

In the modern era, NDEs, or Near-Death Experiences, are a primary form of major spontaneous initiation. Experiences that we don't fully understand on a terrestrial level, such as alien abduction or faery abduction, also catalyze initiatory experiences. One only has to look at the writing and life of Whitley Strieber, author of *Communion*, to see how his contact with nonterrestrial intelligences changed him forever. Hauntings, religious visions, miraculous healings, psychedelic drug trips, and other methods of contact with a non-physical reality can induce an initiation experience.

From a magickal perspective, your first successful experience with magick—whether a manifestation of psychic ability, speaking with a spirit, or any other esoteric phenomenon that awakens you to the magickal, subtle reality—is an initiation. My first initiation was a firsthand experience of psychic diagnosis and healing. I believed there was no way I could do it, but I followed my teacher's training and was open to the experience, yet feared I would fail, or that it wasn't real. I had such a powerful, verifiable experience, with a lot of little experiences leading up to it, that my mind was blown wide open, and I knew I could never go back to being someone who didn't believe in magick and psychic ability. The experience had the profound effect of demonstrating to me that all things are connected, whether we realize it or not. It shocked me into making a significant lifestyle change, and I began devoting much of my time to studying the mystical arts.

Initiation In Ascension

In the overall tradition of ascension, initiation most commonly refers to a series of "steps" described in terms of vibration, light quotient, and advances on the path of ascension. Each step describes a level of awareness and development, and is often compared to the life actions of the masters and mystics of ages past. Ascension magicians also find value in other systems of initiation, marking out levels of awakening and advancement. Systems outlining life initiations are designed to benchmark a person's spiritual progress. I think that initiation is very personal, much like our divisions of magick, and that the lines we draw to divide and categorize initiations are arbitrary; but if you follow a particular system, or point of view on spiritual development, then you can track the changes you are undergoing, and have a map for how to get to the next step. Initiation systems are powerful guides to help us in our spiritual quest, helping us recognize the landmarks, be warned about the pitfalls, and prepare for the coming work.

The systems describing initiation that I have found most helpful have been the traditional Theosophical ascension path, the stages of development from alchemy, the initiations on the Tree of Life, and those outlined on the left-hand path.

THE Initiations OF ASCENSION

In channeled Theosophical material, seven stages of initiation for ascension are outlined, with two preliminary steps and several paths of spiritual development. They are interwoven with our interactions with the Lords and Ladies of Shamballa, who act as our catalysts, guides, and models through the initiations. Initiates are considered to be lightworkers, as the light quotient and vibration are the indicators of what level of initiation one has attained, though there is no objective measurement of such levels, but only psychic impressions from others, or messages received directly from the masters. Though many exercises exist to increase light quotient and refine energy, the best method of walking the path of ascension is to expand your consciousness through the understanding of the triad consisting of divine love, wisdom, and power. Through the proper balancing of the various subtle bodies, and the proper use of love, wisdom, and power, one grows in consciousness and finds the path of ascension.

Probationary Path

At this stage, the potential initiate is not yet aware of initiation, but starts to turn his attention to the higher self and spiritual reality. The individual attracts the attention of a master or group of masters, and the master and higher self stimulate the conscious self with more spiritual light, to see how the individual responds to this energy.

Accepted Disciple

The true initiatory work between the master and disciple begins at this stage. The probationary individual has responded appropriately to the spiritual energy and is accepted by the master as a disciple on the path. The master begins to blend energetically with the disciple, though the disciple might not be completely aware of this connection on a conscious level. Meditation becomes a key practice at this level. The initiate develops spiritual qualities more fully through a meditative practice and the influence of the master. The initiate begins to think about service to the world, the greater good and the divine, and makes an effort to incorporate service into his life.

First Initiation

The requirement of the first initiation is the beginning mastery of the physical body. This could also be seen as mastery of the earth element, from a magickal point of view. The initiate goes through a period of physical cleansing, and may change his diet, restrict toxin intake, and cleanse himself with pure water. The keywords of this stage are moderation and balance, as the initiate masters the physical urges of appetite, sexuality, and sleep. The initiate senses that life is more than just the world of physicality, of the body, and seeks more out of life, soon finding the spiritual path. Appropriate tools for this level include meditation, as well as forms of physical spirituality, such as yoga, martial arts, and fasting.

Second Initiation

As the first initiation requires a certain mastery over the physical body, the second initiation requires a level of mastery over the astral body, or water element. The initiate learns to control his emotions and desires by not identifying with them, and learns to direct his emotional energies into service and self-realization. He becomes inspired by the divine, and develops a more conscious understanding of his higher self and spirit guides. At this initiation level, the initiate ceases to be a victim of his emotions, and learns that his emotions contribute to his reality and that he can control them. Prior to this level, the initiate goes through phases of emotional and psychological healing, understanding his motivations and patterns. Emotional cleansing occurs, and issues of the past that have been repressed will need to be healed. Meditation, counseling, journal writing, affirmations, visualizations, and inner-child work are all powerful tools to prepare for this level.

Third Initiation

The third initiation consists of greater mastery over the mental body and the element of air. The initiate learns to control his thoughts and thoughtforms, no longer being a victim to unconscious thoughts, obsessive thinking, or unclear thought and communication. This process will continue over the next initiations, but a clearer mind is achieved before taking the third initiation. The initiate takes responsibility for his thoughts, and learns to neutralize, and eventually abandon, unwanted thoughtforms and patterns. The transformation of the mind is genuine, and not simply the denial of harmful or unwanted thoughts. Another name for the successful completion of this initiation is the "soul merge," for the personality integrates with the essence of the soul, allowing the initiate to focus more clearly on his spiritual goals in daily life, and to see and think from a soul perspective rather than an ego perspective.

Fourth Initiation

The fourth initiation is one of the most pivotal stages. It is known as the crucifixion or renunciation initiation. The initiate is forced to give up all outer support, letting go of all that is no longer necessary. None of the old mechanisms of support work anymore, and the initiate must rely on himself—not just his personal self, but also his divine self and relationship to spirit. For many initiates, this stage signals the end of career, relationships, family, and friendships on some level. For some, the change is dramatic, and for others, less so. To many, this is the dark night of the soul that precedes a great shift and transformation in consciousness. The initiate may feel like all his earthly accomplishments are being stripped away, and he must truly learn the lessons of nonattachment to the physical world and reliance on the spiritual world. He gives up any sense of self-importance or any self-serving patterns. The initiate's aura is compared to an egg at this point, and upon successful completion of the fourth initiation, it is as if the egg breaks open and a new being emerges. The individually is now fully merged with his higher self, and the monad, also known as the I AM Presence, now fulfills the function that the higher self once did, as the primary inner guide. The spiritual connection of the antakarana, or rainbow bridge, is strengthened to allow direct communion between the individual and the monad. The initiate's aura is viewed no longer as egg-shaped, but as a vortex of light. According to Dr. Joshua David Stone, the individual's light quotient is at 65 percent at this point. Once the fourth initiation has been completed, the initiate can grow by leaps and bounds, fully conscious of the spiritual reality and having a much clearer sense of purpose, or magickal will, in the world.

Fifth Initiation

The fifth initiation is the partial merger of the initiate's consciousness with his monad. This is called the resurrection initiation in Christian mythology, and one who moves through this initiation is known as an adept. In many ways, the initiate seems to become a different person, reborn in the light of his monad. The individual's light quotient is now said to be at 75 percent. The fifth initiation is like a higher octave in experience of the third initiation. Where the third involves merging with the soul level, the fifth is merging with the monadic level.

Sixth Initiation

Ascension, or at least the start of ascension, is the sixth initiation. It represents the full and conscious merger of the initiate's conscious self with his monad while on Earth. The individual becomes a fledgling ascended master after this initiation. Many believe that at this level, the physical body is no longer relevant, and the individual becomes a body of light, living consciously and fully in the lightbody. Light quotient must be between 80 percent and 83 percent at this stage. The initiate experiences full Christ consciousness, or unconditional love, at this point of awareness. He completes his personal earthly mission, his dharma for the physical plane, and is not required to return to Earth.

Seventh Initiation

The seventh initiation completes the earthly ascension process. The initiate merges his conscious self with the seventh plane of reality, with the logoic forces of Earth as embodied by Sanat Kumara and Shamballa. The initiation occurs when the individual's light quotient is at 92 percent, but is not complete until stabilization at 97 percent. The individual becomes a global teacher, whether physically present in the world or in a nonphysical ascended state. The initiate's chakra system is said to transform from an individualized system of multiple points to a unified chakra, a column of light running through the body, as the chakras and the chakra tube, or antakarana, merge, and the initiate receives higher vibrational energy through Sanat Kumara. The individual transcends the laws of the physical universe, and is capable of performing the miracles of saints and gurus. He can be completely liberated from the physical plane, if he so chooses. The initiate becomes a full-fledged ascended master in the courts of Shamballa and begins a new series of learning and a new mission as a master.

Beyond these seven levels of initiation are said to be higher octaves of galactic initiation in a process of galactic or cosmic ascension. The various levels might not be clear-cut in this lifetime, or over multiple lifetimes. The individual continues to refine his mastery of the lower levels, as he works through issues of the body, emotions, and mind in every incarnation. He might have experienced higher levels of initiations in past lives, but feels like he has to repeat or review them in this lifetime before he can advance further.

According to ascension theology, as we move through initiations, we are offered a variety of paths for our personal evolution. We are offered the following choices of paths back to the source after the sixth initiation.

The Path of Earth Service

On this path, a master works in the ashram of a particular chohan, and focuses on helping the Earth from the inner planes. Such masters usually choose to focus on the animal, plant, mineral, or human realm.

The Path of Magnetic Work

A master on this path works to clear the illusions and glamours of the worlds so that all can see clearly and truly.

The Path of the Planetary Logos

A master trains with the Planetary Logos to become a planetary logos, or sub-logos, for one of the planets in this solar system, or another system.

The Path to Sirius

This is the path that most humans follow, as Sirius is considered to be the higher octave of Earth in terms of spiritual development. The Great White Brotherhood of Earth is said to be merely an outpost of the Great White Brotherhood of the spirits of Sirius.

The Ray Path

This path is for those who stay in the ray of their soul, and learn to work with the chohan of that ray, eventually learning to become the chohan of that ray if the work is done properly. This path is similar to the Path of Earth Service.

The Path of the Solar Logos

On this path, a master learns to how to become a solar logos, rather than a planetary logos.

The Path of Absolute Sonship

A master on this path works to connect the Earth with greater cosmic beings.

THE ALCHEMICAL LADDER

The medieval alchemists gave us quite a complex spiritual model, based on the arts of alchemy from ancient Egypt, the Middle East, and Asia, to understand the initiation process. Modern alchemists look to a model of seven alchemical steps, or processes, on a ladder to enlightenment (figure 52). By decoding the alchemical art and wood carvings, we can find a process of spiritual evolution demonstrated in the images of strange animals, esoteric glyphs, kings, queens, and hermaphrodites. Each step is a chemical process the alchemist would place herbal and mineral compounds through, but these laboratory results were said to reflect the changes the alchemist's soul underwent when performing the experiments. The laboratory work is much like that of any magician or mystic. The rituals serve to focus the spiritual energies, using the axiom of the alchemist, "as above, so below," so a change in the material universe corresponds to the change in the alchemist's energy. Each of the seven processes parallels other systems of seven—the seven magickal planets, their seven sacred metals, and the seven chakras. The process of becoming alchemical gold is like the attainment of the true lightbody, another allegory for ascension.

Calcination

The chemical operation of calcination is the process of burning a substance, usually a dry herb, to ash. As a spiritual process, calcination is aligned with the root chakra, the planet Saturn, and the densest metal, lead. Fire is the element of this process. Spiritually, calcination is the first spiritual fire, the first flash of the inner spark that helps the initiate learn that there is more to life than the desires of the ego and simple gratification. The burning fire of calcination helps us understand that life is not simply a series of repetitive, meaningless events. Calcination give us the first glimpse into understanding our spiritual power. It helps burn away the ego, or at least parts of it, to reveal the spiritual energy behind the matter. We experience synchronicity, or magick, at this level. The spark of calcination helps inspire us to have an introspective process, to see more clearly all the time. This process is empowering and is sometimes called an awakening.

Dissolution

Chemically, dissolution involves taking the ash of calcination and dissolving it in a solvent, creating a solution. It relates to the planet Jupiter, the metal tin, and the belly chakra. Water is the element of dissolution. The solution in which the initiate is dissolved is her own emotions. Emotions and traumas that have been repressed are brought up to be faced and healed. The introspection of calcination brings up the shadow, the dark emotions to be faced, understood, and integrated in a healthy manner in the process of dissolution.

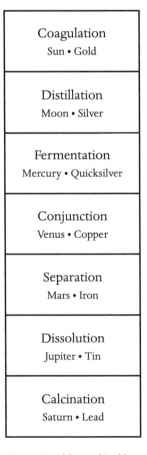

Figure 52: Alchemical Ladder

Separation

Separation is the process of parting the insoluble salts from the solution of the previous process of dissolution. Esoterically, separation is related to the planet Mars, the force that separates and draws boundaries. Its metal is iron, and the chakra is the solar plexus. Air is the element of separation, though the process tends to have some fiery qualities. To the age-old alchemists, air was both warm and moist. During separation, spiritually the initiate becomes separated from many of her peers and family members. The mystic's path can be lonely. The initiate is confronted with how different she is from those around her. She must transform the martial energy of separation into that of the spiritual warrior, the one of right action. The invisible essence that remains in the solution is like the invisible essence of the universe, unseen yet present, guiding and sustaining the initiate, supporting the spiritual self but not the ego. The initiate begins to rely on guidance, seeing herself as an instrument of the universe, rather than relying simply on personal needs and personal power. The power comes from a greater source.

Conjunction

When the salts and solution join together, we have the process of conjunction. It relates to the bridge of the chakras, the heart, situated in the middle of the seven steps. Its planet is Venus, and its metal is copper. Earth is the element of the conjunction. Conjunction creates a new sense of awareness in the initiate that allows the rectification of seemingly opposite traits, making them complements. A balance of two traits, such as logic and feeling, male and female, or light and dark, occurs. The process can involve two seemingly conflicting self-images, such as the desire to be a perfect, holy person while still being very human, experiencing pain, anger, or fear. This union usually results in a rebirth, leading the initiate into a new understanding of her purpose in life, complete with a more peaceful, optimistic, and centered sense of self.

Fermentation

Fermentation is the process of encouraging matter to putrefy, to rot and spoil, which will eventually make a spirit. In the case of grains and many fruits, the spirit is an alcohol that can eventually be distilled and consumed. Fermentation relates to the throat chakra, the planet Mercury, and the metal quicksilver. On a spiritual level, fermentation is the dark night of the soul. The process of introspection started at calcination brings the initiate to a point of disconnection, into her true shadow self. Many individuals face fear, anger, guilt, depression, despair, and suicidal impulses. The fermentation process is the abyss of human experience, a vast gulf to face and cross in order to reach a new level of understanding. Fermentation is the first operation that doesn't have an elemental association to it, raising the experience to the celestial level and beyond the terrestrial realm of elements. Chemical fermentation can create a rainbow oil-slick image, similar to looking at a drop of gasoline in a puddle. The spiritual initiation of fermentation is said to create such an oil slick, also known as the Peacock's Tail, in the soul of the initiate, allowing the initiate to bridge the gap between the terrestrial and celestial worlds, like the rainbow bridge image found in Norse mythology, connecting the world of mortals to the world of the sky gods.

Distillation

Distillation is the process of separating the spirit from the fermented matter. It is associated with the brow chakra (the chakra of psychic ability or higher powers), the Moon, and the Moon's metal, silver. In spiritual terms, the initiate, having crossed the abyss of the dark night of the soul and passed through the veil of the Peacock's Tail, is now able to contact, connect with, and even identify with the higher mystical forces of divinity, though this can happen in many ways. The initiate might identify with her own higher self, an ascended master, god, or other divine spirit. Sometimes the initiate temporarily loses her ability to function in the material world while so enraptured in the spiritual. Some individuals recover, while others sink deeper into mystical delusions, identifying themselves as savior figures or godlike beings. Rather than recognize their divinity and recognize that they are still material beings, they instead neglect their anchor to the material world and physical life. Some exhibit cult-like behavior, encouraging others to worship them and recognize their powers, and because of this level of awareness, they may have formidable psychic or magickal abilities, but not necessarily the enlightenment to use them wisely. Those who successfully navigate through the distillation process rise up and use this contact to expand their consciousness and develop their spiritual abilities further, without losing reason or the ability to remain grounded.

Coagulation

Coagulation is the final step on the seven rungs of the alchemical ladder. It is the union of materials, creating something new with the best assets of the materials used to create it. This process is identified with the crown chakra, the Sun, and the metal gold. Pure gold doesn't tarnish or rust. It is bright colored and solid, yet malleable. It contains the best qualities of all the metals, without their drawbacks. On the spiritual path, coagulation is the union of the highest realms of consciousness with the ability to function in the objective world. One who lives at this level not only functions, but demonstrates the highest spiritual ideals in everyday functioning. Many people would consider the process of spiritual coagulation as enlightenment, self-realization, or ascension.

The important thing to remember is that the ladder goes on infinitely. One rises from the material world and descends again. One refines to the point of coagulation and then begins again with calcination. You might have experiences echoing all seven of these operations, but not necessarily achieve ascension. You continue to refine while you are incarnated in a body. When you are no longer in the material world and no longer need to return, then perhaps you will have a different set of alchemical operations to refine yourself.

Initiations on the Tree of Life

The system of initiation used in the orders of ceremonial magick is based on the Tree of Life. Each sphere on the Tree of Life represents a level of consciousness, a level of initiation to be mastered. This system can represent both inner- and outer-world initiations, as the ceremonial orders have their own initiation rituals and requirements for each level that are said to be objective measures of the inner spiritual development the magician has obtained.

In terms of Qabalistic lore, each sephira has a "vision," or experience, that helps one understand and achieve that level of consciousness if the vision is integrated into waking consciousness. A magician will demonstrate the "virtue" of that sephira when that level is attained and balanced, or a "vice" if that sphere's energy is unattained or unbalanced. Furthermore, there is an "obligation," or a path, to attain this level of awareness, as well as an "illusion" that prevents true attainment.

In terms of initiation levels, each rank is described with two numbers. The first number describes the initiatory step in the group. The second is the number of the sephira on the Tree of Life that corresponds with that initiation's energy. This code is found primarily in ceremonial orders, and gives you an idea of not only what initiation step it is, but also to which part of the tree the step relates. The title of each level can vary depending on the order.

Neophyte—⓪=⓪

The neophyte grade is not on the Tree of Life, but represents a decision to enter the spiritual path. The Greek word neophyte means "newly planted" and shows the initiate as a seed beginning to sprout in a new life. In the outer world, the initiate begins the study of the mystical and magick. The initiate also begins a process of purification and preparation, both through ritual and life experience.

Initiate—①= 10

The first step of the initiation process corresponds to the tenth sphere, Malkuth. The vision of the tenth sphere is Knowledge and Conversation of your Holy Guardian Angel, or, in simpler terms, establishing a conscious relationship with your higher self as your guide and guardian. The obligation to receive this vision is discipline, which is needed to maintain a spiritual practice to make this first step. The illusion of this sphere that distracts you from this goal is materialism, not looking beyond the physical world. The virtue of this sphere is discrimination, discernment of the material world, while the vice of this energy when unbalanced is inertia, or laziness, the lack of discipline to perform the work. The first degree relates to the element of earth and all things physical, so all physical steps necessary to continue the process of initiation and self-realization are taken. One gains greater control over the physical body and the physical world.

Zealot—②=⑨

The second step on the path aligns with the ninth sphere, Yesod. Yesod relates to the Moon, and while some see it as a rank of mastering the element of air, many modern practitioners relate it to the element of water and the emotional realm. The vision of this level of consciousness is the Vision of the Machinery of the Universe, an understanding of how things work, that there are no spare parts in the universe, and that you have a place in the universe. The obligation to get to this level is trust, trust in the divine. The illusion is security, for the rise in consciousness burns away the illusions about security of the astral plane. As we rise from the security of the earthly realm, we must take risks. The virtue of this sphere is independence, while the vice is its opposite, dependence.

Practitioner—③=⑧

The third step on the path works with the eighth sphere, Hod. The planet Mercury relates to the faculties of communication, logic, and memory in astrology, and here we find a level related to the element of air, of the mind, though some traditionalists associate Hod with water. The vision is the Vision of Splendor, the splendor of the universe. To find this splendor, you need the obligation of learning. The illusion of this sphere is order, for while there is pattern, there is no absolute order. The virtue of this sphere is honesty, for our words have power, and the vice is dishonesty.

Philosopher—④=⑦

The fourth step in the realm of initiation relates to the seventh sphere, Netzach. The last of the four elemental steps, this realm deals with fire, with passion and desire. Venus, the planet of love and attraction, is the sphere of Netzach. One achieves the Vision of Beauty Triumphant. It is not the beauty of physical perfection, but the beauty one sees in the highest of emotions, and in nature. The obligation of this sphere is responsibility, while the illusion is emotional projection, seeing the things we dislike in ourselves in others, or seeing what we want to see in others. The virtue of this sphere is unselfishness, while the vice is selfishness.

Adept—⑤=⑥

The sixth sphere, Tiphereth, the sphere of the Sun, relates to the fifth step on the ladder of initiation. Here one crosses a veil and achieves an understanding beyond the elemental steps. One achieves the Vision of Harmony through understanding the nature of sacrifice. All the sacrificed godforms and solar figures are associated with this initiation. On a spiritual level, this step is like a crucifixion or sacrificial experience. One goes beyond the limited identity of the ego. One exhibits the virtue of devotion to the Great Work, to enlightenment, and releases the vice of false pride. The obligation of this level is integrity, and the illusion is identification. One learns to identify not only with the limited self, but also with the higher self and the universe. Some practitioners see this initiation as a step beyond the classic "Knowledge and Conversation of the Holy Guardian Angel," beyond a simple relationship with it, but rather a union or merger of the personal self with the Holy Guardian Angel.

Advanced Adept—⑥–⑤

The sphere of Geburah, the fifth sphere on the Tree of Life, aligns with the sixth step, that of the advanced adept. Geburah is the sphere of mastering power and corresponds with the planet Mars. The vision of the sixth step of initiation is the Vision of Power, and requires courage as both its obligation and virtue. The illusion of this sphere is invincibility, for no one is invincible, and the vice is wanton cruelty and destruction.

Perfect Adept—⑦=④

The perfect adept aligns with the fourth sephira, Chesed, the sphere of Jupiter. The perfect adept's vision is of Love—true spiritual compassion, not romantic love. To find this love, one must be humble. The illusion of this sphere is self-righteousness. The balanced initiate at the Perfect Adept stage exhibits the virtue of obedience, but obedience to the divine, to the higher will, not to any human agency. The vices of Chesed are many, including gluttony, bigotry, hypocrisy, and tyranny. The image is of either the benevolent king or the selfish tyrant, depending on if the enlightened or unenlightened aspect is manifesting.

Master—⑧=③

The level of master crosses the abyss of the Tree of Life, and aligns with the third sphere, Binah. To the ascensionist, the shift from the perfect adept to the master is the shift to ascension, to becoming a first-rank ascended master. Binah is beyond the abyss of the physical universe of the seven spheres below it. Binah, corresponding with Saturn, grants the Vision of Sorrow, the sorrow of the world. It is an understanding of the world, and a sense of compassion. There is no obligation to this sphere, or to any other sphere above it. The virtue of this sphere is silence. The illusion is death, since nothing dies, but is reborn in another form. Ascension is simply a shift into another level of reality. The Master rank is also known as the Master of the Temple, who is called to tend a "garden" of students.

Mage—⑨=②

The ninth initiation level is related to the second sphere, Chokmah, and the zodiac. Here one becomes the true mage, a true force of nature. One receives the Vision of the Source, the primal power of Kether. The illusion of this sphere is independence, which was the virtue of Yesod and is now transformed, for at this level, nothing is separate and independent.

Ipsissimus—⑩=①

The tenth and final initiation step relates to the first sphere on the Tree of Life, Kether. Ipsissimus is usually translated to mean the "very very self," "very own self," or true self, beyond all image or illusion. The last stage of initiation, the union with the source, with Kether, is not embodied by any vision, but by actual reunion with the source, and the completion of the Great Work. The illusion of this sphere is attainment, for we never reach the ultimate end until everyone receives this level of initiation. That is the mystery of the bodhisattva. We have initiation upon initiation to experience, in different forms and functions. The Ipsissimus is beyond all understanding of those in the ranks below and is a master of all forms of consciousness.

Initiation on the Left-Hand Path

Initiation occurs on all paths and in all traditions. One of the most clear, sound, and grounded outlines of the inner initiation a magician undergoes comes from a book entitled *Uncle Setnakt's Essential Guide to the Left Hand Path*, by Don Webb. Grounded in the traditions of the Temple of Set, which many modern lightworkers would initially view as evil, it nonetheless is quite helpful in understanding the path of initiation.

Wandering

The potential initiate wanders through life, perhaps guided unconsciously, but unaware of the true nature of the universe. Surface perceptions are believed to be the truth. Non-ordinary reality is not experienced. Belief systems are gathered at random due to circumstances of life and culture. Stress causes most people to regress into more primal behavior, such as addictive or escapist activities, while a few potential initiates use that stress to develop more complex systems of behavior and begin the path of initiation.

Shock

A life circumstance acts as a shock to the initiate. The circumstance awakens the initiate to the fact that her familiar reality is not quite what it seems. The shock knocks the initiate off the path her life was on. The shock can be of an emotional or intellectual nature, such as the betrayal of a loved one, the end of a relationship, the loss of a career, or a medical illness. Sometimes it's even a spiritual shock, to a new, unseen reality. Many people never recover from the shock, and go back to sleep. Those who do recover will be initiates on the path and do not fall asleep completely.

Daydreaming

The initiate rebuilds her life through daydreaming. She works in a fantasy world stirred by the desires awakened in her by the shock experience. During this daydreaming phase, the initiate develops minor occult skills, such as self-hypnosis and visualization. She is able to break out of the cages of society and follow her own desires and bliss, having some success despite the odds against her. She learns that if she has sufficient will, then she can create a change in her life, even if it seems unlikely. Many people stay at this artistically awakened level, never going on to any further awakening or initiation, and are often unaware that there are more steps on the path.

Second Shock

The initiate is then exposed to a second shock. While the first shock was of a more mundane nature, the second one is of a more magickal nature. The initiate is shocked by the possibility that the world is much stranger, and there is much more potential, than the daydream stage allowed. The shock might consist of meeting someone of genuine occult ability, a talented magician or healer, or of having a manifestation of her own higher self or a spiritual being. Something that cannot be explained occurs, and the initiate is forced to look outside conventional means for an explanation. This is a very difficult and dangerous time for the initiate. Now, because the normal, conventional rules of the world, the world of science and the image of the world presented by the media, do not fully explain reality, the seeker might discard all logic and reason. People at this stage get stuck in obsessive thinking, focusing on bizarre theories, government and alien conspiracies, and new spiritual and occult fads. There is a lack of critical thinking and solely a vision of intuition and feeling, without a healthy balance or check. Many people get oriented in blame toward others, rather than feeling empowered, because they don't yet know how this new reality works. They become afraid and give away their power. The second shock prepares the initiate for the next level.

School

The spiritual seeker finds a school. It might not be a literal building, but it is a system of teaching. This system of spiritual teaching must be of sound metaphysical principle, and consistent in its philosophy, concepts, and ethics. It must have living teachers who show the way by bettering themselves through the teachings of the school. Usually, the seeker will pick a school because she can identify with the quest and struggles of the teacher, and she hopes to emulate the teacher's path. The school must attract a wide variety of students who can benefit from the teaching, and it also must have a series of levels, ranks, or some other orderly format of advancement, with objective criteria. A good match between school and student will help the new student eventually contact the teacher within. Through the school, the initiate experiences true awakening and enrichment of life on every level. The concept of awakening assumes that until this time, even despite the previous shocks, the initiate has been asleep, as most of humanity is asleep to the true nature of the world.

Third Shock

The student in a school will project her idealized self onto her teacher. Though the teacher may live up to those ideals for a time, the student will eventually realize that the teacher is human, like the student. The seeker learns that when an initiate of the mysteries makes a mistake, the consequences are usually on a larger scale than when ordinary people make mistakes. The student might feel that the teacher or school is corrupt or evil, and break away. She might turn her back on the process of spiritual initiation, feeling that it's all a sham because her ideals were not lived up to by another. She may even pursue any evils or perceived evils performed by her teachers, feeling that initiates such as her teachers, and now herself, are above ethics and morals. Here is where we have the many dramas of the esoteric communities, including the pagan "witch wars." Students profess that their teachers are shams and false prophets. They may feel that those who have been closest to them are now psychically attacking them. They may become disenchanted with their gurus, or feel used by a teacher. They may find people in power who are experiencing mystical delusions. Sometimes when they find these things, they are right, but sometimes it's just their perception. Those who make it through the sixth stage and continue onward reach the seventh stage of initiation.

Work

At this stage, the initiate moves past her own personal work, while maintaining a program of self-improvement, and begins to focus on her work in the world, on how to manifest her will in the world. The initiate maintains a link to her school, to her tradition, but seeks to make her own mark on the world. After attaining a certain level of mastery in her tradition, the initiate will seek out other philosophies and concepts to refine them and integrate them into her worldview. Many who dabble in and sample many traditions, but never learn a core philosophy or consistent set of ideas, symbols, and practices, never really move through the sixth stage of schooling, so they cannot come to the seventh. Those who do attain the work stage become the experts of their professions and enjoy satisfying lives. They continue the process of self-empowerment, truly becoming all they desire to be in this lifetime. They refine their philosophies and ideas, to pass them on to their students, students of their lineage or school, and their other spiritual descendants. Their work continues long past their physical lifetime, and acts as a seed for future generations.

These descriptions have been modified slightly to suit the awakening of any mystic, and not just those who identify as left-hand practitioners. Though outlined in seven stages, these stages are not necessarily linear, and the shocks, in particular, might not be single momentous events, but a course of events over time that move the initiate into change.

What I love about this system, and why I think it applies to mystics universally, is that it not only explains spiritual awakening and evolution in real-world terms, but it also shows the pitfalls, the places where one can go wrong on the path. Few systems point out the dangers of initiation in a practical way. Few prepare us for the shocks, and there are many. No one warns you where you might get stuck, so with a lack of knowledge, you might think you are on the last step.

I know many ascensionists who have been hanging out in the daydreaming phase, the Second Shock phase, and never seem to put the time into attending a school of training. They dabble, but never anchor themselves in a paradigm, even a consistent Theosophical ascension paradigm, to move to the work, where they can successfully synthesize new ideas. Many in particular get hung up on the fearful conspiracies, and forget the spiritual path. Even if the conspiracies are real, they shouldn't distract you from your own evolution, healing, and empowerment. In ascension, the more you expand your consciousness, the more you help the world. If you are stuck in fear, then you are only adding to the fear of the world. This Setian model actually gives you a road map out of the fear. From a practical point of view, I find this model of initiation as helpful, or even more helpful, compared to all the others outlined in this book.

By comparing the ascension levels, alchemical process, Tree of Life, and left-hand initiations, you can see a lot of commonality among them. As you review your life, you might find many initiation experiences, and see how they fit into these various models. When comparing your life experiences to systems of initiation, it is important to realize that these systems are not made to flatter your ego or to berate you for not being more spiritually advanced. Wherever you are is perfect for you. These systems provide maps to prepare you for where you are going.

initiation magick

Initiation magick is any act that sets into motion these transformative forces. Joining a group can be an act of initiation magick. Transforming hardship into a hard-won lesson is another act of initiation magick. Communing with the universe and the divine emissaries, such as the gods, spirits, and masters, and asking for initiation into the mysteries is also a form of initiation magick.

To those on the ascension path, the masters are available to aid our own spiritual evolution and advancement. One simply needs to ask for an initiation from the masters. Sometimes the masters will tell you no, and refuse you a further initiation because you are not yet prepared for it. Other times, initiation will happen spontaneously without request, occurring in your meditations, dreams, and rituals. If you are seeking spiritual initiation, ask your masters and guides, and they will help you prepare for it. Initiations come in many forms. There can be an initiation into working with a specific ray of light, attuning you to one or more of the twelve rays. Violet-flame initiations are the most common. You can be initiated into the Order of Melchizedek, which is believed to be a terrestrial branch of the Great White Brotherhood. Many lightworkers are consciously and subconsciously working in this order.

Though this next exercise is called a self-initiation ritual, it is really a ritual to invite the masters more fully into your life and aid your spiritual development. For some of you, it will be the first step of initiation. For others, it will deepen your experience of spiritual initiation and elevate your awareness to a new level.

EXERCISE 22:

Ascension Self-initiation

For this exercise you will need some Abramelin oil and eight candles, colored red, blue, yellow, green, orange, indigo, violet, and white. You will also need a pin or ritual blade to carve the candles.

1. To prepare for the ritual, carve the master symbol (see figure 24 in chapter 8) corresponding to each chohan of the rays for the appropriately colored candle. If you spiritually resonate with a particular symbol, such as a cross, ankh, or pentacle, or if you work with another master who has a particular symbol,

then carve that symbol on the white candle. Anoint all the candles with the Abramelin oil.

2. Cast a magick circle, as in exercise 13. Do the ritual up to the "work" section in step 8.

3. For the working of the ritual, you will be inviting the masters into your life, by lighting their corresponding candles. Light them one by one, and take a moment to meditate, to listen, to feel the power of each master. You are not necessarily evoking each ray, but are asking for its power to come into your life, if this is right for you.

> *I light this red candle and ask for the blessings of El Morya.*
> *I light this blue candle and ask for the blessings of Kuthumi.*
> *I light this yellow candle and ask for the blessings of Serapis Bey.*
> *I light this green candle and ask for the blessings of Paul the Venetian.*
> *I light this orange candle and ask for the blessings of Hilarion.*
> *I light this indigo candle and ask for the blessings of Sananda.*
> *I light this violet candle and ask for the blessings of Saint Germain.*
>
> *I ask for the masters who are appropriate to work with me to make their presence known. I ask for the angels, ancestors, and guides who are appropriate to work with me to make their presence known.*
> *I ask for the divine light to guide my way.*

4. Then light the final white candle.

> *I light this white candle, and call upon my higher self and my highest guidance. I call upon the divine Creator, the Divine Mind, Mother-Father-God, that flows through all things in the web of life. I ask for the ascension flame to be light within my body, heart, mind, and soul. I ask to expand my consciousness and raise my vibration, in a manner that is correct and for my highest good, harming none. I ask to ascend in this lifetime, gaining all the knowledge, wisdom, humility, and power I need to then serve the whole world.*

Some practitioners will then read the Great Invocation (see chart 4 in chapter 7). You can also do a meditative journey. Of all the masters, Serapis Bey has the strongest associations with initiation, particularly the initiations of the temples of

Egypt and the Great Pyramid. You might find yourself being led by one of the masters to an inner-world experience or past-life memory of an initiation ritual.

5. You can end the ritual with the mystical sacrament of wine and cakes, or simply release the four directions, and release the circle.

Because it is easy to get caught up in focusing on initiation rituals, degrees in various systems, and what our own personal "ranking" is (which defeats the whole point of spiritual initiation), I always try to remember a teaching attributed to occultist and author Dion Fortune that shows up in many works: "All the gods are one god and all the goddesses are one goddess and there is one initiator." The one initiator is the higher self, the divine self, and all other beings, systems, and decrees are only tools through which the one self initiates us. The work and the rewards of initiation belong to us, and can be conferred by another only if there is personal, spiritual work and evolution present.

19

incarnation and
past lives

As the Eastern traditions have highly influenced the modern New Age movement, the theory of reincarnation has become a staple teaching to most of us involved in modern esoterics. Reincarnation is the belief that after death the body may decay, but the soul is eternal and will spend a period of time in the spirit worlds and then be reborn, integrating with a fetus to experience life again. The soul travels from lifetime to lifetime, gaining more direct experience and understanding of life through living on the material plane. Some teachings see this as a great blessing or gift, while others see it as a punishment or prison. Most, on both sides, believe that the soul is "learning" something through these material experiences

The most complete doctrines on reincarnation come from Hinduism, but we find similar, if not identical, thoughts on reincarnation in many other spiritual traditions. The teachings made their way into the Greek mysteries, particularly those of Pythagoras and Plato, as well as the Orphic mysteries, and many believe that the Greek scholars received this information from the priest-magicians of Egypt. Though not explicitly found in the Hebrew Bible, various doctrines of reincarnation, gilgul or gilgul neshamot, are found in esoteric lore of the Kabbalah. Likewise, reincarnation is not a part of traditional Christianity, but evidence of reincarnation theories can be found in the very early Christian church and the various branches of Gnosticism. Some people believe this passage in the New Testament is a holdover from early Christian beliefs in reincarnation, referring to John the Baptist as the reincarnation of Elias: "For all the prophets and the law prophesied until John. And if ye will receive it, this is Elias, which was for to come. He that hath ears to hear, let him hear."—Matthew 11:13–15. Exoteric Islam has no reincarnation doctrine, but reincarnation is a part of the esoteric Sufi traditions. Rumi, in *Masnavi*, speaks of the seventy-two forms he has worn.

Ceremonial magicians have borrowed heavily from Kabbalistic lore as well as the ancient Egyptian and Greek mysteries, and often make some form of reincarnation a theme in their teachings. Modern pagans usually believe in reincarnation, borrowing heavily from the ancient classical pagan world of Greece, as well as a report from Julius Caesar, on the Celts, stating that the warriors have no fear of death because the Druids have taught them about rebirth and the immortality of the soul. The ancient Celtic concepts of reincarnation were probably very different from our modern ideas about reincarnation. The Celts, like many tribal people, most likely believed in being reborn among their cultural descendants, other Celts in their tribe. They didn't look at the potential of the soul crossing cultures to be reborn, as their concepts of reincarnation were intimately tied with tribal bloodlines. The idea of a Celtic warrior being reborn to a Roman family was most likely alien to them during that time period. Yet modern pagans who learn the mysteries of the Descent of the Goddess learn that magick, love, and rebirth are key mystical teachings, and there are no genetic or tribal stipulations. Others look to the teachings of shamanic cultures, of aboriginal tribal people in various parts of the globe, and see similar teachings of reincarnation in their lore. Many believe that the soul comes in many parts, and that some reincarnate and others do not. This multiple-soul approach definitely influenced the early mystery schools in their concepts of the soul and consciousness.

In the modern era, reincarnation concepts are becoming more and more widely known, but are influenced by so many theories, modern and ancient, that there is no one set dogma or paradigm. Some people believe in the literal transmission of the soul, while others believe that memories can be passed along genetic lines and we can experience what our ancestors knew. Those of a scientific mind talk about the collective consciousness and morphogenetic fields as an explanation for reincarnation experiences. In the end, more and more people are exploring theories on reincarnation because they are having experiences of past lives. Be it from spontaneous memories surfacing or directed hypnotherapy sessions, the reality of past-life memories is becoming well-known. I know my first memories came to me as a child, watching a documentary on the Trail of Tears with my mother. We both started crying spontaneously, and I asked her, "Do you remember being there?" Later, when we both studied esoteric lore, we came to the conclusion that we had had a Native American life together during that time period, and that television show had triggered the memories for us. Since then, we've used meditation to uncover more past-life memories. A classic book on reincarnation in the modern New Age field is Brian Weiss's *Many Lives, Many Masters*, a true story of a therapist using traditional hypnotherapy who spontaneously begins exploring the past-life memories of his clients and sees vast improvements in their well-being.

The belief in reincarnation and past lives is integral in the ascension movement. A key concept of ascension is that of the soul moving from lifetime to lifetime, eventually reaching a state of perfection and enlightenment where it is free to no longer return to the material world. The soul has reached ascension, moving beyond any need or desire to be attached to the material plane. The soul isn't really "learning," but "awakening" or "remembering" its own divine state through a variety of experiences. The soul is learning how to create and be a part of creation simultaneously. Once the soul fully remembers or awakens, ascension occurs, and the various initiation experiences outlined in the previous chapter are just benchmarks in learning to awaken fully. In fact, a past-life memory can be the first contact with the non-ordinary world and trigger an initiation experience. Exploration of past incarnations, past lives of various stages of enlightenment, can further illuminate your current situation, explain mysterious maladies and fears, and give you a fresh perspective on what patterns you are following.

Ascensionists have a very global view of reincarnation, believing that the immortal self will reincarnate in many different places and roles, varying gender, class, health, and status, to experience all that life has to offer, without judgment of a particular situation as "good" or "bad" based on how personally pleasant or unpleasant it is. From a soul perspective, nothing is good or bad, but is simply a material experience. A blessing of this global view is that we see the similar teachings of spirituality in all the world's traditions.

Ascension lore has adopted some classic concepts associated with reincarnation, such as karma, and added to the lore some unusual concepts, such as twin flame walk-ins. There is no one set theology on reincarnation for the modern era, but rather a collection of ideas based on inner guidance and personal experience.

KARMA

Karma literally means the results of your actions. It is the spiritual or psychic energy associated with your actions that returns to you. Magick effectively operates because we are able to send out energy, and such psychic energy returns to its source, often stronger than it left, manifesting a tangible result. On a small scale, we see our magickal spells working according to this principle. On a larger scale, the universe is an emanation of the divine Creator, and the creation then returns to its source. The Tree of Life descends from the top sphere, and the magician then seeks to climb the tree from the bottom sphere and return to the source, greater, wiser, with more actual experience than when he left. That is the return process on a cosmic scale and a basic principle of ascension. It's not simply our magickal intentions that are amplified and then return, but all our thoughts, words, and deeds. Karma is a word used to describe the process of this return.

Many people think of karma as the moral judge, as it is often equated with Galatians 6:7: "For whatsoever a man soweth, that shall he also reap." In the end, though, both are axioms on taking responsibility for your actions. They do not say that the Creator is meting out divine justice as reward or punishment. Many people think that karma means that if you do something good, you'll get something good, and if you do something bad, you'll get something bad. That is not the case. Karma means that there is a reaction for every action you take. If you don't like the results in your life, then change your actions. Magicians and witches call it the Law of Return. Some describe it as the Law of Three, believing that the results of one's actions are amplified, times three. Though most people try to accrue "good" karma, to get benefits, from a Hindu perspective, good karma is as much a problem as bad karma. Both keep you entangled in the daily drama of life, rather than being free to pursue your divine work. Karma is said to be the force that draws us into further incarnations, to work out the karma and have a zero "balance." The ascended masters have no karma, good or bad. They are operating in the force of dharma.

Dharma is the flip side of karma. Some would translate dharma as "destiny," but from a magickal point of view, dharma is more like your true will, your life's work as an instrument of the divine. You must partner with the divine to fulfill your dharma. It doesn't simply happen. You have to invite it and be willing to do it, to work with it. Magicians call this your true will. Ascensionists would call it your spiritual will, the will of your spirit, of your soul, of the divine higher self. It is your monadic blueprint. When you are clear of karma and are operating in your dharma, in all areas of life, you reach the potential of ascension. We can fall in and out of our dharma, or find it in some aspects of our life and not in others. When we are totally in our dharma, we are ready for enlightenment.

contracts

Many in ascension use the term *contract*, referring to a soul agreement. It is the agreement you make first and foremost with your soul, as to what you plan on accomplishing in this life. It is like the microcosmic version of "the Plan" for Earth. The contract is your personal plan in the greater pattern. It is the agreement between your soul and your monad to fulfill the monadic blueprint. Many people feel that those in our oversoul "families" share a similar purpose, and we incarnate together, or those who are not incarnate act as guides, helping us learn and experience what we want to learn and experience. From the perspective of spiritual, or esoteric, astrology, the birth chart encapsulates not who we are in this lifetime, but who we are learning to be. The chart is like our curriculum for this lifetime, and encoded in it are all the most perfect experiences, but we choose how we manifest those experiences.

 Some say we make soul contracts with others—our parents, siblings, lovers, spouses, children, friends, and even enemies. Every person on the divine plane is a great ally and helper, though they may take more difficult roles in this lifetime, as we play out a variety of experiences in the flesh. Even those who harm us are said to have a contract with us, and in the end, all of it is done in love.

 I'm not sure I agree with all the concepts surrounding soul contracts. The most important aspect of the teaching is that we have free will in how we manifest these contracts. Our spirits, planning out our lives, have the ideals of these experiences in mind, yet we all know that our lives often fall short of the ideal manifestation. We must choose the ideal manifestations of things. On a human consciousness level, we might not be able to choose what happens to us, but we can decide how we respond to experiences, from the blessings to the traumas of life. They are all blessings, even if we don't understand their blessing at first.

SOUL MATES AND TWIN FLAMES

Our soul group physiology of the monad, oversoul, and soul always leads to the discussion of soul mates and twin flames, and how they fit into the equation. There's not a lot of agreement on the definition of both those terms. The popular opinion is that a soul mate is your "other half," the parts of you that "complete you." People project a romantic idea of soul mates and soul-mate relationships as perfect ideals. This person is your twin flame, your divine match, either in your oversoul group or in another oversoul group belonging to your monad. The problem is that once a person finds the human individual that she believes to be her soul mate, it can be a disaster, because neither one wants to put any human effort or communication into the relationship, believing that the perfect partner should just "know" what they want and need. Life doesn't work that way.

A soul mate may be a spiritual partner, but the relationship might not be romantic. A soul mate might be a platonic friend, a sibling or other family member, or even a beloved pet. I know twins who felt they were soul mates, and it obviously wasn't a romantic relationship. I have a very strong soul-mate relationship with my mother. You might find that several people have this soul bond with you, and that you have more than one soul mate.

Other people think of the twin flame or the soul mate as the other half of you, one-half of your polarity. If you incarnate as a female in the world, then on the other side of the veil, your male twin flame will be guiding you. If you are an incarnated male, your female twin flame will be your otherworldly guide. Though this theory parallels some of the polarity teachings in both Eastern and Western magick, as well as the popular psychology theories of the anima/animus, I am not a fan of this interpretation of the soul mate or twin flame. It makes any earthly lover or friend pale in comparison to this spiritual love.

I think it's far healthier to think of a soul mate as a soul who resonates with you, one with whom you might have a past-life or otherworldly connection. You have the potential to form a deep spiritual relationship, but you have to put physical, real-world effort into the relationship to maintain and grow it. You have potentially many beings in your oversoul and monad group, so you have many potential soul mates or twin flames.

UNUSUAL INCARNATIONS

Though the concepts of souls, oversouls, and monads form a great paradigm, it's not the only one. Many ascensionists believe that the Earth is in such an exciting and dynamic state of transition, and so many beings want to be present, that all the traditional "rules" have been thrown out the window, and those in this world might not belong to the traditional structure of soul/oversoul/monad. Doreen Virtue outlines some of the different types of incarnations in her book *Earth Angels*. She describes a variety of beings incarnated on Earth at this time, including angelic beings, faeries, and elementals. Others, too, have shared their firsthand experiences and channeled information on a variety of unusual incarnation possibilities.

Angels

Though traditional lore says that angelic beings cannot incarnate in the physical world, many people claim that they are angels incarnated in this world. Classical lore says that angelic beings don't have free will, but follow the divine plan. Those who find themselves incarnated here from the angelic realm can find free will, choices, and personal relationships very difficult, though they have a strong sense of service to the divine plan and an urgency to fulfill it.

Faeries

Some people believe that there are incarnated faeries, who have a strong reverence for nature and great magickal ability. They are playful tricksters, are easily angered, and may have an androgynous nature.

Elementals and Nature Spirits

Elementals are the consciousness guiding the four classical elements of earth, fire, air, and water. These elementals are depicted as gnomes, salamanders, diminutive faeries known as sylphs, and merfolk, known as undines, respectively. According to certain traditions, elementals have two paths of evolution. Some people believe that the elemental must climb the hierarchy of its element, becoming an elemental king or ruler, and eventually becoming an angelic being. Others feel that an elemental must master all four elements, and then it becomes a nature spirit, guiding the formation of plants, trees, and minerals. Some associate their evolution through nature with dragon spirits. Many people resonate with a particular element and feel a call to the soul lineage of the elemental beings. In classical magickal lore, elementals are not human and don't become human, yet some Wiccan traditions recognize those with a strong connection to a particular elemental realm, using the terms Air Child, Earth Child, Fire Child, and Water Child when a person has characteristics similar to those of a sylph, gnome, salamander, or undine. Often the person's astrological chart will have strong associations with that element.

Wise Ones

Doreen Virtue also outlines the return of "wise ones," those who have mastered magick and mysticism in the past, with a long soul history on Earth, who have answered the Earth's call to aid in this transition time. They are the wizards, witches, sorcerers, Druids, shamans, priestesses, and priests of the ancient ways. The resurgence of paganism and of interest in magick and mysticism is seen as potential evidence of the return of the wise ones from many cultures. The renewal of pagan traditions and magickal spirituality helps the newly incarnated wise ones remember their purpose in aiding the planet and gives them a framework to teach the Earth-honoring ways to the rest of the world.

Returned Masters

Some people feel that those who have previously completed ascension have volunteered to enter back into the wheel of karma and share their gifts. These ascended masters return for another turn in the "game" of human life, but like anybody who masters a game, they can teach their skills to others by demonstrating them. Some people claim to be fully aware of their mastery in this incarnation. Though I'm sure there are some who do indeed have the mastery of a true saint or ascended guru, many in the New Age world who feel the need to repeatedly tell others that they are an ascended master really aren't. True ascended masters will demonstrate their mastery to us by their actions and love, rather than a press release or promotional advertisement.

Starseeds

Some people feel that beings from other star systems are incarnating, with a sense of mission to help the ascension of the Earth. These beings are known as starseeds, star people, or starborns. Some have no conscious memory of where they come from, while others have quite a strong sense of origin and memories from these previous incarnations. Many people believe that there are physically incarnate races in other parts of the universe, and their souls are coming here for experience, in what many consider to be "School Earth." Others feel these star civilizations are not incarnated beings, but are beings that exist in a higher dimension and choose to incarnate in a physically denser dimension than their home to participate in Earth life.

Indigo Children

Much of the New Age literature refers to indigo children. Some people say that this term refers to the hue of the children's energy body, their aura, when glimpsed by those with psychic talent. All agree that a special breed of children is being born in the world, and will potentially lead us into a new era in humanity. Though there is dispute as to the date when these children began incarnating, most agree that the first trickle of indigos occurred during the seventies, and more and more have come through during the eighties, nineties, and beyond, though one common error is to assume that any special, spiritual child is an indigo child. Indigo children have certain characteristics, abilities, and issues. Indigo children are coming in with an awareness of their divinity and a sense of purpose to "bust" the old paradigms of the past and help create new ways of thinking and being in our society. They shake things up and challenge authority.

Many indigos claim that they also have difficulties in this world. Some have physical challenges in life, and some manifest learning disabilities and attention deficit disorders because their thought processes and interface with their physical body are different. Don't be quick to label every child with such issues as an indigo, particularly if the child was born to "spiritual" parents. Don't assume that you are an indigo because you were born in the right time range and you are interested in ascension. Many indigo children have no concept of ascension, but they are fulfilling their purpose. Some people assume that all young starseeds are indigos, yet one doesn't have to be a starseed to be a part of the indigo current of consciousness. Others think indigos are very old souls who have been on this planet for a long time, yet have not been here recently, and that is why they have both a new perspective and some difficulty being in the world. As with any other tradition, let everyone find their own path, and own identity and label, without having to associate them with a specific paradigm. Self-determination is a powerful experience. And allow those who identify as indigo children to grow with the concept, helping them define for themselves the concept of indigo adults.

Walk-ins

Another interesting transition to the pattern of incarnation in the world is the experience of "walk-ins." Some people on the ascension path feel that they are incarnated beings who didn't go through the birth process. The original soul in the body finishes its work in this lifetime, though rather than exiting this incarnation through the death process, the soul makes an agreement with another soul, another being, who wants to be a part of the earthly experience. That new soul takes on the memory, responsibilities, karma, and body of the exiting soul. This is not possession. It is not demonic. It is not an involuntary process. Both souls have, on this higher level of consciousness, completely agreed to the process. Possession and soul dominations manifest in a very different manner.

When the new being enters, he or she can feel out of sorts, in unfamiliar territory, reintegrating the old soul's memories and experiences yet not feeling a depth of connection and emotion to them. Some simply wake up one day and feel like another person. Others have a traumatic experience, such as an accident, and that time is used for the transition. When they have recovered, they feel like someone else. Others have a longer, more gradual transition state. Other people notice a marked change in the individual who is known as a walk-in. The new soul may experience a difficult transition period of reintegrating and readjusting this life to suit his or her own needs. Usually, the new being claims to be of greater spiritual maturity or awareness when coming into the body. Often great shifts in relationships occur, and new career and life paths begin, because it is literally a new soul operating this body.

My first introduction to walk-ins was through a walk-in who claimed to be an ascended master from another star system. The situation wasn't explained very well to me, so I was immediately suspicious. Since then, I've met several walk-ins. Some were amazing individuals who really lived their spiritual truths. Others may have been either delusional, desperately hoping to be a walk-in because they were unhappy with life, or true walk-ins having a hard time adjusting. I must admit that now, when I walk by a salon, I never look at the sign "Walk-ins Welcome" quite the same way anymore.

Soul Braids

Soul braids are a phenomenon often confused with walk-ins. Many who are in fact soul braids, which is a more common occurrence, identify as walk-ins. Instead of the entire original soul walking out of the body and a new one coming in, a higher aspect of the individual, a part of the person's higher self, becomes integrated more fully into the conscious self. The experience can feel as profoundly life-altering as a walk-in, but the identity and the soul link remain the same, even if the individual is disoriented by the process.

Otherkin

A similar phenomenon, yet one that is outside the traditional ascension paradigm, is the otherkin. Otherkin are a diverse group of individuals who believe that their souls come from a nonhuman descent, originating in another plane of existence. Some believe that they were recently dragons, faeries, vampires, or demons, or one of the more New Age models—angels, elementals, or ancient ones. Such fantastic beings, including dragons, vampires, and the elder faces of the faery folk, exist in the nonphysical realms, though some are choosing to participate in the human drama at this time for a variety of reasons.

People who subscribe to the otherkin belief are usually anchored in a Western meta-physical or occult paradigm, rather than the more socially palatable New Age paradigms. Those in more of the New Age world refer to otherkin as incarnated angels/elemen-tals, while those in Western occultism usually refer to them as otherkin or other souled. Though many would relegate both ascension beliefs and the beliefs of otherkin to the fan-tasies of popular RPGs (role-playing games), the identity of being "other souled" is very real for those experiencing it. Each offers a lens to help people understand past memories and experiences in a manner that serves their current incarnation.

Incarnation on Earth is in a pretty unique state of being, and no one paradigm or belief is going to fit your experience. The best thing to do when thinking about past incarnations is to let your experience and intuition guide you, but also to temper your thinking with logic and common sense.

Perform the following exploration into your own past lives and soul origin only if you feel called to do so at this time. Past-life memories awaken differently for different people, and there is no need to rush. This meditation is great to do with a partner. It is helpful to have someone to guide you down by reading the meditation to you, and to be present to aid you in integrating these memories.

If you do desire to experience past-life recall, then taking a few drops of comfrey flower essence or holding a piece of selenite, a phantom quartz, a fossil, or a piece of jet can be very helpful in unlocking the past.

EXERCISE 23:
PAST-LIFE REGRESSION

1. Sit before your altar in a comfortable position. Call upon the divine, in what-ever form you prefer—God, Goddess, Great Spirit, Divine Mind, Mother-Father-God. Ask to be consciously connected to your source, for guidance and protection, and to all your spirit allies who are appropriate for you at this time. Do Exercise 1: Basic Meditation Technique up to step 6 (see page 81) to get into a meditative state.

2. Acknowledge the power of the four directions. Bring your attention to the north, then the east, south, and west. Bring your attention to the heavens above and the space below you. Then bring your awareness to your heart. Feel a shaft

of light descend from the heavens, from the highest dimensions, surrounding you in a column of light and finding its anchor in the heart of the planet. You are now aligned with the twelve dimensions and are capable of interdimensional contact and journey.

3. Ask your higher self and guides to be present. Ask for a guide to aid you specifically in past-life recall. You might find a familiar master or one who is unknown to you but specializes in this work. Ask your guide to take you to the past life that is most perfect for you at this time, and for you to experience it with ease, grace, and gentleness.

4. Imagine the pillar of light around you become either like a spiral staircase, as you descend, or like a more modern image of an elevator, descending floor by floor. Your guide is present and shows you how to descend.

5. When you reach your destination, you find yourself stepping out and into your past life. Look down at your feet. What do you see? Look at your body. What are you wearing? What is your gender? Look around your space. Where are you? Let your first impressions come to you, and follow your gut instinct, without trying to analyze the experience or place it in a specific time period based on your intellectual knowledge.

6. With the power of your will and the aid of your guide, you can fast-forward or rewind your past-life memories. Whenever you are getting stuck, ask to be taken to the next significant event in your life, and count from five to one. At one, you will be at the next event that has something to show you. Ask your guide to help you understand whenever things are not clear. Remember that nothing can hurt you. These events have already occurred. If you don't want to experience them directly, then at any time you can "step out" of the life, and ask to see it like a movie on the screen of your mind, rather than have the point of view of your past-life self.

7. If you are experienced in past-life work and naturally grounded and settled, you can take yourself to the moment of death in this past life. If this is new to you, I suggest not going that far unless directly asked to do so by your guide.

8. When you are done with this past-life exploration, imagine stepping out of the life and back into the pillar of light, either rising in the elevator or taking the spiral stairs upward, back to where you began. Ask your guide any questions

you have about the life and what it was meant to teach you. Ask how to apply the wisdom of the past to your current life.

9. When you are done, say your farewells to your guide. Release the guide, and bring your awareness back to your body. Acknowledge the four directions around you again, north, east, south, and west, then above, below, and center. Thank the divine Creator for guidance and protection. Thank your guides and allies. Perform steps 9 and 10 of Exercise 1: Basic Meditation Technique (see page 82) to return to normal waking consciousness. Write down any impressions or messages you received, before you forget them.

One of the criticisms of past-life regression work is that everybody who does it thinks they were famous in a past life. Everybody believes they were Cleopatra or Joan of Arc. Everybody can't be the same person, so is regression work made up? I don't think so. I think we tap in to that collective consciousness, and retrieve the impressions that best serve us now. In that collective consciousness, there is no separation. We are patterns in the hologram. Each part of us contains all the information of the universe. Scientists call it the holographic theory of the universe. Occultists would say that the macrocosm is in the microcosm, and the microcosm is in the macrocosm. We have all been Cleopatra and Joan of Arc, and none of us have been. But the experiences of Cleopatra and Joan serve us all collectively. Whatever their own life lessons were, we can share in those lessons and messages collectively, so we don't necessarily have to repeat them. Some ascensionists believe that our souls "imprint" the memories of certain famous lifetimes in order to take their lessons with us into the material world. So as you explore your memories, you too might share memories of a famous incarnation, even one that has been attributed to a current ascended master. That shared archetypal experience might lead you to work more closely with that master.

20

THE HiDDEN HiSTORY

Deeply entrenched in the ascension paradigm, particularly from the Theosophical material and the Edgar Cayce readings, is the belief in a secret history of the world, not known or acknowledged by modern history or science. The history entails facts that seem too fantastical to actually be true, things that could never be accepted by mainstream society, yet the history lingers around the edges of our perception, with unexplained mysteries and artifacts teasing and tantalizing those who take the time to really look.

The mysteries of the ancient world engage us. We want to explore them. We want to believe something other than what we've been told, for there seems to be so much more to all aspects of life than what we've been told, not just our history. Shouldn't our past reflect this?

Where does this hidden history come from? Who is its keeper? Why doesn't everybody know it, and accept it, like our mainstream history records? The answer depends on whom you ask. Some people will cite conspiracy theories, ancient or modern, whose purpose is to keep us in the dark about our true heritage so some mysterious secret society can rule the world. Others will say that the mass consciousness is not ready for such facts of life, that our past global traumas have created a situation similar to posttraumatic stress disorder, stretching over lifetimes and affecting us now, even though we have no conscious memory of the trauma. Those ancient and ascended beings hold the entire records, and help us access them when we are ready. And the vast majority of people rooted in traditional history will say it's all made up, pure falsehood.

Our knowledge of something more than what most record books give us comes from two sources in our New Age. As in all our disciplines, we find the twin strands of modern, received knowledge paired with ancient lore. Yes, there is ancient lore, ancient records of the hidden history, if you know where to look. We find the strongest account in Plato's story of Atlantis. Here we have a great scholar, still recognized to this day for his contributions to the world, yet his more esoteric doctrines are almost completely forgotten by the mainstream academics and swept under the rug. His concepts of mysticism, magick, and ancient wisdom are ignored in favor of his more socially acceptable teachings. Among the lesser known and less-respected teachings is information on Atlantis, a fabled land to the west of Greece that sank due to a great cataclysm. This information is found in Plato's documents *Timaeus* and *Critias*. Most people today assume that he created a fictional land to illustrate his teachings, or that it was some reference to the destruction of an ancient Mediterranean culture. Scholars who take this esoteric information seriously, as potential fact and not as symbolic, are deemed quacks in their respective fields for wasting time on such theories. Yet there is still a call deep within us to seek out the wisdom of Atlantis.

Plato is arguably the ancient source most aligned with modern Western-world thinking, so if his account is not taken seriously, then the references to previous worlds and civilizations found in the sacred texts of various cultures have even less credence. Plato claimed to gather his knowledge from the mystery schools of the Egyptians. The Greeks divided mythical history into several ages, each based on a type of metal, tracing the world's history to an almost perfect Golden Age. The fall from grace of the Golden Age has a parallel to the biblical expulsion from the Garden of Eden, as well as the fall of the angels in the war of heaven.

The deluge of the Bible, based on far older sources of myth, is well-known, but is assumed to be a fable, not fact. We need only to look to the Sumerian flood story to find the foundation of the biblical Noah. Most ancient cultures the world over, however, have flood myths, stories of the destruction of the world by water, and its subsequent rebirth. These stories usually note that the flood was only one of many ways the world has been destroyed in the past, and they contain prophecies of how the world will be destroyed again in the future.

The Hindu texts describe the worlds of the past, great ages of the ancient world, and predict coming ages based on spiritual cycles. The Hopi have marked several worlds, each of which has been destroyed so a new world could be born from the death of the previous world. Their prophecies are based on these teachings, as they state that we are entering the fifth world. The Mayans, master timekeepers, mark one more world than the Hopi, stating that we are entering the sixth world, the world beyond time. Their myths outline the battles of the gods, as a different deity rules each epoch, and each comes to an end in a disaster that almost wipes out all traces of the previous worlds.

Today, the tales of the ancient world, of Atlantis and Lemuria, are found in print more than ever before, due in part to modern research, but more often thanks to divinely inspired, channeled works, detailing the author's past-life memories and stories told by the ascended masters. This resurgence in popularity is due partly to the Theosophical works starting with Blavatsky, but even more importantly to Edgar Cayce, who made the material even more accessible, since he didn't have a particular belief in the ancient teachings to begin with. Some approach it from a historical view, surveying the evidence of the ancient worlds, the mysterious artifacts, along with the mythologies. Now many modern authors are lending their voices to repaint the picture of the ancient past, and to tell their soul's story in the drama. Many use Atlantis, Lemuria, Hybornea, or other pre-cataclysmic worlds as a "fictional" setting for their fantasy novels and movies. Others are reclaiming what they see as fact through their psychic explorations.

I have found that the more inspired and personal the story, the more the storyteller's current beliefs color the story being told. Even the purest and deepest trance channels are not immune to personal bias. In the stories of Blavatsky, the fabled times have a flavor inspired by the ancient world we know, that of the Hindus, Egyptians, and Greeks. The records of Cayce have a Christian bias, even though much of the specific Judeo-Christian theology that was said to be a part of the fabled lands did not survive into the ancient cultures they supposedly seeded. In Plato's account, which is said to be a historical account rather than a channeled one, we see a definite polytheistic pagan orientation to Atlantis.

When a writer colors a story with his or her own beliefs, it doesn't make the account false—it simply makes it the writer's version of the story, not the absolute and objective truth for all to believe. Imagine us all trying to remember an event that occurred ten years ago that none of us wrote down. We could have fifty people who were present together ten years ago who each experienced the same thing. Yet now, when we each retell the story, I guarantee that we will have fifty different stories, all with similar themes, but each having its own bias, its own point of view, its own perspective of time clouding the objective reality. Now imagine trying to remember a story tens of thousands of years old. Imagine how much it could change. That is the process of digging in the hidden history of our world. Each storyteller may add the strands to the story that he or she is most interested in now, and if a detail is missing, then the subconscious mind will fill it in, even if it's not true, just to make a better story. It doesn't mean that many of the facts are not there, or that the purpose of the story has been lost. In fact, the purpose of the story is more important than the details.

Initiation Through Secret Knowledge

I have found that the purpose of any hidden history story is to aid the initiation process. Secret histories and creation stories are the basis of initiation rituals in mystery societies, where what you comfortably know as fact is ripped away. Your foundation is pulled out, and you must sink or swim. You must find the story that will keep you floating, yet be open to the possibility that it is one of many stories. If you explore many mystery schools, you will find many different stories in your rebirth experience. Each tradition will give you its version. It is the purview of the mystery school to keep its history secret, veiled from the eyes of the uninitiated, while the institutional religions put forth the story that is for everyone. Now, in the dawning New Age, everyone will be an initiate. Everyone is ready for the mystical secrets. All the stories are coming to light.

Dogmatic religions tell you what to believe. The stories of the exoteric institutions are the stories for the masses, the general public, be it the religious tale of Genesis as a literal truth or the most commonly accepted scientific theorem. Mystic traditions give you the opportunity to listen, to explore and hear the whispers of symbolism in the exoteric tales. They encourage you to experience your part of the story, to claim or reclaim it. Ascension teachings can sometimes be dogmatic. Many people know only a dogmatic form of thinking and structure their new spirituality around their old ways of operating, but ideally ascension is an individual mystic tradition, a mystery school. We each climb the mountain alone. Perhaps we walk side by side, but we each have our own path.

When you open to the possibility that everything is not known by science, is not written down by historians, that there are wonders to explore, then your consciousness expands. Suddenly the lack of foundation shows you that you are ready to fly, not fall. The possibilities revealed through secret knowledge create a mystery. Potential initiates can explore secret esoteric techniques, past-life memories, and foreign philosophies to create their own mystery story. This story gives the initiates a platform to understand spiritually how they have arrived at this point in history, and how the world has arrived at this point. The exploration of the mystery gives you a grander mythos to work in, whether you believe it's all fiction, a mythical play and ritual drama to explore, or whether you believe your own story is immutable fact. As long as you are open to both possibilities, then the mystery is still alive.

A good teacher in the ascension paradigm will help you unlock your own story, and the truths and teachings it brings you, rather than have you get caught up in his or her own story. If you meet anybody who says that you were his or her disciple in Atlantis during a past life, and you are now destined to be again, then run screaming out the door. But if you resonate with something said—an idea, a name, a place—then use that resonance to unlock your own soul's story, and let it unfold before you, while remaining grounded. If your story ever becomes so dramatic that you cannot take care of yourself or live up to your normal worldly responsibilities, then you must take a step back and reintegrate before proceeding.

Sometimes the revelation of a secret history without a spiritual discipline or technique can be destructive. Those who seek the truth, yet have no spiritual method for contacting the inner truth, can be destroyed by the new knowledge, falling and never learning to fly. I think of the popular character Fox Mulder from the television show *The X-Files*. The reality of a greater history, filled with mystery, monsters, and aliens, was revealed to him. But not having a spiritual context for it, the reality made him an outcast in his field and quite obsessive about "proving" his reality to others. In the end, the truth hurt him more than helped him.

I know that like many things in the New Age world I was quite skeptical of this secret history of the world, yet over the years I've seen many things point toward the possibility of its existence, or toward one of the many possibilities presented in this paradigm. I studied the ancient stories and modern commentaries on them. More importantly, I experienced past-life memories that didn't exactly match the mainstream history writings that I had read, yet found people with past-life memories that were very similar to mine, which helped validate my experiences. I later had students whom I know had not done any of the intellectual research on Atlantis, yet were having memories and visions of things described in detail in the accounts of Atlantis that I had read.

Now, looking back on my uncertain plunge into the waters of unknown history, I found it a spiritually liberating experience, yet I cannot tell you what is fact, fantasy, or speculation. Many ideas have come to me, through books, other people, and personal experience, and some are quite plausible in my mind. Quite a few other ideas are just too far out there for me to swallow as fact. Just because one is open-minded does not mean one has to be foolish and take everything as literal truth. Some things are symbolic, or are true as a multidimensional experience, in a mythical, energetic sense, but are not true in a physical, literal sense. Truth can be found on many levels. There is objective truth, facts and figures proven through third-dimensional reason and logic, and there is subjective truth, the truth of the spirit, found in other dimensions, and open to interpretation because it is based on a person's relationship with these otherworldly dimensions.

The following account is a version of my truth, my understanding of the hidden history, found by weaving together several cultural myths. It's told while looking through my rose-colored glasses, my personal biases as a modern gay man, currently based in a pagan tradition of spirituality, with leanings toward both tribal cultures and the ancient East, and the feeling that while Judeo-Christianity is a huge piece of the ascension mosaic for some, it is not the dominant piece for me. I draw from both ancient tales and modern Theosophy, with its theology of root races and undiscovered lands. This tale weaves together my own thoughts and experiences with the work of many other authors and researchers. I take what feels and seems plausible to me, using both head and heart, to create a story that has worked for me. What of it is fact? I'm not entirely sure. Are there fictions? Probably, in the sense that we might never prove them without a doubt in objective reality. Does that bother me? No. And when you find your story, it should not bother you either. As the story progresses, we enter a realm of historical figures and verifiable events, but the characterizations of such events are always subjective.

Don't take my story, my truth, my inspirational sources for the secret history as your own. Be inspired by it, if the exploration of the secret history interests you. Be open. Be objective. Be critical. Find the truths that resonate with you. Be open to changes as you change. When you put the pieces together, what kind of picture do you get?

THE AGES OF CREATION

There have been many creations before this world, and many creations will follow. The inhabitants of each world see themselves as the center of their own cosmos, their own drama, even when we know we are on a small planet, orbiting a star, which orbits the galactic center. From our view, the Sun appears to rotate around us, and the stars rise and set from our horizons. Our stories are told from the stars in the night sky, and we tell them from the perspective of our home. Our creation stories follow that pattern.

Each stage of creation manifests an age, an epoch. These epochs have been charted and calculated by those who keep the sacred calendars. Different cultures start the story at different ages, with perhaps the Mayans having one of the most complete views of the great ages. As one age ends, the "world" is said to be destroyed and born again. While the world, or that age of the world, is destroyed, one should not assume that world and planet are synonymous. Each age has its mythical lessons and strengths, as well as drawbacks and challenges. They can be related to specific elements, in the manner in which they were created, and how they are destroyed.

Each age is dominated by a particular Mayan god who presides over it, and the rise of another Mayan god spells its demise, ending the cycle and beginning another one. It is important to realize culturally that light or creation does not equate with good, nor does darkness or destruction equate with evil. These deities are not personifications of a struggle of good versus evil, as some people have interpreted it, but more of the necessary qualities of creation, like yin and yang, each of which is needed to balance the other. Mystical cultures have similar stories of the ages of gods marking out the epochs. Though their time cycles may not always match evenly in the way we currently account for time and history, symbolically there are many parallels. In fact, when we look at the first "worlds," they are very much beyond our concept of traditional time.

According to Theosophy, each world is populated with a particular "root race" of beings who dominate the learning cycle. The term race is used loosely, as not all of these races are of a biological nature. Many are more spiritually oriented, rooted in the ethers and having little to do with physical life, while we, current humanity, are rooted in the physical and learning to expand our consciousness into other dimensions. The root races are by no means the only beings in each world, as life occurs on a multitude of planes, but this Theosophical view gives humanity a spiritual lineage, to understand where we have been, where we are, and where we are going. We can see traces of the root races in our ancient mythologies, in the gods and monsters of ages past. Each root race evolves into the next, yet has the potential to attract souls from other realms into the unfolding drama. Each world is like a school. Those who want to experience the lessons and teachings of that era, of that school, are welcome to attend.

Because of this view of spiritual evolution, Theosophists are sometimes depicted as anti-science or out of touch with what most of the world believes to be true based on scientific evidence, much like fundamentalists who look at the biblical story of creation as literal truth, rather than myth and symbol. H. P. Blavatsky was a vocal critic of Darwin's evolution theory, a concept now accepted by the majority of the educated world. The misunderstanding between the two schools was not that Blavatsky denied the evidence of biological evolution, but that she looked to the spiritual impetus behind evolution. On page 429 of *Isis Unveiled*, Blavatsky wrote, "Darwin begins his evolution of species at the lowest point and traces upward. His only mistake may be that he applies his system at the wrong end." From her point of view, we didn't evolve up from no consciousness, but rather our physical vessels evolved under the guidance of our spiritual consciousness, to be the perfect vessels for us in this world. We descended down from a point of spiritual perfection into manifestation, and will ascend again, to evolve our consciousness back up, finding union with the source. Blavatsky's root races trace this evolution, giving each race and epoch character and form, though we find similar concepts of manifestation through the dimensions and reunion with the source in Qabalah, Hinduism, Buddhism, and alchemy.

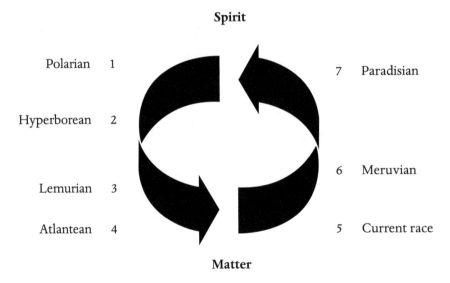

Figure 53: Root Race Cycle

The root races follow a cycle of spirit descending into matter and reintegrating those experiences back into spirit (figure 53).

In the end, the search is for the truth. In the introduction of *The Secret Doctrine*, Blavatsky said, "There is no religion higher than truth." But spiritual truths can be subjective, told from a specific point of view. The ages and epochs are described from a very human point of view, seeking to know the past in order to understand the future.

In the Beginning

In the beginning, only the void existed—the void, the first, formless power. Like a watery chaos, an undefined primordial soup of energy, it formed the fertile pool from which our creation took life. It is the cosmic egg, from which hatched creation. From this void was born the first light, the first Sun of the first age. The light brought into existence the first word of creation, known to some as OM, which reverberated throughout the void, manifesting worlds upon worlds. The divine force manifested as the Mother and Father of creation. Together they divided light from dark and heaven from Earth. Together they sang the songs of creation, creating the spheres of life, the harmonies of dimensions. Together they populated the worlds with their children. To the Greeks, this was the era of creation, in which Gaia (as not only the Earth Mother but also the mother of all form) and Uranus gave birth to the universe as the cosmic Mother and Father. Only later were they identified solely as the physical Earth and sky.

According to the Mayans, each "Sun" of an age is ruled by one of the first gods. In their myths, the first Sun was ruled by Tezcatlipoca, the god of the smoking mirror, of obsidian, and the dark brother of the feathered serpent, Quetzalcoatl. Tezcatlipoca ruled an age of giants. To the Theosophists, our ancestors of the first world were known as the Polarians, and they ruled over the vast land mass known as Pangea, the first motherland. The Polarians were not flesh and blood as we are today. As our most distant spiritual ancestors, they were the least like us. They were gigantic, like the people described in the world of Tezcatlipoca, but they were etheric. As ephemeral beings, they were not rooted in the material plane at all. They were immortal and androgynous. They were the archetypal, first race, the first ancient ones, beyond all our current knowing and understanding. The Polarians were our seeds. From them we grew. From the ethers, they guided the development of the planet. They were the first guardians of and stewards to the planet Earth. Their history goes so far back that we have little knowledge of them, yet their past is a part of many of our own soul stories.

But all cycles must come to an end. The dark void presided over by Tezcatlipoca gave way to a new age. Quetzalcoatl rose up to fight the dark god, changing the ages. As he did, jaguars rose up and devoured the world of the giants, giving birth to the next age.

The next world was one characterized by air and wind, or clarity and clear perceptions. Here we have the first true golden age, though many other later epochs, such as Atlantis, would be considered the Golden Age. The blessings of these ages are simply echoes throughout time, originating with this golden age. In the Mayan cycle, this is the second world, the second Sun, ruled by Quetzalcoatl. The god of light ruled over an era of enlightenment. This parallels well with the Krita Yuga, the Golden Age of the Vedic cycles, and the first world of the Hopi. The Hopi do not count the first world of the void as a world at all, but begin their count here, with the Tokpela, the age symbolized by the fire pit in their ceremonies.

To the Greeks, it was the Golden Age of Chronos, known as Saturn to the Romans. A god of golden grain, Chronos ruled over a world where the Titans walked the Earth with golden men, perfected beings. Are we to think of these humans as literally made from gold, as the legend says, or is the term symbolic of the shining light of their spiritual bodies? Are they made from the "first matter" of the alchemists, and not physical at all, but rather made from the perfected gold the alchemist sought in the quest for the Philosopher's Stone? The Theosophists would agree that people of the second age were not made of metal or flesh. Known as the Hyperboreans, and their land known as Hyperborea, these beings were still etheric, like the Polarians, yet slightly denser, slightly more physical, more in tune with the material world. Like the Polarians, we know little of them.

In traditional Greek mythology, the Hyperboreans were the "people beyond the north wind," as Boreas is the spirit of the north wind. They were said to live in a paradise to the north, beyond the European mountains, where the Sun shone twenty-four hours straight. These people did not die from injury or old age, but consciously chose when to end their existence after living a full life. The land was full of gold and guarded by griffins. The Greek god Apollo was said to spend his winters in Hyperborea, and various Greek heroes have visited in their myth cycles.

The name Hyperborea has been associated with a setting in Robert E. Howard's *Conan the Barbarian* story cycles, as well as in the H. P. Lovecraft horror mythos. Hyperborea has also been linked to the myths of Thule, originally part of Greek mythology, and in physical terms has been associated with Norway. The Thule mythology was adopted as a part of Nazi and neo-Nazi mysticism as the root of Aryan mysticism. The Theosophical Hyperboreans have little to do with modern fantasy writings and esoteric Nazi theology, though it's unclear how much of the Greek writings about Hyperborea is actually connected to this race or time. It's possible that Blavatsky borrowed this name from Greek mythology to describe this race, and the Greeks were actually referring to a land and people that today we would call Lemuria or Atlantis.

Like the world before, this second Sun also set. There are conflicting mythologies concerning the end of this world of air. The Hopi say it was destroyed by fire. Tezcatlipoca summoned winds to topple Quetzalcoatl and destroy this world. With the Greeks, we had the war of the Olympians and Titans, in which Zeus rose up against his father, Chronos, and led his siblings to rule. The golden men who passed in this age were said to become the holy spirits of the heavenly realms.

THE SILVER AGE OF LEMURIA

The second world was followed by the third great world, born from the forces of storm and fire. Following the Golden Age, it was known to the Greeks as the Silver Age, and the storm gods ruled. To the Mayans, the presiding figure was Tlaloc, the god of rain and water. He acted as caretaker and guide to this world. Zeus took over rule from Chronos, leading his brothers and sisters, the Olympians, against the chthonic Titans. The Olympians claimed victory after a long war, and divided up the realms between them, with Zeus ruling the heavens, Poseidon ruling the seas, and Hades ruling the Underworld. Most of the Titans were imprisoned in a section of the Underworld known as Tartarus. It is interesting to note that one of the remaining free Titans, the goddess Hecate, was given a portion of the heavens, seas, and Underworld by the three ruling brother gods. The Olympians' success moved creation from the Golden Age of the grain god to the Silver Age of the storm king, ruling from high above, on Mount Olympus. Chronus's image moved from that of the wise father, a veritable Father Time figure, to that of the Grim Reaper, the figure of death. The golden immortality was lost, and there was now a time of change and strife.

To the Theosophists, this third world was characterized by the lost land of Mu, or Lemuria. Some think of Lemuria and Mu as the same place, in different epochs. Others think of them as two distinct places, with Mu being in the Pacific and Lemuria in the Indian Ocean. Though the Lemurian myths are not as popular as those of Atlantis, Lemuria was said to be the first true motherland, preceding Atlantis, and potentially coexisting with it for a time at the transition of ages.

Modern seekers have named the land Lemuria after the lemurs, unusual animals that are found in several places unconnected by land bridges. Lemurs are small mammals described as a cross between a squirrel and a monkey, who live chiefly in Madagascar but also in Africa, India, and Malaysia. Some theorize that Lemuria was the connecting land of these diverse places, envisioned as a large continent or perhaps several large islands. If this is a literal truth, though, you might wonder why there wasn't a broader migration of animals in these same territories. Lemuria was named by Philip L. Sclater, an English ornithologist and a contemporary of Charles Darwin. Others scholars of his day suggested that Lemuria was most likely the primal home of humanity, granting us the ancestral memory of the paradise, or Garden of Eden, that many of our traditions hold.

Compared to Atlantis and other civilizations to come, Lemuria truly expressed the "mother" land principle, as its inhabitants and culture were described as being more intuitive, creative, magickal, and nurturing. It is interesting that the metal silver, characterizing this age, is the metal of the Moon, the mother, and the feminine principle. According to Blavatsky, the Lemurians were considered to be gigantic and ape-like, with very little intelligence. W. Scott-Elliot expanded upon Blavatsky's vision, describing them as "far from beautiful" and fifteen feet tall, with brown skin and elongated noses. The Lemurians were said to have a third eye on the back of their heads and extended heels that allowed them to walk backward or forward. They started as hermaphrodites, but over time they evolved into separate sexes and eventually progressed toward what we would recognize as humanity. They bred with beasts, creating a variety of the monsters we find in our mythology books. The Lemurians were said to be aided by advanced beings from Venus who guided their evolution.

More recent channelings paint a prettier picture of the Lemurians, saying their spirits, if not their bodies, were advanced, and their spirits could physically precipitate a body, fragile and primitive as it was, to experience the physical world. The Lemurians experimented with genetics and animal forms. Their spirits were insightful and magickal, and Lemuria was both their playground and laboratory. Eventually the Lemurians got trapped in their bodies, unable to rise back into the world of spirit. They dealt with their "fall" from spirit into matter, and used their psychic knowledge to guide the development of the growing plant, animal, and mineral kingdoms.

The Hopi tell us that tribes and villages prospered during this time, but like all worlds, it eventually came to an end. The Hopi say that it was destroyed by ice, while the Mayans and Aztecs speaks of a fiery rain, brought about by Quetzalcoatl. Many in the Theosophical current feel that Lemuria quietly sank beneath the waves, and its inhabitants, with their natural intuitive abilities, understood the signs and were able to leave without incurring any major loss of life. According to the Greeks, the mortals destroyed at the end of the Silver Age, the silver men, became the spirits of the Underworld. From this destruction we have the birth of the fourth Sun, or fourth world, and enter the more familiar territory of Atlantis.

THE ERA OF ATLANTIS

The fourth great age is known by many names. The Hindus called it the Copper Age, while it was Bronze to the Greeks. Both denote something less than the stellar shining of the Golden and Silver Ages, though compared to today's world, many see the fourth age as a golden age. The Hopi's name for it was the third world. To the Mayans, the fourth Sun was ruled by Chalchiuhtlicue, the Goddess of the Jade Skirt. In this era, cities grew and civilization was created. The first of all such civilizations—in fact, the archetype upon which those that would follow built their model—was the nation state of Atlantis. Upon a great island in the Atlantic Ocean, beyond the Pillars of Hercules or the Straits of Gibraltar, flourished a land like no other. Known as the Motherland of the ancient world, Atlantis eventually leaned more toward the masculine energies and may have even introduced the concept of war to our collective human consciousness.

Named after Atlas, the son of Poseidon, Atlantis in the early periods was said to be a great kingdom that created what might even be seen as another golden age, free from want, suffering, or turmoil, even though the root race of this age was more fully incarnated in the physical world, following the Lemurian culture. Was this race physically incarnate, like humanity is today? Some say yes, and some say no. Perhaps one of the reasons we have found such little physical evidence of Atlantis is that this civilization existed in the ethers so close to the physical realm, we would be hard-pressed to tell them apart, but it was not quite at the same frequency as physical life today, off by a few overtones in dimensional harmonics. This would also explain the great achievements in science, medicine, and magick in ancient Atlantis described by modern channelers. Accounts describe incredible temples channeling energy, lights, running water, crystal technology, healing springs, and ships that traveled through the air, following lines of Earth force. At any rate, all accounts of Atlantis have the population clearly divided into male and female sexes, and appearing basically as human, with beautiful features and graceful and strong bodies, distinguishing them from the Lemurians.

Some historians of the secret past speculate that the early Atlantean civilization was more Goddess-oriented than God-oriented, or it at least found a balance between the two. Feminine divinity was seen in the great seas, oceans, and rivers, for water was a main theme of the island nation. At later times, the island was depicted as several small islands, with rivers and waterways separating them. The main city was said to be divided into several concentric rings, with waterways separating them. Other channeled information reports that the nation had ten major centers, possibly corresponding to the ten spheres of the Qabalistic Tree of Life. The society, politics, and traditions of Atlantis were believed to interweave religious tradition with science and magick, where the differences between these three disciplines were not neatly separated. Temples played a major role in society, which was divided into several castes, and the mystics enjoyed much prestige and power. Plato's tales of the last epoch of Atlantis included its trading with other civilizations, the nautical advancements of its people, wars, and its eventual end, rapidly sinking beneath the waves after a great cataclysm.

To the Greeks, this age was one of mythical heroes. Gods walked the Earth with creatures of myth, and inspired mortals could carve a name for themselves in the history books and possibly achieve the status of an ascended being. Some see the myths of many of the ancient gods as tales of the Atlantean priest kings and queens. Many channeled tales involve Atlantean science and magick, breeding creatures as a worker caste that would fit the stories of our mythical monsters. Edgar Cayce talked about this era as a time in which monstrous animals of gigantic proportions ravaged the land and people, and a council of the world leaders, moving in great flying ships, came together to do something about this. Similar descriptions of monstrous animals come from old hereditary witchcraft histories, reportedly taught by the controversial witchcraft figure George Pickingill. Old George's teachings on the matter, in *The Pickingill Papers*, echoed those of Cayce's, but it's unclear if we are seeing these teachings through a post-Cayce framework, or if there were two very similar teachings on massive animals taking over the world and humanity, occurring independently of each other in the modern era.

Though the civilization of Atlantis started with the best of intentions, eventually the caste system broke down into a method of social and political control, rather than a tool to aid people in finding their calling, much like the caste system in India. Some people believe that the higher class bred a slave race of man-monsters. Tales of the noble Atlanteans' fall from grace, into depravity and "black magick," led to their doom, but they flourished for many generations before their fall. The soul that was said to later become Saint Germain was reported to be the high priest of the temple of violet flame in Atlantis. Through his connection with the Creator, he manifested the system that later became known as Shamballa Reiki, to aid those of the lower castes attain a higher spiritual vibration and heal their DNA of monstrous defects. He took the systems and symbols to various sacred sites, such as Tibet and India, seeding the cultures with esoteric lore. Many of our current masters, including Master Jesus/Sananda, are said to have started their incarnations in Atlantis.

Atlantean knowledge and structure are said to be the roots of many seemingly disparate civilizations' similarities, such as the pyramids of Egypt, the step pyramids, or ziggurats, of Sumer, and similar buildings in the Americas. Many people think that the religions of the ancient world stem from a similar root source. If that source is physical, and not a spiritual inspiration, then perhaps it was Atlantis. Many myths credit Atlantis as the source of wisdom for the Mayans, Aztecs, Incans, Native Americans, Celts, Egyptians, Basques, Tibetans, and Hindus. As the Atlantean civilization ended, the refugees seeded new lands with their advanced knowledge. Some believe there were several waves of Atlantean immigration, and that these refugees were seen as gods by the natives. In the Irish Celtic traditions, the Tuatha de Danaan, the Children of the Goddess Danu, a race of godlike beings, were said to sail on magickal flying ships from the west, from the land beneath the waves, or come from the four corners of the globe. Some think the accounts of Avalon, the mythical land of the Goddess, or of the various Fortunate Isles of Celtic myth, sunk beneath the waves, come from tales of Atlantis.

The one fact that all accounts agree upon is the end of this world and the Atlantean civilization. The flood was the method of ending. Some accounts have Atlantis flooding several times, each flood getting progressively worse, while others see it disappearing in one single catastrophe. The populace was said to have been shown signs, to have been warned, but in its pride, to have ignored the warnings. In the study of astrological ages, Atlantis was said to fall during the reign of Leo, the sign of ego and pride when manifested in its lowest form. All the old flood stories of Sumer, Greece, and most popularly the Hebrew Old Testament are really telling of this pivotal time of transformation and the end of the last age, and the beginning of the next. The few who survived the Great Flood became the fathers of the next civilizations.

OUR WORLD

We live in the fifth great age, in what most people consider the "real" history of the world. This age starts with human civilization emerging from the Stone Age and the beginning of the ancient world. The age is marked with the rise of humanity with great technological achievements, and the apparent spiritual decline of humanity as we become more separated from our spiritual heritage. Because it is our commonly accepted history, this age can be subdivided into many periods, but all bear the stamp of the fall of the Atlantean Age and the promise of the coming Aquarian Age.

Theosophists say that from the Atlantean root race, our next race was broken into five physical types, like the points of a pentagram. This may have already occurred well before the literal end of the Atlantean Age, as many argue as to what the Atlanteans really looked like, most often citing red skin or white skin. Humanity in the physical realm had developed into a variety of types, or what would later be known as five races of the fifth age. The races were based on skin color. The Red Race was most often thought to have settled in North America, and the Brown Race was strongly related to the Lemurian race and settled in the Andes and the remnants of Lemuria in the Pacific. The Yellow Race settled in Asia and the Gobi desert, the Black Race in Africa and Sudan, and the White Race in what is now Iran and the Carpathian Mountains. The five races as a whole were called the Aryan race by Theosophists, but this term referred to the epoch and not specifically to white ethnicity, and was later corrupted by the Nazis. The whole system may seem archaic or politically incorrect to the modern reader, but it formed a strong basis for occultism at the turn of the twentieth century.

The hallmark of the fifth age is physical denseness. We are the most manifested race, anchored in this physical world, when compared to any other. The Mayans call the fifth Sun the Sun of Motion, because dense time will speed up by the end of this age. The Hopi call it the fourth world. The metal associated with this age, in a metaphysical sense, is iron. The Iron Age is also associated with the Kali Yuga, the yuga, or epoch, of the Hindu goddess Kali, goddess of nature but also destruction. She is pictured as black-skinned, fanged, with many arms, wearing a necklace of severed heads and a skirt of severed arms. Kali is the destroyer. This age is said to be the dark night of the soul that humanity must endure to transform and find the light.

The people of this world have gone through many cycles of development and decline. Rather than have our development be limited to any one geographic location, like the centralized Lemurian or Atlantean cultures, it has spread throughout the globe, with many different races and cultures. We have seen the rise and fall of a variety of cultures, each with something to offer our collective consciousness. The cultures that most affect ascensionists are the Greek, Egyptian, Hindu, American, and Celtic. In our age, we have had the visitations of three major masters who greatly affected history—Buddha, Jesus, and Krishna—though the historical personages of each are still debated by scholars. Their teachings, however, have been instrumental in the development of humanity. Still, even after their dispensations, we have had massive killings and wars, from the Inquisition's assaults on the pagans, healers, Jews, and homosexuals of Europe to the rise of the world wars and the current conflicts in the Middle East.

In this age, many people believe that reality is being controlled and even distorted by a shadowy council that secretly rules us all. Known as the Illuminati—not because they are enlightened, but because they keep the hidden knowledge of the world—they pull social, economic, and political strings to keep the world off balance. Some feel they are the dark brothers and sisters, purposely slowing down our evolutions. Many think they are they are in league with evil aliens or demonic forces. Some skeptics of the ascended masters even think that the secret chiefs and ascended beings are really the Illuminati and, through both politics and the New Age movement, are controlling both sides of the chessboard. Whether the world wakes up, or doesn't, from the spell of the secret government ruling the world will determine how we manifest the next age.

The fifth age has not yet been destroyed, though the sacred calendars tell us the end is looming. Some say it has already happened, and this is what the end looks like for those living it. Years such as 1972, 1987, 2000, 2005, 2010, 2012, 2020, and 2080 have been given as the benchmark for the sixth age. Some mark the year 1904, for Aleister Crowley's Equinox of the Gods, as the end of the age. Others see the Summer of Love, in 1967, as the transition point. The Aztec calendar was said to end in 1987, commemorated by the Harmonic Convergence. Christian apocalyptic groups favored 2000, the end of the millennium. The Golden Dawn's astrological teachings give us 2010. Most ascensionists favor the specific time of the winter solstice in 2012, which is also the end of the Mayan calendar.

THE FUTURE IS NOW

We will soon enter the sixth great age, the age of light, the age of Aquarius, the Hopi fifth world, and the Mayan sixth Sun. We enter the Aeon of Horus, according to Thelemites. The root race of the sixth age is the Meruvian race, which is said to be developing primarily in the United States, as a global melting pot, but also in all countries with ethnic diversity. The Meruvian root race is to be a blend of all cultures and colors, as the five races meld into one again, richer for the experience of individuality. This parallels some Native American teachings of the Rainbow Warriors, in which their four primary races—red, black, white, and yellow—come together, like the points on a medicine wheel, to fulfill the ancient prophecy of peace, prosperity, and harmony with the Earth and spirit worlds. The stories of the Rainbow Warriors have been adopted by many in the New Age, particularly those who live near the sands of Sedona, Arizona, a place of power and many energy vortexes, where, it is said, the prophecy will be fulfilled.

The qualities of the sixth age will include a focus on spirituality and healing. A group consciousness is said to be developing, creating the conditions of unconditional love and world peace. New lessons, cooperation, and harmony will have to be learned. The sixth age is to bring paradise to Earth, grounding heaven into the world. All esoteric secrets will be revealed in this age of light, and any who seek the mysteries will find them. It is said that various records from the Age of Atlantis will come to light during the turning of the age, from the information encoded in the ancient crystal skulls to a supposed hall of records beneath the Sphinx in Egypt.

The last epoch predicted by the Theosophists is a seventh great age ruled by a seventh root race known as the Paradisians. The Paradisians will lead us back to the spirit world, ascending from the physical world and even the lower etheric levels of reality to reside solely in the highest dimensions. Some feel that we will then begin a new cycle of descent and ascent on another planet, such as Mercury, or in another galaxy.

LONG, LONG AGO, IN A GALAXY FAR, FAR AWAY . . .

The last part of our secret history is really said to be a first. Modern channeled lore has traced a whole history of humanity, giving us an origin beyond the Earth. Such teachings state that we came from another realm and entered this galaxy from the star system Lyra, eventually manifesting bodies on some dimensional level and existing in the stars and planets of the Lyra system.

From Lyra, we branched out, settling on various planets. The beings from other star systems, physical and spiritual, are truly our ancestors, as we settled on Arcturus, Sirius, and the Pleiades. Some of us fell out of harmony with the rhythms of life, becoming disconnected from health and wholeness. Eventually, these races devolved into the various species of Grays who are seeking new forms for life sustainment. The Pleiadians and Sirians in particular took great care in seeding life upon Earth, and watching and guiding our development. But the beings that are most relevant to our consciousness now are those who settled on Orion.

Orion proved to be a battleground for the forces of light and darkness in ascension channeling. Many people see both our thoughts of futuristic science fiction and high fantasy worlds of fantastical magickal feats as experiences that occurred, on some dimensional level, in the Orion system. Many lightworkers have thoughts, dreams, and visions from this time in their soul history. Many modern ascensionists think George Lucas drew his inspiration for the *Star Wars* series from this epoch in our collective history. The polarity consciousness of the conflict permeated the soul's memory. It is believed that souls from the Orion Wars began to integrate into Earth's evolutionary pattern, particularly during the time of Atlantis. Some believe that Mars was the first site of an ancient civilization, and upon the destruction of Mars, the Orion souls then migrated to Atlantis, and re-created the Martian conflict there all over again. We have been living with the conflict ever since.

Our hidden history is filled with perceived "enemies" who have played various roles in our worldly drama. The central players vary, depending on the version of the history you hear. Some tales play upon the ancient astronaut theory, stating that the gods of the ancient world, specifically the Sumerian gods, were not gods at all in a spiritual sense, but rather were aliens from a twelfth planet, beyond the orbit of Pluto, with a monumentally long and highly unusual orbit. At various cycles, this twelfth planet makes its way into the inner solar system, and its inhabitants create havoc in our world. Some theories depict them as physically incarnate beings, responsible for the genetic advancement, or missing link, of humanity's evolution and the propagators of the original Garden of Eden. Others see them as 4D aliens, beyond our linear understanding. Their programming and plan have kept us asleep, in bondage and not realizing our true magickal and spiritual heritage. Pseudo-historians of the secret world claim these twelfth-planet aliens have been most active from the end of the Atlantean era to our current time. Some say their members are still here, ruling in secret.

WAS ANY OF IT REAL?

This is a question I often find myself asking when hearing about the secret histories and conspiracy theories. Could be. I guess it depends on how you define "real." Folk history is very real, but when you talk to the keepers of folklore, they may have different interpretations of events, or recount entirely different events, from those in the standard textbooks.

Sometimes our secret histories can be codes for larger themes that were understood in a mythical sense by mystics, but now science has given us a different view. Were the Titans who ruled the Earth in the ancient days an allegory for the age of the dinosaurs? We did have giants walking the Earth, but in forms we could not have recognized before. Are the tales of fire from the sky images of comet strikes, changing the biosphere? Could the tales of water and ice destruction be based on images of the various ice ages the world has undergone? Could be. We don't know, but they make quite a bit of sense when looked at in this light. And in terms of dimensional reality, it doesn't make the Theosophical stories and the Edgar Cayce readings any less true. While the physical reality of our planet experienced the age of titans we now call dinosaurs, on the etheric levels of reality, the souls of those who would be the first humans to incarnate on the planet might have been experiencing a reality of mythical Titans and a golden age. Things we think of as symbolic in the physical world might actually stem from literal events in a supernal world from which we draw inspiration. All magicians know that on the astral plane thoughts and symbols do not represent things. On that plane, they *are* things.

In an effort to "prove" our ancient history, New Age practitioners are accused of practicing poor science, of seeing what they want to see. And that can be true. But there are also some genuine mysteries for those who are involved in the search for the hidden history. There are strange cultures, facts, and discrepancies that can't be explained. There is a core mythology about a pre-flood civilization, found in most cultures, from East to West. And sometimes, just sometimes, things that mainstream science and archaeology have dismissed as fiction, such as the city of Troy, turn out to be literal fact. Who is to say that Plato's Atlantis won't bear similar fruit, accepted by all at some point? There are many who feel that discoveries off the coast of Bimini are already moving us in that direction.

The point of the hidden histories is to awaken you to the possibility the world is not quite what it has always appeared to be. It may not be exactly the way you were told. Other truths are possible. If you have never heard of any of these concepts, and then you go out to research them and find some interesting "proof," it can be quite mind-blowing. I know my experience was. Let these secrets chip away at the comfortable illusion that is your reality, to let in a greater truth of more possibilities. Learn from the lessons of the past, so you can choose your future wisely.

EXERCISE 24:
EXPLORING YOUR SOUL HISTORY

1. Begin Exercise 23: Past-Life Regression on page 417. At step 3, ask for an ascended master to guide you in reading the akashic records of your own soul history. Hold the intention of exploring a past incarnation beyond this age, in one of the previous ages. If you feel ready for it, you can ask for your first incarnation in the Earth cycle of creation. If you identify as a starseed, walk-in, or otherkin, then this might be your first life in the Earth cycle of creation. You might be taken to a past life in a different realm. Stones that can help you access the akashic records include apopholite, fossils, lepidolite, merlinite, moldavite, Pietersite, phantom quartz, phenacite, and zoizite. You can hold them or place them on your altar or near you when doing this exercise.

2. Continue on at step 4 in exercise 23, though you might find yourself ascending rather than descending. The akashic records might not manifest the information in the same way as a past-life regression. Instead of being inside the experience, you might watch it on a screen, or even read about it in words. The akashic records themselves might manifest to you, in your inner sight, as a futuristic computer terminal or a vast old-time library filled with books and scrolls. It might be a library of floating crystals or geometries of light. Allow the images of your incarnation to appear in a book or on a scroll, crystal, or visual screen. As you watch the story unfold, ask your guides questions to help you understand what has happened, and what significance the events have for your life now. You might find the akashic record projecting a three-dimensional reality, that you feel you've been "sucked" in to, to experience firsthand. Follow your guide and your intuition. Use the same questions to explore who you are in this incarnation. The answers may be unusual if you find yourself in a non-human life. Ask your guides to show you how to access this information in a manner that is correct and for your highest good.

3. Complete the exercise, then return, ground yourself, and record your experiences.

ASCENSION TIMEKEEPING

One of the key facets of the secret history is prophecy. Everybody has a prophecy as to what will happen next. Theosophists spell it out with their future root races and worlds. Other traditions base their prophecies on the timekeeping devices known as the sacred calendars. Many sacred calendars exist, and each one is a paradigm, a way of looking at history and time, past, present, and future. None of them are completely right, but they give us a new viewpoint. By understanding what has been and what is to come, we have a greater sense of our future, and can truly be futurists, actively participating in the building of our future world while still enjoying each moment of our daily lives.

I've found the greatest aid in looking at the ages of the zodiac. The Great Ages of the Zodiac refers to a system of timekeeping measured in roughly 2,000-year periods. It is believed that in each of these "great years," one sign's lessons, characteristics, and pitfalls dominate the world and, in particular, human evolution. The sign that dominates is determined through a process known as the "precession of the equinoxes." In reality, there are two distinct zodiacs. One is known as the sidereal zodiac, based upon the stellar constellations. The second is known as the tropical zodiac, in which the sky is divided into twelve sections based upon the cycles of the seasons and the alignments of the Sun and Earth. At one point, there was no difference between the sidereal and tropical zodiacs. Due to a slight wobble in the Earth's axis, the two slowly moved out of sync, until the tropical signs no longer matched those of the stars. Many uneducated critics will say that astrology is not even based upon the constellations, but Western astrology has always been based upon the tropical zodiac and has always worked quite well, while Hindu astrology has always been based upon the sidereal zodiac. At the spring equinox, the Sun enters the sign of Aries in the tropical zodiac (and always has), but in the sidereal zodiac, the Sun currently enters the sign of Pisces at the spring equinox, and will eventually enter Aquarius. Whatever sidereal sign is at the vernal equinox is said to dominate the current age, or great year. Each "year" lasts for about 2,166 of our years, but because the measurement is so large, people disagree as to the beginning and end of these cycles.

We can gain an interesting perspective by looking at human history through the lens of the Great Ages.

The Age of Cancer

The beginning of human civilization, as most people measure it, was in the Stone Age, in what we would now call the Age of Cancer. The previous age, the Age of Leo, was said to be the end of the Age of Atlantis, due to pride and ego. Cancer, the sign ruled by the Moon, signals nourishment and mothering energies. Many people believe that the Stone Age cultures were great matriarchies, honoring the Goddess. From the Atlantean period, we were reborn in the Stone Age through tribal shamanic cultures honoring the Earth and sky, Sun and Moon. Modern scientists reject this utopian matriarchal image of the past, but there is enough evidence to show that many feminine images are from this period of history, and surviving tribal cultures today still honor the Earth and mother.

The Age of Gemini

The Age of Gemini marks the start of what many consider to be sophisticated society, as humans developed more advanced communication and language skills, including the development of writing beyond pictographs. Though some believe those in the Age of Cancer possessed a form of communal telepathy, others feel they communicated through primitive body language and basic grunts. For whatever reasons, we developed into a species that used complex language skills. Gemini is an air sign, ruled by Mercury, the messenger, and its hallmarks are writing, speaking, and social skills. With the advancement of society in this direction, we began the agricultural revolution, adapting from the hunter/gatherer traditions to farming the land. Along with improved communication came the development of hand tools and technology that increased the success of our farming efforts.

The Age of Taurus

Next came the Taurean Age, marked by the builders. This age saw the creation of the first great structures and the start of the bull and calf sacrifices in religious rites. Horned agricultural gods, along with Earth and Moon mothers, were the popular divine images. The ancient Egyptian pyramids, the Sumerian ziggurats, and the Minoan temples were all hallmarks of this time period. The people of this age carved out territories and adapted them to suit their needs, working with the land and stone to create vast monuments to the culture and, often, to the divine powers.

The Age of Aries

The Age of Taurus was replaced by the Age of Aries. Ruled by Mars, the god of war, Aries is the sign of the warrior. The technology of human culture grew to include the finely crafted point of the sword or spear. Ram sacrifices replaced bull sacrifices. This age was marked by the rise of the patriarchal gods, of the sky and war gods. The focus on war, particularly in the Roman Empire, was a key sign of this age.

The Age of Pisces

The birth of Christ, and the subsequent rise of Christianity as a world power, was said to be the birth of the Age of Pisces. The current of Pisces had been growing long before, in the fertility cults of the sacrificed gods and solar gods that predated Christianity. Most cultures have an image of the sacrificed god, but Christ was the uniting figure under which this concept spread across the globe. Pisces is the sign of the two fish, and has a strange dichotomy, as one fish swims toward the world, and the other toward spirit. Both are linked, so they never get far from each other. The highest end of Pisces is associated with unconditional love, noble sacrifice, and a merging with the divine self. The lowest end of Pisces is expressed as delusion, illusion, religious fanaticism, institutional hierarchy, depression, and escapism.

In the last 2,000 years, we have seen both of those currents entwined with the rise of Christianity. We have seen the polytheism of paganism give way to the monotheism of the Judeo-Christian-Muslim worldview of one god. The dogmatic religions of the end of the cycle of Pisces are slowly being replaced by the "god" of science, yet the teachings of science are also helping bring mystical concepts back to our consciousness. The rise of rationalism and atheism, as well as the Industrial Revolution, inspired those who found the world bereft of deeper meaning to seek out Spiritualism, Theosophy, and ceremonial magick. They, in turn, provided the foundation for the resurgence of shamanism, paganism, and eventually ascension, where the practitioners found greater understanding through the development of quantum physics. The merging of science and mysticism marks the turn to the Age of Aquarius.

The Age of Aquarius

The fabled Age of Aquarius is promised to be the Golden Age reborn. The reason for this is that Aquarius is the sign of universal sisterhood/brotherhood. Aquarius is the sign of freedom and individuality, where all are able to freely express themselves. The new religious movements of spirit are personal and eclectic, demonstrating that paradigms like ascension will be the midwives to the next age. Aquarius is also the sign of inspiration, marking leaps in consciousness. As the Water Bearer, it is not a water sign (despite the name), but is the one who bears the waves of consciousness. We receive those waves as nonlinear insights, as we are connected to this great cosmic river of life. Some people describe the flashes of insight from Aquarius as the lightning bolt, or the "eureka" experience. Like Einstein, we might receive the answer nonlinearly, just as he received $E = mc^2$, but have to go back and figure out the steps in between.

The Aquarian mind is concerned with social responsibility and envisions a utopia where all of society's ills are vanquished. Social, political, and environmental equality are at the forefront of Aquarius. Known for revolutionary action, Aquarius can bring swift changes in word and action. There are still quite a few drawbacks to Aquarian energy. As an air sign, Aquarius can appear to be cold and detached. As a revolutionary power, it also rules violent revolution, so as we manifest the next age, we must be on guard against the lower forms of Aquarian change. All sudden, swift, and violent changes are Aquarian in nature, including earthquakes, floods, and tidal waves, leading many to believe that the next age will be heralded by a great natural or humanmade disaster.

One of the greatest challenges of Aquarius is finding a balance between individual needs and the needs of society. As we look to the great society, to create the utopia, how do we not sacrifice the individual for the greater society? Will some people have to conform their visions in order to be a part of the great society? Ideally, no. The whole lesson of Aquarius is that each of us has something to contribute to the world, and without it, that part of the world, that thread in the web, is missing. Each of our contributions, through our higher will, is a valued part of this world. Our job is to find out how we can contribute, and then do so. We can make a contribution only if we are following our true will, if we are being our authentic, individual selves. Conforming to someone else's vision destroys our ability to perform our true will, and our piece of the greater picture will be missing. If each of us really finds our true will, it will not conflict with another's. Just as two stars do not fight to occupy the same point in space, so two wills are not in conflict if they are in harmony with the divine.

Much of our esoteric lore on astrology is aligned with ascension. Doreen Valiente, in *An ABC of Witchcraft Past & Present*, states that originally the zodiac energies were divided into only ten signs, before the hermaphrodite beings of Lemuria were divided into two distinct sexes. Our consciousness could understand and recognize only ten signs. Upon the division of the sexes, our perception of the zodiac signs changed, dividing into twelve signs. Modern esoteric astrologers believe the additional signs were found by dividing the area of Virgo, Libra, and Scorpio. This aligns well with our lore on Lemuria.

In the Thelemic forms of ceremonial magick, the great ages are divided into archetypes of Egypt. The first age was the Age of Isis, roughly correlating with the matriarchal Age of Cancer. It continued on through the ancient civilizations that were very Goddess reverent, at least initially. The second age was the Age of Osiris. In this age, the death and resurrection gods ruled supreme, starting with the war and sky gods and culminating in the advent of Christianity in the Age of Pisces. Crowley, through the reception of his *The Book of the Law*, ushered in the advent of the Age of Horus, the son of Isis and Osiris, who expresses the best qualities of both. The event was known as the Equinox of the Gods, in which the god who was guiding humanity, Osiris, gave up his seat on the cosmic throne to his son. The Age of Horus was the age of the defender, the age of the child, marked by childlike optimism and the ability to play. According to the Horus legend, our savior will be not only our child, but our inner child, come to the forefront. Horus can blend the best of his mother and father, magick and wisdom, strength and power, synthesizing the needed qualities of the next age. Horus has to face his shadow, and triumph, integrating it into his life, yet not letting it dominate.

In Theosophy, each age is said to be ruled by one of the rays of light, and guided by a particular chohan. We are leaving the Age of Pisces, ruled by the sixth ray, indigo, and guided by Sananda, Jesus Christ. We are entering the Age of Aquarius, ruled by the seventh ray, violet, ruled by Saint Germain, the alchemist and magician, until he abdicates to become the Mahachohan.

Other timekeeping systems are popular in ascension. Personal timekeeping by following the cycles of the day, as well as the Moons of the year and the equinoxes and solstices, can align you with the power of the Earth and heavens. The Mayan calendar is one that has definitely come into prominence, being one of the most advanced and accurate systems of timekeeping we have, accurately predicting sunspot cycles. It is famous for predicting the shift of ages and the end of this world on the winter solstice of 2012. The Mayan calendar aligns very well with the teachings of author and psilocybin-psychonaut Terence McKenna. Through his research on the patterns of the I Ching, he created a "Time Wave Graph" that also predicts the end of our current consciousness and world on 2012. Some think that McKenna's Time Wave Graph and the ancient yet incredibly accurate Mayan calendar both spell out a sort of "singularity" of consciousness, in which whatever is coming next in the world is so unlike whatever we've experienced before that it's off the graph, off the calendar, and cannot be measured with the tools we have today. I think that's a good way to describe ascension.

EARTH CHANGES

One of the recurring themes in the hidden histories, sacred calendars, and ancient prophecies is the concept of Earth changes. The belief is that in the transition from one age to the next, some terrible catastrophe occurs to remake the planet, and that is why there is so little evidence of these previous worlds in our current world. Some people theorize that the magnetic poles of the planet actually move or flip, "resetting" the electromagnetic grid, and altering our consciousness, memory, and perspective. Along with this pole shift comes the readjustment of the tectonic plates of the Earth The shifting plates will cause some lands to sink, while others will be raised from the ocean. The pole shift will cause severe changes in weather, increased volcanic activity, tidal waves, and a variety of environmental effects to radically change our planet. The ancient lands that we see today as sacred sites are often believed by mystics to be remnants of the previous civilizations. They are considered to be zones of safety and holiness because they have been spared in ages past. Some believe that we must gather at these sacred sites during the coming Earth changes, for we will be safe there.

Each of the ancient prophecies says this world will end, leading to a new golden age, though they all don't necessarily agree on how the world will end. Fear is a great motivator for many people in the ascension paradigm. They want to be "good" enough to be saved from the cataclysm or spiritual enough to receive an inner psychic warning of where to be and when it will occur. Though fear is a low vibration, it can be a powerful stimulus. Many of the ancient initiation rituals put you in a fearful situation, to see how you handle it. It's part of facing your shadow. If you handle it poorly, will your desire to never experience that fear again bring you to true love and spirituality? I know that was a key motivation for me.

When I first got deeply involved in the ascension paradigm, I was greatly concerned about the Earth changes, for myself, my family, and my friends. I thought about moving to high ground. That may seem silly to some people, but I know quite a few other lightworkers who had similar thoughts. Many have created world maps of what they think the world will look like after 2012, with Atlantis and Lemuria rising, and vast portions of the United States and Europe underwater. Though meant to be helpful, such maps inspire fear in those of us who live in the parts of the world that are shown underwater. The thought that the merkaba meditation would be a "key" to surviving the Earth changes was a motivation for me to study this technique. But I soon realized that neither I, nor anybody I knew who practiced it, was literally transferring their body from one dimension to another. Perhaps they were moving their consciousness, but their body didn't disappear. Yet, the merkaba proved invaluable to me because it focused the entirety of my life and spiritual practice on love. I was never quite the same afterward.

I now believe that the Earth changes are nothing to fear. I don't know if they will manifest as a cataclysm. I hope not, but if they do, I know I will be exactly where I need to be, whether safe from harm or directly in line with whatever may happen. I truly believe that humanity and the world do not have to experience a physical cataclysm. We have done it before. It's old news. It worked in the past, but there are other ways to experience the transition of the ages. Our level of consciousness is directly proportional to the experience we have. If we all raise our collective consciousness, then perhaps the cataclysm will be a "little earthquake" within our minds, hearts, and souls, rather than a catastrophe in the physical world. It might not be any easier to withstand than a physical earthquake, but it could be more beneficial, shifting our spiritual foundation. Perhaps it will be a flood not of H_2O, but of the esoteric principles of water, of love and healing, washing us all in their power. Nobody knows how the Earth changes will manifest, but we do know that we create our own collective reality, and it is humanity's choice as to how those changes will manifest. We simply have to choose wisely.

21

MERKABA MYSTICISM

My fascination with the merkaba was what led me to ascension spirituality. The mysterious geometry associated with this meditation mesmerized me. It called me home. I wanted to know everything about it. It was a mystery I needed to explore. And I did. Although there wasn't a lot of public information on the subject available at the time, I found several different versions of the merkaba meditation. I explored the history, from information from channeled sources to historical references. I learned a version of the meditation technique and made it a regular part of my spiritual practice.

In many ways, the merkaba became the most important part of my spiritual practice. My first activations of the merkaba were spiritually purging, putting me in touch with all the parts of myself that were in need of healing. It cleared away many of my spiritual blocks, from this life and from past incarnations. I had visions of who I was in the past and who I will be in the future. The activation cleared my "channeling circuits" to be able to hear my guides, ascended masters, angels, and patrons with new clarity and vision. The process triggered an intense period of spiritual and physical sickness, which left me as suddenly as it came on, without medical explanation, like the classic shamanic sickness. When an initiate awakens from shamanic sickness, he or she is forever changed. I have to say that viewing my merkaba illness in terms of shamanic sickness really struck a cord with me. I was changed.

Continued daily practice of the merkaba meditation allowed me to anchor this new level of consciousness into my life. That's not to say I never had another problem, never got angry, or never felt sorrow or pain, but my consciousness did ascend to another level. The practice did bring an awakening that I took into my daily life. I still had my ups and downs, but something was very different. My consciousness expanded to the next evolution that was right for me. The regular practice of the meditation reaffirmed this new awareness and continued to give me opportunities for healing, guidance, and clarity.

Most importantly, as the merkaba is a technique, and not a religion, it brought this new consciousness to my own religion. I found my practice of witchcraft and magick completely transformed. I made the merkaba something I performed before my rituals. My focus was on the key words of my craft, Perfect Love and Perfect Trust, the witch's unconditional love. My magick was transformed. I know of many other practitioners who have gone through a similar process, in which the practice of merkaba mysticism brought them back to the heart of their own religion. Those who had left the institutions of Christianity found the true heart of Jesus's message clear in their lives, and put it into action. Jewish mystics found themselves connected to the heart of their tradition, as the merkaba is historically connected to Judaism. Ceremonial magicians found the technique to be much like the Abramelin Operation, giving them contact with their own Holy Guardian Angel and understanding of the True Will. The merkaba cuts through all traditions to find the shining heart in each of them.

WHAT IS THE MERKABA?

The merkaba technique is a meditation to activate the sacred geometry of light that is a part of your energy bodies. This geometry is viewed around and interpenetrating the physical body, but usually remains inactive unless consciously activated. The meditation is described as a "lightbody" activation. When you have your lightbody activated, you are able to "ground" more "light" into your physical body and energy fields. You unite your body with your mind, heart, and spirit. What does that mean? In practical terms, you are able to be more fully conscious, to live more from your higher self in day-to-day life. You live in a state of greater unconditional love, closer to Christ consciousness.

Technically, the merkaba itself is the geometry of light, the energetic structure that the meditative technique activates. Through the meditation, you unite all aspects of yourself, your four-body system, to activate this geometry of light. There are many forms of lightbody activation, including affirmations, meditation, energy work, and body-work techniques, but the merkaba is a particular form of lightbody activation. I describe the meditation itself as "yoga for the aura." Unlike many meditations in which I guide a student and let him have his own experience without direction, with no "wrong" way to do it, the merkaba meditation involves some very specific steps that remind me of a yogic practice. The steps are what activate the energy, just as yogic postures create physiological and psychological changes in us. Although we think of yoga as an exercise system from the East, yogic disciplines entail far more than that. The word yoga means "to yoke" and refers to yoking, or uniting, yourself with the divine through your practice. Merkaba is much the same. Like yogic exercises, the merkaba meditation requires specific breathing patterns, hand positions called mudras, visualizations, and phrases to fully activate the lightbody.

Once activated, the geometry of light, described in terms of the sacred geometry shapes known as the Platonic solids, is a "vehicle" of light. Described as a chariot, the lightbody allows us to traverse the realms of creation, exploring all levels of consciousness. Merkaba sessions create a form of "soul travel" that is different from other types of psychic journey, going beyond what people call astral travel, remote viewing, or mental projection. Rather than only projecting our consciousness from one point to another, the merkaba allows us to expand our consciousness. Activation of this "engine of light," as it has been described, accelerates our spiritual learning, as it creates a sacred vortex of energy through its movement, attracting the energies we need and transforming those we do not. But when we go beyond simple activation and use the light vehicle to traverse the other dimensions and encounter beings who have lessons and information for us, personally, and new paradigms to potentially share with the world, we have come to the heart of merkaba mysticism.

WHERE DOES THE MERKABA COME FROM?

The merkaba light vehicle is already present in us. Though we talk about "building" the lightbody, or "building" the divine chariot of light, it is already there, fully formed within us, a part of our divine nature. The merkaba is a geometric structure that is already a part of your energy field. It is part of the geometry that creates your physical structure, from the basic formation of your cells to the proportion of your limbs. The "building" aspect of the meditation involves the repetition of specific visualizations to strengthen your conscious connection to the merkaba and activate it. Otherwise, the vehicle just lies dormant.

Merkaba activation has become very popular in ascension literature and media, from books to audio/video multimedia. Practitioners claim an ancient lineage to this technique. If you look hard, you can see the threads of the merkaba in ancient cultures. Despite our channeled lore on the origins of the merkaba, what we are practicing today is most likely not quite what was practiced in ancient times. Though there are many variations of meditations and rituals to activate the merkaba, the most prevalent forms seem to be a mix of several different cultural techniques, using geometric imagery from the ancient Greeks of Plato's time, Hindu mudras, pranic breathing, and ritual gestures.

The strongest historical current of the merkaba comes from Hebrew mysticism. The merkaba, merkavah, or merkava is said to be the chariot of light or throne of light in which Elijah ascended into heaven, described as a whirlwind of fire: "And it came to pass, as they still went on, and talked, that, behold, there appeared a chariot of fire, and horses of fire, and parted them both asunder; and Elijah went up by a whirlwind into heaven."—2 Kings 2:11.

Some say the Hebrew word for whirlwind is purposely misspelled in this story. When the word whirlwind is used in other biblical passages, it is spelled correctly. The author of Elijah's story intended a different meaning than whirlwind. The Hebrew letters that spell the word merkaba are Mem-Resh-Caph-Beth, from the root word, spelled Resh-Caph-Beth, meaning "to ride." Here we have the chariot and wheel imagery. The root word is the same as the root word for cherub, a form of angel, as angels were believed to use these chariots of light to travel from heaven to Earth and back again. Angels are associated with the wheels, light, fire, and lightning. The merkaba seems to be a means to travel to the heavens and back again. Though I'm not a scholar of ancient Hebrew, I find this to be an interesting theory.

When one "rides," one leaves one place to go somewhere else. When it is said that the Creator, or any divinity, "rides," it means that it leaves its natural state of mystery, of being unknowable, to travel to a new state, where humanity can visualize and experience divinity. The mysticism of the merkaba is to attain a state of consciousness where one can experience visions of the divine, like the prophets of the Old Testament. Here is the vision of Ezekiel (from Ezekiel 2: 13–28) that is often associated with the merkaba due to the wheel and crystal associations:

They were dreadful; and their rings were full of eyes round about them four. And when the living creatures went, the wheels went by them: and when the living creatures were lifted up from the earth, the wheels were lifted up. Whithersoever the spirit was to go, they went, thither was their spirit to go; and the wheels were lifted up over against them: for the spirit of the living creature was in the wheels. When those went, these went; and when those stood, these stood; and when those were lifted up from the earth, the wheels were lifted up over against them: for the spirit of the living creature was in the wheels. And the likeness of the firmament upon the heads of the living creature was as the color of the terrible crystal, stretched forth over their heads above. And under the firmament were their wings straight, the one toward the other: every one had two, which covered on this side, and every one had two, which covered on that side, their bodies. And when they went, I heard the noise of their wings, like the noise of great waters, as the voice of the Almighty, the voice of speech, as the noise of an host: when they stood, they let down their wings. And there was a voice from the firmament that was over their heads, when they stood, and had let down their wings. And above the firmament that was over their heads was the likeness of a throne, as the appearance of a sapphire stone: and upon the likeness of the throne was the likeness as the appearance of a man above upon it. And I saw as the color of amber, as the appearance of fire round about within it, from the appearance of his loins even upward, and from the appearance of his loins even downward, I saw as it were the appearance of fire, and it had brightness round about. As the appearance of the bow that is in the cloud in the day of rain, so was the appearance of the brightness round about. This was the appearance of the likeness of the glory of the LORD.

The Talmud, a Hebrew holy text, mentions the merkaba in reference to Prince Judah, who forbade mention of it in the text of the Mishnah. Many of these mystical teachings were shrouded in secrecy at the time, because people were told that casual practice of such techniques would lead to madness or death. Later, access to the Kabbalah itself was restricted to only married men over the age of forty, hoping that the social stability of such men would prevent the mystical teaching from imbalance and madness.

Merkaba mysticism is said to be the root of the Kabbalistic teachings, using this form of spiritual travel, though it has never been clear if merkaba mysticism meant the experiences of astral travel, shamanic journey, or pathworking familiar to us today, or, if biblical sources are to be believed, physical full-body travel to other dimensions. The Kabbalistic understanding of levels of consciousness, the hekhaloth, or heavenly halls of God's palace, and their various associations were said to be recorded by the ancient merkaba mystics, as they explored each level. Unfortunately, there is no historical record telling us exactly what their techniques were, though many assume this was a form of early Hebraic core shamanism, probably combining prayer and chanting the names of God with other trance-inducing techniques and perhaps postures akin in spirit to those of Eastern yoga. We know that Hebrew mysticism and magick were part of a healthy cross-pollination with many other Middle Eastern cultures, so it's possible that merkaba mysticism and its Kabbalistic teachings didn't originate within the Hebrew culture, but grew out of their associations with other magickal traditions. The *Greater Hekhaloth*, from the first century CE, is the main visionary text associated with merkaba mysticism.

In the Hindu sacred texts, several references to the divine chariot exist. The image of the chariot is used as a metaphor for the body, for human existence, as the divine part of the self is what guides and controls the chariot and the animal self. This quotation is from the *Upanishads*: "Know the self to be sitting in a Chariot, the body to be the Chariot, the intellect (buddhi) the charioteer, and the mind the reins."

In the *Mahabharata* are references to the Vimanas, translated as chariots, flying chariots, flying cars, or even spaceships. Many people look at the references to the Vimanas, as well as Ezekiel's vision, as proof of advanced technology in the ancient world and the ancient astronaut theory. They interpret the war of the gods in the *Mahabharata* as a potential nuclear war in pre-history. Others have a more spiritual interpretation, seeing the ships not as physical vessels but as chariots of light. The following two quotations are from the *Mahabharata*.

The gods said, "Gathering all forms that may be found in the three worlds and taking portions of each, we will, O Lord of the gods, construct a car (vimana) of great energy for thee" . . . The Mind became the ground upon which that car stood, and Speech the tracks upon which it was to proceed . . . With lightning and Indra's bow attached to it, that blazing car gave fierce light . . .

Bhima flew along in his car, resplendent as the sun and loud as thunder . . . The flying chariot shone like a flame in the night sky of summer . . . it swept by like a comet . . . It was as if two suns were shining. Then the chariot rose up and all the heavens brightened.

Figure 54: Sri Yantra

This quotation is from the Hindu sacred text Ayodhya Kandam, XVI:

> The splendid chariot, made of silver and coated with tiger-skin, and bright like the fire itself, making a noise like the roaring of the clouds; defying all obstacles, adorned with jewels and gold, dazzling to the eyesight and bright . . . went speedily on, making space resound like unto the muttering cloud in the sky. He issued out of his abode like the beautiful moon passing through a huge cloud.

The spinning geometry of the merkaba is sometimes interpreted as a flying disc or flying globe, much like the popular science-fiction images of spaceships and UFOs. The concept has led some to believe that flying saucers from advanced civilizations do not have advanced technology, but rather they have advanced spirituality, which we interpret as technology because we have no other explanation in our day and age. Modern occultists link the energy of the merkaba to a form of spiritual UFO, and believe that advanced beings travel in energetic vehicles rather than metal ships. We interpret them as ships because that is the only frame of reference we have.

The meditation practices of Hinduism bear a striking resemblance to modern-day merkaba meditations, with an emphasis on mudras and pranayama, or energized breathing. One meditation aid, a visual focus known as the Sri Yantra (figure 54), evokes a sense of the merkaba's interdimensional geometry, even though it's a two-dimensional drawing.

In Hermetic magick, drawing deeply upon the Kabbalistic tradition, the merkaba chariot of light is associated with the sphere of Geburah, whose image is a warrior on a chariot, prepared to travel or fight. The tarot card named the Chariot is associated with the path between Binah and Geburah, on the pillar of severity. The general meaning of the card is one of travel, be it physical movement or spiritual movement, and the overarching theme is the decisions we must make before we set course. Shamanism is associated with this card, the ability to travel to other worlds. The Hebrew letter associated with this card is Cheth, which means "fence" or "enclosure." It is the enclosure we must transcend in order to rise above. It is ruled by the astrological sign of Cancer, symbolized by the crab, with its protective, enclosed shell.

The magicians look to the vision of Ezekial as the four living creatures being the four elemental powers, as embodied by ox–earth–Taurus, lion–fire–Leo, eagle–water–Scorpio, and human–air–Aquarius, combined within their wheels, to make the chariot or throne of light, the protective enclosure that guides the magician through the planes of reality to commune with the angels, archangels, and the Creator.

Hermetic magicians, drawing upon Jewish, Egyptian, and Greek mysticism, build a "body of light" as the merkaba vehicle through the use of the Middle Pillar and the Circulation of the Body of Light techniques. Not only are these healing and energizing, similar to chakra meditations, but they help prepare the magician for all manner of psychic travel. The body of light becomes the chariot of our consciousness to other planes of existence. Such Hermetic exercises are not necessary for learning the modern merkaba meditation, but are valuable as a practice by themselves.

In Blavatsky's landmark work *Isis Unveiled*, the merkaba is mentioned among the mysteries of the world. She refers to the "awful knowledge" of the merkaba, again with the allusion to the merkaba mysteries as having powerful consequences. On page xxxiii of volume 1 she writes: "Every nation had its Mysteries and hierophants. Even the Jews had their Peter—Tanaim or Rabbin, like Hillel, Akiba, and other famous Kabbalists, who alone could impart the awful knowledge contained in the Merkaba."

In our more modern ascension lore, the merkaba is said to be an ancient technique dating back to Egypt, Atlantis, and Lemuria. Back then, all humans were living with an activated merkaba, living a multidimensional existence. All were aware of the realms of spirit that were not a part of the physical plane. Then, with the trauma of the shifting of the Earth, and the disasters that led to the end of Atlantis, humanity was so traumatized that our merkabas were no longer consciously activated in us. We no longer understood the invisible realms, and stumbled through a post-apocalyptic, post-Atlantean stone age.

The ancient Egyptian civilization was responsible for the revival of merkaba mysticism, but eventually the information was lost until it was revived by the 18th dynasty in the mystery school of the controversial Pharaoh Akhenaton. Supposedly, he created a series of mystical trainings, balancing the emotional and mental sides of the initiate. Upon completion of this training, the inner mysteries of the merkaba were taught.

The syllables of the term merkaba are mer, ka, and ba. Ka and Ba are considered parts of the Egyptian soul (see chapter 5). The word merkaba can be pronounced with equal stress on all three syllables, MER KA BA, though some people emphasize the second syllable, mer KA ba. Because the word merkaba is phonetically related to parts of the Egyptian soul, modern practitioners speculate that merkaba mysticism originally came from Egypt and was later learned by the Hebrews.

Aleister Crowley, in *The Book of the Law*, observes something about the Egyptian model of the soul that is demonstrated perfectly in our merkaba mysticism: "The Khabs is in the Khu, not the Khu in the Khabs," meaning the soul is not in the body, but rather the body is in the soul. Our physicality is the denser, and more central, expression of our divinity. The body is the center of the auric field, the subtle bodies, and the divine geometries of the merkaba energy fields.

Differing from traditional Egyptian teachings, the new lore says that the Ka means "spirit" while the Ba refers to either "soul" or "body" or even "reality." Some think of the Ba as the physical body, while the Ka is the spiritual body. Mer refers to a special form of light, and together, as *merkaba*, they are counter-rotating fields of light, fields of spirit and soul, forming a new level of consciousness. Strict etymologists would take issue with the use of these words in this context, with no real facts to back it up, but this definition helps us understand the merkaba in the modern context.

Although the earliest references to the merkaba in New Age lore can most likely be found in *Isis Unveiled*, we owe the most recent understanding of the merkaba to Drunvalo Melchizedek and his Flower of Life workshops. Melchizedek's teachings on the merkaba have been the foundation stone of the modern interpretations. He claims the information was given to him by the Egyptian master Thoth. His version of the merkaba meditation is based on the shape of the star tetrahedron, a three-dimensional version of the six-pointed star. His teachings were first revealed to the world through his student Bob Frissell, in *Nothing in This Book Is True, but It's Exactly How Things Are*. Later, Melchizedek published two books on the topic, called *The Ancient Secrets of the Flower of Life, Volumes I and II*.

The monumental work of future science known as *The Keys of Enoch* by J. J. Hurtak refers to the merkaba as an interdimensional vehicle, and includes diagrams of various merkaba geometries around the human body. Other variations have been based on the Drunvalo material, inspired by *The Keys of Enoch* and other sources. Drunvalo Melchizedek claims several other people of Melchizedek consciousness are living on the Earth at this time. Soon, some people publicly claimed to be of Melchizedek consciousness, including Sheckenah Melchizedek and Hari Das Melchizedek. Though not acknowledged by Drunvalo directly, they have contributed to the modern experiences of merkaba. Sheckenah is credited with expanding the geometry of the star tetrahedron to include other sacred geometry shapes. The teachings of Sheckenah were used by Gary Smith to develop the Sacred Merkaba Techniques and several versions of the meditation. The Sacred Merkaba Techniques influenced my own merkaba teachings, which I refer to as the Mystic Merkaba, just to differentiate them from other traditions and teachings. Students of Sai Baba have shared a merkaba meditation very similar to Drunvalo's and Gary Smith's.

A gentleman named Alton Melchizedek, also known as Alton Kamadon, taught a simple three-breath merkaba technique known as the Hologram of Love lightbody activation in 1997. The simplicity of it contrasted greatly with the other merkaba techniques and trainings. It was shared freely through articles and Internet postings, but eventually became part of his multi-tiered training known as the Melchizedek Method. Hari Das Melchizedek, the founder of the Shamballa Multidimentional Healing tradition, teaches a technique based solely on visualization and affirmation, making the activation even simpler. In a similar vein, the channeled being Lazaris released a technique known as the Double-Tetrahedron Technique & Meditation. Though not specifically called the merkaba, its geometry and intention are the same. The technique is for both journeying and releasing unwanted energies.

Since then, various meditations named for the merkaba have been disseminated to the public. Many produce similar effects. Many are very different, and do different things. The merkaba teachings of this book are those that I was spiritually guided to practice after studying several of the traditions just mentioned, but they vary from the "standard" versions. They are not the exact meditations from the Flower of Life or the Sacred Merkaba Techniques schools.

Figure 55: Flower of Life

SACRED GEOMETRY

Sacred geometry is the basis of the merkaba activation. Sacred geometry differs from traditional geometry, as it's the study of shape and form and how they relate to the spiritual dimensions of creation. In the ancient world, particularly in Greece, the study of geometry was practical, artistic, and sacred, forming a part of the ancient mystery-school teachings.

By understanding the patterns of geometry that underlie all of reality, rooted in our sixth-dimensional patterns, we understand the interconnection between ourselves and all of creation. In merkaba traditions, the study of geometry gives the logical, rational mind an understanding of what the heart knows to be true—that we are all connected. There is a logical pattern, a blueprint of creation, guided by spirit. The formation of the universe, and life within it, did not happen by random chance, but was part of many corresponding patterns.

We are greatly indebted to Drunvalo Melchizedek for making the merkaba geometry widely known, as well as the pattern known as the Flower of Life (figure 55). The Flower of Life, sometimes abbreviated as the FOL, is said to be an ancient pattern that holds the geometry of all creation. Some refer to it as the Seed Blueprint for Life, as it symbolizes

Figure 56: Flower of Life and Tree of Life

the divine pattern, the divine plan for life, in its highest expression. Images of the pattern, of the nineteen interlocking circles, are found in the art of the ancient world, in places such as Egypt and China.

The geometry of the Flower of Life implies many shapes. Drunvalo points out several patterns that can be drawn out of the FOL symbol. In the flower itself, you can perfectly map the proportions of the Tree of Life (figure 56).

There is also the Seed of Life, the core of the flower, seven interlocking circles that serve as the basic pattern for the entire flower (figure 57). Then there is the Fruit of Life, thirteen circles in a six-pointed pattern (figure 58).

By connecting the centers of the circles in the Fruit of Life with straight lines, one creates the shape known as Metatron's Cube (figure 59). Metatron is one of the most powerful angels of creation, responsible for shape and form in the universe.

In Metatron's Cube, we can find the three-dimensional Platonic solids (figure 60). Attributed to the philosopher Plato, these are geometric shapes in which each facet of the shape is the same. All shapes are combinations of the geometry found in the Platonic solids. The ancients attributed special powers and attributes to the shapes, associating them

Figure 57: Seed of Life

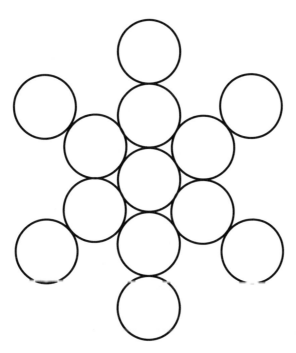

Figure 58: Fruit of Life

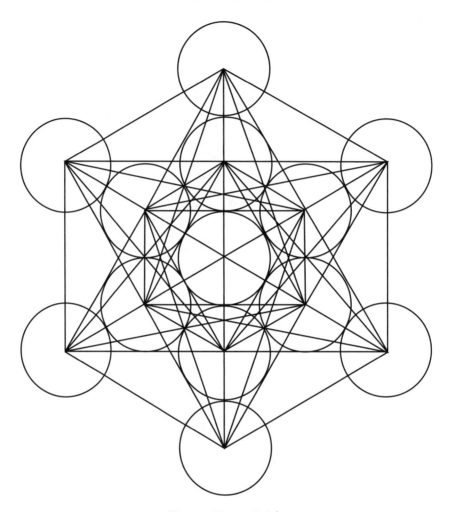

Figure 59: Metatron's Cube

with the classical elements. It was said that meditation on these shapes would help unlock the secrets of the universe. For those involved in modern role-playing games, or RPGs, you might notice some of the shapes as familiar dice used in games.

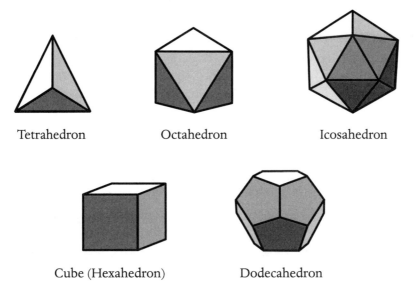

Figure 60: Platonic Solids

Tetrahedron

The tetrahedron is a four-sided shape with triangular faces. It is often mistaken for the shape of the Egyptian pyramids, which are actually one-half of an octahedron. Tetrahedrons are associated with the element of fire, the primal powers of creation, and the polarity of energies.

Octahedron

The octahedron is an eight-sided shape with triangular faces. Octahedrons, or the pyramid shape, are powerful constructs for protection and for concentrating energy. The element of air is connected with the octahedron, and in modern lore, the "diamond" association of the lightbody comes from the octahedron diamond shape. The octahedron is associated with the seven sacred directions of ritual magick and medicine traditions—the four directions and the points above, below, and in the center.

Icosahedron

The icosahedron is a twenty-sided figure with triangular faces. The element of the icosahedron is water.

Cube (Hexahedron)

The cube, also known as the hexahedron, is a six-sided figure with square faces. This solid foundation is associated with the element of earth. In certain ceremonial magick traditions, the altar is always shaped as a double cube, with one cube symbolizing the realm below, the material realm, and one symbolizing the upper realm, the nonphysical realm, relating "as above, so below."

Dodecahedron

The dodecahedron is a twelve-sided figure with pentagonal faces. The fifth Platonic solid is linked to the element of spirit. The dodecahedron is associated with the concept of Christ consciousness, the principle of unconditional love, as the Earth grid geometry associated with Christ consciousness is said to be formed in a dodecahedron.

Sphere

Though technically not a Platonic solid, the sphere is the last shape associated with the previous five. It has no element, but is associated with the void. The circle and the sphere are associated with sacred space in indigenous cultures and Earth-reverent traditions all around the world.

Star Tetrahedron

The star tetrahedron is the powerful shape drawn out of the Platonic solids that sparked my ascension quest. The star tetrahedron is composed of two interlocked tetrahedrons, one pointing up and one pointing down, forming a three-dimensional Star of David, or three-dimensional hexagram (figure 61). It has eight points and is still associated with the element of fire, the spark of the soul. The shape triggers powerful energies in the consciousness, just seeing it drawn on paper or carved in crystal.

The hexagram is the two-dimensional representation of the star tetrahedron. The hexagram is usually associated with Jewish mysticism, but its lore goes far further. Many place the hexagram in the heart chakra in Hindu mysticism, as the two triangles represent the merging of Shiva descending and Shakti rising, God and Goddess, merging in the heart. In Qabalistic ceremonial magick, the hexagram is found in the sphere of Tiphereth, the solar heart of the tree. The hexagram represents the seven magickal planets—Moon, Mercury, Venus, Mars, Jupiter, and Saturn, with the Sun in the center. Lastly, the alchemical images

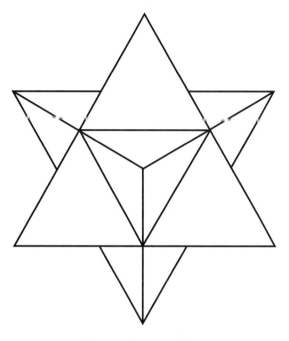

Figure 61: Star Tetrahedron

of the four elements are depicted as four triangles. Putting the symbols together creates the hexagram, an amalgam of all the elements.

The star tetrahedron is the primary shape of the merkaba, the first energetic field of the merkaba in the more advanced activations. In his Flower of Life workshops, Drunvalo Melchizedek states that the first eight cells of our being, of all cellular beings, form the star tetrahedron, and those original eight cells remain at the base of the spine. The star tetrahedron shape is the geometric foundation of our energy field.

The star tetrahedron merkaba is oriented around the physical body, with its measure affecting our own length and width (see figure 62). The edge of each single tetrahedron is the length of the fully outstretched arms, measured from the middle fingertips of each hand. The top point is exactly one hand length above the head. The apex is the "soul star" chakra of our modern chakra lore. This upward-pointing tetrahedron is called the Sun or Sky tetrahedron. When standing straight, the bottom point is exactly one hand length below the feet, etherically reaching into the floor or ground. The point ends at the "Earth star" chakra, our anchor to the world. The downward-pointing tetrahedron is known as

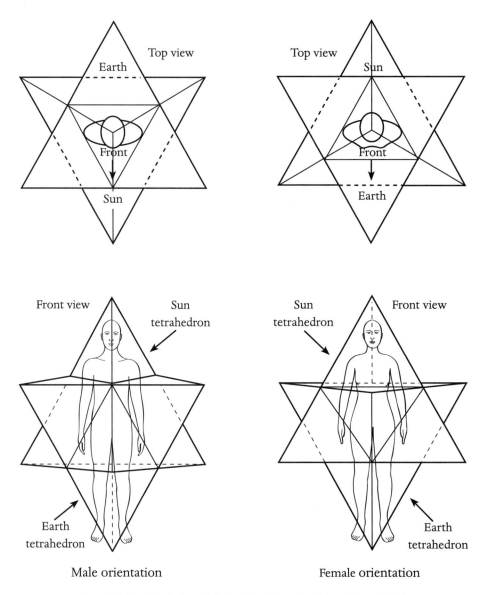

Figure 62: Star Tetrahedron Merkaba Orientations for Male and Female Bodies

the Earth tetrahedron. Some refer to the Sun tetrahedron as male and the Earth tetrahedron as female, but such terminology makes later parts of the meditation more confusing. The flat upper surface of the Earth tetrahedron is at the level of the sternum. The flat lower surface of the Sun tetrahedron is at the knees when standing up. In workshops with several people, I measure out yarn and, with people holding the "points" of the tetrahedrons, mark out each student's tetrahedron so they really have an idea of how big this shape is.

The axis of the tetrahedron is always roughly aligned with the spine, with the top point at the top of the head despite what the legs are doing. If you are sitting cross-legged on the ground, the geometry of the star tetrahedron interpenetrates the ground. The tetrahedrons remain together and consistent. They do not bend as the body bends.

The tetrahedrons are oriented differently on different genders. On a male, the Sun tetrahedron is oriented with edge and point forward, and the Earth tetrahedron is flat side forward. On a female, the Sun tetrahedron is flat side forward, and the Earth tetrahedron is edge and point forward.

Many people ask if these orientations are absolute, or based on sexual orientation or gender identity. I have found them to be based on physical genetic identity, and not sexual orientation and social or spiritual gender identity. Some people believe that those who identify as homosexual simply have their star tetrahedrons on backwards, and that correct visualizations of the star tetrahedron will lead to heterosexual identity. I have to say from personal experience that that's not the case. Homosexuality, or queer spirit, is a part of spiritual identity in a given lifetime, and cannot, nor should it, be changed through a visualization technique. Ideally, the balanced energy fields would make everyone bisexual and androgynous, yet we all still retain our gender and sexual identities after merkaba activation. For some people, if an issue of sexuality is repressed, it can be brought up for healing, but this won't change a person's basic orientation and identity. In the end, you must unite heart and mind and discover how your own merkaba is oriented. Follow your intuition.

The most important thing to keep in mind about the geometry of the star tetrahedron is that it acts as a single unit, like the other shapes. The two tetrahedrons, Earth and Sun, always remain locked together as a unit, forming the star tetrahedron. Although during the meditation you may focus on one tetrahedron at a time, the other one is implied, but invisible, since your attention is not on it. Even when we discuss the rotation of the star tetrahedron, the star tetrahedron rotates as a unit. The two individual Earth and Sun tetrahedrons do not separate and rotate independently of each other.

THE SPIRAL OF LIFE

The spinning geometry of the merkaba is activated by the rotation of the spiral, the infinite swirling of energy. Since the spiral is truly infinite, in order to find it in the material world, which is not infinite, its geometry must be approximated. The true infinite spiral is based on the golden ratio. It is represented by the Greek letter phi (ϕ), and the decimal is written 1.6180339887499, but could continue infinitely. We find the phi ratio in life, and in art. The proportions of various measurements of human limbs closely approximate the phi ratio. The measurements in the five-pointed star, the pentagram, are proportioned according to the phi ratio.

To create the phi ratio in life, a sequence of numbers comes close to approximating it. The higher the numbers in the sequence, the closer it approaches the infinite ratio. The sequence is known as the Fibonacci sequence, named after the man who is credited with discovering it, based upon the observation of leaves on a newly growing plant. We get the next number in the sequence by adding the previous two numbers in the sequence.

1	
1	
2	1+1
3	2+1
5	3+2
8	5+3
13	8+5
21	13+8
34	21+13
55	34+21
89	55+34
144	89+55
233	144+89
377	233+144

When we divide the two numbers in the sequence, we come closer and closer to the phi ratio.

$$1/1 = 1$$
$$2/1 = 2$$
$$3/2 = 1.5$$

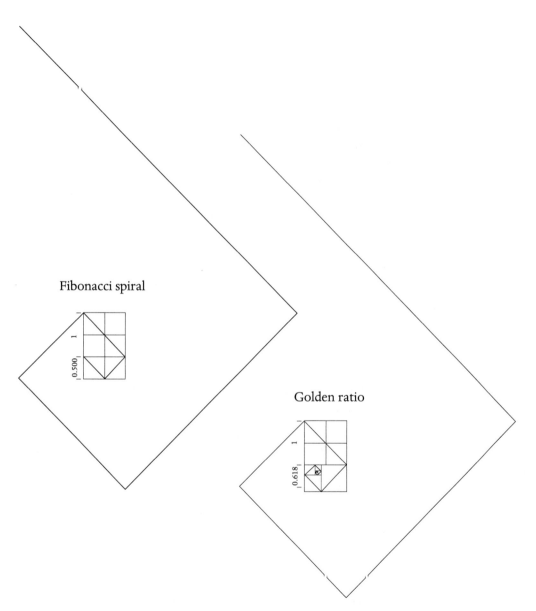

Figure 63: Golden Ratio and Fibonacci Spirals

$5/3 = 1.6666\ldots$

$8/5 = 1.6$

$13/8 = 1.625$

$21/13 = 1.61538\ldots$

$34/21 = 1.61904\ldots$

When we look at spirals plotted on a graph, the Fibonacci spiral comes closer and closer to our graphic representation of the infinite golden ratio spiral (figure 63). The Fibonacci spiral is found in nature, from the spiral seashell to the sunflower and pine cone. The merkaba meditations use this sequence of numbers as command codes to start the spinning of the merkaba fields in harmony with spirals of life. The spinning fields, as they come closer and closer to infinity, allow the dynamic consciousness expansion attributed to the merkaba.

For those interested in a deeper exploration of sacred geometry in general, I suggest *Sacred Geometry: Philosophy and Practice* by Robert Lawlor, and for the merkaba in particular, I suggest *The Ancient Secrets of the Flower of Life, Volumes I and II* by Drunvalo Melchizedek, *Sedona: Beyond the Vortex* by Richard Dannelley, and *Nothing in This Book Is True, but It's Exactly How Things Are* by Bob Frissell.

THE MERKABA MEDITATION

The merkaba meditation takes all this information on sacred geometry and puts it into action. Although the meditation may appear complicated, it can be quite easy and natural with regular practice. You are not learning something new, but remembering something that is a part of you. By balancing your logical and rational functions of technique with the emotional and intuitive aspects, you create a bridge of unconditional love between both sides of yourself. Though it follows technical steps, the focus on unconditional love is the most important part of the experience. Love is the key to consciousness expansion.

The merkaba meditation can be divided into three basic parts: clearing, pranic breathing, and rotation. Once you have completed those three sections, you can use the merkaba in a variety of practical and meditative ways. The merkaba is a devotional practice, focusing your attention on the bridge of love, but it is also a tool for further mystical exploration.

Hand Position	Name	Planet	Element	Power
First finger and thumb	Gyan mudra	Jupiter	Water	Wisdom
Second finger and thumb	Akash mudra	Saturn	Earth	Patience
Third finger and thumb	Prithvi mudra	Sun	Fire	Energy
Fourth finger and thumb	Varuna mudra	Mercury	Air	Communication

Chart 12: Mudras and Associations

Clearing

The clearing aspect of the meditation involves the first thirteen breaths. They serve to cleanse the chakras and energy circuits, though not everyone agrees on which breath cleanses which chakra. Some practitioners look at the first thirteen breaths as cleansing the seven major chakras along with the "new" chakra points in between the traditional chakras. Other practitioners say that the breaths cleanse the seven main body chakras along with the Earth star chakra below and four chakras above the crown. Still others feel that the thirteen breaths clear chakra points outside the normal systems, believing that the points of the star tetrahedron are also chakras. A popular version of this meditation uses six breaths, not thirteen, stating that it cleanses the six chakra points of the star tetrahedron, not including the soul star and Earth star points of the star tetrahedron.

The thirteen breaths are said to connect us to the Tree of Life, the map of reality encoded in our body, much like the Flower of Life. By doing this, we intuitively prepare for travel into the higher dimensions of consciousness. These breaths clear the main channel to connect to the heavens, and also allow the kundalini energy, the energy of consciousness at the base of the spine, to rise safely. The merkaba's geometry is centered around the base of the spine, around the supposed eight original cells in the star tetrahedron shape.

Although all of this lore is subjective and not clearly based on metaphysical principles, and with no historical documentation, I can tell you from experience that the breaths do clear the energy field. They clear the mind and emotions to be centered on unconditional love. They help induce an altered state of consciousness.

Each of the breaths utilizes a different hand position, known as a mudra in Eastern lore. Mudras create energetic circuits in the body. Each finger relates to a different element and planet in palmistry (see chart 12). The first breath uses the mudra of the thumb and the first, or index, finger. The second breath is the thumb and the second, or middle, finger. The third breath is the thumb and the third, or ring, finger, and the fourth breath uses the thumb and the pinky, or fourth, finger. The pattern repeats on the fifth breath.

Inhale through your nose with your eyes closed at least nine-tenths of the way, and visualize the upward-pointing Sun tetrahedron only. Make sure the orientation is correct for your gender (see figure 62). As you inhale, bring your eyes up, with your eyelids still closed, as if you are trying to stare at your third eye. Imagine the Sun tetrahedron filling with light, usually starting with white light and then letting the white light change to whatever color it desires. The colors indicate the energies you are cleansing. Any color, no matter how beautiful, indicates a need for cleansing. The more often you do this cleansing, the clearer the colors will become, eventually being only white, light blue, or violet. You can do this exercise for the first thirteen breaths alone, without continuing on to the rest of the merkaba, to simply clear your energy field.

As you exhale, imagine the Sun tetrahedron disappearing, as if a light switch in it has been turned off while at the same time a light has been turned on in the downward-pointing Earth tetrahedron. Make sure the Earth tetrahedron is oriented correctly for your gender. With your eyes still at least nine-tenths closed, if not fully closed, look down at the ground on the exhale. Imagine the Earth tetrahedron filling with the color that previously filled the Sun tetrahedron. At the end of the exhale, bring your eyes, still closed (or almost closed), to center, looking forward beneath your eyelids. Then bring your eyes together, like you are crossing them. Then quickly look up and then down, and on your last bit of breath exhaled, imagine "pulsing" the colored light of the Earth tetrahedron on the quick downward look with your eyes, moving the energy down through the bottom point of the Earth tetrahedron, "flushing" it into the Earth. The Earth Mother will transmute the unwanted energy into something that will aid the Earth, much like dead leaves and compost are transmuted into soil. Continue this pattern with each breath, changing mudras as you go.

For these cleansing breaths, some people use a word or mantra on the in and out breaths. This is not mandatory, but you might find it helpful. Some use a sequence of words, like love, truth, beauty, and harmony, repeated over and over. I used to inhale and think "love," and then exhale and think "love." My favorite is a kundalini yoga mantra, Sat Nam, which means "true name." It is a call to your higher self. On the inhale, I think "Sat," then on the exhale, I think "Nam." If you have a spirit name that you identify with your higher self, you can use that as a mantra too.

The eye movements are said to activate different parts of the brain and the upper energy centers. In yoga, such eye movements change consciousness. In merkaba, they are said to build a "bridge of light" between the pineal gland and the pituitary gland, the physical correspondents to the third eye and crown chakras. Connecting and strengthening the flow of energy between the upper chakras allows for greater consciousness expansion.

Pranic Breathing

Running through the axis of the star tetrahedron is the pranic tube, which terminates at the top and bottom points of the tetrahedron and has a diameter similar to that of your thumb or middle finger. The pranic breathing section of the merkaba meditation starts a flow of energy through your cleansed system, simultaneously from the top and bottom of the pranic tube, meeting in the heart chakra to bring your focus to unconditional love. The tube draws pranic energy not just from this third dimension, but from the dimensions above and below you, forming a pure sphere of prana in your heart center. The hand mudra for the pranic breathing starts with the thumb with the first two fingers.

The sphere of prana in the heart becomes energized with several breaths, growing larger in the heart center until it reaches a "critical" energy level and ignites in a white pranic flame. The sphere then expands into a larger sphere of prana encompassing the entire star tetrahedron, while still keeping a small sphere in the heart center, appearing much like a spherical cell with a central nucleus. This expansion of the pranic sphere is an excellent technique to aid those people who have a much weaker aura behind them, being slightly collapsed when compared to the front section of the aura. Those with a weaker back aura are prone to physical back problems as well as emotional betrayals that could be described as being "stabbed in the back," because they are less aware of people and situations that are not clearly evident. The sphere strengthens the auric shield all the way around the body, on all sides, saturating it with energy. You continue to breathe through the tube, radiating energy from the smaller heart sphere to fill the larger sphere, unifying your aura and filling it with vital life force. This is known as spherical breathing, or dolphin breathing.

Once the outer sphere is stabilized with three breaths, then you raise the smaller sphere at the heart chakra up to the throat center and then the third eye in a series of physical ritualized movements with your hands. They are similar to some movements found in ceremonial magick. By raising the sphere up the chakra column, you raise your consciousness to a higher level of awareness. In reality, the ritual motions serve to create additional spheres of prana, one each in the heart, throat, and third eye. You perceive it as raising a single sphere. The movements simply open the pathway to expanded consciousness. This pranic breathing and consciousness raising "primes the pump" of your merkaba light vehicle and prepares you for rotation. You can practice spherical pranic breathing without the first cleansing breaths, although it's not recommended, and you can do it without continuing on to the activation and rotation phase.

Rotation

The last steps of the merkaba activation are probably the most confusing, due to the multidimensional nature of the merkaba. There is not one star tetrahedron, but three complete and distinct star tetrahedrons, existing simultaneously in space. They are in the same space as we perceive them, but in different vibrations of reality. Just as radio waves, television waves, gamma waves, and visible light can occupy the same space without conflict, so too do these three star tetrahedrons.

One star tetrahedron is said to be magnetic in nature, relating to the feminine energy. It rotates to the right, or clockwise, around the body. The second star tetrahedron is electric, or masculine in nature, and rotates counterclockwise, or to the left, around the body. The third star tetrahedron is stationary, relating to the physical nature. It doesn't move at all, remaining in the orientation for your gender. These are distinct star tetrahedrons, and not individual tetrahedrons. The Sun and Earth tetrahedrons that compose each of the star tetrahedrons always remain locked together in position, rotating as a unit.

In the descriptions of dimensional science, lightworkers equate the magnetic quality of the merkaba as a symbol for energies that resonate with the earthly realms of the first and second dimensions. The electric quality symbolically relates to the realm of the fourth dimension. Together, the electromagnetic quality relates to the fifth dimension, unity through unconditional love, allowing access to all realms through love.

The counter-rotating fields of energy united in love can be seen in a similar light to the sacred space of the magick circle, but they create a permanent temple of sacred space that moves with the creator, rather than a stationary one. The magick circle is cast clockwise, though when participants hold hands in a ceremonial group, with right hands over left, they are sending energy out of their right hands, creating a counterclockwise flow. These

Figure 64: Extended Merkaba Field

two flows are like the counter-rotating fields of the merkaba, opening the space beyond space and time beyond time. The merkaba creates a temple of living light around you.

The magnetic and electric star tetrahedrons are dormant until they are activated through will and intention. You will use command codes that include number ratios of the Fibonacci sequence to approximate the spin of infinity. You will also use breath work, in which you inhale, usually through your nose, and think of the command code and purse your lips together, like blowing a kiss or whistling, and then exhale forcefully. My yoga teacher calls it cannon breath, as it is used to release the energy of the prana, and with it, the command code, starting the rotation. The same technique is used in spherical breathing, to expand the pranic ball around the body. The fields are said to rotate in proportion to the speed of light, though obviously these rotations are not scientifically measured, and might be more of a symbolic reality than a literal scientific reality.

During the basic activation, you might feel your energy field expand outward, further than the star tetrahedron and pranic sphere, creating a disc centered on your root chakra that expands to a diameter of roughly fifty-five feet (twenty-seven and a half feet on each side), creating a shape reminiscent of a flying saucer (figure 64). Once the star tetrahedron fields are activated and rotating properly, you have created the living merkaba vehicle of light. From the basic star tetrahedron activation, there are further activations based on different geometric shapes, increasing the size of the field considerably.

EXERCISE 25:
Basic Merkaba Meditation

You can do the merkaba anywhere, with no tools or props, but when starting out, it can be helpful to set the space, doing it before your altar, with candles lit and incense burning. Kyphi incense is said to help us create and feed the lightbody vehicle, though it's not mandatory. When I first learned the merkaba, I took three drops of yarrow flower essence made in moonlight to aid lightbody activation. Certain gemstones also aid merkaba activation, including merkabite (white merkaba calcite), white aragonite, phenacite, labradorite, sugilite, moldavite, tektite, diamond, celestite, azeztulite and Herkimer diamond. You can have them in your lap, on your altar, in your pockets, or around your meditation space.

I like to begin with a prayer to the divine, a call to the masters and angels, to safely guide me in the correct activation of the merkaba, for my highest good. I often chant the Qabalistic god name Eh-heh-yeh, meaning "I am that I am," three times. Some people recite the Monadic Prayer or the Great Invocation. Close your eyes. Take a deep breath in and then out to prepare, and then begin.

Clearing—First Thirteen Breaths

Breath 1: Thumb and first finger together.

Inhale into the Sun tetrahedron, eyes up. Imagine it filling with light, usually starting with white light and then letting the white light change to whatever color it desires. Think of your love of the sky and all people.

Exhale into the Earth tetrahedron, eyes down. Let it fill with the colored light from the Sun tetrahedron. Think of your love of the Earth and all of creation.

Eyes center, eyes together, up, down, and pulse the energy down through the bottom point of the tetrahedron.

Breath 2: Thumb and second finger together.

Inhale into the Sun tetrahedron, eyes up. Let it fill with light, and the light will change to any color it wants. Think of your love of the sky and all people.

Exhale into the Earth tetrahedron, eyes down. Let it fill with the colored light from the Sun tetrahedron. Think of your love of the Earth and all of creation.

Eyes center, eyes together, up, down, and pulse.

Breath 3: Thumb and third finger together.

Inhale into the Sun tetrahedron, eyes up. Let it fill with light, and the light will change to any color it wants. Think of your love of the sky and all people.

Exhale into the Earth tetrahedron, eyes down. Let it fill with the colored light from the Sun tetrahedron. Think of your love of the Earth and all of creation.

Eyes center, eyes together, up, down, and pulse.

Breath 4: Thumb and fourth finger together.

Inhale into the Sun tetrahedron, eyes up. Let it fill with light, and the light will change to any color it wants. Think of your love of the sky and all people.

Exhale into the Earth tetrahedron, eyes down. Let it fill with the colored light from the Sun tetrahedron. Think of your love of the Earth and all of creation.

Eyes center, eyes together, up, down, and pulse.

Breath 5: Thumb and first finger together.

Inhale into the Sun tetrahedron, eyes up. Let it fill with light, and the light will change to any color it wants. Think of your love of the sky and all people.

Exhale into the Earth tetrahedron, eyes down. Let it fill with the colored light from the Sun tetrahedron. Think of your love of the Earth and all of creation.

Eyes center, eyes together, up, down, and pulse.

Breath 6: Thumb and second finger together.

Inhale into the Sun tetrahedron, eyes up. Let it fill with light, and the light will change to any color it wants. Think of your love of the sky and all people.

Exhale into the Earth tetrahedron, eyes down. Let it fill with the colored light from the Sun tetrahedron. Think of your love of the Earth and all of creation.

Eyes center, eyes together, up, down, and pulse.

Breath 7: Thumb and third finger together.

Inhale into the Sun tetrahedron, eyes up. Let it fill with light, and the light will change to any color it wants. Think of your love of the sky and all people.

Exhale into the Earth tetrahedron, eyes down. Let it fill with the colored light from the Sun tetrahedron. Think of your love of the Earth and all of creation.

Eyes center, eyes together, up, down, and pulse.

Breath 8: Thumb and fourth finger together.

Inhale into the Sun tetrahedron, eyes up. Let it fill with light, and the light will change to any color it wants. Think of your love of the sky and all people.

Exhale into the Earth tetrahedron, eyes down. Let it fill with the colored light from the Sun tetrahedron. Think of your love of the Earth and all of creation.

Eyes center, eyes together, up, down, and pulse.

Breath 9: Thumb and first finger together.

Inhale into the Sun tetrahedron, eyes up. Let it fill with light, and the light will change to any color it wants. Think of your love of the sky and all people.

Exhale into the Earth tetrahedron, eyes down. Let it fill with the colored light from the Sun tetrahedron. Think of your love of the Earth and all of creation.

Eyes center, eyes together, up, down, and pulse.

Breath 10: Thumb and second finger together.

Inhale into the Sun tetrahedron, eyes up. Let it fill with light, and the light will change to any color it wants. Think of your love of the sky and all people.

Exhale into the Earth tetrahedron, eyes down. Let it fill with the colored light from the Sun tetrahedron. Think of your love of the Earth and all of creation.

Eyes center, eyes together, up, down, and pulse.

Breath 11: Thumb and third finger together.

Inhale into the Sun tetrahedron, eyes up. Let it fill with light, and the light will change to any color it wants. Think of your love of the sky and all people.

Exhale into the Earth tetrahedron, eyes down. Let it fill with the colored light from the Sun tetrahedron. Think of your love of the Earth and all of creation.

Eyes center, eyes together, up, down, and pulse.

Breath 12: Thumb and fourth finger together.

Inhale into the Sun tetrahedron, eyes up. Let it fill with light, and the light will change to any color it wants. Think of your love of the sky and all people.

Exhale into the Earth tetrahedron, eyes down. Let it fill with the colored light from the Sun tetrahedron. Think of your love of the Earth and all of creation.

Eyes center, eyes together, up, down, and pulse.

Breath 13: Thumb and first finger together.

Inhale into the Sun tetrahedron, eyes up. Let it fill with light, and the light will change to any color it wants. Think of your love of the sky and all people.

Exhale into the Earth tetrahedron, eyes down. Let it fill with the colored light from the Sun tetrahedron. Think of your love of the Earth and all of creation.

Eyes center, eyes together, up, down, and pulse.

Pranic Breathing

The spherical breathing can be divided into three parts. In the first part, you create the ball of prana at your heart chakra, and expand it. In the second part, you stabilize it. In the third part, you raise consciousness from your heart chakra to your throat and then to your third eye.

Breath 14: Keep your eyes relaxed. Thumb and first two fingers together.

Inhale. Visualize the pranic tube drawing in energy on both the inhale and exhale, from above and below, meeting in your heart space, forming a golden ball of light roughly the size of your fist. Some refer to this as the Moon sphere.

Exhale. The ball of light continues to grow.

Breath 15:

Inhale. Continue breathing through the pranic tube.

Prana flows on both the inhale and exhale as the golden ball of light at your heart chakra grows larger.

Exhale. The ball of light continues to grow.

Breath 16:

Inhale. Continue breathing through the pranic tube.

Prana flows on both the inhale and exhale as the golden ball of light at your heart chakra reaches its maximum size, about two hand lengths across.

Exhale. The ball continues to fill with energy.

Breath 17:

Inhale. The ball of light in your heart chakra ignites into white fire.

Purse your lips and blow out, expanding the ball into a sphere around your body, while the smaller sphere remains at your heart center. Your entire body and star tetrahedron are surrounded by a sphere of blazing white light. Some refer to this as the Leonardo da Vinci sphere, because it fits perfectly around his Canon of Proportions.

Breath 18:

Inhale the first stabilizing breath. Energy continues to flow through the pranic tube, into your heart chakra, and then radiate from your heart to fill the sphere around your body on both the inhale and exhale.

Exhale. Energy continues to flow. Do not stop at this point until you have stabilized the sphere around you.

Breath 19:

Inhale the second stabilizing breath.

Energy continues to flow through the pranic tube, into your heart chakra, and then radiate from your heart to fill the sphere around your body on both the inhale and exhale.

Exhale. Energy continues to flow.

Figure 65: Diamond (Octahedron) Position

Figure 66: Triangle (Tetrahedron) Position

Breath 20:

Inhale the third stabilizing breath.

Energy continues to flow through the pranic tube, into your heart chakra, and then radiate from your heart to fill the sphere around your body on both the inhale and exhale.

Exhale. Energy continues to flow.

Breath 21:

Inhale. Bring your hands out of the mudra, and imagine holding the heart pranic sphere with your hands, as if holding a ball. With the inhale, raise your hands to your throat center, raising the pranic sphere, and then create the diamond, or octahedron, position with your fingers (figure 65). Do this by holding the tips of your fingers together with your thumbs pointing down.

Exhale. Hold your hands in place over your throat center.

Breath 22:

Inhale. Raise your hands in the diamond position at your throat to your third eye, and create the triangle, or tetrahedron, position, similar to the triangle of manifestation in ceremonial magick (figure 66). Do this by moving your thumbs up into a horizontal line, creating a triangle image.

Exhale. Let your hands slowly fall into your lap. No other mudra or hand positions are necessary.

Rotation Activation

Breath 23:

Inhale.

Think, "Merkaba equal speeds."

Purse your lips and blow out. This activates all three star tetrahedrons, and sends the magnetic and electric star tetrahedrons spinning in opposite directions in an equal and balanced manner. This means that for every one rotation of the magnetic star tetrahedron, there will be one opposite rotation of the electric star tetrahedron. The field is said to reach one-third the speed of light.

Breath 24:

Inhale.

Think, "Merkaba 34–21."

Purse your lips and blow out. This activates the ratios in the Fibonacci sequence and revs up the rotation to a higher level. Many people often feel a slight nausea at this point, particularly if they are working on heart chakra issues. Usually the next activation step, breath 25, alleviates it. The nausea is partly caused by the fact that the fields are spinning at different rates. For every 34 rotations of the electric star tetrahedron, the magnetic star tetrahedron rotates 21 times. The electric star tetrahedron is said to reach two-thirds the speed of light. The field will not be stable at this point.

Breath 25:
   Inhale.
   Think, "Merkaba nine-tenths the speed of light."
   Purse your lips and blow out. At this point, you may feel the merkaba expand to a horizontal disc-shaped field from the center (see figure 64).

This completes the basic activation. You can meditate at this point, contact your guides and masters, or simply ground yourself and open your eyes. The active basic merkaba should last from twenty-four to thirty-six hours before another activation is needed, though most practitioners suggest regular daily activation of the merkaba.

EXTENDED MERKABA ACTIVATION

Our energy fields are like Metatron's Cube. They contain all the Platonic solid shapes, and not just the tetrahedrons in the star formation. We have additional merkaba fields based on these geometries. The activation of these fields is known to some as the "advanced merkaba techniques," but I have found them to be an integral part of my daily activations. Each shape corresponds to a different level of consciousness, a different type of awareness, and by activating its corresponding merkaba fields, spinning them clockwise and counterclockwise, you awaken that level of consciousness and can expand more fully.

Different merkaba traditions activate these fields in a different order, or visualize them differently. Some practitioners say it is dangerous to activate them, or they are used solely for planetary healing, but I have found only beneficial results from this work. I suggest you follow your own guidance on whether or not to do this extended activation. Some people feel it's not necessary, as all the shapes are implied in the original star tetrahedron. Others have abandoned the star tetrahedron to focus solely on the octahedron or dodecahedron. I feel that all the fields are important parts of the meditation. Like chakra meditations, you don't focus on one chakra, but balance them all. Here you activate all the shapes in a balanced way. In the version I teach, the fields are activated in an elemental order, moving from the least dense to the most dense. We start with the star tetrahedron, as that corresponds to the fire element. The next activation is the octahedron, for the air element, followed by the icosahedron for water, the cube for earth, and then surrounded by the dodecahedron for spirit. I have found this to be the most powerful activation sequence.

As you activate each shape, these additional fields operate much like the star tetrahedron merkaba fields. Each shape has three distinct units: one corresponding to the magnetic nature, one to the electric nature, and one to the physical. One rotates to the right, the other to the left, and one remains stationary, just like the star tetrahedrons. Each additional shape takes only one activation code, one breath blown out. The fields will automatically go from one-third the speed of light to two-thirds and then to nine-tenths.

In this series of activated shapes, the activation codes from the numbers of the Fibonacci sequence alternate the ratio from lower to higher number, then higher to lower, switching back and forth with each merkaba field shape. The magnetic and electric fields of the merkaba shapes alternate which is moving faster before reaching nine-tenths the speed of light. This alternating sequence is said to create a double helix of these two energies, much like a DNA spiral, or the rising of kundalini energy from the base of the spine, creating a caduceus shape (figure 67).

Shape	Ratio	Electric	Magnetic
Star tetrahedron	34–21	Faster	Slower
Octahedron	34–55	Slower	Faster
Icosahedron	89–55	Faster	Slower
Cube	89–144	Slower	Faster
Dodecahedron	253–144	Faster	Slower

When visualizing these shapes, there is no set, mutually agreed-upon orientation among all teachers. They are seen as stationary only for a few moments, and then the one-breath activation sets them spinning. With the possible exception of the octahedron, they do not appear to be oriented based on gender, like the star tetrahedron. I have described the orientations here as I view them. For many people, seeing the whole shape is difficult. Imagine that you are looking out the "window" of a shape, and focus on the image directly in front of you until it starts to rotate.

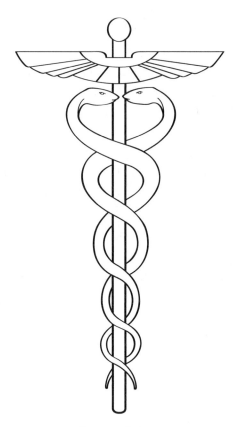

Figure 67: Caduceus

Some people visualize each successive shape as larger and larger, containing the previous shape, like hollow wooden dolls. Others see them as roughly occupying the same space, with the top a hand length above the head and the bottom a hand length below the feet, all fitting together, much like Metatron's Cube. The shapes are already there, and I believe there are multiple geometries around us in all different sizes. Simply let them appear with your will and intention as they do, and then activate them.

EXERCISE 26:

EXTENDED MERKABA ACTIVATION

Perform the Basic Merkaba Activation (exercise 25), breaths 1–25, and go directly on to breath 26. Eyes are still closed.

Breath 26:

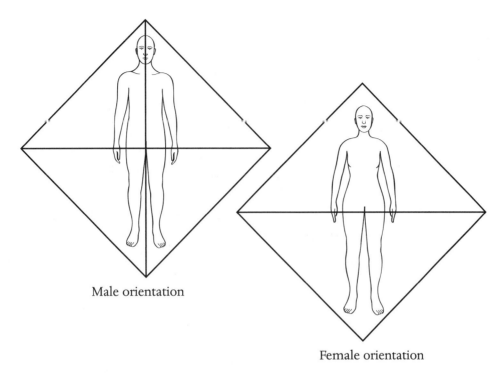

Male orientation

Female orientation

Figure 68: Octahedron Orientation for Male and Female Bodies

Inhale.

Think, "Merkaba octahedron, 34–55, nine-tenths the speed of light."

Purse your lips and blow out. Visualize the set of three octahedrons, two rotating in opposite directions and one remaining stationary. Most people imagine the four points of the octahedron facing in front, behind, to the left, and to the right (figure 68). If you connected them all, you would be in the center of a cross, with a point at the top of your head and another below your feet. When viewed while looking forward, imagine the two triangular faces of the top front half of the octahedron angled before you. Some practitioners suggest that this is the orientation for men, while women would have the flat faces of the octahedron before them. The octahedron merkaba is known as the diamond lightbody. While the star tetrahedron is often associated with shifts in dimensional space, the octahedron is related to our ability to travel in time, and perceive all time as one time, a cyclical spiral rather than a linear form. Some people visualize the octahedron in golden light, while others see it as dazzling white.

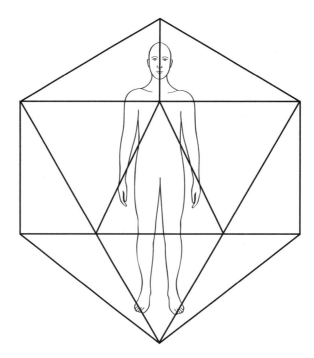

Figure 69: Icosahedron Orientation

Breath 27: Inhale.

Think, "Merkaba icosahedron, 89–55, nine-tenths the speed of light."

Purse your lips and blow out. Visualize the set of three icosahedrons, two rotating in opposite directions and one remaining stationary. Visualize the icosahedron with points at the top and bottom, creating a top-like motion as it spins (figure 69). When viewed from above, I see one of the five angles on top facing forward in relationship to the body.

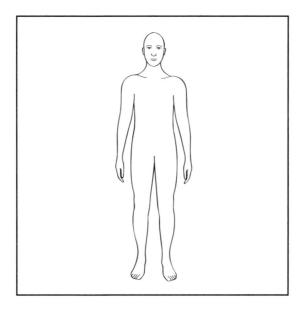

Figure 70: Cube Orientation

Breath 28:

Inhale.

Think, "Merkaba cube, 89–144, nine-tenths the speed of light."

Purse your lips and blow out. Visualize the set of three cubes, two rotating in opposite directions and one remaining stationary. Visualize the cube with a square face in front and in back, on each side, and above and below (figure 70). You may feel like you are looking out a large, square glass window or door.

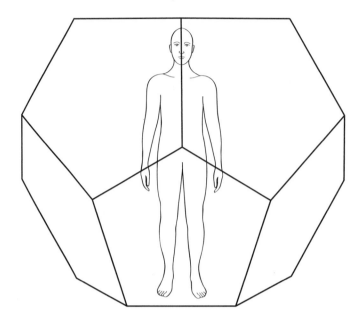

Figure 71: Dodecahedron Orientation

Breath 29:

Inhale.

Think, "Merkaba dodecahedron, 233–144, nine-tenths the speed of light."

Purse your lips and blow out. Visualize the set of three dodecahedrons, two rotating in opposite directions and one remaining stationary. If seen from above, the top face is a pentagon with the point facing forward in relationship to the body (figure 71), similar to the icosahedron. The dodecahedron is said to be the "true merkaba," for it is the shape of the element of spirit, the purest of the shapes, and coincides with the Christ consciousness grid, the energy shape around the Earth created by the ascended masters who attain this state of perfect love.

Breath 30:

Inhale.

Think, "All merkaba fields, faster than the speed of light."

Purse your lips and blow out. Visualize all the merkaba fields rotating in the proper manner, faster than the speed of light, creating the "wheels within wheels."

Breath 31:

Inhale.

Think, "All merkaba fields, light . . . lock."

Exhale. Visualize a beam of light from the eight original cells at the base of your spine, rising through the pranic tube, reaching your heart and extending out in all six directions—front, back, left, right, above, and below, locking all of the fields in the correct place and spin. Your merkaba is perfectly aligned, and your consciousness has expanded. As all the fields are spinning in perfect harmony in the same space, you may feel the merkaba take on the form of the Flower of Life sphere (figure 72), or literally feel as if you are in counter-rotating Metatron's Cubes.

At this point, you are able to travel in all dimensions and all realms of consciousness in this universe. You have activated all the sacred shapes within you and balanced all the elements of your being. Though it appears quite long, once done fluidly, the entire activation can take under eight minutes. It is only 31 breaths. If you add the next step on consciousness grid activation, it can be only 34 breaths.

Figure 72: Flower of Life Sphere

The active extended merkaba, once light-locked, should last up to five days before another activation is needed, though I suggest regular daily activation. Some practitioners suggest that with regular practice, you will eventually create a permanent active merkaba field that will not require reactivation. Though this is possible, I suggest doing the meditation regularly. As with any other spiritual practice, you need to perform it to truly reap the benefits. It would be like getting a sense of enlightenment from doing yoga and then never doing yoga again. Even those who are considered to be great yogic masters still do yogic meditation. Merkaba is like yoga for your lightbody.

The extended disc of the merkaba extends from the 55 feet of basic activation out to several miles. As the field interacts with other people, it helps uplift and fill them with unconditional love, even if they are not consciously aware of it. Some teachers suggest activating your merkaba and then walking around a major city to help uplift others.

---

consciousness grid activation

The last part of merkaba training is orienting your merkaba fields to align with the various consciousness grids relating to humanity and life on Earth. This step is not mandatory, but can be used to enhance the spiritual and meditative experiences. You can go on to other forms of meditation and magick once you have done the 31 breaths, or choose to align with the consciousness grids first and make them a part of your meditations.

Ascensionists most often talk about the Christ consciousness grid, as it's the level of consciousness we are all aspiring to reach, but everything has a consciousness grid. All species have their own consciousness grid. Normal humanity has its consciousness grid. Beings beyond our normal vision have their consciousness grid, and the merkaba lets us attune our energy to whatever level of consciousness we desire. The levels most attuned to in ascension magick are the Earth consciousness grid of Mother Earth, the Christ consciousness grid of the ascended masters, and the solar consciousness grid to extend our awareness toward the stars. These consciousness-grid alignments can be shortcuts to attune to the various dimensions, as the Earth grid is attuned to the first three dimensions, the Christ consciousness grid is anchored in the fifth but also attuned to the fourth and sixth dimensions, and the solar consciousness grid helps us connect with the seventh dimension and beyond.

I prefer to activate these levels of consciousness with a full breath blown out through pursed lips, but this is not necessary. You can simply silently think each command. Between each activation, you can meditate at that level of consciousness. You can stop after any one without continuing onward. You can do all three in three breaths, to expand your consciousness without attempting to communicate with any beings at that level of consciousness.

Exercise 27:
Aligning with the Consciousness Grids

Perform the Basic and Extended Merkaba Activations fully (exercises 25 and 26). Eyes remain closed.

Breath 32:

Inhale.

Think, "Consciousness expand to the consciousness of Mother Earth."

Purse your lips and blow out. Here, you may communicate with Mother Earth, do Earth healing, and locate anyone or anything on the planet. Meditate as long as you wish, and then, if you choose, go on to the next step. Even if I don't stay long at this level, I always like to say hi to Mother Earth.

Breath 33:

Inhale.

Think, "Consciousness expand to the Christ consciousness."

Purse your lips and blow out. Here, you can open even further to unconditional love, experience healing, or speak to the ascended masters and teachers of Earth. Meditate as long as you wish, and then, if you choose, go on to the next step.

Breath 34:

Inhale.

Think, "Consciousness expand to solar consciousness."

Purse your lips and blow out. Here, you can communicate with celestial beings and galactic masters from other planes of existence, including the archangels and starry ones.

When done, say silently to yourself or out loud, "Return, return, return." Ground yourself as needed, particularly by using the pranic tube as an anchor extended into Mother Earth, and when ready, open your eyes.

AFFIRMATION ACTIVATION

For many lightworkers, the meditations given in this chapter are just too complicated. Though the point of the merkaba meditation is to balance the logical with the intuitive, as many of us land too strongly on one side or the other, there are many other techniques that can be used in merkaba mysticism. I don't find them as powerful as the thirty-four breaths, but I do find them effective. To me, it's like the difference between doing a full yoga set or visualizing yourself doing a full yoga set. The combination of physical movement and breath, coupled with intention, is more powerful than just visualization, because it aligns you in all dimensions, including the physical. But if the meditation truly doesn't suit you, then try this affirmation activation instead.

The merkaba is activated through love and intention. If you can hold this love energy and intention, then you can activate and reactivate your merkaba using these simple commands, or whatever calls to you. Trust your highest guidance. Affirmations are very effective using repetitions in sets of three, such as 3, 9, or 33 repetitions.

Prayer or Intention of Unconditional Love

I affirm that all merkaba fields are activated and rotating in an equal, balanced way.
I affirm that all merkaba fields are rotating at one-third the speed of light, in a balanced way.
I affirm that all merkaba fields are rotating at two-thirds the speed of light, in a balanced way.
I affirm that all merkaba fields are rotating at nine-tenths the speed of light, in a balanced way.
I affirm that all merkaba fields are rotating faster than the speed of light, light-locked, in a manner that is correct and for my highest good.

MERKABA MAGICK

Merkaba magick is putting the merkaba to practical use in your life and spiritual practice. The technique itself is beneficial, but as you explore it, you will find that a whole world of applications opens up to you and your magick. The merkaba creates a living temple of light that moves as you move, and you can direct this energy in a variety of ways.

Altered Consciousness

Just performing the merkaba activation technique induces an altered state of consciousness, expanding your awareness and clearing your energy field. You can do this meditation prior to any other ritual or exercise to receive the full benefit of that ritual or exercise.

Cleansing

Merkaba activation not only clears your personal energy field, but also clears the environment around you. Use it to clear your room, home, or other space of unwanted forces. The Lazaris channelings give us an additional emotional clearing technique, encouraging us to visualize our troubles literally as baggage and packages inside our star tetrahedron fields. As we spin the star tetrahedrons, the baggage becomes like water and spins out of the field, never to return.

Manifestation

As the merkaba is crystalline in nature, it can be programmed with intention, much like a quartz crystal. The living vortex will amplify whatever intention you place in it. Like the sacred space of a magick circle, whatever you say, do, or think is likely to manifest in this living light temple. So be careful of all your thoughts and intentions once you activate your merkaba. Think of a clear goal you wish to achieve. Ideally, use the "I AM" form for it, and once your merkaba field is activated, state your affirmation in your mind. Visualize the goal or outcome. Ask that it be for the highest good, harming none. Take a deep breath, reflect on your goal, and then purse your lips and blow out. As you blow out, imagine the intention entering all your merkaba fields. Now, all your energies are working toward the outcome of your goal. You can put many goals into your merkaba simultaneously, but according to traditional magickal lore, it is most effective to focus on no more than three at a time for best results.

Protection

One of the main uses of the merkaba is for protection, both physical and spiritual. The merkaba is naturally protective, but its powers can be enhanced by programming it with a direct intention for protection. I program it to protect me from all harm, including harmful environmental energy and electromagnetic pollution.

Psychic Ability

Merkaba activation heightens our psychic abilities and allows for easier communication between us and our spiritual guides. By attuning to the consciousness grids, we can talk more easily to Mother Earth, the masters, and other spiritual beings. Channeling abilities also increase after merkaba activation.

Dimensional Journey

The merkaba is a chariot of light, and you can use it to journey through the universe in any manner you choose, intensifying what would be considered shamanic journey or astral travel. One technique for dimensional travel is to imagine the pillar of light from the Great Central Sun aligning you with the dimensional spire. Imagine drawing down from this sun the Flower of Life in a spherical shape. Draw down the number of Flower of Life spheres that corresponds to the number of the dimension you wish to visit. If you wish to travel to the sixth dimension, then drawn down six spheres and proceed to journey. Some merkaba travelers will draw down twelve spheres with every activation, to align themselves with all the dimensions.

Time Travel

Just as the merkaba can travel in different dimensions, it can also travel in time. You can do past-life regression work in the merkaba, or travel to any period in the history of the planet. The merkaba gives you access to the entire space-time continuum.

Initiation

As the merkaba opens up your consciousness, the masters might perform an inner-world initiation after successful activation of the merkaba. They might take you on a journey to Shamballa or a sacred ancient site, where you will experience a ritual to expand your consciousness even further and attain greater self-mastery. After my merkaba activation, I was called by Quan Yin to the pyramids in Giza. I found it interesting that an Asian would call me to Egypt, but the experience showed me that all the ascended masters have access to all the sacred sites across the world, regardless of the culture they are traditionally associated with. There, inside a chamber within a pyramid that was not physical, at least not on any physical diagram of that pyramid that I have ever seen, celestial energy from Sirius was funneled through my merkaba. My physical body image and identity seemed to dissolve into a puddle of silver liquid, and I was "rebuilt" by Quan Yin and her helpers, inside the crystalline field of my merkaba lightbody. Afterward, many of my physical ailments seemed to have disappeared.

Healing

Though the merkaba meditation itself has inherent healing properties, naturally granting vitality and health, the technique can be used in specific ways. During the pranic breathing, you can pause before rotation, or return to the pranic breathing after rotation, and direct prana to a specific area of the body in need of healing using your will. To heal others, you can direct the prana from the sphere in your heart through your shoulders, arms, and hands, to do hands-on healing without draining your personal energy in a method similar to forms of traditional pranic healing or Reiki. You can use the merkaba to gather and direct Mahatma energy, both for yourself and others. Ideally, during any healing you would want to make contact with a healing guide or ascended master to help you regulate the flow of energy, preventing you from overloading the recipient or yourself. You can amplify this energy through a healing wand.

Merkaba Surrogate

The merkaba meditation can be used as a form of "spiritual CPR." Instead of activating the cardiopulmonary system, it resuscitates the energy system and restores the true sacred geometry that underlies the energy fields and body. By proxy, you can activate another person's merkaba, either in person or distantly, to jump-start the self-healing process. This is not a simple task, or one to be taken lightly. Usually, it should be done only in cases of extreme need, where you have the recipient's conscious permission or encouragement from your own guides and permission from the recipient's own higher self. Unlike other forms of healing, merkaba activation is also one of consciousness expansion, and it can bring a physical clearing and an emotional/mental clearing, restore past-life memories, and facilitate contact from other dimensional beings. Many people don't want or need those experiences to be part of their healing process. I have used this technique rarely, only in critical situations, but when I have, it has yielded amazing results. You should not do this technique when there is no need, to simply "spiritually advance" another whom you feel should be doing the merkaba meditation, but isn't. At times, we can feel so enraptured by our own tools for ascension that we think that everybody should be using them, but at this time, the merkaba, like all techniques, is not for everyone. We each have our own way up the mountain. If you assume that you know what is best for another, and move against that person's will, then you are acting from ego, not from love, and are not following the path of ascension and free will.

Once you have activated your own merkaba, call upon your guides and the higher self of the recipient. Imagine the recipient before you, inside the star tetrahedron. Repeat your merkaba activation, but rather than seeing your own star tetrahedrons activate, imagine that whatever physical motions you are performing are activating the star tetrahedrons of the recipient. You can stop after the cleansing breaths, if you just wish to clear the recipient's energy field. You can also stop after the spherical breathing, to get energy into the recipient's system. You should continue on to rotation only if you feel directly guided to do so. In fact, I suggest checking in between each section, asking the recipient's higher self and your own guides for permission to continue. I usually stop after the basic activation and do not pursue the extended fields of activation. Wherever you choose to end in this healing, make sure you ground yourself, with the intention of grounding the recipient as well. The fields will last as long for the recipient as they normally do for you. To keep the fields rotating, you will need to repeat the process for your recipient of healing. You should not get into the habit of activating other people's merkabas for them when there is no healing need or crisis. If they find the technique works for them, then teach them to be conscious participants in the process by learning and doing the meditation themselves. There is no need to spiritually carry anyone else.

Earth Healing

You can use the merkaba to aid the healing of the planet as well as yourself. Attune yourself to the Earth grid first, and ask permission of Mother Earth before doing any Earth healing. Use the merkaba to draw down higher dimensional energies, such as the Mahatma energy, and ground them into the heart of Mother Earth for her healing. You might be directed to ground energies in specific places, such as places of current or pending natural disaster or political conflict, "carrying" them in your merkaba vehicle and grounding them in the area. Many people send such healing to places in the Middle East, Africa, and the United States. You could draw down a globe-sized Flower of Life sphere from the Great Central Sun, to surround, protect, and heal Mother Earth and all beings on the planet. If you are working with a space that is filled with chemical, energetic, or spiritual pollution, then you can create a surrogate environmental merkaba. It is just like the surrogate merkaba for healing, but rather than focus on a person, you construct one for a place, and, once the merkaba fields are rotating, program it for environmental healing, peace, protection, clearing, or love.

DAΠGERS OF MERKABA

A lot of fear-based material has emerged regarding the merkaba because it is such a powerful technique. Just look at the short mention of it that Blavatsky gives us. Some cite the merkaba as the reason for the fall of Atlantis or the end of life on Mars, but just because it's powerful doesn't mean you shouldn't explore it if you feel called to do so. Likewise, if you don't feel drawn to perform a merkaba activation, then no teacher or group should expect you to do so. It's an individual choice. Trust your guidance and intuition to determine if it's right for you. Merkaba has been such a huge part of my ascension experience that I had to include it, but it doesn't mean you have to explore it if, after reading the material, it doesn't resonate with you.

Some people will say that if you don't learn merkaba from a certified teacher, then you will not learn it "right," you will not have a proper activation, and all sorts of things could befall you. After speaking to some certified merkaba teachers, I realized that many did not have any greater knowledge or understanding of the complex steps in the meditation, or their significance, than I did. Many could not answer my questions with anything other than "that's the way I learned it." They told me their training took place on a higher dimensional level and they intuitively knew everything they needed. They didn't need to know the technical information on the steps or geometry, but through the training, they had the ability to unconsciously pass on the information safely to the student with just the minimal amount of instruction. Though I agree that much teaching can occur interdimensionally, that is only one way to learn.

You can make your own connections to the ascended masters, and receive their guidance and protection in this activation process. You do not need a teacher to transmit the information directly, particularly if the techniques are written down. Such rituals are gateways to facilitate even deeper contact with the masters. The rituals and meditative guides from any tradition are like the keys etched in the ethers that guide the way. Those who first receive spiritual information and build institutions around any tradition or technique must have received it from somewhere to begin with. As with the rituals of ceremonial magick and Wicca, many practitioners take oaths that bind them from openly teaching the merkaba, but in the New Age of Aquarius, many needed teachings are coming to the light, and we all must take personal responsibility as to how to use them. We are all connected to that same source of spiritual information. In the next age, we are all our own prophets. We honor the community, teachers past and present, but there is no one right way for all. That lateral relationship is a key to the Age of Aquarius.

Unlike an initiation into a magickal order or such traditions as Reiki, there is no merkaba "current" that is passed along from teacher to student through ritual. Some merkaba teachers teach the merkaba as an attunement, and perform a merkaba attunement on the student similar to a Reiki attunement, but that misses the point of integrating the meditation into your daily spiritual practice. Merkaba activation can increase healing ability and give new options for energy work, but it is not a method of automatically channeling healing energy. Merkaba is based on the contemplation of sacred geometry, intention, breath, and will, all of which are techniques that many people have learned successfully on their own, like any magickal technique.

Stories of full-body interdimensional travel abound in the ascension community. One person told me that someone had activated his merkaba lightbody improperly and disappeared from his London apartment, reappeared in the middle of the Antarctic, and died. She was afraid the same thing would happen to her. I wondered how we could know this person had had a lethal merkaba experience since he couldn't come back to tell us. Some say that if you don't use the merkaba under the auspices of a proper teacher, you attract the M.I.B., or Men in Black, who come take you away for being too spiritual and threatening the world order, or you attract satanic forces prepared to do battle. Though the techniques can bring up memories and even spiritual attachments in need of healing that can be perceived as demons, they are not going to take you away to hell. Perhaps these are just urban legends used to control the technique and who uses it.

There are some advantages to studying merkaba with a qualified person, just as there are advantages to studying with any mage, mystic, or healer. You get to ask questions, have things explained in detail, and get a "feel" for the merkaba with others. In group classes, you share your experiences and build a group consciousness. Some traditions of merkaba require you be trained by their certified teachers if you plan to continue on to learn their "advanced" techniques or other modalities dependent upon the merkaba meditation. For consistency's sake, that is understandable, and if you desire these teachings, then you might have to subscribe to a specific school of thought.

Just because I give no credence to the urban legends of merkaba dangers doesn't mean there are no real dangers. The merkaba is an intense and powerful meditation. The breath work is very cleansing. Such an influx of pure prana can induce a powerful purging effect on all levels, from the psychological and emotional to the physical. You have to be prepared for both the physical and psychological ramifications of the merkaba on you and those around you. Many who have done a lot of personal cleansing work do not find the merkaba to be that intense of a purge, but it does expand your consciousness. You have to be prepared for the messages you might receive. They can be life changing. After my second major activation in a group setting, I was very sick with digestive purge for three days, racked with violent dreams of being torn apart and resurrected in the traditional shamanic context, but then suddenly I felt better, like a new person. My partner and family didn't quite know what to do during those three days. I also remember that particular large-group merkaba activation affecting the local weather patterns, inducing a huge rainstorm when the weather report called for none. Mystics, and in particular witches, are known for their ability to cause storms with magick. Medicine people are known for their rain dance ritual. Though modern Westerners think of sunny and clear as "good," ancient cultures look at rain as a blessing, though it freaked out a lot of participants in the group.

Some people fear that if they don't have the most "advanced" activation techniques, then they will not reap the benefits, and are either wasting their time or actually doing harm. As the world shifts in vibration, some believe that the ways we activate the merkaba must be altered to match these change. Endless "updates" to the techniques are added, making them overly complicated and unwieldy. The meditation can be complicated enough without more steps added to it. I like to think of merkaba as akin to a yogic mystical practice, but there is no Hatha Yoga 2.0 or 2.1, as there is with a computer program. Although there are many variations of yoga, they all work for the practitioner. The challenge is to find the right type of yoga for you. Modifications and additions will always be made to a living tradition, and that is to be celebrated, but the older traditions work very well too.

If you fear the merkaba meditation and its ramifications, but want to learn the technique in order to overcome this fear, then I believe that clear intention, a prayer for guidance, and a focus on unconditional love are the true keys of the meditation. With them, your experience will be perfect for you

22

THE DARKNESS
AND THE LIGHT

One of the key focuses of ascension lore is on "the light." People on the ascension path talk all about the light. A self-chosen label for many is the term lightworker. Light is a term for energy or for consciousness. One can't discuss the light without discussing the dark, however. In fact, for some lightworkers, a focus on the dark has become just as powerful as a focus on the light. Usually, the focus manifests as a fear or hatred of what is deemed "dark," and that misunderstanding becomes a hindrance on the path of ascension.

The concept of dark is muddled in modern ascension lore. During one of my first lightworker experiences, I was told that "black is not a healing color." But in the traditions of the Goddess, black is one of the most healing colors. Lightworkers, so focused on the light as a part of their identity, become polarized around their concept of the dark, rejecting anything they consider dark. As in any balanced system of mysticism, there must be a rectification of all forces, a balance and synthesis, for all things come from, and return to, the divine source. In many older systems of mysticism, the dark was revered as much as the light. It was seen as a complement to the light. Dark was not a synonym for evil. One cannot exist without the other in this world.

In this chapter, we'll explore both the misconceptions other communities have of ascensionists and lightworkers, and common misconceptions and blind spots found in the lightworker community. As someone who came to the lightworker community from a paradigm outside of it, modern witchcraft, and with a background in comparative religion and other magickal traditions, I have an unusual perspective in understanding issues surrounding ascension and offer suggestions on the path to fully integrating all aspects of the divine into our lives. Most mystic traditions encourage the integration of the shadow, of the unknown, to become fully conscious. Ascension cannot be an exception.

MISCONCEPTIONS OF THE ASCENSION PATH

Many people, including many lightworkers, make assumptions based on some erroneous preconceptions about ascension. A lot of people ignore the wonderful lore and wisdom of ascension theology because of these assumptions.

There will always be people in any tradition who embrace ideas that are discriminatory against others, but we cannot assume that such people represent the views of the entire community, or that such ideas are a reflection of the tradition's mystical theory. Many horrible acts have been committed by Christians, but we should not assume that those acts were based on the teachings of Christ. Many battles have been fought by indigenous people, yet we cannot assume that shamanism teaches the doctrine of war. In this modern era, we have to be well aware that extremists, from social and political extremists to more spiritual ones, are not representative of the greater whole.

Here are a few basic points that are often confused by people looking at the ascension paradigm. They are all phrased as negative statements, in an effort to emphatically clear up misconceptions of what many people think ascension theology is.

Ascension Is Not a Religion

Ascension is a paradigm, a set of philosophies in which modern mystics test their theories and frame their experiences. It transcends any one religion and absorbs wisdom from many world traditions, modern and ancient. Some branches of ascension lore have been strongly influenced by Christian, Jewish, Hindu, and Buddhist sources, but ascension does not promote any one path over the others. You can remain a practitioner of your own religion and still subscribe to the ascension traditions. Ascension seeks to separate the religious and political dogma of a religion from the essential core of truth that all religions share. Any conflict you feel regarding ascension and religion is based upon your own understanding of the tenets of your religion or the orthodox views of your religious institution. Many people might feel that ascension lore and Catholicism are not compatible, and I'm sure the Catholic Church would not encourage its members to put their time, effort, faith, and money into ascension practices, but I know many Catholics who work with the ascended masters quite successfully, and personally have no conflict in their own hearts, discerning the fundamental core of their religion from the institutions that govern its worldly body.

Ascension Is Not Racist

Many people fear the use of the terms *black* and *dark* as negative influences on the spiritual path, and also fear the pitting of *white* against *dark* or *black*. The term Great White Brotherhood, used for the ascended masters, conjures an image of the Ku Klux Klan. I have a friend who met someone who said he was a channel for the Great White Brotherhood, but didn't explain to her what that meant. Being entirely new to ascension spirituality, she wanted to discreetly leave the premises before the robes and burning crosses came out.

The term white is not a commentary on race, but refers to the inclusion of all colors and is a symbol of consciousness. The Great White Brotherhood is not a euphemism for Aryan superiority. When teachers such as Blavatsky, in the Theosophical paradigm, used the term Aryan race in the context of the root races, they were referring to the modern race of men, *Homo sapiens*, divided into five sub-races, based on skin color—white, black, red, yellow, and brown. Such divisions today seem politically incorrect, but in her era, Blavatsky was trying to convey a mystical idea. Aryan is also used in a linguistic sense, associated with the Indo-European languages and races, which would also include a link to the dark-skinned Hindus. Some older texts, referencing the four or five colors of race, list characteristics and rank white among the top strata for intellectual and spiritual development, but this is a prejudice of the age in which the material was written, and not necessarily a teaching of ascension. Ascension values the entire spectrum, the whole rainbow of color, and includes ascended masters from all races and religions.

Ascension Is Not Anti-Semitic

Many people have misinterpreted the Christian and Eastern symbolism in ascension lore as anti-Semitic. Some make a reasonable argument that early ascensionists were anti-Semitic, and it's quite possible that they were a product of their time and culture, yet anti-Semitism is not part of modern ascension lore at the start of the twenty-first century. Some look at the seal of the Theosophical Society with the swastika, and automatically see a Nazi symbol, but the seal, as well as its use in Buddhism and Germanic magick, predates the Nazis. Others interpret the reference to the "plan" in the Great Invocation, being very Christianized, as a reference to having no tolerance toward Jews. Modern ascension lore includes Hebrew, the Tree of Life, and merkaba mysticism, as well as a reverence for Jewish Old Testament prophets as masters and teachers.

Ascension Is Not Anti-Feminist

Because of the use of the term ascended master, many people ask, where are the ascended *mistresses*? While it is true that many of the early Theosophical masters were perceived as male, there is a greater showing of ascended masters who are recognized as female in the modern era. The term master was just used as a gender-neutral term because many feared that mistress was a derogatory term. Sometimes the title "Lady" is given to a female master, much as the Goddess is referred to as "the Lady" in many traditions of paganism. Now, the title of "Lords and Ladies of Shamballa" is used more than "Great White Brotherhood." In truth, ascended masters are beyond gender, yet manifest in ways we can relate to, usually through the most recent physical past incarnation.

Some believe that the body of the ascended incarnation is preserved or reconstructed from light in the realm of Shamballa. In certain forms of magick, it is interesting that the inner plane is said to have opposite polarity in terms of gender energy. Often a priestess is a conduit for a god's male energy, and a priest is a conduit for a goddess's female energy. It is also interesting to note that the two people best known for introducing the ascended masters' popular teachings were women, H. P. Blavatsky and Alice Bailey, channeling male masters, while two men, Gerald Gardner and Alex Sanders, are most noted for reviving the Goddess traditions of Wicca, though Gardner was strongly influenced by priestess Doreen Valiente.

Ascension does, however, have far to go in recognizing and integrating feminine and Goddess spirituality in its paradigm to be truly holistic. Most practitioners use the default pronoun *he* to refer to the divine Creator, beyond shape and gender. Some have tried to use the term Mother/Father/God to offset this bias. The mythologies of the Goddess, and in particular of the dark goddess, also have to be integrated into ascension lore more fully to have a balanced tradition.

Ascension Is Not Anti-Pagan

Though many people involved in ascension focus on the monotheistic lore, and see it as an improvement over, or evolution of, polytheistic traditions of the past, most ascension lore values the pagan scholars of the ancient world, particularly of Egypt and Greece. Though they would not use the word pagan in their own time period, they practiced paganism as the word is understood today. Some claim that the writings of ancient pagan scholars, such as those attributed to Hermes Trismegistus, are monotheistic at heart and even echo Christianity. Yet if this is so, then their monotheism was more akin to the teachings of Hinduism, with one creative essence, one divine reality beyond the illusion, or maya, manifested as many gods and spirits. The sacrificed-god motifs found in many pagan cultures echo Christianity. Most ascension lore values the "paganism" of the East, found in Hinduism and Tibetan Buddhism and Bon, as well as the apparent pagan polytheistic views of many tribal cultures and ancient Western civilizations, such as the Aztecs, Mayans, and Incans. It appears that the prejudice against polytheism remains only in the traditions of Europe and the Middle East, where the Christian religion persecuted such views. If prejudice against paganism is found in ascension lore, it is simply a holdover from these thought patterns.

Ascension Is Not Homophobic

Some esoteric writings, usually from more conservative time periods in which homosexuality was not generally accepted, condemn homosexuality or simply look at it as a spiritual or energetic "imbalance" in need of "fixing." This is another Judeo-Christian holdover in thought. Most ancient and tribal cultures honored or accepted people of homosexual orientation. Many of these people in those societies were mystics, set apart and "between the worlds" in more ways than one. The lore in the Old Testament condemning homosexuality included a long list of other pagan practices, such as the use of idols or statues in ritual, to set the Jewish people apart from those practicing the pagan religions, who often worshipped a goddess. Modern ascensionists look at homosexuality as just as valid a life path as any other. Many esotericists see true bisexuality as the ideal, as one loves and is attracted to both forms, and unattached to either one.

Ascension Is Not Anti-Sex

Though many on the ascension road take a path of the ascetic, withdrawing from the world and living minimally, imitating the practices found in both Eastern ashrams and Western cloisters, it is not mandatory. Many look to the practices of sacred sexuality, found in Eastern tantric texts, as well as Taoist sexual alchemy or Western sex magick, as a path to enlightenment. Ascension is not necessarily a path of moderation, so some practitioners go to extremes in their spiritual practice. Many others believe that they should live in moderation and not be attached to sensation. They understand that while life in the physical world is transitory, they can enjoy what the physical world has to offer while they are here.

Ascension Is Not Anti-Earth

Due to a huge Gnostic influence, much of the ascension lore depicts the material world as corrupt or debased, and not inherently divine. In other doctrines, from paganism to Qabalah and Native teachings, the material world is seen as the expression, the fruit, of all the other spiritual worlds. It is divinity in its densest state. Dense is not bad, but simply different from the ethereal. This has led some ascensionists to believe that we do not need to care for the world because we will eventually "escape" the third dimension and be in the higher dimensions. Others believe that the dimensions overlap, and what happens to one influences the others. These practitioners have a strong environmental ethic, for both spiritual and practical reasons. Many ascensionists are devoted to Mother Earth and work with the devas and faeries of nature, doing rituals to cleanse the world of pollution as well as taking part in political environmental activism, recycling and living "green." We find the "furry Buddhas" in our animal relationships. We find masters of healing in plants. Both the animal and plant beings know they are a part of divinity. The green current of modern ascension lore is growing due to the interest in Goddess studies, paganism, and Native shamanism within the tradition.

Ascension Is Not Anti-Government

Many people believe that the transitions of the New Age require a transformation in the political systems founded in the Age of Pisces, usually through the dismantling of old systems and the building of new ones. Ascension practitioners usually call for a peaceful, rather than violent, transformation. Though some advocate the overthrow of the government, or consider the world governments to be puppets for a shadow organization, most don't see the need for a violent revolution, but instead promote a revolution in consciousness. Many believe that the influence of the ascended masters in the founding of America has created one of the more Aquarian forms of government that can be both practical and idealistic, and set an example in the world. Many looking at the practice of politics in America might disagree, but in its highest form, democracy, with its roots in the pagan Greek philosophy, is an Aquarian value.

Ascension Is Not Fraudulent

Ascension lore and the teachings of the ascended masters have become genuine and positive contributions to the Western occult traditions, but we'd be remiss in not mentioning that ascension, in its relatively short history, has had its share of ups and downs. Many practitioners associated with the fringes of the teachings have been exposed as charlatans, cult leaders, and money seekers. Even founders of the theologies, such as Madame Blavatsky, are surrounded in controversy. Like many other traditions, mainstream or otherwise, ascension has had its share of scandals, but this makes it no less legitimate. One can find similar scandals in mainstream institutions, such as the Catholic Church, among various Eastern gurus, and in occult lodges, such as the Golden Dawn. Leaders and founders of traditions are faced with misunderstanding and scandal, making it difficult to discern what is truth and what is fabrication, but in the end, it is the teachings, not the personalities, that matter most.

PROBLEMS ON THE ASCENSION PATH

Now that we have a better understanding of what ascension philosophy is not, from an outside perspective, it's time to tackle the thorny issues of the paradigm from the inside perspective. Following are some of the concepts not fully understood even by many who subscribe to ascension, because many of the historical and spiritual contexts of these ideas are usually glossed over in most books and classes in favor of a solely intuitive approach. Here are the places where we are most likely to get caught on the thorns and suffer without attaining the knowledge that can come with suffering. We can acquire the same knowledge while bypassing the suffering, to ease our way into a greater understanding of the world and our spirituality.

Divine Immanence versus Divine Transcendence

One of the major sticking points in understanding ascension is the paradox of divinity. For most people in the ascension world, divinity is simultaneously immanent in the world, in people, in all of nature, and transcendent, or otherworldly, beyond the confines of what we perceive of as the universe. Spirituality is filled with such paradoxes, such as the fact that we appear to be separate beings, yet from a spiritual perspective, we are all one. The possibility of ascension means that we are already divine, yet need to ascend to a conscious knowing and experience of that higher perspective. From that perspective, we can do anything.

Mystery school lore and ancient teachings parallel our modern understanding that we are spirit, we are light, we come from the stars, yet we acknowledge the place of the world, of flesh, and do not see it as evil or harmful. Due to the influence of Zoroastrianism, some interpretations of Judaism, and forms of Gnosticism and Gnostic Christianity, there is a sense that the Creator, divinity, is outside and beyond us in some way. There is the Creator and the Creation, and they are separate. In light of modern ascension practices, the two views can be looked at through the historical lens of theurgists in the Neoplatonic and Gnostic schools of thought. Ascension is a form of theurgy, of god magick. What separates the Neoplatonic ceremonial theurgists and the Gnostic sacramental theurgists is that the Gnostics saw the divine forces as supernatural, outside of creation, above us and unnaturally intervening in the course of events. Being dualistic with the Zoroastrian influence, divinity was seen as separate and above the laws of creation. The Neoplatonists saw divinity as part of the natural world order. The world emanated out of the divine, as in the Qabalistic Tree of Life. The divine raised their worshippers to the divine level, while still having their feet rooted in the material world, while the dualist must either have the divine descend into the material, or escape the material to be one with the divine. In the end, both schools of thought are working with the same forces. It just depends on what you call natural and supernatural.

Many people of mainstream faiths today are grounded, often unconsciously, in the Gnostic view of divinity being beyond us, and not ever present, though many mystics, even of those same mainstream faiths, understand the paradox and have a view more in alignment with the Emanationists, even if that view is unconscious and not articulated. This disconnection is the source of our "fall" mythologies, separating us from the heavens. It is across the abyss of the fall we must ascend, but if we choose to embrace both transcendence and immanence, and realize the material universe is within the soul of the universe, then the void is much easier, and much healthier, to cross, because we know divinity is with us every step of the way. This fundamental misunderstanding of the paradox, the truths, of both transcendence and immanence, and the view of absolute dualism has caused much of the pain, confusion, and suffering in the world in the name of religion.

Fundamentalism

Though many people believe fundamentalism is found only in mainstream institutional religions, some New Agers have a fundamentalist slant. With the excitement and zeal one finds in entering a new paradigm, sometimes people forget it's a paradigm, and feel it's an absolute truth. They have the attitude of "if it works for me, it must work for everybody." They get swept up in the excitement. Their views become dogmatic and rigid, rather than flexible, synthesized, and inclusive. Some forget that ascension, like all spiritual traditions and ways of thinking, is a paradigm, a way of looking at something. They are so excited by it that they assume it is "the truth" and the only way of looking at something, and can't imagine why others don't share their viewpoint.

I've had students who started with me in Wicca go on to ascension work, and can't understand why I stay grounded in Wicca. My roots are in Wicca, and the New Age is about bringing the Old Age back to the modern era. One of my students who got involved in ascension lore with her teenaged daughter almost left her husband because he "wasn't getting with the program quickly enough" or, in her mind, raising his vibration and consciousness in the manner she felt was necessary. Some people take the patterns, prejudices, and dogma from their core religion and apply them to ascension lore. Many accuse ascensionists of having a strong Christian bias, and forcing their Christianity on those in the community who don't want it. Though that might be true in some cases, we could say the same for practitioners of all traditions. Many feel that an Eastern slant is pressed on Western seekers. You may read this text and feel I'm pushing a pagan/ceremonial-magician slant. Everybody is biased in some way, but if they feel their own bias is the absolute truth, the only way for everybody, then it becomes a fundamentalist view.

Naiveté

Many people in the various New Age paradigms are considered naive, on a variety of levels. Though we can hold an ideal of the most perfect world, we also have to remain grounded in the physical world, where everything and everyone are not perfect. One of my favorite stories that demonstrates this fact is a tale about Yogananda, guru and founder of the Self-Realization Fellowship. As Yogananda and his students were getting ready to enter an event together, he urged his students to make sure they locked their cars. The students got upset and echoed back his teaching, that we are all of God. Yogananda answered, "Yes, we know that, but not everybody else knows it, so lock your car." Many people do not discern that there is harm in the world. Many are hindered by their sense of political correctness. Even those in the polarity of light and dark often won't even use the term "dark," but instead say "not of the light." There is a denial of the reality of the world, and without a sense of that reality, one cannot transform the world.

Love and *light* are often the watchwords of the New Age movement, but few people realize that these two *L* words are but two of four major principles representing the ideals of the four elements. Light is for fire, the principle of the soul, energy, and will. Love is for water, for emotion. The other two are *life*, for air, the breath of life, and *law*, for earth, the divine structure. Living according to only two leaves you unbalanced. Lightworkers are often unclear about or unversed in their own basic metaphysical principles, relying solely on intuition and having no use for logic. We are given the label of being a "fluffy bunny," cute and cuddly, but lacking substance and depth.

Folklore is often confused with, or equated with, fact. While folklore, myth, and intuitive information have great value, it is important in many arenas to discern what is provable fact and what is an idea or metaphor. Many assume that the romantic tales of King Arthur were indeed fact, but if King Arthur were a living person, or based upon a living person, his reality, his court and Camelot, would be quite different from the popular notions we have of them. Some lore will speak of Jesus Christ visiting Egypt, India, France, Spain, and Britain. Though they are nice ideas and great speculations, few serious historians have found any credible evidence to support them. We could debate whether there even was a physical person matching the descriptions of Jesus Christ, though most people in the Western world accept his existence as fact because of the institutions of Christianity.

Lastly, many ascensionists, having such a strong belief in the power of divine intention, magick, and psychic ability, often fail to follow up their intentions with real-world action. According to basic spell theory, you must follow up your spells with real-world action, to open the door to allow the effects of your magick into your life. If you set your intention to get a job, then be sure to send out applications, network, look through the newspaper and online, and go on interviews. If you have the intention to have a relationship, then go to parties and clubs, get set up by friends, answer personal ads, or attempt to date. Those who simply wait for things to happen without making any practical efforts are not living in the real world. Sometimes that type of magick works, but usually it fails.

Ego

For a tradition that seeks to transcend the ego in universal love and union with the divine, we collectively have a large ego, but the same could be said for almost any spiritual tradition. Each will have various personalities, and people will be attracted to those personalities, on a large and small scale. The very nature of ascension is surprisingly egotistical. One major step along the path, the step glorified by the very term ascension, is the individual becoming an ascended master. One potentially becomes known by spiritual seekers, and one's last incarnation is revered almost to the point of deification. There is nothing wrong with this practice. We've done it for centuries with our ancestors, heroes, and figures of folk myth. But from the perspective of one seeking this step and knowing this veneration could potentially come with it, I think that this type of hero worship does create an environment where personal ego is encouraged.

This personal ego is exactly what distracts a person from the path of ascension and self-mastery. While our Theosophical foundation has a huge Buddhist slant, the reverence of ascended masters actually conflicts with a lot of fundamental Buddhist thought. There is a saying, "If you see the Buddha on the path, kill him." This is not a call to violence, but a warning that we can get obsessed with a figure, a personality, and not follow the path to completion. Buddha, the awakened one, is simply a guide, and not a figure to be worshipped.

Unfortunately, many convince themselves that they have moved beyond the personal ego. Whenever I find someone running around claiming to be an incarnated ascended master who chooses to be here on Earth, I am always skeptical. On some level, aren't we all spiritual masters who choose to incarnate here on Earth? But I'm not sure that if a person were truly consciously enlightened while here on Earth, that revealing this fact in casual conversation would be a sign of that enlightenment. I think that if someone is truly spiritually aware, then he or she lets other people figure it out on their own and live by example. Many people enter what is considered "mystical delusion." Those who do invocation or channeling work start to identify so strongly with the forces they mediate that they begin to think they "are" those forces, rather than a conduit for them. Suddenly, they take on the qualities and values of the masters, angels, or gods in their own mind, and feel like they are beyond "human" concerns and morals. This can be a form of escapism. It's easier to identify with a perfected being than to deal with an unperfected life and the consequences of one's actions. It's also a form of ego expansion to identify oneself with these archetypal forces. We can witness this same phenomenon among rock stars and actors. Through their craft, they channel these forces, like a ritualist or channel, and some become humble, knowing the forces are being channeled through them. Others become arrogant, feeling that these forces come from their own personal consciousness.

At one workshop, I met two people who believed that in a past life they were inhabitants, in another galaxy, during the Orion Wars, who were archetypally the figures on which George Lucas based the *Star Wars* characters of Luke Skywalker and Princess Leia. "Luke" even had his crystal lightsaber with him at the workshop. Though archetypally those figures can be helpful, and who knows what, if anything, really happened a long time ago in a galaxy far, far away, it didn't seem healthy for those two to identify so strongly with these figures. In my opinion, it inhibited their development in this life. Their sense of mission now, and the ego attached to its importance, probably prevented them from working on a lot of more mundane, current-life issues that needed to be addressed.

During episodes of mystical delusion, it is easy for a teacher, healer, or channel to get caught up in the "guru" mentality, as it is seen in the West. Rather than helping others find their own healthy stories, the teacher gets trapped in her own story, her own drama, and imposes it upon her students. The teachings begin as universal truths, but are turned into a foundation built upon a cult of personality. The channel doesn't have messages for herself, but for all others, even when others don't ask for that message in the first place. The lines and boundaries of relationships start to blur, and service is no longer being provided, but rather a drama is unfolding. Fear and misdirection are used. I recently spoke to a woman who was being indoctrinated daily with fear and paranoia from the "secret government," and her teacher had told her that only she had special techniques that could heal and save her, that traditional shamans, witches, and magicians didn't know how to work with these energies. The teacher was the only one with the special knowledge. When this student questioned her teacher's prophecies that had failed, such as that a walk-in would be the next president of the United States and there would be peace, the teacher's response was that the black government had manipulated the election. Finally, this woman said to me, "I feel like I am becoming dependent upon my teacher." All I could say was, trust your feelings. A good teacher, a good mystery school or path, will eventually empower you, and not create fear-based dependence or build your faith around one living individual who holds all the power.

Pseudo-Science

Many of the metaphysical terms in ascension are couched in scientific jargon. Perhaps when they were coined, the concepts were not as clearly defined and well-known scientifically. But now, in an age in which science and spirituality are not so far apart, with quantum physics, morphogenetic fields, holographic universe theory, and superstring theory, we need to be clear in our terminology. Many people, working in a space-age style paradigm, find comfort in scientific terms, but to those uninitiated in the ways of ascension, these terms sound rather strange. I once spoke to a healer who talked about how his method of healing generated photons to pass through the body. I asked him if the room lit up when he did it. He said of course not. Well, photons are discrete packets of light. They are part of the visible light spectrum. Perhaps his healing technique generated a subtle force, an invisible energy, an etheric energy or astral light, but it didn't generate photons. I've heard channels say that our planet is going to enter a photon belt, and we will have daylight twenty-four hours a day until we pass through it. I'm skeptical. When ascensionists speak in terms of photons, vibration, dimension, light quotient, and electromagnetic and quantum energy, it is important that we define our terms, so our meaning is clear, rather than confusing the listener. Perhaps this will lead to the rise of a new system of terminology in harmony with modern science.

The Power of Channeling

Since much of the modern Theosophical foundation came from channeled sources, reportedly right from the masters, there has been an outpouring of channeled material, yet there is quite a difference between the early channelings of Theosophy and the plethora of modern channeled material. This reliance on channeling has weakened the sense of scholarship, research, history, and critical thinking in the New Age metaphysical movement. As we enter the Age of Aquarius, it is important to know that Aquarius is ruled by Uranus, for innovation, with a lingering influence from the old ruler, Saturn, representing discipline, history, and respect for the past. The New Age is really the Old Age brought back into consciousness and adapted to the next world. We mustn't disregard our ancient wisdom. We must reconcile it and synthesize it along with our modern teachings.

Channeling encourages people to seek answers directly from the masters, which is very empowering, though many don't stop to ask questions for themselves, but feel they have the messages for others. In mystic orders, those who channel the masters reportedly have gone through a variety of initiations and rituals to purify themselves and to understand their shadow, so the master's message is not distorted through the ego and the message can be more universal, divine information and wisdom to be shared. Many who start channeling have done little introspective work, so unless they are naturally a clear channel for an entity, the messages they receive can be muddled or poorly written to convey practical information for those on the path. The messages, even when they are clear, are almost always colored by the personal views, or paradigms, of the channeler. Many of these messages contribute to the idea of channeling being a pseudo-science. Channeled information is often accepted as divine fact, and is not subjected to any process of critical discernment. The original Theosophical writings were anything but fluff. If anything, they were too packed with information and hard to decipher, much like the medieval grimoires. Others will say the modern channelings might lack information for the 3D world, but their cadence and vibration induce altered states, heal, and awaken the spark of life when listened to or read, and that could be true as well.

The excess of channeling can also encourage people to focus on channeling information instead of experiencing the spiritual world. A friend of mine who manages a local metaphysical bookshop was discussing the works of both Alice Bailey and Dion Fortune and their contributions to the New Age. He favored Fortune. Though both women were highly influential and left a great legacy of work, many who follow Bailey's work simply read it, or then attempt to channel more information, but are often unclear as to how to apply it. Those who read Fortune's work are more likely to do the pathworkings and rituals to experience the various levels of consciousness on the Tree of Life. They have a direct experience, using their will, rather than passively listening to or only pondering the information. Though the Bailey material can definitely be applied, I see his point. I encourage people to ask for both lofty and practical information when communing with the masters and angels, and to find ways of applying that information. Look to the rituals of the past, and if they don't work for you, then ask the masters for guidance on adapting those rituals to suit the next aeon.

Escapism

Many people with escapists tendencies are drawn to ascension lore. The concept of leaving the physical world for a perfected world of pure light, of consciousness, is appealing to those who have difficulties with the material world. Sometimes this view is encouraged by teachers and teachings with a heavily Gnostic view of the material world. Their sole view of ascension becomes the literal and physical transcendence of the physical plane, rather than merging with the authentic higher self and creating a paradise on Earth. In applying the doctrines of nonattachment, many try to be so beyond the physical world that they find no joy in the material world. They distrust their primal instincts in regard to personal safety, deny the need for medical help, and do not take care of their bodies. Some sects have encouraged students to go a step further from the vegetarian/vegan line and become breatherians, or those who exist solely on the life force of breath, on subtle energy. Though I do believe that this is metaphysically possible, I think many try it without having the spiritual and magickal awareness, the level of enlightenment, to accomplish it, and end up starving themselves.

Some people become detached from the world in other ways, seeking to escape the society and responsibilities of community. They focus so much on the higher dimensions that they cannot deal with the third dimension. They can't hold a job, pay bills, or maintain a home, relationships, or their health. Though the classic examples of escapist addictions are drugs and alcohol, anything can be taken to an extreme, including meditation and reading. Some people are not grounded in this time period, always looking back to past lives and blaming people in their current life for past-life issues. Past-life memories serve to increase your own awareness, to help you work out your issues rather than take them out on others in this life. You should have compassion for both yourself and those in this life whom you have known in past incarnations. The point of nonattachment, of being free of the wheel of life, is to identify with the center of the wheel, and realize that your personal self has highs and lows, ups and downs, but your divine self sits balanced in the center. You can live from both points of view, and eventually merge them, so you are "in the world, but not of it," as the popular spiritual saying goes. This is another one of our strange divine paradoxes. Even those Eastern traditions that stress nonattachment the most also stress being in the present moment and paying full attention to the reality around you.

Lastly, some escapists are seeking to be "saved." We cannot seek salvation from an outer source. Aliens are not going to physically land and take over, making things perfect. The masters are not going to manifest and control the world's governments. We must be our own saving force.

Addictions

Though many in the lightworker community work hard to rid themselves of any physical addictions—cigarettes, coffee, white sugar, and even certain other foods—many have addictive behaviors bent toward seemingly positive pursuits. But if it's still an addiction, it can be dangerous, or at least distracting from the focus of your spiritual work. Some escapists are addicted to excessive meditation, spiritual books and websites, or entertainment that plays to their spiritual ideas and even fantasies. After giving up many physically addictive behaviors, many become addicted to the "peak experiences" provided by group workshops, rituals, and meditations. Each peak experience gives you "work" to process and do, to integrate the experience into your life. Many do not consciously integrate these experiences, but continue to seek out the next energy "high" or spiritual buzz under the veil of an epiphany. Many seek out energetic attunements, such as those found in Reiki, and continue to get one attunement after another, without working with the self-healing that attunement offers. When we increase our vibrations, we may feel that our techniques are no longer working. We can't feel the intensity of energy or spiritual forces, because what was once a great expansion is now the everyday level of energy we carry. Some people seek out greater and greater experiences, without regard to doing the work associated with those experiences. Some become addicted to these energy expansions and are constantly on the lookout for the "latest and greatest" technique, teacher, meditation, or healing attunement.

In the end, the hunt for the next technique distracts you from using any of the tools to have a greater sense of health, peace, and alignment with your soul. This addiction to energy and power is not unique to lightworkers. The yogis warn of practitioners becoming so focused on the psychic powers of the siddhis that they get distracted from the path of enlightenment.

Fatalism

Many people in the ascension movement are not magicians at all, and that's fine, though some take it to an unhealthy extreme. They hold a philosophy of non-interference, believing that whatever is "meant to be" will be, and they don't want to unduly influence the world. Such people don't realize that their every thought, word, and deed influences their world already, and setting an intention, or making magick, is simply aligning with the soul to do our work here in the world. If we had nothing to do, nothing to share, to add to the greater web of life, then we probably wouldn't be incarnated here.

From a magickal point of view, nothing is completely predestined. Many in the metaphysical community use the concepts of karma, fate, higher will, and the soul's contract, but those are ideals of how things could manifest. Our choices, our actions, are what bring potentials into being. You might have the "karma" to have an accident, but it might manifest as a toe stubbing or a car crash, depending on your clarity, your energy, your sense of divine connection and protection. Some with such a fatalistic view seek to focus on just "being" and not doing, not having to be goal-oriented, and feel that simply showing up for life is all that is required.

Most of us have to balance our time "doing" with our time for just "being." We have to learn how to just "be" while we are doing and living our lives. This balance is another of the mystical paradoxes. I find that the execution of the magickal will is our practice of being, of simply existing, while simultaneously offering our service to the world. When in service to our true will, we often show up and simply "be," and find ourselves "being" a divine instrument to be played by the universe. But we had to make the conscious choice, to take the action, to show up and make ourselves, our instrument, available to the divine.

Hierarchy

The very basis of the Theosophical lore is actually anathema to what the New Age is supposed to be about. In detailed channelings, we receive information about a hierarchy, yet hierarchy is said to be the failing hallmark of the Piscean Age. The Age of Aquarius will be marked by councils, by teamwork, by lateral, not hierarchical, relationships. The concept of hierarchy breeds the idea of higher being better and lower being worse. People take that prejudice into every situation. Even our view of the chakras leaves many ascensionists thinking that the lower structures, the lower chakras, are bad in favor of the higher, more spiritual ones. It's much like saying that the foundation of a building is worse than the penthouse. The foundation might not be luxurious, but if you cut it out because you think it's "bad," then the whole building will collapse. Many have taken the hierarchies of conventional religions and placed them within their own New Age organizations. We are working from old models. We can interpret the messages of the masters based only on the paradigm in which we are operating. Though channels like Alice Bailey were great pioneers, they were still looking at the world through Piscean eyes, even though those eyes were aimed at Aquarius. We must pick up where they left off, and create new models with the masters, to understand the reality of our Aquarian relationship with them and the universe.

Lack of Structure, Tradition, or Religion

Since ascension lore is a synthesis of many different traditions, it can be hard to find solid ground. Though each spiritual tradition is telling a similar truth, from a different point of view, most successful mystics have worked well in a specific tradition, and then with a level of success, branch out and become much more inclusive of other lore and traditions. Though ideally ascension helps us transcend religion, most mystics begin firmly rooted in a tradition. Mother Teresa was a devout Catholic. Many look to her works, and see that it was her devotion to Christ, in the context of Catholicism, rather than the Catholic Church itself, that inspired her work. Gandhi was a peaceful warrior, yet was rooted in the Hindu traditions and the lore of the Bhagavad Gita. The Dalai Lama once said, "Compassion is my religion." That might be true, but he started as a Tibetan Buddhist to get to a place to understand that compassion is the true undercurrent of all religions and then act upon it. It is his practice of his tradition that gives him the structure, awareness, and support to endure as a leader in exile.

Some teachers compare taking the immediate multicultural approach, without grounding in a specific tradition, to digging many shallow wells that yield no water. If a person digs one well and strikes water, and has a reliable source of water, then he or she can then go explore other things. Many people purposely break away from their original well. I know I did when I left Catholicism. But many don't dig another well, and fear to commit to another tradition, because they don't want to be betrayed or become disillusioned. When they look for the truths of all traditions, without having a strong foundation in any one as a daily practice, they can become very philosophical yet never apply any of the teachings to daily life.

Power, Morals, and Ethics

Since ascension is not a specific religion, there is not one moral code guiding it. Many people look to the moral code of their previous religious tradition to guide them, yet the waters of morality and ethics can be murky. Many practitioners feel they don't need any specific education on morality, because the path of ascension is the path of the highest moral integrity. I agree, yet many get tripped up on how exactly one defines power, morals, and ethics. Some on the path feel that if they have the spiritual power to do something, then the divine is allowing it, and it must be okay, because the divine would not allow spiritual power to be abused, particularly by a good, spiritual, evolving person. I only wish that were so, but good people get into all sorts of difficult situations in life, ranging from psychic/magickal harm to physical-world dangers.

Power is power, and the only thing that differentiates it is the conscious or unconscious use of it. Electricity is neutral. We can light up a room or electrocute someone. The electrons don't make a judgment call and say, "No, we don't want to be used for harm." A gun can protect us, or murder someone. A tool can be used to carve a beautiful piece of art, or smash someone's face. Good people do morally dubious things all the time, and we never really stop to think about it. Using the dualistic approach of the light and dark sides in *Star*

Wars, we find this in a very subtle way. The Jedi Knights, the "good" guys, use their popular "Jedi mind tricks" to subvert the will of another to their own will. In magick, we would see the subversion of someone's will as a form of harmful magick, yet we all applaud the Jedis in the movies.

I once knew a lightworker and crystal healer who was a wonderful woman, and told the story of how she was pulled over for speeding. She had a crystal in her car, and when the officer went back to his vehicle to run her license and registration, she pointed the quartz at him and sent "waves of love" to melt his heart and help him feel compassion for her, so she wouldn't get a ticket. Was that the right thing for her to do? His job at that time was not to feel compassion, but to uphold the law. Even with the best of intentions, with her waves of love, I found her actions to be morally suspect and controlling.

We can reason our way into justifying our motives and actions, particularly if we haven't given time to contemplate our own moral and ethical code. Spiritual powers can be even harder to contemplate in an ethical context. In the magickal tradition of Wicca, we have the Wiccan Rede, popularly summed up in the last two lines: "An' it harm none, do what ye will." It's similar to the Christian Golden Rule: "Treat others as you wish to be treated," or more formally, "All things whatsoever ye would that men should do to you, do ye so to them; for this is the law and the prophets."—Matthew 7:12. Variations of this saying can be found in many cultures. Think about your own sense of power and responsibility, and the morals and ethics that guide your life.

THE DARKNESS

As lightworkers sometimes consider themselves to be in conflict with the forces of darkness, or to be healing the darkness, it is important to look at what constitutes these dark forces, real and imaginary. Understanding our perceived "enemy" is like going through an introspective process, to better know ourselves, our own faults and our own needs. Only then can we create a lasting peace.

The Shadow

In looking at the problems facing the ascension movement, the single greatest difficulty revolves around the shadow. It is the darkness within us, and not the perceived darkness outside of us, that causes the greatest problems. Heal one and you automatically heal the other. The shadow is a concept popularized by modern psychology, but found in the initiatory process of almost all mystic traditions. The shadow is all the forces within the individual that the conscious self wishes to disassociate from, to suppress, confine, or otherwise deny. It is the parts of ourselves that we don't like and can't accept on a conscious level. The shadow comprises every unwanted feeling, thought, and action, and like a closet in the back of our soul, we stuff these forces deep within. What can happen is that one day we seek to stuff one last thing inside this bursting closet, and the contents come crashing down upon us, creating a spiritual crisis in our life, as we are forced to deal with all that we have repressed. Those who have a thorough knowledge of the items in their closet, who keep it organized, need never fear a collapse.

The shadow has power. It dwells in the unconscious and holds the keys to much of our power. It uses that power to get our attention, really seeking to be healed, but knowing it cannot without our attention and focus. The self-saboteur, escapist, addict, and masochist are all part of the shadow. Most lightworkers believe they create their own reality. I agree, yet when people create something they don't like in their lives, such as illness, injury, or poverty, many are quick to cite karma as the reason. Well, our karma is a part of our shadow. What is termed "negative karma" is the consequence of harmful actions in this life and past incarnations. When we don't own up to our past mistakes and rectify them as best we can, often neutralizing the karmic energy, we reap the results of our past.

This shadow self is the mechanism that manifests much of our karma. It is our Dweller on the Threshold, the guardian that we are required to master before we come into even greater spiritual mastery and awareness. Many never come to this abyss, let alone cross it. When we are not conscious of the shadow, or are actively denying its influence, we project our shadow self onto others. Have you ever noticed how the people who upset you the most are the ones who, upon deeper reflection, often mirror back things about yourself that you don't like? Many people never stop to reflect on and face the problems they see in other people that are simply representative of their own internal problems. The difference between the mystic and everybody else is that the mystic actively works to come to terms with the shadow, and learns to heal through self-awareness.

While incarnated, we each have an individual shadow. It's only when we ascend to a higher state on another plane that we renounce our physical vessel and cast no shadow, literally and metaphorically. While we are in body, with karma, life lessons, and experiences, we have a shadow. Like the ego, it is a natural part of us at this level. Even if we aspire to transcend our shadow, we will not succeed in doing so by ignoring it. Part of the mystical process of initiation is to integrate all aspects of the self into the greater whole, including the parts we don't like.

The Devil

If we each have an individual shadow, then our culture, our community, our race, has a collective shadow. We project that collective shadow onto the "other" somewhere outside of ourselves, and see conspiracies, aliens, and evil magicians. There can even be people and forces that play out those roles. And like the shadow self, they call for our attention, to take a look at the parts of the world we don't like. They have the power to draw our attention, but it is a power we have given them by casting them out in the first place.

The popular image we've given our collective shadow is the Devil. The Devil is an amalgam of several different ideas. The fusion of these ideas occurred in Christian mythology, and many non-Christian mystics feel the concept of the Devil was far more a political tool than a spiritual truth. During the troubles of the Dark Ages, the dominant Christian institution needed a scapegoat for rampant economic collapse, social inequality, and the spread of the plague. Taking concepts of a spiritual antagonist from many mythologies, the Devil was born. Though there are spiritual truths to each of these antagonistic figures, including Lucifer, Sataniel, Set, Angra Mainyu, Ahriman, and the Gnostic Demiurge, their union, and subsequent interpretation as an ultimate being of evil, is not in alignment with the spiritual teachings dating before this time. The hysteria, persecutions, and crimes committed in the name of punishing the servants of the Devil conflict with the very heart of Christianity. Unfortunately, many in the ascension paradigm, versed in Christian mythology, adopted the Devil image as an anti-god and source of ultimate evil, rather than a mystic symbol.

The concept of the devil comes from the Greek *diablos*, meaning to "throw something in your way or path." A devil was one who crossed your path, offering you challenges, but was not necessarily a force of evil. The Devil card in the tarot teaches us about liberation, breaking self-constructed cages, and freedom. As mystics, we know that our separation, the "other," is an illusion. We are all one, but appear to be separate and individual. Just as an individual cannot be separate from the shadow, so too can our race, our community, not be separate from the shadow. Our initiation as part of the ascension process will be the integration of all the parts of us, reflected in the universe, that we don't like. It doesn't mean that these parts conform to what we want them to be. If they did, then we would simply be able to banish them, which is not possible. Integration requires synthesis—taking the best from all points of view and creating a harmonious whole that is balanced, healthy, and, most of all, *real*. Union with all of creation requires the union of all, not just the parts we like.

Left-Hand Paths

Left-hand path is a term used by some to denote the practice of dark or evil traditions, though the term has many different meanings, depending on who is using it. In the most simplistic sense, the right-hand path is considered to be a "good" spiritual path, or the practice of white magick, while the left-hand path is considered to be a "bad" path, or the practice of black magick. This term is an insult against the minority of people in society who are left-handed, as being left-handed was considered a "sinister" orientation in some traditions. Some of our prejudice against left-handedness actually comes from social customs in which eating was done with the right hand and hygienic practices were done with the left hand.

Though some practitioners do subscribe to these roles, seeing the left-hand-path practitioner as the stereotypical Satanist rebelling against mainstream religion and values, most practitioners, including most self-identified Satanists, have a deeper theology. Some look to Eastern definitions of the left- and right-hand paths, which have nothing to do with good and evil. The right-hand path stood for masculine mysteries and a sense of the ascetic, one who renounces and withdraws from the material world to achieve greater spirituality. The left-hand path was one of feminine, goddess, and sexual mysteries. Rituals often went counterclockwise, symbolizing a deepening into the Earth and orientation with the Moon. The body and senses were stimulated to find the spiritual level. Though most people don't realize it, these orientations influence the good/bad set of definitions above. Many practitioners are apt to see the more male-influenced traditions as "good," and the sensual female ones as "bad."

In a more intricate approach, the right-hand path is said to be one of merging with the divine. The goal is to give up your sense of self to find blissful union with the creative force of the universe. Practitioners of the left-hand path do not seek this union, but rather they seek individual immortality. They seek not to become one with God, but to become God. Divinity becomes an example to follow, rather than something to unite with. Various rebellious divinities, such as Set, Lucifer, and Lumiel, have led the way. One way the left-hand path has been described is that the practitioner is a seed, who goes on to produce his own plant, rather than become a seed rooting at the base of the plant, eventually decomposing and feeding the parent plant, merging with it.

Most ascensionists don't look at the intricacies of these theologies, and usually see left-hand-path practitioners as Satanic, and often label many traditions as Satanic that would not identify themselves as such. Theosophy has long postulated the existence of a lodge of "black brothers," the antithesis of the Great White Brotherhood, yet there is little historical evidence of such an organized group. The modern Church of Satan, and its offshoot, the Temple of Set, are both self-identified as left-hand paths, yet we can see similarities between their theologies and the theologies in the ascension community. Setians, members of the Temple of Set, look to the keyword and principle of Xeper (pronounced "Kheffer") to spiritually guide them. Coming from the Egyptian, Xeper means, in a Temple of Set context, "I Have Come Into Being." This concept is not too far off from the ascension principle of the Might I Am Presence, or of divinity being an expression of "I Am that I Am." Xeper has a more rebellious connotation, that coming into being upsets the status quo, while the I AM teachings are more about union with the status quo. Yet at heart, there are some similarities between the two.

Left-hand-path practitioner Stephen Flowers, in his book *Lords of the Left-Hand Path*, actually sees Blavatsky's Theosophy as having more in common with the left-hand path than her perception of the right-hand path. Perhaps, on some level, she thought so too, because she named her public journal *Lucifer*. Skeptics think of Theosophy as a cover for a sinister left-hand path. They look to the Planetary Logos, Sanat Kumara, as Lord Sanat, or a variation of Lord Satan. When we look at the myths of Lucifer in a Gnostic sense, they might not be far off, yet the Theosophical concept of Satan is quite different from the mainstream Christian version. Aleister Crowley's Thelema religion is often erroneously labeled Satanic, but practitioners of it do not identify as such. Crowley identified as a member of the Great White Brotherhood, doing the spiritual work of the gods and masters for the next aeon. He simply wasn't afraid of dark imagery or upsetting the status quo of the previous age. The traditions of Wicca, Voodou, Santeria, necromancy, Goetic ceremonial magick, and Chaos magick have all been misidentified as Satanic or wholly left-hand at one time or another.

Ascension War

The polarity teachings of ascension are often framed in terms of a war, which I feel is the most debilitating metaphor for this spiritual paradigm, even though at times, to many of us, the shift of ages can feel like a war. The other side of the polarity we don't identify with is divided, separated, and demonized. We see it on a small scale in partisan politics in the United States and elsewhere, but we shouldn't see it on the scale we do in spiritual lore.

Ascension is seen as a heroic path, a path of trials and sufferings through initiation, rather than a gentle, soothing, wise-woman path. To "earn" our advancement, we feel there needs to be conflict. A whole mythology has been created around a dark brotherhood, and kept as our secret history. If there is a Great White Brotherhood, then there must be the antithesis, a Great Dark Brotherhood, working against the white. It's a nice theory for a box-office blockbuster, but other than in Zoroastrianism and aspects of Gnosticism, as a spiritual philosophy, it doesn't hold much water. Yes, there are forces of harm, of evil, causing destruction intentionally, but to see the universe in a polarized war of ultimate good and ultimate evil is not real. There are a lot of gray areas. There are a lot of points of view. Those labeled evil rarely think of themselves as evil. They do so only in comic books and movies.

Things are not always as they appear, yet we have a theology of the evil masters, evil secret governments, and evil aliens bent on causing our destruction unless we fight back. Where is the unconditional love in that theology? Where is the spiritual union we speak about? Many religious people are always gearing up for the end of the world, be it stories from Atlantis, the Book of Revelations, Nostradamus's prophecies, the Rapture, or the end of the Mayan calendar. In a metaphysical sense, the end of the world is not the end of the planet, but rather the end of an age, a cycle. The fervor of feeling as if "time is running out" is prone to create paranoia and misunderstandings. We see conspiracies everywhere and overreact. Forces in polarity do not, and should not, be in conflict. They can be complementary. Yin doesn't battle with yang, because in the end, we all know that yin contains yang, and vice versa. One cannot exist without the other. One is the seed for the other. The acceptance and integration of the opposite is a part of working with the shadow self in a healthy and balanced manner. It takes effort from all sides.

One of the things that completely changed my understanding of "enemies," or those whom we might perceive as doing evil or acting as the evil empire, was the concept of the struggle being a game. Hari Das Melchizedek explained the conflict to me as a game. Rather than viewing the conflict around us as a war, with such dramatic energies surrounding the word war, life is really a game, with many players. Some players are wearing light T-shirts, and some are wearing dark T-shirts. (Light and dark are two terms I still dislike, but they were the symbols given to me.) When the game is over, we will all take off our team uniforms and go home. We all come from a similar place, with similar families and similar hopes and needs. We're all the same beneath the T-shirts, after the game. When we get so involved in the game, we can forget all else, and we can truly fight to prevail against the other side, but it's just a game, it's not everything. Sometimes we win and sometimes we lose, but it's a game. When we're off the field or court, these people are still our brothers and sisters, and who knows, in the next game, we might get traded and be wearing a dark T-shirt. Don't take life too seriously, because from this higher perspective, it's just a game. When you reach that higher perspective, you can step in and out of the game anytime you'd like.

The concept of darkness and light is simply one way of looking at ourselves. To quote one of my favorite fictional mystical scholars, Obi-Wan Kenobi, "Many of the truths that we cling to depend on our point of view." Mystics often divide, by their own definitions, into left- and right-hand paths, seeing their own path as the only path, but there is another way. People, particularly those in the Piscean Age, have a natural tendency to polarize, but we know that each pole cannot exist without the other. There is a middle path. As with any art and craft, we have the capacity to use both hands. The use of both hands makes our job clearer, simpler, and safer. Using only one hand, when both are available, puts us at a disadvantage. There is both a left and right energy, both a yin and yang, a dark and light, and a power to ascend and descend. As the Earth turns, we take time to be awake and active, and we take time to rest and relax.

Many people see the serpent as a symbol of evil and the dove as a symbol of good, yet in mystical lore, the serpent, the kundalini goddess, is the force that rises through the body, to bring enlightenment through the awakening of the chakras. Jesus said, "Be wise like serpents," yet the serpent continues to be a symbol of evil in mainstream traditions. The dove actually descends from the heavens, to bring light into the material world, imitating the fall of the divine into the material world to bring redemption. Both animals, both principles, are needed in the spiritual evolution of all. Many traditions are not as cut and dried, left or right, dark or light, as they appear to be.

We each need to find our own way and what works for us. Contrary to the popular image, many left-hand-path practitioners are successful, healthy, happy, and well-adjusted members of society. Many right-hand-path practitioners, and self-identified "holy" leaders, often do not live up to the moral code they preach. We see this in both mainstream and New Age traditions. Most of us, intuitively or consciously, walk a middle path. We might stray to one extreme or the other at times, but the middle path offers us the opportunity to explore both sides and find what works best for us.

HEALING THE SHADOW

Now that we've explored the ideas and traditions involving light and shadow, what do we do? We must face, build a relationship with, and eventually integrate the shadow's energy into our being. Only then can we be whole and ready for ascension. To the alchemists, this is the putrefaction process, where we face the dark, dead matter, and through the oil of the peacock, the multi-prismatic oil that gathers through this initiation, we find our light and transform. In the Middle Eastern Yazidi tradition, their god, Malak Ta'us, is identified with both the peacock, as the peacock angel, and the "devil."

Why do we need to balance the shadow? Why isn't it all right to be at one end of the polarity all the time? Why isn't the light, and only the light, our sole focus and the key to spiritual enlightenment? The dark is a part of the light, and the light is a part of the dark. If the key to the lightworker's path is this divine, unconditional love, what I was taught as Perfect Love, then you cannot have unconditional love if you do not love and accept the parts of you, and the parts of other people and the universe, that you don't like. This doesn't mean you should condone misbehavior or allow your boundaries to be violated, but it does mean truly expressing a sense of unconditional love, and not just talking about it. In the end, most spiritual traditions focus on a sense of balance and harmony.

One of our most modern yet profound archetypal teachings, coming in the form of the popular *Star Wars* movies, gets lost in the flash and special effects of the films. The story of *Star Wars*, of the Force, is not the story of the winners, the light side of the Force, but of the one, either Anakin Skywalker or Luke Skywalker, who brings balance to the Force. Everyone in the story, Jedi and Sith alike, has their own interpretation, their own point of view, of what balance is. In the end, the balance doesn't manifest in the way anyone expects. The fiction of novels and comics that follow the sixth episode detail Luke starting a Jedi school that incorporates both sides of the philosophy of the Force. Ultimately, Luke has to learn both to find peace and to use his passions to defeat the Empire and redeem his father.

Darth Vader/Anakin Skywalker, much like our Luciferian figures, can be considered a redeemer, for it is he who ultimately defeats the Emperor Darth Sidious, and redeems himself in the process. So many fans forget that the key to the teaching is balance, not that the light side is the winner. The Force got out of balance in the first place because everything was so polarized. The Jedi, as they grew in power, grew in arrogance as well, and came to believe that their way was the only way. In many ways, they set themselves up for their fall from power. As their arrogance grew, their power waned, and they hid this loss of power. The dark side was able to grow unchecked because of this imbalance, but eventually, the growth of the dark side, and all the destruction it caused, allowed the universe, the Force, to right itself by fulfilling the age-old prophecy.

People think the opposing forces of polarity that create the greatest conflict are light and dark, but they are not. The most difficult polarity is love and fear. Many think of hate as the antithesis of love, but if emotion is depicted as circular, then love and hate are more alike that you might think. That is why it is so easy to have such strong emotions for some-one, be it love or hate, and switch from one to the other in passion or rage. Fear, on the other hand, is on the opposite side of love. While love expands, fear contracts. In the popu-lar *Star Wars* theology, we have a line from Master Yoda that sums up the problems of fear: "Fear is the path to the dark side. Fear leads to anger. Anger leads to hate. Hate leads to suffering."

When we talk about the polarity of consciousness, light and dark are two sides of the same coin. They are of a similar nature, and much closer to each other than most people think. The stars in the night sky show us that. The light is at home in the dark. It is fear that prevents the two from coming together—the fear of being consumed by the unknown, the dark, the unseen and unconscious, and the fear of being blinded and exposed by the shin-ing light, with no sense of personal individuality, privacy, or freedom.

In a very magickal tale told in a comic book series with a strong Gnostic influence, called *The Invisibles*, we are given a great teaching. The premise of *The Invisibles* fuses magickal wisdom, Gnostic philosophy, ceremonial magick, ascension lore, Eastern teach-ings, H. P. Lovecraft fiction, alien abductions, and futuristic science into a great spell de-signed to awaken the reader. The two opposing forces are depicted as the Invisibles and the Outer Church. The Invisibles, based in an extradimensional college, are a loose network of magickal freedom fighters dedicated to liberty. The innermost leaders are seen as akin to ascended masters, though they are not the traditional, white-light ascended masters of modern New Age lore. The Outer Church, a hierarchy dealing with dark monsters and government conspiracies, stands in conflict with the Invisibles, seeking order and control of everyone. They seek to enslave the world as "food" for their atrocious masters, the Archons. At one time in our fiction, the good guys were the forces of order, and the bad guys were the forces of chaos. *The Invisibles* shows this switch. We see the same switch in *Star Wars*, with the wild rebels and the evil Empire seeking to control all. In *The Invisibles*, the characters are told two key points that transform the war for humanity: "The Outer Church and Invisible College, same address," and "This is not a war. It's a rescue mission." When we stop framing our experience as a conflict, as a war, between the self and other, but instead look at it as people helping people, people helping the world and all things, then we can truly do the work. To be able to accept the other outside of ourselves, we need to first accept the other, the shadow, inside of ourselves.

Getting over denial of the shadow is the first step. Many who are immersed in the ascension paradigm choose to ignore their shadow. Some lightworker teachers suggest that you "not think much about the evil lodges of hidden masters, and focus on love and light." The idea behind this is that what you focus on can grow, particularly if you are afraid of it and feed it fear energy, but also what you ignore can grow. To heal the rift between your light and shadow, you must acknowledge the shadow. You must pick up the rock and find your monsters beneath it. You must face your fears, angers, hatreds, jealousies, insecurities, and petty thoughts until they no longer hold any energy for you. You must integrate their energy so it holds no power over you. Only then can you heal yourself. As you heal yourself, the world heals. Then the shadow, and all those who embody the shadow, can never harm you again.

Many seek to help others with their shadows, or fight the shadow forces in the ascension war without dealing with their own shadow. For those tempted to do so, I offer one of my favorite biblical verses, from Luke 6:41–42: "And why beholdest thou the mote that is in thy brother's eye, but perceivest not the beam that is in thine own eye? Either how canst thou say to thy brother, Brother, let me pull out the mote that is in thine eye, when thou thyself beholdest not the beam that is in thine own eye? Thou hypocrite, cast out first the beam out of thine own eye, and then shalt thou see clearly to pull out the mote that is in thy brother's eye." Similar passages can also be found in the Gospel of Matthew, illustrating the concept that you should take care of your own problems, the things that cloud your own vision, before presuming to help another. Only then can you be a clearer channel for divinity and a better guide for others.

While ascension theology gave me amazing healing techniques, particularly physical healing techniques, and opened my heart chakra in ways I had never before experienced, it didn't give me a lot of tools for dealing with the shadow, with my dark emotions, with my fear. I had to find these tools through witchcraft, and the mystery schools of both

Eastern and Western lore. Some of the primary fears that motivate all people, but in particular those involved in ascension, are the fear of death, the fear of suffering, and the fear of empowerment and the potential abuse of that power. To address these fears, I look to the initiation rituals of dismemberment, which are found in shamanism, the Egyptian and Greek mystery schools, the Goddess's descent, and the Tibetan Chöd rituals. Dismemberment helps us move beyond the personal limitations of the self, and identify consciousness beyond the body. Only by passing through this gate of death and resurrection can we no longer fear the shadow, and reconcile our seemingly opposing parts.

Through contemplation of the dark mysteries and asking the Underworld gods to be our teachers and initiators, we can understand our own shadow selves. If we continue to look at the image of the Devil, then we must realize that part of our healing path is to integrate the Devil back into harmony—our own personal Devil, or diablos, the one who works against us, as well as the collectively created images of a Devil for humanity. We can look to older shadow images, such as the dark mother, for aid in understanding the full spectrum of the shadow and facing the unknown.

Use the following ritual to successfully evoke your shadow self. Through direct contact, you can become aware of your hidden issues and work directly with this part of yourself to heal your own fears, traumas, angers, and other "negative" experiences, to achieve a greater sense of health and happiness.

Exercise 28:
The Shadow Rebirth Ritual

Start this ritual seven days before you actually plan to perform the main section of the ritual. Ideally, you would start seven days before the new Moon. Check an astrological calendar or almanac to find out when the next new Moon will occur.

1. Begin the ritual by journaling on the shadow. Use a notebook or paper for the journal that you don't mind destroying. If you don't want to rip out pages of your favorite journal, then use a cheaper notebook. I find it most effective not to journal written sentences and paragraphs, but to brainstorm on the shadow, writing down all the things about the shadow that I can think of. Focus on your own shadow, all the things about yourself that you don't like, don't trust, and are not proud of. Write short phrases on things that have happened to you, or have been done by you, that evoke your shadow. No one but you is going to

read this, so feel free to write whatever comes to mind. Be honest. Be intro-spective. Each session should yield at least a page. Do this every day for seven days. Don't look back to see what you wrote on previous days. Start each ses-sion fresh, when contemplating your shadow. Just journaling on the shadow can bring up intense emotions that will not necessarily be cleared immediately, but the shadow rebirth ritual, done on the seventh day, will give you tools to work with those feelings.

2. On the first day of journaling, make a vibrational essence (see exercise 19) with obsidian, garnet, and black tourmaline. Bottle it and keep it in a dark place until the seventh day, when you will perform the main ritual. Before the main ritual, dilute the mother essence into a stock bottle and then a dosage bottle.

3. On the seventh day, perform the shadow rebirth ritual. Tear out the pages of your shadow journal exercise, and have a flameproof vessel, such as an iron cauldron, in which to burn them. Some practitioners doing this outside will dig a small fire pit. You can also use a metal bowl filled halfway with sand. Prepare your altar to cast a magick circle, and make sure your dosage bottle of gem-stone essence is ready.

4. Cast your magick circle, and create your sacred space.

5. For the work of the circle, take 7 drops of your gemstone essence orally, or apply 1 drop to each of the seven chakras. This essence will not only help you attune with your shadow, but also protect you from harm.

6. While in the circle, perform Exercise 2: Dimensional Travel—First Dimension, and travel to the chthonic depths of the Mother, where you shall face your shadow. Travel through the first garden, the first jungle, taking notice of the plants and animals from the past, present, and future. Look for a place of dark-ness within the inner world of the first dimension. Look for a cave, deep for-est, dark grove, or pool of dark water. In this place, ask for the shadow, your Dweller on the Threshold, to appear to you. Invite it into your life. When the shadow self appears, commune with it. It might frighten or anger you. Move through these feelings. Don't deny them, but don't get stuck in them. Talk with the shadow self. Share your feelings. Listen to the shadow's feelings and thoughts. How can you work together in partnership? Take as long as you need to build a relationship with the shadow, taking it out of the fear, out of the

unconscious realm, and inviting it into a healing relationship with you, for better understanding and integration.

7. If you feel ready at this time, ask the shadow for the ritual of dismemberment. If you are not ready, you can continue to build your relationship with the shadow. If you choose dismemberment, and the shadow self agrees, then you will have a vision of yourself being killed, violently, and usually your body will be ripped apart. You may feel physical pain as psychological torment, but your essence will remain, even without a "body" or self-image. Then, after a time, you will be guided by your inner wisdom to resurrect yourself. Perhaps a deity or master will aid you. Perhaps you will simply use your force of will and imagine reconstituting your body, resurrecting yourself. Added to the mix will be a "new" symbol or tool for your body—perhaps a stone, bone, or crystal, or perhaps a dark sphere, as you add the "shadow" to your matrix, to integrate it into your self-identity.

8. When you are done, say your farewells to any beings who have aided you. Return to where you began, and climb the vertical axis of light, through the dimensions. Come back to where your sense of your three-dimensional body is. Ground yourself in your body. Relax. Take a few breaths. Open your eyes. Complete your ritual, releasing the circle. As you return to 3D consciousness, write down any impressions or messages you got, before you forget them.

Now, because I am looking at the shadowy mystic traditions in a positive light, going beyond gross generalizations into the theology and philosophies, and dissecting some of the sacred cows of the New Age, I'm sure some will accuse me of being a black brother, a practitioner of the left-hand path, or a twilight master. They will see my arguments in favor of the less accepted traditions as a subtle way of seeking to sway others to the "dark" side. I hope such people take comfort in knowing that traditional practitioners of the left-hand path would be just as aghast to find that I support so much of what they consider New Age babble and wouldn't consider me a left-hand practitioner by any stretch of the imagination.

I do advocate an understanding of both practices, and don't necessarily describe myself as a practitioner of a left- or a right-hand path, by any set of definitions. I like to use both hands. I don't describe my magick as black or white, but as containing all the colors of the spectrum. I value the dark as a place of learning and healing as much as the light, as both contain the other. I find the term twilight master, one who is between and not wholly of the light, to be interesting, because my traditions see twilight as a sacred and holy time, not a time of fear or evil. It is powerful and dangerous, but it is also full of possibility and wonder. If you enter twilight with respect and love, amazing things can happen. The doors between the worlds open, and magick is afoot. I wouldn't consider the term twilight master to be a negative title, but potentially exactly what the next age needs.

All I'm advocating is a greater understanding between the two "sides." I think the magick of the next aeon that will be most helpful will be created by those who use both hands and find balance, integration, and synthesis. The new aeon will be an exploration of the mysteries, of the seeming paradoxes, in a personal way. I know my own paradox is that although I come from an Earth-based, nature-reverent tradition, Gnostic teachings have sneaked into my worldview, even though personally and theologically, I'm not comfortable with any teachings that look at the physical world as an "evil" place to be escaped. But the universe evolves in its own way, and I have to assume that in some manner, Zoroastrianism, Judaism, Gnosticism, and the various branches of Christianity and Islam have contributed to the evolution of humanity, even though I prefer the pagan faiths. In many ways, my understanding of paganism has improved after having examined and compared it to these other faiths. But the next step is to learn to integrate all these views, to take ascension theology to the next level. I offer this information to expand your worldview, to help you find what works for you and encourage you to think for yourself and discern what is true for you, so you can truly find peace and harmony with all aspects of life to create the next golden age.

23

PERSONAL AND PLANETARY ASCENSION

As I was finishing the writing of this book, I was speaking to a friend who manages a metaphysical bookstore, and he told me about an interesting customer. She had bought a variety of books on ascension, and she called up very unhappy. She was yelling at him, "Why haven't I ascended yet? I've done everything in these books! It's time for me to go. Why am I still here?!" She wanted to return the books because they were obviously defective. My friend politely tried to explain to her that ascension is a paradigm, influenced deeply by Tibetan Buddhism, and from his point a view, a symbolic truth, not a literal truth, no matter what the books said.

Though we think of the ascended masters as transcendent beings, and they are, I doubt that people physically disappear through practicing the techniques in a New Age book, though they might have a greater awareness of and control over their energy, and find spiritual practices that expand their consciousness. Many people get lost in the idea of physically disappearing, and use it as a measure of their spirituality, or seeming lack thereof. The idea of ascending becomes less about transcending and consciousness expanding and more of an escape from reality and the collective consequences of humanity. One of things that I found to be a guiding mantra was the title of the first book I read on the ascension paradigm and merkaba, *Nothing in This Book Is True, but It's Exactly How Things Are*. The very title is a paradox, and for quite a while, before the whole merkaba and associated Flower of Life workshops caught on in America, I questioned whether the book was a hoax or a practical joke. All the "craziest" aspects of the book, and of ascension lore, are metaphors. Others would disagree, and some feel they are literal truths. Until they happen, we can't be sure. But if you keep this view—nothing is true, but it's exactly how things are—as your lens for looking at all things in ascension lore, you will see the paradox of how two or more seemingly divergent realities can exist at the same time. You will see how an infinite number of realities can coexist, as we each have our own reality, our own worldview, that is at least slightly different from that of the person next to us. Such a view helps us stay grounded in the consensus reality of our society while exploring the fringes of consciousness, because we don't have to prove one reality is right at the expense of another.

ASCENSION IN THE MEDIA

Ascension as a topic has entered the media, primarily through less mainstream outlets, yet it is still seeping into our consciousness. Through understanding various writers' and artists' visions of ascension, some serious and some merely for entertainment, we can see the symbols and ideas that are informing our understanding of ascension, consciously and unconsciously.

One of the most visible media forums discussing ascension is the *Stargate* series. The movie *Stargate* tackled the topic of the ancient astronaut theory set in Egypt. In the movie, the gods of Egypt were parasitical aliens posing as divinities. In the television series *Stargate SG-1*, and its spin-off, *Stargate Atlantis*, the story continued, and included concepts of ancient beings who had ascended, yet influenced ancient humanity and other planets. These ascended ancients were seen as noble, wise, moral, and spiritual. They were seen as literally transcended, yet still able to make contact with physically incarnate humans.

A variety of sci-fi media outlets hold views similar to those of ascensionists in terms of humanity's place in a galactic brotherhood. Many would say that perhaps modern New Agers adopted this idea from science fiction. Many *Star Trek* concepts, including that of the Galactic Federation, show up in tone and character in modern channelings of the star people. The concept of the Q Continuum, also employed in *Star Trek*, is a plane of existence inhabited by advanced beings beyond space and time, whose culture is unfathomable to humanity, yet on some level, they seek to guide the evolution of humanity.

On a more metaphysical level, both in more standard ascension lore and this book, are the philosophies of *Star Wars* and the Jedi Knights. The polarity war of the *Star Wars* series, along with its Buddhist tone, relate well to ascension lore. Many see the channeled information about the Orion Wars relating strongly to George Lucas's vision of the *Star Wars* universe, to the point of believing that he unconsciously channeled it. Literal truth or not, *Star Wars* and the Orion Wars depict classic archetypal themes found in world mythologies, and they continue to serve us today. Several Jedi masters, merged with the Force, appear much like ascended masters and teachers. Luke Skywalker is guided by the non-corporeal form of Ben Kenobi. Though none of the characters use the term ascended master, the Jedi masters serve the same function in the story, guiding the spiritual initiate on the path of awakening and empowerment.

Lesser known are some underground media sources, namely role-playing games, or RPGs, and comic books. Role-playing games are pen and paper games, based on various fantasy and science fiction premises, in which a story is told through a judge and a variety of players. One important game in the ascension paradigm is a version of *Mage* called *Mage: The Ascension*. The premise of the game is that reality is mutable, and that the rules of reality are a consensus of the collective consciousness. The rules of science were not the only rules in ages past. A special, relatively small group of people have "awakened" to the true nature of reality, and have become will-workers, capable of working their own will on the collective reality, performing magick.

This role-playing game is a reality war between four factions: the Technocracy, or our modern economic and scientific paradigm; the Nephandi, the worshippers of the monstrous creatures from the outer dark; the Marauders, the mad mages who can control reality to match their wild deliriums; and lastly the Traditions, an order of nine different traditions of magickal practitioners, including Pagans, Christians, Taoists, Shamans, Hindus, and Hermetics of various types. This last group has banded together because its members have more in common than those of any of the other groups. Each mage personally, and as a Tradition, is seeking ascension, but none of the Traditions agree upon exactly what ascension means. They each have their own paradigm that shapes their view of ascension. They have ascended beings, mages who have reached a personal ascension, who have become what are called oracles, like the ascended masters. In general, personal ascension is seeking enlightenment on the path of your Tradition. Each has a different view toward understanding the mysteries, based on a specific "sphere," or type of magick, the Tradition focuses on. Global ascension is promoting your paradigm to mass consciousness, so that your paradigm can be a large part, if not the dominant part, of mass consciousness. To the Verbena, the witches of this game, ascension could be re-creating a mythical time when the veil between worlds was not so thick and magickal creatures walked with men. To the Christian Celestial Chorus, ascension is total union of all with the one Creator. To the members of the Cult of Ecstasy, it would be stepping out of time and body to perceive the true reality, permanently.

This game is one of the few fictional accounts of ascension that has a strong parallel to real-world esoterics and mystics. The lesson from it, and these Traditions, is that there is more than one view of ascension, and these views are not mutually exclusive. The current version of *Mage* is named *Mage: The Awakening*, and focuses less on ascension and more on a traditionally Gnostic view of reality and magick.

In the comic world, we have two strong examples exploring ascension. The first is the three-volume series of Vertigo comics known as *The Invisibles*, written by Chaos magician Grant Morrison. Taking a strong Gnostic view, the Invisibles constitute an organization dedicated to the fight for freedom, consisting of cells of both physical fighters and esoteric/mystic warriors, fighting the forces of order and oppression known as the Outer Church, represented by a military industrial complex of the world government. The story races through time and space, magick, and technology, toward the ever-fated 2012 singularity, in which everybody can win, creating their own version of Utopia beyond space and time, as the "healthy" meta-universe, unhinged from the terminally ill meta-universe and our reality, collapses.

The main characters, a cell of Invisibles consisting of the future Buddha, a tantric sex assassin, a cybernetic witch from the future, a martial artist, and a transsexual shaman, fight the forces of the world government, embodied by both British and American operatives. The story itself is very un-New Age, filled with sex, magick, violence, UFOs, time machines, and a variety of esoteric cultural references, but it encapsulates many of the spiritual issues of the ascension "war," showing us that the only solution is one in which everybody wins, and that the fight against oppression will be far more subtle than conventional wars. Like *Mage: The Ascension*, it's a battle for reality and consciousness, not territory or money. The Invisible cells are seen as terrorists by the Outer Church, but they eventually learn to use subtle forms of reprogramming, through the media and culture, to turn the tide. Ultimately, the forces of this epic battle realize that there is no "other." The Invisibles and the Outer Church are two sides of the same coin, and everybody is going "home." The mystical Barbelith, never fully explained as a being or object, acts as an initiator and guide from its orbit just beyond the Moon. It seeks to get all the players to "wake up" and "try to remember" through experiencing traumatic initiations. They must remember that they are beings beyond this time, space, and form, and remember their true nature beyond the third dimension.

Promethea, a comic written by magician Alan Moore and published by America's Best Comics, teaches the foundations of Western magic to the reader through each issue as the main character, Sophie Bangs, learns how to become the heroine Promethea. Promethea is described as a walk-in, though she operates slightly differently than our New Age concept of a walk-in. She eventually climbs the Tree of Life, and her lessons lead up to the spiritual Apocalypse, but it isn't like any apocalypse that most people would expect, with missiles or natural disasters, but rather is a worldwide epiphany, in which the mass consciousness ascends the 32nd Path of the Tree of Life, corresponding to the World or Universe card in the tarot. The real question is what will happen afterward, when the epiphany of mass consciousness is over and "normal" reality returns.

Out of all the views of ascension, the story in *Promethea* is the one that resonates the most with me. I think something profound may happen to the world in 2012, or at any other apocalyptic point, but I don't think it will be the end of the world that many expect, or an ascent to pure light, or at least not a permanent ascent to pure light, as many people think. I believe it will be an opportunity to transform our world and find unity, but there is still physical work to be done. I imagine that our planet can reach a critical mass of consciousness and take a leap forward, as proposed in more advanced models of consciousness using the idea of the consciousness grids. I love the *Promethea* story, because it raises the most important ideas, to prepare us for this transformation.

> I mean, it's not like there weren't going to still be questions and choices after the apocalypse. What did we think, we'd all just go to heaven and there'd be no more problems or diseases or earthquakes? No, we all woke up, the day after the world ended, and we still had to feed ourselves and keep a roof over our heads. Life goes on, y'know? Life goes on. It's not even like there aren't still wars and murders and rapes. Everybody had the revelation, but not everybody understood it, or took any notice of it. Though maybe enough people did. Things are changing.

—*Promethea*, No. 31, page 17.

The truth is, we don't know what ascension will look like, personally, because we haven't experienced it yet in this lifetime. Even if we experienced it in the past, past-life memories are quite subjective. We don't have any idea of what it will look like globally, for it has never happened globally here on Earth.

The whole point of magick is to set an intention, put energy into it, and co-create with divinity. But as I've said before, you must follow it up with real-world action. I don't know if it is possible for us to disappear and become just light. I'm not even sure that is desirable. But I do know it's possible to have a global culture free of hunger, disease, poverty, war, crime, and prejudice. I know it because I envision it. It's a physical possibility. The only thing stopping us is the change in consciousness, and I've seen so many ascensions in consciousness through healings, workshops, prayers, rituals, and living life that I know it is possible to raise the mass consciousness of this planet to create a vision in which everybody can win. I don't know how that will look. I simply know that we must act, magickally and mundanely, to make it happen. As we ascend, we soon learn that the magickal and the mundane are not as sharply separated as we think. Every action becomes a ritual, a prayer, a devotion to the divine, to ascend the consciousness of the planet and create a truly healthy, loving world. To me, ascension is creating heaven on Earth. Though I'm unsure of how this will manifest, I am open to my role in it, and am certain it will manifest.

PERSONAL ASCENSION

The first step we can all take in manifesting heaven on Earth is to follow our own personal ascension path. The religions, spiritualities, and experiences you have incorporated into your worldview inform your ascension path. I believe that, like the characters in *Mage: The Ascension*, we can follow a multitude of spiritualities and traditions, yet work together for a common good.

Several key points transcend tradition, and apply to us all on the path.

Walking Your Talk

One of the biggest factors in all spiritual practices is to "walk your talk," or live your truth. If you profess to believe something, then live your life in accordance with those beliefs. As you become more in tune with your truth and reflect the truths in the world, you raise your vibration. The higher a vibration you hold, the more you help others. Walking your talk can be very easy, but also very hard. If you are influenced by the mainstream world, it is easy to justify little things. If you believe, as a spiritual being, in truth, yet you are okay with telling little white lies to make your life easier in certain circumstances, then you are lowering your vibration because you are not living in your truth. Sometimes it is difficult to say that you don't want to do something rather than make up an excuse, but the honesty transforms your relationship with others, and with yourself. Holding your vibration in the face of societal pressure, among people who do not share your truth, can be difficult. We want to fit it and belong, yet when we don't, we have to be okay with not belonging to the group, for we belong to our soul, our higher I AM Presence. That is the only one we should seek to satisfy. If you believe in prosperity and the ability to create your own reality, then no one should hear you complaining or whining for long. It's okay to feel down. It's okay to take time to be gentle with yourself and feel compassion for the situation, but it's not okay to wallow in self-pity. If you believe your thoughts, emotions, and magick can change your situation, then do so, rather than complain. If the situation doesn't change, then look into why—was it harmful for you? Was it not an expression of your true will? If you know your true will, then enact it to the best of your current ability.

Synchronicity

The more conscious we become of all the connections of life, the more synchronicity occurs. Synchronicity is when two seemingly unrelated events or experiences are meaningfully connected. There is synchronicity when you are thinking of or speaking about someone you know, and he or she suddenly calls. Synchronicity is when you say you need a new, inexpensive car, and then you run into someone who is selling a great car for a low price. Synchronicity is the universe's way of showing us that everything is connected, and it is always listening and a part of our interactions. We are all part of the divine web of life.

Compassion

Compassion is a key concept of my spiritual traditions. We all aspire to reach the unconditional love of the fifth dimension. Through compassion for yourself and others, you find this unconditional love, and new worlds open to you. Compassion is not pity or charity, but rather the recognition that spiritually, we are not only all connected, but we are all one. The person whom you have compassion for is an extension of the same force that manifests you. To have compassion for another is to have compassion for yourself. Compassion can often be stimulated by working on the heart chakra and having a heart-chakra awakening.

Detachment

Detachment goes hand in hand with compassion. Though many see it as an Eastern ideal, detachment is found in the traditions of both the East and the West. To the mage, detachment is letting go of your intention once you send it out, and being open to your divine will, over your personal will. You still act upon what you want to create, for you are a co-creator with the divine. You do not do it all, yet you don't expect the divine to do it all either. For the partnership to work, you have to show up, and act on your part, but you are not attached to the fruits of your action. You are detached from how it manifests, simply knowing you are doing what you need to be doing in any given moment, and the outcome might not be what you personally expect or want. Detachment doesn't mean having no desires, but means not being attached to the desires. You don't become passionless. In fact, you might find yourself with more intensity and passion than ever before, because the divine powers flow through you, touching everything you do. You can still enjoy the world and all its pleasures. Doreen Valiente, in her classic book *Witchcraft for Tomorrow*, discusses this idea in a commentary on the Hindu and Buddhist philosophies in her chapter on ethics (page 45):

> They imply that once a person has attained spiritual enlightenment, and become in their heart a true follower of the Dharma, the ancient wisdom-religion which was from the beginning of time, and of which all the Buddhas have been exponents, then it matters not whether that person observes conventional codes of conduct or no, and whether or not he or she takes part in worldly activities and pleasures. Having attained mastery of mind, such a person will act from non-attachment, and therefore will not err.

It's important to keep in mind the phrase "attained spiritual enlightenment," because many will convince themselves they have attained this state, to justify their own vices and obviously not be in a state of nonattachment. It takes a very self-aware individual to walk that fine line.

Healing

Walking a healing path is a critical part of the ascension path. We have all been wounded, in this lifetime and many others. We all carry old programs about religion, sexuality, poverty, power, obedience, and our bodies that are unhealthy to us and our society now. Removing them from our consciousness is called cleansing, and occurs through a variety of psychological and energetically based therapies. Ritual, Native teachings, yoga, and prayer also initiate a healing process. Through our healing process, we explore our past and present, to understand our motivations and what has influenced us previously and what is influencing us now. "Know thyself" is the inscription at the oracle's temple in Delphi, and it is as good advice today as it was in ancient Greece. We explore our consciousness, bringing the unconscious aspects of the self to light. When traumatic experiences, of this life and past lives, are accepted, they can be reframed in terms of the "lesson," of the gift or blessing, they had to offer. Merkaba teacher Gary Smith refers to them as "blessons," because they can contain a bit of each. With this reframing, potentially damaging experiences can become empowering ones. Ascensionists are sought out as healers, but we cannot be healers unless we seek out aid in our own healing processes. As we heal, we help the world heal, for as we rise in consciousness, so does the world. As others heal, they help us rise a little more. Healers sometimes refer to healing as "doing the work," for we all have a part of ourselves, and therefore a part of the world, to heal. Through this healing, we are better able to merge with our higher selves, monads, and the creative source.

Freedom from Glamour

A deeper understanding of healing detachment comes when we are freed from what is known in Theosophy as "glamour." Not to be confused with faery bewitchment or a spell to make yourself look different, the glamours of Theosophical lore are entrapments of the material world that take you off the path of ascension. They are considered delusions. If you can be in the world, yet not be enticed by these glamours, then you are truly detached from their entrapment, yet able to act from a place of clarity and compassion. There are many manifestations of glamour. Here are a few of the formalized and codified challenges we face. If you look at the seven rays in chapter 13, you will find that each ray has a potential glamour to beware of.

The Glamour of Devotion

This glamour is created when one is so devoted to cause or ideal that the commitment reaches an unhealthy, fanatical extreme, where no other possibility is considered. Extremes and absolutes blind us to the path of ascension.

The Glamour of Materiality

This glamour is the enticement of the material world, of possessions, money, and sensory experiences. One becomes so immersed in the material world that no other reality can be focused upon.

The Glamour of Sentiment

This glamour is the illusion of sentimental love, the process of falling in love, loving another or being loved and adored by another. This glamour doesn't encourage healthy, adult romantic relationships, but those that are characterized by excessive drama and an illusionary view of oneself and one's partners.

The Glamour of the Pairs of Opposites

When under this glamour's power, one swings quickly back and forth between opposite qualities without ever finding balance or an even center. One is attached to people or things, not realizing that the nature of this world is transition, a gentle flow from one polarity to the next, a cycle of life to death to life, or light to dark to light. The nature of the material world is change, and we cannot be attached to things that will change.

Wise Choices

In the end, however you define ascension, it's a choice you make every day. Every choice you make, every thought, word, and deed, can either raise your vibration and expand your consciousness, or lower your vibration and contract you. When you are faced with a situation, do you react to it, unconsciously, or do you respond to it, with your full awareness? If you can train yourself to respond rather than simply react to something, you will have the opportunity to make wise choices to expand your consciousness. This can happen in little and big ways. When cut off in traffic, do you respond with anger, or realize that anger isn't productive? When faced with a challenging person, do you blame the person for how you are reacting to him or her, or look at yourself as playing at least a small part in the drama? When you are faced with greater life challenges, such as illness, death, or crisis, do you see the potential lesson in the situation, or simply react with anger, sorrow, or pity? A wise choice doesn't mean denial, however. When you feel these emotions, they are perfectly normal and a part of being human. The difference between a person who chooses ascension and one who doesn't involves how conscious the individual is of these emotions and thoughts, and whether the individual processes them or gets trapped in them.

SPIRITUAL NAMES

Those who have been walking the ascension path for a time often find that their given birth name no longer suits their identity. They choose to take a spiritual name. All generations and traditions of spiritual seekers do this. Some have formal name-taking traditions, or are given a name from a teacher. Those in Catholicism take confirmation names. Tribal traditions might have naming ceremonies or vision quests to gain an adult name and identity. Wiccans often take the name of a god or hero they aspire to emulate upon initiation. Magicians of the Golden Dawn era had magickal names and mottos. Dion Fortune's name came from her family motto, "Deo, non fortuna," meaning "God, not fate." Crowley had many magickal names, though his motto was "I will endure," and he certainly did, as his material is far more popular today than it was in his lifetime.

Such magicians are often concerned with the numerological correspondences in their magickal names. The Latin noms de plume are not as popular these days among the ceremonialists. Eastern seekers take Hindu names, or are named by their guru, getting the essence of their energy from the guru. Ascensionists can take the names of ascended masters, or words from a variety of foreign languages, such as Egyptian, Sanskrit, Hebrew, or Greek. Sometimes these names make sense in an earthly language, and sometimes they don't, being a "language of light." Ascensionists often say that they don't feel they are taking the name of someone whom they wish to emulate, as many mystics do, but rather are taking a name that reflects who they really are.

PLANETARY ASCENSION

Though our personal ascension aids planetary ascension, if we are to manifest the new society of the Age of Aquarius, then we have global issues to explore. The first is to realize that there is no savior coming to rescue us. Neither Christ nor the aliens are going to come and do the work for us. We can't wait for a last-minute rescue from on high.

The mystical truth is that we all must be our own saviors, and collectively be our world saviors. The Christ force comes on many levels, including planetary, solar, galactic, and cosmic. Global ascension is raising the collective mass consciousness of the planet to the level of Christ consciousness, the fifth dimension, perfect love or whatever term you want to use. When we ascend to this level, individually and collectively, we become the world savior, the world redeemer, and usher in the next age. But we can achieve this only if we do the work to prepare for it.

The global community has to look at a number of paradigms and how they will work in the next age. We are going to have to restructure and rebuild our society, and many light-workers feel that those of us involved in spiritual pursuits will be creating the templates for the new world. We have to start exploring these issues in detail now, to transform the way we think about them, to create the new paradigms.

Environment

Though some ascensionists are not concerned about the environment, feeling we are ascending to a higher plane and leaving the physical world behind, most of us are concerned about humanity's relationship with the planet. Our seemingly destructive behavior toward Mother Earth is of great concern, and many Gaian-oriented lightworkers are doing rituals to heal the planet and prevent catastrophic Earth changes. Many of us also believe in following up that work with responsible decisions in the physical world, such as recycling, conservation, political action, and living "green."

One of the fundamental paradigms that must shift is coming to understand that there is no separation between us. We are part of a greater whole. The world is not ours to be used. We are like cells within the greater being of the Earth, but what kind of cells are we? Some have compared the movement and behavior of humanity to cancer—moving about with no pattern and creating destructive constructs. That is only one view. We could be more like the immune system if we choose to be. Much of our channeled lore states that the whales and dolphins are the guardians of the seas, and that humanity was meant to be the guardian of the land. We are shirking that responsibility and need to step up and act as guardians and keepers of the land. Grant Morrison, in *The Invisibles*, compares humans to caterpillars, greedily devouring everything in our path before entering the cocoon and transforming. That may be true, but as we consume now, we have to consume consciously and choose what we are transforming into, and how, as butterflies, we will relate to the planet. We have to create models of sustainable living for all of us, using both high-tech and low-tech resources. Though we are waiting for the invention of machines to produce the right food and neutralize pollution, and that is a possibility, we have to find new ways of living that won't lead to these situations in the first place.

Medicine

Our models of medicine are just beginning to embrace the mind-body-spirit connection. Our medical models must continue on that path, treating the whole individual and incorporating the medicines of the past—such as traditional Chinese medicine and Indian medicine—with modern allopathic medicine. Frontiers of homeopathy, vibrational essences, crystals, meditation, and energy healing must work hand in hand with more mainstream and technologically oriented systems of healing. Rather than just masking symptoms, we must learn to get to the true root, on a spiritual level, of the illness if healing is to occur. Our views of medicine, from pharmaceuticals to herbs, must be reevaluated. Sometimes distilling the active compound in an herb is wonderful, while at other times we lose so much of what the herb has to offer in the process. We must get back in touch with nature and our natural rhythms, and also move out of our current model of modern medicine that says we must fix people as machines, instead of viewing people as holistic beings needing care on all levels. People must be educated about their own health, and given access to proper food, herbs, and supplements, in a regime of preventive medicine. We can strike a balance between alternative and traditional care.

Politics

Our political systems, particularly in America, have to be redesigned. Though from an Aquarian perspective, America is a veritable birthplace of Aquarian, revolutionary ideas for humanitarian principles, the current political system completely emphasizes the polarity consciousness that epitomizes the Age of Pisces and resists the changes we need to move toward the Age of Aquarius. A multiparty system is one remedy to bring us into the New Age. Lateral rulership and councils rather than hierarchical democracy seem to be the hallmarks of the next aeon. The one-leader, one-identity model is almost over. Even in communities, the one leader, from school principal to mayor, is being replaced with councils and governing bodies. Though American democracy has many of these ideals at heart, the bureaucracy prevents them from being properly executed at times, and the machinery of the government needs to be altered to make these ideals more tenable.

Society

As we enter the new aeon, a lot of our societal taboos and restrictions will have to be lifted. The key to the new aeon, according to Crowley, is "Do what you will is the whole of the law. Love is the law. Love under will." This influenced the popular Wiccan Rede: "An' it harm none, do what ye will." Though the Rede is often misinterpreted to mean anything goes, while it really means fulfill your true will in all things, I do believe that all of our social restraints will be lessened, as long as they harm no one. The concept of the family might be altered from the small nuclear family for some to a more polyamorous structure. Some people have been advocating communal living since the 1960s, and many have made such experiments work. Sexuality of a once nontraditional nature, such as homosexuality and bisexuality, as well as transgendered identity, will become more accepted.

Our view of our elders must also change. Tribal society revered the elders, while today we feel burdened by them. We can transform our elder population into a resource of wisdom, mentoring, and aid for the younger generations. Lastly, our restrictions on drug use, particularly ethogens for spiritual awakening, must lessen. Drugs that cause spiraling addictions and destroy lives are one thing, but both recreational use, and spiritual use, have a place in our society, as long as the actions of the users do not harm others. We have legalized far more addictive and destructive drugs, such as alcohol, commercialized tobacco, and white sugar. If we expect adults to deal with those drugs appropriately, then we must be allowed to choose others of a mind-expanding quality as well.

Economics

Our economic system must also be revamped. One of the lessons I take from the *Star Trek* series is a world in which money is no longer necessary. Everybody has all the resources they need, yet at the same time contributes to society as a part of their duty. Our current model of economics creates a paradigm of win/loss rather than situations of win/win for all. Ultimately, there is no need for some people to be poor, ill, or homeless in order for the rest of us to feel empowered and wealthy. We should all have access to basic resources, from food, shelter, and clothing to education and recreation. The drive to acquire money prevents many people from truly finding their gifts and what they have to offer to the world.

Activism

The way we voice our opinions and handle opposition must be altered as well. Though political protests can be quite effective in certain circumstances, ultimately, the more time you spend fighting *against* something, the less time you have to fight *for* something. There is a huge difference between force and power. Force comes from an outside strength or cohesion. Power comes from an innate truth. When you fight against something, you are using force. You don't create whatever vision you have, because you are trying to stop another's vision from manifesting rather than presenting an alternative scenario. True power sets an example and raises the vibration of a situation. It is said that one enlightened person can do the work of ten armies. Imagine the power of a whole group of enlightened individuals to change the world.

Our job is to reach that level of vibration, starting with the enlightenment of the self. We don't need to win a revolution of politics or the military and set the rules for a new empire. We simply need to aid the enlightenment, the personal revolution process, of as many people as we can. Then, our job is to expand the consciousness of our "enemies" so they can see our point of view without distortion. In the end, this encapsulates the idea that our ascension utopia creates a world where everybody wins, where everybody's voice is heard and can be expressed clearly. But if those with the restricted worldview continue to rule, on both the left and right sides of the political spectrum, then the larger views will never be understood or manifested without distortion. Our spiritual healing and utopia is for everybody, not just a chosen few who agree with us. From the spiritual view, we all succeed or none of us succeeds. We are all one.

These are only a few places where the spiritual thinkers and co-creators of the New Age need to be looking to reweave our society into a holistic paradigm, as all of these factors, seemingly separate, are connected. Our attitudes toward society, politics, economics, and the environment are all tied together. What we do to one affects the rest.

THE NEW MYTHOS

Part of our personal and planetary ascension is living with the divine paradox. We are both spiritual and material beings. The material world is the densest expression of the spiritual world. The spiritual forces are the roots of the material world. As above, so below. Qabalists would say Kether is in Malkuth, and Malkuth is in Kether.

Western consciousness in particular has had great difficulty with the divine paradox. It seems to be something that is more easily understood in Hinduism and forms of tribal belief. We can see in those systems that divinity is both transcendent and divine.

One of the ways we learn to embrace the paradox and heal the schism is by making new myths. While many of the themes of the old myths still serve us, we are coming together as a global society, and need global myths to address the needs of a global people.

Our story gives us a sense of belonging and motivates our future actions. Individually, when we retrace and reframe our story, we are transformed. As a people, we are called to reframe our story. The old myths, the old religious dogmas, are what created the schisms in the first place. Even our science-fiction and fantasy myths play out the same tale of light versus dark. Recently, I've noticed a trend, particularly in comics, in which villains are being redeemed as heroes. I think that is part of the new trend—where everyone and everything is redeemable. As long as we write our myths to reflect that, it can be a reality. We are calling upon artists, writers, and musicians to create the new mythos.

What is happening to our planet? As we move into an age of information, instant connection, and global identity, how do we reframe the experience? Some frame it in terms of the Armageddon, the destruction of the world. I don't disagree with that concept as long as we realize the destruction of the world doesn't mean the destruction of the physical planet. It is the destruction of the age we live in, and the death of the limiting concepts and mindsets of that age, to make room for the birth of a new age, a new world. The apocalypse is the end of *a* world, not *the* world. The world and the planet are two different things, and the planet is far older and wiser than we are, and will be here far longer than we will, no matter what we do.

Some people give us a mythology of a great planetary council. All the planets are alive and conscious, like Gaia. The council is ruled by the Solar Logos, Helios, or whatever name you wish to give to the Sun. Earth, although old and wise, and seen as mother or grandmother to humanity, is undergoing an initiation into this council of elders in the solar system. Our awakening global consciousness and all our "growing pains" in the world have been the full awakening of the Earth, on all levels, including our human level. Much like making a life transition from childhood through puberty, or adulthood to elderhood, our planet is going through a shift, and taking us with her. Our changes reflect her changes, and vice versa. Now our mythical experience must be framed not only in global terms, but in terms of the solar system and then the galaxy.

Another ascension mythology framing our vision is the thought of the New Universe. The entire universe is ascending, and we are to be the seeds of life in a new universe. The diversity on Earth reflects the fact that we are like a living library for this universe, containing some of the most important patterns of life and creation. Our energy will create the templates to seed the next universe with a variety of forms on all levels of creation. This universe will have a whole different set of rules and challenges compared to what we have experienced here, and it will not necessarily be aligned with the polarity consciousness that we experience in the lower dimensions.

These are only a few of the myths to explain where we are going. The mysteries of hidden history are some of the mythical takes on where we are now, where we have been, and where we are going. Some are seen as literal truths, and some as symbolic. As mages, we know that in the higher dimensions, on the astral plane and beyond, a symbol does not stand for something, but rather it is something. On a higher level, symbolic truths and literal truths are not easily distinguished. As long as they serve a higher purpose, the distinction doesn't matter. Did the ancient gods walk the Earth, or only the ethers of Mount Olympus or Heliopolis? Did the Grays physically take you away and experiment, or did that happen on an etheric level, in your spirit vision? If either of these experiences uplifts and transforms you, then it doesn't matter.

We must be the new mythmakers for this age. Some of us will keep the old traditions pristine and clear or reconstructed, which is important to know our history. We must have our traditional Buddhists, Wiccans, Hindus, and Christians. At the same time, others must forge the new holistic traditions and myths that will keep us sane and spiritual in the coming age. We are explorers, forging a new way, so of course we may seem crazy at times, or depressed, much like the shamans of ages past. We have this potentially insane view, overwhelmed by uniting all the world mythologies into one whole, inclusive mythos. To survive and to succeed in our self-appointed task, we must stand between the worlds, and be visionaries, seeing the overall pattern that unites the world religions. We have to bring the healing powers of the other worlds, through our stories and songs, to our people.

MAGICKAL ASCENSION

For a lot of practitioners, magick is not their spiritual path. For many others, magick is the very lifeblood of our spiritual practice. Magick starts as spells and rituals. Corrupted magick becomes our superstitions, leading us to do things while not understanding why. Magick can evolve into a religious practice, honoring seasonal shifts and the patterns of the Moon, Sun, planets, and stars. Magick opens the gateway between worlds, and we realize that it is not a religion, or only a religion, but a spiritual partnership with the unseen. We move toward what magicians of all ages in their various tongues have called the Great Work. All magicians seek to perform the Great Work—enlightenment, the Philosopher's Stone, ascension.

On the path, we reach a point where we stop doing magick. The rituals, symbols, and tools don't matter; they are the hardware and software of our magickal machine. We stop being people who do magick, using those hardware and software tools, and instead we become magick. We identify directly with the current that flows through those tools, that flows through all things. We stop doing magick and start living magick, eventually becoming magick.

The next age is the age of magick, and is ruled by the seventh, or violet, ray of ceremonial order, magick, ritual, and alchemy. As Saint Germain, the chohan of the seventh ray, moves to the position of the Mahachohan, the Lord of Civilization, the master magician and alchemist will inform and color our entire perspective in the New Age. Magick will take its place among all the other arts, sciences, and religions as an aid to civilization and all of humanity. The seeds have already been planted through a partnership between incarnated humanity and the ascended masters. These seeds are taking root. They are growing. Magick is the power of growth, of evolution, leading to the fulfillment of the Great Work. Magick is ascension.

BIBLIOGRAPHY

Agrippa, Henry Cornelius. *De Occulta Philosophia, or Three Books of Occult Philosophy*. Edited by Donald Tyson. 1655; reprint, St. Paul, MN: Llewellyn Publications, 1993.

Alchemy: Alchemistic Philosophy Module One. Sacramento, CA: ETX Seminars, 1999.

Alexander, Karen. *A Gift from Daniel*. New York: Perigree Books, 1996.

Andrews, Shirley. *Atlantis: Insights from a Lost Civilization*. St. Paul, MN: Llewellyn Publications, 1997.

———. *Lemuria and Atlantis: Studying the Past to Survive the Future*. St. Paul, MN: Llewellyn Publications, 2004.

Bailey, Alice A. *Esoteric Astrology*. New York: Lucis Publishing, 1951.

———. *Esoteric Psychology, Vol. I*. New York: Lucis Publishing, 1936.

———. *Esoteric Psychology, Vol. II*. New York: Lucis Publishing, 1942.

———. *The Rays and the Initiations*. New York: Lucis Publishing, 1960.

Blavatsky, Helena P. *Isis Unveiled*. Wheaton, IL: Theosophical Publishing House, 1972.

———. *The Secret Doctrine*. Adyar, India: Theosophical Publishing House, 1888.

Brennan, J. H. *Occult Tibet: Secret Practices of Himalayan Magic*. St. Paul, MN: Llewellyn Publications, 2002.

Cabot, Laurie, with Tom Cowan. *Power of the Witch: The Earth, the Moon and the Magical Path to Enlightenment*. New York: Dell Publishing, 1989.

Church, W. H. *Edgar Cayce's Story of the Soul*. Virginia Beach, VA: Inner Vision, 1989.

Cicero, Chic, and Sandra Tabatha Cicero. *The Essential Golden Dawn*. St. Paul, MN: Llewellyn Publications, 2003.

Clark, Rosemary. *The Sacred Magic of Ancient Egypt*. St. Paul, MN: Llewellyn Publications, 2003.

Clow, Barbara Hand. *The Pleiadian Agenda: A New Cosmology for the Age of Light*. Santa Fe, NM: Bear & Company, 1995.

Clow, Barbara Hand, with Gerry Clow. *Alchemy of Nine Dimensions: Decoding the Vertical Axis, Crop Circles, and the Mayan Calendar*. Charlottesville, VA: Hampton Roads Publishing, 2004.

Conway, D. J. *The Ancient & Shining Ones*. St. Paul, MN: Llewellyn Publications, 1993.

Cooper, Diana. *A Little Light on Ascension*. Forres, Scotland: Findhorn Press, 1997.

Cooper, Phillip. *Basic Magick: A Practical Guide.* York Beach, ME: Samuel Weiser, 1996.

Courtenay, Edwin. *The Ascended Masters' Book of Ritual and Prayer.* Freiburg, Germany: Prince of the Stars, 2004.

———. *Reflections: The Masters Remember.* Freiburg, Germany: Prince of the Stars, 2004.

Crowley, Aleister. *Magick in Theory and Practice.* New York: Dover Publications, 1976.

Cunningham, Scott. *Cunningham's Encyclopedia of Crystal, Gem & Metal Magic.* St. Paul, MN: Llewellyn Publications, 1992.

———. *Cunningham's Encyclopedia of Magical Herbs.* St. Paul, MN: Llewellyn Publications, 1985.

———. *Incense, Oils and Brews.* St. Paul, MN: Llewellyn Publications, 1989.

Dalichow, Irene, and Mike Booth. *Aura-Soma: Healing Through Color, Plant and Crystal Energy.* Carlsbad, CA: Hay House, 1996.

Dannelley, Richard. *Sedona: Beyond the Vortex.* Sedona, AZ: Vortex Society, 1995.

Davidson, Gustav. *A Dictionary of Angels, Including the Fallen Angels.* New York: Free Press, 1967.

DeKorne, Jim. *Psychedelic Shamanism: The Cultivation, Preparation, and Shamanic Use of Psychotropic Plants.* Port Townsend, WA: Loompanics Unlimited, 1994.

Diagram Group. *The Little Giant Encyclopedia of Spells & Magic.* Compiled by Jane Johnson. New York: Sterling Publishing, 1999.

Donnelly, Ignatius. *Atlantis: The Antediluvian World.* New York: Harper, 1971.

Doreal, Dr. *The Emerald Tablets of Thoth-the-Atlantean.* Sedalia, CO: Brotherhood of the White Temple, 2002.

Duirin. *Ancestors: Not Just for Samhain Anymore.* Self-published booklet. Salt Lake City, UT: 2005.

DuQuette, Lon Milo. *The Magick of Aleister Crowley.* Boston, MA: Weiser, 2003.

Dyer, Dr. Wayne W. *Real Magic: Creating Miracles in Everyday Life.* Audio cassette. New York: Harper Audio/HarperCollins Publishers, 1992.

Ea. *Understanding the Bornless Rite.* Class handout from Pagan Spirit Gathering. Wisteria, OH: 2004.

Eliade, Mircea. *Shamanism: Archaic Techniques of Ecstasy.* Princeton, NJ: Princeton University Press, 1972.

Farrar, Janet, and Gavin Bone. *Progressive Witchcraft.* Franklin Lakes, NJ: New Page Books, 2004.

Flowers, Stephen E., Ph.D. *Lords of the Left-Hand Path.* Smithville, TX: Runa-Raven Press, 1997.

Fortune, Dion. *The Goat-Foot God.* New York: Samuel Weiser, 1971.

———. *The Sea Priestess.* York Beach, ME: Samuel Weiser, 1972.

Fries, Jan. *Cauldron of the Gods: A Manual of Celtic Magick.* Oxford, UK: Mandrake Press, 2003.

Frissell, Bob. *Nothing in This Book Is True, but It's Exactly How Things Are.* Berkeley, CA: Frog, 1994.

———. *Something in This Book Is True.* Berkeley, CA: Frog, 1997.

Goddard, David. *The Sacred Magic of the Angels.* York Beach, ME: Samuel Weiser, 1996.

Grattan, Brian. *Mahatma I & II: The I Am Presence.* Sedona, AZ: Light Technology Publishing, 1994.

Greer, John Michael. *The New Encyclopedia of the Occult.* St. Paul, MN: Llewellyn Publications, 2003.

Grimassi, Raven. *Hereditary Witchcraft: Secrets of the Old Religion.* St. Paul, MN: Llewellyn Publications, 1999.

Guiley, Rosemary Ellen. *The Encyclopedia of Witches and Witchcraft.* New York: Checkmark Books, 1999.

———. *Harper's Encyclopedia of Mystical & Paranormal Experience.* San Francisco: HarperSanFrancisco, 1991.

Haich, Elisabeth. *Initiation.* Santa Fe, NM: Aurora Press, 2000.

Hardin, Jesse Wolf. *Gaia Eros: Reconnecting to the Magic and Spirit of Nature.* Franklin Lakes, NJ: New Page Books, 2004.

Harner, Michael. *The Way of the Shaman.* Third edition. New York: HarperCollins, 1990.

Hay, Louise H. *Heal Your Body A–Z.* Carlsbad, CA: Hay House, 1988.

Heath, Maya. *Ceridwen's Handbook of Incense, Oils, and Candles.* San Antonio, TX: Words of Wizdom International, 1996.

Heselton, Philip. *Leylines: A Beginner's Guide*. London: Hodder & Stoughton, 1999.

Hine, Phil. *Condensed Chaos*. Tempe, AZ: New Falcon, 1995.

Hope, Murry. *Practical Atlantean Magic*. London: Aquarian Press, 1991.

Hurtak, J. J. *The Book of Knowledge: The Keys of Enoch*. Los Gatos, CA: Academy for Future Science, 1977.

Jenkins, Elizabeth B. *Initiation: A Woman's Spiritual Adventure in the Heart of the Andes*. New York: Berkeley Books, 1997.

Jensen, Paul. *Introduction to Vogel Healing Tools*. Foundation for the Advancement of Vogel Healing Techniques, 1999.

Johnson, Kenneth. *Witchcraft and the Shamanic Journey: Pagan Folkways from the Burning Times*. St. Paul, MN: Llewellyn Publications, 1998.

Joseph, Frank. *The Atlantis Encyclopedia*. Franklin Lakes, NJ: New Page Books, 2005.

Kaminski, Patricia, and Richard Katz. *Flower Essence Repertory*. Nevada City, CA: Flower Essence Society, 1994.

Kaplan, Aryeh. *Meditation and Kabbalah*. York Beach, ME: Weiser Books, 1989.

Kelly, Maureen J. *Reiki and the Healing Buddha*. Twin Lakes, WI: Lotus, 2000.

Kharitidi, Olga. *The Master of Lucid Dreams*. Charlottesville, VA: Hampton Roads, 2001.

King, Godfré Ray [Guy Warren Ballard]. *Unveiled Mysteries*. Chicago, IL: Saint Germain Press, 1934.

Kraig, Donald Michael. *Modern Magick: Eleven Lessons in the High Magickal Arts*. St. Paul, MN: Llewellyn Publications, 1988.

The Kybalion: Hermetic Philosophy by Three Initiates. Chicago, IL: Yogi Publication Society, 1912.

Lawlor, Robert. *The Sacred Geometry: Philosophy and Practice*. New York: Crossroad, 1982.

Lazaris. *The Lazaris Material: Letting More Love into Your Life: The Double Tetrahedron Technique & Meditation*. Audiotape. Orlando, FL: NPN Publishing, 1998.

Liddel, W. E., and Michael Howard. *The Pickingill Papers: The Origin of the Gardnerian Craft*. Somerset, UK: Capall Bann, 1994.

Lindsay, Phillip. *Masters of the Seven Rays: Their Past Lives and Reappearance*. Newport Beach, Australia: Apollo Publishing, 2000.

———. *The Shamballa Impacts*. Newport Beach, Australia: Apollo Publishing, 2000.

MacLaine, Shirley. *The Camino: A Journey of the Spirit*. New York: Atria Books, 2001.

Mage: The Ascension RPG. Atlanta, GA: White Wolf Games Studio, 2001.

Marciniak, Barbara. *Bringers of the Dawn: Teachings from the Pleiadians*. Santa Fe, NM: Bear & Company, 1992.

Marciniak, Barbara, with Karen Marciniak and Tera Thomas. *Earth: Pleiadian Keys to the Living Library*. Santa Fe, NM: Bear & Company, 1995.

Margold, Harlan. *The Alchemist's Almanach: Reweaving the Tapestry of Time*. Santa Fe, NM: Bear & Company, 1991.

McKenna, Terence. *The Search for the Original Tree of Knowledge*. Audio cassette. Boulder, CO: Sounds True, 1992.

Melchizedek, Drunvalo. *The Ancient Secrets of the Flower of Life, Vol. 1*. Sedona, AZ: Light Technology Publishing, 1998.

———. *The Ancient Secrets of the Flower of Life, Vol. 2*. Sedona, AZ: Light Technology Publishing, 2000.

Melody. *Love Is in the Earth*. Wheat Ridge, CO: Earth-Love Publishing, 1995.

Michael, Kevin. *Merkaba*. Class notes. Santa Fe, NM: Santa Fe Mystery School, 1997.

Michell, John. *The New View Over Atlantis*. San Francisco: Harper & Row, 1983.

Milanovich, Norma J., with Betty Rice and Cynthia Ploski. *We, the Arcturians*. Albuquerque, NM: Athena Publishing, 1990.

Mitchell, Karyn K., N.D., Ph.D. *Reiki Mystery School*. Oregon, IL: Mind Rivers, 1998.

Moore, Judith, and Barbara Lamb. *Crop Circles Revealed*. Flagstaff, AZ: Light Technology Publishing, 2001.

Morrison, Grant. *The Invisibles: Counting to None*. New York: DC Comics, 1999.

———. *The Invisibles: Bloody Hell in America*. New York: DC Comics, 1998.

Morton, Chris, and Ceri Louise Thomas. *The Mystery of the Crystal Skulls*. Santa Fe, NM: Bear & Company, 1998.

Neighly, Patrick, and Kereth Cowe-Spigai. *Anarchy for the Masses: The Disinformation Guide to The Invisibles*. New York: Disinformation, 2003.

Newcomb, Jason Augustus. *Conjuring the Goetia Spirits: A Simple Advanced Key*. Arlington, MA: Smite! Press, 1999.

———. *The New Hermetics*. Boston, MA: Weiser, 2004.

Penczak, Christopher. *The Inner Temple of Witchcraft: Magick, Meditation and Psychic Development*. St. Paul, MN: Llewellyn Publications, 2002.

———. *Magick of Reiki*. St. Paul, MN: Llewellyn Publications, 2004.

———. *The Outer Temple of Witchcraft: Circles, Spells and Rituals*. St. Paul, MN: Llewellyn Publications, 2004.

———. *Spirit Allies: Meet Your Team from the Other Side*. Boston, MA: Weiser, 2001.

———. *The Temple of Shamanic Witchcraft: Shadows, Spirits and the Healing Journey*. St. Paul, MN: Llewellyn Publications, 2005.

Perry, Robert. *Life with the Little People*. Greenfield Center, NY: Greenfield Review Press, 1998.

Prophet, Elizabeth Clare. *Violet Flame to Heal Body, Mind & Soul*. Corwin Springs, MT: Summit University Press, 1997.

Prophet, Mark L., and Elizabeth Clare Prophet. *Lords of the Seven Rays: Mirror of Consciousness*. Corwin Springs, MT: Summit University Press, 1986.

———. *The Masters and the Spiritual Path*. Corwin Springs, MT: Summit University Press, 2001.

Red Star, Nancy. *Legends of the Star Ancestors*. Rochester, VT: Bear & Company, 2002.

———. *Star Ancestors*. Rochester, VT: Destiny Books, 2000.

Redfield, James. *The Secret of Shambhala*. New York: Warner Books, 1999.

Royal, Lyssa, and Keith Priest. *The Prism of Lyra*. Scottsdale, AZ: Royal Priest Research Press, 1989.

Sams, Jamie, and David Carson. *Medicine Cards: The Discovery of Power Through the Ways of Animals*. Santa Fe, NM: Bear and Company, 1998.

Sanchez, Victor. *The Teachings of Don Carlos*. Translation by Robert Nelson. Santa Fe, NM: Bear & Company, 1995.

Sarangerel. *Chosen by the Spirits: Following Your Shamanic Calling*. Rochester, VT: Destiny Books, 2001.

Satchidananda, Sri Swami. *The Living Gita: The Complete Bhagavad Gita*. Yogaville, VA: Integral Yoga Publications, 1988.

Schneider, Petra, and Gerhard K. Pieroth. *LightBeings Master Essences*. Twin Lakes, WI: Arcana Publishing, 1998.

Silva, Freddy. *Secrets in the Fields: The Science and Mysticism of Crop Circles*. Charlottesville, VA: Hampton Roads Publishing, 2002.

Sitchin, Zecharia. *The 12th Planet*. New York: Avon Books, 1976.

Slesinger, Andrea T. *The Diamond Galaxy*. Sagus, MA: JG Thomas Communications, 1996.

Smith, Kalila Katherina. *New Orleans Ghosts and Vampires: Journey into Darkness*. New Orleans, LA: De Simonin Publications, 1997.

Starhawk. *The Spiral Dance: A Rebirth of the Ancient Religion of the Great Goddess*. San Francisco: Harper & Row, 1989.

Stone, Joshua David, Ph.D. *A Beginner's Guide to the Path of Ascension*. Sedona, AZ: Light Technology Publishing, 1998.

———. *The Ascended Masters Light the Way: Beacons of Ascension*. Sedona, AZ: Light Technology Publishing, 1995.

———. *The Complete Ascension Manual*. Sedona, AZ: Light Technology Publishing, 1994.

———. *Hidden Mysteries*. Sedona, AZ: Light Technology Publishing, 1995.

Stone, Joshua David, Ph.D., and Sarayon Michael White. *The Ascension Names and Terms Glossary*. Lincoln, NE: iUniverse. com, 2001.

Strieber, Whitley. *Communion: A True Story*. New York: Beech Tree Books, 1987.

Twyman, James F. *Emissary of Light*. New York: Warner Books, 1997.

Valiente, Doreen. *An ABC of Witchcraft Past & Present*. New York: St. Martin's Press, 1973.

———. *Witchcraft for Tomorrow*. Blaine, WA: Phoenix Publishing, 1978.

Virtue, Doreen, Ph.D. *Archangels & Ascended Masters*. Carlsbad, CA: Hay House, 2003.

———. *Earth Angels: A Pocket Guide for Incarnated Angels, Elementals, Starpeople, Walk-Ins and Wizards*. Carlsbad, CA: Hay House, 2002.

Wall, Vicky. *Aura Soma: Self-Discovery through Color*. Second edition. Rochester, VT: Healing Arts Press, 2005.

Wallis, R. T. *Neoplatonism*. Cambridge, MA: Hackett Publishing, 1995.

Watkins, Alfred. *The Old Straight Track*. London: Sago Press, 1970.

Webb, Don. *Uncle Setnakt's Essential Guide to the Left Hand Path*. Smithville, TX: Runa-Raven Press, 1999.

Weiss, Brian. *Many Lives, Many Masters*. New York: Simon & Schuster, 1988.

Whitcomb, Bill. *The Magician's Companion*. St. Paul, MN: Llewellyn Publications, 1993.

Wilcox, Joan Parisi. *Keepers of the Ancient Knowledge: The Mystical World of the Q'ero Indians of Peru*. London: Vega, 2001.

Wilson, Robert Anton. *Sex, Drugs & Magick*. Second edition. Temple, AZ: New Falcon Publications, 2000.

Wolkstein, Diane, and Samuel Noah Kramer. *Inanna: Queen of Heaven and Earth: Her Stories and Hymns from Sumer*. New York: Harper & Row, 1983.

Wright, Machaelle Small. *MAP: The Co-Creative White Brotherhood Medical Assistance Program*. Jeffersonton, VA: Perelandra, 1990.

———. *The Perelandra Garden Workbook*. Jeffersonton, VA: Perelandra, 1987.

———. *The Perelandra Garden Workbook II*. Jeffersonton, VA: Perelandra, 1990.

Yin, Amorah Quan. *The Pleiadian Workbook: Awakening Your Divine Ka*. Santa Fe, NM: Bear & Company, 1996.

Yogananda, Paramahansa. *Autobiography of a Yogi*. Los Angeles: Self-Realization Fellowship, 1946.

ONLINE RESOURCES

http://drunvalo.net/melchizedek.html. Drunvalo Melchizedek's website.

http://en.wikipedia.org/wiki/Super_string_theory. "Superstring theory," *Wikipedia*.

http://homepage.mac.com/scarab1/incense.html. "Breath of the Gods." Website of Nikki Wieleba.

http://religiousmovements.lib.virginia.edu/nrms/Spiritsm.html. "Spiritualism." Religious Movements homepage at the University of Virginia.

http://searchlight.iwarp.com/articles/na_plan.html. Hannah Newman, "The Rainbow Swastika: A Report to the Jewish People about New Age Anti-Semitism: The Plan of the New Age."

http://searchlight.iwarp.com/articles/na_transform.html#invocation. Hannah Newman, "The Rainbow Swastika: A Report to the Jewish People about New Age Antisemitism: The Transformation of Society."

http://skepdic.com/steiner.html. Robert Todd Carroll, "Rudolf Steiner," *The Skeptic's Dictionary*.

http://user.cyberlink.ch/~koenig/early.htm. Peter R. Koenig, "Ordo Templi Orientis Early Years and Development," *The Ordo Templi Orientis Phenomenon*.

http://www.creationspirituality.com/matthew.html—*Creationspirituality.com*.

http://www.crystalinks.com/sanatkumara.html. "Sanat Kumara," *Crystalinks*.

http://www.drjoshuadavidstone.com/wist/angelheart.htm. "Activating the Angels of the Heart." Website of Dr. Joshua David Stone.

http://www.earthlinkmission.org/stargate.htm. "Stargates," *Earth Link Mission 2005*.

http://www.earthtransitions.com/products/history_genese_crystals.htm. "Genesa Crystal," *EarthTransitions*.

http://www.fortunecity.com/roswell/chaney/191/id53.htm. "Incense Spells," *Wicca*.

http://www.heavenandearthjewelry.com. Heaven & Earth crystal company.

http://www.hermetic.com/egc/aisha-cakes.html. Aisha Qadisha, "Cakes of Light," *The Hermetic Library*.

http://www.jcf.org. *Joseph Campbell Foundation*.

http://www.kheper.net/topics/Neoplatonism/Iamblich-theurgy.htm. "Theurgy," *Kheper*.

http://www.kheper.net/topics/Theosophy/Hierarchy.html. "Hierarchy," *Kheper*.

http://www.letusreason.org/NAM20.htm. "The Plan," *Let Us Reason*.

http://www.lightparty.com/Spirituality/StGermain120904.html. "St. Germain: Human Beings Did Not Originate on Earth, 12.09.04," *The Light Party*.

http://www.mahatma.co.uk. *The Mahatma Shamballa Multidimensional Healing Network*.

http://www.matthewfox.org/sys-tmpl/door. *Friends of Creation Spirituality*.

http://www.merkaba.org. *The Sacred Merkaba Techniques*.

http://www.pantheon.org/articles/v/valkyries.html. Micha F. Lindemans, "Valkyries," *Encyclopedia Mythica*.

http://www.pinenet.com/~rooster/bailey.html. "Anti-Semitic Stereotypes in Alice Bailey's Writings." Homepage of Rabbi Gershom.

http://www.seizethemagic.com/lol/05worldinfo/05alpha.html. "Questions about the Order of Melchizedek."

http://www.thelemapedia.org/index.php/Cakes_of_Light. "Cakes of Light," *Thelemapedia*.

http://www.treeofthegoldenlight.com/Wakeup%20Call/MWmesages/December2004/SG12-02-04.htm. "Wakeup Call Message, December 2, 2004," *The Tree of the Golden Light*.

http://www.uncletaz.com/hubbstein.html. Tarjei Straume, "Scientology vs. Anthroposophy," the official Uncle Taz home page.

http://www.wisdomsdoor.com/wb/hwb-arc.shtml. "Archangels Chart," *Wisdom's Door*.

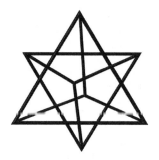

INDEX

tO wRite tO tHe AutHoR

If you wish to contact the author or would like more information about this book, please write to the author in care of Llewellyn Worldwide and we will forward your request. Both the author and publisher appreciate hearing from you and learning of your enjoyment of this book and how it has helped you. Llewellyn Worldwide cannot guarantee that every letter written to the author can be answered, but all will be forwarded. Please write to:

Christopher Penczak
℅ Llewellyn Worldwide
2143 Wooddale Drive, Dept. 0-7387-1047-4
Woodbury, Minnesota 55125-2989, U.S.A.

Please enclose a self-addressed stamped envelope for reply,
or $1.00 to cover costs. If outside U.S.A., enclose
international postal reply coupon.

Many of Llewellyn's authors have websites with additional information and resources. For more information, please visit our website at http://www.llewellyn.com.